PENGUIN BOOKS

THE PENGUIN HISTORY OF EARLY INDIA

Romila Thapar was born in India in 1931 and comes from a Punjabi family, spending her early years in various parts of India. She took her first degree from Punjab University and her doctorate from London University. She was appointed to a Readership at Delhi University and subsequently to the Chair in Ancient Indian History at the Jawaharlal Nehru University, New Delhi, where she is now Emeritus Professor in History. Romila Thapar is also an Honorary Fellow of Lady Margaret Hall, Oxford, and has been a Visiting Professor at Cornell University and the University of Pennsylvania as well as the Collège de France in Paris. In 1983 she was elected General President of the Indian History Congress and in 1999 a Corresponding Fellow of the British Academy.

Among her publications are *Ashoka and the Decline of the Mauryas*, *Ancient Indian Social History: Some Interpretations*, *From Lineage to State*, *History and Beyond*, *Sakuntala: Texts, Readings, Histories* and *Cultural Pasts: Essays on Indian History*, as well as a children's book, *Indian Tales*.

D1153836

ROMILA THAPAR

The Penguin History of Early India

FROM THE ORIGINS

TO AD 1300

PENGUIN BOOKS

PENGUIN BOOKS

Published by the Penguin Group
Penguin Books Ltd, 80 Strand, London WC2R ORL, England
Penguin Putnam Inc., 375 Hudson Street, New York, New York 10014, USA
Penguin Books Australia Ltd, 250 Camberwell Road, Camberwell, Victoria 3124, Australia
Penguin Books Canada Ltd, 10 Alcorn Avenue, Toronto, Ontario, Canada M4V 3B2
Penguin Books India (P) Ltd, 11 Community Centre,
Panchsheel Park, New Delhi – 110 017, India
Penguin Books (NZ) Ltd, Cnr Rosedale and Airborne Roads,
Albany, Auckland, New Zealand
Penguin Books (South Africa) (Pty) Ltd, 24 Sturdee Avenue,
Rosebank 2196, South Africa

Penguin Books Ltd, Registered Offices: 80 Strand, London WC2R ORL, England

www.penguin.com

First published as *Early India* by Allen Lane The Penguin Press 2002
Published under the present title in Penguin Books 2003

1

Copyright © Romila Thapar, 2002
All rights reserved

The moral right of the author has been asserted

Typeset by Rowland Phototypesetting Ltd, Bury St Edmunds, Suffolk
Printed in England by Clays Ltd, St Ives plc

For Sergei: in memoriam
and
remembering Kaushalya and Daya Ram
and our many years together

Contents

List of Illustrations

FIGURES

MAPS

The external boundaries of India as depicted in the maps are neither correct nor authentic.

Preface

It has been almost four decades since the first version of this book was written and in that time there have been substantial changes in the readings of Indian history. These have come about as a result of some new data, together with many fresh interpretations of the known data. My attempt here has been to incorporate the essentials of the new data and interpretations while retaining some of the older arguments where they are still relevant.

A major amendment to this book lies in its chronological span. It now closes at *c*. AD 1300 instead of AD 1526 as in the earlier version. After many years, I have finally persuaded Penguin that the history of India should be covered in three volumes and not be restricted to two. The earlier division of two volumes did not do justice to the important period from *c*. AD 1300 to 1800 and this is now being corrected. The final volume will bring the narrative up to contemporary times. This change also provides more space for each volume. An introduction already exists to the pre-history and proto-history of India in the volume by F. R. and B. Allchin, *The Birth of Indian Civilisation*, revised in 1993, also published by Penguin, as well as *The Origins of a Civilization* by the same authors and published by Viking in 1997 (Penguin, 1998). I have therefore given only a brief overview of prehistory and protohistory.

In the course of writing this book I have drawn on many friends for comments on various chapters of an earlier draft. Among them I would like to thank R. Champakalakshmi, Madhav Gadgil, Dennis Hudson, Xinru Liu, Michael Meister, Vivek Nanda and K. N. Panikkar. My special thanks go to Susan Reynolds, not only for observations on specific chapters but also for many conversations about the book. I was delighted when Ravi Dayal suggested that he might like to read the penultimate draft and ploughed his way through it, with helpful remarks on what he had read. Naina's postings of 'not clear' have hopefully made the narrative more lucid. Lucy Peck gallantly agreed to do rough drafts of all the maps, thus allowing me to include maps relating to every chapter. I would also like to thank the Homi Bhabha Fellowships Council for the award of a Senior Fellowship. The research carried out during this period contributed to the shaping of the earlier half of this book. And I would also like to thank David Ludden for arranging a series of lectures at the University of Pennsylvania which broadly covered the same themes.

Gene Smith was fantastically generous with time and effort when he painstakingly scanned the earlier version onto disk and this made the mechanics of rewriting much easier. Shirish and Gautam Patel and Chris Gomes have been unruffled by my frequent cries for help when the computer behaved unpredictably, and have patiently set me right, a patience also shown by Vivek Sharma. Rajani was the one person who over the years kept insisting that I revise the earlier book, and finally her insistence has had effect.

Romila Thapar
New Delhi
2001

Acknowledgements

Every effort has been made to contact copyright holders. The publishers shall be happy to make good in future editions any errors or omissions brought to their attention. The author would like to thank the following for permission to use copyright material in this book: extract from *The Universal History of Numbers* by George Ifrah published by the Harvill Press and used by permission of the Random House Group Ltd; extract from R. Parthasarathy's translation of *The Tale of an Anklet* by permission of Columbia University Press; extract from S. Radhakrishnan's translation of *The Principle Upanisads* by permission of HarperCollins Publishers; extracts from Nilakantha Sastri's *The Colas* and Romila Thapar's *Asoka and the Decline of the Mauryas* by permission of Oxford University Press, New Delhi; extract from Ronald Latham's translation of *The Travels of Marco Polo* by permission of Penguin Books Ltd; extracts from A. K. Ramanujam's translations of *Hymns for the Drowning* by permission of Princeton University Press; extracts from A. L. Basham's *The Wonder that was India* by permission of Macmillan Publishers; extracts from Indira V. Peterson's *Poems to Siva: The Hymns of the Tamil Saints* by permission of the author; illustration of Nagara-style temple by permission of Michael Meister; Circular Deri temple plan by permission of Vidya Dehejia; Circular Devi temple plan by permission of Nilakanta Sastri and A. K. Ramanujan.

Note on the Bibliographies

A General Bibliography is included at the end of the book, with a broad coverage of books providing introductions to major aspects of the subject.

Select Bibliographies in the nature of further readings and specific to each chapter are grouped according to chapters and their subheadings. Books are listed in the order of the subject matter discussed within the text.

Bibliographies are limited to monographs as these are more accessible than articles in journals. However, since much of the new research is in papers in journals these journals are also listed for those who may wish to consult them.

Chronology

c. 1000 BC – AD 1300

The chronology of the earlier part of Indian history is notoriously uncertain compared to that of China or the Mediterranean world. Literary sources can belong to a span of time rather than a precise date. However, this ambiguity is offset in the data from inscriptions that are usually precisely dated, often in a known era. Most of the important dynasties of the early period used their own system of reckoning, which resulted in a number of unconnected eras. But among the more widely used eras are the Vikrama era of 58–57 BC and the Shaka era of AD 78. The Vikrama era was known earlier as the Krita or the Malava era. Others include the Gupta era of AD 319–20, the Harsha era of AD 606, the Vikrama-Chalukya era of AD 1075 and a variety of others. Buddhist sources generally reckon from the year of the death of the Buddha, but there are three alternative dates for this event – 544/486/483 BC. It is more usual to use either of the two latter dates, the first being generally doubted. Lately, there has been much discussion on the date of the Buddha and suggestions have taken this chronology to almost a hundred years later. But as yet there is no generally accepted agreement on a date, other than the traditional.

BC

c. 2600–1700	Harappan urbanization: Mature and Late Harappan
c. 1500–500	Composition and compilation of the Vedic corpus
	Neolithic and chalcolithic cultures in various parts of the subcontinent
	Megalithic burials, largely in the peninsula
c. 1000	Availability of iron artefacts
	Use of iron artefacts gradually increases in range and number after the sixth century BC

c. 6th century	Urbanization in the Ganges Plain
	Formation of the earliest states
	The rise of Magadha
	Mahavira
	Gautama Buddha
519	Cyrus, the Achaemenid Emperor of Persia, conquers parts of north-western India
c. 493	Accession of Ajatashatru
486	Death of the Buddha
c. 362–321	Nanda dynasty
327–325	Alexander of Macedon in India
321	Accession of Chandragupta, the founder of the Maurya dynasty
268–231	Reign of Ashoka
c. 250	Third Buddhist Council held at Pataliputra
185	Termination of Mauryan rule and accession of a Shunga king
180–165	Indo-Greek rule in the north-west under Demetrius
c. 166–150	Menander, the best known Indo-Greek ruler
c. 94	Maues, the Shaka King, in north-western India
58	Azes I, thought to have founded the Vikrama era
c. 50	Rise of Satavahana power in the Deccan
c. 50	Kharavela, King of Kalinga

AD

c. 50 BC–AD 50	Peak period of Roman trade with India
1st century AD	Kushana power established
? c. 78	Accession of Kanishka, Kushana King of the north-west Founding of the Shaka era
c. 125	Gautamiputra and subsequently Vasishthiputra ruling the Satavahana kingdom
c. 150	Rudradaman, the Shaka Kshatrapa King ruling in western India
319–20	Accession of Chandra Gupta I, founder of the Gupta dynasty
335	Accession of Samudragupta
375–415	Chandra Gupta II
405–11	Visit of Fa Hsien
c. 455	Skandagupta, in whose reign the Hunas attack north India

Introduction

A book originally written when one had just been initiated into the profession, now being revised late in life, has elements of an autobiography. Returning to a book of almost forty years ago has brought home to me the substantial changes in the readings of early Indian history, some arising out of new data and many more from new interpretations of the existing data. There has been much discussion on these readings and my participation in these has shaped my own understanding of this period. The attempt here is to incorporate such readings that I think are valid without writing an entirely different book. Inevitably, however, there is much that is different in this book. Many ideas that were merely glanced at in the earlier version have now been further drawn out. One may not have been aware of it at the time, but the earlier version was written at a nodal point of change when early Indian history, which had begun essentially as an interest in Indology, was gradually becoming part of the human sciences – a change that I hope to demonstrate in the first chapter on historiography. I have stayed largely within the framework of the earlier book since I thought it was still viable and did not require radical alteration. Chapters have been re-oriented so that some contain more new material, while in others the emphasis is on new interpretations. The reading of early Indian history has seen considerable changes in the last four decades and I have sought to capture these in the narrative that follows.

The new readings emerged from various ongoing assessments. Some were of colonial interpretations of the Indian past, which also had to contend with the attitudes to Indian culture that were prevalent in the period just after Indian independence. In the popular imagination of Europe, India had been the fabulous land of untold wealth, of mystical happenings and of an association with ideas that reached beyond mundane experience. From gold-digging ants to philosophers who lived naked in the forests and meditated on the after-life of the soul, these were all part of the picture of India formed by the ancient Greeks, for example, and these images persisted in Europe into more recent centuries. As in every other ancient culture, wealth in India was limited to the few. Publicizing myths, such as that of the rope trick, was also the preoccupation of just a handful of people. It is true, however, that acceptance – sometimes bemused – of such notions was more extensive in India. Whereas in some cultures the myth of the rope trick would have been ascribed to the prompting of the devil, and all reference to it suppressed, in India it was received with a mixture of belief and disbelief. A fundamental sanity in Indian civilization has been due to an absence of Satan.

Other reactions contending with earlier colonial and nationalist views of Indian culture were different. One was the rather simplistic reaction of annulling or reversing negative statements about Indian civilization and exaggerating the positive statements – a reaction that now seems to be capturing some part of the popular Indian imagination. The more serious concern with history was its recognition as a discipline with a method, including the search for readings that incorporated viable alternative ways of explaining the past. It is the latter that is being set out in this book.

To begin at the beginning then, is to start by asking how histories of India[1] came to be written, who the historians were, why they were writing and what were the intellectual and ideological influences that shaped their histories, in short, that which is now called historiography. History is not information that is handed down unchanged from generation to generation. Historical situations need to be explained and explanations draw on analyses of the evidence, providing generalizations that derive from the logic of the argument. With new evidence or fresh interpretations of existing evidence, a new understanding of the past can be achieved. But interpretations have to conform to the basic requirements of using reliable evidence, analytical methods and arguments drawing on logic. Following from these, a sensitivity is needed to the ways in which people from earlier times led their lives and thought about their past. Historiography therefore becomes a prelude to understanding history as a form of knowledge.

Interpretations frequently derive from prevalent intellectual modes. These constitute shifts in the way history is read. Looking at how histories are written is in part the intellectual history of the period under discussion and can therefore be vibrant with ideas and explanations. The starting point in the history of a society, therefore, has to be a familiarity with its historio-

1 This book covers the early part of the history of pre-modern south Asia. Terms such as 'India' and 'Indian' apply to the subcontinent, except where specified as referring to the modern nation state of India.

graphy – the history of historical interpretation. This provides recognition of the intellectual context of history, instead of setting this aside with a preference for just a narration of events. Familiarity with the context encourages a more sensitive understanding of the past. This awareness of historiography has contributed substantially to the change in understanding Indian history over the last half-century.

Historiographical change incorporates new evidence and new ways of looking at existing evidence. The inclusion of perspectives from other human sciences such as studies of societies, economies and religions has led to some important reformulations in explaining the past, resulting primarily from asking different questions from the sources than had been asked before. If earlier historical writing was concerned largely with politics, today it includes virtually all human activities and their interconnections. These are crucial to the argument that the image of reality, as reflected in the human sciences, is socially and culturally controlled and that actions have multiple causes. Advances in knowledge would inevitably change some of these perspectives. Historical explanation therefore creates an awareness of how the past impinges on the present, as well as the reverse.

Among the new sources of evidence, quite apart from the occasional coin, inscription or sculpture, have been data provided by archaeology, evidence on the links between environment and history, and the insights provided by historical and socio-linguistics. Aspects of the oral tradition, when used in a comparative manner, have often illustrated the methods that are used to preserve information, either by societies that are not literate or by those that chose to use the oral form in preference to the literate. The possibility of applying these methods to an earlier oral tradition has been revealing.

In recent years the early history of India has increasingly drawn on evidence from archaeology, which has provided tangible, three-dimensional data in the artefacts and material remains discovered through survey and excavation. These were once used to corroborate the evidence from literary and textual sources (and in some theories about ancient India they continue to be thus used). But archaeological data may or may not corroborate literary evidence, and, where they do not, they provide an alternative view. In the absence of written evidence, or where the written evidence remains undeciphered, artefacts can fill lacunae. The corroboration is not one-to-one since archaeological data are substantially in the form of artefacts, whereas textual information is abstract, and both are subject to the intervention of the historian's interpretation. The relationship of archaeological data with literary evidence is complicated and requires expertise in each category.

Reacting against the earlier tyranny of the text, some archaeologists today would deny the use of texts, even in a comparative way.

Sophisticated methods of excavation and the reading of excavated data are far more complex than in the days when an archaeologist had merely to dig and to discover. Various techniques from scientific disciplines are being used in the analyses of archaeological data, and the scope of the information provided by these has expanded enormously to include data on climate, ecology, settlement patterns, palaeo-pathology, flora and fauna. Palaeo-botany – the study of plant and seed remains from an excavation – relates to flora and environmental conditions, and therefore adds another dimension to the understanding of human settlements. Some of this data can lend itself to a modicum of statistical analysis.

India still sustains an extensive range of societies, some even suggesting a stone age condition. This 'living pre-history', as it has been called, underlines the continuity of cultural survivals. Attempts are now being made in the cross-discipline of ethno-archaeology to correlate ethnographic studies with the excavations of human settlements. The correlating may raise some doubts, but the usefulness of such studies lies in the asking of questions, for instance, on forms of social organization or on the functions of artefacts. In areas where there are some cultural survivals, these procedures can endorse the assistance occasionally provided by fieldwork as an adjunct to textual studies, and, as has been rightly argued, this is particularly pertinent to the study of religion in India. Fieldwork provides insights that can enhance the meaning of the text. The changes that occur, for instance, in rituals incorporate elements of history, particularly in societies where for many people ritual activity or orthopraxy is more important than theology or orthodoxy. The entirely text-based studies of religions are now being supplemented by comparative studies of the practice of various religions.

Impressive evidence, both in quality and quantity, has come from sites dating to the second and first millennia BC excavated during the past half-century. It is now possible to map the settlements of the period subsequent to the decline of the first urban civilization in north-western India and this provides some clues to the successor cultures. This raises questions of whether there were continuities from the earlier cultures. Equally significant is the identifying of the nature of successor cultures. There is also evidence on some of the precursor settlements in the Ganges Plain and its fringes in central India, providing clues to the nature of the second urbanization of the mid-first millennium in the Ganges Plain. However, these questions can only be answered after there have been horizontal excavations of the major sites, an activity that awaits attention. Megalithic burials of various kinds, dating from the late second millennium BC, are especially characteristic of the peninsula. Their origins and relationships to settlements remain somewhat enigmatic, but at least they provide evidence of cultural levels and networks prior to the information from inscriptions, coins and texts.

Recent studies of archaeological data have led to an interest in the environment as a factor in the making of history. This began with the long debate on whether the decline of the Indus cities was substantially due to environmental degradation. To this has been added the evidence of the drying up of the Ghaggar-Hakra River in northern India, with related hydraulic changes and their historical implications. Archaeological evidence has also been used to suggest a decline in urban centres during the Gupta period, thus questioning its claim to being an age of considerable urban prosperity. Artefacts can be examined as pointers to technology, leading to the examination of the role of technological change in history. There has been an extended discussion, for example, on the role of iron technology – particularly in the clearing of forests and the use of the iron ploughshare as processes related to urbanization in the Ganges Plain.

Archaeological evidence has also underlined the significance of geography to history, particularly in understanding the location of settlements, the movements of peoples and the creation of states. Large unitary kingdoms were more easily hosted in the northern Indo-Gangetic Plains. The southern half of the subcontinent, the peninsula, was divided into smaller regions by mountains, plateaus and river valleys – a topography that made the functioning of expansive kingdoms more difficult. In an age of empires, as the nineteenth century was, the large kingdoms of the north attracted the attention of historians. Periods when such kingdoms flourished were described as 'Golden Ages' and those that saw the growth of smaller and more localized states were viewed as the 'Dark Ages'. The history of the peninsula received far less attention, except when it too could boast of large kingdoms. It suffered further from the fact that political strategy in the peninsula and its economic potential differed from that of the north. This is particularly noticeable in the deployment of maritime commerce as part of the economy in some states.

Among the more interesting departures from earlier views has been the realization that particular geographical regions do not remain pivotal to historical activity permanently. They can and do change, as do the regions that are their peripheries. Sometimes multiple centres share the same history and at other times the centres have diverse histories. Why such regions change and how this affects historical evolution is in itself a worthwhile exploration. The recognition of the region and its links with geomorphology and ecology is drawing the attention of historians. However, a region in the Indian subcontinent cannot become an isolated historical entity, and regional histories inevitably have to be related to larger wholes. Detailed studies of regions have inducted an interest in landscape and how it has changed. The agencies of change are dependent on geology, geomorphology and human activity, but what needs to be looked at more closely is the effect of a change in landscape on history. The most obvious examples of this are changes in river courses or deforestation. We still tend to presume that the landscape of today was also the landscape of yesterday.

Associated with fieldwork is the study of oral traditions, which has been used by anthropologists in deriving material for analysing myths and for kinship patterns. Although myths need not go back to earlier times, they can in some cases carry forward earlier ideas. But because of their fluid chronology, and the fact that they are generally not records of actual happenings, myths can only be used in a limited way. Mythology and history are often counterposed and myth cannot be treated as a factual account. Yet the prizing out of the social assumptions implicit in a myth can be helpful to reconstructing some kinds of history. The interpretation of myths, if handled with caution, can invoke some of the fantasies and subconscious beliefs of their authors, while the structure of the myth can hint at the connections and confrontations in a society of those sustaining the myths. Since history now reflects many voices, some from sources other than those from the courts of rulers, the oral tradition or the more popular traditions are no longer dismissed as unimportant. Obviously the survival of the oral tradition is from a recent period, but a familiarity with the techniques of assessing an oral tradition has been helpful in re-examining texts that were once part of an early oral tradition. Oral sources were sometimes preserved through being so carefully memorized that the text almost came to be frozen, as in some of the Vedic ritual compositions. Alternatively, the memorization was less frozen and more open, with a composition such as the epic poetry of the *Mahabharata*, and many interpolations became possible. The ways in which oral traditions work provide a variety of approaches to such texts.

Linguistics is another field that is proving helpful to historians of early India. Analysing a word helps to explain its meaning and, if it can be seen in a historical context, much is added to the meaning. Words such as *raja* – initially meaning chief and subsequently king – constitute a history of their own and have a bearing on historical readings. Socio-linguistics provides evidence of how words can point to social relationships through the way in which they are used. Given the connection between languages and the fact that languages change, both through use and through communication between speakers of different languages, such change becomes a significant adjunct to other historical evidence. The study of a language from the perspective of linguistics is not limited to similarities of sound or meaning, but involves a familiarity with the essential structure of the language – grammar, morphology, phonetics – and this is more demanding that just being able to read and write a language.

Linguistic diversity may well have been registered in the Indian subcontinent from earliest times, which might explain part of the problem in attempting to decipher the Indus script. Among the many languages used in India, Tibeto-Burman, for example, has been associated with the north-eastern and Himalayan fringes. The Austro-Asiatic group of languages, particularly Munda, clusters in parts of central and eastern India. It could have been more widespread if one believes the mythology of its speakers or, for that matter, the evidence of some of the linguistic elements which occur as a substratum in the earliest Indo-Aryan compositions. Dravidian is likely to have been more extensively used than it is now, with groups of speakers in central India and with four major languages derived from it in the peninsula, not to mention the pocket of Brahui in the north-west of the subcontinent. The reason why, or the way in which, a language either spreads or becomes restricted, has historical explanations.

Indo-Aryan spread gradually over northern India, incorporating some elements of Austro-Asiatic and Dravidian. It bears repeating that Indo-Aryan is in fact a language label, indicating a speech-group of the Indo-European family, and is not a racial term. To refer to 'the Aryans' as a race is therefore inaccurate. The racial identities of speakers of Indo-Aryan languages are not known. When textual sources refer to *arya* the reference is generally to an identity that involves language, social status and associated rituals and custom. It is in this sense that the term is used in this book.

Other than archaeological data, there have been no major sources of new evidence that would radically change our understanding of the period. The recent discovery of important inscriptions and coins has clarified some ambiguities. The exploration of textual data has led to evidence being gathered from texts of historical importance, but in languages other than Sanskrit. Perhaps the most significant change with regard to textual sources is a greater recognition that important authoritative, didactic texts, or even the epics, as we have them today, were not necessarily written at a precise point in time. They have been edited over long time periods and inter-polations have been incorporated. A single authorship for a text is not insisted upon. The tradition of writing and using texts in the early past was different from the way in which we view authorship and texts today. It was recognized that a succession of authors, generally of the same persuasion, could edit the same text. The authorship, audience and purpose of a text are also now receiving attention when data is gathered.

The problems of the chronology of these texts remains as complicated as before, and this prevents their being closely related to a particular period. A large number of texts of other genres, for instance creative literature, are of single authorship, even if their chronology is sometimes uncertain. These have been used in making comparative linguistic analyses. Some attempts have also been made in sifting linguistic style and usage to ascertain the history of the compilation of a text. Such sifting has been facilitated on a few occasions through the use of computers, although this technique is not entirely without hassles.

One of the current debates relating to the beginnings of Indian history involves both archaeology and linguistics, and attempts to differentiate between indigenous and alien peoples. But history has shown that communities and their identities are neither permanent nor static. Their composition changes either with the arrival of new people in an area, and the possible new technologies that are introduced, or by historical changes of a more local but far-reaching kind. Some areas are more prone to change, such as borderlands, mountain passes and fertile plains, whereas densely forested areas or deserts may retain their isolation for a longer period until such time as there is a demand on them for resources. To categorize some people as indigenous and others as alien, to argue about the identity of the first inhabitants of the subcontinent, and to try and sort out these categories for the remote past, is to attempt the impossible. It is precisely in the intermixture of peoples and ideas that the genesis of cultures is to be found. Such arguments arise from the concerns of present-day privilege and power, rather than from the reading of history.

It was not just the landscape that changed, but society also changed and often quite noticeably. But this was a proposition unacceptable to colonial perceptions that insisted on the unchanging character of Indian history and society. The concentration on dynastic histories in the early studies was due to the assumption that in 'Oriental' societies the power of the ruler was supreme even in the day-to-day functioning of the government. Yet authority for routine functions was rarely entirely concentrated at the centre in the Indian political systems. Much that was seen as essentially centralized in theories such as 'Oriental Despotism' was in actual fact localized through the functions of caste and of other organizations. The understanding of political power in India involves analyses of caste relationships and institutions, such as the guilds and rural and urban councils, and not merely a survey of dynasties. That the study of institutions did not receive much emphasis was in part due to the belief that they did not undergo much change: an idea derived from the conviction that Indian culture had been static, largely owing to the lethargy of the Indian and his gloomy, fatalistic attitude to life. Yet even a superficial analysis of the changes in social relationships within the caste structure, or the links between politics and economic systems, or the vigorous mercantile activities of Indians throughout the centuries, points to anything but static behaviour or an unchanging socio-economic pattern. At certain levels there are aspects of cultural traditions in India that can be traced to roots as far back as a few thousand years, but such continuity should not be confused with stagnation. The chanting of the *gayatri*[1] hymn has a history of three millennia, but its current context can hardly be said to have remained unchanged from earlier times, and for the historian the context is as important as the content of the hymn.

In common with all branches of knowledge, the premium on specialization in the later twentieth century has made it impossible to hold a seriously considered view about a subject without some technical expertise in the discipline. Such expertise enhances both the pleasure and the understanding of what is under study. To be able to read a text or a coin legend or an inscription is the bare minimum of knowledge required: some familiarity with the mathematics of numismatics, the semiotics of symbols and the contextual dimensions of a text make history a far richer discipline than it was thought to be. The interpretation of a text draws on its authorship, intention, audience, historical context and its interface with other texts of its kind. As a result there is a distance between the professional historian and the amateur writing history. The function then of a history such as this is to provide some flavour of the richer taste emerging in historical research.

My attempt in this book is to treat political history as a skeletal framework in order to provide a chronological bearing, even if chronology is not always certain. This also introduces a few names of rulers as a more familiar aspect of early Indian history. However, the major focus of each chapter is the attempt to broadly interrelate the political, economic, social and religious aspects of a period with the intention of showing where and why changes have occurred and how these in turn have had an effect on each aspect. Where there are continuities these will become apparent. The subdivisions in each chapter, therefore, are not meant to suggest separate entities, but

1 A hymn from the *Rig-Veda*, evoking the solar deity, and regarded as particularly holy.

are pointers to what is significant in that period. The contents of the chapters do not exactly match the periods listed in the first chapter in my reconsideration of periodization, but the book does follow the pattern suggested.

The pattern of change moves from small societies and states with a relatively uncomplicated organization to the emergence of more complex societies, often accompanied by large states and the requirements of such states. In summary form, the latter included a variety of facets, such as: the need to administer extensive territory, literally, in terms of the reality on the ground; agrarian and commercial economies of varying kinds; diverse social forms, some of which were viewed as part of a uniform caste organization, while others were described as deviant forms; the structures of knowledge and the way in which their ideological formulations were linked to other aspects of society and culture; manifold religious sects expressing social concerns, as well as incorporating ideas that ranged from mythology to philosophical notions; creative literature of various kinds; the location of sacred sites that gave a tangible presence to religious sects and their varied forms of worship. Implicit in the listing of these items are the ways in which they are linked, and their forms are either influential or fade away. The discussion of these links and the changes they bring about, in other words the explanation of historical change, will hopefully unfold in the narrative.

It is assumed that much of the history that is discussed here emerges out of the existence of states, or at least the recognition of forms of political organization. The formation of a state is a recognized historical process, accompanied by concentrations of settlements that can evolve into towns. The presence of the state introduces more complexities into a situation than in societies where states are yet to evolve. This also introduces the notion that there can be varieties of states in early history. The patterns taken by a state can differ in accordance with its constituents. Ascertaining the particular pattern of the state, or the way in which the state functions, also becomes a way of observing the history of the period and place. The emergence of states need not be simultaneous in every area, for this transformation can also occur in other times and places. Periodization therefore tends to describe a significant change over a substantial area, but in earlier periods it need not necessarily have applied to every region. The change gradually becomes more uniform.

The structure of administration that helped to define the nature of the state began as a rudimentary form of ensuring the functioning of a particular form of government, for instance chiefship or kingship. It tended to become increasingly complex as it had to be adjusted to the environment – forests, pastures, deserts, fields, mountains, seas – and the environment could be diverse in the large states, which sometimes prevented a neat, uniform administration. The notion of governance, therefore, was modified up to a point by local requirements. The balance between the concentration and the distribution of power was another determining factor of administration, as was the control over resources. Theories of governance would both have influenced, and been influenced by, the form of administration. Territory included within a state could be defined by campaigns where a successful campaign brought in more territory, or else the existing territory could be eroded if the campaign failed. Such demarcations derive from politics, but also, although to a lesser extent, from terrain.

Economies were matched to the patterns of states and to the power that they wielded. Agrarian economies varied in relation to ecology, crop patterns, methods of irrigation and the hierarchy of control over agricultural land. The latter was initially diverse, but slowly evolved into forms that extended over large areas. The forms grew out of matters relating to sources of power, resources for the economies and the diverse methods of obtaining and controlling human labour. The growth of cities is also a pointer to commerce, with trade being the most effective economy in some areas. Histories of India in the past have been essentially land-locked, with maritime trade playing a marginal role. This is now being corrected by the attention given to maritime trade, both in terms of the commercial economy and the creation of new social identities involving traders who settled in India.

There has been a tendency to treat caste as a uniform social organization in the subcontinent. But there are variations in terms of whether landowning groups or trading groups were dominant, a dominance that could vary regionally. The hierarchical ordering of society became uniform, but there were ways of handling the hierarchy that introduced regional variations. Both agriculture and commerce allow a different set of freedoms to, and restrictions on, castes. This raises the question of whether in some situations wealth, rather than caste-ranking, was not the more effective gauge of patronage and power. The formation of castes is now being explored as a way of understanding how Indian society functioned. Various possibilities include the emergence of castes from clans of forest-dwellers, professional groups or religious sects. Caste is therefore seen as a less rigid and frozen system than it was previously thought to be, but at the same time this raises a new set of interesting questions for social historians.

The manifold expressions of structured knowledge are generally seen as tied to philosophical notions, as indeed they were. But not all categories of knowledge were invariably divorced from technological practices and texts. The techniques of preserving knowledge or the methods of advancing knowledge are diverse, ranging from the oral to the literate, and incorporate, at various levels, the technological as well as the theoretical. Equally important are the intellectual contestations between the heterodoxy and the orthodoxy, between the nature of belief and the nature of doubt.

Creative literature is characteristic of every period, but the predominant forms that it takes would appear to vary. The great oral compositions, such as the epics, date to earlier times, while the more courtly literature of the educated elite became more frequent from the early centuries of the Christian era. Nevertheless, even if courts fostered poetry and drama of a sophisticated kind, the popularity of the epics continued. This popularity is demonstrated from time to time in the choice of themes for courtly literature, selected from the popular literature, but of course treated in a different manner.

Similarly, religious literature ranges from ritual texts to the compositions of religious poets and teachers intended for a popular audience, and the intricacies of the philosophical discourse intended for other audiences. Since the sources are largely those of the elite, we have less information on the religions of ordinary people, and what we do know comes indirectly from the sources. Possibly the excavation of settlements in the future will provide more data on popular religion. But from what can be gathered there appears to have been a considerable continuity at the popular level, for example in the worship of local goddesses – as would be expected.

Apart from the study of texts, on which the initial understanding of Indian religions was based, the history of religions in India has been studied by investigating cults with information on ritual and belief, and working on the history of sects that extends to the social groups supporting particular beliefs and forms of worship. Arguing that Vedic Brahmanism – drawing its identity from the Vedic corpus – was a religious form associated with socially dominant groups, supporting practices and beliefs that could be seen as an orthodoxy, there have been studies of movements that have distanced themselves in various ways from Vedic Brahmanism. The Shramana group – Buddhism, Jainism and various 'heterodox' sects – is one such well-established group. More recently, sects within the Hindu tradition deriving their identity from the texts known as the *Agamas* and the *Puranas*, variously linked with or distanced from the orthodoxy, are being seen as constituting what some historians of religion prefer to call Puranic Hinduism or the Puranic religions. The distinguishing features relate to differences in belief and ritual from Vedic Brahmanism. The history of these sects points to processes that either retain their distinctiveness or else encourage an accommodation with Vedic Brahmanism, although the two are not equated.

Close identities between religious sects and castes are frequent in Indian religion and the multiplicity of reasonably independent sects has led some scholars to speak of the Hindu religions (in the plural). The term 'Hindu' to describe a religious identity came into currency as late as the second millennium AD. Prior to that, sectarian identities were more frequently referred to, since the over-arching term *Dharma* included not only sacred duties but also a range of social obligations. Sects are not invariably formed by breaking away from a historical religious mainstream, but are at times born from a mosaic of belief, worship and mythology coming together. Relating religious sects to castes as segments of society provides pointers to where religious and social concerns overlap. What is of greater interest is the manner in which some of these popular manifestations of religion find their way into the religious activity of the elite.

This last aspect also introduces a dimension relating to the history of art that perhaps requires a fuller integration into history. The history of art is no longer confined to discussing an image isolated in a museum or a structure seen as an entity by itself. Each is part of a larger history. Architecture, for instance, has also to be viewed as representing an institution, and both institutional and aesthetic needs would determine form. In many ways narrative art provides a bridge, whether it be stories relating to the life of the Buddha or the mythology surrounding deities. At one level these are representations of reality, but are not merely that, and their other meanings also have to be read. Similarly, there remains the perennial question of whether the icon of a deity is to be viewed primarily as an aesthetic object or a religious representation, or both, or much more. There is also the question raised by art historians as to when an image becomes a stereotype. This is related to the question of the identities of artists or architects. These remain largely anonymous in the earlier periods, barring an occasional name, and it is only in the later period that names are mentioned more frequently so that we learn something about them. But even this information is limited, although we know relatively more about their patrons. Our contemporary aesthetic concerns become primary, although these are different from the aesthetics of earlier times. As has been rightly said, we have to assess how much was routine and how much was inspired by the ideals of their time, which means that historians have to recover 'the period eye'.

Implicit in these lists of items, and in their narration and discussion as aspects of the past, are theories of explanation. My attempt to address these aspects leads to a presentation of how history moved and societies changed in the Indian subcontinent. There is now far greater sensitivity among historians of early India about the way in which early history is written and the intellectual dimensions of this historiography. Four decades ago, this was a preliminary inquiry but it has since become a theme of considerable historical interest. This has also made historians more aware of their own location on the historiographical map. To that extent, historical argument has become more demanding and more taut. Given the centrality of theories of explanation in the historical research that has followed, the narrative of history has been encouraged to present connections between the personalities of the past, their activities and the degree to which they made or were made by their historical context where information is available. However, barring a few exceptions, it is the historical context that has primacy, which is evident also in the shift of focus to the group. Inevitably, the range of players has increased with some attention to groups earlier thought to be insignificant and to activities earlier thought to be marginal. The change aims at a more integrated understanding of a complex society, its various mutations, its creativity and its efforts at enhancing its contributions to civilization.

I

Perceptions of the Past

Colonial Constructions: Orientalist Readings

The modern writing of Indian history began with colonial perceptions of the Indian past that were to be seminal to its subsequent interpretations. It took shape with the beginnings of colonial rule in various parts of the subcontinent from the eighteenth century onwards. European scholars searched for histories of India but could find none that conformed to the familiar European view of what a history should be, a view influenced in part by the thinking of the European Enlightenment. The only exception according to them was the twelfth-century history of Kashmir, the *Rajatarangini*, written by Kalhana. They saw India only as a Hindu and Sanskritic civilization, so they set aside the numerous chronicles written largely in Persian by court poets and chroniclers of the Turkish, Afghan and Mughal rulers. These were regarded as alien to Indian civilization, even though their contents concerned Indian society and politics and the people whom they wrote about had settled in India to become part of Indian society. There was as yet little familiarity with other sources in Sanskrit such as local chronicles or, for that matter, the lengthy inscriptions issued by various rulers that were in effect dynastic annals.

Hindu and Sanskritic elements were highlighted as the contribution of India to world history and the presence of other religious and linguistic cultures, such as Buddhism, Jainism or even Islam as it evolved in India, were barely recognized in terms of constructing Indian civilization. Concession to the importance of Buddhism came later. The initial hostility to Islam was doubtless aggravated by European antagonism due to historical reasons, beginning with the Crusades. If the role of Islam was conceded at all, it was said to be negative, and such judgements were based on little or no evidence since the history of Islam in India had not been investigated at this point.

That there could be other ways of perceiving the past or that Indians might have seen their history in a different manner was discounted. Societies were divided into those who have a sense of history and those who lack it. Indian civilization was described as a-historical. Not only were there no histories of India, but the absence of history was also explained by arguing that the concept of time in early India was cyclic. Therefore, all human activities were continually repeated in each cycle. This was inimical to a historical perspective that required each event to be seen as unique, a view endorsed by a linear concept where time moves not in a circle but in a straight line, from a given beginning to a stipulated end. Ways of looking at the Indian past in the form of genealogies, chronicles and annals, which conformed to linear time, were certainly studied for the reconstruction of the chronology of rulers, but their obviously linear dimension was ignored in discussions on the concept of time. That there is evidence of both linear and cyclic time in early India, and that the most insightful way of appreciating this would be to see the intersections of the two, was an idea alien to these scholars.

Since there was no recognizably connected narrative of the happenings in the Indian subcontinent since earliest times, the modern writing of history began with narratives constructed from this early European inquiry: hence the references to the 'discovery' or the 'rediscovery' of the Indian past. History as a distinctive discipline was coming into its own in Europe and was being moulded by a variety of practitioners. The sense of the past that emerged from ideas fostered by the European Enlightenment gave shape to the writing of history, as did influential historical works such as the narrative of the Roman Empire by Edward Gibbon. Inevitably, the imprint of the European image of India drew on these earlier reconstructions, an imprint that has now faded with the questioning of these readings.

Initially, there were two major strands in the European interpretation of Indian civilization, which came to be known as the Orientalist and the Utilitarian. These developed from the studies made by British officials working for the British East India Company, trading with India, some of whom held office in India and some in England. The administrative functions of the East India Company required that its officers be knowledgeable about Indian practices and norms, particularly when parts of India came under the administration of the Company and eventually became colonies. This led to the officers studying Sanskrit, Persian, Bengali, Tamil and various other Indian languages, as well as writing grammars in English that became essential tools for this study. Administrative requirements also encouraged the translation of what were believed to be legal codes, such as the *Dharma-shastras*, which were actually not codes of law but norms relating to social obligations and ritual requirements.

Much of this activity was fostered by the belief that knowledge about the colony would enable a greater control over it and would provide a firm foundation to the power that the colonial authorities exercised. This was thought to be 'the necessary furniture of empire' and the recasting of this knowledge became as important as its acquisition. In the course of investigating what came to be called Hinduism, together with various aspects of its belief, ritual and custom, many were baffled by a religion that was altogether different from their own. It was not monotheistic, there was no historical founder, or single sacred text, or dogma or ecclesiastical organization – and it was closely tied to caste. There was therefore an overriding need to fit it into the known moulds of familiar religions, so as to make it more accessible. Some scholars have suggested that Hinduism as it is formulated and perceived today, very differently from earlier times, was largely born out of this reformulation. In India, diverse and multiple religions were practised, with royal patronage extending to more than one. This was a contrast to the European experience where a single religion – Christianity – and sometimes only a single division within this religion, either Roman Catholicism or Protestantism, received royal patronage.

Such activities encouraged what have come to be called Orientalist studies, and the major British scholars initially associated with them were William Jones, Henry Colebrooke, Nathaniel Halhead, Charles Wilkins and Horace Hyman Wilson. Some of their initial research and seminal papers were published as monographs, with many more in *Asiatic Researches*, a periodical of the Asiatic Society of Bengal established in 1784. There was much discussion at the meetings of the Asiatic Society in Calcutta, focusing largely on the origins and reconstruction of language and on religion and custom. But, curiously, membership of the Society was not open to Indians for many years, even though those presenting their findings were being trained by Indian scholars.

European missionaries and visitors to India in preceding centuries had noticed the similarities between Sanskrit and some European languages. William Jones now set the connections in a more systematic framework. He also suggested the monogenesis of these languages, tracing them back to a common ancestor. Grammars and analyses of Sanskrit confirmed connections between Sanskrit, Greek and Latin, and led eventually to the discipline of comparative philology. Some attempts were also made to relate the chronology of the ancient texts, the *Puranas*, with Biblical chronology, but this was not successful. A son of Noah was said to have migrated to India to establish the Indian population but the evidence for this was found wanting! Comparisons between Greco-Roman and Indian deities were among the early attempts at comparative religion, and Indian mythology fired the romantic imagination of Europe.

Interpretations of the Indian past, growing out of these studies, were inevitably influenced by colonial concerns and interests, and also by prevalent European ideas about history, civilization and the Orient. Orientalist scholars studied the languages and the texts with selected Indian scholars, but made little attempt to understand the world-view of those who were teaching them. The readings therefore are something of a disjuncture from the traditional ways of looking at the Indian past. European preconceptions imprinted on the readings gradually came to influence the way in which Indians themselves viewed their own culture. This reordering of Indian culture facilitated the direction given even to the self-perceptions of Indians.

Orientalism fuelled the fantasy and the freedom sought by European Romanticism, particularly in its opposition to the more disciplined Neo-Classicism. The cultures of Asia were seen as bringing a new Romantic paradigm. Another Renaissance was anticipated through an acquaintance with the Orient, and this, it was thought, would be different from the earlier Greek Renaissance. It was believed that this Oriental Renaissance would liberate European thought and literature from the increasing focus on discipline and rationality that had followed from the earlier Enlightenment. This in part accounts for the enthusiasm for India in the writings of German authors, such as Herder, or the brothers Wilhelm and Auguste Schlegel, or Novalis. Others, such as the English poets Wordsworth and Coleridge, were apprehensive of the changes introduced by industrialization and turned to nature and to fantasies of the Orient.

However, this enthusiasm gradually changed, to conform with the emphasis later in the nineteenth century on the innate superiority of European civilization. Oriental civilizations were now seen as having once been great but currently in decline. The various phases of Orientalism tended to mould European understanding of the Indian past into a particular pattern. In the late nineteenth century it also influenced the emerging Indian middle class in its understanding of its own past. There was an attempt to formulate Indian culture as uniform, such formulations being derived from texts that were given priority. The so-called 'discovery' of India was largely through selected literature in Sanskrit. This interpretation tended to emphasize non-historical aspects of Indian culture, for example the idea of an unchanging continuity of society and religion over 3,000 years; and it was believed that the Indian pattern of life was so concerned with metaphysics and the subtleties of religious belief that little attention was given to the more tangible aspects.

German Romanticism endorsed this image of India, and it became the mystic land for many Europeans, where even the most ordinary actions were imbued with a complex symbolism. This was the genesis of the idea of the spiritual east, and also, incidentally, the refuge of European intellectuals seeking to distance themselves from the changing patterns of their own societies. A dichotomy in values was maintained, Indian values being described as 'spiritual' and European values as 'materialistic', with little attempt to juxtapose these values with the reality of Indian society. This theme has been even more firmly endorsed by a section of Indian opinion during the last hundred years. It was a consolation to the Indian intelligentsia for its perceived inability to counter the technical superiority of the west, a superiority viewed as having enabled Europe to colonize Asia and other parts of the world. At the height of anti-colonial nationalism it acted as a salve for having been made a colony of Britain.

Colonial Constructions: A Utilitarian Critique

The other strand in the European interpretation of the Indian past was a critique of Indian culture. It drew from the Utilitarian, legalistic philosophy current in Britain, and was largely the contribution of those writing on India but based in Britain. This interpretation is best represented in the views of James Mill and Thomas Macaulay and was partially endorsed, but for quite other reasons, by the Evangelicals among the Christian missionaries. Mill, writing his *History of British India* in the early nineteenth century, was the first to periodize Indian history. His division of the Indian past into the Hindu civilization, Muslim civilization and the British period has been so deeply embedded in the consciousness of those studying India that it prevails to this day. It is at the root of the ideologies of current religious nationalisms and therefore still plays a role in the politics of south Asia. It has resulted in a distorting of Indian history and has frequently thwarted the search for causes of historical change other than those linked to a superficial assessment of religion.

Indian civilization was said to lack the qualities that Europe admired. For instance, the perceived emphasis on the values of rational thought and individualism was said to be absent, and India's culture was seen as stagnant.

This attitude was perhaps best typified in Macaulay's contempt for things Indian, especially traditional Indian education and learning. The political institutions of India, visualized largely as the rule of Maharajas and Sultans, were dismissed as despotic and totally unrepresentative of public opinion. And this, in an age of democratic revolutions, was about the worst sin. Mill's *History of British India*, in which he argued these propositions, became a hegemonic text in the nineteenth century which influenced many commentators and administrators associated with India. Mill's views were echoed in aspects of colonial policy, increasingly concerned with the conquest of the subcontinent and the restructuring of its economy to suit colonial requirements.

The Utilitarian critique of India argued that backwardness can be remedied through appropriate legislation, which could be used by the British to change the stagnant nature of Indian society that had prevented its progress. Mill's insistence on these negative features reflected his use of this description as part of his campaign to legislate change in Britain. Many of the debates assessing the condition of India can be better explained through a familiarity with the current debates on political economy in Britain at that time.

A theory often associated with the Utilitarian view of Asian civilizations was that of Oriental Despotism. This visualized a system of government consisting of a despotic ruler with absolute power, said to be characteristic of Asian societies. Such societies featured the existence of isolated, self-sufficient village communities whose surplus produce was creamed off by the despotic ruler and his court, governing through an autocratic bureaucracy. The latter controlled irrigation, which was a prerequisite for agriculture dependent on water management, and also organized the collection of surplus produce. Much of Asia was thought to be arid and dry, irrigation being provided by the state and controlled by the bureaucracy to ensure a surplus agricultural income providing revenue for the despot. The peasant was kept subjugated and had little freedom; cities were largely administrative centres and there was hardly any commercial exchange; the association of divinity with kingship strengthened the status of the king. According to this theory, Oriental Despotism encapsulated the political economy of Asian empires.

This view can be traced to early Greek sources perceiving the Persian Achaemenid Empire of the mid-first millennium BC as despotic. The Greeks themselves were not averse on occasion to despotic behaviour, but their view of Asian societies as culturally alien led to exaggerated accounts. To this was added the vision of luxurious Oriental courts, a vision deriving in part from the luxury trade with the east since early times, and partly on the fantasy world of the east as described by Greek visitors. The Greek physician Ktesias at the Persian court, for instance, let his imagination run riot in describing the marvels, mysteries and wealth of the eastern lands. The Crusades and the ensuing literature on the Turks would have strengthened these notions, many of which were exaggerated to impress European audiences.

Given the concerns of eighteenth-century France and England, the central question was seen as private ownership of land. The theory of Oriental Despotism assumed there was no private ownership of land in Asia and that the king owned all the land. There had been a controversy between Voltaire, supported by the Physiocrats, arguing against the state ownership of land in Asia and Montesquieu, who held the contrary opinion. The standard text on the traditional economy of India used in Haileybury College, where administrators were trained before going to India, was that of Richard Jones who endorsed the theory. The standard history was that of James Mill who also did not question this idea. Those who came to administer India assumed the essential viability of the theory, and some among them were also the pre-eminent historians of the period writing on India.

The theory became axiomatic to the interpretation of the Indian past in the nineteenth century, particularly that aspect which concerned land relations and the rights of the state over the cultivator. The nature of ownership of land was debated, as was the question of who was the owner – the king/state, the individual cultivator or the village community. The village community was sometimes projected as an autonomous republic or as a collective for gathering and paying taxes. These debates were reflected in the writings of administrators and historians, such as Henry Maine, Baden-Powell, Munroe and Montstuart Elphinstone. In the process of answering these questions, conditions in pre-colonial India began to assume importance. Land ownership and revenue collection by the state became themes of historical study, but the exploration of these questions was influenced by the prevailing preconceptions about the Indian past.

India as 'The Other'

Trends such as these, deriving from Orientalist and Utilitarian notions about Asia, led, in the latter part of the nineteenth century to treating Asia as significantly different – 'the Other' of Europe. The central question related to the lack of a capitalist system in Asia, and the answers were thought to lie in the pre-modern history of Indian society and religion. The analyses of Karl Marx, in what he called the Asiatic Mode of Production, envisaged despotism and stagnancy as key characteristics which nullified movements towards change parallel to that of Europe. In the absence of private property there were no intermediary groups between king and peasant, nor classes or class conflict of a kind that would lead to dialectical change. This was further nullified by the absence of commercial centres and cities specializing in production for a market which, if they had existed, might have encouraged economic change. The theory of the Asiatic Mode of Production has been resorted to from time to time in the last century for reasons of current politics to explain the inability of Asian societies to develop capitalist systems. Accepting the idea of Oriental Despotism, Karl Wittfogel argued that the control of the irrigation system – the hydraulic machinery – lay in the hands of the bureaucracy in Asian states, and this allowed the ruler to be despotic. The theory was widely discussed by Asian Marxist historians, who pointed out that there was little historical evidence to support it. The question of technologies, such as irrigation and their impact on Indian history, is in any case far more complex than the simplistic notion of bureaucracies controlling water management and thereby the entire economy.

Another area that brought forth debates among those involved with Indian administration in the nineteenth century concerned the origins of caste. The possible genesis was said to be from regulations of kinship and marriage or occupation, religious functions or political hierarchies. Caste was linked to religion and the close connection between the two was seen as a barrier to economic change. This was discussed in Max Weber's study of the religion of India, focusing on Hinduism. Castes were projected as distinct and separate, with no social action across castes being possible. Max Weber was also concerned with the non-emergence of capitalism in India, but his perspective was different from that of Karl Marx. He surveyed a variety of religious sects, and the underlining feature that he emphasized was the absence of a Puritan ethic in their belief and function. This for him was a crucial factor in the emergence of capitalism in Europe. The Puritan ethic favoured frugality, saving and investment of wealth, a commitment to a vocation and a concern with the salvation of the soul. Economic rationality had to be present in the religious teaching of the ethic. The economic rationality of a number of Hindu, Buddhist and Jaina sects was thought to have played a marginal role. Even those Islamic sects in India that were significant to its commerce, and whose religious perceptions were heavily infused with the local religious interests of commercial castes, were excluded, since India was seen as a Hindu civilization. Curiously, the contribution of colonialism to the emergence of capitalism in Europe was given no attention in this analysis. The intention was to depict a situation in contrast to the European, even if the depiction had to be exaggerated.

Weber's study of Indian society in terms of its caste components and its interface with religious activity was not an isolated interest. This was an area in which a number of philologists, sociologists and specialists of religious studies of the late nineteenth and early twentieth centuries had developed an interest, often seeing the Indian evidence as indicative of a different system from those now familiar to European scholars. Emile Durkheim's studies helped to recognize survivals from earlier societies in the rituals of later historical periods. His demarcation between beliefs and rituals was significant to later studies of Vedic sacrifice, and the centrality of deity to religion and its absence in Buddhism was also a matter of considerable debate in defining religion. Marcel Mauss and H. Hubert analysed the ritual of sacrifice in some detail, particularly in attempts to separate the sacred from the profane. Mauss's work on gift-giving was pathbreaking in examining the links between social and religious relationships, and early Indian texts were central to these studies. Celestin Bougle raised the question of whether caste was characteristic of Hindu society alone, or whether it could be found in other societies. This led him to define caste as more pertinent to *jatis* – hereditary groups arranged hierarchically, with unequal rights, a separation based on taboos of marriage rules, food and custom, and a resistance to unification with others. This was a different analysis from that of many Indologists, for whom the definition of caste was restricted to *varna* or ritual status and viewed in terms of brahmanical culture. *Jati* and *varna* did not annul each other, but had different origins and functions.

'Discovering' the Indian Past

When European scholars in the late eighteenth century first became curious about the past of India their sources of information were largely brahmans, who maintained that the ancient tradition was preserved in Sanskrit works about which they alone were knowledgeable. Thus, much of the early history of India was reconstructed almost entirely from Sanskrit texts, and reflected views associated with their authors. Many of these works were texts on religion or manuals of ritual, which coloured the interpretation of early Indian culture. Even texts with other concerns often had brahman authors and commentators, and were therefore biased in favour of those in authority, generally adhering to brahmanical theories of society irrespective of whether or not they had widespread historical applicability. For example, caste as described in texts such as the *Dharma-shastras* referred to *varna* distinctions, a hierarchy of ritual status creating a closed stratification of society, apparently imposed from an early period and thereafter preserved almost intact for many centuries. The lower castes were seen from the perspective of the upper-caste brahman authors of the texts. Yet the actual working of caste in Indian society permitted of variation, in accordance with local conditions, which the authors of the *Dharma-shastras* were reluctant to admit.

It is curious that there were only a few attempts to integrate the texts studied by Indologists with the data collected by ethnographers. Both constituted substantial but diverse information on Indian society. Presumably the bifurcation was influenced by the distinction between 'civilized' and 'primitive' peoples, the latter being said to have no literature. Those who studied oral traditions were regarded as scholars but of another category. Such traditions were seen as limited to bards, to lower castes and the tribal and forest peoples, and as such not reliable when compared to the texts of the higher castes and the elite. Had the two been seen as aspects of the same society, the functioning of caste would have been viewed as rather different from the theories of the *Dharma-shastras*.

The use of evidence from a variety of different sources that were later to become dominant was a challenge to certain aspects of textual evidence, but a corroboration of others, thus providing a more accurate and less one-sided picture of the past. Evidence from contemporary inscriptions, for example, became increasingly important. A small interest developed in genealogies and local chronicles. James Tod gathered information from bards and local chronicles for a history of various Rajput clans, but this did not lead to greater interest in collecting bardic evidence or assessing the role of bards as authors of local history. Tod tended to filter the data through his own preconceptions of medieval European society, and was among those who drew parallels with European feudalism, albeit of a superficial kind. He popularized the notion that the Rajputs were the traditional aristocracy and resisted Muslim rule, disregarding their political alliances and marriage relations with Muslim rulers. L. P. Tessitori made collections of genealogies and attempted to analyse them, but these never found their way into conventional histories. He too consulted local bards in Rajasthan and collected their records.

Those interested in studying the Indian past and present through its languages and literatures, its ethnology and religion, gradually increased. The nineteenth century saw considerable advances in what came to be called Indology – the study of India by non-Indians, using methods of investigation developed by European scholars in the nineteenth century. In India the use of modern techniques to 'rediscover' the past came into practice. Among these was the decipherment of the *brahmi* script, largely by James Prinsep. Many inscriptions pertaining to the early past were written in *brahmi*, but knowledge of how to read the script had been lost. Since inscriptions form the annals of Indian history, this decipherment was a major advance that led to the gradual unfolding of the past from sources other than religious and literary texts. Epigraphic sources introduced many new perspectives that have as yet not been exhausted. They were used for firming up historical chronology but their substantial evidence on social and economic history, as also on the history of religious sects, was recognized only subsequently. Numismatics took off from reading bilingual coin-legends, some in Greek and *brahmi* on the Indo-Greek coins minted at the turn of the Christian era. The name of the king written in Greek had an equivalent written in *brahmi*, which provided some clues to the decipherment of *brahmi*. Alexander Cunningham explored the countryside searching for archaeological remains, using the seventh-century itinerary of the Chinese Buddhist monk, Hsüan Tsang, as a guide, and summarized his explorations in *The Ancient Geography of India*. Professionally, many of these scholars were surveyors and engineers, charting the colony in more senses than one. Textual analyses, which had begun with Sanskrit texts, were now slowly including Pali texts associated with Buddhism and, later, Prakrit texts of the Jaina tradition. This was careful, meticulous work and enlarged the data on the Indian past. The interpretation of what was found was of course most often within the framework of a colonial perspective on the Indian past.

Many who had visited India from afar in the early past recorded their impressions for various purposes, and these are available as Greek, Latin, Chinese and Arabic writings, which provide different perspectives from the Indian. The descriptions of the visitors can sometimes be correlated with the more tangible remains of the past made possible through excavations. The corpus of evidence on Buddhism, for instance, was increased with the availability of the chronicles from Sri Lanka. Buddhist Canonical texts translated into Chinese and various central Asian languages filled in lacunae, in some cases providing significant variant readings. Similarly, texts in Arabic and Persian relating to the history of India began to be studied in their own right, and ceased being regarded only as supplements to Islamic culture in western Asia. Strangely, Indians travelling outside the subcontinent do not seem to have left itineraries of where they went or descriptions of what they saw. Distant places enter the narratives of story-telling only very occasionally.

Notions of Race and their Influence on Indology

Linguistic studies, especially those of Sanskrit grammarians, helped develop the discipline of comparative philology in Europe, which in turn led not only to encouraging the study of the early languages of Asia but also to re-reading the early history of Eurasia. The study of Sanskrit and the ethnography of India also fed into what was emerging as a new perspective on human society, the discipline of 'race science' as it came to be called. Race was a European invention that drew from a variety of contemporary studies and situations, such as the categorizing of plants by Linnaeus, Social Darwinism arguing for the survival of the fittest, and the triumph of imperialism that was used to claim superiority for the European.

Social concerns, which later incorporated racial attitudes, governed the British approach towards their empire. Traditional aristocracies were regarded as racially superior and their status upheld prior to their being incorporated into the new colonial hierarchy. This also enhanced the status of the colonizer. Traditions could be invented, drawing on a supposed history and legitimizing authority. But theories of race were also applied to larger categories of people, believed to be the authors of civilizations.

F. Max Müller is one example of a scholar who reflected on race while studying Sanskrit. His major contribution to the interpretation of Indian history was the reconstruction of a perceived Aryan presence, or even on occasion a race, from his study of the *Vedas*. Like Mill, Max Müller did not think it necessary to visit India, yet he projected Indian society as a reversal of the European, evidenced by his books *India, What Can it Teach Us?* and *Biographies of Words and the Home of the Aryas*. His fanciful descriptions of Indians made of them a gentle, passive people who spent their time meditating. His study of Vedic Sanskrit and philology brought him to his theories about the Aryans. In showing the similarities between Sanskrit, Greek and Latin, William Jones had argued for a monogenesis of language, suggesting that they had all descended from an ancestral language. Indo-European was now projected as such a language, a hypothetical language reconstructed from known languages that were related to each other within a structure of linguistic rules. This was often incorrectly extended to equating all those who spoke Indo-European languages with membership of an Aryan race. In the latter half of the nineteenth century discussions on social inequality were often projected in racial terms as in the writings of Gobineau.

Max Müller maintained that the Aryans had originated in central Asia, one branch migrating to Europe and another settling in Iran, with a segment of the Iranian branch subsequently moving to India. He dated the earliest composition of the latter, the *Rig-Veda*, to about 1200 BC. The Aryans, he maintained, had invaded in large numbers and subordinated the indigenous population of northern India in the second millennium BC. They had introduced the Indo-Aryan language, the language of the conquerors who represented a superior civilization. The latter emerged as Vedic culture and became the foundation of Indian culture. Since a mechanism for maintaining racial segregation was required, this took the form of dividing society into socially self-contained and separate castes. The racial imprint may also have been due to the counterposing of *arya* with *dasa*, since it was argued that in the earliest section of the Vedic corpus, the *Rig-Veda*, the *dasa* is described as physically dissimilar to the *arya*, particularly with reference to skin colour. This was interpreted as the representation of two racial types. Race was seen as a scientific explanation for caste and the four main castes or *varnas* were said to represent the major racial groups. Their racial identity was preserved by the strict prevention of intermarriage between them.

The equation of language and race was seen to be a fallacy even by Max Müller, but there was a tendency to use it as a convenient distinction. In his later writings he clarified this fallacy, but by then it had become common currency. That Aryan should have been interpreted in racial terms is curious, since the texts use it to refer to persons of status who speak Sanskrit and observe caste regulations. The equation had still wider ramifications. It appealed to some of those working on Dravidian languages, who proposed that there was a Dravidian race speaking Dravidian, prior to, and distinct from, the Aryan. They quoted in support the fact that Indo-Aryan is an inflected language, and therefore quite distinct from the Dravidian languages which are agglutinative. Gradually, Proto-Dravidian was projected as the original language and came to be equated with Tamil, which is not a historically or linguistically valid equation. Proto-Dravidian, like Indo-European, is a hypothetical language reconstructed from known Dravidian languages of which Tamil was one, and therefore Tamil would have evolved later. The theory of a Dravidian civilization prior to the coming of the Aryans was to be reinforced in the 1920s by the discovery of the cities of the Indus civilization, Mohenjo-daro and Harappa, dating to the third millennium BC.

The reaction in India to the theory of Aryan race was wide-ranging, even among those who were not historians. It came to be used – and continues to be used – in the political confrontations of various groups. This is demonstrated by two examples at the extreme ends of the spectrum. Jyotiba Phule, an authority for the Dalits, argued in the late nineteenth century that the Sanskrit-speaking brahmans were descended from the Aryans who were alien to India, and that the indigenous peoples of the lower castes were therefore the rightful inheritors of the land. This argument assumes a conflict between the dominant upper caste and the conquered, oppressed lower castes. This was the foundation of caste confrontation and an explanation for caste hierarchy. It was later to be used extensively in those political movements that sought to justify their non-Brahmin and anti-Brahmin thrust, especially in south India.

At the opposite end, some are now propagating an interpretation of Indian history based on Hindu nationalism and what has come to be called the Hindutva ideology. Since the early twentieth century, this view has gradually shifted from supporting the theory of an invasion to denying such an event, now arguing that the Aryans and their language, Sanskrit, were indigenous to India. The amended theory became axiomatic to their belief that those for whom the subcontinent was not the land of their ancestors and the land where their religion originated were aliens. This changed the focus in the definition of who were indigenous and who were alien. The focus moved from caste to religion: the aliens were not the upper castes, but Muslims and Christians whose religion had originated in west Asia. The Communists were also added to this group for good measure! According to this theory only the Hindus, as the lineal descendants of the Aryans, could be defined as indigenous and therefore the inheritors of the land, and not even those whose ancestry was of the subcontinent, but who had been converted to Islam and Christianity.

Mainstream historians of an earlier period differed from both these interpretations, particularly the second. They accepted the theory of an invasion, with the introduction of Indo-Aryan and its speakers as the foundation of Indian history. This appealed to members of the upper castes who identified themselves as the descendants of a superior race – the Aryans – some insisting that membership of this race implied a kinship connection with the British! The theory provided what was thought to be an unbroken, linear history for caste Hindus. However, the discovery of the Indus civilization and its city culture in the 1920s contradicted this theory of linear descent. The cities of the Indus civilization are of an earlier date than the composition of the Vedic corpus – the literature of the Indo-Aryan speaking people – and do not reflect an identity with this later culture. The insistence on a linear history for the Hindus is now the reason for some attempts to take the Vedic culture back in time and identify it with the Indus civilization. Today mainstream historians argue that despite little archaeological evidence of a large-scale Aryan invasion with a displacement of the existing cultures, there is linguistic evidence of the Indo-Aryan language belonging to the Indo-European family, having been brought to northern India from beyond the Indo-Iranian borderlands and evolving through a series of probably small-scale migrations and settlements.

A close affinity can be observed between the present-day Hindutva view of 'the Aryans' and nineteenth-century colonial views, in particular the theories of some Theosophists. Colonel Olcott, for example, was among the early Theosophists who maintained that the Aryans were indigenous to India, as was the language Indo-Aryan; that Aryan culture as the cradle of civilization spread from India to Europe; and that the Aryan literature – the Vedic corpus – was the foundation of knowledge. Such Theosophical views attracted some of the nineteenth-century Indian socio-religious reform movements, such as the Arya Samaj. The Theosophical movement in India had a number of British and European members, some of whom may have endorsed these ideas as a form of sympathy for Indian nationalism. The late nineteenth and early twentieth centuries were times when there were links between various wide ranging or alternatively narrowly focused assortments of ideas, some of which involved theories of race, of the Aryans, of Theosophy and of nationalisms.

By the mid-twentieth century, the notion that language and race can be equated was found to be invalid, and indeed the entire construction of unitary races was seriously doubted. The concept of an Aryan race fell apart. Race is essentially a social construct, although initially it was claimed to be based on biology. Recent genetic studies have further invalidated this claim. It is therefore more correct to refer to 'the Indo-Aryan speaking peoples' than to 'the Aryans', although the latter term can be used as a shorthand. It is important to emphasize that it refers to a language group and not to race, and language groups can incorporate a variety of people.

History and Nationalism

As we have seen, those who were most directly concerned with India in the nineteenth century were the British administrators, many of whom wrote on the history of India. Such histories tended to be 'administrators' histories', recounting the rise and fall of dynasties and empires. This was also the predominant subject of historical study in Europe at that time. Admiration for the Roman Empire was imprinted both on those involved with the British Empire and on historians, such as Vincent Smith, writing on Indian history at the turn of the century; the first empire provided the model for the second. The protagonists of history were kings and the narration of events revolved around them. The autocratic king, oppressive and unconcerned with the welfare of his subjects, was the standard image of the Indian ruler, with a few exceptions such as Ashoka, Chandra Gupta II and Akbar. As for actual governing, the underlying assumption was that British administration was superior and a centralized bureaucracy was the best form of administration.

In the late nineteenth century Indian historians followed the model of political and administrative history, producing dynastic histories highlighting the lives of rulers. But colonial explanations of the Indian past were not always acceptable to Indian historians. Historical theories were part of the growing political contestation, particularly now that the close relationship between power and knowledge was being tacitly recognized. The evolution of an Indian middle class familiar with the English language indicated more communication between the colonizer and the colonized.

Most Indian historians of the early twentieth century were either participants in the national movement for independence or influenced by it. Prominent among them, and expressing varying degrees of nationalist sentiment, were R. Mitra, R. G. Bhandarkar, R. C. Dutt, A. S. Altekar, U. N. Ghoshal, K. P. Jayaswal, H. C. Raychaudhuri, R. K. Mookherjee, R. C. Majumdar, K. A. Nilakanta Sastri and H. C. Ojha. Historical interpretation often drew from existing views but could be changed to what was now regarded as a legitimate nationalist interpretation. Nationalist historians tended to endorse the more favourable views from colonial readings of the early past, but criticized the unfavourable. Thus, it was asserted that some institutions such as democracy and constitutional monarchy were familiar to the Indian past. References to the *mantriparishad*, the council of ministers, were compared to the working of the British Privy Council. Non-violence was praised as a special Indian contribution to civilization, yet at the same time the Gupta King, Samudragupta, was described as the Napoleon of India and his conquests much lauded. Nationalism was taken back to the fourth century BC with the opposition to Alexander's campaign and the creation of the Mauryan Empire that extended over virtually the entire subcontinent. Aryan Vedic culture was viewed as the foundation of Indian civilization, its antiquity taken back to the second millennium BC. The emphases on indigenous origins of many past achievements were gradually becoming visible. There was an objection – not surprisingly – to the theory of Oriental Despotism, but an endorsement for the ancient past being a 'Golden Age'; such an age being a prerequisite for claims to civilization. This view was an inevitable adjunct to nationalist aspirations in the early twentieth century. The Golden Age was either the entire Hindu period that was seen as unchanging and universally prosperous, or else the reign of the Gupta kings which historians, both Indian and British, had associated with positive characteristics and revival of the brahmanical religion and culture.

Cultural achievement was measured in terms of the arts, literature and philosophy, with less attention to descriptions of social realities. It also put a premium on Sanskrit sources compared to those in Pali, Prakrit or other languages. Sanskrit had been the language of the courts and of upper-caste Hinduism. What were regarded as lesser languages were assumed to have been used by people of lesser status. Sanskrit texts were given priority even where there were variants of the same narrative in other languages. Such variants, although known, were seldom analysed in a historically comparative way, a case in point being the different versions of the story of Rama. The Buddhist telling of the story in the Pali *Jatakas*, or the Prakrit versions of Jaina authors, were discussed in the context of the study of the *Jatakas* or of Jaina texts but seldom in a comparative way with similar works in Sanskrit, such as the *Ramayana* of Valmiki.

Linked to this was a *bête noire*, casting its shadow on much of the early writing on ancient India. European historians working on this period had been brought up on the classical tradition of Europe, believing that the greatest human achievement was the civilization of the ancient Greeks – *le miracle Grec*. Consequently, every newly-discovered culture was measured against the norms set by ancient Greece and invariably found to be lacking. Or, if there were individual features worth admiring, the instinct was to try and connect them with Greek culture. Vincent Smith, for some decades regarded as the pre-eminent historian of early India, was prone to this tendency. When writing of the murals at the famous Buddhist site at Ajanta and particularly of a painting supposedly depicting the arrival of an embassy from a Sassanian king of Persia, unconnected with Greece both artistically and historically, he states:

The picture, in addition to its interest as a contemporary record of unusual political relations between India and Persia, is one of the highest value as a landmark in the history of art. It not only fixes the date of some of the most important paintings at Ajanta and so establishes a standard by which the date of others can be judged, but also suggests the possibility that the Ajanta school of pictorial art may have been derived from Persia and ultimately from Greece.

Early History of India (Oxford, 1924), p. 442

Indian historians reacted sharply to such statements. Attempts were made to prove either that India had not derived any part of its culture from Greece or else that the culture of India paralleled that of Greece, manifesting all the qualities that were present in the latter. That every civilization emerges out of interactions with others, but nevertheless creates its own miracle, was not yet recognized by either European or Indian historians. The notion of the osmosis of cultures shaping histories was still to come.

While European historians of the early twentieth century attempted to discover patterns of change and evolution, Indian history was seldom approached from this perspective. It was treated as a series of islands in time, each named after a particular dynasty. This is not to suggest that studies on other aspects were ignored, but these tended not to be integrated into the history of a period. Valuable and interesting information was collected on various aspects of Indian society and religious practices, but this information rarely found its way into standard historical works, or even into the histories of religion, and tended more often to be indexed as studies pertaining to particular tribes, castes and communities. An Indologist with a more open approach to Indian culture, interested in the new influences then entering the study of ancient Indian history, was A. L. Basham. His awareness is evident from his sensitive and historically rigorous handling of Indian cultural history in his classic work, *The Wonder That Was India*. This was also an early attempt at extending the parameters of history.

Emphasis on dynastic history endorsed the division of Indian history into three major periods, Hindu, Muslim and British, with a later change of nomenclature to Ancient, Medieval, and Modern, which is still prevalent as a periodization. Since the time brackets remained the same, the earlier division prevailed despite the change of nomenclature. The Ancient period begins with the Indus civilization, which replaced what was termed 'the Aryan period' in earlier histories, and concludes with the Turkish raids on northern India in the eleventh and twelfth centuries and the establishing of the Delhi Sultanate in the thirteenth century AD. This inaugurates the Medieval period, lasting until the coming of the British in the mid-eighteenth century. The equation of Ancient with Hindu, and Medieval with Muslim, was based on the fact that many dynasties of the first period were Hindu while those of the second were Muslim. The Muslim period was imbued with a distinctive character that distinguished it from the earlier period by emphasizing the separateness of Muslim and Hindu culture at all levels. Justification for this thesis was sought in the writings of the theologians and court chroniclers of Muslim rulers. At the best of times, court interests are distant from those of the populace and all the more so when the chronicler or the historian focused on eulogizing the ruler as an exemplary patron of his religion. Court chronicles the world over have to be decoded and cannot be taken as factual accounts. In any case, the political trends dominant in early twentieth-century India justified the separate religious nationalisms by referring to (among other things) the Hindu and Muslim periodization, endorsed by many Indian and non-Indian historians. Only a few questioned its validity. But such a periodization of Indian history is misleading in its emphasis, apart from being questionable in its assumptions. The religious affiliation of rulers was not the pre-eminent motivating factor of change in Indian history, as these categories would imply: it was one among a number of factors.

Indian historians initially tended to follow the pattern established by European historians and wrote largely on dynastic history. But, with the growing presence of a nationalist ideology, the nationalist interpretation of Indian history gained importance. Seminal to this approach was the Indian liberal tradition of the early nineteenth century – as in the writings of Rammohun Roy – and the questioning of negative features attributed to the Indian past, as in the theory of Oriental Despotism. History, as a major component in the construction of national identity and culture, became a subject of contestation between the anti-colonial nationalists and those supporting colonial views, although some colonial views such as those of the Orientalists found a sympathetic echo in nationalist writing. Nationalism seeks legitimacy from the past and history therefore becomes a sensitive subject. Even if nationalist history did not introduce a new explanation of the Indian past, it was nevertheless a powerful voice in the debate on the past.

The Seeding of Communal History

Indian nationalist history challenged aspects of colonial historiography and thereby helped to release historical writing from the imprint of the more negative colonial theories about the Indian past. But by endorsing other theories that provided positive images of the Indian past some historical interpretations emerged even more deeply embedded in these colonial theories. Instead of being reassessed they became foundational to yet other kinds of histories claiming to be nationalist. 'Nationalist' histories of this latter kind are defined by a single category, for instance, that of religion. Muslim and Hindu nationalisms drew from anti-colonial, nationalist ideology for legitimacy, but converted their interests into a nationalism that confined itself to the articulation of a single concern – interpreting history in terms of monolithic religious identities. These ideologies have their roots in the nationalist phase of historical writing but are generally more effective as sources for political mobilization following the success of anti-colonial nationalism. These tendencies, because their appeal is to emotion and to faith, can threaten the intellectual foundations of historical discourse. This has happened with attempts to write both Muslim and Hindu nationalist histories (not to mention others at regional levels). Their refusal to countenance other approaches to explaining the past results in contentious views of history.

Identity in pre-colonial India was dependent on various features such as caste, occupation, language, sect, region and location. As late as the eighteenth century caste was often given primacy over religion, although caste and the religious sect could overlap. But in the colonial reconstruction of Indian society religion was given primacy, particularly as the imprint of identity. Colonial historians argued that, with the arrival of groups professing Islam, there was a confrontation between Hinduism and Islam which led to the crystallization of two communities, the Hindu and the Muslim. Social and political interaction was therefore perceived in terms of the two communities and this duality governed the interpretation of Indian history. Further, it was believed that the importance of caste segmentation of Hindu society was set aside and Muslim society was thought not to have caste identities. Both these propositions are now being questioned. The history of India of the second millennium AD is no longer seen in terms of the confrontation between two religious communities, and social identities drawn from caste, occupation, language and region are being recognized as equally important to these religious communities.

Nevertheless, the influence of interpretations conditioned by what is called communal history, or history based on religious nationalisms, continues. This is different from anti-colonial nationalist history, despite an occasional overlap. Whereas the nationalist perspective was wide-angled and inclusive, that of communal historical writing is narrowed down to projecting the history of a particular community, identified by a monolithic religion being pre-eminent, and excludes the study of others. Muslim religious nationalism sees Indian history in terms of the role of the Muslim community *vis-à-vis* the Hindu, while Hindu religious nationalism projects the Hindu community as confronting the Muslim, despite the large percentage of the population regarding an identity in these terms as ambiguous in the past. Communal history does not attempt to analyse the nature of communities and their changing history. Each community is seen as a homogeneous whole and defined as a uniform, monolithic, religious community functioning as a unit of history.

Religious nationalism retains the colonial periodization of Indian history and the fundamental interpretation that India consists of the majority Hindu community and the minority Muslim community, with other lesser minority communities. Historical causes are explained as arising almost entirely from matters of religion, which are frequently assumed to be confrontational. For some, if the 'Hindu' period was an unblemished Golden Age, the 'Muslim' period was a Dark Age, and this imagery is reversed by those of the alternative persuasion. The justification for the two-nation theory that led to the partition of India in 1947 was facilitated by the belief that the Hindu and the Muslim communities have, from the start of their relationship in Indian history, constituted two distinct nations; therefore a Muslim and a Hindu nation-state in our time were historically inevitable.

The 'Hindu' period having been described as a Golden Age, there is a hesitation to accept critical evaluations of events and people during this time. The normative texts are taken at face value and read as descriptions of the perfect harmonious society. It is stoutly maintained, for example, that pre-Islamic India was a tolerant society, and references to religious and social intolerance are dismissed as incorrect readings of the source or are ignored.

Some of the limitations of nationalist history were also reflected in regional history when histories of regions were first written in the early twentieth century. The periodization of Hindu, Muslim and British was assumed to be universally applicable. The chronology of this application was far from uniform, with Muslim rule registering a start in the eighth century AD in some areas and a millennium later in others. Regional history developed partly as a reaction to projecting Indian history from the perspective of the Indo-Gangetic Plain, as was often the case in early writing. It was further encouraged by the attention given to local source material with the establishing of new states in the Indian Union after 1947, each anxious to claim its own history. The definition of a region in accordance with the boundaries of present-day states is self-defeating, since such boundaries are themselves the result of historical actions. It would be more appropriate for regional history to use regions as defined in the geography of India.

Research on regional sources is increasing, some of which has modified the earlier perspective of subcontinental history. It also helps in analysing historical problems at greater depth. For instance, because the pattern of caste configurations varies from region to region, instead of searching for the fourfold castes everywhere it would be more helpful to investigate the variations. Similarly, the variant patterns in the environment, resources and economies of the regions can assist in defining aspects of regional history. A more recent trend, again borrowing from one of the concerns of nationalist history, is the introduction, in some instances, of the history of the currently dominant community as coinciding with the history of the region. This tends to warp the overall history of the region. Ideally, the importance of regional history is not only to provide more information about an area, but also to signify variations and similarities, so that generalizations about historical change at the larger level can be more precise.

Marxist Histories and the Debates they Generated

A paradigm shift in the understanding of historical change in India was introduced by Marxist interpretations that began as historical debates from the 1950s onwards. The historical writings of D. D. Kosambi, in particular, encapsulated this shift. An interest in social and economic history rather than dynastic history alone had been initiated and this was now intensified, calling for a different periodization drawing on social change. There was a questioning of Marx's own model for India, contained in his Asiatic Mode of Production, and this was by and large set aside, although there were some historians and sociologists who thought that even if it was not applicable in its entirety it raised worthwhile questions. Its weakness was common to many nineteenth-century theories about Asia, in that early nineteenth-century sources for Asian history available to European scholars were very limited while the available sources had not been explored in any depth.

Kosambi, in his *Introduction to the Study of Indian History*, moved away from dynastic history to describing what he perceived as the dynamics of economy and society in various phases of Indian history. He underlined the importance of what he called 'living prehistory' and cultural survivals that enable us to reconstruct archaeological and historical cultures with greater empathy. His familiarity with the Maharashtrian countryside gave him an insight into the readings of early texts, which led him to new perspectives of the ancient past. His essays in *Myth and Reality* were an even more innovative exploration of the social basis of ideological concepts, resulting in creative analyses of a range of themes from mother goddesses to microliths, pilgrimage routes and the *Bhagavadgita*. Kosambi's intention was to indicate the stages through which he thought Indian society had moved, and the reasons for the change. There may be a debate today about the stages, a debate that has been influenced by other theories of social change, but it cannot be doubted that a pattern of change existed. There is an increasing range of explanations for this change, with some suggesting additional causal features.

The critique of the Asiatic Mode of Production did not lead to the dismissal of Marxist analyses. Attempts were made to see whether other modes of production, such as the Slave Mode of Production or the Feudal Mode of Production, could be used to explain aspects of pre-modern Indian history. The maximum discussion and the most intensive debate was generated over the question of whether there was a Feudal Mode of Production or even feudalism in the Indian past. This opened up a number of new perspectives on the nature of the state, changing economies at different times and the interrelations between religions and social groups.

Earlier comparisons with feudal Europe had tended to be based on rather impressionistic readings which did not provide an explanation of how such societies could have functioned in India. The first systematic analysis was that of Kosambi, who viewed the period as embodying a form of the Feudal Mode of Production, rather than being just a period of small states. Seminal to his discussion was his modification of the Marxist model – what he called feudalism from above and feudalism from below: that from above was where feudatories were directly subordinate to the ruler without the intervention of other intermediaries; and feudalism from below created a hierarchy of landowning intermediaries between the king and the peasant. The two phases have not generally been accepted, but the broad argument endorsing feudalism has been discussed. It was said that the existing land economy was restructured through the ruler giving substantial grants of land to religious beneficiaries, or to officers for their services. In time, the grant was accompanied by a transfer of fiscal and juridical rights from the ruler to the grantees, which converted the latter into landed intermediaries with extensive rights to exploit the labour of the peasant. Whether the form of exploitation was the equivalent of serfdom remains debatable. Charters that had earlier been read only for information on dynasties, kings and chronologies were now being analysed for social and economic data. Cultural and ideological dimensions of feudal society were also introduced into the discussion.

Both the application and the critique of the feudal mode initially came from Marxists. The concept of Indian feudalism was discussed in a number of spirited controversies, eventually attracting both Marxists and non-Marxists. A lively debate was thus initiated on the decentralization of state power and the use of resources and labour, as well as on the religious expressions that arose at this time. Feudalism, as a historical process, is still debated among historians writing of this period, and draws on various models. The Marxist concept of the Feudal Mode of Production is the more familiar category as a starting point. It focuses on the distinct categories of landowners and peasants with family holdings, the relationship between the two being characterized by coercion or a threat of force by the former, who appropriate surplus from the latter and demand labour taxes of various kinds. There is however the problem that its genesis does not lie in the transition from slavery to serfdom, as in Marx's sequence for Europe, since although there was slave labour in India, a Slave Mode of Production that some associated with Europe did not prevail and there is no unanimity regarding the prevalence of serfdom in India. The genesis of feudalism has to be sought in other changes.

Some have preferred other models of feudalism, such as that which seeks to follow the more general description of medieval Europe with its society of fiefs and vassals, but with variations. This was not necessarily replicated in India, but approximations could provide fresh readings of a comparative kind. Thus many medieval societies functioned through coercing a subject peasantry, which was in turn controlled through service tenures since land was the basis of relationships and power was decentralized in such societies. The term 'feudal' has been applied to such diverse situations that it is difficult to provide a single definition, applicable to all.

The recognition of variants in modes of production drew from the idea that a dialectical method could be used to arrive at formulations about history, but it need not follow the stipulated five stages or modes as described by Marx, of which primitive communism, slavery and feudalism would pertain to pre-colonial history. Thus some theories derived from Marxism have departed from the framework of the modes defined for Europe and have also been influenced in their methodology by other innovatory forms. Illustrative of this are some studies of the formation of states, particularly in the first millennium BC, and the manner in which ruling clans and chiefs acquired the characteristics of states and kings. The discussions of this process show a familiarity with anthropological analyses of the early state, although the utilization of such models is limited. Among anthropologists at the time there was considerable interest in questions relating to the control over irrigation, labour, resources and technologies, and these questions are reflected in the early notions of the state.

Discussion on various aspects of the evolution of a state has included changes that led to this, just prior to 500 BC in north India. Transitions to state systems, together with urban centres, have been analysed with reference to the kingdoms of the Ganges Plain of the mid-first millennium BC, with an emphasis on locating the agencies of change: the identification of territory; rituals enhancing the notion of conquest and power; the use of iron technology; the production of an agricultural surplus; the beginnings of administrative control; and new ideologies confronting those already established. With the emergence of empire in the Mauryan period, a distinction has been suggested between empire and kingdom, a distinction moving away from the arbitrary use of the label 'empire' and seeking to explain the distinctive structure of an empire. This also has some relevance to the definition of kingdoms.

Other theories explaining the state, particularly of the period subsequent to the eighth century AD, do not subscribe to the Marxist model but their critique of the model has been the starting-point of their own formulations. One view is that the states of the post-Gupta period differed from the previous ones, but that this change did not constitute feudalism. Territories emerged under new names and ruling lineages were associated with territorial names, rather than with clan names. Pre-state polities were transformed into states, and the creating of a centre of power involved the colonization of an area by settling subordinate branch lineages of the main dynasty in new areas. Rather than a decentralized feudal system, this is seen as spreading monarchy into pre-state societies and introducing what has been called an 'integrative polity'. The theory has been discussed mainly with reference to Rajasthan, but how widespread it may have been has yet to be ascertained. And of course every polity is integrative in some way. The process could be pertinent to areas where new states were being formed but may be less applicable to areas with old, established states. The extent to which the new process differs from the old would also have to be investigated.

Yet another model is that of the segmentary state. As originally formulated, it referred to societies in Africa following a segmentary form of social organization and without a clear state system. Segmentary societies are generally associated with systems where lineages determine the identities of descent groups. A segmentary state is therefore something of a contradiction in terms. The Alur in East Africa was said to be an emerging state system still rooted in segmentary forms. This model was applied to kingdoms in India, and particularly to the southern kingdoms. It assumes the separation of political sovereignty from ritual authority, arguing that the former is confined to the central or core area of the state whereas the latter holds for the peripheries. Unity is sought through the control of the centre at the apex, but more broadly through ritual conformity. The theory does not explain the pattern of political economies and has found little support, although in this case, too, the initial arguments in the debate led to some interesting explorations of south Indian history.

The arguments and evidence used in these theories, and more particularly the critiques that they evoked, have moved away from seeing a uniform pattern applicable to every state. This has led to clarifying some aspects of the history of this period. For example, the impressive statistical research by Japanese and south Indian scholars, using computer-based analyses of inscriptions, has refined methods and generalizations pertaining to this history. The emerging picture of agrarian and commercial structures, with their relationship to governmental authority and the administrative networks that it fostered, is central to the discussion. Attention has also been directed to other processes, such as the creation of new castes and new religious beliefs and practices. These historical interests will be discussed in greater detail in the relevant chapters (11 and 13). The intention here is merely to provide a pointer to the directions they have taken.

History as a Social and Human Science

The writing of Marxist histories began at the same time as other developments in Indian historiography, evident from the discussion above. In India, the 1950s and 1960s saw the earlier germination of the social sciences being transmuted into established disciplines. This was in part linked to the post-independence period when realistic assessments of Indian society were being called for. Related subjects such as growth economics, demography, social anthropology and sociology, socio-linguistics, archaeology and history developed independently, with the growing interest in their subject matter, across disciplines in interdisciplinary research. Questions asked in one discipline began to interest the practitioners of another.

History was pivotal, since there was always a curiosity in comparing the past with the present. Historians began to ask a different set of questions from those that had been asked previously and expanded the range of the theories of explanation. History relating to society, economy, culture and religion was explored, and the interconnections between them attracted interest. Historical research continued to require technical expertise in the handling of a range of source materials from artefacts to texts, but in addition also required some understanding of theoretical procedures of analysis. This differed from the approach of those for whom history was just a narrative about the past with a focus on providing information. Historical imagination shifted from the romance of reconstructing the past to a more creative exploration, asking a wide spectrum of questions and searching for answers.

The Marxist intervention, quite apart from introducing new perspectives into historical studies, also encouraged a range of new themes considered legitimate to historical analyses. The influential writings on history by the French Annales School, which became available in English and began to be widely read a few decades ago, coincided with these explorations. These were historians who helped move history further towards studies of society, economy, population, environment and the ideas and attitudes of people to the world surrounding them. Inevitably, this involved using the methodology of disciplines such as social and economic anthropology, the sociology of religion, economics, ecological studies and intellectual history to ask new questions of existing data or to formulate new ways of analysing evidence. Interconnections were made, linking many facets that had earlier been treated in isolation or ignored.

The interests that characterize the kind of history of those who contributed to these changes grew in part from the notion of the social sciences, or the human sciences as some would prefer to call them, as a legitimate method to explore the human past. This required a wider recognition of what constitutes historical data. It included not only the representation of actions, but also the way in which they were represented through words, objects or the intervening landscape with virtually everything that reflected the presence of the human. The focus was less on reconstructing reality and more on making the past intelligible. This required transcending the single event to view actions as not just individual articulations, but part of a wider context of human and social activity. Hence the emphasis on society, economy, religious articulations, art, literature and systems of knowledge. The necessary multiplicity of causes in such studies added to the dimension of historical explanation. Thus the social dimension of culture introduces questions such as who created the form, what was its function, who was the audience and how was it disseminated. Such a perspective not only enlarges historical space, but also prevents time being restricted to a linear narrative. The coexistence of different concepts of time becomes possible: Fernand Braudel writes of the historical moment of the event, the conjuncture of its broader social and economic context, and the long duration of the landscape and geology within which the event is enacted.

Such studies are also providing a comparative perspective on Indian history, not along the old lines of declaring one culture to be the norm and judging others by its standards, but rather in terms of comparative analyses of forms and their functions across more than one culture. This approach has made historical studies of other parts of the world relevant to the intellectual equipment of the historian of early India. Some notable examples are: those of Moses Finley and Arnaldo Momigliano on the Greco-Roman world; Marc Bloch on medieval Europe; Joseph Needham on the history of scientific thought and practice in China; Nathan Wachtel's study of the Peruvian perception of the Spanish conquest; and Jan Vansina's recent work on the oral tradition. The debates initiated by their work among a wide range of historians from various societies and cultures provide comparative ways of approaching the understanding of Indian history as well, although obviously the particularities of Indian history will remain.

The purpose of indicating the changing outlook of historical writing on India is not to dismiss the work of the early historians as being without value or to denigrate the importance of their scholarship. The inadequacies of their interpretations were often the inadequacies of their times, for historians are frequently far more representative of their age than they are aware. Despite such shortcomings, these studies laid the foundations of the history of India, providing a chronological and historical framework around which fresh interpretations could be constructed and which would place the ideas and institutions of Indian civilization in what was believed to be a significant perspective. Changes in the requirements of a historical approach now place less emphasis on chronological and dynastic reconstruction and more on understanding the layered nature of past societies.

Social history is now taking cognizance of the studies of diverse forms of kinship and of gender relations in the multiple societies of the Indian past. These have been encouraged by anthropological studies, and also by historians working on gender. Earlier studies on the status of women were largely collections of information on the life of women, with a general approval of their status, as given in the *Dharma-shastras* and other norma- tive texts. This was part of the assumption of a Golden Age. It was also an encouragement to women to participate in the national movement, and the underlying argument was that even in the early past they were respected partners. Only later did their condition worsen. The new work is far more searching, attempting to explain the variations in the status of women in terms of different periods, regions and castes, and relates these to historical change. Social aspects that determined status, such as rights to property, marriage regulations and the use of women as labour, inevitably point to discrepancies in the earlier uniformly positive representation. There is a growing understanding of the implications of patriarchy, not only in determining gender relations, but also as a condition of society and in the manner of its assertion through social norms, religious beliefs or the work carried out by women. Women were not a distinct and separate category but an integral part of the social process. Hence the status of women becomes a commentary on society.

Lower castes, marginalized groups and untouchables now enter historical narratives, sometimes as significant players, as for example in religious movements governed by social concerns. Those who laboured were not thought of as playing a part in historical change, perhaps because those who did not labour wrote the sources that were quoted. It is sometimes possible, however, to infer the life of those who laboured from passing references in the texts. But the recognition of labour as an essential precondition to activities that are admired from the past has encouraged historians to look for such references in order to complete the picture of society.

The historian of India was once regarded primarily as an Orientalist, or an Indologist, in the days when the studies of the languages and cultures of Asia were fragrant with exotica. This concept of Oriental studies has been mutating in the last century, both in India and elsewhere. In the contemporary world, the history of early societies is being approached from many perspectives, rather than being limited to the periods said to have created 'classical cultures'. Political histories and dynastic studies remain an important aspect of historical interpretation, but these are also viewed in the light of other features that make a society and a culture. Changes in the political pattern are inextricably entwined with changes in the economic structure and in social relationships. If a religious movement finds a large following, then its attraction must have some relevance to the kind of people who support it. A new language and a new literature can only emerge if they fulfil a need for the society in which they are rooted. It is not enough for the historian to present the ideas of those who attempted to create the contours of the history of India. It is essential to attempt to know how these ideas arose and the extent of their acceptability within Indian society.

Reconsidering Periodization

A reconsideration of periodization becomes necessary, both because of the discussions on the nature of historical change and because of the introduction of new categories of sources. Archaeological evidence, for instance, defines a society from viewpoints different from the literary. These perspectives of the past have inevitably led to questioning the current forms of the periodization of Indian history. The terms Ancient, Medieval and Modern were taken from European history and applied to the existing tripartite division of Indian history. European history made a distinction between Antiquity/Ancient referring to the Greco-Roman civilization, and Medieval, which was essentially the period of Christian Europe. Both Ancient and Medieval had specific connotations in European history, which were not relevant to Indian history.

'Ancient' in Indian history remains an imprecise term, conveying little of the nature of the period, and 'Medieval' merely means the middle. In addition, the Ancient period covers a large enough span to include major changes within it. Accommodating variant patterns of historical change in the subcontinent to a uniform pattern also presents problems. In recent years this tripartite division has been modified to suit Indian history. The first period is described as Early Historical and terminates in about the eighth century AD. Subsequent to this is the Early Medieval – from the eighth century to the thirteenth century. The Medieval begins with Turkish rule or the Sultanates and ends with the decline of the Mughals. The fourth and last period is the Modern, marking the establishment of British rule in the eighteenth century.

Although an improvement on the tripartite division, this tends to remain vague. The start of the Early Historical period is generally associated with the emergence of urban centres and states in the Ganges Plain in about 500 BC, marking a major change from that which preceded it. But this does not accommodate the previous lengthy period of pre-state and pre-urban society, subsequent to the decline of the Indus civilization and different from what emerged in the mid-first millennium BC. Contemporary written documents are available only from the third century BC, still leaving the earlier period without an appropriate label. A break around the eighth century AD is certainly called for, given the socio-economic changes and new developments in religions registered in the subcontinent, but whether the label Early Medieval conveys an impression of these changes is another matter. Periodization, if it is not merely to be a chronological division, should give some indication of social mutations and project a sequence involving what came before and what follows. Advances in historical knowledge could therefore alter the periodization. The ambiguity of the term 'Medieval' is now being debated for European history and it might be better to consider a more definitive term.

A possible alternative periodization, although using more descriptive terms, could be as given here. This is far from definitive, has no easy labels for quick reference, but directs attention to substantial points of historical change. The divisions as listed below would not be of equal length. For purposes of grouping them into larger periods the focus would be on a central theme, towards which historical activities may be directed or from which they may lead. The attempt here is to suggest some ideas towards a more realistic view of change and to indicate what the characteristics of this may be.

The following is a suggested periodization:

1 Hunter-gatherers, pastoralists and early farmers
2 First urbanization: the Indus Plain and north-west India
3 Megalithic settlements of the peninsula
   (*The focal point of these three periods was the Indus urbanization with cultures that led up to it and others that diverged after its decline. Archaeological data provides the evidence for this period.*)

4 Chiefships and kingships 1200–600 BC
5 Second urbanization and state formation in the Ganges Plain c. 600– 400 BC
   (*The focal point here is the formation of states and urbanization in the Ganges Plain. Period 4 discusses the factors that led up to this. Evidence comes from archaeological data and oral traditions recorded later. The difference in the nature of this urbanization from the earlier calls for attention.*)

6 The Mauryan state, c. 400–c. 200 BC
   (*The earliest attempt at an imperial system. The possibility of interrogating a range of sources increases.*)

7 The rise of the mercantile community and cross-cultural contacts, c. 200 BC–AD 300
   (*This period saw a range of states and a variety of economic and religious networks in which the role of the mercantile community and cross-cultural contacts had greater significance than before, and contributed to transcontinental cultures.*)

8 The creation of Sanskritic cultures, c. AD 300–700
   (*Characteristics of this period were elements of cultural integration through the evolving of a court culture, recognizable in many parts*)

of the subcontinent, that also reflected the potentialities of creating new states.)

9 Distributive political economies and regional cultures, *c.* AD 700–1300
(*Both the state structures and the cultural contacts became more predict-able from region to region because of the widespread influence of Sanskritic cultures correlated to distributive economies in the form of grants of land. In emphasizing the emergence of regional cultures, the intention is not to present a picture of political fragmentation but to underline the reformulation of politics, society and culture in a pattern that differs from the earlier pre-Gupta period.*)

10 The assertion of regional identities, *c.* AD 1300–1550
(*An assertion of regional identities becomes more evident in political economies and cultures, but not to the point of preventing the establish-ment of a powerful suzerain state.*)

11 The Mughal state and subsequent regional kingdoms, *c.* AD 1550–1750

12 British colonial rule and the Indian nationalist response

Defining periods in history is important, but it is equally important to determine the cause of change, a question sometimes referred to as that of the transition from one period to another. Even specific changes may begin casually, but if they occur with sufficient frequency they can give a new direction to the way society functions and this encapsulates historical change. The nature of the transition therefore becomes a significant aspect of periodization. The distinction between the different periods is determined by characteristics of polity, economy, technology, society and religion that were prevalent at the time, as well as some reference to the makers of events wherever available. Inevitably, there is more information on elite groups since they were the authors and patrons. A corrective to this is sometimes available when archaeology provides evidence of the material culture of ordinary people.

Cultural Histories of a
Different Kind

A summary of historical trends such as this should at least mention the questioning of the discipline of history by theories that focus on language, or what has been called 'the literary turn'. Some have argued that as language is the medium of knowledge, that which comes in the form of language constitutes a text; since language is interpreted by the individual, the reading by the individual gives meaning to the text; therefore each time a text is read by a different individual it acquires a fresh meaning. Taken to its logical conclusion, this denies any generally accepted meaning of a text and is implicitly a denial of attempts at historical representation or claims to relative objectivity, since the meaning would change with each reading. However, the prevalent views are more subtle.

Readings can be hegemonic or there can be attempts to ignore alternative readings, but readings with little or no structures of how to read a text can be self-defeating in terms of acquiring knowledge. The more acceptable historical argument would be that there is space for greater sensitivity to alternative texts and readings, and to multiple voices, but that these should observe the procedures of historical analysis. The focus on culture, beliefs and ideologies could be a necessary addition to the earlier historical emphases on politics and the economy, but it is not in itself definitive history since history requires a correlation between the reading of a text and its multi-layered historical contexts. This enables an understanding of what is directly stated in a text and, equally important, that which is implied.

These developments have been paralleled by the continual return to theories of explanation, some of which have been explored and developed, while others have been replaced. For example, Marxism, once thought of by some as synonymous with economic determinism, can no longer be described as such, given the debates that have been generated in recent times through its many varieties – humanist, existentialist, structuralist. Theories arising from colonial readings are being replaced by more analytical studies using a wider range of data and explanation. Nationalist interpretations are also being more rigorously sieved. Paradigms, or frameworks of understanding, are reformulated and in history this change relates most closely to the question of facts and concepts. The reformulation often comes about through the contemplation of the surrounding world and the attempt to comprehend it.

A wider interest in cultural history has led to analytical studies of texts, not just to arrive at alternative or variant readings but also to view the text as an artefact of history. This requires comparative studies of variant versions as well as placing it in its context. Priority is given to the intention of the author and of the patron if there is one. The close connection between patronage and culture, both literary and artistic, is an essential component of cultural history. This has often raised questions such as who constitutes the audience of the text and what is its intention? This in turn has made historians sensitive to particular audiences determining artistic or literary form or providing variants.

Ascertaining the audience and the intention has been useful in attempts to locate texts that incorporate historical perceptions of the past, in what is now sometimes called the *itihasa-purana* tradition. *Itihasa* literally means 'thus it was' and *purana* refers to that which belongs to the past. This takes a variety of forms. In the early *Puranas* there are genealogies, some quite fanciful, gradually moving towards more realistic lists of dynastic succession. Subsequently, there are historical biographies of kings and even the occasional minister, largely hagiographic but encapsulating some aspects of historical events. And there are chronicles of regional histories, of which Kalhana's *Rajatarangini* is certainly the finest example. A few chronicles of Buddhist monasteries are also seen as historical narratives. The recording of the rule of a king or the history of a dynasty in the form of inscriptions began just prior to the Christian era, becoming common in the period after the eighth century AD, and these constitute the annals of early Indian history.

Such texts are not histories in any modern sense, but are attempts to capture the past in particular forms and to use it to legitimize the claims of the present. The narratives are set in linear time. Their writing involves the patron ordering the history, the authors formulating it, and an audience whom they seek to address and who acquiesced in the presentation. The forms are not disjointed, and they attempt to borrow from and adapt what has gone before. The *itihasa-purana* tradition presents a narrative of events, their explanation and an attempt at summation. These are not acceptable to modern notions of analyses and arriving at historical generalizations, but they provide insights into how the past was viewed at various points of time many centuries ago.

Linked to the historical tradition, although not classified as such, are the many thousand inscriptions earlier used to reconstruct dynastic history and now being re-read for information on a variety of other facets of history. As texts they sometimes contain alternative statements to those of the normative literature. Those subsequent to the mid-first millennium present a meshing of the culture of the mainstream and the region. If read analytically, such evidence can provide clues to voices other than those of the authors of mainstream texts.

A historical study is not a juxtaposition of islands or fragments of historical facets which are lined up: political, environmental, technological, economic, social, religious and other histories. A historical analysis requires recognizing the fragments, but relating them to a whole that determines what causes events, and formulating an explanation. The complexities of each of these can be fine-tuned by a more accurate attention to the reading of the text, illuminating the reading through perspectives other than the well-known, but these remain the essentials of a historical analysis.

History is concerned with change and historical change, and, although it may not be determined, it is also not arbitrary or purposeless. The formation of varied societies in a region surfaces through historical analysis, and in this surfacing the historian points out the players and the context. Theories of explanation assist in understanding the context and such theories differ. For some, power relations may be fundamental; for others it may be the dialectic of who controls resources and labour and who labours, for still others it may be the relationship between socio-economic structures and the ideologies that they spawn, or the inversion of this. For a few historians it can also be the interlocking of all these.

Theories of interpretation as presented in this chapter are not intended as inevitably sequential, although there are causal links between them. They are the articulation of particular contexts of time, place and events. They have their own histories and constitute many strands in historical thought. Since they are not merely an extension or reversal of data, but are intended to explain complex problems, they have varied existences. Some theories decline or die out. Others persist, generally in a modified form. Some surface aggressively if their function as ideologies of political mobilization is more important than their function as historical explanation. Yet others generate new theories, and these tend to extend the reach of historical analysis.

In this book an attempt is made to anticipate a few of the themes and questions that are significant to understanding the Indian past, and to indicate the people, events and institutions that have contributed to the making of Indian society through time. But the tendency to evaluate Indian history and culture in absolute terms, and to make categorical judgements, has been avoided since such an evaluation within the space of this brief history would merely result in platitudes. In the course of tracing the evolution of certain aspects of Indian life – the environment and the economic structure, changing social relationships, the historical context of religious movements, the emergence and growth of languages, to mention but a few – identifiable patterns have emerged. These patterns have been described and interpreted along lines that appear to me to be the most convincing, given the evidence available and the logic implicit in its analysis. In a survey of this kind the aim is to present the features of the Indian past, hopefully in an intelligible manner, given the complexities of these features. As a historian, I am aware that I too am part of the historical process, and that the paradigm will shift in the future. The direction of the shift may draw on the way history is viewed in present times.

2

Landscapes and Peoples

Time and Space

Speaking metaphorically, time and space are said to be the warp and woof of history. In India the perception of time includes abstract concepts, such as cyclic time as a component of cosmology, and linear time which is born of human action. Cyclic time is a part of cosmology in various texts, such as the epic the *Mahabharata*, the *Dharma-shastra* of Manu and the *Vishnu Purana*, and the elaboration of this cosmology probably dated to the early Christian era. The last of these texts also has a section on genealogies and dynasties, providing indications of linear time, but this was overlooked in modern studies of time concepts and Indian civilization was said to be familiar only with cyclic time.

The imaginative vastness of cycles of time, where the great cycle – the *mahayuga* – extends to 4,320,000 years, provides a cosmological frame. The immensity of the span was required for calculations in astronomy. It encapsulates four lesser cycles, each smaller than the previous and declining in an orderly, arithmetical progression. The four cycles or ages are the Krita or Satya – the Age of Truth – the Treta or the third, the Dvapara or the second, and the Kali. We are now in the Kali Age, the start of which has been calculated as equivalent to 3102 BC and which is to last for 432,000 years. Apart from the decline in the number of years, the quality of life also diminishes in each cycle. It is said to be like a bull that initially stands on four legs, but with each age loses a leg and now stands on one! With the exception of the first, the names of the cycles follow the throws of dice introducing an element of chance into the concept of time, and the Kali Age has therefore been appropriately translated as the age of the losing throw.

Linear time is circumscribed by what is viewed as the beginning and the end of time in human history. It can take the form of the shallow or deep descent of the genealogy of a clan or a dynasty: the human lifespan of a biography; or the innumerable chronicles written to assert the authority of kings and dynasties, with the multiple eras they established from the first millennium AD. Unlike the Judaeo-Christian tradition, where there is a precise beginning and a definite termination in the Day of Judgement, the Indian form has a weaker eschatology. Nevertheless, the concept of linearity as the basic approach to recording the past is unmistakable. Linear time is the immediate context for heroes and kings, and for the chronicles of institutions and states. It would seem that cyclic and linear time had variant functions and the exploration of their interface as reflected in Indian texts is still in its initial stages.

Regions enclosing space are active players in historical events when seen from a historical and geographical perspective. Regions are not uniform nor do they emerge simultaneously. They surface in an uneven pattern, the differences being determined both by a pre-existing landscape and environment and by the shape given to it through human action. This would incorporate conditions of physical geography and be modulated by climate, soil, water resources, crops, drought and flood, as well as the impact of those technologies that alter environment and landscape.

There are also spaces pertaining to how a geographical entity is viewed historically. Geologically the subcontinent was formed through the shifting land mass of Gondwanaland, as it has been called, and the filling in of the seas which have now become the northern plains. Once the subcontinent was formed geographically, it remained an entity for millennia. But its historical identity is dated to relatively recent times. Even within this recent identity, the names used for the historical identity referred to different concepts of space that moved from the narrower to the broader. These were, for example, the *heptahindu* used in the *Avesta* and the equivalent of the Rigvedic *sapta sindhu* (the Sindhu/Indus and its tributaries); *hi[n]dush* in Iranian Achaemenid inscriptions (referring to north-western India, the name being taken from Sindhu); the *aryavarta*, essentially the Ganges Plain and its fringes (although sometimes expanded to include more of northern India); *hndstn*, read as Hindustan, although it did not refer to the subcontinent but only to the north-west (in a Middle Persian Sasanian inscription of Shahpur I in the third century AD); and, in Arab sources, *al-Hind* (the land beyond the Indus).

Cosmology describes the earth as flat and circular, with Mount Meru in its centre. Surrounding Mount Meru were the four continents or *dvipas*, literally islands, separated by oceans. The southern continent was *Jambud-vipa* (literally, the island of the rose-apple tree, and also referred to by the Mauryan Emperor Ashoka in his inscriptions), and within this, in the area to the south of the Himalaya, was *Bharatavarsha*, named after the ruler Bharata. Permutations on this scheme included projections incorporating several continents and oceans.

Consciousness of space is also implicit in the listing of places of pilgrimage and the gradual expansion of these lists. The formulaic mention of conquered lands in the claims of those who took the title of *digvijayin*, conqueror of the four quarters, in the post-Gupta period also invoked space. The relationship between regions and larger entities changed as the peripheral and the unknown gradually became part of the mainstream. The latter was subject to still wider pulls: from central Asia in the north; from west Asia along the western coastal areas; and towards south-east Asia from various directions. To see the subcontinent only in terms of regions oriented to the cardinal directions may therefore not be historically apposite, however convenient this view is for handling its history.

As part of the interest in the land–man relationship, regions are said to be either areas of attraction where human activity is evident in attempts to shape the landscape, or areas of isolation where human settlements tend to be remote and the landscape unchanging. This dichotomy should not be taken too literally. There are also areas of relative isolation that over time are incorporated into the territory of kingdoms. Forests and deserts, for example, would be areas of isolation, although forests provided many resources used by neighbouring states, such as timber, elephants, and semi-precious stones; and the use of routes across deserts led to quicker communication between surrounding regions. Access was often obtained through negotiation with those who dwelt in each region.

The Northern Mountains

Geographically, the subcontinent has been divided into three major regions: the northern mountains, the Indo-Gangetic Plain and the peninsula. The northern mountains have been described in the past as a barrier to communication that isolates northern India from Asia. But in effect they were rarely barriers and the north-west of the subcontinent was in continuous communication with peoples and places in western and central Asia. It was almost as if such communication focused on the passes in the north-western mountains and intensified cross-cultural activities.

The northern plain is bounded by the Hindu Kush and the Sulaiman and Kirthar Mountains to the north-west, and by the Himalaya to the north and north-east. The Hindu Kush is also a watershed, an elevated area that provides the geographical interface between the Oxus and the Indus Valleys. When seen from this perspective it ceases to be the barrier cutting off access to central Asia which it was once thought to be.

The passes in the north-west mountains, although arid, were less snow-bound than those of the higher Himalaya and therefore more frequently used. These included the Bolan, Gomal and Khyber passes. The fertile Swat Valley formed another route, as did the Hunza and Upper Indus Valley. The Khyber played an important role in the British attempt to control Afghanistan and contain the Russian presence in the nineteenth century, and has therefore been much romanticized in literature, becoming the focus of historical attention. But the Bolan may have been the more important route in the earliest period. It led to the Seistan area and the Helmand valley in Afghanistan, which in turn gave access to north-eastern Iran and central Asia. The Swat Valley attracted attention in modern histories because of its connections with the route of Alexander of Macedon.

Pastoralists arriving from and returning to Afghanistan, or even central Asia, travelled regularly through the passes and the valleys. They continued to do so until a few years ago, as did immigrants coming from central Asia, Iran or Afghanistan, or large groups of Indians trading and settling in these distant places. Missionaries from Persia, caravans of merchants and, from time to time, invading armies used the same routes. Settlements at both ends point to the importance of controlling the passes. In early times the towns of Taxila and Begram controlled the Khyber Pass and, later, Peshawar and Kabul. The junction of the pass with the plain forms an area particularly sensitive to the politics and trade of the local regions. These passes were used so frequently that it is incorrect to project the north-western mountains as barriers. They were corridors of communication. Contact with what are now referred to as central Asia, Iran and Afghanistan goes back to the third millennium BC, the period of the Indus cities, and the passes are likely to have been used by people in even earlier times. There was a historical continuity of peoples entering northern India, such as with the migrations of the Indo-Aryan speakers, sporadically with the armies of Alexander of Macedon and more consistently with the Indo-Greeks, Parthians, Shakas, Kushanas, Hunas and Turks. The most regular movements were those of herders and of trading caravans.

The Himalaya mountains to the north are somewhat different and although not a barrier had less communication with the world beyond. The plateau of Tibet was itself somewhat distanced from central Asia and China. The passes here are high and inhospitable in winter, generally snow-covered. Nevertheless, they have seen traffic and trade. The directly northern route to central Asia lay in the recently discovered Karakorum Highway via Gilgit, Chitral and Hunza, which tied into what came to be called the central Asian Silk Route. In the last couple of centuries these areas caught public attention as part of the backdrop to 'the Great Game', the British attempt to open up central Asia and Tibet.

Further to the east, contact with Tibet was linked to the transhumance of pastoral groups moving to summer pastures through the passes. Still further east, the mountains of what is today referred to as north-eastern India were difficult to cross, given the direction of the ranges that made a west-to-east access less usable. The frequency of migrations and trade, and the role of these in history, varied therefore from region to region.

Differences in the terrain of the mountain systems, and of the cultures beyond them encouraged a cultural divide between the north-east and the north-west. This was emphasized in the interaction between the plains and the mountains, with the north-west mountains that constituted the Himalayan region of the north being very different from those of the north-east. Whereas in the north-west there was a continual influx of peoples, patterns of living and languages, the northern Himalayan valleys tended to be more sequestered. This was despite the link between the *doab* and the middle Ganges Plain lying along the *uttarapatha*, the northern route which followed the foothills of the Himalaya, known as the *terai*. With eastward extensions from the watershed into the Ganges Plain in the first millennium BC, it was probably easier to cut a route through the more elevated and less densely forested foothills than through the heavy monsoon forests of the Ganges Plain. In the first millennium AD, adventurers seeking to establish kingdoms in the northern valleys started arriving from the plains. This led to greater interaction between the kingdoms of the plains and areas further in the mountains. The north-east had areas of relative isolation and some in which political power drew on those from across the mountains.

The Indo-Gangetic Plain

A perennial supply of water to the rivers of the north comes from glaciers, which have also changed the landscape of the northern mountains by creating deeper ravines or reducing elevations, opening up meadows at high altitudes. Geologically, the northern plains have resulted from the filling in of earlier seas, and rivers have played their part in this. These rivers are partially a blessing to cultivators where they spread a cover of fertile silt, but some such as the Sutlej, Kosi, Tista and Brahmaputra frequently change course or flood on a large scale, bringing disaster. The elevation of the northern plains is not uniform as there is a gentle gradient from the west to the east, starting from the Punjab Plain and the watershed before descending along the Ganges Plain to its eastern section and the Brahmaputra Plain.

The northern plain is bifurcated into the river systems of the Indus and the Ganges. The Indus rises beyond the Himalaya, flows north through a furrow in the mountains and then turns towards the south-west when it enters the plains. The middle Indus is essentially the area of the confluence of the Indus and its major tributaries that flow from the northern Himalaya through the Punjab plains: the Jhelum, Chenab, Ravi, Sutlej and Beas, of which the Sutlej has frequently changed course. The lower Indus culminates in the Delta, which because of the silting up of its channels tended to cut short the life of its ports. To the west is the inhospitable Makran coast, the traversing of which became a nightmare for Alexander's army returning to Babylon.

Another river whose history was linked to the Indus Plain was the Hakra. It is thought to have once been a significant river flowing almost parallel with the present-day courses of the Sutlej and the lower Indus, with its estuary in the Rann of Kutch. However, the waters of its upper reaches, sometimes called the Ghaggar, were diverted through natural hydraulic changes. Rivers originally flowing into the Hakra were converted to the Sutlej, becoming a tributary of the Indus and linked to the Beas and the Yamuna, flowing to join the Ganges. This was accompanied by the gradual drying up of the Hakra, of which virtually all that remains are the disjointed streams of the present-day Ghaggar. That there were settlements on the dry river-bed of the Hakra by about the late-second millennium BC would date the desiccation to this period, so it is clear the hydraulic changes would have occurred earlier and these are generally dated to the early second millennium.

The identification of the Ghaggar with the Sarasvati, mentioned in the *Rig-Veda*, is controversial. Furthermore, the early references to Sarasvati could be to the Haraxvati Plain in Afghanistan. The identification is also problematic as the Sarasvati is said to cut its way through high mountains and this is not the landscape of the Ghaggar. Although the Sarasvati is described in the *Rig-Veda* in glowing terms, the Sutlej and the Yamuna were already separate rivers and not flowing into the Ghaggar. This would indicate that the hymns were composed subsequent to the changes affecting the Hakra/Ghaggar. Once the river had been mythologized through invoking the memory of the earlier river, its name – Sarasvati – could be applied to many rivers, which is what happened in various parts of the subcontinent.

The elevated area of the Indo-Gangetic watershed separates the Indus system in the west from that of the Ganges in the east. The separation is further emphasized by the Aravalli Hills that separate the arid lands of Rajasthan from the western Ganges Plain. The Indo-Gangetic watershed also acts as a frontier to the Ganges Plain in the face of intrusions from the north-west. The Ganges, rising in the Himalaya, flows south and then towards the east, with tributaries providing a viable network used until recently as routes for river transportation. The Yamuna flows approximately parallel to the Ganges, but then joins it, and the area between the two is known as the *doab* – literally, between two rivers. Further east the important tributaries of the Ganges are the Gomati, Sarayu, Ghaghra and Gandak, flowing southwards from the Himalaya. The Son, Betwa and Chambal (the ravines of which have been famous as dacoit country) flow northwards from the Vindhyan Plateau. Still further east are the dual streams of the Ganges – the Bhagirathi flows south and is known to change its course, attested to by geology and reflected in mythology, while the Padma flows towards the south-east.

At its eastern extremity the Ganges Plain merges into the plains of the Brahmaputra River. Rising beyond the Himalaya, the Brahmaputra flows west to east across Tibet, as the Tsang-po, for an immense distance, then does a U-turn and continues through the plains of north-eastern India in an approximately east–west direction. In the plains it is a vast but slow-moving river with scattered islands. Both the Indus and the Brahmaputra rise from proximate sources but flow in different directions over immense distances. The lake, Manasarovara, and the nearby mountain of Kailasa have come to be regarded as sacred. In the east, the Brahmaputra meets the Padma, as does the Meghna further along. This creates an immense expanse of water during the monsoon, and the boatmen of this area have a prominent cultural place in the folk literature of the region.

River valleys or the plains created by a river and its tributaries are often optimal areas for the rise of urban centres, particularly at or near nodal points such as the confluence of rivers. The urban civilization of the Indus system dates to the third millennium BC, that of the Ganges system to the first millennium BC. Urban centres developed somewhat later in the plains of the Brahmaputra. Possibly the ecological and technological conditions did not encourage an early clearance and settlement of land. This is not altogether unassociated with the mountains of north-eastern India supporting many groups of 'tribal societies', as they have been called, since they remained an area of relative isolation for a long period. Land to the east of the Ganges Delta was also cleared, with settlements gradually being established in the first millennium AD. The Indus Plain appears to have been less densely forested than the Ganges Plain, although the Harappan seals depict tigers and rhinoceroses which are generally associated with tropical forest. It is hard to believe that in earlier times the Ganges Plain was covered with monsoon forests, so effectively have these been cleared. The fertility of these plains, particularly the flood plains of the rivers, attracted agriculture despite the virtually annual damage caused by floods.

The northern plains however were not uniformly fertile. The Thar desert of Rajasthan and the semi-arid regions encircling it did not allow for much cultivation. But as is characteristic of deserts, these became areas conducive to routes which were used extensively by traders whose goods were carried by camel caravans. Small centres of exchange or staging points gradually emerged, and a few grew to be towns. With attention to irrigation, some of these areas also became agriculturally viable.

The Peninsula

The third major region is that of the peninsula. Lying to the south of the Vindhya Mountains, the Satpura Ranges and the Narmada River, it is largely a plateau region but with hilly terrain in the Western and Eastern Ghats. The plateau in the northern half of the peninsula is known as the Deccan, a name given to the area by northerners and derived from *dakshina*, meaning the south. A major route going south in historical times, the *dakshinapatha* – literally, the southern route – is frequently mentioned in texts. The plateau consists of volcanic rock, very different from the northern mountains. Such rock is somewhat easier to cut into, hence the frequency of rock-cut monasteries and temples in the Deccan.

The Western Ghats rise sharply close to the western coast, tapering eastwards into the plateau of the peninsula. They are cut by a series of passes similar to those at Junnar, Kanheri, Karle and Karad, which linked the trade routes traversing the plateau with the ports along the west coast. The passes were points where Buddhist rock-cut monasteries were clustered. At the southern end, the Palghat Gap was the pass that allowed access from the west coast to the Kaveri Valley and was important to Indo-Roman trade.

The Ghats on the east merge more gradually into the plateau and the coastal plain. The major rivers are approximately parallel, apart from the Mahanadi at the eastern end of the peninsula. Whereas the more northern ones – the Narmada and the Tapti – run east to west, those further south such as the Godavari, Krishna, Tungabhadra and Kaveri flow the other way, west to east. Rivers are generally regarded as sacred and some, such as the Ganges, more sacred than others. Places of pilgrimage are often located on river banks. Pilgrimage on the Narmada involved starting at the source and walking along one bank, then crossing over to the other bank and walking back to the source, a pattern less common for other rivers.

The peninsula is broken up by the topography of rivers and elevations, making expansive agrarian states similar to those of the northern plains a less common occurrence. Urbanization in the peninsula dates to the late Mauryan period and the start of the first millennium AD, but there is considerable and impressive pre-urban activity in many areas. The Deccan, as the more northern part of the peninsula, inevitably became the bridge area linking the north and the south, as is reflected in language and architectural styles.

The mountains and plateaux of central India, with their dense forests, tended to get bypassed by migrants and settlers for many centuries. The major settlements were along the more frequented routes from the northern plain southwards to the Deccan. These settlements made only a marginal impact on the forest dwellers until later centuries when encroachments into the forests for timber and elephants, as well as cultivable land, became more common. Central India was regarded as the major habitat of 'tribal societies' and forest peoples, even though such societies were scattered throughout the subcontinent. Pockets of these continue to the present. The population size of such 'tribal societies' or forest-people varies today from about a hundred for a society such as the Onge in the Andaman Islands, to over a million among the Munda, Oraon, Bhil, Gond, Santhal and Mina. Living patterns range from hunting-gathering, shifting cultivation and horticulture to farming. A distinction between these societies and the neighbouring peasant societies had been the centrality of plough agriculture and tenancies among the latter, although this has entered the lives of the former in recent times. Ecological regions were not sharply demarcated and there were symbiotic relations of interdependence between adjoining regions. Forests and savannas were much more extensive in the past than they are now. This in part accounted for densities of forest populations in certain areas, and only gradually were peasant villages settled among such populations. Early texts refer to traversing forests as part of travelling from town to town. Brigands, who also treated the forest as their habitat, added to the apprehensions about undertaking a long journey.

Coastal Areas

The peninsula, with its extensive western and eastern coasts, inevitably has a history of maritime activities. These have not been given their due recognition, largely because the historical perspective of the subcontinent has been land-locked. The monsoon was a dominant feature since the monsoon winds, when used at the appropriate time and with the correct technology, powered sailing ships. Long-distance routes were mid-ocean routes requiring knowledge of winds and currents. Coastal routes were networks that remained reasonably constant. The coasts in each case constitute regions of their own through sea links. The geomorphology of the coastline and the technology of navigation and shipping often led to the continuity of ports and harbours over many centuries. A striking example is the port of Muziris in Kerala which, if identified as it generally is with Kodangallur/Cranganore, would have remained active from the turn of the Christian era to the coming of the Portuguese, fifteen centuries later.

Equally active for much of history were the pirates all along the western coast from Gujarat to Kerala. There are frequent references to the threat of pirates, with memorials to heroes who had resisted them. Piracy is in part a gauge of exchange and a form of redistribution of wealth from plunder. The threat from piracy was that if it remained uncontrolled it could lead to the termination of the trade. Piracy on the sea had a parallel in the brigands on the land. Early societies tried to curb both, but often had to live with them.

The Indian Ocean is divided by the Indian peninsula into two arcs: the Arabian Sea and the western coast of India; and the Bay of Bengal and the eastern coast. The western coast can best be viewed historically as having various foci or core areas: the Indus Delta, Gujarat and Saurashtra, Thana (in the vicinity of Mumbai), the Konkan (south of this) and Malabar (in Kerala). The foci on the eastern coast were: the Ganges Delta, Kalinga (in Orissa), the Deltas of the Godavari and Krishna, and the Coromandel coast with a concentration in the Kaveri Delta (in Tamil Nadu). These core areas were often the nuclei of kingdoms that also had maritime ambitions and economies.

Over many centuries the rise or fall in sea level has also introduced changes along the coasts. A rise in sea level meant that an area such as the Rann of Kutch in western India was once a shallow sea, open to small ships. A fall in sea level would leave some ports high and dry, although the emergence of new land was useful to human and animal populations. These changes particularly affected low-lying coastal areas, such as the Sundarbans in the Ganges Delta, and estuaries in Bangladesh where some parts of the land could either be submerged or silted up, with land forms constantly changing.

The east coast provides evidence of the movement of Buddhism from eastern India, following the coast to south India and Sri Lanka, from approximately the late-first millennium BC. East-coast traders also took the initiative in establishing trade with south-east Asia and southern China. Maritime contacts between the western coast and west Asia go back to the third millennium BC, with seafaring between the Indus cities and Mesopotamia. The south Asian presence in the Gulf has been almost continuous. In later times, beginning in the first century BC, the trade with the eastern Mediterranean provinces of the Roman Empire through the ports of the Red Sea was highly profitable. It was doubtless the success of this trade that took the links further to the eastern coast of Africa in the first millennium AD. The western coast has been home to a number of trading communities, including Christians, Parsis, Arabs and Jews. Another geographical formation, not altogether historically irrelevant as it was once thought, is the cluster of coral islands off the coast of Kerala and Sri Lanka – Lakshadvipa, Minicoy and the Maldives. They broke the fury of the incoming monsoon, and could be used as outposts for traders sailing in both directions.

Far to the east are the Andaman and Nicobar islands, closer to south-east Asia than India. They could have been staging points along the Indian Ocean routes, but seem not to have been used as such. Perhaps the people living there were not so welcoming. In the last couple of centuries the people of the islands have been studied by colonial anthropologists, attempting to define the 'primitive'.

Frontiers

Geographical features are sometimes said to serve as boundaries between states. The concept of the boundary of a kingdom was different in early times from what it is today. In the absence of maps, there was also an absence of a clearly drawn cartographic line marking a boundary. Features of the landscape, such as a mountain range, forest, river, coast or desert, could act as frontier zones rather than boundary lines. Frontier zones were areas of interaction between those who lived within a jurisdiction and those outside it. A frontier was probably more often recognized through changes in language and custom. This flexibility allowed for diplomatic leeway. It also facilitated the crossing of frontiers as a normal part of travelling. Both merchants and traders travelled extensively, while metalsmiths and pastoralists had their own circuits. After the mid-first millennium AD, brahmans also became increasingly mobile, travelling from court to court in search of employment. Pilgrims journeying to sacred places probably had greater immunity to frontiers, since the purpose of their travel was regarded as uplifting or fulfilling a vow.

Frontiers also relate to the curious phenomenon of how some languages spread, while others remain in one place. Indo-Aryan, as Sanskrit, initially had a limited elite status. The use of Sanskrit became more widespread across north India when various dynasties gave it preference over the popularly used Prakrit as their official language. It became part of the demarcation between cultures, the *marga*, or Sanskrit-using mainstream, and the *deshi*, using the regional language. Sanskrit became the language of the court, of classical literature and philosophical works, in short of the subcontinental elite. It was edged out of the court when the administration of an area used Persian or the regional languages. Regional languages, some derived from a Dravidian source and some from Indo-Aryan, remained within approximate regional boundaries even when a few became court languages. The change of language was not a matter of linguistics alone, but had to do with where the writ of authority ran and the identity of that authority.

Geography and landscape come into focus in the area of religious belief. Places of pilgrimage – *tirthas* and *ziarats* – are scattered all over the subcontinent. Pilgrimage crosses frontiers and carries cultural idioms from one place to another. Some sites are specific to a religion and retain their prominence as long as they can count on the patronage of that religion. But many more places acquire an association with the sacred and this brings about a cluster of religious connections, sometimes in succession and at other times simultaneously. Somanatha and its vicinity in Gujarat were home to places of worship revered by Vaishnavas, Buddhists, Shaivas, Jainas and Muslims. Patterns such as this cannot be explained by simply maintaining that there was religious tolerance, as there were expressions of intolerance at some places. Evidently there were other concerns that made such places attractive. Sacred sites could also be taken over by a winning religion – thus a megalithic site was appropriated for the building of a Buddhist *stupa* at Amaravati, a Buddhist *chaitya* was converted into a Hindu temple at Chezarla, a Hindu temple was converted into a Muslim mosque at Ajmer, and there are many more examples. Possibly some sites were thought to be intrinsically sacred and therefore attracted new religions, or perhaps taking over a sacred site was a demonstration of power. Sacred groves and trees, mountains, caves in hillsides, springs and pools are part of popular worship where landscape and belief come together. When they are appropriated by the powerful and the wealthy, then the landscape has to host monuments.

Transportation

Both human porterage and animals were used to transport goods on land. The animal changed according to environment. The most widely used were pack-oxen, mules and asses, as well as some locally bred horses, such as those bred in later periods in western India. For specific terrain, the animal changed to elephants in forests, camels – the dromedary – in arid lands, and sheep, goats, yak and dzo in the mountains. Animal caravans moved along tracks, but ox-carts required a minimal road. Rivers could be forded with ferries and boat bridges. From the ninth century AD stone bridges with corbelled arches were introduced. The Emperor Ashoka, as early as the third century BC, took pride in building rest-houses, digging wells and planting shady trees along the highways. The transportation of goods was possible for most of the year, but was difficult during the three-month period of the monsoon rains.

Until the nineteenth century it would seem that water transport was preferred for bulk items wherever possible and most rivers were navigable, particularly in their lower reaches. River ports were therefore important as nodal points. The confluence of the Ganges and the Yamuna, for instance, was the point at which the Ganges became a waterway of significance. The major city of Kaushambi may have been closer to the confluence in the mid-first millennium BC. For short distances or river crossings the most commonly used forms of transportation were floats, rafts, coracles, dug-outs, basket boats and suchlike. For heavier duty, boats built of timber were used more regularly, the local timber being not only river-worthy but, as in the case of teak, eminently suitable even for ships sailing the seas. The size of such craft varied, as did the space and accommodation on the boat and the nature of the sails. Coastal craft were sometimes elaborate dug-outs or else large logs tied together, as in the famous *kattamaram*, or planks sewn together. Mid-ocean ships were larger and built at special shipyards. The navigation of these required a good knowledge of winds and currents – particularly if the south-west monsoon was being used – of coastal landmarks and, inevitably, of astronomy based on observing the stars. The knowledge of astronomy tended to advance during times of considerable maritime trade.

Climate and Agriculture

Agriculture and climatic conditions are dominated by the monsoon – the seasonal rain. The south-west monsoon moves across the Arabian Sea and over the subcontinent from June to September, and the lesser north-east monsoon blows briefly in the opposite direction from December to February, affecting mainly the north-east and the peninsula. This leads to high humidity in the north-eastern area and in Bengal, Orissa and Kerala, with heavier rains and a dense growth of plants and trees. In contrast, parts of the Deccan Plateau and Rajasthan are semi-arid regions for most of the year. The variation in climate and rainfall also contributes to regional differentiation. The high Himalaya acts as a barrier against the cold winds from central Asia, and also stops the monsoon from crossing the initial Himalayan barrier.

It is likely that some changes in climate affected agricultural production, but mapping such changes is not always possible or even precise, given the paucity of evidence for early periods. Analyses of plant remains and soil from excavations have suggested increasing aridity in north-western India in the post-Harappan period. A change in climate has also been suggested for the mid-first millennium AD.

Climatic conditions, together with ecological and environmental variations, account for the range of settlement patterns and domestic architecture that also influenced other architectural forms. One type of village is nucleated, with a concentration of houses surrounded by fields, and grazing grounds for livestock further away. This tends to be the pattern in some of the areas that have a generally dry or arid environment. In areas that are wetter and given to rice cultivation, such as eastern and southern India, the pattern of linear homesteads is often preferred. Houses could be constructed using bamboo beams and woven stalks and matting, or wooden posts and a mud plaster over small branches of trees, the simplest huts being round, square or rectangular. Timber infrastructures gradually replaced these in urban centres, where mud-brick was also used by the better off, while the relatively affluent used kiln-fired brick. House-plans were often rooms around a courtyard, and this remained the standard architectural form in the plains until recent times. Buildings intended to last for a long period, such as palaces and temples, were built more often in stone. Roofs also changed according to the climate of the region, from flat roofs to sloping roofs with thatch or tiles. Vaulted timber ceilings, sometimes imitated in stone, gave way to flat ceilings. Those with a higher elevation, as in temples, took the form of a corbelled construction.

The same preconditions of regional difference made the subcontinent one of the richest areas in floral diversity. This included a range of forests from pine and fir to tropical deciduous forests and, in some wetter places, extensive rain forests. The dry, deciduous forests of the Indus Plain were different from the dense forests of the Ganges Plain. Timber from the teak tree became famous for its durability, ebony for its colour and sandalwood for its fragrance. Drier regions hosted savannas, bush growth and coarse grasses. If there are alpine meadows in the lower Himalaya, there are sand dunes in the desert of Rajasthan and majestic rock formations in the central plateau. Many estuaries had mangrove swamps, among them those of the Indus, the Ganges and the Mahanadi, as well as the coasts of the Andaman Islands.

Climatic conditions relate closely to agricultural production, which in turn is frequently governed by knowing the best time for sowing and harvesting: a connection which the local brahman often calculated on the basis of a lunar–solar calendar. The agricultural and lunar calendar also served for calculating the dates of festivals. The determining of time was initially connected to the twenty-seven stellar constellations, and the phases of the moon provided clues to temporal points in the lunar month. To this were later added calculations based on solar reckoning, such as the equinoxes and the solstices. Such linking of information was important to the cultivator and partially explains his dependence on those who made the calendar, quite apart from his dependence on the quality of the soil, the seed and irrigation.

Soil quality is judged by its natural nutrients, its ability to retain water and the degree to which it facilitates ploughing. Soils vary enormously from region to region, with alluvial and black-cotton soils as well as red soils and laterite. Generalizations on agrarian history have to consider these variations. It has been rightly said that durable boots are essential to the equipment of an agrarian historian required to walk in the countryside! In many areas, better soils are closer to rivers that tend to silt over their flood plains. These are often the preferred though hazardous locations of farming communities. The more established settlements move to elevated areas. Where the richer soil tends to be found below the topsoil, or is heavy, deep ploughing is called for. This has occasioned a debate among historians as to when the iron ploughshare was first used, how extensively and with what historical consequences. The use of wooden ploughshares in many parts of the subcontinent, particularly the peninsula, makes an interesting counterpoint to this discussion.

Given the common practice of rain-fed agriculture in the north-west, wheat and barley were the preferred food crops. In drier regions, as in parts of the peninsula, a variety of millets were cultivated. Wet-rice cultivation provided the staple in larger areas of the middle Ganges Plain and eastern India, the broader valleys of the peninsula and in coastal areas. Wet-rice cultivation yields a considerably higher surplus than other cereal crops and perhaps is thus able to sustain complex societies with large numbers of people not engaged in cultivation for longer periods. The drier areas were home to cattle-breeding, with the buffalo taking precedence in wetter areas. Cultivation processes range from shifting cultivation/slash-and-burn/ swidden, known locally as *jhooming*, and hoe cultivation, to the use of the plough. In limited areas *jhooming* has destroyed primary forests and all that remain are secondary forests, growing in areas now fallow. Shifting cultivation produces enough to live on but no more. It does not always imply a shifting settlement as the shift may only be in the land under cultivation. Nevertheless, the settlements tended to be temporary, as is still the case with some shifting cultivation of north-eastern India. Clearing forests to provide permanent cultivable land and extend agriculture has been an ongoing process in the history of the subcontinent. But the *Artha- shastra* of Kautilya, a text on political economy dating to the Mauryan and post-Mauryan period, advises rigorous state control over this activity, doubtless to keep a check on the revenue brought in by extending agriculture and possibly to prevent over-exploitation of the land. While the population was small the extent of damage was limited, but in recent centuries regular and intensive clearing has depleted the forest cover.

Methods of irrigating fields were not uniform, being dependent on natural conditions and the control of irrigation works. Extensive farming was tied to a regular supply of water. Irrigation systems ranged from the simple to the complicated: water taken from rivers and diverted into channels for irrigation; water-lifts working on wells and rivers; wheels fitted with pots and attached to wells; Persian wheels with a gearing mechanism; small hillside channels bringing water to terraced fields; tanks; embankments with weirs to hold water in reservoirs; enclosures at catchment areas; canals and anicuts; underground conduits; and small dams. The system adopted was specific to particular environments, the acreage of land under cultivation and the person or institution that took the initiative in setting up irrigation works. The theory that the hydraulic machinery was controlled by the bureaucracy of the state, with the peasant dependent on it being subjected to the despotism of the ruler, has been quoted as characteristic of agriculture and politics in pre-modern India. Studies of agrarian history have proved this theory to be erroneous. State-controlled irrigation works, such as large reservoirs, dams or anicuts, were few and far between. The more common forms were established either through private initiatives by wealthy farmers and landowners, or through the co-operation of the community of villagers. A failed monsoon may have brought a drought, and there is mention of famines. But the constant flooding of rivers and changes in river courses were as catastrophic as earthquakes and famines. Small-scale irrigation was the attempt of the cultivator to bypass disaster.

Population

In the relation of human activity to the landscape, the question of the number of human beings involved remains enigmatic for the Indian past. The immense variation in environment, climate and crop patterns presents problems in projecting figures. The numbers would certainly have been much smaller than those for later times and therefore susceptible to frequent change because of epidemics, campaigns and natural catastrophes. Some surveys linking habitation to humans on the basis of excavations have been attempted but these inevitably remain tentative. Despite some approximate estimates of population in the Harappan cities, based on the size of each city, there is no consensus on the figures. The lower town at Mohenjo-daro, more densely populated than the citadel, is thought to have had a population of about 42,000, but this is regarded by some as too low a figure.

An estimate of 181 million as the population of the subcontinent had been suggested for the late fourth century BC but this figure was obviously far too high. It had been calculated on the size of the Mauryan army, based on figures from Greek sources. These are almost certainly exaggerated since the intention was to project a formidable military strength to oppose Alexander should be have campaigned in the Ganges plain. More recent attempts, calculated on the archaeology of two districts, one in the western Ganges Plain and one in north-western Maharashtra, suggest considerably smaller numbers. These have been further calculated for the mid-first millennium BC as around 20 million. The population for the city of Kaushambi during this period has been estimated at 36,000, which makes an interesting comparison with that of Mohenjo-daro.

Variation in population numbers would have been affected by catastrophes, some of which have been mentioned above. What has not been investigated for early Indian history is the occurrence of disease and epidemics. It has been suggested that one of the causes for a large number of deaths at Mohenjo-daro was the prevalence of severe anaemia. The frequency of floods may well have been followed by epidemics of malaria or similar diseases. It is now being argued that the stalling of animals together with humans in the same hut, as often happens in agrarian societies, would be conducive to the spread of viruses. Urban congestion, which characterized some of the smaller towns in the declining period of the Indus civilization, is a well known cause of a variety of devastating diseases.

Estimates for the early seventeenth century hover around nearly 150 million for the Mughal Empire. The first census of the British Indian administration, carried out in 1881, put the population at a little over 253 million. The argument that there was a stasis between *c.* 500 BC and AD 1500 would therefore not be supported by these recent views. Population growth would be closely associated with human activity and the earliest forms of this would have involved small populations, gradually increasing in number as the activities became more complex and food more readily available.

Categories of Societies

The Indian subcontinent has been the habitat of many societies, ranging from those with a relatively simple organization to others with more complex organizations, the range disallowing easy generalizations. Complex societies were obviously the more dominant and elbowed their way into history. Others were forced to be more reticent but they did not disappear. It is often in the interface of such differing societies that the patterns of Indian culture were forged. As the 'living prehistory' of India, their survival – albeit even in forms that have changed somewhat over time – and their presence in history has to be recognized.

The understanding of early societies has been helped by anthropologists studying pre-modern societies and by those analysing pre-capitalist systems. These studies have not only attempted to explain the difference between early societies and those of the present, but have encouraged historians to ask more incisive questions about the nature of past societies. The attempt here is to understand and differentiate between some of the categories that have been focused on, as a prelude to the historical delineation of Indian society from the early past. These societies still exist in various parts of India, some quite marginally, and are part of what has been called a cultural survival. It would therefore be possible to speak of them in the present tense. But since it is their role in history under discussion here, it is more appropriate to use the past tense.

For convenience, the categories of societies may be listed as hunter-gatherers, pastoralists, peasants and townsmen. In setting out these categories the intention is not to suggest that they were demarcated and separate throughout history. These were predominant categories in different ecological regions, but there were overlaps and changes alongside the historical change that the region underwent. Nor is it intended to set these out in a strictly evolutionary order, each experiencing the previous stage and evolving into the next. Nevertheless, hunter-gatherers had a minimal organization, whereas urban societies were far more complex. Their activities and their relationships with each other need explanation when they surface both in the historical sources and as part of historical events. It was not characteristic of these societies to be invariably self-contained and isolated, for there were overlaps as, for example, in systems of kinship or in the interdependence of some. Even the normative texts that present a homogeneous society have to concede variations in occupation, patriarchy, matriliny, marriage forms and inheritance rules. The importance of these categories is underlined by the fact that until recent centuries such communities could be found juxtaposed in many parts of the subcontinent, although particular categories were predominant in each area. Now that they have been recognized, their contribution to the making of Indian culture is also beginning to receive attention.

Hunter-gatherers

As the term implies, hunter-gatherers lived by hunting animals for food and other requirements, and by foraging for edible plants. Breeding animals or growing crops were not part of their activity, so they were distinct from pastoralists and peasants. They were organized in small bands, sometimes constituted of a few families, and were unfamiliar with matters of status distinction or social organization beyond the family or a larger group linked through kinship. They used the forest and the scrublands as their resource. Hunting grounds may have been nominally demarcated, but such territories were large enough to accommodate more than one group. Such groups could therefore have lived in isolation, provided there were no demands on the territory within which they hunted. When such demands occurred, as when the cultivators from nearby villages or the neighbouring state began to clear forests and start cultivating the cleared land, the existing hunter-gatherers understandably resorted to a ferocious defence of their territory. It is possible that descriptions of those outside the pale of caste society – such as the Shabaras or even the demonic figures said to inhabit the forest, against whom the heroes of the epics had to fight – could be exaggerated accounts of such forest-dwellers resisting intruders. The *rakshasas* of the texts were projected as supernatural beings, and, as part of the unknown wilderness, some were also demonized forest-dwellers.

One of the most graphic descriptions of clearing a forest to establish a settlement occurs in the *Mahabharata*, where the burning of the Khandava Forest to clear land for the settlement of Indraprastha led to large numbers of animals, as well as human and demonic inhabitants, being burnt to death. The presentation of forest-dwellers as demonic would have emphasized their being alien to caste society. The Shabaras, Pulindas, Nishadas and so on, frequently mentioned in early texts, would have been the prototype. The conventional description is that they were stocky in build, dark in complexion, with bloodshot eyes and speaking a strange language. Bana-bhatta, writing in the seventh century AD, described such groups in his *Harshacharita*, but some among them had been acculturated and their activities were similar to those of neighbouring peasant societies.

As this description indicates, forest-dwellers were not confined to being hunter-gatherers. Some were shifting cultivators, or were horticulturalists, and some practised sedentary cultivation. Their societies were organized in clans and the larger unit was the tribe; this organization distinguished them from peasant cultivators and caste society. Social hierarchy received little attention and generally the differentiation was only between the chief, who had the highest status, and the other clansmen. Status and bonding based on kinship relations were more common. They had a preference for living in forests and used a limited technology, their religion was largely animistic, their rituals and beliefs created by shamans, and their isolation permitted them to use their own language.

Awareness of such groups is apparent from early sources, and they were not entirely excluded from the dichotomy underlying much of the thinking about the environment and human activity. The demarcation between what was called the *grama*, village, and the *aranya*, forest or wilderness, and later the *kshetra*, literally field, and the *vana*, forest, reflects a perceived opposition between the two systems. In actual practice the dichotomy was not so sharp and the one faded into the other, but the divide was maintained in theory. The forest was the unknown, the wild, the unpredictable, whereas the settlement was predictable and subject to known laws. Fantasies about the people of the forest, be they *apsaras*, celestial maidens, or *rakshasas*, demons, occur more frequently in the earlier literature.

But there was a perceptible shift in attitudes towards forest-dwellers from earlier to later times. Initially, the forest was the habitat of those regarded as outside the social pale. Subsequently, the establishing of hermitages in the forests and the preference of ascetics for forest retreats led to some romanticizing of the forest. But, parallel to this, the state and the rulers treated forest-people with some suspicion. The *Arthashastra* of Kautilya advised the king not to trust forest-chiefs and verged on regarding them with hostility. From the mid-first millennium A D onwards there were references to the uprooting of forest-dwellers, or to their conquest or assimilation becoming necessary to the foundation of new kingdoms. Encroachments were doubtless intensified from this period, what with clearing forests for cultivation or cutting routes through them. The persistence of such societies to the present time, and in appreciable number, is an indication of their having been resilient as a population and distinctive in culture.

In recent times there has been a debate on whether or not they should be regarded as the *adivasis*, the earliest indigenous inhabitants of India. The game of 'who was there first' played by those claiming to speak on behalf of Aryans, or Dravidians or Austro-Asiatics, or whatever, is historically not viable. Not only are the claims to these identities as being historical and having an immense antiquity untenable, but the paucity of the required evidence to prove this makes it impossible to give answers with any certainty. *Adivasi* societies are not fossilized societies. The historical legitimacy of groups such as forest tribes lies in recognizing their way of life and in analysing the significance of their contribution to the creation of Indian culture since early times. Given that the precise meaning of the term 'tribe' remains controversial and is not uniformly defined, it becomes even more difficult to deduce an authentic history. Confrontations between forest-dwellers and migrating peasants, or with the armies of a kingdom, would result – if the former were overcome by the latter – in the conversion of the former to caste society.

Pastoralists

Another category, more frequently met with in Indian history than historians admit, is that of the pastoralists. Some pastoralists were nomadic, their circuits varying in distance, while others were semi-sedentary, occasionally practising a minimal agriculture as well. Most pastoralists were part of a system of exchange that brought them into contact with cultivators and others. Hence the preference for the term agro-pastoralism, which registers the presence of agriculture even in predominantly pastoral societies. Some acted as carriers of goods and this widened their range of contacts. Pastoral circuits encouraged possibilities of migration and the exploration of new grazing grounds, and therefore involved the history of the movements of peoples.

Pastoral societies generally had a fairly conventional organization, with marginal variations. The family formed the core and patrilineal descent was often traced from a common ancestor. Kinship, whether actual or fictive, was essential to identity and to loyalty, with a premium on the latter. This ensured the coherence of the larger unit, the clan, which because of constant movement would otherwise tend to get dispersed. Charisma grew out of defending the clan when attacked. The clan was relatively egalitarian with a sharing of the produce, although a better and bigger share was collected by the chief. Where herds were acquired through raids, as described in the *Rig-Veda*, the clan chief had to be a successful raider to retain his status. A group of clans constituted what have been called tribes, although this word can cover diverse forms of social groups. Among pastoralists, membership of a tribe generally included those claiming common grazing grounds and descent from a common ancestor, with a common language and customs, as well as rituals. The creation of a tribe could be occasioned by political needs when searching for new pastures or attacking sedentary societies. The tribe can be viewed as segmentary, moving away from the family as the nucleus to larger entities such as lineages which were identified by a common, mythical ancestor. Where descent was unilineal the emphasis was on kinship, whether actual or fictive.

Pastoralists from central Asia intervened from time to time in the history of India, often because of disturbances in central Asia that resulted in migrations and incursions or invasions further south. Such disturbances are thought to have led indirectly to the arrival of the Indo-Aryan speakers and to the Parthians, Shakas, Kushanas, Hunas and Turks. But other pastoral groups within the subcontinent were also important, such as the cattle-keepers in the peninsula. As a component of agriculture and exchange, these filled in the spaces between peasant societies. Cattle-keepers, apart from providing dairy produce, also acted as carriers of commodities for exchange. The *banjaras* continued to perform this role until quite recently. The frequency of memorials to local heroes defending cattle herds in western India and the peninsula is a pointer to the importance of pastoralism.

In the upper reaches of the mountains where agriculture was scarce, transhumance became a practice regulated by the change of season, as it is in many parts of the world. The animals were taken up to pastures at higher elevations in the summer and then brought back in the autumn. This regular movement encouraged incipient trade, as, for example, in the exchange of rice from the Indian side in the Himalayan region for tea from Tibet, an exchange that has elsewhere been called 'a vertical economy'.

Transhumance provided the additional pasturage that at lower altitudes came from cultivating fodder crops or from an arrangement with farmers. There was considerable interaction between pastoralists and peasants, unlike the societies of hunter-gatherers and others, between whom such links were lacking. Pastoralists generally had (and continue to have) a symbiotic relationship with agriculturalists. When the crop was harvested a herd of sheep, goats or cattle was brought by herders to feed on the stubble. The animal droppings manured the land. As a by-product some exchange of essential items also took place. The effectiveness of this system required that the annual circuit of the pastoralists and its timing remained relatively unchanged, so that it was co-ordinated with harvesting activities. The relationship between the herder and the farmer was almost contractual. Such symbiotic relations of agro-pastoralism could have a considerable antiquity.

Societies with a strong clan organization or those determined by lineage identity were frequently chiefdoms; these could be small and simple or could be larger confederacies. The emphasis was on relationships based on kinship bonds. The determining of marriage circles, namely the regulations regarding the taking and giving of women in marriage, were worked out in terms of relationships between various clans. Rules of inheritance could also mark the status of the clan. More complex systems would exclude those who were not members of the clan, but who nonetheless had other connections with the clan. These could be religious functionaries, such as shamans and priests, or could be those who provided labour. The former defined the belief systems and rituals of the clan. The latter were sometimes enslaved persons who had been captured after a raid or those who were not members of the clan. The change from a chiefdom to a kingdom, or the emergence of a state, with its attendant characteristics of the concentration of political power, rudimentary administration, revenue and other such changes, was usually accompanied by a greater reliance on peasant agriculture.

Peasants

The predominant category was that of peasant society. Historians have underlined the role of peasants as producers of food and providers of revenue. The revenue was a stipulated amount of agricultural produce claimed by the ruling group. The change from the categories of hunter-gatherers to pastoralism to agriculture involved using a decreasing area of land, but an increasingly more intensive use of the land. Whereas in the earlier two categories the landscape remained substantially unchanged, agriculture required clearing and cultivation. If the clearing was on a part of the grazing grounds or forested areas there could be confrontations between the societies living in each. It is generally thought that agriculture resulted in an increase of the population, the relative predictability of agricultural produce supporting larger numbers. Surplus food feeds non-producers and therefore elites, priests, soldiers and traders become viable. Unlike pastoral produce that cannot be stored for too long, grain was more easily stored and could therefore be used over a longer period. It has also been argued that density of population and a constant proximity to animals can result in the more rapid spread of disease, so that the increase in population could be offset to some extent by vulnerability to disease.

Peasants, unlike the earlier categories, were sedentary and permanent occupants of the land they cultivated, and the cultivation was not dispersed. This perhaps made them less autonomous than pastoralists. Up to a point this also assisted in holding them down and peasants have generally had a subordinate status in social hierarchies. Peasant discontent was expressed most commonly in India through migrating to new lands, and only in the early second millennium AD is there evidence for what some have interpreted as revolts. In this, the situation is different from that of the Chinese peasant, given the frequency of peasant revolts in early Chinese history. Peasants were much more dependent on the land, a dependence that was also expressed in the worship of deities, generally goddesses, symbolizing what mattered most to the peasant – the earth and fertility.

Peasants were more frequently identified by castes, which were distinct from clans as they were generally not kin-related, nor did they necessarily own resources in common. Peasant society was of various kinds, with differentiation of status based on ownership or arrangements regarding tenure with either superior owners or the state. At the simplest level, those who cultivated their own land paid a tax to the state, and those who cultivated land owned by landowners paid them a rent. Historical analyses involve assessments of the extraction of revenue from their labour and the degrees of unfreedom to which they were subjected. Peasant agriculture was also a necessary precondition of the formation of states and the evolution of cities, since it could produce the agricultural surplus to maintain populations that were not tied to producing their food.

Peasant societies were closely linked to the emergent state. This could have been a primary state, newly formed in an area, or else a secondary state where it had earlier been part of a larger state system and then become an independent state for the first time. Apart from claiming a demarcated territory, the state had legal authority over the population and over resources, was sovereign in governing and exercised power through a hierarchy of administration. The institutions of the state such as the treasury, the administrative structure, the focus of power encapsulated in the army or in systems of coercion, were concentrated in the capital which was generally the most important town.

Townsmen

The genesis of towns varied: some began as administrative centres, with a focus on the location of the treasury where the tribute was brought; some as centres of craft production more specialized than in villages; some as pilgrimage centres; and some as centres of exchange. An area could have a hierarchical network of villages and small towns culminating in a central city. The physical plan of a town focused on a defence circuit and the central location of those in authority, and reflected economic linkages of production and exchange. The consumption of wealth was also thought of as characteristic of some cities. The concentrations of people were generally those involved in the production of specialized items and their exchange: they were artisans and merchants. But a number of them retained links with rural areas, and towns also housed groups that were transitional between village and city. Townspeople depended on the countryside for much of their food. This encouraged rural–urban relationships that varied and were not uniform.

There was a more marked division in the specializations characteristic of towns as compared to villages. As the loci of craft production and of exchange there was a premium on quantity, since production catered to more than a single village; and, given the concentration of specialists and the more extensive distribution of products, there was also an emphasis on quality. Both these demands frequently led to some organization or association of craftsmen and artisans where occupational requirements had priority. This was extended to associations of merchants whose occupation was to transport and distribute the items produced for exchange. Such associations, similar to guilds, became central to urban life. The bond began as an occupational one, but came to include marriage circles if the association became sufficiently large. Its identity was further established when it began to receive investments and property. Such associations also became patrons of religious sects and, where there was wealth, donations from them were recorded at sacred centres.

Exchange relations varied according to the products involved. Barter, or the direct exchange of item for item, was negotiated in terms of the value of each item. It tended to be a localized exchange with a limited choice of items. Exchange centres as incipient markets conducted trade in a large variety of goods, including those of high value, and the choice could in theory have been more entrepreneurial. Sometimes the underpinnings were determined more by social considerations than economic. Thus, goods of high value were also a mark of status and were often exchanged outside the commercial circuit as gifts among families of high status or as objects of patronage. Trade converted the item into a commodity that could be transported to distant places. Sale generally involved a money transaction. Coined metallic money radically changed the nature of exchange. Commodities were valued in terms of a common medium – money. Issued by an institution such as a guild or a state, it could be of varying value depending on the metal and the weight, and could be easily carried, thus facilitating long-distance exchange. This encouraged the accumulation of wealth and forward speculation. Complex exchange furthered the growth of markets.

The heterogeneity of urban life distinguished it from the village. Towns were closely packed settlements with populations larger than in a village. Norms of social behaviour tended to be more flexible, and heterodox ideas were often developed in urban centres or in places associated with these. Early brahmanical normative texts tend to disapprove of the town, although in later works this view changes. Sophisticated Sanskritic culture came to be city-based and the man-about-town was the central figure in many writings, an implicit contrast to the simple country yokel.

The Creation of Castes

Reference to these categories of societies ties into a process of social organization that is fundamental to understanding Indian society. This was, and is, the prevalence of group identities referred to as castes. The word as used in modern European languages comes from a root meaning 'pure' and reflects the application of what is termed as *varna*, a concept now often translated as ritual status. In a hierarchy of status the highest and purest was that of the brahmans. Interestingly, an account of Indian society written by the Greek, Megasthenes, in the fourth century BC, merely refers to seven broad divisions without any association of degrees of purity. He says that the philosophers are the most respected, but includes in this group the brahmans as well as those members of heterodox sects – the *shramanas* – who did not regard the brahmans as being of the highest status. Elements of caste have been noticed in some other societies but the pattern they take in Indian society is different.

As a construction around ritual status the ranking of the brahman had to be the highest, as ritually the brahman represented the purest category. The evolution of this idea can be seen from the Vedic corpus, and since this constitutes the earliest literary source, it came to be seen as the origin of caste society. This body of texts reflected the brahmanical view of caste, and maintained that the *varnas* were created on a particular occasion and have remained virtually unchanged. Control over ritual not only gave authority to the brahman *varna*, but the assertion of purity set it apart. In the *varna* ordering of society notions of purity and pollution were central and activities were worked out in this context. *Varna* is formulaic and orderly, dividing society into four groups arranged in a hierarchy – the brahman (priest), *kshatriya* (warrior aristocrat), *vaishya* (cultivator and trader) and *shudra* (who labours for the others), the fifth being the untouchable and therefore beyond the pale.

However, there have been other ways of looking at the origins and functioning of caste society. A concept used equally frequently for caste is *jati*. It is derived from a root meaning 'birth', and the numbers of *jatis* are listed by name and are too numerous to be easily counted. The hierarchical ordering of *jatis* is neither consistent nor uniform, although hierarchy cannot be denied. The two concepts of *jati* and *varna* overlap in part but are also different. The question therefore is, how did caste society evolve and which one of the two preceded the other? According to some scholars, the earliest and basic division was *varna* and the *jatis* were subdivisions of the *varna*, since the earliest literary source, the Vedic corpus, mentions *varnas*. But it can also be argued that the two were distinct in origin and had different functions, and that the enveloping of *jati* by *varna*, as in the case of Hindu castes, was a historical process.

The origin of *varna* is reasonably clear from the references in the Vedic corpus. The origin myth describes the primeval sacrifice and the emergence of four groups – brahman, *kshatriya*, *vaishya* and *shudra* – which were subsequently called the four *varnas*. *Jatis* are not mentioned until the later sections of the corpus, and then rather cursorily, which is not surprising since the corpus is essentially a collection of ritual texts. Yet it is possible that the formation of *jatis* may even have been the earlier process. The genesis of the *jati* may have been the clan, prior to its becoming a caste.

For a society to become a caste-based society there have to be three preconditions: the society must register social disparities; there has to be unequal access of various groups within that society to economic resources; inequalities should be legitimized through a theoretically irreversible hierarchy and the imposition of the hierarchy claim to be based on a super-natural authority. The latter takes the form of a ritual demarcation dependent on degrees of assumed purity or pollution determined by those controlling the religious ideology. The first two features would be present in a minimal way in many societies. These would be essential characteristics of a *jati* and might even occur in a lesser form in some clan organizations. The ideological factor derives from *varna* and is characteristic of Hindu society. The insistence on the absolute purity of one group requires the counter-weight of the absolute impurity of another – in this case the untouchable.

There are close parallels between the clan as a form of social organization and the *jati*. *Jati* derives its meaning from 'birth' which determines membership of a group and the status within it; it also determines rules relating to the circles within which marriage could or could not take place and rules relating to the inheritance of property. These would strengthen separate identities among *jatis*, a separation reinforced by variance in ritual and worship as well as the acceptance of a hierarchy among *jatis*. Therefore, these are entities which gradually evolve their own cultural identities, with differentiations of language, custom and religious practice. A significant difference between clans and *jatis* is that occupation becomes an indicator of status, since *jatis* emerge in conditions of a wider range of occupations than clan-based societies. The differentiations would be influenced by contact with other societies.

Systems of social organization take a while to evolve. The nature of pre-Vedic societies has not been investigated in sufficient detail since the evidence is archaeological and therefore not easily readable for this purpose. Inevitably explanations remain hypothetical as is the one being suggested here. Chalcolithic societies are sometimes said to be chiefships and this would assume a clan organization of some kind. The urban Harappan cultures indicate more complex systems, probably with a clear differentiation between those in authority controlling the production of the cities and those who laboured for them. The theory that might have legitimized this is not easily discernible from the excavated data, but the social hierarchies are evident. Peasant cultivators and pastoralists fed the cities, labour of various kinds was involved in their construction and maintenance, artisans were the producers of goods for exchange and there was the overall authority controlling distribution and asserting governmental powers. Such a society may well have been based on a hierarchy of *jatis* and the differentiation between those who produced and those who controlled was doubtless legitimized through an ideology, probably religious. Social hierarchy requires an ideological legitimation. When the urban system collapsed the legitimation might well have disappeared, although the basic social organization of some clans and some potential or actual *jatis* may have continued in various forms.

Segmentation and hierarchy made it easier to control such a society, but the continuance of both required an ideological explanation. Occupations also had to be brought into the hierarchy to assist control over the system. Labour, for instance, had to be placed at the lowest level to ensure its availability and continuity. It is possible therefore that in the post-Harappan period, with the emergence of Vedic culture, the ideological legitimation was encapsulated in *varna* which underlined hierarchy, occupation and purity. The ideology of *varna* was then imposed on societies that may have been familiar with the notions of *jati*. The idea of purity and pollution, derived from religious sanction and knitted into the *jati* structure, made it difficult to change the system.

The clue to the formation of at least some early *jatis* may lie in tracing back the relationship between settled societies and others. For example, a differentiation between forest-dwellers and *jati* society is that the former do not conform to caste rules. An interface between them was created through historical pressures, such as hermitages or kingdoms encroaching into the forest, routes cutting through the forest or demands for forest resources from local administrations. According to caste rules, the forest-dwellers were regarded as *mlechchha* – those outside the social pale of caste society. If they were given a caste status, either when they were converted into peasants or into craftsmen, then they would become part of an acceptable hierarchy. Such a status would be conferred upon them where there was need for closely controlled labour to produce the requirements of a society that functioned as a state.

Hypothetically, a forest-clan would generally be a group of people sharing defined space, kinship relations, material culture, a near egalitarian status, custom and ritual. Where such a group begins to concede that there can be unequal access to resources among its members, and treats this differentiation as a hierarchical status inherited at birth, the elements of *jati* begin to surface. The change would be encouraged through new attitudes to resources and authority or through close and continued contact with a society differentiated by caste. *Varna* status would follow, with such groups performing rituals and observing, at least in theory, a hierarchy according to certain prescribed rules of the *Dharma-shastras*, as well as accepting notions of purity and pollution among the castes. The families of chiefs would aspire to *kshatriya* or aristocratic status, while others would fill the range of lower *shudra jatis*. Where Hinduism had to incorporate a local cult, the priest of the cult could be inducted into brahman status or a lesser status could be given to priests of less important cults.

The conversion from tribe or clan to caste, or from *jana* to *jati* as it is sometimes called, was one of the basic mutations of Indian social history and, whether it was the result of persuasion or confrontation, would have varied with individual situations. For those being converted it would have affected all aspects of their life. Certain foods, such as beef and alcohol, would become taboo to such members of the tribe who were inducted into higher-caste status, and eating together – which had been a form of bonding among clans – would be disapproved of; the assertion of women as equal members of society would be curtailed, forcing them to accept the subordinate part; religious rituals were new and strange as were some of the deities to be worshipped – although in this matter substantial concessions might have been necessary, with the Puranic aspects of the Hindu religion incorporating the deities and rituals of such new castes; the introduction of ownership of land and revenue collection could have resulted in the oppressive experience of debt bondage for some; and the notion of hierarchy in caste was opposed to the more egalitarian ethos of the clan. New activities encouraged the breaking apart of some earlier clans.

The conversion of clan to *jati* was not the only avenue to creating castes. Since caste identities were also determined by occupations, various professional associations, particularly urban artisans, gradually coalesced into *jatis*, beginning to observe *jati* rules by accepting a social hierarchy that defined marriage circles and inheritance laws, by adhering to common custom and by identifying with a location. Yet another type of *jati* was the one that grew out of a religious sect that may have included various *jatis* to begin with, but started functioning so successfully as a unit that eventually it too became a caste. A striking example of this is the history of the Lingayat caste in the peninsula.

This process of *jati* formation was primarily a change in social identity and ways of social functioning. Subsequent to this change, a *jati* was also inducted into a religious identity. Where the religious identity was of Vedic Brahmanism or, later, of Puranic Hinduism, there was a shuffling of *jatis* into hierarchies and the *varna* hierarchy was imposed. Ritual status meant observing rules of purity and pollution, where the brahman was regarded as the purest and the others in descending order down to the most impure, who was untouchable. The process became apparent when members of the same group, for example, the Abhiras, were given different *varna* statuses – brahman or *shudra*.

It was not that an existing *varna* was invariably subdivided into *jatis*, but that *jatis* were often allotted *varna* statuses. This might also explain why *jatis* are universally recognized in India as functional social units even if their names vary from region to region, but *varna* statuses are not uniformly observed, barring the brahman and the untouchable. Intermediate castes have a varying hierarchy. Thus, in some historical periods the trading caste of *khatris* in the Punjab and the landowning *velalas* in Tamil Nadu were dominant groups. *Jati* identities therefore often provide more incisive information on social reality than do *varna* identities. Nevertheless, references to *varnas* as a shorthand in the texts act as pointers to social disparities. Since the status of the higher *varna* was protected, the maximum recruitment of new *jatis* would have been into the *shudra* status. This would accommodate varieties of professions. Therefore some existing practices would also be accommodated in the new *varna* identity of *shudras*.

The creation of *jatis* as the primary step in the making of caste society also meant that *jatis* could be converted to religions other than the Hindu. An interesting characteristic of caste society in relation to religion is that, apart from hunter-gatherers, shifting cultivators and forest-dwellers (who were regarded as beyond the pale of caste), many religious communities other than Hindus have also observed rules similar to caste. *Jati* identities were frequently continued even on conversion to religions that theoretically rejected caste, such as Islam or Christianity. This was particularly so when an entire *jati* or a substantial part of one, in a village or town, was converted. The continuities among such groups pertained to regulations of kinship and inheritance, and to the observance of marriage circles, and less to ritual. This was largely because there was continuity in social custom even after conversion.

This also raises the issue of religious conversion. It would seem that the conversion of an individual to Hinduism would present difficulties and it would be easier to convert the larger group – the clan or the *jati* – and allot it a *varna* status. Other religions such as Buddhism, Jainism, Christianity and Islam were more flexible in encouraging individual conversion. This is not to suggest that the conversion of the individual was not possible, but it was more problematic for Hinduism because of the intermeshing of caste and religious sect.

The categories of societies described here do not exhaust the permutations inherent in social forms. Variations of these coexisted in a region in the same historical period. With some of these categories being transmuted into castes, a new dimension is added to social history. However, at particular times and in particular regions, some among them could be dominant and the need to explain the structure of social relationships sharpens the historical image of place and time. Although the historical reconstruction of a region or a period focuses on the predominant forms, the roles of the lesser ones require integration. Societies in India evolved and changed. Understanding these processes involves understanding situations of assimilation and confrontation, of tolerance and intolerance, of social incorporation and contestation, all of which become essential to historical analyses. These call for not just a familiarity with the evidence from the past, but also an explanation and understanding of this evidence. Data on the earliest forms of societies are more easily observed in the archaeological record.

3

Antecedents

Prehistoric Beginnings

The interest in the archaeology of India is rooted in the activity of the late nineteenth century, focusing on the collection of historical remains to help in understanding the past and illumine the present. The search for antiquities that constituted pre-history was encouraged by comparative studies with other parts of the world, and the recognition of similarities or of deviances. To begin with, antiquities of the historical period were mainly objects that were later classified as art remains. Interpretations of excavated data became current during the last century and these have undergone change from time to time.

The excavation of the Indus cities in the 1920s and 1930s led to a re-orientation in Indian archaeology, their origin being initially attributed to possible colonial transpositions from west Asian civilizations. Even later, when the methods and techniques of excavating were altered and made more rigorous by Mortimer Wheeler, the shadow of this imprint did not disappear. The pendulum has now in part swung the other way, for some archaeologists would like to explain the Harappa culture as entirely indigenous and a lineal ancestor to subsequent cultures.

In the intervening half-century between these two interpretations, new ways of examining archaeological data were adopted by other archaeologists. The questions asked of the data have moved away from being confined to discussions of origins and chronology and have begun to explore the nature of various archaeological cultures and the changes manifested by them or by successor cultures. The context of the artefact demands attention more than just the artefact. Hopefully this approach will help shift the interest away from merely fuelling the search for origins. This will, however, require more empirical data, from a range of cultures, collected through controlled surveys and systematic excavations and motivated by questions that relate to explaining the various societies that created the Indian past.

The history and identity of human settlements in India goes back to prehistoric times, when there was a gradual spread from the sporadic settlements of the old stone age to the more densely distributed habitations of later stone ages, followed by the even later societies of a more complex kind. The question of the identity of the earliest settlers is linked to the evolution and early history of *homo sapiens* and their dispersal from Africa. The earlier geological conditions assume that the Indian subcontinent was linked to east Africa in remote times.

The contours of societies in India evidenced by archaeology broadly conform to those recorded for adjoining parts of the world, although of course there are differences that derive from specific environmental contexts. The tracks can be traced through the recognized patterns of the settlements and cultures that have been labelled as the palaeolithic, mesolithic, neolithic, chalcolithic and iron ages. Not all societies evolved from one to the next in a series, nor were they uniform in time throughout the subcontinent. Nevertheless, a brief survey of what has come to be called pre-history and proto-history provides the antecedents to the earliest history.

Archaeological data is in the form of tangible, material remains. This becomes the basis for calculating chronology. Methods of dating have undergone impressive improvements in the last half-century and are among the many areas of archaeology in which modern scientific techniques have made enormous contributions. For many very early periods there are methods such as spectrometric dating, or measuring potassium or radio-active decay, for arriving at an early date. For periods of the last 10,000 years, the three most commonly used techniques are radio-carbon dating (Carbon-14), based on measuring the loss of carbon in organic material; dendro-chronology, which refers to the number of tree rings in wood; and thermoluminescence (TL), which can be applied to artefacts of particular materials that have been put through fire, such as pottery. Given the range of techniques, it is possible to calibrate chronology, as was done a couple of decades ago for Carbon-14. Dates for archaeological data therefore tend to be reasonably secure and can also help in ascertaining historical chronology, provided archaeological evidence is available.

Terms such as culture and civilization, when used in an archaeological context, have a somewhat different meaning from their general use. Culture refers to the pattern of life of a society, so there are multiple kinds of cultures. Such patterns would include the use made of the habitual environment, social relations, language and ritual. Typologies of cultures were earlier made on the basis of the tools used by human groups. These were largely of stone, changing from the older and larger tools of the palaeolithic to the smaller ones of the mesolithic, and the polished ones of the neolithic, to the use of both stone and metal in the chalcolithic. Tool typologies are sometimes added to or substituted by types of pottery (when it comes into use), characteristic of certain kinds of settlements. The pottery label is used to identify the people who made it. Labels such as hunter-gatherers, cattle-keepers and early farming communities are also used, since they are more descriptive. Similarities in cultures do not necessarily indicate that they evolved from the same people. Patterns of life and the artefacts that go with them can take similar forms, even if those who make them are unconnected. But where there are connections, similarities have to be differentiated from imitations.

Civilization implies a pattern that is thought of as more complex and sophisticated, incorporating urban living and all that it connotes, a conscious aesthetic awareness, sophisticated religious beliefs and the use of texts. City societies are stratified and the wider context is the state, with its unequal social divisions. Ruling groups need not be based on kin connections. A civilization can cover a wide area, recognized by the similarity of artefacts, and its extent often arises from the interdependence of peoples who are affected by its systems in various ways.

Palaeolithic and Mesolithic

Evidence for hunter-gatherers of the palaeolithic comes from various parts of the subcontinent. The initial studies focused on the north-west, in terraces of the Soan River and in the Potwar Plateau. Since then sites have been found scattered across the subcontinent. Habitations tended to be in rock shelters, frequently located in Madhya Pradesh as at Bhimbetka but also found in other parts of India, or in caves such as at Sanghao (north-west Pakistan), or in Kurnool (Andhra Pradesh), or even sometimes as camps in the open, although there is less evidence for the latter type of settlement than for rock shelters. Shelters in the open were sometimes made of foliage and would therefore not survive, but stone tools and signs of settlement provide clues to such shelters. Sites are generally located near water sources and where plants are readily available. Fossil remains are another source of information and fossil animals include some that were eventually domesticated, such as cattle, sheep, goats and others that remained in the wild, including the cat family and deer. In the earliest stage food was obtained by hunting animals and gathering edible plants and tubers. Settlements tended to be close to scrub jungles and watering places as, for instance, at Hungsi. The hunting of large animals would have required the combined effort of a group of people, whereas smaller animals could be more easily ensnared or hunted by individuals.

The sites date from before 30,000 to about 10,000 BC. Stone tools, hand-sized and flaked-off large pebbles, are among the more obvious characteristics of palaeolithic sites. Large pebbles are often found in river terraces, such as those of the Soan Valley or the upper reaches of rivers as in the Siwalik Hills of the north. A skull found in the Narmada Valley is likely to yield interesting evidence. Various techniques of analysing plant and animal remains help in the reconstruction of environment and climate. Variations in climate were an additional challenge to the small bands of hunter-gatherers. Their way of life moved gradually towards attempts to domesticate animals and plants and make some crude pots. Evidence of their perceptions of the world around them is rare. We know little about how they communicated and next to nothing about the languages they spoke, nor much about what constituted their concerns beyond the obvious. A few paintings on rock at Bhimbetka, discovered alongside other later paintings, are thought to be of this period and reflect a concern with success in hunting and with fertility. At Baghor I (Madhya Pradesh) a natural stone, shaped like a triangle, has been interpreted as a symbol of female fertility. Parallel to it, is the worship of a similar stone as a goddess in neighbouring villages today.

Improved technologies of obtaining food would have enabled some hunter-gatherers to settle. Sites of the mesolithic – the middle stone age that succeeded the palaeolithic – show the use of a different type of stone tool. These are tiny stone artefacts, often not more than five centimetres in size and therefore called microliths, consisting of flakes, blades, burins, points, scrapers, crescents and various geometrical forms. The technique of making these was also through flaking off pieces by striking the larger stone at an appropriate angle. The small microlith was used in a greater variety of ways than the bigger stone artefacts because it could be hafted to many more functional tools, for instance to make knives and sickles. An increase in small arrowheads points to the use of the bow and arrow. This meant that the close stalking of animals was becoming less frequent than shooting an arrow from a distance. This also reduced the fear of animals attacking the stalker. In order to make the small tools it was necessary to change from using pebble-stones to a different kind of stone, such as quartz, chert, agate, chalcedony and suchlike, which are easier to flake as small tools. This change indicates a greater confidence in relation to the environment and in controlling technology, but also points to a shift in habitat closer to the new raw material. River pebbles were now less in demand and the new kind of rock was more easily available in hills and forests. That the transition was extremely gradual is evident from the many centuries between the earlier and later patterns. The new technology introduced a change in living patterns, and hunting and gathering were initially supplemented by the use of wild grains and then by domesticated animals, horticulture and primitive cultivation. A tendency to settle for longer periods in an area can be surmised. Hunting and gathering continued to a lesser degree into later times, but dependence solely on these activities for food began to gradually decrease.

If the sites excavated so far are an indication, mesolithic activities took place away from heavy monsoon forests and remained on the drier uplands. Ranging between the tenth and the fifth millennia, this period again witnessed variations of wet and dry climate. Many settlements were in or near rock shelters, as in Madhya Pradesh, but, judging by postholes – in one case indicating circular huts – and habitation areas, some were more daring in venturing beyond the caves and shelters. Mesolithic remains have also been found in Langhnaj (Gujarat), Adamgarh (Madhya Pradesh), Rajasthan, Sarai Nahar Rai and Mahadaha (Uttar Pradesh), and in Bihar. Primitive querns and rubbing-stones at some sites suggest a more varied preparation of wild grains and plants as food. This is reinforced by the presence at one site of what seem to be potsherds of crude handmade pottery, together with an object identified as a storage bin. Animal bones in the habitation area become more frequent and include deer, boar and the now extinct ostrich, and some are bones of what were to become domesticated animals, such as bovines, sheep and goats.

Burials are occasionally within the habitation area and grave goods – such as microliths, shells and an ivory pendant – are placed in the grave. Some ideas of an after-life seem evident from the grave goods. The location may have developed from attachment to the person, but could have been due to more functional considerations, such as protecting the grave from animal predators. Very occasionally there are double burials, but not invariably of male and female. The skeletons suggest they were people who died between the ages of fifteen and forty, the average life expectancy being half-way. This would be usual for those times, but by our standards life expectancy was short. Some skeletons show evidence of osteo-arthritis.

Such early societies would have been organized as bands of people, with possibly some demarcation of families. Constant migration in search of food limited the numbers in a family, since children, tiring easily from walking long distances, could be an impediment to movement. Given that the population sizes were small, a disease could wipe out an entire settlement.

Rock shelters and caves in Madhya Pradesh and elsewhere that were habitation sites with paintings and engravings on the rock surface, continue to be found after careful exploration. Some are of the mesolithic period, but at other more extensive sites such as Bhimbetka the practice of painting continued into historical times. The latter can be dated from scenes depicting horses and elephants in processions and in battle. The themes of the earlier art focused on the life of hunters and gatherers. The hunting of animals, particularly varieties of deer, was a major enterprise. Both man and animal are represented in an abstract style, while the bodies of the animals often have cross-hatching and other designs. Presumably this was part of the ritual of the hunt, where the depiction of a successful chase became a talisman to ensure such a hunt, the assumption being that the representation would actually materialize. Such representation is the expression of cognition in which sympathetic magic is thought to be unfailing. Figures of men and women symbolizing fertility are also frequent. It would be interesting to speculate whether these communities scattered across the hills of central India shared cults and rituals.

The geographical extent of prehistoric rock art is impressive. Rock engravings, believed to be associated with the later stage of the neolithic, occur in the Edakal cave in the Western Ghats in Kerala and depict human activity in an unusual style of engraving. Recently, in the exploration of the Gilgit and Baltistan area in the far north, engravings of male figures and depictions of masks have been found, but the largest in number are of ibexes and others with highly stylized horns. It has been suggested that some of these engravings might link the upper Indus to central Asia, going back to the third millennium BC.

Neolithic

The change to a neolithic pattern, where the beginnings of agriculture and the domestication of animals becomes crucial, introduced what Gordon Childe once argued was a revolution through the practice of agriculture. This was not a sudden, radical change, and some activities of the earlier age had anticipated these developments. It may have been accelerated in areas experiencing a change in the environment as also by the ingenuity of men and women attempting improvements in their way of life. But its ultimate effect, inasmuch as it changed the processes of obtaining food and establishing new types of links between humans, animals and land, was revolutionary. A larger, and up to a point predictable, production of food may perhaps have been required by and resulted in a growing population. Together with this came the possibility of storing food – at least for a short time – which would have further encouraged the making of pots for storage. A higher density of population in places where agriculture was practised might also have brought about a more sedentary population. It is thought that gradually those practising settled agriculture may, on occasion, have overwhelmed hunter-gatherers and shifting cultivators. Habitats might have tended to encourage a concentration of people. This would eventually have made urbanization possible, but after a considerable experience of cultivation and sedentary occupations.

Neolithic sites occur in diverse parts of the subcontinent: in Galighai in the Swat Valley, Sarai Khola further to the south, and in the loess plateau of the Kashmir Valley that allowed pit dwellings; in Chirand in Bihar and in sites in the Belan Valley of Uttar Pradesh, such as Chopani Mando and Koldihva; eastwards to Pandu Rajar Dhibi, and further to Daojali Hading and Sarutaru; and in a cluster of sites spreading out from the Raichur doab and the Godavari and Krishna Valleys in the peninsula at Utnur, Piklihal, Maski, Tekkalakota, Brahmagiri, Hallur, Paiyampalli and T. Narsipur. Some of these sites were active into the historical period when a few had elements of urbanism.

Initially the cultivators are likely to have moved from place to place before more intensive agriculture made them sedentary. There may well have been confrontation between hunter-gatherers and shifting cultivators, some of the latter having only recently been hunter-gatherers themselves, although now wishing to subordinate other activities to agriculture. Ultimately, the dominance of the latter was established and the dependence on hunting and gathering would have declined. The suggestion that the transition to agriculture was made by women, who stayed home while the men hunted, is plausible. This gave women the opportunity to sow and then to tend what they had sown. But the more extensive change came with plough agriculture which was handled by men. Agriculture provided some predictability to the supply of food. The extension of cultivation required a sedentary society, and with technological advances it was possible to produce more food than the minimum required by the the band of people. This surplus food had the potential of being used, as it was in later times, for a variety of exchanges – some for other items or some even for obtaining labour. This use of the extra food gradually introduced stratification into a society where some controlled the food and used it for exchange, while others were left to produce the extra food.

Technologically there was a substantial improvement in tools, which were now polished. The removal of rough edges increased their functional effectiveness, as in the case of polished stone axes. The technological improvement of the polished axes as compared to the earlier ones is quite striking. Gradually, at some sites grass huts gave way to wattle-and-daub huts (constructed from branches of trees and foliage plastered with mud), and these in turn to mud-brick structures, small granaries and water storage. Hand-turned pottery later gave way to wheel-thrown pottery, and the production of a few ornaments. Sites such as Mehrgarh, because of the extensive horizontal excavations, show a well-demarcated transition from early agriculture to the preliminaries of urbanization. The spread of agriculture has been explained as moving from west Asia to north-west India, but the evidence from sites in the latter area suggests that the transition to agriculture may have occurred more locally.

Wheat, barley, rice and millet began to be cultivated in different areas and at different times. The provenance of rice cultivation appears to have been in eastern India. Gradually, the domestication of sheep, goats and cattle was established. This provided dairy produce and some meat when required, reducing the dependence on hunting. Pastoralism and agriculture were interdependent at this stage, although the changes carried the potential of a bifurcation. The cultivation of crops permitted some predictability and control over obtaining food, but required permanent settlement to make a qualitative change. The domestication of animals provided food more readily. Larger animals were used additionally for traction and for transportation. The increasing use of pottery allowed for storage of food, which encouraged cooking, and the range in the size of the pots enabled their use in other ways. Where grave goods were buried with bodies, pots were sometimes included as items of ritual value. Large urns were also used as coffins for the burial of infants whose mortality is noticeable in these earlier cultures.

The increasing emphasis on farming in neolithic cultures draws attention to parallels observed by anthropologists studying similar societies. Farming anticipates the potentiality for chiefdoms where initially cultivation is carried out by family and clan labour. In many early societies the family as a unit, or as a constituent part of a clan, herded animals and cultivated crops. Younger members were expected to labour for the elders. This was labour performed because of a kinship link and is prior to the induction of non-kin labour, which marks a significant social departure but which probably becomes a resource in the more developed farming associated with later, socially stratified cultures. When societies became more complex and the system changed, non-kin labour was added or replaced kin-based labour. This was the labour of those who were not kinsmen but were willing to labour for recompense, or, possibly, if they were captives they could be forced to labour for those who had captured them. The use of non-kin labour also ushers in the possibility of an increase in produce and this would have raised the question of how the increase was to be distributed. Controlling and organizing labour in such situations, whether kin-based or not, would become a major source of authority and one of the functions of the chief.

Neolithic sites are scattered in various places and evolve at varying times. Among the early sites is Mehrgarh near Quetta in Baluchistan, one amid a number of village sites. This is a more impressive site than many others as it provides evidence of the continuity of the settlement over a few millennia and the gradual evolution of the settlement from agriculture towards urbanization. Some parallels are evident at sites in the north-west, which can be attributed to a cross-fertilization of ideas and activities in the region. Settlements were not isolated and the interaction between them could have been through an exchange of goods associated with even a minimal specialization in the production of exchangeable items, such as beads, through pastoral circuits and migrations and through confrontations. These would have created networks to channel exchange on a more regular basis, together with marriage circles and new ritual practices.

The origins of Mehrgarh have been dated to *c.* 7000 BC. The cultivation of wheat and barley, the herding of cattle, sheep and goats, habitation in mud-brick huts with hearths, a possible granary, pit burials with personal effects, beads of turquoise and lapis, and a scatter of clay figurines are aspects of a cultural pattern that was established by the sixth millennium. By the fourth millennium wheel-thrown pottery was introduced. Sites of the sixth to fourth millennia BC – also in the north-west at Kile Gul Mohammad, Rana Ghundai, Sheri Khan Tarakai, Gumla and Rehman Dheri – were similarly centres of pastoral and agricultural activities, as well as being located along routes crossing the area. The Nal culture in Baluchistan and the Kulli culture to the south were also part of this scene. Some of these sites change from agro-pastoralism to farming, then to the beginnings of towns, and are therefore precursors of Harappan urbanization.

Close to the Indus River in the plains were the settlements at Kot Diji and Amri, with features which were the forerunners of some of the characteristics of the Harappa culture. The painted designs on the pottery at Kot Diji, for example, were based on the leaf of the *pipal/ficus religiosa* tree, and on fish and fish scales similar to those on Harappan pottery. Kot Diji features are also evident in some of the pottery from what have been called the Sothi sites in Rajasthan, such as the pre-Harappan settlement at Kalibangan. Further east, there are some similarities in artefacts from Kunal and Banawali (Haryana). The Aravalli Hills are rich in copper, and places essentially involved in the production of copper, such as Ganeshwar, were important. Practices in the alloying of metal were to become a legacy from the Harappans. Further south in Gujarat there is evidence of pre-Harappan settlements, some at places that were preludes to important Harappan towns such as Dholavira.

Some of the settlements in Rajasthan and Punjab also carried features associated with the Hakra Plain, particularly present-day Bahawalpur and Cholistan. The Hakra River, which gradually dried up, was once a substantial river although all that remains of its upper reaches now is the Ghaggar in the Punjab. The question has been raised whether the Indus-Hakra area was more pertinent to the rise of the Harappan cities, given the dense cluster of sites in the area, than was Baluchistan and the north-west; and, if this was so, perhaps the civilization should be called the Indus-Sarasvati civilization. However, the crucial factor is not the number of sites but the nature of the sites. Judging the nature of a site does not lie in merely listing artefacts, but assessing, in this case, the role of the site in encouraging the change from pre-urban activities to urbanization. Given the earlier and more widespread evidence for the evolution towards urbanization in the north-west, the initial impetus for the transition to urban centres lay, more likely, in the Indus plain and the north-west. In terms of access to the raw materials used in craft production and in controlling trade, which provided the impetus to urbanization, the centres in the north-west and the Indus Plain were certainly better situated than those in Cholistan. The former were more active, and with the potential of having connections beyond the borderlands.

Although the evidence from the north-west provides some indicators of the emergence of urbanism, in other areas, such as Gujarat, it has been described as a relatively sudden mutation accompanied by a notable increase in the size of urban settlements. This could have followed from the earlier Harappans reaching out into new areas and the latter adapting to the demands of the former. This might account for the seeming uniformity combined with a continuing presence of some regional features. It would also have allowed for the spread of Harappan material culture, which makes it the most expansive civilization of its time.

The evolution of cities in north-western India has to be viewed not only in the local context, but also in the context of archaeological change and the movement of peoples in the borderlands and beyond, with whom there had been earlier contacts. This does not, however, preclude the possibility of areas with a potential for urbanization, such as Kutch, coastal Gujarat or Cholistan, developing this potential on the heels of the first urbanization. The large urban site of Ganweriwala in Bahawalpur remains to be excavated and the stages towards urbanization in these parts have yet to be determined. It is more appropriate therefore to continue referring to the civilization as the Indus civilization or the Harappa culture, the latter name deriving from the initial site which was one of the earlier cities of the civilization.

Chalcolithic

The innovation in the chalcolithic cultures was the use of copper and bronze, which forged the new technology of smelting metal ore and crafting metal artefacts. Obtaining raw material could now necessitate long-distance travel, which was encouraged due to the high value placed on the production of metal. The networks of chalcolithic cultures therefore widened. The use of stone tools was not abandoned and some of the microlithic forms, such as the parallel-sided blades, continued as essential items. Copper and bronze introduced yet another improved technology, which in turn encouraged a specialization in crafts in particular areas, often where the raw material was easily available and craftsmen would gather. The inclusion of metal technology introduced some complexities into the patterns of living, for instance determining who was to control the new technology, since those who were producing the artefacts were not necessarily the same as those in authority. Where the use of a script accompanies chalcolithic cultures, they are sometimes referred to as proto-historic and are differentiated from prehistoric cultures which were prior in form and lacking both metal and a script. When the incidence of the use of bronze increases perceptibly, some prefer to call it the bronze age.

The First Urbanization – the Cities of the Indus Civilization

The earliest excavations of the cities of the Indus civilization were at Harappa (Punjab) and Mohenjo-daro (Sind) and these remain the most important urban complexes, larger than the other towns. Many of the latter – large or small – have been excavated, some only partially, such as Kot Diji (Sind), Kalibangan (Rajasthan), Rupar (Punjab), Rakhigarhi,

Banawali, Mitathal (Haryana) and the ports of Lothal and Dholavira, and Surkotada (Gujarat). Ganweriwala (Bahawalpur) awaits excavation. The larger cities are approximately a hundred hectares in size and the lesser towns come close to half that size. It has been suggested that if the extensions of the city are included Mohenjo-daro could cover an area of 200 hectares.

The time period of the civilization has in the past been divided into the pre-Harappan (starting in the late fourth millennium and continuing to 2600 BC), the Mature Harappan (from c. 2600 to 1900 BC) and the Late Harappan (to c. 1750 BC). There is sometimes a preference for the term Early Harappan rather than pre-Harappan, since it suggests continuity into the Mature Harappan. Other labels have also been used in recent studies but there is no final consensus. The cluster of sites in the Bolan area – Mehrgarh, Pirak and Nowshehra – as well as the settlement at Harappa, show an impressive continuity from the pre-urban to the mature urban, and finally the declining phase of the civilization.

The Indus civilization was the most extensive of the ancient riverine civilizations, with sites as far north as Shortughai in the Pamirs, and some activity across the sea southwards in Oman in the Arabian peninsula. It incorporated the north-western mountains and came as far east as the upper *doab*, although the actual area of control is likely to have been more limited. Southwards there was much activity in present-day Gujarat, and some settlements going further into northern Maharashtra. In the first two instances the Harappans, as entrepreneurs in trade, were doubtless searching for valuable raw materials. Lapis lazuli from the Pamirs and the Chagai Hills of eastern Iran was much valued in the trade with Mesopotamia. Copper deposits in Oman were perhaps what attracted the Harappans, given that copper was much in demand further west. Trade with Mesopotamia is evident from the recovery of a few Harappan seals, beads and weights at Mesopotamian sites, and some, which are thought to be Harappan, at sites in the Persian Gulf. The Mesopotamian references to the land of Meluhha and its people might have been intended for the Indus civilization, the products of this land being listed as ivory, carnelian, wood, lapis and gold, all familiar to the Indus cities. Other areas to the east mentioned in Mesopotamian sources were Dilmun and Makan. Coastal shipping from western India along the Gulf to the Tigris-Euphrates delta has been continuously involved in the exchange between India and the Gulf. Contacts with Afghanistan and Iran were maintained through the passes in the north-west mountains, and particularly the Bolan Valley. Other contemporaries were the people of the Sothi-Siswal cultures in Rajasthan and Haryana, as well as the Kayatha culture in central India. The locations of the cities appear to have been chosen with an eye to the availability of resources and the transportation of goods by river or by sea.

Harappan artefacts, or artefacts influenced by Harappan forms, designs and functions, have been found over an extensive area. But this is not an indication that the area had a uniform culture and identical observances. It seems evident from the variations discovered that local cultures functioned and took shape beneath the Harappan system. This interface between the local culture and a wider ranging one is an aspect of the subcontinental cultural life throughout its history.

The cities were maintained from the surplus produced in the countryside, together with other resources gathered or mined in various regions. This process seems to have resulted from co-ordination in obtaining raw materials, working them into commodities and trading them in a systematic manner. Closer to home, copper would be mined in Rajasthan and Baluchistan. Semi-precious stones were available in large quantities from western India, lapis from the Chagai Hills or the Pamirs and were crafted into beads, some perhaps being traded as raw material. Timber such as teak was available in Gujarat, and other wood elsewhere; shell and chank came from the coast and were cut to make ornaments; and there was a range of other items. Harappan pottery is distinctive, with designs in black, of plants, birds and abstract forms, frequently painted on a red surface. Pottery is a clue to locating Harappan sites, but it is likely to have been made, after a fashion, in many local areas.

The cities were centres for the production of crafted items that were traded both overland and across the seas. This was not the work of casual craftsmen and required considerable skill and organization. Bead-making was an extensive industry, using gold, copper, shell, semi-precious stones, steatite, faience and ivory. Bronze and stone tools were largely functional but some were useful for exchange. Workshops for the production of beads and similar objects were located in Harappan cities and the etched carnelian bead was to become a characteristic Harappan object. Such workshops are often identified by the presence of a quantity of unfinished items. Carefully graded weights made of chert occur at Harappan sites, as well as rods for measurement, again suggesting functions linked to exchange and a sophisticated system of weights and measures. Lothal has evidence of a structure that has been described as a dockyard, although this description remains controversial. In its vicinity was a warehouse which was probably a hub of exchange and a place where the finished products of the craft workshops were gathered, stored and transported. Doubtless the profits from trade both within the northern and western areas of the subcontinent, and between the people of this culture and those of the Persian Gulf and Mesopotamia, kept the cities economically viable.

The cities demonstrate a sophisticated sense of civic planning and organization. In most cases the city was divided into the smaller citadel area, frequently to the west, where the essential institutions of civic life were located, possibly together with some places used for public rituals, and the larger residential area to the east. This bifurcation was not continued in the planning of cities of the later historical periods, although the tendency in civic planning to concentrate professions in particular areas remained characteristic. The impression given by the Harappan cities is one of a concern with maintaining urban order and an efficient economic system managing land, labour and water.

Huge man-made brick platforms formed the foundation for the buildings of the citadel, possibly to make them secure against floods and other damage since most of the cities were on the banks of rivers, probably to facilitate the transportation of goods. These structures may also have given direction to the plan of the cities. City-planning roughly followed a grid pattern, with roads oriented approximately to the cardinal directions, which assisted civic facilities, particularly the carefully articulated drainage system where house drains were linked to those of the street. House-plans generally had a courtyard as the focus, with rooms opening on to it. Most houses had individual wells, bathing places and drains. Drains and structures of importance were largely constructed of kiln-fired brick, whereas the houses were of mud-brick. The brickwork shows experience and expertise. Stone was used more extensively in Dholavira. The quarrying, dressing and transporting of stone was more labour-intensive and would have required considerable management. The city-plan of Dholavira differed from that of the other cities. Elaborate arrangements were made, but less for the storage of food and more for the storage of water. Large water reservoirs were built within the fortified part of the city. Architectural requirements for the building of the Harappan cities would have included a knowledge of surveying and geometry. The making of a calendar was necessary for agriculture and this in turn incorporated some knowledge of astronomy.

The citadel area of the city generally had defence walls and bastions, with elaborate entrances that were no doubt appropriately guarded. Sometimes the city was also fortified. Was this demarcation from the surrounding countryside expected in early cities? As a new phenomenon, the city was the focus of wealth that was different in quantity from that of the village, and its management also differed. It required a distinctive way of life unfamiliar to non-urban societies. In comparison with other contemporary cities, the Harappan cities do not display any spectacular wealth in either the houses or the graves. A few impressive gold objects have recently been excavated from a Harappan site, but the totality of jewellery remains small when compared, for instance, to the volume from Mesopotamian cities. The demarcation between town and countryside may also reflect the management of the cities. Did the control over agricultural production, labour and raw materials require that those exercising this authority be protected? Such control would have been more extensive than that based on kinship connections and clan loyalties. This is not to suggest that those inhabiting the cities were aliens, but rather that they gave expression to the kind of authority that had not existed before, and that it was the concept of this authority that may have seemed alien to rural life.

Clearing the surrounding tropical savanna forest around each city may have been necessary in order to extend cultivation sufficiently to support the urban population. This may have resulted in fairly large-scale deforestation. A ploughed field of the period just prior to Harappan urbanization was excavated at the site of Kalibangan, with the field coming up to the edge of the city. Wheat and barley were the staple crops, although rice and millet were also grown where possible. Water conduits, some of which were underground in certain areas, and small-scale inundation canals leading off rivers directed water to where it was needed. These would have required constant maintenance and supervision.

The monumental buildings of the citadel areas have been variously interpreted: granaries, warehouses, collegiate buildings and possibly a ritual centre at Mohenjo-daro, including a tank and its surroundings. The constructing of the platforms and the buildings would have required a large deployment of organized labour with an equally effective system of obtaining and controlling labour. Possibly this was done through regular labour services rather than a tax or tribute. The form that this may have taken remains uncertain, although some attempts have been made to reconstruct the foci of authority. Supervision and control involved many aspects of administration: agriculture to ensure food for the city population; the production of items for trade, such as copper ingots and beads, and seals for stamping goods; labour for the building and maintaining of cities; and above all the organization of the trade itself.

In describing the governing authority it was earlier suggested that it consisted of a single imperial system, with twin capitals at Mohenjo-daro and Harappa, a suggestion that has been superseded by others. The recent idea that the Indus cities were city-states and were the prototypes for the 'autonomous' cities of historical times carries little conviction, given the essential differences in the concept and planning of the early and later cities. It might be more plausible to consider flexible relationships between the cities, given their differentiated size and their authority systems that are apparent, for instance, if the city-plan of Kalibangan is compared with that of Dholavira or Harappa. Governed by chiefs of clans in the early phase, this system would have given way to a more complex one by the Mature period, when representatives of city authorities probably coalesced to ruling jointly in assembly to control a sophisticated system of obtaining labour and co-ordinating urban activities. The structures at Mohenjo-daro point to complex authority systems. Possibly a more centralized administration was adopted and adapted in various regions, interacting with city centres.

The kind of evidence that is associated with the archaic states of west Asia is hardly recognizable in the Harappan state or states. Distinctive buildings cluster in one area in most cities, and there is a striking absence of monumental graves or well-demarcated sacred centres. Even a palace is difficult to discern. The availability of weapons appears to have been limited, with little evidence of disturbed strata to indicate physical destruction arising from warfare. The usual supporting evidence for an organized administration in the form of designations, codes and accounting is unavailable, unless some of the pictograms when deciphered contain information on titles and formal functionaries. The seals may well be tokens of identity of such authorities.

Among the many remains of the Harappan culture, the most puzzling are the seals. They are generally small, flat, square or rectangular, often made of steatite, with a pictorial motif that depicts humans and/or animals or composite figures, and an inscription which remains undeciphered. If the script is pictographic or logographic and not alphabetic, as has been suggested, it could point to the use of more than one language. The possible languages that have been considered include Proto-Dravidian, Indo-Sumerian, Elamo-Dravidian, Indo-Aryan and Austro-Asiatic. Some systematic work in linguistic patterns suggested by the script has attempted to use Proto-Dravidian, but so far without success in decipherment. Attempts to read it as Indo-Aryan are as yet far from systematic. The one certainty is that the signs should be read from right to left. A perforated boss at the back of the seal helps in its handling. Seal impressions on clay indicate that among other uses seals were used to stamp packages. They could therefore have been tokens identifying civic authorities, supervisory managers of long-distance trade, merchants or those bringing raw materials to the cities, or clan affiliations. Signs of identification could relate to professions, religious associations or social organizations. The script also occurs on objects thought to be copper amulets, apart from occasionally being scratched on pots, bangles and suchlike. A short inscription in large-sized letters was unearthed at Dholavira and has been described as a signboard.

Equally puzzling are some of the animals and the scenes depicted on the seals. The most common animal is one that is thought to be a mythical unicorn, although a more mundane identification describes it as a stylized rhinoceros. It is often depicted together with an object that has been variously interpreted, often described as an altar or even a brazier. Among single animals the bull and the elephant were popular. Tigers occur less frequently and more often as part of a scene. The depiction of the horse is absent on the seals. A few bones, said to be of the horse, and small terracotta forms occur in late levels at Pirak (Baluchistan) dating to the early second millennium BC. The claim that horse bones occur at Surkotada, and at a few other sites at earlier levels, has met with doubt, the bones being identified as those of the ass and the onager. The late arrival of the horse in India is not surprising since the horse is not an animal indigenous to India. Even on the west Asian scene, its presence is not registered until the second millennium BC. The horse was unimportant, ritually and functionally, to the Indus civilization.

A noticeable difference between the Harappan cities and those of other ancient civilizations is the absence of recognizable religious buildings and of elaborate burials. If there were temples they are difficult to identify, for there is neither the presence of magnificent icons nor specially decorated structures. Temples therefore were not the focus of social bonding. Traditions of ancestral rituals are also not apparent, for people tended to migrate away from the cities when they declined. The cities may not therefore have been the focus of religious worship. Female figurines from the more westerly sites have been viewed as icons for worship with a prevalence of a goddess cult. This possibility is based in part on the continuing worship of various goddesses later in Indian history. Some emphasis on fertility rituals seems evident, but whether these were elaborate ceremonies remains uncertain. Fertility rituals would not be unusual given the prevalence of these in other chalcolithic cultures of the subcontinent. Some small oval structures containing ash have been interpreted as fire altars, but they could equally well be hearths. A shamanistic religion has also been suggested, but the urban character of the civilization is unlikely to have been conducive to shamanism.

A few motifs continue from Harappan times into later history, such as the *pipal* – as a leaf decoration on pottery and as a tree on seals – which was revered by some later religious sects. Much speculation focuses on whether a seated figure on a seal represents a proto-Shiva. The identification of the figure is uncertain and the evidence for the link with Shiva is tenuous. It would perhaps be more apposite to regard these representations as contributing to the evolution of a later religious mythology and iconography, rather than insisting that a later icon be imposed on an earlier period. To explore the meaning of such an icon in its own context would perhaps be more meaningful than to give it an instant label derived from an icon of a much later period. The figure could equally well be identified as depicting a yogic position, as indeed female figures in trees on some seals could be linked to the evolving of the idea of *apsaras*, celestial maidens associated with trees.

Sculptures in stone and bronze have been found, but in sporadic locations not indicating an assembly of images in a temple. Such sculpture shows a refinement of technique and concept that is striking. A small bronze figurine, probably not a ritual object, has the pleasing stance of a young and spirited woman. One among the portrait heads sculpted in stone is evidently of a person of consequence, given the band around his head and the trefoil design on his shawl, together with his curiously semi-closed eyes. Popular interpretation describes him as a priest, but this remains unproven. Terracotta forms range from children's toys to larger representations of animals. There is a noticeable absence of figures reflecting grandiose self-representations, in common with many other civilizations of this period.

Another striking contrast is the simplicity of the burials compared to the tombs of rulers further west. Grave goods are mainly the pottery of daily use with a scatter of other small items. Clearly, they did not expect huge demands on the dead in the after-life, nor were burials occasions for demonstrating status.

Post-Harappan burials of the late second millennium BC in what has been called the Cemetery H culture, largely confined to Harappa and the Punjab plains, were accompanied by pottery that was different from the Harappan. The ritual of burial continued even if the culture of these later people was not identical. These burials may point to new arrivals or the emergence of some new traits in the cultures of the region. Such suggestive links through a few items reflect similar hints from earlier times, although the artefacts differed. For instance, connections have been suggested between artefacts found in the Bolan Valley and in the Indo-Iranian borderlands, and still further in Afghanistan and Iran, in the area now being referred to as the Bactria Margiana Archaeological Complex.

The decline of the cities was once ascribed to invading Aryans. However, there is little archaeological evidence for the type of massive invasion that would have led to the collapse of a well-established political and economic system, resulting in a displacement of culture, although the denial of an invasion does not preclude the possibility of migrants bringing the Indo-Aryan language into India. The argument supporting an invasion was based on the subsequent culture of the Vedic corpus, using a language – Indo-Aryan – that had affinities with central Asian Indo-European, particularly with Old Iranian. That this language gained currency in northern India was thought to be the result of a conquest of the local population by Indo-Aryan speakers, the evidence being drawn from the hostility of the *arya* towards the *dasa* in the *Rig-Veda*. The reference to Indra attacking the *pur*, enclosed settlements of the *dasas*, was erroneously read as referring to the cities of the Indus civilization. However, there are alternative explanations for the introduction of Indo-Aryan into India and its gradual spread across northern India. These explanations have more to do with the historical context of urban decline, the coexistence of differing cultures or languages, and the filtering of Indo-Aryan speakers into north India through small-scale migrations, than with the overly simplistic theory of an invasion as a historical explanation; or for that matter with the current attempts being made by some enthusiasts to prove the indigenous origin of the Indo-Aryan speakers even though, as we shall see, the evidence points to the contrary.

The skeletons in habitation areas at Mohenjo-daro were earlier interpreted as demonstrating the massacre of citizens, which endorsed the theory of an invasion. But analyses of the skeletons revealed that most of these people had died of diseases such as severe anaemia, indicating a different set of reasons for urban decline. Violent deaths in a limited area do not necessarily mean widespread invasion and could be evidence of local disturbances. Diseases or severe environmental changes as factors in weakening a population have not been sufficiently examined in the context of early Indian history.

Other explanations generally advanced are that the cities declined largely because of environmental changes, such as the long duration of the severe flooding of the Indus in the vicinity of Mohenjo-daro, and climatic change leading to greater desiccation, deforestation and a more generalized de-urbanization with the dying out of trade requirements and a consequent political collapse. The extent to which the degradation of the environment caused the decline of the cities remains unclear. Urban decline can only be properly explained by multiple causes, and these were not uniformly applicable to each region. This is also evident from the variant patterns that followed urban decline. Squatters from the countryside occupied some cities in the lower Indus Plain, bringing about a ruralization of the erstwhile urban system. Elsewhere there were migrations away from Harappan centres, as in the migration from the Hakra Plain towards the Ganges-Yamuna *doab*, or from Gujarat to northern Maharashtra. Some settlements in the north-west and Punjab might have been subjected to raids and skirmishes, such as are described in the *Rig-Veda*, or for which there appears to be occasional evidence at some sites, for example Kot Diji.

The decline of the cities did not mean that the Harappan pattern of culture disappeared. Although many urban functions would have ceased, people in rural areas would have continued their activities with marginal changes. The Harappan system was a network linking the urban to the rural and some features could have been maintained in the rural areas, even if these areas suffered administratively and economically from the removal of this protective system. Some archaeological cultures were contiguous in time and space with the Harappan; at other places there were overlaps between the Late Harappan and subsequent cultures. Continuities would therefore not be unexpected, but it is more likely that these were restricted to myth-ologies, rituals and concepts of tradition, since the material culture does not show continuities.

The second millennium also saw activity along the Indo-Iranian border-lands, including the arrival in north-western India of the horse and the chariot with a spoked wheel, both of which were new to the subcontinent. Occasional comings and goings across these borderlands were gradually to accelerate, a pattern that remained effective until recent times.

Neolithic and Chalcolithic Cultures, Other Than in the North-West

The evolution of an urban culture in the north-west did not envelop or sweep away all other pre-urban societies. Those in the vicinity were incorpor-ated into the Harappan system. There were still, however, large numbers of hunter-gatherers, pastoralists and farmers whose lives were either untouched or only marginally affected by the changes in north-western India. The potential for change now lay with the chalcolithic cultures, using artefacts of stone and metal – primarily copper, until the early first millennium when iron was introduced.

Chalcolithic societies of the second–first millennium BC emerged in many parts of the subcontinent, sometimes incorporating an earlier neolithic society. The sites of Burzahom and Gufkral (Kashmir), dating to the third–second millennium BC, feature pit dwellings cut into the loess soil of the plateau. Evidence of some carnelian beads, and the depiction of a horned animal on pottery, have both been taken as links with the Indus civilization. This need not imply a direct connection, since the artefacts could have come through a chain of exchanges. A stone engraving depicts a hunting scene. Stone implements for harvesting grain and approximating a sickle-shape are thought to have similarities with such harvesters from central Asia, but connections beyond this have not been established. Burials within the hut, sometimes together with an animal – such as a dog – occur both at these sites and elsewhere in India. Burzahom also has large upright stones or menhirs. Sites with some similarities are located in the hills of Almora (Uttaranchal). The more northern settlements of the Gandhara Grave culture in the Swat Valley were familiar with the horse by the late second millennium BC, and show evidence of the use of iron weapons in the early first millennium. The Swat Valley was one of the routes linking north-west India to Afghanistan and central Asia.

One tends to look at the Ganges Plain for a larger spread of settlements, since this was to be the location of the second urbanization. There is a different sequence of cultures between the western and the eastern parts of the plain. The earliest culture in the western plain is that of the Ochre Colour Pottery (OCP) also found in the watershed, and this has been excavated at sites such as Atranjikhera, Lal Qila and Hulas. This pottery was earlier linked to poor quality Harappan ware, but the link remains tenuous despite some evidence of Late Harappan remains in the early levels at Hulas. At some sites in Haryana and Punjab there is an overlap between Late Harappan pottery and that of the people of the subsequent Painted Grey Ware (PGW). This would suggest an introduction of the Painted Grey Ware somewhat earlier than the first millennium. The later phase of the Painted Grey Ware is associated with the use of iron. Perhaps the most significant aspect of this evidence is that it reveals a minimal continuity from Harappan ideas in this area, although the cultures of the western Ganges Plain show little similarity with Harappan artefacts. The notion of urban centres, however, remained unfamiliar to these cultures since the preconditions were absent.

Yet there seems to be a further connection eastwards as well. Copper objects with an impressive technical proficiency – spearheads, harpoons, celts, antennae swords and what are thought to be anthropomorphic figures – have been found buried as hoards in this area. Occasionally they occur in a stratified context, but more frequently in caches in fields. A link has been suggested with similar objects found in Chhotanagpur and further east, dating to the second millennium.

The Painted Grey Ware culture, of which some sites were located in the Hakra Plain in a post-Harappan context, was predominant in the western Ganges Plain in the first millennium BC, spreading from the Indo-Gangetic watershed to the confluence of the Ganges and Yamuna. Metal technology in this culture includes the early use of iron, which was more fully developed prior to and during the urbanization in the Ganges Plain, generally dated to the mid-millennium. Characteristic of many iron age cultures, the earlier use for iron was in weaponry but this gradually extended to other objects, particularly household ones. As agricultural communities they cultivated wheat and barley, although some rice was found and the domestication of cattle is attested. That cattle provided food other than milk products is evident from the proximity of cattle bones near domestic hearths, bearing marks of having been cut that indicate their flesh was eaten. Important settlements of the PGW include Ropar (Punjab), Bhagwanpura (Haryana) and Atranjikhera, Hastinapur, Ahicchatra, and Jakhera (Uttar Pradesh).

Some sites of the second millennium in the middle Ganges Plain emerge more definitively in the first millennium – such as Piprahwa and Ganwaria (associated still later with Buddhism), Sohgaura, Narhan and Khairadih. The cluster of sites south of the Mirzapur area could be explained by their access to the Son Valley and the route going southwards. Settlements in the Belan Valley, south of Allahabad, have yielded rice grains and it was claimed that the domestication of rice went back to the sixth millennium BC. However, this has been questioned and a later date is preferred. Domestication of plants and animals is evident at Koldihva and Chopani-mando. Settlements in the Ganges Plain go back to about the third–second millennium BC, some having begun as neolithic sites, such as Chirand at the confluence of the Ganges and the Sarayu, which remained important until the early Christian era. Huts of wattle-and-daub contained functional artefacts, including polished stone axes and microliths, bone implements, pestles and querns for grinding grain, and terracotta animal figurines, among which the bull was common. The later phase included copper artefacts, and still later there is evidence of some iron objects. Chirand provides useful information on the evolution of cultures in the Ganges Plain.

The Northern Black Polished Ware, characteristic of the urban centres of the Ganges Plain, which was also the area of its provenance, is thought to have developed from high-temperature firing techniques used in smelting iron and from the use of local haematite soil. Its extensive distribution as a luxury ware helps the tracking of exchange and trade in various parts of the subcontinent.

Further east in Bengal the chalcolithic sites seem to have been concentrated in the valleys to the west of the Bhagirathi, particularly in the Damodar and Ajay Valleys, perhaps because of access to the copper-producing areas in Chhotanagpur. Some settlements, such as Pandu Rajar Dhibi, Mahisdal and Mangalkot, began as neolithic sites but gradually began to use metal. Burials occur in the habitation areas. Further to the east, the Assam neolithic includes sites such as Daojali Hading and others in the Garo hills and the Cachar area. Neolithic settlements have also been found in Orissa at Kuchai and Golbai Sasan, and in Manipur. Connections with cultures in south-east Asia and eastern Asia have been suggested, but await further investigation. Similarities with neolithic cultures of these areas have been noticed in artefacts such as axes and harvesters, and in the stone used (such as jadeite), as well as in cord-impressed pottery.

There may have been a few indirect links between Harappan sites and those in southern Rajasthan, such as Ahar, Gilund and Balathal, where Harappan beads have been found. The proximity of copper ore in the Aravallis doubtless encouraged settlement and the links led to mining copper. A wide distribution in Gujarat, Rajasthan, the fringes of the *doab* and the middle Ganges Valley, extending to parts of Bengal, is recorded for a pottery technique that resulted in double colours of black and red which has been labelled the Black-and-Red Ware. This was not the pottery of a single, uniform culture, nor was it the sole pottery at these sites, although it often predominated. The earliest dates for this pottery range, according to region, from the second to the first millennium BC.

Beads of carnelian and lapis lazuli sometimes occur at sites of the Malwa culture in Madhya Pradesh, again hinting at links with the Late Harappan. Both the major sites of Kayatha and Navdatoli, going back to an earlier period, suggest a degree of complex living. Navdatoli faces Maheshwar across the Narmada, and these could have been crossing-points on the river. Salvage archaeology in Madhya Pradesh prior to the completion of the dam on the Narmada River has yielded evidence of sites with impressive chacolithic levels, such as Sabatpur, Peethanagar and Mandsaur. Some are linked to the Malwa culture and others appear to have been on a route going south through the Hoshangabad area, a route that comes into prominence in later times.

The curious and impressive find of four bronze objects, thought to be reminiscent of the Late Harappan style, has surfaced at Daimabad in northern Maharashtra. A rider driving a yoke of oxen, and three animals – a rhinoceros, a buffalo and an elephant, each on wheels – are unusual sculptures for a chalcolithic site. It could point to Harappan contacts through Gujarat, if the identity of the style is accepted. Such contacts have also been suggested for the chalcolithic site of Jorwe (Maharashtra), which was actively involved in the smelting of copper and the making of copper artefacts. Equally interesting is the chalcolithic site at Inamgaon (Maharashtra), dating to the second millennium BC, which was extensively excavated. It is thought to have been the hub of a chiefdom.

The people of Inamgaon practised both farming and livestock breeding, with barley and millet as commonly grown crops, in a system of crop rotation. Cultivation was not dependent on rainfall alone for there is evidence of embankments to hold water. Villages of round or square huts, built of wattle and daub, were surrounded by a mud wall. The nature of this barrier may not have kept attacks by other villagers at bay but could have acted as a defence against animal predators, of which there were plenty in the adjacent forests. The presence of predators is depicted in a scene on a jar. Female terracotta figurines were found, some curiously headless but with prominent breasts, emphasizing ritual and symbolic aspects, and some placed in clay containers. By comparison, male images are fewer. The disposal of the dead was largely in the form of burial, often in a pit in the floor of the hut accompanied by some grave goods. Children were buried in urns. What is puzzling is that in some cases of adult burial the feet had been deliberately cut off. Vidarbha (Maharashtra) has provided evidence of cairn burials with Black-and-Red pottery, horse bits and copper and iron objects at places such as Junapani and Mahurjhari. These have links with some megalithic burials further south.

The river valleys of the Godavari, Krishna, Tungabhadra, Pennar and Kaveri were settled by farming communities as early as the third millennium BC. The Raichur *doab* between the Krishna and the Tungabhadra Rivers becomes a focus of attention. Hallur, Kupgal, Maski (Karnataka) and Nagarjunakonda (Andhra Pradesh) had farming communities. The semi-arid areas were suitable for cattle-keeping villages, and it is thought that the large ash mounds at Piklihal (Karnataka), Utnur (Andhra Pradesh) and Kupgal resulted from burning cattle dung. Budihal (Andhra Pradesh) was a cattle-keeping village where an abattoir was unearthed. Sheep and goats were also bred, with the later addition of buffalo. Millet was widely cultivated and rice was grown later, being confined to wet, low-lying areas. Initially, these cultures were not metal-using and were limited to a range of stone artefacts, some used for polishing and grinding and some for more refined work through sharp-edged tools. Hand-turned pottery was gradually replaced by the technically more advanced wheel-thrown pottery.

Towards the end of the second millennium there is some limited evidence of copper and bronze artefacts. This is developed further at Paiyampalli (Tamil Nadu), an earlier neolithic site, Hallur and T. Narsipur, with a bigger array of bronze and copper objects, beads, terracotta figurines and wheel-thrown pottery. A similar development is noticed at sites such as Sangankallu in Karnataka. Some among them are places for megalithic burials. Hallur and Kumaranhalli provide an early date for the use of iron, the sites going back to the late second millennium BC.

The study of chalcolithic cultures suggests certain common characteristics. The close connection between a settlement and the environment is now an established perspective in archaeology. The interplay of locality and region that underlines some of these settlements becomes an important feature of later historical change. The imprint of early settlements did not continue unchanged, but nevertheless this interplay remains a consequential feature.

Settlements occur in river valleys, although semi-arid areas may have been preferred for livestock breeding. Since stockbreeding and agriculture are interdependent, the semi-arid areas would have encouraged the cultivation of millet, apart from the northern plain where wheat and barley were more common, or in more eastern areas where rice was grown. It has been argued that areas given to the cultivation of wheat have different social patterns from those primarily cultivating rice. The latter tend to be associated with a more hierarchical authority and possibly greater stratification. This perspective has yet to be examined for the history of the subcontinent, but at an impressionistic level there does seem to be a difference, for example, between the north-west and the middle Ganges Plain in terms of social patterns. However, the difference need not have been caused by this one factor.

The organization of a village, and subsequently a hierarchy of villages within a cluster, required some form of authority and regulations of control. This could have evolved from social stratification, with families coalescing into clans which maintained a hierarchy or at least sustained the notion of a semblance of authority by a chief or by elders. The political and social structure would have been far more complex than that of bands. Chiefdoms would presuppose not just surplus food but the control of a few families over what was produced, demarcating the chief from the clan. The handling of what were thought of as luxury goods, such as beads and certain kinds of symbolic daggers, would mark the status of such families. Their power would draw on their access to weapons, to maintaining stratification and allotment of resources, and on claims exercised through ritual.

The worship of female figurines is in some ways remarkable. It not only parallels the Harappan figurines, but almost anticipates the extensive worship of female cult figures and goddesses in later history. But this need not point to the prevalence of a matriarchal system. Matriarchies would have been unlikely to approve of headless female figures, even as objects of worship. But it does point to a greater social presence of the female than in later times, which may also have been a generally more assertive presence.

Burial within the hut is in some ways strange, although it occurs in many regions. Was this a sign of the status of the family, which treated the burial as a claim to that status? Or was it an attempt to keep those who had died close to the family, a sentiment known to some other societies, and suggested here by the cutting off of the feet? Or was there also a fear that wild animals would ravage the pit graves since the dead were not buried in coffins?

Megalithic Burials

The style of burial changed dramatically in the first millennium. Burials moved out of the habitation huts to be located in specially demarcated sanctuaries. These are the megalithic sites with a large variety of megalithic markers, and are most commonly located in the peninsula providing it with a distinctive cultural phase. Some sites go back to about 1000 BC or even a little earlier. Whether the megaliths are characteristic of a distinctively different cultural pattern, or are a burial fashion adopted in the first millennium as part of chalcolithic activity, had been a controversial question. The paucity of settlement sites that can be correlated with the burials makes the assessment less definitive. Nevertheless, attempts were made to identify them as a distinctive culture. It was even argued that because they were associated with the horse they might have been Indo-Aryan speakers settling in the peninsula. But such identities have found little support. Nevertheless the extent and range of megalithic burials are striking.

The forms and styles of megalithic burials are diverse and range from the single standing stone to rock-cut chambers. Simple cairns or a heaping up of stones were found in Baluchistan and Makran, in the Vindhyan region and parts of the peninsula. Other indicators were the marking of a location with a single, extremely large, stone marker or menhir. Such markers have led to the name *mega* + *lithos*, the large stone. The dolmen consisted of a number of large stones placed in formation. Or there could be a capstone balancing over upright stones, marking a pit. Pits often have what is referred to as a cist burial. This was frequently a circle demarcated with stones, enclosing a pit within which was constructed a cist, a rectangular box made of stone slabs to contain bones and grave goods. Sometimes there is a circular hole in one of the side slabs, referred to as a porthole. This would suggest that the burial chamber was used more than once. The more impressive range and forms of these burials occur in the peninsula where they are widely distributed. The cists occasionally contain pottery sarcophagi. Even more elaborate are the rock-cut caves in the Western Ghats, such as those in Kerala. The cutting of caves was difficult and required the softer laterite rock. The heterogeneity in form would suggest that the megalithic burials do not constitute a single culture, but settlements with cultural habits having similarities in concepts even though they were not identical in form.

The megalithic burials of the peninsula south of the Narmada, at sites such as Hallur, Piklihal, Brahmagiri, Maski (Karnataka), Nagarjunakonda (Andhra Pradesh) and Adichannallur (Tamil Nadu), have characteristic forms similar to those of non-Indian megalithic cultures, but their origins remain somewhat unclear. It is feasible that they evolved from the earlier neolithic and chalcolithic cultures of the peninsula with some small intrusion of forms from elsewhere. Brahmagiri has a habitation site with megalithic objects. Parallels have also been drawn with practices among forest tribes, many of which have *sarnas*, sanctuaries, where large upright stones are erected to commemorate people, a practice which continues to the present. Similar megalithic burials also occur in Sri Lanka at approximately the same date, which would suggest links with south India.

Grave furnishings were primarily Black-and-Red pottery and impressive iron artefacts, such as hoes and sickles, small weapons and horse trappings. Were these ritual objects deliberately buried with the dead, or were they objects of daily use thought to be helpful to the dead in the after-life? Could this have been a cult of ancestor worship if the burial sites were the focus of rituals? Some of the graffiti on the pottery resembles the signs of the Harappa script, which provides yet another dimension to identification. The communities involved in these memorials appear to have depended on the cultivation of millet and rice, with some regional variation, and to have domesticated cattle, sheep and goats.

The categories of objects from megalithic burials are also often typologically similar, for instance artefacts of iron, and the question therefore is whether blacksmiths originating in a particular location traversed the peninsula, or whether there was an extensive network of exchange. The blacksmith clearly had an important function in the production of iron artefacts and, judging by the quality of the objects, could well have been a specialized craftsman. The presence of the horse would suggest an extensive network, drawing in suppliers of horses from northern and western India. This would endorse the idea that the control over the exchange would lie with heads of clans, who were most likely the ones buried under these stone markers. There appears to have been a continuing connection between burial and status.

The association of iron artefacts and the range of forms are striking. These markers are generally found in the vicinity of fertile land, which may have been irrigated from tanks specially built for storing water. This would suggest co-operative effort on the part of the builders, an effort that would have been required even for the setting up of the burial monuments. Yet there are few settlements linked archaeologically to the megalithic memorials. If the area designated for burials was associated with both status and continuity it could well be at some distance from the settlement. The status is further underlined by the fact that at some sites the top levels have early Roman imperial coins, thus providing a terminal date of around the turn of the Christian era. The presence of a coin links the archaeological evidence to the historical. It is also suggestive of the range of exchange networks in which the local societies were involved.

This all-too-brief survey of the archaeological evidence, prior to the textual, makes apparent the presence of multiple vibrant cultures in various parts of the subcontinent, particularly in the second and early first millennia BC. The nature of these cultures establishes that, whatever contemporary records there may be of a textual kind in later periods, the archaeological data has to be kept within historical vision. It also contradicts the idea of scattered primitive cultures that were easily edged out to the periphery when a superior culture came to establish itself. The history of the subsequent predominant cultures is modulated by both the continuities and the disjunctures underlined by the excavated evidence. The location of what is sometimes called the second urbanization shifts from the Indus Plain to the Ganges Plain. The process leading up to the formation of states and the emergence of towns can be observed in some depth for the Ganges Plain, where there is literary evidence marking the process. However, the more detailed literary evidence relates to the mature period of urbanism, and here the archaeological evidence has to be teased out by the textual. One hopes there will be more excavation of sites in the Ganges Plain, particularly horizontal excavations, as this will provide the necessary evidence for observing the process of change. The nature and the formal plan of the cities in the Ganges Plain differed substantially from those of the Indus civilization. This was partly due to environmental differences, but also to the economic functions of the cities and their political roles.

4

Towards Chiefdoms and Kingdoms

c. 1200–600 BC

Narratives of Beginnings

Narratives of the period subsequent to the Indus civilization are thought of as the beginnings of history, since they come from textual sources. The beginnings are reconstructed as usual from archaeological and textual data, but the interweaving of these is immensely complicated. Archaeology reveals the existence of many diverse cultures, mostly chalcolithic, either inter-locking or in juxtaposition. Evidence of the material culture of the late-second and early first millennia BC is relatively clear, and on occasion can even be used as cross-evidence for descriptions in the texts. The complication arises from trying to identify these cultures with groups mentioned in the texts. And there is a large range of texts with varying narratives and of different dates, all thought to have references to the beginnings. Those that came to constitute the Vedic corpus and were contemporary with this period began as an oral tradition to be memorized with much precision, which was eventually written many centuries later. Other texts claiming to reflect the past, such as the epics – *Mahabharata* and *Ramayana* – and the *Puranas*, also began as oral tradition, were more informally memorized and frequently added to, and were converted to their present textual form in the early first millennium AD.

The *Puranas* were the religious sectarian literature of later times, but some of the earlier ones included narratives of how the past was perceived. As records they are later than the Vedic corpus. The epics are also later, but unlike the *Vedas* they have a well-defined perception of the past. It might therefore be of interest to quote their version of the genesis of Indian civilization before entering the world of the *Vedas*. The *Puranas* do at least have an integrated view and, even though it is not acceptable as history, it provides some useful perspectives on how the past was seen in the mid-first millennium AD.

Puranic accounts narrating the beginnings of Indian history are largely variations on a well-known theme and are narrated, for example, in the *Vishnu* and *Matsya Puranas*. The earth was ruled by the Manus, of which the first was Manu Svayambhu (the Self-born Manu), born directly of the god Brahma. It was during the time of the seventh Manu that the great flood occurred, when everything was submerged. The god Vishnu had warned Manu of the flood, and told him to build a boat to carry his family and the seven sages of antiquity. Vishnu took the form of a large fish, the boat was fastened to its horn and it swam through the flood until the boat was lodged on a mountain peak. Here Manu remained until the water had subsided and they could all safely return home. The progeny of Manu became the ancestors to many lineages. Later kings seeking aristocratic status traced themselves back to these. In some versions, Manu's eldest son – Ikshvaku – was ancestor to the Suryavamsha or Solar line, and the youngest child – Ila – a daughter, or a hermaphrodite in some accounts, gave rise to the Chandravamsha or Lunar line.

The flood supposedly occurred many thousands of years ago and is a time-marker in the narrative. The sequence of descent is in the form of genealogies that were obviously fictional since they cover almost a hundred generations. The descent is unbroken and the pattern suggests an attempt to present a continuous narrative of the past. A point of culmination is the war at Kurukshetra, described in the *Mahabharata*, which acts as another time-maker, after which the present cycle of time – the Kaliyuga – commences. The date for this is given in the form of a planetary configuration. It was calculated many centuries later for astronomical purposes, probably by Aryabhatta, and is equivalent to 3102 BC. There seems to have been a conflation of the date for the Kaliyuga with the date for the war, as 3102 BC would be far too early for such a war and would be in conflict with historical evidence suggesting a later date. After the account of the war, the narrative goes on to chronicle the dynasties of the historical period. The listing of the dynasties and their kings brings the account up to about the mid-first millennium AD. At this point the narrative in the *Puranas* comes to a close and this is thought to be the final date of the composition of the early *Puranas*.

Such traditional accounts were collected and written many centuries after the events they claim to record. As long as the Puranic genealogical tradition was the monopoly of the *sutas*, bards, it was oral. When the tradition came to be used to legitimize kings of later times, it was shuffled, compiled, edited and given a written form for easy reference. It therefore encapsulates a late perspective on the past. As with all such traditions, it cannot be taken literally. These sections of the *Puranas* are not entirely mythical, since they contain some references to historical dynasties. But claims to factual history need to be used with circumspection, more so than with some other textual data. Such texts raise many historical problems about authorship, date, interpolations and veracity. It is difficult to ascertain the veracity of the genealogical sections, since only a few names find mention in other sources and there are substantial differences between the genealogies in various texts. Genealogies are known to be stretched and contracted as required, and to have legends woven in.

The name Manu is linked to the generic base for *manava*, meaning 'mankind'. The myth about the first ruler, Prithu, clearing the forests and introducing cultivation and cattle-herding has echoes of early settlements, familiar from archaeology. The story of the flood in all its details immediately brings to mind the earlier Mesopotamian legend, also borrowed by the Hebrews in the story of Noah's Ark. In Indian sources it may have filtered down from Harappan traditions that in turn could have been derived from the Mesopotamians. At the time the *Puranas* were finally revised and edited royal families began tracing their origin to the Solar and Lunar lines, and there was naturally an attempt to connect these with what were believed to be the earliest rulers.

The link between the *Puranas* and the epics is that the descent of Manu's progeny comes down to the heroes and clans who are the actors in the epics. Inevitably, there are also parallel narratives which could have been borrowed or taken from a common source. Narrative literature, where it is initially preserved as an oral tradition, is frequently stitched together from bardic fragments. Hence the insistence on single authorship, even if the text is far too long to have been composed by a single author. This also permits constant interpolation, making it difficult to give a date to the composition. Epic literature is not history but is again a way of looking at the past. A later age looks back with nostalgia at an earlier one and depicts it in terms of ideals and activities now receding. The social assumptions implicit in the narratives are of value to the historian even if the events are fictional.

The *Mahabharata* brought into the story the many segments of the Lunar line and its narratives were pre-eminently stories of societies adhering to clan and lineage organization. References to complexities of administering kingdoms would be later interpolations. The *Ramayana* is more clearly an endorsement of monarchy and the heroes are of the Solar line. Within each epic, societies that do not conform to monarchy are also visible. The epics therefore give us a glimpse of that which had receded or was different from conventional kingship. They are each concerned with events that are difficult to date since many passages were added at times later than the original composition. The versions we have today are generally placed in a chrono-logical bracket between the mid-first millennium BC to the mid-first millen-nium AD. Therefore they can hardly be regarded as authentic sources for the study of a narrowly defined period. Hence historians have abandoned the concept of an 'epic age'. Incidents from the epics, in the nature of bardic fragments, can have some historical authenticity provided supporting evidence can be found to bear them out. Attempts are therefore being made to correlate archaeological data with events described in the epics. An example of this is the flood at Hastinapur, evident from archaeology and mentioned in the epic, which has been used to date the war to *c.* 900 BC. But such correlations remain tenuous since chronologies and locations pose insurmountable problems. Poetic fantasy in epic poetry, undoubtedly attractive in itself, is not an ally of historical authenticity.

The *Mahabharata* as it survives today is among the longest single poems. The main action revolves around what has become famous as the contest between the Kauravas and the Pandavas, and is set in the fertile and strategic region around Delhi. The Kauravas, with their capital at Hastinapura, were the hundred sons of Dhritarashtra, and the Pandavas – the five sons of Pandu – were their cousins. The Pandavas became heirs to the Kuru territories, since Dhritrashtra was blind and therefore not eligible to rule. But Pandu had a skin ailment that made the succession of the Pandavas uncertain. This was a culture in which he who ruled was required to be free of any physical blemish, at least in theory. Dhritrashtra, in the hope of avoiding a conflict between the cousins, divided the territory and gave half to the Pandavas, who ruled from Indraprastha (in the vicinity of Delhi). But this arrangement did not satisfy the Kauravas, who challenged the Pandavas to a gambling match. The latter staked all their wealth including their patrimony and their joint wife, and lost, but as a compromise were permitted to retain half of the patrimony and their wife, provided they first went into exile for thirteen years. At the end of this period the Kauravas were still unwilling to allow them to rule, so the matter had to be settled through a war. They battled for eighteen days on the plain at Kurukshetra, resulting in the annihilation of many clans, including most of the Kauravas. The Pandavas, after ruling long and peacefully, renounced rulership, installed a grandson and went to the City of the Gods in the Himalaya.

The ambience of the *Mahabharata* is that of clan-based societies, particu-larly in the case of the Yadavas. Intervening frequently in the narrative, as a close friend and adviser of the Pandavas, is a Yadava chief, Krishna. Where the Pandavas and Kauravas were descendants of Puru, the Yadavas were traced back to Puru's elder brother, Yadu. There was therefore a distant kinship connection. The geography of the *Mahabharata* focused on the Ganges–Yamuna *doab* and adjoining areas, involving the Kauravas and Pandavas, and also Saurashtra in Gujarat, where the Yadavas were based. Incidentally, these were two of the more active areas after the decline of the Harappan cities.

Originally the *Mahabharata* may have been the description of a more localized feud, but it caught the imagination of the bards and in its final form virtually all the clans and peoples known to the bards were said to have participated in the battle. One reading of the symbolism of the war could be that it marked the termination of clan-based societies, since subsequent societies tended to support kingdoms. But as in all epic poetry, it has layers of meaning enriched by frequent additions. Its composition is traditionally ascribed to Vyasa, who also plays various enigmatic roles in the story, but it is not the work of a single person. It is no longer only the story of the feud and the war, but has acquired a number of episodes (some of which are unrelated to the main story) and a variety of interpolations, many of which are familiar in themselves, such as the *Bhagavadgita*. A distinction has been made between what is called the epic and the pseudo-epic, or between what have also been called the narrative sections – believed to be older – and the didactic sections added later. But even this is not invariably a reliable chronological divide.

The *Ramayana* is much shorter than the *Mahabharata* despite later additions. The scene is set further east into the middle Ganges Plain and the Vindhyan forests. The original version is attributed to the poet Valmiki, who probably brought together bardic fragments and crafted them into poetry that was to become a hallmark of early Sanskrit literature. The many parallels to segments of the story from other narrative literature, such as the Buddhist *Jatakas*, would tend to support this. The language of the *Ramayana* is more polished and its concepts more closely related to later societies, although it is traditionally believed to be the earlier of the two. It is frequently described as the first consciously literary composition, the *adi-kavya*, a description not used for the other epic.

Rama, the heir of the King of Kosala, married Sita, the Princess of Videha. Rama's stepmother wanted her son to succeed to the throne and successfully contrived to have Rama banished for fourteen years. Accompanied by his wife and his younger brother Lakshmana, the exile took them into the forests of the peninsula where they lived as forest-dwellers. But Ravana – the demon King of Lanka – kidnapped Sita. Rama organized an army, taking the assistance of Hanuman, the leader of the monkeys. A fierce battle was fought against Ravana, in which Ravana and his army were destroyed and Sita was rescued. Sita had to prove her innocence by undergoing a fire ordeal, and was eventually reunited with Rama. The fourteen years of exile having ended, Rama, Sita and Lakshmana returned to Kosala, where they were warmly welcomed. Rama was installed as king, his father having died during his exile, and his reign has been mythologized as associated with prosperity and justice. To this day the term *ramarajya* (the reign of Rama) is used to describe a utopian state.

The narrative follows the recognized forms of the morphology of a folk-tale, with contests, heroic deeds, obstacles and their resolution. There are many variants of the basic story, some with a different ethical message such as the Buddhist and the later Jaina versions, and some of a still later date with striking changes in the narrative relating to Sita. In one Buddhist version Rama and Sita are brother and sister who on their return from exile, ruled for many thousands of years. In the Buddhist tradition sibling origin symbolized the purest ancestry and therefore this assumes the highest status for Rama and Sita. An early Jaina version had a rational explanation for the unconventional descriptions of the Valmiki version and the major actors in the story were all Jainas.

These variations and their treatment in the divergent narratives point to the story being used as a means of expressing diverse cultures rather than conforming to a single homogeneous cultural tradition. The story travelled widely all over India and Asia, wherever Indian culture reached, and these variations reflect the perceptions of the story by different societies who interpreted the idiom and the symbols in their own way. The widespread appropriation of both epics is reflected in the tendency to link local topography all over the Indian countryside with the characters and events from the stories.

The original version of the *Ramayana* is generally dated to the mid-first millennium BC. The conflict between Rama and Ravana probably reflects an exaggerated version of local conflicts, occurring between expanding kingdoms of the Ganges Plain and the less sedentary societies of the Vindhyan region. The kingdom of Kosala represents the sophistication of the newly emerging monarchies and is a contrast to the society of the *rakshasas*, or demons, where the latter might be an exaggerated depiction of the forest tribes who were demonized because their pattern of life was so different from that of the monarchies. The dichotomy of kingdom and forest is an illustration of the vision of the world divided into *grama* and *aranya* – the settlement and the wilderness – which underlies much of the tension in

Indian epic literature. The transference of events to a more southerly location may have been the work of editors of a later period, reflecting an expanded geography, as was possibly also the case in the depiction of Lanka itself as a city of immense wealth.

Epic literature has an imagined space, central to its imagery, which is inhabited by people whose culture could be either alien or worth imitating. Such imagined space had a vague geographical location because it was used as a way of incorporating new peoples into the ambit of the culture of the epic. If the sea was the space of exile in the *Odyssey*, the forest plays the same role in the Indian epics. The theme of exile is virtually predictable as it represents the migration and settling of communities in forested areas, which could bring them into conflict with existing communities. Exile also provides scope for the poet to prolong the story in a variety of ways.

The Vedic Corpus

Had these been the only sources available, the reconstruction of the beginnings of Indian history would have been relatively simple. But two other kinds of evidence have contributed to our understanding of historical beginnings, both predating the sources discussed above. In the nineteenth century the reading of the Vedic corpus and subsequent philological studies led to a different reconstruction of the past, at variance with the traditional story. European scholars of Sanskrit had recognized that it was related in structure and sound to Greek and Latin. This led to the theory of a common ancestral language, Indo-European, used by the ancestors of people speaking these languages.

The focus of this research was on the Vedic corpus, the composition of which was earlier than that of the epics and *Puranas*, and the language was a more archaic form of Sanskrit that is now called Old Indo-Aryan. This differentiated it from the later form of Sanskrit referred to as Classical Sanskrit. The *Vedas* were primarily manuals of rituals and commentaries on these, the narrative being incidental. Epic literature was the narrative of the society of heroes and the *Puranas* were sectarian literature of later times. Therefore the purpose of the epics, the *Puranas* and the *Vedas*, was different. Since the last were the earliest in time, Indian history was said to begin with the information that they contained. Unlike the *Puranas* and the epics, which have some explanation of the past, the Vedic corpus has little of this, but is a collection of compositions contemporary with the period from the mid-second millennium to the mid-first millennium BC. The reconstruction was therefore based on the readings made by modern scholars of the evidence in the corpus.

Indo-European and Indo-Aryan are language labels, but in the nineteenth century these were also incorrectly used as racial labels and this confusion persists. The correct usage should be 'Indo-European-speaking people' and 'Indo-Aryan-speaking people', but the shortened labels, Indo-European and Indo-Aryan or Aryan, are commonly used. Language is a cultural label and should not be confused with race, which, although also a social construct, claims that it has to do with biological descent. Indo-European is a reconstructed language, working back from cognate languages, and its speakers had central Asia as their original habitat. Gradually, over many centuries, they branched out and as pastoralists spread far afield in search of fresh pastures. They also worked as carriers of goods intended for exchange. Some migrated to Anatolia, others to Iran, and some among the latter, it is thought, migrated to India. In the texts composed by them, such as the *Avesta* in Iran and the *Rig-Veda* in India, they refer to themselves as *airiia* and *arya*, hence the European term, Aryan. Vedic literature in the Indo-Aryan language has been studied intensively, as an early textual source of an Indo-European language which was concerned with rituals and their explanation, and was regarded as the most sacred. The beginnings of Indian history were associated with the coming of the 'Aryans', some time in the second millennium BC.

But this picture of the past was again to be disturbed in the twentieth century. In the 1920s archaeology revealed the existence of an urban civilization, dating to a period prior to the *Rig-Veda*, in the north-west of India: the Indus civilization or the Harappa culture. This discovery took the formative period of civilization back to the third millennium BC. Archaeology has provided evidence on the evolution of cultures from pre-Harappan societies, and this goes back still further in time. The Harappa culture provides no clues to the rule of Manus, nor does the Vedic corpus.

There are clearly many sources of information on the beginnings of Indian history. Archaeological evidence is chronologically more precise, but cannot be used to identify any culture as 'Aryan' since archaeology, in the absence of a script, cannot supply information on a language. Unfortunately, the Harappan script remains undeciphered. The theory of an Aryan invasion no longer has credence. The *Rig-Veda* refers to skirmishes between groups, some among those who identify themselves as *aryas* and some between the *aryas* and *dasas*. The more acceptable theory is that groups of Indo-Aryan speakers gradually migrated from the Indo-Iranian borderlands and Afghanistan to northern India, where they introduced the language. The impetus to migrate was a search for better pastures, for arable land and some advantage from an exchange of goods. The migrations were generally not disruptive of settlements and cultures. There is also the argument that these were dissident groups that had broken away from the speakers of Old Iranian, whose language and ideas came to be encapsulated in the *Avesta*. There is a significant reversal of meaning in concepts common to both the *Avesta* and the *Rig-Veda*.

There is a tendency among those who oppose the idea of Aryan speakers coming from outside India to equate invasion with migration. Historically the two are distinctly different processes in terms of what would have been the preconditions of either, such as the activities and organization involved, or the pattern of social and historical change that ensued. The migrant groups would have remained small as there is little evidence of the substantial cultural replacements associated with massive migrations. Migration raises different questions from those of invasion, relating to cultural interactions, linguistic changes and the defining of social status among both the host groups and those arriving.

The linguistic evidence remains firm. Indo-Aryan is of the Indo-European family of languages and there is a linguistic relationship with some ancient languages of west Asia and Iran, as well as some that took shape in Europe. Indo-Aryan is a cognate of Old Iranian, dating to the second millennium BC, with which it has a close relationship. Indo-Aryan also incorporated elements of Dravidian and Munda, languages known only to the Indian subcontinent. The incorporation increases in the texts composed in locations eastwards into the Ganges Plain. This points to a considerable intermixing of the speakers of these languages.

The sequence of events seems to have been as follows. The cities of the Indus civilization had declined by the mid-second millennium BC and the economic and administrative system slowly petered out, the emphasis shifting to rural settlements. It was probably around this period that the Indo-Aryan speakers entered the north-west of India from the Indo-Iranian borderlands, migrating in small numbers through the passes in the north-western mountains to settle in northern India. Small-scale migrations have the advantage of not being dramatically disruptive and these could have started even earlier, although the cultural differences would have been registered only after the decline of the Harappan cities. Although archaeological confirmation of textual information is not possible, there are no strikingly large settlements in the area during this period. Textual sources suggest that initial settlements were in the valleys of the north-west and the plains of the Punjab, later followed by some groups moving to the

Indo-Gangetic watershed. Such continuous small-scale migrations may have followed earlier pastoral circuits. The search was for pastures and some arable land, as they were mainly a cattle-keeping people. Myths in the *Avesta* refer to repeated migrations from lands in Iran to the Indus area, explaining these migrations as arising from a pressure on the land through an increase in human and animal numbers. The *Rig-Veda* suggests the close proximity of other peoples inhabiting the area.

During this period of the early first millennium the hymns of the *Rig-Veda*, composed in the previous centuries, were compiled in the form known to us today. The compilation is thought to be later than the composition, which adds to the problems of dating the hymns. Central to this compilation are what have been called the 'family books', said to have been among the earliest hymns, attributed to those belonging to the more respected families. They were claimed as inheritance by those who also claimed descent from the eponymous ancestor said to be the author of the book. Among the later commentaries on the *Rig-Veda*, the best known is that of Sayana, written in the fourteenth century AD and illuminating as a late perspective, but prior to modern analyses.

The Context of the *Rig-Veda*

The aim of this brief summary is to indicate the nature of the evidence from a variety of sources and organize it in a historical order. The diverse textual sources make it difficult to provide a neat reconstruction and there are inevitably loose ends. These are complicated further when attempts are made to correlate this evidence with non-textual sources.

The earliest dated evidence of a form of Indo-Aryan, which, although not identical to Rig-Vedic Sanskrit is nevertheless close to it, comes not from India but from northern Syria. The evidence is brief and scattered and consists of names and words that are in a form of Indo-Aryan. A treaty between the Hittites and the Mitannis dating to the fourteenth century BC calls upon certain gods as witnesses and among these are Indara/Indra, Mitras(il)/Mitra, Nasatianna/Nasatya, and Uruvanass(il)/Varuna, known to the *Rig-Veda* and the *Avesta*. Curiously, there is no reference to the dominant deities of the *Rig-Veda* – Agni and Soma. A text of a similar date on the training of horses includes some words that are a close variant of Indo-Aryan. The horse and chariot, introduced from central Asia, became common in west Asia in the second millennium BC, suggesting a correlation between the arrival of horses and of Indo-Aryan speakers. The Kassite rulers of Babylon, who seem to have come from the Iranian plateau in the middle of the millennium, also mention gods, a few of whom have close parallels in Sanskrit, such as Surias and Maruttas. The Kassite language was not Indo-European despite some names sounding Indo-Aryan. The Indo-Aryan of west Asia is referred to as Proto-Indo-Aryan to differentiate it from Vedic Sanskrit and to indicate that it appears to be more archaic.

It would seem that sometime in the second millennium there were people in northern Syria who spoke a language that was Indo-Aryan in form, judging by what is referred to as the Hittite–Mitanni treaty of the fourteenth century BC. It is not clear how this language reached the western end of west Asia when there is no archaeological or linguistic evidence of contact between north India and these areas in this period. One possibility is that the language originated in a region from where Indo-Aryan speakers could have travelled either westwards or to the south-east. This could have been north-eastern Iran, which would explain how people speaking an Indo-European language and using horses and chariots arrived in lands to the west. What is of historical interest is that, although the treaty suggests the military success of these people, Indo-Aryan nevertheless had a precarious presence in Syria and disappeared from this region after a while. Yet in India, where it arrived through migration, its presence came to be firmly established. Conquest, therefore, is not necessarily always the mechanism for the spread of a language. A more advanced technology, control over nodes of power and claims to ritual authority can be far more effective.

The connections between Iran and north India on the other hand are close. The language of the *Avesta* and Indo-Aryan were cognates, descended from the same ancestral language. The date of the *Avesta* – the text of Zoroastrianism – has been controversial, but a mid-second millennium date is now being accepted. The linguistic relationship between the two includes not just words but also concepts. The interchangeability between 'h' and 's' is one of the differences, but there is a consistency in this change such as *haoma, daha, hepta hindu, Ahura* in Avestan, and *soma, dasa, sapta sindhu, asura* in Rig-Vedic Sanskrit. In terms of religious concepts the attributes of gods are often reversed. Thus Indra is demonic in the *Avesta*, as are the *daevas* (*devas* or gods in Sanskrit) and Ahura/*asura* emerges as the highest deity. This has led to the theory that originally the Old Iranian and Indo-Aryan speakers were a single group but dissensions led to their splitting up. It was then that the Indo-Aryan speakers living in the Indo-Iranian borderlands and the Haraxvati (Sarasvati) area of Afghanistan gradually migrated to the Indus plain, bringing with them their language, rituals and social customs, to settle as agro-pastoralists in the *sapta-sindhu* area, as described in the *Rig-Veda*, later merging with the local population.

This reconstruction tallies up to a point with the archaeological evidence. If the presence of Indo-Aryan speakers is indicated by the presence of the horse – which was central to both action and ritual in the *Rig-Veda* – then it dates to the early second millennium in the subcontinent, having been virtually absent in the Mature Harappan period. Some horse bones and terracotta representations of the later period have been found at sites adjoining the borderlands. The paucity of bones and representations points to its being an unfamiliar animal. Other items, small in number, turn up in excavations along the Indo-Iranian borderlands at sites that were entry-points to the Indus plains, which parallel those found in southern Afghanistan and north-eastern Iran. Among these areas is that of the Bactria Margiana Archaeological Complex (BMAC). Terracotta models of horses carrying riders sometimes with beaked faces, pottery recalling that of central Asia and Iran, compartmented seals, bronze dirks and axe-adzes hint at connections. These could be items of gift exchange limited to high-status families, but they suggest more than just accidental coming and going. The trickle of migration may have had its beginnings at this point but gained momentum later.

Evidence of Proto-Indo-Aryan in Syria has a bearing on the date of the *Rig-Veda*. If the Indo-Aryan of the Hittite–Mitanni treaty was more archaic than the Sanskrit of the *Rig-Veda*, the compositions of the latter would date to a period subsequent to the fourteenth century BC. Even if they were of the same date, the language of the *Rig-Veda* would not be earlier than the second millennium BC. Such a date would also corroborate its closeness to the language and concepts of the *Avesta*. The closeness gradually decreases as the location of Vedic Sanskrit shifts into the north Indian Plain. This date would also suit the composition of the *Brahmanas* as texts interpreting the ritual. The *Brahmanas* were post-Rig-Vedic, generally dated to the first millennium BC, and revealed familiarity with the western and middle Ganges Plain, referring to migrations into this area.

Recently, it has been argued that the date of the *Rig-Veda* should be taken back to Harappan or even pre-Harappan times, and its authors equated with the creators of the Indus civilization. This would support the 'Aryan' authors of the *Rig-Veda* being indigenous to northern India, and also the Indo-Aryan language. By calling it the Indus-Sarasvati or Sarasvati civilization, the Vedic contribution is evoked – even if it is in fact absent.

This view overlooks the data from linguistics, and does not present an analytical understanding of the archaeological evidence. There are two aspects to this evidence: one is whether the artefacts and monuments of the

Harappa culture are described in the *Rig-Veda*; the other is whether the concepts implicit in organizing the Harappan system of urban settlements find their counterpart in the *Rig-Veda*. Many scholars have described what they regard as the essential characteristics of Harappan urbanism, which they have found to be absent in the *Rig-Veda*. Among these may be listed cities with a grid pattern in their town plan, extensive mud-brick platforms as a base for large structures, monumental buildings, complex fortifications, elaborate drainage systems, the use of mud bricks and fired bricks in buildings, granaries or warehouses, a tank for rituals, and remains associated with extensive craft activity related to the manufacturing of copper ingots, etched carnelian beads, the cutting of steatite seals, terracotta female figurines thought to be goddesses, and suchlike.

The second aspect calls for a conceptual familiarity with the use of these objects and structures. The *Rig-Veda* lacks a sense of the civic life founded on the functioning of planned and fortified cities. It does not refer to non-kin labour, or even slave labour, or to such labour being organized for building urban structures. There are no references to different facets or items of an exchange system, such as centres of craft production, complex and graded weights and measures, forms of packaging and transportation, or priorities associated with categories of exchange. Rituals are not performed at permanent ritual locations such as water tanks or buildings. Terracotta figurines are alien and the fertility cult meets with strong disapproval. Fire altars as described in the corpus are of a shape and size not easily identifiable at Harappan sites as altars. There is no familiarity from mythology with the notion of an animal such as the unicorn, mythical as it was, nor even its supposed approximation in the rhinoceros, the most frequently depicted animal on the Harappan seals. The animal central to the *Rig-Veda*, the horse, is absent on Harappan seals. There is no mention of seals or a script in the *Rig-Veda*. Sculptured representations of the human body seem unknown. The geography of the *Rig-Veda* is limited to the northerly Indus Plain – the *sapta-sindhu* area – and is unfamiliar with lower Sind, Kutch and Gujarat, and with the ports and hinterlands along the Persian Gulf that were significant to Harappan maritime trade.

Societies in the Vedic Corpus

The *Rig-Veda* is the earliest section of the Vedic corpus. The composition of the later Vedic corpus – the *Sama*, *Yajur* and *Atharva Vedas* – is generally dated to the first half of the first millennium BC. The *Samhita* section of each is a collection of hymns and the *Brahmanas* are exegeses on the ritual. The *Upanishads* and the *Aranyakas*, essentially philosophical discourses, also form part of the corpus. The *sutra* section which is often included in the corpus has three categories of texts: the *Grihyasutras*, concerned with domestic rituals; the *Shrautasutras*, concerned with public rituals performed for establishing status; and the *Dharmasutras*, stating the rules of what was regarded as sacred duty in accordance with caste regulations and social obligations. The latter were probably composed from the middle of the first millennium BC and, as normative texts on social and ritual obligations, had a different purpose from the hymns. There appears to be only a small distance in time between the *Rig-Veda* and the later *Vedas* in terms of purpose and content. This would further endorse a date of the second millennium for the former, since the latter are dated to the first millennium.

The hymns were memorized meticulously and transmitted orally over many centuries before being written. A number of devices were used for memorization and for the correct articulation of the sound, which determined its efficacy – a prime requirement in ritual texts. This also ensured that they would be confined to a small, select group of brahmans, who on the basis of knowing the *Vedas* claimed superior knowledge, and they alone were allowed to perform the major rituals. The epics were also recited orally to begin with, but they were popular literature and each recitation could result in a modification or addition to the composition. This was a more open transmission. The tighter control over the *Vedas* related to their position as ritual texts, the preservation of which had to be ensured in as precise a manner as possible.

The geographical knowledge of the authors of the Rig-Vedic hymns can be ascertained by their reference to various rivers. The *Rig-Veda* shows greater familiarity with eastern Afghanistan, the Swat Valley, Punjab and the Indo-Gangetic watershed – largely what came to be called the *sapta-sindhu* region. The Yamuna was referred to as the twin of the Ganges and the Sutlej is associated with the Beas, so neither were tributaries of the Ghaggar-Hakra. Their movement away from the Ghaggar was due to hydraulic changes that have been dated to the start of the second millennium BC. The Rig-Vedic references would therefore be subsequent to this. Climatically, the region was wetter than it is today and forests covered what are now vast plains, although some parts of the Punjab are likely to have been semi-arid and conducive to cattle-rearing. Cultivation during the Harappan period would already have led to some deforestation, and settlements in the Ganges Plain would have required further clearing. The introduction of iron artefacts, in addition to those of copper and bronze, would have assisted in the process.

But iron, other than for weapons, does not appear to have been commonly used until about 800 BC.

There was earlier thought to be a racial difference between the *aryas* who spoke Indo-Aryan and those whom they met with, whom they called *dasas*, *dasyus* and *panis*. The statement that there were two *varnas* – the *arya-varna* and the *dasa-varna* – was quoted as evidence. *Varna* literally means colour and this was taken to be skin colour. But, more likely, judging from the references, colour was used as a symbolic classifier to express differences. This is supported by the paucity of specific descriptions of the skin colour of the *dasas* and many more references to differences of language, ritual, deities and custom. The *panis* are said to be cattle-lifters and therefore disliked. Interestingly, the *Avesta* refers to *daha* and *dahyu* (the *dasa* and the *dasyu* of the *Rig-Veda*) as meaning other people. The word in the *Rig-Veda* indicating the flat nose of the *dasa* has been alternatively read to mean those who have no mouth, that is, do not know the language. Perhaps it would be more viable to argue that the *Rig-Veda* depicts various societies adhering to different cultural forms, but since the hymns were composed by Aryan speakers it is their society that emerges as dominant. There is both a fear of and contempt for the *dasas*, whose immense wealth, especially their cattle wealth, made them a source of envy and the subject of hostility. Later, the term *dasa* came to be used for anyone who was made subordinate or enslaved. But this change of meaning took some centuries and was therefore different from the original connotation of the word. The change in meaning would also be a pointer to the decline of pastoralism since pastoral societies have problems in controlling slaves, given the opportunities for running away when grazing animals. *Arya* continued to mean a person of status, often speaking an Indo-Aryan language.

The authors of the *Rig-Veda* were initially pastoralists, but practised some agriculture. Since pastoral migrants often have close relations with local sedentary communities, the situation would at times have led to confrontations and at other times involved negotiating relationships. Thus some *dasa* chiefs, for example Shambara, are described as enemies, and raiding the cattle of the wealthy *dasas* was a justified occupation. Other *dasas*, such as Bribu and Balbutha, are obviously won over as they are described as patrons of the rituals performed for them by Vedic priests. Possibly some of the pastoral chiefs became the protectors of local agricultur-alists, given that the Harappan administration had ceased to exist. This would have given the Indo-Aryan pastoral chiefs considerable authority, which would have ensured the more widespread use of their language. Combined with the claims made for the efficacy of the rituals, this would have added to the prestige of the language. Pastoralists and cultivators have a symbiotic relationship, where cultivators allow the herds to feed on the stubble after the harvest and this manures the fields. They are also linked by exchanges of produce, the more so where pastoralists are carriers of goods for exchange. Some overlap evolves between pastoralists and cultivators that permits the more established pastoral chiefs to claim territories and cultivated land. Other identities would be subordinated to those of status and the control of resources.

A two-way relationship is expressed in the language change that is reflected in Vedic Sanskrit. Indo-Aryan was introduced and adopted, so evidently those who spoke it or adopted it associated it with some advantage, such as authority, technological change or ritual power. At the same time Vedic Sanskrit itself underwent changes. Linguistic elements from Dravidian and Austro-Asiatic (for example, Munda) were introduced into Vedic Sanskrit. A period of bilingualism has been suggested when more than one language was used in the communication between various communities. Alternatively, the non-Indo-Aryan languages could have been substratum languages, elements from which were absorbed into Indo-Aryan. The Vedic corpus is the statement of the dominant group, but this does not preclude the presence of others. These linguistic elements are apparent in Indo-Aryan but are not noticed in cognate languages such as Old Iranian.

Evidence of migration comes in various forms. The most unambiguous are references in the *Avesta* to a distant homeland and the list of places through which the *airiia* migrated. The geographical direction goes from central Asia to northern India, and among the places mentioned towards the end of the itinerary is the *heptahindu*. Even if this section dates to a later part of the *Avesta*, the story of an early migration and its geography was not doubted. The original homeland remained mythical, but the areas through which the *airiia* are believed to have travelled are geographical locations. Geographical names from Afghanistan mentioned in the *Avesta*, such as Haraxvati and Harayu, seem to have been repeated in a more easterly direction in northern India, as in Sarasvati and Sarayu. Important clans, such as the Turvasa and the Bharatas, migrated from the mountains to the plains or from the Ravi to the Beas.

Lack of familiarity with flora and fauna is another indication of migration. Rice, for instance, was not known to begin with, although it occurs at certain Harappan sites. Of the wild animals, the lion was known earlier than the tiger or the rhinoceros. Yet the latter animals had been depicted frequently on Harappan seals, although they are both absent in the *Rig-Veda*. This would point to the earlier habitat of the authors of the *Rig-Veda* being further west and north. The elephant was looked upon as a curiosity and was described as the animal with a hand, *mrigahastin*.

References to the horse meant not only the introduction of the animal, but also of equestrian activities. Pastures had to be adequate for feeding horses, since there is no mention of a fodder crop. Cattle raids are mentioned with noticeable frequency. For migrating pastoralists, there would not only be references to the movements of peoples, but raids would be an important source of increasing livestock. Clans therefore not only raided the *dasas*, but also fought each other over pastures and lands in which to settle. Pastoral movements explored new areas appropriate for hosting settlements. These would not have been isolated places, as some exchange with sedentary agriculturalists was necessary for the initial procurement of grain and other items.

Many clans are mentioned in the *Rig-Veda*, especially where there are references to inter-tribal conflicts. In one case we are told that Sudas was the raja or chief of the Bharata clan settled in western Punjab, and associated with both Vishvamitra and Vasishtha, who were in turn his chief priests and who had ensured successful campaigns for him. Sudas was attacked by a confederacy of ten clans on the banks of the Ravi but was victorious. Conflicts arose from stealing cattle, disputes over grazing grounds or controlling river water. Families or clans often owned herds but the pastures were used in common. A rapid increase in livestock or its re-allocation could be achieved through a raid. Skirmishes and raids involved physical confrontations, both among the clans claiming an *arya* status and between them and the others.

Migrations continued into the Ganges Plain and are mentioned in the *Brahmanas*. Videgha Mathava led his people along the Himalayan foothills eastwards as far as the Gandaka. The land across the river had to be cleared by fire before it could be settled. The Panchalas confederated and then re-confederated into the powerful Kuru-Panchalas, controlling parts of the western Ganges Plain. Even as late as the first millennium BC they were said to be conducting raids lasting a few months at a time. They were also significant players in the *Mahabharata*. Although the western Ganges Plain is not important in the *Rig-Veda*, the heartland shifts later from the Punjab to the territories of the Kuru-Panchalas in the western Ganges Plain. The Kuru-Panchalas became patrons of the more elaborate rituals that were evolving, and began to assert a new form of political authority. It is said that the best Sanskrit is spoken in this area. The north-west and the east are later said to be the habitat of the *mlechchha*. This word originally referred to those who were unable to speak Sanskrit correctly, and later to those who were outside the pale of caste society and therefore regarded as impure. This is an early example of a shift in the geographical focus of a culture, which probably occurred around the eighth–seventh centuries BC. It also points to a possible change in the connotation of *arya*: the language spoken was increasingly incorporating non-Aryan, and the intermingling with non-Aryan speakers, who were the authors of the neolithic and chalcolithic cultures of the Ganges Plain, would have been much greater. The compositions of the later Vedic corpus reflect this change.

Agro-pastoralism remained the main occupation of the Aryan speakers for some time. The cow was a measure of value. Many early linguistic expressions were associated with cattle. Thus *gavishthi*, literally 'to search for cows', came to mean 'to fight' – the obvious implication being that cattle raids and lost cattle frequently led to armed conflicts. Perhaps the cow was regarded as a totem animal and in that sense an object of veneration. The eating of beef was reserved for specific occasions, such as rituals or when welcoming a guest or a person of high status. This is a common practice in other cattle-keeping cultures as well. The economic value of the cow further enhanced its veneration. This may have contributed to the later attitude of regarding the cow as sacred and inviolable, although association with the sacred need not require rational explanations. The question relates to livestock breeding, grazing grounds and ecological changes. Eventually it became a matter of status to refrain from eating beef and the prohibition was strengthened by various religious sanctions. Significantly, the prohibition was prevalent among the upper castes. Of the other animals the horse held pride of place. The horse was essential to movement, to speed in war, and in mythology it drew the chariots not only of men but also of the gods. And it was easier to herd cattle from horseback where the grazing grounds were extensive.

Tending herds of cattle did not preclude agriculture. Archaeology provides evidence of varied societies in the *sapta-sindhu* region – the Cemetery H culture, the Gandhara Grave culture, the Ochre Colour Pottery culture, to mention just a few. The authors of the Rig-Vedic hymns may have been familiar with some of these. Chalcolithic cultures practised agriculture, so there would have been a combining of agriculturalists and pastoralists, some pre-existing and some arriving. But for agriculture to be extended, the clearing of land was required. Fire played its part in this process and the burning of forests is described, perhaps initially in imitation of shifting cultivation. However, cutting down rather than burning forests was probably a more effective means of clearing the land, particularly after the later introduction of iron axes, since cutting enabled a greater control over the area to be cleared. The use of the plough goes back to pre-Harappan times and one of the words frequently used for the plough – *langala* – is from Munda, a non-Aryan language. The range of agricultural terms borrowed by Indo-Aryan from non-Aryan languages would suggest that plough agriculture was more common among the pre-existing communities.

Agricultural products came to be more frequently mentioned, even in the offerings made during sacrificial ritual. Yokes with six and eight oxen were used to plough the land. The plough became an icon of power and fertility, as shown in this hymn:

Let the plough, lance-pointed, well-lying with well-smoothed handle turn up cow, sheep and on-going chariot frame and a plump wench. Let Indra hold down the furrow; let Pushan defend it; let it, rich in milk, yield to us each further summer.

Successfully let the good ploughshares thrust apart the earth; successfully let the ploughmen follow the beasts of draft; Shunashira, do ye two dripping with oblation, make the herbs rich in berries for this man.

Successfully let the draft-animals, successfully the men, successfully let the plough, plough; successfully let the straps be bound; successfully do thou brandish the goad.
Atharva Veda, 3.17. 3–6, tr. W. D. Whitney

One innovation in agriculture in the Ganges Plain was the gradual shift from wheat cultivation to rice, and, in animal herding, the presence of the buffalo. Wet-rice cultivation was a dramatic change as it produced a larger yield which allowed a bigger surplus. The *vish*, or clan, was pressed into making more frequent prestations and offerings, and sacrifices dependent on these increased in number, as well as the gift-giving to priests in the form of *dana* and *dakshina*, gifts and fees.

To begin with, land was worked in common by the clan or the community. Eventually the decline of clan identity, and the prevalence of rights of usage and the demarcation of fields, led to land being divided among smaller groups, probably families. The greater dependence on agriculture rather than pastoralism led to a wider range of occupations. The carpenter remained an honoured member of the community, for not only was he the maker of the chariot but he was now also the maker of the plough, not to mention the framework required for building huts. The increasing availability of wood from the forests made carpentry a lucrative profession, which must have given it additional status. Other essential members of the village community were the metalsmiths – using copper, bronze, and later iron – as well as the potter, the tanner, the reed-worker and the weaver.

The location of the later Vedic corpus in the Ganges Plain describes conditions that are a prelude to urbanization. Chalcolithic cultures encouraged specialization and some of the settlements were eventually to become urban centres. Cultures just prior to urbanization are sometimes differentiated by the use of Painted Grey Ware in the western part and Black-and-Red Wares in the middle and eastern part. These cultures tended to be closely placed small settlements, largely agricultural. Some correlations have been suggested in the material culture of the Painted Grey Ware and that described in the later corpus, although it would not be accurate to label these archaeological cultures as Aryan or non-Aryan. Parallels with the corpus would suggest evolving societies and norms emerging out of many interactions. Incipient urbanism is noticeable by about the early sixth century BC at some sites, and at other places somewhat later. Links between the Punjab and the Ganges Plain were through routes along the Himalayan foothills and along the rivers of the Ganges system. The former may have been attractive because the foothills had relatively less dense vegetation, and were possibly sources of metal ores. The rivers of the Ganges system provided an easier means of communication than cutting paths through the forest.

When agrarian produce became available as surplus this led to exchange, which later resulted in trade. Initially exchange was in the form of barter, the cow being the unit of value in large-scale transactions, which limited the geographical reach of those wishing to exchange produce. The *nishka* is also mentioned as a measure of value, perhaps of gold, since later it came to be the name of a gold coin. With settlements increasing eastwards in the Ganges Plain, particularly along the banks of rivers, the rivers became natural highways, even if the river trade was of a rather basic kind to begin with.

Chiefs and Kings

The smallest segment of society was the *kula*, family, which among the higher status groups tended to be patriarchal. A number of families constituted a *grama*, a word used later for village, suggesting that the families in the early settlements were related. Another view holds that *grama* was the formation made up of wagons used by the mobile pastoralists. The family as a social entity generally extended over three generations, with the sons often living together in the parental home. Very early marriages were not customary. Both dowry and bride-price were recognized as distinctive systems. The birth of a son was especially welcome, for the son's presence was increasingly important in various ceremonies.

Within the confines of a patriarchal system the status of women veered, according to occasion, from being relatively free to being restricted. Women as depicted in the *Vedas* have been much romanticized, but a realistic view suggests varied conditions, especially when the mores of the clan gave way to the norms of the caste. The participation of wives was required in many rituals but it carried little authority. Curiously, in contrast to the presence of Harappan figurines, some of which may have represented deities, the Vedic texts did not attribute much power to their goddesses, who remained figures in the wings. It is thought that a widow had to perform a symbolic self-immolation at the death of her husband and this may have been a sign of status. In later centuries this was cited as the origin of the practice of becoming a *sati/suttee*, with a small emendation of the text, which made it possible to insist that a widow actually burn herself on her husband's funeral pyre. That the ritual was symbolic in the early period seems evident from the remarriage of widows, generally to the husband's brother – a custom referred to as *niyoga* or levirate. Monogamy was common, although polygamy was known among the rajas and polyandry was not unfamiliar. These divergences of marriage and kinship patterns, as well as of social codes, would question the universal applicability or the rigid observance of the regulations of the normative texts. There are three variants among the Pandavas alone: endogamous marriages among *kshatriyas* as in the marriages of Pandu; polyandry in the five Pandava brothers marrying Draupadi; and cross-cousin marriage between Arjuna and Subhadra. All of these point to a range of prevalent social patterns. If mythology is an indication of attitudes towards norms relating to kinship and marriage, then evidently there was flexibility.

The worship of Agni, as the god of fire, gave symbolic importance to the hearth as the most venerated part of the homestead and the nucleus of the home. Houses were built around a wooden frame. There were posts at the corners of the room, and crossbeams, around which were constructed walls of reed stuffed with straw. These later gave way to mud-plastered walls. Brick structures are not associated with buildings and the use of mud bricks was more frequent in the construction of the large altars for the major sacrifices. The use of bamboo ribs to support thatch provided a roof. The house was large, with family and animals living under the same roof. The staple diet included milk, *ghi* (clarified butter), vegetables, fruit, wheat and barley in various forms, and rice where it was grown. On ceremonial occasions, or on the arrival of a guest, a more elaborate meal was customary, including the flesh of cattle, goats, and sheep, washed down with the intoxicating *sura* or *madhu* (a type of mead). Clothes were simple, but ornaments were more elaborate and a source of pleasure to their owners.

Interest in music can be seen not only from the variety of instruments mentioned, but also from the highly developed knowledge of sound, tone and pitch, which was used particularly in the chanting of the *Sama Veda*, and a familiarity with the heptatonic scale. Schools of music in later times have frequently traced their origins to these beginnings, an ancestry that in many cases was more a matter of prestige than of history. Nevertheless, where legitimate, it provided the possibilities for complex musical structures that became central to later forms of music. Leisure hours were spent mainly in playing music, singing, dancing and gambling, with chariot-racing for the more energetic. Chariot-racing was a sport of the rajas, sometimes included as part of their ritual of initiation. The chariots were lightly built with spoked wheels, and were drawn by horses. Gambling was a favourite pastime. The gamblers lamented but played on, and the hymns provide details of the dice and the rules of the throw.

Clans were organized as patriarchal groups, and in the early stages the raja was merely the leader. When the need for protection and for social regulation became necessary, the most capable protector was selected as chief. He gradually began to assume privileges that were later incorporated into kingship. However, the concentration of power was checked by various assemblies of the clansmen, in particular, the *vidatha*, *sabha* and *samiti*. The *vidatha* was the gathering at which, among other things, the booty acquired in a raid was distributed. These were occasions when the bards composed eulogies on the exploits of the chiefs and were rewarded with generous gifts. The *dana*, gift, began as an appreciation for a hymn immortalizing the hero, and praise was therefore showered on the magnanimous givers of wealth, such as the chief, Divodas. These were the *dana-stuti* hymns of the *Rig-Veda*, eulogizing the gift. Sometimes exaggerated quantities of wealth were listed, such as 60,000 head of cattle or 10,000 head of horse. This was to shame those who gave small gifts. Increasing occasions for gift-giving led to the idea of the patron of the sacrifice giving a *dakshina*, a fee in the form of a gift, to the person performing the ritual. The gift and the fee established a relationship between the patron and the priest, which could be competitive or in tandem.

Gift-giving was deeply embedded in these societies and not only assumed social forms, but acted as a mechanism for the distribution of wealth, often at clan assemblies. The *sabha* was the council of the select and exclusive, whereas the *samiti* was an assembly of the clan. The emerging political organization can be traced in some of the legends on the origin of government: the gods and the demons were at war, and the gods appeared to be losing, so they gathered together and elected a raja from among themselves to lead them, and eventually they won the war.

The word raja, which has been translated as 'king' from its earliest occurrence, is better translated as 'chief' in the earlier references until the time when it clearly refers to a king. It is derived from a root which means 'to shine' or 'to lead', although its etymology in the epics, thought to be less accurate, is associated with another root – 'to please' – suggesting that the raja gratifies the people. The change to kingship is generally linked to two phases: there is first the performance of major sacrifices – *yajnas* – as discussed in the later *Vedas*, when the priests not only initiated the chief into a status above the ordinary but also imbued him with elements of divinity; the second phase has to do with the emergence of the state, which was a departure from the earlier organization of society and governance on the basis of clans. Associated with these changes was the gradual receding of the notion of the *vish*, clan, selecting a raja, which implies that the clan was subordinated. The telling simile is the statement that the raja eats the *vish* as the deer eats grain.

To begin with, the raja was primarily a military leader. His skill lay in protecting the settlement and winning booty, both essential to his status. He received voluntary gifts and prestations in kind, for which the term *bali* came to be used – an extension of its meaning as an offering to the gods. There was no regular tax that he could claim, nor had he any rights over the land. He was entitled to a portion of the booty from successful cattle-raids after the *bhaga*, shares, had been sorted out, and he would obviously claim a larger one. Mention is also made of *shulka*, literally the value or worth of an item. In later times, after the establishing of states, all three terms were used for various taxes.

When the functions of the priest became distinctive, and the raja claimed greater authority, he emerged as the patron of the sacrifice. There was now both a competition and an interweaving of the authority of the raja, the one who wielded power, and that of the brahman, the one who legitimized this power through ritual – a competition in which the brahman eventually emerged as the one with the highest ritual status. A later legend tells us that not only did the gods elect a raja to lead them to victory, but that he was also endowed with distinctive attributes. Similarly, mortal rajas were invested with attributes of divinity. Special sacrifices were evolved to enable the priests, regarded as the intermediaries between men and gods, to bestow this divinity. This empowered the priest and was the beginning of the interdependence of temporal and sacral power, sometimes involving a con-testation over status. The *Mahabharata*, unlike the Vedic corpus, depicts a situation where the concerns and status of the *kshatriyas* are primary. Not surprisingly there was now a tendency for the office of the raja to become hereditary and primogeniture began to be favoured. The occasional and shallow genealogies of the chiefs of clans in the *Rig-Veda* gave way to genealogies of greater depth, to legitimize rajas through lineage – irrespective of whether the genealogies were actual or fictive. The status of the assemblies also underwent a consequential change: the *sabha* could act as an advisory body to the raja, but he was the final authority. The larger assemblies gradually declined. These were pointers to the coming of kingship.

The raja was the pivot in a rudimentary administrative system. Chiefship began to be associated with territory, incorporating the families settled in the villages, the wider clans and the still larger unit of the tribe. These constituted the *janapada* – literally the place where the tribe places its foot – significantly named after the ruling clan. This could be either a single clan, such as the Kekeyas, Madras, Kurus and Kosalas, or a confederacy such as that of the Panchalas. A more complex confederacy involved the coming together of the Kurus and the Panchalas. The *purohita* or chief priest, who combined the function of priest, astrologer and adviser, and the *senani* or military commander are among those more frequently mentioned as assisting the raja. Later, a more elaborate group surrounded the raja, including the charioteer, the treasurer, the steward and the superintendent of dicing. The last is not surprising, considering the love of gambling among both royalty and commoners. But the throwing of dice may have been linked to lots, involving wealth or access to grazing lands and fields, in the absence of effective rights to the ownership of land, illustrated, for example, in the *Mahabharata*.

Some ceremonies were originally intended to establish the status of the chief, but were gradually made more elaborate until they eventually became a necessity for the raja claiming the status of a king. Once the chief had been initiated and his legal status established, he was eligible to perform the year-long *rajasuya*, or consecration, investing him with divinity brought from the gods by the magic power of the priests. The ritual involved rites of purification and symbolic rebirth. Towards the end of this ritual the raja was required to make an offering to the twelve *ratnins*, jewels, in return for their loyalty. Some of these were members of his household and others were craftsmen and specialists. The inclusion of the latter underlined the growing importance of specialization in daily life. After some years the consecration ceremony was followed by sacrifices, intended to assist in his rejuvenation.

Perhaps the best known of the spectacular sacrifices was the *ashvamedha*, or horse sacrifice, not unknown to other cultures such as those of the

Romans and the Celts. Starting as a rather simple ritual, it incorporated more elaborate ones, as is evident from the description in the later corpus. References to large numbers of rajas having performed the *ashvamedha* provide us with lists of possible rajas, together with a brief ancestry, where some may have been historical. After due ceremonies, a raja released a special horse to wander at will, accompanied by a substantial bodyguard. The raja claimed the territory over which it wandered. This sacrifice was theoretically permitted only to those who were powerful and could support such a claim, but in effect it was to become a ritual of kingship. Many minor chiefs performed the sacrifice and doubtless some manipulated the wandering of the horse to save face. These sacrifices were conducted on a vast scale, with many priests and sacrificial animals, and a variety of objects used in the ceremony. On the return of the horse, the second part of the ritual focused on rites of fertility that involved the sacrificed horse and the chief wife of the raja. Such rituals reinforced the special status of raja and brahman. When the claim to status explicitly incorporated political and economic power not necessarily based on kinship connections, then it initiated the notion of kingship and the incipient state.

Incipient Caste

Some of the clans were given the status of *aryas*, but there were also other respected rajas, such as Puru, whose antecedents are ambiguous. He is described as *mridhra-vac*, not speaking the language correctly, and later as being of *asura rakshasa*, demon, descent. Even where a *dasa* ancestry is mentioned the ambiguity remains; for example in the presence of what were called *dasi-putra* brahmans, whose mothers were of the *dasa* community. They are referred to in the later sections of the *Vedas*, by which time some mixing of communities had occurred. They were initially reviled, but, on demonstrating their power as priests, were respected. This would have been an avenue for various local rituals to be assimilated into Vedic worship, which is thought to have been the case with many of the rituals described in the *Atharvaveda*. If ritual specialists were accorded high status, then others from the existing societies would also have been adjusted into the social hierarchy. The Nishada, for example, were of a different culture but were associated with some Vedic rituals.

The *Vedas* subsequent to the *Rig-Veda* (barring one late hymn in the latter) mention the four *varnas*: brahman, *kshatriya*, *vaishya* and *shudra*. This is not a division of the two – the *arya varna* and the *dasa varna* of the

Rig-Veda – into four, since the basis of the four is different. The first three have an occupational function as priests, as warriors and aristocrats, and as the providers of wealth through herding, agriculture and exchange. Occupations and marriage regulations were among the factors identifying these categories. The latter are also apparent from references to *gotra*, the literal meaning of which was a cowpen although it was later used to segregate groups for identification relating to permitted marriage circles and, in later times, property rights.

The inclusion of the fourth category, the *shudra*, reflected a substantial change. Kinship connections and lineage rank had initially determined who controlled labour and who laboured, the division sometimes taking the form of senior lineages demarcated from cadet lines or lesser lineages. Economic relations were therefore embedded in kinship relations and age groups. Where stratification had come to be recognized, chiefly families demarcated themselves from others and claimed a particular lineage. This changed to a householding system where the family of the lesser clansman became the unit of labour. The further change was introducing non-kin labour. Some who were unrelated through kinship were inducted as labour. This assumes a shift towards agriculture and increased social demarcation. Permanency was given to this change through establishing a group whose function was to labour for others. This was a radical departure from the earlier system. The term *dasa*, which in the *Rig-Veda* was used to designate the other person of a different culture, was now used to mean the one who laboured for others. This was also the function of the *shudra*, who began to provide labour for occupations ranging across the agrarian and craft specializations and other less attractive jobs.

Social divisions became sharper and degrees of labour became part of the assessment of social rank. Whereas the *vaishya* is described as tributary to another, to be eaten by another, to be oppressed at will, the *shudra* is said to be the servant of another, to be removed at will, to be slain at will. The expansion of agriculture and the emergence of craftsmen required greater specialization, as well as occupations that further encouraged separate categories of craftsmen, cultivators and labourers. Each of these was said to be of low status and treated as a separate *jati*.

Jati comes from the root meaning 'birth', and is a status acquired through birth. *Jati* had a different origin and function from *varna* and was not just a subdivision of the latter. The creation of *varnas* appears to be associated with ritual status, a status denied to the *shudra* who was debarred from participating in all rituals. Whereas the three higher *varnas* were said to be strict about marrying within regulated circles, the *shudra varna* described in the normative texts was characterized as originating in an indiscriminate marriage between castes, creating mixed castes – a category abhorrent to those insisting on the theoretical purity of descent. This sets them apart and they were often labelled as *jatis*. This was an attempt to explain a low category of mixed castes and can hardly be taken literally. Once they had been recognized as categories, both *varnas* and *jatis* were required to observe specific marriage regulations and rules regarding access to occupation, social hierarchy and hereditary status. Marriage had to be regulated within marriage circles, an essential requirement for the continuation of caste society. It was also a method of controlling the exchange of women and thus keeping women subordinated.

By the mid-first millennium this status was reiterated in the theory that the first three *varnas* are *dvija*, twice-born – the second birth being initiation into the ritual status – whereas the *shudra* has only a single birth. This was also tied to the notion of grading the purity of the statuses, theoretically according to occupation. Thus, the brahman was the purest and the *shudra* the least pure. Subsequently, a fifth category came to be added, that of the untouchable (now referred to as Dalit), and this was regarded as maximally polluting. A system that combined status by birth, determined by access to resources, social status and occupation, with notions of ritual purity and pollution was doubtless thought to be virtually infallible as a mechanism of social control.

The question posed earlier in Chapter 2 becomes relevant here: in the transition from clan status to *varna* status – a transition familiar to Indian history – did *varna* status precede *jati* status as has been generally argued? Or is it possible to suggest an alternative system where, if clans were the earlier forms of social organization, they were first transmuted into *jatis*, with *jatis* retaining some features of clan organization such as observing the rules of which circles a *jati* could marry into? Such *jatis* would be the result of people being conquered, subordinated or encroached upon by caste society already observing *varna* distinctions. Was there then a re-allocation of statuses? Whereas a few were incorporated into brahman, *kshatriya* and *vaishya* status, were the large residual groups given *shudra* status? *Varna* would be necessary as a ritual status in the hierarchy of caste society. *Shudras*, because they were excluded from participating in most Vedic ritual, would have had their own rituals and worshipped their own gods. Vedic rituals would remain the religion of the elite.

This division of society made it easier in later centuries to induct new cultures and groups of people. New groups took on the characteristics of a separate caste and were slotted into the caste hierarchy, their position being dependent on their occupation and social origins, and on the reason for the induction. Such groups could be migrants as were pastoralists and traders, or could be clans of cultivators, or invaders who came and settled, such as the Hunas, or even those scattered in various regions such as the forest-dwellers and other groups on the margins of settled society. This was in some ways a form of conversion.

The brahmans were not slow to realize the significance of these social divisions and the authority which could be invested in the foremost caste. They claimed the highest position in the ranking of ritual purity, thereby insisting that they alone could bestow the divinity essential to kingship, and give religious sanction to *varna* divisions. A frequently quoted hymn from the *Rig-Veda*, although a later addition, provides a mythical sanction to the origin of the castes:

> When the gods made a sacrifice with the Man as their victim . . .
> When they divided the Man, into how many parts did they divide him?
> What was his mouth, what were his arms, what were his thighs and his feet
>   called?
> The brahman was his mouth, of his arms were made the warrior.
> His thighs became the *vaishya*, of his feet the *shudra* was born.
> With Sacrifice the gods sacrificed to Sacrifice, these were the first of the sacred
>   laws.
> These mighty beings reached the sky, where are the eternal spirits, the gods.
>
> *Rig-Veda*, 10.90, tr. A. L. Basham, *The Wonder That Was India*, p. 241

The continuance of caste was secured by its being made hereditary, linked to occupation, with a taboo on commensality (eating together), and the defining of marriage circles leading to elaborate rules of endogamy (marriage within certain groups) and exogamy (marriage outside certain groups). The basis of caste as a form of social control, and its continuance, depended on the ritual observance of the fourfold division and an insistence on the hierarchy that it imposed. Eventually, *jati* relationships and adjustments acquired considerable relevance for the day-to-day working of Indian society, and for a wide range of religious groups, even if some hesitated to admit to this. *Varna* status was the concern of the twice-born Hindus, but *jati* was basic to the larger society. The division of society into four *varnas* was not uniformly observed in every part of the subcontinent. With caste becoming hereditary, and the close connection between occupation and *jati*, there was an automatic check on individuals moving up in the hierarchy of castes. Vertical mobility was possible to the *jati* as a whole, but depended upon the entire group acting as one and changing both its location and its work. An individual could express his protest by joining a sect which disavowed caste, or at least questioned its assumptions, many of which evolved from the fifth century BC onwards.

Sacrifice as Ritual and as a Form of Social Exchange

Despite the fact that the Harappans had used a script, writing did not develop in this period, hence the premium on oral memory and instruction. There is a delightfully humorous hymn in the *Rig-Veda* describing frogs croaking at the onset of the rainy season, echoing each other's voices, an activity that is compared to pupils repeating lessons after the teacher or ritual recitations of brahmans. However, the method of memorizing was not simple and was fine-tuned to the point of making the composition almost unalterable. By the mid-first millennium the institution of the *brahmacharin* was well established. The student was expected to live with a teacher in the latter's hermitage for a number of years. The good student was expected to shun urban life when cities became an attraction. Education was in theory open to the twice-born, although the curriculum of formal education was useful largely to brahmans. Arithmetic, grammar and prosody were included as subjects of study. Some of the Rig-Vedic hymns incorporated the recitation of dialogues, thus constituting the rudiments of a dramatic form.

There were no legal institutions at this stage. Custom was law and the arbiters were the chief or the king and the priest, perhaps advised by elders of the community. Varieties of theft, particularly cattle-stealing, were the commonest crimes. Punishment for homicide was based on *wergeld*, and the usual payment for killing a man was a hundred cows. Capital punishment was a later idea. Trial by ordeal was normal, and among the ordeals was one where the accused had to prove his innocence by placing his tongue on a heated metal axe-head. Rules of inheritance came to be formulated gradually, doubtless when changing notions of what constituted property became problematic. Increasingly, caste considerations carried more weight, with lighter punishments for higher castes.

The Harappans seem to have looked upon certain objects as sacred, and some were perhaps associated with fertility, such as female figurines, the bull, the Horned Deity and trees like the *pipal* (*ficus religiosa*). These reappear in later worship. The *dasas* in the *Rig-Veda* are castigated for not observing the proper rituals and instead practising a fertility cult. The more abstract brahman systems of belief, founded on the *Vedas*, appealed to a

limited few and, whereas their impact can be seen in subsequent philosophies, most people preferred more accessible forms of religion and worship. A hierarchy emerged in the categories of rituals. Those that were lavish
required a considerable expenditure of wealth, but others were pared down
to essentials. The number of priests grew with the expansion of the ritual,
requiring that they be sorted out according to function. The Vedic corpus
reflects the archetypal religion of those who called themselves *aryas*, and
which, although it contributed to facets of latter-day Hinduism, was nevertheless distinct. But inevitably some belief and practice would have been
transmuted because of the proximity of those with other religious practices.
Possibly the rituals, particularly those of the major sacrifices, were more
closely observed once the corpus came to be compiled.

Mythologies were continually created or revised and these provide clues to
changing beliefs. The enmity between *devas* and *asuras* is often the starting
point of a myth. A gradual reversing of the values associated with these two
groups can be noticed from the *Avesta* to the late *Rig-Veda*. The *soma* sacrifice, a key ritual, was specific only to Iran and India among the cultures of
Indo-European speakers. The *soma* plant, although deified, was also said to
grow in the north-western mountains. It is generally thought that the plant
was ephedra, although this identification was contested when the fly agaric
mushroom was thought to be *soma*. The juice of the *soma* plant was drunk
on ritual occasions and acted as a hallucinogen. An entire book of the
Rig-Veda was dedicated to *soma* and inevitably carries a complicated symbolism. The worship of fire was central to ritual in Iran and India although
it was also more widely practised. Fire altars changed from small domestic
structures, associated with a habitation, to include impressively large structures especially constructed as altars for the more elaborate rituals. Built at
this time with mud bricks, none have survived, but a couple of altars built of
fired bricks at the turn of the Christian era are still visible. Rituals were held
on specific days and times thought to be auspicious. The patron of the
sacrifice – the *yajamana* – was consecrated for the period of the ritual. The
sacrificial ground was also initially consecrated and finally desanctified at
the termination of the ritual, leaving no permanent location for acts of
worship. Nor is there mention of the worship of images.

Deities mentioned in the *Rig-Veda* include some that go back to Indo-
Iranian origins, such as Mitra and Varuna. These gave way to Indra and
Agni. Indra was the ideal hero, foremost in battle, always ready to smite
demons and to destroy the settlements of the *dasas*, and willing to aid those
who propitiated him. His help against the enemy is constantly called for.
He was the god of storms and thunder and, as the rainmaker, fulfilled an

important symbolic function in these societies. Agni, the god of fire, inspired some beautifully evocative hymns. The fire was the focus of multiple domestic rituals, such as the solemnizing of marriages. Thought to be the purest of the five elements, it was the appropriate intermediary between gods and men. Other gods included Surya (Sun), Savitri (a solar deity to whom the famous *gayatri mantra* is dedicated), Pushan and Yama, the god of death. For the rest, the cosmos was peopled by a large variety of celestial beings – Gandharvas, Maruts, Vishvadevas – and the numbers of these could be multiplied as and when desired. Hymns were also dedicated to the power residing in the sacrificial implements, especially the sacrificial altar, and to the stones used for pressing the *soma* plant, as well as to the plough, the weapons of war, the drum and the mortar and pestle.

The central ritual was the *yajna*, sacrifice. The domestic rituals with small oblations continued to be performed, and remained intimate. Gradually the more spectacular rituals attracted patronage, as they had a public function, and only the upper castes could participate. They were also the arenas for the competition between sacred and temporal authority. It has been argued that insistence on performing rituals was more important than the dogma of belief, that orthopraxy was more elevated than orthodoxy. The ritual of sacrifice was believed to sustain the well-being of the clan and the system. Thus the devaluing of the *yajna* by heterodoxy in later times was a significant challenge. Domestic prosperity, requiring an increase in the herd and good crops, had to be prayed for, as well as success in skirmishes and raids. Gods were believed to grant boons and even to participate unseen in the rituals. Small oblations were restricted to the domestic sacrifice, but from time to time larger sacrifices were organized for which the clan brought substantial prestations. The public sacrifice was a solemn occasion, but it also released energies through the general conviviality that followed at its conclusion. The wealth collected by the raja through voluntary tribute and prestations from the *vish* was consumed in the ritual and in the distribution of gifts at the end to other rajas and to the priests.

With the elaboration of the ritual the role of the priest assumed greater importance, hence the designation of brahman, applied to one who possessed the mysterious and magical power, *brahma*. It was also thought that the god, the priests and the offering passed through a moment of complete identity. The giving of gifts was believed to ensure a return of gifts in even greater amount. Sacrificial rites tended to increase the power of the priest, without whom the sacrifice could not take place, and of the raja who possessed the wealth it required. Collecting this wealth meant pressurizing the *vish* to part with their produce. The sacrifice assisted the *kshatriya* to assert greater power over the *vish* and the *shudra*. No wonder it is said that the *vish* is the food for the *kshatriya* and the *kshatriya* eats the *vish*. The later corpus refers frequently to *kshatriya* in place of the earlier terms such as *raja* and *rajan*. Derived from *kshatra*, meaning power, it points to the greater authority now associated with the chief transmuting into kingship.

The public sacrifices were occasions when the wealth of a raja was collected and displayed via the rituals. This wealth was consumed, and whatever remained was gifted, with some even being deliberately destroyed through forms of ritual which were part of the display. The patron of the sacrifice, the *yajamana*, was generally a raja, and each competed with his peers in the magnificence of the occasion and the generosity of the gifts. Such competitions in the display of wealth, spurred on by those who eulogized the rajas, established the status and power of the *yajamana*, encouraging his belief that even more wealth would come his way. Comparisons have been made with the similar expectations of the potlatch, a ceremony characteristic of the native Americans of the north Pacific coast. The raja's gifts to the priests enriched and empowered the brahmans. The sacrifice prevented the raja from accumulating wealth to the point where his status would be based on economic power rather than ritual sanction. Yet the former was necessary to create the type of kingship associated with the notion of a state in which the king controlled the accumulation and distribution of wealth, among other things.

In order to accumulate the required wealth for these sacrifices, the raja would have made bigger demands on the *vish*, in the form of offerings and prestations, and would have needed to create a rudimentary administration for support. The point at which wealth could be accumulated and spent on a variety of adjuncts to authority marked the point at which kingship was beginning to draw on political authority, rather than ritual authority alone. However, the ritual of sacrifice as a necessary precondition to kingship could not become a permanent feature. Once kingdoms were established there were other demands on the wealth that went to support the kingdoms. At one level the questioning of the centrality of the ritual was encouraged by new perceptions of the relationship between the human and the divine. At another level the greater production of wealth in the middle Ganges Plain on the eve of urbanization, not all of which could be consumed in rituals, did allow for rajas accumulating wealth and this contributed towards a change in the requirements of society and polity. It is significant that ideas questioning the *yajna* were developed initially by the *kshatriyas*, as commented upon in the *Upanishads*. As patrons they were affected by a decline in the necessity of these rituals as this would have given them an edge, influencing not only religious practice and philosophical theories but also social ethics and economic viability.

The ritual of sacrifice resulted in some interesting by-products. Mathematical knowledge was developed as a result of the calculations required for demarcating the precise locations and size of structures and objects in the large sacrificial arena. Basic geometry was used to work out the size and number of mud bricks required for building the altars. It has been suggested that the use of bricks and the calculations may have come from a Harappan tradition harking back to the construction of platforms. Rituals of the *Rig-Veda* did not require large-scale brick-built altars and these were introduced in the later corpus. The Harappans would have had advanced knowledge of building brick structures far more monumental than the altars. If there had been such a tradition, then the assimilation of earlier ideas would have bypassed the Rig-Vedic period and surfaced later. Methods of measurement were useful in much later times when land had to be measured for assessment of taxes. A concern with numbers became important to priestly practice. Observations of lunar movements and constellations came to be used to calculate time and the calendar. The frequent sacrifice of animals led to some knowledge of animal anatomy, and, for a long time, anatomy was more advanced than physiology or pathology. Yet the physician was initially declared to be an impure person and unfit for participating in the ritual.

The dead were either buried or cremated, the former being the earlier custom that gave way to the latter. It was, however, continued among groups of people even when cremation became the norm. The association of fire with purification may have led to the preference for cremation. (Although a practical method of disposing of the dead, for the historian this was an unhappy choice since graves, together with grave furnishings, provide excellent historical evidence, as demonstrated in the data available from the megalithic burials of the peninsula.)

Life after death was envisaged in terms of either punishment or reward. Those to be punished went to the House of Clay. Those to be rewarded, such as heroes, went to the World of the Fathers. The later Vedic corpus has occasional hints of metempsychosis, of souls being reborn in plants, but the idea of the transmigration of souls was initially vague. Its currency in the *Upanishads* led it to be tied into the theory that souls were born to happiness or to sorrow, according to their conduct in their previous life. This was to evolve into the doctrine of *karma*, action, and *samsara*, rebirth, which has ever since been influential in Indian thought.

The questioning of the centrality of sacrifice, hinted at by thoughtful brahmans was developed in depth among *kshatriyas* and led eventually to alternative ideas. Among these was the notion of the *atman*, the individual soul, seeking unity with the *brahman*, the universal soul – unity which could require many cycles of rebirth of the soul. An attempt to move away from the sacrificial ritual could have been liberating for the raja. It was, however, soon muted by the idea of *karma* and *samsara*. The measure of quality in the reborn life came to rest on conforming to the social codes of caste and caste hierarchies. Thus it is said that:

Those whose conduct here has been good will quickly attain a good birth [literally, 'womb'], the birth of a brahman, the birth of a kshatriya, the birth of a vaishya. But those whose conduct here has been evil, will quickly attain an evil birth, the birth of a dog, the birth of a hog or the birth of a Chandala.

Chandogya Upanishad, 5.10.7, tr. S. Radhakrishnan

The doctrine of *karma* came to be systematized in the broader concept of *dharma* – social and sacred obligations – which in conservative circles was seen as maintaining the social order, in fact the laws of *varna*.

Metaphysical concepts gave rise to various explanations for the universe and its origin. One was that it grew out of a vast cosmic sacrifice and was maintained by the proper performing of sacrifices. Yet this idea was not entirely accepted, as is evident from what has been called the Creation Hymn, which doubts any certainty about the birth of the universe and even postulates creation emerging from Nothingness:

> Then even nothingness was not, nor existence.
> There was no air then, nor the heavens beyond it.
> Who covered it? Where was it? In whose keeping?
> Was there then cosmic water, in depths unfathomed? . . .
> But, after all, who knows, and who can say,
> Whence it all came, and how creation happened?
> The gods themselves are later than creation,
> So who knows truly whence it has arisen?

Rig-Veda, 10. 129, tr. A. L. Basham,
The Wonder That Was India, p. 247

The doubts expressed in the Creation Hymn were symptomatic of a wider spirit of inquiry. Local beliefs and customs were now being incorporated into Vedic practice. The resulting concepts were not the expression of any 'pure tradition', but were an amalgam from many varied sources. Some have argued that the concepts of the *Upanishads* and of asceticism grew not from a single, brahmanical tradition, but from the thinking of the many and varied groups that constituted Indian society at the time. This may be so. But it is perhaps more valid to look for inspirations and intentions as they emerged from the actual situations faced by various groups, with their search for answers in what they seem to have perceived as a world of almost bewildering change.

Some changes encouraged ideas of asceticism, of people withdrawing from the community and living either as hermits or in small groups away from centres of habitation. Asceticism could have had either of two purposes: to acquire more than ordinary powers by extraordinary control over the physical body, as in *yoga*, and through *dhyana*, meditation; or to seek freedom from having to adjust to an increasingly regulated society by physically withdrawing from it, evidenced by the practice of renunciation at a young age being regarded as a distancing from Vedic ritual and from the rules of the normative texts.

The intention was not a life-negating philosophy through an escape from social obligations, but an attempt to find an alternative style of life conforming to a philosophy and an ethic different from what had now become the conventional. The impact of this possibility is frequently imprinted on events and situations in the history of India. This is sometimes taken for an impassive spirituality, whereas in effect it assisted on occasion in giving a radical turn to Indian society, or at least to accommodating radical ideas and behaviour. Renunciation of social obligations, implicit in asceticism, encouraged a kind of counter-culture and this became an accepted strand of religious and social thought in India. Some forms of Indian asceticism, although not all, have a socio-political dimension and these cannot be marginalized as merely the wish to negate life.

Ascetics did not invariably spend all their time isolated in forests or on the tops of mountains. Some returned to their communities and challenged the existing social and religious norms. This may have been seen as a threat. The normative texts advocated a sequence in which the life of a man was divided into four stages, called *ashramas*, refuges. He was first to be a student, then a householder with a family, then a renouncer withdrawn from social life and, finally, a wandering ascetic. Asceticism was placed at the end of a man's life because his social obligation to his community had priority. Needless to say, this pattern applied largely to the upper castes, which could afford to follow it, but it remained essentially an ideal. And, even in theory, such a curriculum was intended only for men.

Some among the ascetics and the rajas continued to seek answers to fundamental questions, as is evident from the *Upanishads*. How did creation come about? Through a cosmic sexual act? Through heat? Through asceticism? Is there a soul? What is the soul? What is the relation between the human soul and the universal soul? And, above all, there was the question of how one defines the Self.

> 'Fetch me a fruit of the banyan tree.'
>
> 'Here is one, sir.'
>
> 'Break it.'
>
> 'I have broken it, sir.'
>
> 'What do you see?'
>
> 'Very tiny seeds, sir.'
>
> 'Break one.'
>
> 'I have broken it, sir.'
>
> 'Now what do you see?'
>
> 'Nothing, sir.'
>
> 'My son,' the father said, 'what you do not perceive is the essence and in that essence the mighty banyan tree exists. Believe me my son, in that essence is the self of all that is. That is the True, that is the Self. And you are that Self, Shvetaketu.'
>
> *Chandogya Upanishad*, 6.13, tr. A. L. Basham,
> *The Wonder That Was India*, p. 250

The period from 1200 to 600 BC is popularly thought of as the Golden Age of the Vedic period. This has tended to give uncritical emphasis to one category of historical source material and its interpretation. The historical reconstruction of these centuries is full of uncertainties and lacunae. By the end of the period the corpus had been compiled. Being essentially concerned with ritual and belief, the most fulsome descriptions are of the societies of those who were the performers and the patrons of rituals. Reading between the lines to obtain information on other segments of these societies, or on other societies, requires analytical investigations of the corpus. Significant new evidence can also come from archaeology. Excavations of sites and particularly horizontal excavations in the Ganges Plain will help clarify the evolution of these societies. Studies that illuminate social and political institutions, as well as investigating the evolution of religious forms, provide themes of immediate historical interest.

The question of whether 'the Aryans' were an indigenous people or an alien people relates to concerns of the nineteenth century. Its revival today has more to do with political intentions than with history. The historically more germane questions focus on processes of acculturation, the evolution of social forms and the emergence of varying ideologies. The answers to these questions will illumine what the texts mean when they refer to the *aryas*.

The societies of the Indo-Gangetic Plains, where the substantial changes of this period took place, generated ideas and institutions that helped shape Indian society. Some resulted from the coming of the Indo-Aryan speakers and their interaction with existing cultures; others evolved through the changes referred to earlier in this chapter. We can no longer regard the early first millennium as a period of Aryan conquest that resulted in the spread of a homogeneous Aryan culture across northern India; nor can it be described as the articulation of an indigenous culture called Aryan that was untouched by anything extraneous. The historical picture points to a range of societies with varied origins attempting to establish a presence or dominance in the mosaic of cultures. The cultures change continually as cultures always do. Our literary evidence from the *Vedas* is from the perspective of brahmanical authors, and their perspective has to be juxtaposed where possible with other sources that have a different perspective, or with a reading of the *Vedas* open to the possibility of hearing other voices.

This encourages a more incisive questioning of the sources. Archaeology is often a useful counterbalance as it provides evidence of material culture, on the basis of which one can observe some of the changes towards new social forms. The time-dimension of this change is often overlooked by modern commentators. It was a slow mutation over almost a thousand years. Initial attempts at maintaining a distance between societies were gradually eroded and, although cultures remained distinct, they also registered change from early to late periods. One of the more obvious but complex examples of this is illustrated in language changes.

In the course of its evolution Vedic Sanskrit incorporated elements of Dravidian and Austro-Asiatic. This borrowing, it has been argued, was based on bilingualism or on the interrelations between the diverse groups that constituted the many societies of this time, even those who referred to themselves as *aryas* – those who used Indo-Aryan and were regarded as respected members of society. The historically relevant question is: how did Indo-Aryan become the dominant language of northern India, given the currency of other distinctly different languages? Dominance tends to be associated with power, effective technologies and claims to ritual superiority. These were claims made by the *aryas*, but why and how they were so widely accepted needs investigation.

The grammar of Panini, the *Ashtadhyayi*, written in the fifth century BC, was an attempt to regulate the more familiar form of Sanskrit and structure its grammar. The upper castes were familiar with Sanskrit, although it is likely that Prakrit was preferred for routine usage and for general speech by that time. If there is evidence of borrowing from other local languages in the language used for ritual, then the borrowing must have been greater in everyday speech. Mixed languages would have partially blurred the linguistic demarcation between Aryan and non-Aryan speakers. At one level Sanskrit was to become a unifying factor in the subcontinent, but it also tended to isolate its speakers from those who used other languages. That some aspects of Vedic Sanskrit had already become obscure to its speakers is indicated by the need for etymological explanations, such as are contained in the *Nirukta* of Yaska. The codifying of the language in a grammar could also have been a way of preventing further linguistic change, or else of enabling those unfamiliar with the language to learn it more easily.

Stratification through caste led increasingly to the upper castes having access to resources and subordinating the lower castes. It gave a ritual sanction to a variety of inequalities. The permanency or otherwise of this inequality varied according to group and occasion. Interrelationships between castes were influential in public life, which sometimes tended to divert attention away from distant political concerns and towards local loyalties. Where central political authority became remote, the nature of local functioning had clearer contours.

The centrality of the *yajna* became a characteristic of Vedic Brahmanism. The contesting of this centrality released a range of new philosophical concepts and religious articulations. This is evident from the *Upanishads*, and from the ideologies that drew on these in the subsequent period, as well as from a range of other teachers who introduced new forms of belief and worship. The brahmanical contribution to the discussion in the *Upanishads* – what became the interconnected notions of *karma* and *samsara* – also became pivotal to the confrontation of the Shramanic sects such as the Buddhist and the Jaina, with Vedic Brahmanism, albeit in a differently defined form; and it was foundational to many sects of an even later period, giving rise to what has come to be called Puranic Hinduism, which was in many ways a departure from Vedic Brahmanism.

It was also a time when various social groups left their imprint on the physical landscape. Small patches of forests and wasteland were cleared for cultivation to feed not only the growing population, but also to provide for the incipient centres of exchange. Some of these grew into towns by the mid-first millennium and were the base for urbanization in the Ganges Plain. The people who saw themselves as *aryas* were essentially unconcerned with whether they were indigenous or alien, since *arya* comes to be used as signifying status and culture. The difference is apparent from the *Rig-Veda* and the later *Vedas*. In the former, the divide between the *arya* and the *dasa* relates to language, ritual and custom. In the latter, there appears to have been a reshuffling of these and the divide changes to the *arya* being the respected one and *dasa* being a member of the subordinated group, but irrespective of origins. The words are taken from the earlier *Veda* but have by now acquired another meaning.

Underlying these developments was the contestation between those who claimed the social status of *arya* and those who were excluded from this status, resulting in a continuous modification and transmutation of both. New people of diverse backgrounds were either recruited into the status or were excluded. The status was not biologically or racially determined but was recognized by other characteristics: by speech-forms deriving from the Indo-Aryan language; by belief systems and rituals as initially encoded in the Vedic corpus; and by the acceptance, at least in theory, of certain social codes eventually gathered together in the *Dharmasutras*. The identification of the *arya* was therefore of a status that was modified from time to time by historical contingencies. It was neither a homogeneous nor a permanent ancestry. What was permanent to their self-perception was that they saw themselves as the dominant group, with the right to demand subservience or respect from others. By the mid-first millennium BC the societies of northern India had moved a long way from the agro-pastoral communities of the *Rig-Veda* and were now ensconced in the politically effective territories ruled by clan aristocracies or kings.

5

States and Cities of the
Indo-Gangetic Plain

c. 600–300 BC

States and Cities

The sixth century BC witnessed a transition to a new historical scene in north India with the establishment of kingdoms, oligarchies and chiefdoms, and the emergence of towns. Attention now shifted from the north-west and Punjab to the Ganges Plain, although the former area continued its activity. Changes in polity had begun somewhat earlier, but where they were accompanied by urbanization they were to become foundational to the flow of history in the Indian subcontinent. The preceding period had been one of accommodation or confrontation between polities based on clan organization and others experiencing the beginnings of kingship. Permanent settlement in a particular area gave a geographical identity to a clan, or a confederacy of clans, and subsequently this identity was given concrete shape by its claiming possession of the territory, then naming it after the ruling clan. Maintaining this possession required political organization, either as a *gana-sangha*, chiefdom, or as a kingdom. Polities of the earlier period, deriving their identity from the lineage of the ruling family, were gradually giving way to identification with territory and new forms of political authority, although traces of the continuity of descent from a particular ancestry can be found in the names given to the territories. The change to kingdoms was a more pronounced departure in the formation of states.

The emergence of the *gana-sangha* might be better seen as a form of a proto-state. It was unlike a kingdom, since power was diffused, the stratification of its society was limited, and the ramifications of administration and coercive authority were not extensive. The persistence of the *gana-sanghas* in Indian history was quite remarkable, especially in the northern and western regions. Despite being conquered periodically, their resilience was demonstrated by their reappearance and continued presence until the mid-first millennium AD.

A state has been described as a sovereign political entity and its rise assumes a complex network of conditions. These would include a density of population with a concentrated drawing on resources, agricultural or other; control over a defined, recognized territory; an urban centre as the location of authority, which could also be the location for craft activities that were produced for both local consumption and commercial exchange; diverse communities coming within a network of stratification and accepting unequal statuses; a political authority managing the incoming revenue from taxes and their redistribution through at least a minimal administration; the assertion of authority through a monopoly of the agencies of coercion, both of armed force and the imposition of regulations and obligations; the awareness of diplomacy; and the sovereignty of the state being represented in the king as the focus of authority. The emergence of a state system frequently coincides with unequal power relations and access to resources and some social disparity. Such changes would also have sought support from various ideological justifications.

Reference is made to the *mahajanapadas*, or the great *janapadas*, larger and more powerful than the earlier multiple *janapadas*, and some of these conformed to the definition of the state. Sixteen of them are listed in Buddhist texts as those of Anga, Magadha, the Vrijji confederacy and the Mallas in the middle Ganges Valley; Kashi, Kosala and Vatsa to its west; Kuru, Panchala, Matsya and Shurasena further west; Kamboja and Gandhara in the north-west; Avanti and Chedi in western and central India; and Assaka in the Deccan. This was the geography known to the early Buddhist Pali Canon. In Vedic sources Magadha and Anga are described as impure lands, but Magadha was to dominate the politics of the Ganges Plain. Assaka's importance is related to the southern route to the peninsula, the *dakshinapatha*. The Vrijjis were a confederacy of eight clans, said to have 7,707 rajas; the Mallas were said to have 500 rajas; and the Chedis even more, these being *gana-sanghas*. The *mahajanapadas* listed in Jaina sources take in a wider geographical area, the list probably having been compiled later. This shift parallels the boundaries of the *aryavarta* – the land of the *arya* – which move eastwards in Jaina and Buddhist sources, since the epicentre of these religions was more easterly than the heartland of Vedic culture. Of the clans mentioned in the *Mahabharata*, many were closer to the *gana-sangha* system than to kingdoms, for instance Vrishnis, the clan to which Krishna Vasudeva belonged. The lynchpin of the *janapada* had been the ruling clan, after which it was named, and this in turn ensured some linguistic and cultural commonality. But the *mahajanapada* was also incorporating varied cultures.

The Second Urbanization: the Ganges Plain

The emergence of states and proto-states was a process frequently locked into urbanization. If various degrees of state formation are evident in the polities, degrees of urbanization are similarly reflected in different kinds of towns as they grew out of earlier settlements. The genesis of towns was not uniform and this gave them diverse features. Some grew out of political and administrative centres and were the hub of this power, such as Hastinapura. Somewhat later references mention the capitals of kingdoms, such as Rajagriha in Magadha, Shravasti in Kosala, Kaushambi in Vatsa, Champa in Anga and Ahicchatra in Panchala. Others grew out of markets, each catering to a variety of villages usually located where there was an agricultural surplus that could regularly enter an exchange nexus. Such exchanges were, to begin with, of mundane but essential items such as grain or salt. The exchange could be extended to goods from more distant places if the market was on a trade route, as at Ujjain. These were different from the rituals of exchange of expensive items or prestige goods conducted by elite groups on special occasions. Towns also grew from being sacred centres where people gathered, as is thought to have been the case with Vaishali. These various functions could also be combined in one place. Kaushambi became a town fairly early. The raja is said to have shifted the capital from Hastinapura to Kaushambi because of floods at the former location. The new location was more central to controlling river traffic on the Ganges. Later, it hosted one of the earliest Buddhist monasteries. A concentration of people and the scope for a range of occupations and products were obviously conducive to the growth of towns.

Unfortunately, the details of these processes of change can become available only when horizontal excavations of urban sites of the Ganges Plain are carried out, exposing more extensive layers of occupation in an attempt to answer the more complex questions related to urbanism. Most excavations at such sites have so far been vertical sections that provide a chronology, but other information is limited. The contrast with the excavation of Harappan cities is only too apparent. Thus, although the earliest dated evidence comes from archaeology, it is difficult to discuss the genesis, growth and function of towns from the kind of data available. Bhir Mound, the section of the city of Taxila in the north-west that is dated to this period, has been excavated horizontally, but is a little too distant for use as evidence for the middle Ganges Plain.

Inevitably, information is gleaned from texts, but these are not always contemporary and, in some cases, even though they reflect on the past, some of the data could be of the immediately subsequent period. Evidence of a more definitive kind about chiefdoms and towns comes from the grammar of Panini, generally dated to the fifth century BC and therefore contemporary with urban centres. The Buddhist Pali Canon, primarily the *Tripitaka*, narrates events relating to the Buddha and records his teaching, and these are often set in an urban context which encourages their use as data on urbanization. This Canon was initially an oral tradition, the writing of which began a couple of centuries after the death of the Buddha. It therefore does not coincide with the earliest phase of urbanization, but with the more mature period. Nevertheless, it can suggest the trends that led to the growth of cities.

Two areas with a concentration of population in the Ganges Plain were the chalcolithic societies of the *doab* and of the middle Ganges Plain. States and urban centres emerged in both areas, but there was a difference. The *doab* and the western Ganges Plain was home to the cultures associated with the Painted Grey Ware/PGW (*c.* 1200–400 BC). Further east, the settlements associated with the Black-and-Red Ware/BRW cultures and the subsequent lustrous, luxury ware known as the Northern Black Polished Ware/NBPW (*c.* 700–200 BC), suggest what in comparison might be called a thicker urbanism, especially from the mid-millennium, although this impression could be due to the imprint of Buddhist texts as well.

The population of the *doab*, though small, slowly expanded. From staying close to the banks of rivers, some settlements moved into the interior where they cleared land for cultivation. This may have been an escape from floods or a more venturesome encroachment into forests. The small settlements linked to Ochre Colour Pottery were more frequent in the upper *doab*. The Painted Grey Ware settlements had a wider distribution in the *doab* and larger sites often occur on the edge of *jheels*, or lakes formed from natural depressions or as ox-bow lakes. Further east, wet-rice cultivation provided a high yield, even if it was more labour intensive. Although sedentary cultivation came to dominate the landscape, it did not eliminate hunter-gatherers, pastoralists and shifting cultivators. Closely placed, small settlements of the Painted Grey Ware gave way to appreciably larger settlements and, at longer distances these were associated with sites and levels of the Northern Black Polished Ware which herald incipient urbanism.

Apart from pre-existing neolithic and chacolithic settlements in the Ganges Plain, the migration there of people from the watershed is suggested by the Black Slipped Ware associated with the Painted Grey Ware of the *doab*, being the same as that associated with potteries from the middle

Ganges Plain although of a slightly late date. Imitation of some of the technologies of the watershed area may have resulted in the similarity of technique between the Painted Grey Ware and the Northern Black Polished Ware. This does not point to the imposition of a culture from the western plain, but merely to the presence of people and technologies from there mingling with the existing cultures. Hydraulic and climatic change, resulting in some desiccation in the north-west and Punjab, may have encouraged migrations to the *doab*, while further east the attraction would have been the potential of fertile lands. The archaeology of those settlements that developed into urban centres reflects differences when compared to earlier settlements, in addition to the occurrence of Northern Black Polished Ware which was an urban hallmark. Having travelled through trade to virtually every part of the subcontinent by the end of the first millennium BC, the Northern Black Polished Ware provides instant recognition. References to towns of the *doab*, such as Hastinapura, gave way to Kaushambi and Bhita, carrying a hint of the metropolis. Excavation at sites such as Vaishali, Ujjain, Shravasti, Rajghat and Rajagriha date urban beginnings to the mid-first millennium BC. At Kaushambi, the start is somewhat earlier.

Judging by excavated and textual data, there seems to have been a fairly consistent concept of the layout of urban centres, although the plan was not invariably adhered to. The town was enclosed by a moat or a rampart, and was sometimes fortified. Digging a moat probably threw up enough earth for the beginnings of a rampart. These sometimes began as mud-fillings, as at Rajghat, and graduated to include bricks, as at Kaushambi. Since many of the towns were located on river banks the rampart would have been a protection against flood, as well as providing a minimal defence against predators and raids. As it developed, the urban ambience was different from that of the village and this may also have encouraged a demarcation. Towns were the location of what was collected as revenue and placed in a treasury, which would also have made them vulnerable to attack and necessitated some form of fortification. The houses were better built than previously and, in the later stages, were of mud-brick with some limited use of fired brick. They were equipped with facilities that were new, such as drains, ring wells and soakage pits which were to become archaeological markers of the second urbanization and were different in form from those used in Harappan cities. Houses at Bhir Mound consisted of rooms built round a courtyard, and this was the prototype house-plan for many towns in India. Rooms opening directly on to streets may have been shops. Streets were levelled to allow wheeled traffic.

A large range of items was involved in the early trade. Iron objects ranged from hoes, sickles and knives to hooks, nails, arrowheads, vessels and mirrors. Salt was mined in the Potwar Plateau in the north-west, and may have travelled the long distance to the Ganges Plain. Craftsmen and artisans in the towns produced textiles, beads, pottery, ivory objects, ceramics and glassware, and artefacts of other metals, all of which were items of trade. The occurrence of the occasional weight together with some of these items underlines exchange. The distribution through exchange was not limited to the Ganges Plain. Goods were also taken to the north-west, from where presumably horses were brought back, and texts refer to the production of blankets and woollen goods in this area, intended for trade. Human and animal forms in terracotta were in considerable demand, and terracotta moulds are commonly found. Figurines reappear, particularly those with extraordinarily elaborate coiffures. Terracotta was also used for making the impressively precise rings for the wells and for the large jars, fitted one above the other as soakage pits.

The urban settlements of the north-west, pre-eminently Taxila, emerge from cultures that differ from those of the Ganges Plain. The excavation of Hathial, which was prior to this period, and the excavation of Bhir Mound – the part of the city complex of Taxila which dates to this period – underlines the importance of the site. Gandhara, in the north-west, is mentioned in the Iranian Achaemenid inscriptions as one of the provinces of the empire, so Taxila is likely to have been an important administrative centre. This may have provided the initial impetus towards urbanization, although its importance grew when it became a point of exchange between north India and places to its west. It has been suggested that the trend towards urbanization of what were to become cities in Gandhara, such as Taxila and Pushkalavati, may have been tied into the earlier importance of cities further west, such as Kandahar in Afghanistan.

Both urbanization and the formation of states are dependent on the realization of a surplus in production and on the mechanisms by which this was made possible. An agricultural surplus was necessary to townspeople who did not produce their own food and it provided a base for economic diversification. Perhaps the crucial factor was the possibility of two crops a year, in some cases even three. Wet-rice cultivation made a noticeable difference given the substantially larger amount that could be harvested as compared to other crops, and this provided the necessary surplus. This made irrigation a precondition. Converting what was described in the Vedic corpus as the marshland of the middle Ganges Plain to arable land would have involved draining some areas through inundation channels. These may have suggested the idea of cutting channels for irrigation. Irrigation through wells and water-lifting devices would then have been supplemented to a far greater degree. The prerequisite to the cultivation of high-yielding crops and the provision of irrigation would have included the availability of labour, together with a system by which labour could be controlled and directed.

But the production of a surplus is not in itself sufficient, since it has to be gathered and distributed in ways that enable a small group in society to effectively control these activities: a control which also had to be acceptable to the larger society. Surplus produce provides a basis for power only when it can be deployed to enhance the authority of those claiming special status. Since it feeds those who do not produce their own food, it also enables specialization in various professional craft activities. These are no longer geared only to local consumption, but to producing over and above that in order to augment exchange, since exchange also yields revenue. But, again, the augmentation becomes useful only if there are people to organize the availability of raw material and the distribution of the finished product.

It was earlier thought that providing irrigation was the primary pre-condition to producing a surplus, and therefore control over irrigation was the foundation of power. This argument has now been questioned and, although irrigation is important, it is not the primary or only factor. The current debate focuses on whether iron technology was the crucial variable. Iron objects of a rudimentary kind go back to the end of the second millennium BC. The use of iron, especially in weaponry, was known around 800 BC although the quality of the metal was of a low grade. The more systematic use of better quality iron is later, with a quantitative and qualitative increase of iron artefacts, which included implements of various kinds, vessels, nails, and suchlike, as well as an improvement in weapons.

The smelting of iron may have begun with using a technology parallel to that of copper-smelting, but the marked confidence in using iron by the mid-millennium is striking. Higher temperatures began to be possible, which was also reflected in the firing of the Northern Black Polished Ware. Excavation at Jodhpura in northern Rajasthan has revealed furnaces for smelting and forging ore, and other centres of iron production were Atranjikhera and Khairadih in the western Ganges Plain. Efficiency in handling iron was a new experience, given that the chalcolithic cultures of the Ganges Plain do not suggest the extensive use of metal. Judging by the artefacts at sites in many parts of India from this time, it would seem that various societies were experimenting with new technologies facilitating the use of iron. The frequency of iron slag also points to its widespread use. It has been plausibly argued that there are references in the earlier sections of the *Mahabharata* to the quenching of iron and to molten metal for casting.

The argument that iron technology changed agricultural production draws on a series of links; iron axes facilitated the clearing of forests so that land could be used for cultivation, the iron hoe was an effective agricultural implement, and the invention of the iron ploughshare was more efficient in a heavy soil as it could plough deeper than a wooden share. However, very few iron axes have appeared in excavations. Textual evidence seems to prefer burning forests as a method of clearing. Iron ploughshares are still rare from excavated sites, but a much quoted example from a Buddhist text refers to tempering such a share. The efficiency of an iron ploughshare in soils other than that of the Ganges Plain has been questioned.

A function of iron technology, often overlooked in the emphasis on axes and ploughshares, is that of the technical changes which the introduction of iron implements would have brought about in various craft activities. There is a striking increase and qualitative improvement in the making of items from bone, glass, ivory, beads of semi-precious stones and shell, and stone objects, as compared to earlier chalcolithic levels. This is suggestive of a confidence in using the new technology and using it more extensively, for example in various constructions in wood, from the making of beams for ceilings to improving the structure of the chariot, cart and possibly even river craft. Interdependent technologies, such as the firing of superior pottery and the making of glass, were probably also tied into experiments to improve iron artefacts.

Although iron may not have been the crucial variable as a single techno-logical input there is little doubt that as part of a package of change its role cannot be minimized. Since control over the surplus was in the hands of the few, that which enhances the surplus becomes a significant factor. The new technology was diffused through the availability of iron and the fact that blacksmiths were itinerant. To establish a monopoly over the technology was therefore not so easy. Blacksmiths were ranked socially as low. Control therefore could be extended to specific products. Objects made of iron, other than functional ones, could have become status symbols. The state asserted its control over the armoury.

Agricultural expansion and the use of iron are in themselves necessary but not sufficient factors in the creation of a surplus to bring about urbaniz-ation and state systems. An interesting comparison could be made with the contemporary megalithic societies of the peninsula that had both features but remained at a pre-state and pre-urban level. The collecting and redistri-buting of the surplus was yet another necessary component to the change, which was not limited to accessing what came to the treasury but also extended to control over those who laboured in creating these products.

The evolution towards the state required a new relationship between those who laboured and those who managed their labour.

Textual sources point to early urbanization in two ways. One was the description of some villages specializing in professions such as blacksmithing, pottery, carpentry, cloth-weaving, basket-weaving and so on. These were villages close to the raw materials and linked to routes and markets. The availability of the right type of clay, for instance, would attract potters to a particular area, carpenters would head to where timber was available. Specialized craftsmen tended to congregate because this facilitated access to resources and distribution of the crafted items. Such a concentration could evolve into a town, and towns in turn expanded their production and their markets to become commercial centres. Some, such as Vaishali, Shravasti, Champa, Rajagriha, Kaushambi and Kashi, were of substantial importance to the economy of the Ganges Plain. Others, such as Ujjain, Taxila or the port of Bharukaccha (Bharuch), had a wider geographical and economic reach.

A pointer to urbanization also lies in the hierarchy of settlements. The *grama*, village, was the smallest settlement. Places referred to as *nigama* and *putabhedana* were exchange centres and local markets. River ports, such as Pataligrama, and crossing-points on rivers, such as Shringaverapura, facilitated exchange. The *nagara* was the town and the *mahanagara* was the substantially larger, well-established, prosperous, politically important city. Kaushambi could well have been a *mahanagara*, since its size has been estimated at 150 hectares. Buddhist sources sometimes refer to *gama*, *nigama*, *nagara*, in that order, suggesting a hierarchy of the village, the market and the town.

Different wide-ranging identities among townspeople are characteristic of urban centres. In theory, occupational groups are said to have lived and worked in specified sections of the town. Textual sources refer to two highways intersecting at right angles, forming the axis of the town, with the central point being the seat of authority, such as the palace and court of the king, or the assembly hall in the *gana-sangha*. This would be a more monumental building, although such buildings are associated with the mature phase of urbanization, for example the palace at Kaushambi. The religious institution that carried authority would also be associated with the centre of the city, and at this stage would have been the Buddhist monastery. Although both palace and monastery exist at Kaushambi, the latter is not at the central axis of the city. Bhir Mound, where such a city-plan is absent, indicates that cities need not have conformed to the plan. Some attempts at urban coherence were possible through the network of roads, drainage systems and occupational sectors.

Judging by the evidence available so far, it does seem that there was neither remembrance of the city-plans of Harappan times, nor any attempt to imitate them. The structures of the Harappan citadel seem to have been incorporated into the city centre or scattered in the city. Despite the fact that some cities were built on the banks of rivers, which were liable to be affected by floods, there is no evidence of brick foundations to safeguard the buildings. The urban requirements of the Ganges system and its city-dwellers were clearly different from those of the Indus urban centres. Possibly the mobilization of labour for the extension of agriculture took precedence over urban construction.

Townsmen were not kin-related (except perhaps in the towns inhabited by small oligarchies) and, as the town grew, kinship ties declined despite towns being more densely settled than villages. Urban links were therefore based on other features, such as the interdependence of occupation or mechanisms of administration. However, towns were still small enough to allow face-to-face relationships. Apart from the seat of authority, the other important location was where the exchange of goods took place. Later, the locations of religious institutions were added to these. Indian cities generally did not have a central, single market place. Buying and selling were part of the transactions in the locations where items were produced, which may in part account for the concentration of particular products in certain parts of the city. This system may have developed from production and exchange centres growing into cities. Towns, therefore, included a wide span of occupations that allowed experimentation in technologies. They were inhabited by people of varying social strata, permitting varieties of social interchange or social demarcation, and were frequently the location for diverse religious sects.

Gana-sanghas – Chiefdoms and Oligarchies

The *gana-sanghas* were an alternative polity to the kingdoms and may represent the continuation of an earlier system. The connection between the *gana-sanghas* and the growth of various ideologies and belief systems, particularly Buddhist and Jaina, was due to many of these being rooted in the *gana-sanghas*. Buddhist sources therefore mention the working of this system. Panini's grammar refers to both the chiefdoms and the kingdoms, but, owing to the nature of the text, it does not provide detailed descriptions. Brahmanical sources disapproved of the *gana-sanghas* because they did not perform the required rituals or observe the rules of *varna*, therefore they tend to be ignored in the Vedic corpus. Disapproval is extended to towns in general, whereas the Buddhist Canon has more empathy with urban centres, and emphasizes the centrality of the town. Nevertheless, the role of the town seems more active in the kingdoms, particularly where the town is the capital.

Whereas the kingdoms were concentrated in the Ganges Plain, the *gana-sanghas* were ranged around the periphery of these kingdoms, in the Himalayan foothills and just south of these, in north-western India, Punjab and Sind, and in central and western India. The *gana-sanghas* tended to occupy the less fertile, hilly areas, which may suggest that their establishment predated the transition to kingdoms, since the wooded low-lying hills would probably have been easier to clear than the marshy jungles of the plain. It is equally plausible, however, that the more independent-minded settlers of the plains, disgruntled with the increasing strength of orthodoxy in territories evolving into kingdoms, moved up towards the hills where they established communities more in keeping with egalitarian traditions, at least among the ruling clans. The rejection of Vedic orthodoxy by the *gana-sanghas* indicates that they may have been maintaining an older or an alternative tradition. There were also systems similar to the *gana-sangha* in western India, of which the Vrishnis as described in the *Mahabharata* would be one. Since the Buddhist texts focus on the Ganges Plain, little is said about those in western India.

The compound term *gana-sangha* or *gana-rajya* has the connotation of *gana*, referring to those who claim to be of equal status, and *sangha*, meaning an assembly, or *rajya*, referring to governance. These were systems where the heads of families belonging to a clan, or clan chiefs in a confederacy of clans, governed the territory of the clan or the confederacy through an assembly, of which they alone were members. The term has been translated in various ways. It was once thought that they were democracies but this is hardly appropriate, given that power was vested in the small ruling families and they alone participated in governance. The larger numbers of people who lived in the territory had no rights and were denied access to resources. The term 'republic' was therefore preferred, since it conceded social stratification but was distinct from monarchy. Another term used is 'oligarchy', which emphasizes the power of the ruling families. More recently, early forms of such systems are seen as chiefdoms, underlining their particular genesis, suggesting that they might be pre-states or proto-states, and, at any rate, different from kingdoms.

The *gana-sanghas* consisted of either a single clan, such as the Shakyas, Koliyas and Mallas, or a confederacy of clans, such as the Vrijjis and the Vrishnis. The confederacy of the Vrijjis, located at Vaishali, was of independent clans of equal status and the identity of each was maintained despite their having confederated. These were *kshatriya* clans, but the existence of *kshatriyas* did not presuppose the observance of a *varna* society. They retained more of the clan tradition than did the kingdoms, for example the concept of governing through an assembly representing the clan, even if the assembly was restricted to the heads of clans or families. Legends relating to their origin generally refer to two curious features: one was that the ruling families were frequently founded by persons of high status who, for a variety of reasons, had left or been exiled from their homeland; the other was that a claim to high status was encapsulated in a myth tracing the founding family to an incestuous union between brother and sister. Tracing origins back to such parentage was thought to prove purity of descent, and was therefore highly complimentary. This parting from Vedic orthodoxy is also apparent from at least one source, attributed to brahman authorship, which describes certain *gana-sangha* clans as degenerate *kshatriyas* and even *shudras*, because they have ceased to honour the brahmans or to observe Vedic ritual. Honouring the brahmans included accepting *varna* stratification. The *gana-sanghas* had only two strata – the *kshatriya rajakula*, ruling families, and the *dasa-karmakara*, the slaves and labourers. The latter were therefore non-kin labour, which was a departure from earlier clan systems where kinsfolk laboured together. Their non-acceptance of Vedic ritual is also evident in their veneration for sacred enclosures and groves, with other manifestations of popular religious cults.

The corporate aspect of government was held to be the major strength of *gana-sanghas*. The actual procedure involved the meeting of the heads of families, or of clans in the assembly, located in the main city where they lived. The assembly was presided over by the head of the clan. This office was not hereditary and was regarded as that of a chief, rather than a king, although the later gloss on raja tended to treat it as that of a king. The matter for discussion was placed before the assembly and debated, and if a unanimous decision could not be reached it was put to vote. Assisting in the rudimentary administration were those who advised the raja, the treasurer and the commander of the soldiers. Later sources describe an elaborate judicial procedure, the suspected criminal having to face in turn a hierarchy of seven officials.

Social and political power lay with the rajas who sat as representatives in the assembly, and who were ranked as *kshatriyas*. This may account for Buddhist sources often placing the *kshatriyas* first, with the brahmans second in the *varna* hierarchy, since they were more familiar with the *gana-sanghas*, although it could also have been due to Buddhist opposition to Brahmanism. The income of the *gana-sanghas* of the middle Ganges Plain came largely from agriculture, particularly wet-rice cultivation, cattle-rearing no longer being a primary occupation except in parts of the Punjab and the *doab*. However, their cities also attracted traders, which would have been an additional source of wealth. For the chiefdoms of the north-west, however, revenue from trade would have been primary.

Land was owned in common by the clan, but was worked by hired labourers and slaves – the *dasa-karmakara*. This compound phrase makes it difficult to determine the degree to which production was dependent on the *dasas*, slaves, or on the *karmakaras*, hired labour. Most descriptions of slavery suggest domestic slavery, rather than the use of slaves in production. In the two-tier system those who worked the land did so under the control of the ruling clan, so management of labour was comparatively simple provided the cultivators did not resist the control. Thus, when trouble broke out over the diversion of irrigation water between those cultivating the land of the Shakyas and of the Koliyas, the ruling families of the two clans intervened directly. The *dasa-karmakaras* were not represented in the assembly and had virtually no rights.

Judging by descriptions of the *gana-sanghas*, the town functioned rather like a capital and was a familiar part of their life. The landowning clansmen lived in the town and participated in the usual urban activities. We are told of a young man of Vaishali who travelled to Taxila to be trained in medicine, a long and difficult journey, and then returned. The *gana-sanghas* were less opposed to individualistic and independent opinion than the kingdoms, and were more ready to tolerate unorthodox views. It was from the *gana-sanghas* that there came the two teachers of what were to become the most important heterodox sects: Mahavira, associated with advancing Jainism, belonged to the Jnatrika clan which was part of the Vrijji confederacy located at Vaishali, and the Buddha grew up in Kapilavastu, the town of the Shakya clan.

Not having a monarchical system, members of the *gana-sanghas* could also reject brahman political theories. Perhaps the most striking of the non-brahman theories was the Buddhist account of the origin of the state, possibly the earliest theory approaching that of a social contract. There was a time in the remote past when complete harmony prevailed among all created beings, men and women having no desires, as everything was provided for. Gradually a process of decay began, when needs, wants and desires became manifest. These led to the notion of ownership that resulted in the concept of the family, then led to private property, and these in turn to disputes and struggles that necessitated law and a controlling authority.

Thus it was decided that, in order to avoid conflict, one person be elected to rule and maintain justice. He was to be the Great Elect (*Mahasammata*) and was given a fixed share in the produce of the land as a wage. The Buddhist theory attempts to explain the connections between various institutions that were current at the time – the family, private property and caste. Such a theory suited the political systems of the *gana-sanghas* and was different from that prevalent in the kingdoms. In the brahmanical theory of kingship, the king as the protector of the people was appointed by the gods, was the patron of the ritual of sacrifice, and was expected to uphold and maintain *varna* society – the *varnashrama-dharma*. By contrast, the Buddhist theory attempts a rational explanation of the need for governance.

Kingdoms

In contrast to the *gana-sanghas*, kingdoms registered a centralized government with the king's sovereignty as its basis. The polity in the kingdoms was slowly transmuted from chiefship to kingship. The change carried with it a ritual status that added another dimension to the authority of the king. Power was concentrated in the ruling family. Legitimation became an important component, emphasizing claims to *kshatriya* status often bestowed through brahmanical ritual. Kingdoms point to a state system characterized by new features compared to the earlier period. The king enforced laws that could involve coercion. The latter had to be dovetailed into the customary law of the *jatis* and the region – a concern that was to continue throughout history. Governance extended over the territory of the hinterland surrounding the main town, and sometimes much further.

The ruling family became a dynasty, succession to kingship being hereditary, with a premium on primogeniture. Political power was concentrated in the king. He was advised and assisted by ministers, advisory councils such as the *parishad* and *sabha* – both terms continuing from earlier times but now with an advisory connotation – and an administration manned by officers. The latter assessed and collected the revenue, bringing it to the treasury in the capital from where it was redistributed in the form of salaries and public expenses, such as the maintenance of an army and administration, gift-giving to brahmans and religious functionaries and, of course, a personal income for the ruling family. Public works would include ways of enhancing production, for this would increase the revenue. The provision of irrigation works, for instance, was once thought to be the prerogative of the state, but routine irrigation that provided much of the water for agriculture in many areas remained an activity of the individual cultivator or the village. Where labour was required on a scale not manageable by local cultivators, such as building canals or reservoirs, the state would intervene. The existence of a state also involved political relations of varying kinds with neighbours, some friendly and some hostile, with a tendency to erase existing social relations and replace them with new ones, often more amenable to those in authority.

Clan loyalty weakened in the kingdoms, giving way to caste loyalties and a focus on loyalty to the king. The political expansion of the kingdoms over large areas also emaciated the strength of the popular assemblies, since distances prevented frequent meetings. The *gana-sangha* was based on a smaller geographical area, where it was easier to meet the requirements of a relatively more representative government. In the monarchical system the divinity of the king, with its corollary of the power of the priests and of Vedic ritual, had further reduced the centrality of the popular assemblies of early Vedic times. The competition between elites in the kingdom, and the earlier rivalry between brahmans and *kshatriyas*, was gradually having to contend with what was to become a new phenomenon in the towns – the rise of wealthy traders. Insistence on the *varna* hierarchy was an attempt at retaining authority.

A number of kingdoms are mentioned in the literature of the period. Among these, Kashi (the region of Banaras) was initially important. Kosala (adjoining Kashi to the north-east), and later Magadha (in south Bihar), were rivals for the control of the Ganges Plain, a control that had both strategic and economic advantages, since a large part of the early trade in the region was carried by river and was centred on river ports. Finally, there remained only four rival states: the three kingdoms of Kashi, Kosala and Magadha, and the oligarchy of the Vrijjis.

Kings were supposed to be of the *kshatriya* caste, although this preference remained theoretical since kings of various castes were to rule, depending on political expediency. That kingship could acquire attributes of divinity was an established idea. It was reinforced from time to time by elaborate ritual sacrifices, initiated by the king, and observing the instructions of the Vedic corpus. They appear to have been more routinely performed by the rajas of earlier times, as now they were tending to become less common. A king performing these rituals could claim ritual power, but the more realistic foundation of kingship lay in a concentration of political power and in the accessing of resources. For the population, the grand sacrificial rituals were vast spectacles to be talked of for years. No doubt they kept the more critical minds diverted and created the appropriate awe for the king, who was depicted as an exceptional person, communicating with the gods, even if only through priests. The priests too were not ordinary mortals, since they were in effect the transmitters of divinity. Despite the earlier rivalries between the brahman and the *kshatriya*, the throne and the priesthood were mutually supportive.

The battle for political pre-eminence among the three kingdoms of Kashi, Kosala and Magadha, and the *gana-sangha* of the Vrijjis, lasted for a long period. Magadha emerged victorious as the centre of political activity in northern India, a position that it maintained for some centuries. The first important king of Magadha was Bimbisara, who realized the potentialities of a large state controlling revenue. Bimbisara became king some time in the second half of the sixth century BC. Alliances included marriage into a high-status family from Vaishali, as well as into the ruling family in Kosala, and these marriages furthered his expansionist policy. Having thus secured his western and northern frontiers, he went on to conquer Anga to the south-east. This gave him access to routes to the Ganges Delta, the ports of which were potentially important for contacts along the eastern coast.

Bimbisara established the beginnings of an administrative system, with officers appointed to various categories of work, and recognized the need for ministerial advice. The village was the basic unit of administration and has remained so. Officers were appointed to measure the land under cultivation and evaluate the crop. Each village is said to have been under the jurisdiction of a headman – *gramani* – who was responsible for collecting taxes, which were brought to the treasury by the officers.

The voluntary tribute and prestations of the earlier period were now being converted into taxes – *bali*, *bhaga*, *kara* and *shulka*. The terms used were the same as in previous times but the meaning differed. *Bali* is thought to have been a tax on the amount of land cultivated, that is, on the source of revenue, *bhaga* was a share of the produce, and the other taxes were of a variant kind. Taxes were therefore calculated on the size and the produce of the land, with the assessment being carried out by officers who also collected the taxes at a stipulated time, and of a specific amount calculated on the basis of the assessment. These were the seminal activities of later revenue systems of great complexity. Whereas earlier the clansmen or the junior lineages voluntarily provided wealth to the ruling clans, now wealth was being extracted from those who produced it by those who ruled and the two were not connected through kinship ties. A peasant economy was being established. The difference between the ruler and the ruled, between the cultivator and his land, between the rich and the poor was now more easily recognized. The ramifications of governing a kingdom were a contrast to the more direct functioning of the *gana-sanghas*.

The landholdings of individuals varied in size and resulted in categories of owners. The richer ones were *gahapatis/grihapatis*, householders, some of whom became landowners, and the smaller ones were generally referred to as *kassakas/krishakas*, cultivators. An indication of difference was that the former employed non-kin labour in the form of *dasas* and *karmakaras*, while the poorer ones used family labour. When the state began to emerge as the major agency of action and production, there was more frequent mention of *varna* categories as hierarchies of status. The *varna* system was perhaps seen, from an upper-caste perspective, as more homogeneous than that of *jatis*. At the lower end of the social scale, cultivators and artisans were included in the *shudra varna*. Dependence on *shudra* cultivators was to increase, with the status of landless labourers being low even within this category.

Another trend that gained strength was that more and more land was claimed by the state, it being eventually conceded that the state had rights to all wasteland. This influenced the way in which the king was perceived. Initially, he protected his people against external aggression and his qualifications as a warrior were foremost. Subsequently, he was seen as the one who maintains law and order in what would otherwise be a kingless, chaotic society. This was explained by various analogies, the most common being that of what came to be called *matsyanyaya* – the law of the fish. It is said that in a condition of drought, when tanks dry up, the big fish eat the little fish. This is a chaotic condition which requires someone to maintain laws. Kingship was also explained through a contractual act, but in its working out there was usually the intervention of a deity. The person so selected, sometimes referred to as Manu, was appointed by the gods but carried out his functions in return for a wage that took the form of a tax and various other privileges. Control over wasteland was an implied privilege, made explicit in texts of the subsequent period.

Beyond the village were fields and pastures, and still further away lay the wasteland and the jungles. This juxtaposition had been expressed in the duality of the *grama*, settlement, and the *aranya*, forest or wilderness, later to incorporate the terms *kshetra* and *vana*, with the same meaning. That wasteland belonged to the king further underlined his right to take a certain percentage, generally one-sixth of the produce, as tax on the land that had been cleared and was under cultivation. The term *shadbhagin* – he who has a share of one-sixth – was to become a customary term for the king. Actually, of course, the tax could have been higher, as it sometimes was. Land set aside for royal farms, which was an idea that developed later, grew out of the notion of the king controlling wasteland. The king being a symbol of the state, it was probable that his ownership over land was conceded but in a somewhat ambiguous manner. Gradually, as the distinction between king and state became blurred, the king's claim to ownership was not seriously challenged.

Another social category came to be added below the *varna* hierarchy. The Chandalas were reduced to a status lower than that of the *shudras* and were to be designated as the untouchables. They are referred to in various ways in sources that could be of this period, although some would be of a later time, such as the Buddhist *Jataka* stories. It has been argued that the Chandalas, who came to be treated as untouchable, appear to have been people on the edges of settlements, either forced there by encroaching settlers or requiring a habitat where they lived by hunting and food-gathering. They are described as having their own language, incomprehensible to Indo-Aryan speakers. Their occupations, such as weaving rush-mats and hunting, came to be looked upon as extremely low. Others have argued that they were groups who had been increasingly marginalized by the growth of towns, where they were required to perform menial tasks which became the source of their association with pollution in the hierarchy of ritual stratification. Expanding urbanization often trapped people at the margins of settlements into becoming landless and unable to use their skills and thus gradually forced them into performing lowly tasks. The presence of such groups, which became the epitome of social disabilities and prohibitions, points to the increasing authority of the upper castes in the kingdoms. The two categories of brahman and untouchable act as social counterweights, and the power of the higher required the depression of the lower in the *varna* scheme. Untouchability was perhaps the most degrading status clamped on any social group and was ethically quite unjustified. The combination of hereditary status with economic deprivation and social disabilities ensured a permanent and subjugated labour force.

The Pre-eminence of Magadha

Ajatashatru, the son of Bimbisara, impatient to rule Magadha, is believed to have murdered his father in about 493 BC to become king. He was determined to continue his father's policy of expansion through military conquest. The capital of Magadha, at Rajagriha, was an impressive city surrounded by five hills which formed a natural defence. Ajatashatru strengthened Rajagriha and built a small fort at Pataligrama, on the Ganges, which was a centre for the exchange of local produce. This was later to become the famous Mauryan metropolis of Pataliputra. His father having conquered the eastern state of Anga, Ajatashatru turned his attention to the north and the west. The king of Kosala was his maternal uncle, but this did not prevent Ajatashatru from annexing Kosala and continuing the advance west until he had included Kashi in his dominion. The war with the Vrijji confederacy over the control of the river trade, which was also a confrontation between two divergent political systems, one a kingdom and the other a *gana-sangha*, was a lengthy affair. It lasted for many years, with Ajatashatru's minister appropriately named Vassakara – the rainmaker – working towards a rift in the confederacy. A description of this war mentions the use of two weapons that appear to have been new to Magadhan military technology. These were the *mahashilakantaka*, a large-sized catapult used for hurling rocks, and the *rathamusala*, a chariot fitted with a mace for driving through the enemy's ranks to mow them down. Soldiering as a profession, with the need for a standing army, began to surface as a feature of the monarchical state. Finally, when Vassakara's attempts to sow dissension among the Vrijjis succeeded, victory was conceded to Magadha. It was a victory for monarchy in the Ganges Plain. Bimbisara's ambition had been fulfilled.

The rise of Magadha was not due merely to the political ambitions of Bimbisara and Ajatashatru, for, although the latter was succeeded by a series of unsatisfactory rulers, Magadha remained powerful. Magadha controlled nodal points in the Ganges river system that gave it access to the river trade. Fortifying the exchange centre at Pataligrama is an indication of the importance of this revenue. The conquest of Anga linked this trade to more distant places. Magadha was favoured by natural resources: the soil was fertile, especially for the cultivation of rice, and the expansion of agriculture brought in further revenue of another kind; the neighbouring forests provided timber for buildings and elephants for the army, with ivory as a prestige item; and local iron and copper deposits added to the wealth and activity of the area.

Ajatashatru died in about 461 BC. He was succeeded by five kings and tradition has it that they were all parricides. The people of Magadha, finally outraged by this, deposed the last of the five and appointed a viceroy, Shishunaga, as king. The Shishunaga dynasty lasted barely half a century before giving way to the usurper Mahapadma Nanda, who founded a dynasty, short-lived but significant. The Nandas were of low social status, being described as *shudras*, and were the first of a number of non-*kshatriya* dynasties. Most of the leading dynasties of northern India from now on belonged to castes other than *kshatriya*, until about a thousand years later when royalty started claiming *kshatriya* status irrespective of whether or not they were born as such. The reference to the Nandas destroying the *kshatriyas* could be to their incorporation of the *gana-sanghas* of the middle Ganges Plain into their kingdom.

The Nandas are sometimes described as the first dynasty with imperial ambitions, a statement hinted at in the *Puranas*. They inherited the large kingdom of Magadha and extended it to yet more distant frontiers. To this purpose they built up a vast army, although the estimates by Greek writers are almost certainly exaggerated – 20,000 cavalry, 200,000 infantry, 2,000 chariots and 3,000 elephants being the least of the numbers quoted. These figures were intended to suggest a formidable opposition to the Greek army under Alexander, leading to Greek soldiers refusing to campaign further. But the Nandas never had the opportunity to use their army against the Greeks, since Alexander turned back while in southern Punjab and followed the Indus to its delta.

Another factor assisting the consolidation of the kingdom was that taxes were given importance as revenue. The methodical collection of taxes by regularly appointed officials became a part of the administrative system. The treasury was doubtless kept replenished, the wealth of the Nandas being proverbial. The Nandas also built canals and carried out irrigation projects even as far as Kalinga (Orissa). The possibility of an imperial structure based on an essentially agrarian economy began to germinate in the Indian mind. The Nanda attempt was cut short by Chandragupta Maurya, the young adventurer who usurped the Nanda throne in 321 BC. It was under the Mauryas, therefore, that the imperial idea found expression.

North-west India and Alexander

Meanwhile, the scene shifts back to north-western India, which, during the sixth century BC, had been part of the Achaemenid Empire. A little before 530 BC, Cyrus, the Achaemenid Emperor of Persia, crossed the Hindu Kush mountains and received tribute from the people of Kamboja and Gandhara. Gandhara and Hindush/Sindhu are mentioned as satrapies or provinces in Achaemenid inscriptions. Historically, this was to be a region with changing suzerainties, shifting between north India and Afghanistan and Iran.

Herodotus mentions that Gandhara was the twentieth satrapy, counted among the most populous and wealthy in the Achaemenid Empire. Indian provinces provided mercenaries for the Persian armies fighting against the

Greeks in the fifth century BC. Herodotus describes them as dressed in cotton clothes and armed with reed bows, spears and arrows of cane tipped with iron. Ktesias, a Greek physician living at the Achaemenid court in the early half of the fifth century BC, left a description of north-western India, much of which is fanciful writing, such as his description of what was believed to be the tiger:

In each jaw it has three rows of teeth and at the tip of its tail it is armed with stings by which it defends itself in close fight and which it discharges against distant foes, just like an arrow shot by an archer.

Quoted in Pausanius, IX.21: J. W. McCrindle,
Ancient India as Described in Classical Literature, p. 210

Among the more famous cities of Gandhara and the north-west was Takshashila, or Taxila, as the Greeks called it. It rapidly became a cosmopolitan centre where Indian and Iranian learning mingled, to which was later added knowledge from the Hellenistic Greeks. Orthodox brahmans treated this region as impure, since Vedic rituals were no longer regularly performed. That Iranian and Vedic ideas and rituals had once been close seems not to have been remembered. Nevertheless, the mixing of Iranian and Indian forms was felt in various spheres of Indian life: Persian sigloi-type coins were copied in India; perhaps the idea of rock inscriptions used so effectively by the Emperor Ashoka in the third century BC was inspired by the rock inscriptions of the Persian King Darius; the script used widely in north-western India, *kharoshthi*, was derived from Aramaic, current in the Achaemenid Empire. Achaemenid control over some western parts of central Asia, as well as over Gandhara, brought the two areas under a single suzerainty, a connection which was to be repeated by various dynasties in subsequent centuries. Achaemenid ascendancy in north-western India ended with the conquest of the empire by Alexander of Macedon in *c.* 330 BC. Soon after this, north-west India was also to face Alexander's armies.

In 327 BC Alexander, continuing his march across the empire of Darius, entered the Indian provinces. The Greek campaign in north-western India lasted for about two years. It made little lasting impression historically or politically on India, and not even a mention of Alexander is to be found in early Indian sources. Alexander came to India in order to reach the easternmost parts of Darius's empire. He also wished to solve the 'problem of Ocean', the limits of which were a puzzle to Greek geographers. And, not unnaturally, he wanted to add what was already being described as the fabulous country of India to his list of conquests. The campaigns took him across the five rivers of the Punjab, at the last of which his soldiers refused to go further. Reports of the strength of the Nanda army may have been the cause. He then decided to follow the Indus to its delta, and from there return to Babylon, sending a part of his army by sea via the Persian Gulf and the remainder by land along the coast. The latter was a disastrous enterprise, since it was an exceptionally inhospitable coast. The campaign had involved some hard-fought battles, such as the now famous Battle of the Hydaspes against Poros (Puru), the King of the Jhelum region; the subduing of innumerable polities, both kingdoms and what the Greeks called 'autonomous cities', probably the *gana-sanghas*; the wounding of Alexander by the Malloi, and his revenge; and the extreme hardships of the army travelling down the Indus and along the coast of Makran. Alexander left governors to rule his Indian conquests, but his death, following so close on his departure, caused a state of confusion in which his governors soon left India to seek their fortunes in west Asia.

A significant outcome of Alexander's campaign, that was neither political nor military, was that he had with him literate Greeks who recorded their impressions of India, such as the accounts of his Admiral Nearchus and of Onesicritus. These are vignettes of how the Greeks saw northern India. They sometimes provide a corrective to the fantasies in other Greek accounts, although even in these the imagination of the authors is not always curbed. Customs and practices of the north-west were not identical with those of the Ganges Plain. This forms an interesting point of contrast, indicating that the genesis of regional cultures varied, rather than growing uniformly out of a single, homogeneous culture. Furthermore, invasions often open routes of communication and points of exchange, even if inadvertently. The proximity of the post-Alexander Hellenistic kingdoms, some founded by the generals of Alexander, was not insignificant to Mauryan politics and commerce. Frequent references to 'autonomous cities' in the Indus Plain indicate the continuing presence of a variety of *gana-sanghas* in this region. These polities survived and had not yet been affected by the imperialism of Magadha, unlike the eastern *gana-sanghas* that seem to have succumbed to Magadhan power.

The Greek accounts remain a curious mixture of fact and fable, as much a comment on the Greek view of the world as an attempt to describe Indians. Greater familiarity with India in the ensuing centuries corrected some of their more incredible stories, but the attraction of the exotic could not be suppressed. The play on fantasies and marvels is of interest for what they perceived of India, but it also contributed to imprinting the idea of India with the mythical and the extraordinary in the mind of Europe over the centuries. Nearchus, Alexander's admiral, accurately describes the clothes worn by Indians:

The dress worn by the Indians is made of cotton produced on trees. But this cotton is either of a brighter white colour than any found anywhere else, or the darkness of the Indian complexion makes their apparel look so much whiter. They wear an undergarment of cotton which reaches below the knee halfway down to the ankles and an upper garment which they throw partly over their shoulders and partly twist in folds round their head. The Indians also wear earrings of ivory, but only the very wealthy do this. They use parasols as a screen from the heat. They wear shoes made of white leather and these are elaborately trimmed, while the soles are variegated, and made of great thickness, to make the wearer seem so much taller.

Nearchus, quoted in Arrian's *Indica*, 16; J. W. McCrindle,
Ancient India as Described by Megasthenes and Arrian, p. 219

But the bizarre was always present and is repeatedly mentioned even in later accounts:

there are men said to be ten feet tall and six feet wide some of whom have no nose but only two orifices above the mouth through which they breathe. Some were brought to the court who had no mouths . . . they dwell near the source of the Ganges and subsist on perfumes and the savour of roasted flesh. Some had ears reaching down to their feet and they could sleep in them. And then there were ants that dug up gold and left it on the surface so it could be picked up.

Strabo, *Geography*, 15.1.57; J. W. McCrindle,
Ancient India as Described by Megasthenes and Arrian, pp. 74–5

One of the most enduring images was that of Alexander in conversation with Indian sophists, one of whom is said to have accompanied him to Babylon. The subjects of discussion would of course have been embroidered upon with every rendering of the story. This image was seminal to the view that Indian ideas entered the Hellenistic and Mediterranean world subsequent to Alexander and contributed to various schools of thought that did not necessarily conform to established views in the European tradition. Some schools of agnosticism sought ancestry from the east. Neo-Platonism, claiming similar origins, survived for many centuries almost as a substratum philosophy in Europe.

Indians, on the other hand, did not say much about the Greeks, and what they did say varies. The term used for them in Sanskrit was Yavana, a back-formation from Prakrit *yona*, most likely derived from *yauna* – a rendering of Ionia that is mentioned in Achaemenid inscriptions. Yavana became a generic term for people coming from the west and was used as recently as the last century. Some later brahmanical texts were bitterly uncomplimentary and hateful about the Yavanas, perhaps because of a lingering memory of Alexander's hostility to the brahmans during his campaign, or perhaps because the Yavana rulers of the later period tended to be patrons of sects that did not conform to Brahmanism. Buddhist texts, however, were curious about the dual division of Yona society – the masters and the slaves – and saw this as an alternative to caste stratification.

Early Trade

Alexander established a number of Greek settlements in the Punjab, none of which survived as towns. It is probable that the Greek settlers moved into neighbouring towns, becoming part of a floating Greek population in the north-west. The movement of the Greek army across western Asia and Iran to India reinforced or opened up routes between north-western India via Afghanistan to Iran, and from there to the eastern Mediterranean. This was to accelerate east–west trade, and no doubt the small Greek population in India and west Asia played a part in this. As often happens, where there has been an exchange of goods there soon follows an exchange of ideas, and this was to become evident in the subsequent period in styles of art, in medicine and in astronomy. Earlier sources had mentioned the presence of people thought to be Indians scattered here and there in west Asia, but now the presence became more focused.

Routes going south into the Indian peninsula were introducing a new area to northern trade. The presence of the Northern Black Polished Ware as far south as Alagankulam, together with the distribution of punch-marked coins, would suggest at least the start of communication with the peninsula. Ujjain, Vidisha and Tripuri were to be linked to Pratishthana in the Deccan. The main trade routes, however, were along the Ganges River itself, going from Rajagriha as far as Kaushambi, and then via Ujjain to Bhrigukachchha/ Bharuch on the Narmada Estuary, which was to grow into a major port for overseas trade with the west. Another route from Kaushambi, up the *doab*, went across the Punjab to Taxila, the outlet for the overland western trade. Shravasti in the middle Ganges Plain was also a point for exchange.

Goods continued to be transported in ox-carts and on pack animals, but the use of river routes allowed extensive transport by boats. Vaishali, Rajghat, Pataligrama and Champa are mentioned as important river ports.

The texts begin to refer more frequently to coastal ports, such as Tamluk in the Ganges Delta and Bhrigukachchha in western India. The port of Sopara (in the vicinity of Mumbai), which became important in the Mauryan period, had its beginnings a little earlier. The fastest mode of travel for the individual traveller was of course riding a horse, but for greater comfort a light horse-drawn carriage was doubtless preferred.

The appearance of towns made some changes in the landscape. More striking was the varied orientation towards towns in the texts, depending on authorship and world-view. From many perspectives the growth of towns marked a departure. A demarcation between urban and rural, although not sharp at this point, was nevertheless a beginning. Ramparts and fortifications, even if initially unimpressive, symbolize a demarcation. What was earlier a demarcation between the settlement and the forest now takes on a further dimension, with the settlement including the urban. The village had consisted of people often connected through kinship or occupation, but the townspeople tended increasingly to come from varying and unconnected backgrounds. The structures and buildings associated with towns required organized labour on a scale not familiar to village requirements, and this would have been one aspect of a substantial social change.

The town was viewed as much larger than the village. The size of Ayodhya, for instance, as given in the *Ramayana*, is exaggeratedly larger than the sizes obtained from archaeology for urban settlements in the Ganges Plain. Kaushambi, among the larger cities, is thought to have had a population of about 36,000 and covered an area of between 150 to 200 hectares. Most large cities such as Rajagriha, Ahichhatra and Shravasti covered a similar area. The texts were not concerned with giving a precise size, but with conveying the sense of an immensely bigger settlement than the earlier and familiar village. The area covered by the town included houses with gardens, although larger groves and orchards were on the periphery.

Much of the long-distance trade was restricted to luxury articles, the more commonly produced goods finding local markets. Goods were carried by various groups of people – pastoralists, itinerant craftsmen and more regular traders. Some activities associated with towns were to evolve into new professions that became prominent in the subsequent period. From the ranks of the wealthy, landowning householders – the *gahapatis* – there were to emerge the *setthis*, who became entrepreneurs of trade and financiers.

The introduction of coined metallic money facilitated exchange, introducing a qualitative difference in trading activities. Silver punch-marked coins became widespread legal tender, although copper punch-marked coins and cast copper coins also had some currency. The quantity of coins suggests the availability of silver, some of which was mined in Rajasthan. It is unclear who issued the coins, since the punch-marked coins generally carry only symbols. It is thought that they may have been issued by organizations involved in exchange since a few carry the legend *negama*, thought to be linked to *nigama*, connected to market activities. The minting of coins would have been another urban professional activity. The standard coin was the *pana* and the range of greater and lesser units would have been refined with usage.

Coins mark a radical departure in exchange relations. They provide a uniform means of exchange and accounting, and can bring about an increase in the range of goods, all valued within a single system. This facilitates long-distance trade, as well as connections between merchants. Investment bringing an interest becomes part of the financier's profession because coins can be accumulated and treated as capital. This also makes forward speculation financially viable. Another innovation linked to a monetary system was usury, but whether it was common and what the rates of interest may have been are not known for this early period. Brahmanical sources were initially opposed to usury, probably because it was central to the new profession of financiers who were urban-based and generally supporters of the heterodox sects. But the Buddha is said to have endorsed investment, presumably on interest, when he is reported to have said:

> Whoso is virtuous and intelligent.
> Shines like a fire that blazes on the hill.
> To him amassing wealth like roving bee
> Its honey gathering [and hurting naught],
> Riches mount up as ant-heap growing high.
> When the good layman wealth has so amassed
> Able is he to benefit his clan.
> In portions four let him divide that wealth,
> So binds he to himself life's friendly things.
> One portion let him spend and taste the fruit.
> His business to conduct let him take two.
> And portion four let him reserve and hoard;
> So there'll be wherewithal in times of need.
> *Digha Nikaya*, III. 188, tr. T. W. Rhys Davids,
> *Dialogues of the Buddha*, III, pp. 179–80

The need to evolve a script may have been influenced by the use of the Aramaic script in Achaemenid Persia, spreading through Achaemenid administration and trade. A script assists both administrative and commercial activities. The inscriptions of Ashoka, dating to the third century BC, are the earliest examples of writing (other than the Harappan script), and seem to assume some familiarity with a script. The script may therefore go back at least a few generations. Although Panini refers to a script in his famous grammar of Sanskrit, the *Ashtadhyayi*, composed in the fifth century BC, this could have been the Iranian Aramaic which was familiar to the literati of the north-west. The date of potsherds excavated from fifth century BC levels at Anuradhapura in Sri Lanka, with graffiti in *brahmi*, would make this the earliest evidence of *brahmi*, but the find remains controversial. Isolated examples would require more supporting evidence before the date can be accepted.

Methods of memorizing the Vedic hymns involved a series of cross-checks, and analyses of Vedic Sanskrit already had complex rules. The foundation was laid for sophisticated linguistic analyses and it is debatable whether the absence of a script actually assisted this process. The grammar of Panini, although it was not the grammar of the ritual language – Vedic Sanskrit – but of the more commonly used Sanskrit, reflected an unusually advanced understanding of the structure of language and was remarkable in many ways. (It was, incidentally, seminal to the work of Franz Bopp and comparative philology in nineteenth-century Europe, and the birth of modern linguistics.)

At about this time mention was made of variant languages of the Indo-Aryan family. Vedic Sanskrit as the language of ritual developed differently from spoken Sanskrit, or what Panini calls *Bhasha*, and for which he wrote his grammar. This was to evolve into Classical Sanskrit, the language of those with formal learning. Panini's grammar was foundational to later grammars of Sanskrit and of other Indo-Aryan derived languages. It would be worth investigating why the grammar was written at this time. Was it written to prevent further changes in Sanskrit introduced by the currency of non-Aryan languages? Or did it provide a structure for the learning of the language, particularly for those not familiar with Indo-Aryan? Or was it thought appropriate that the oral tradition be given a written form? Panini is said to be from the north-west, yet the best Sanskrit according to some commentators was the language of the Kuru-Panchala area in the western Ganges Plain.

In the towns and villages the more popular speech was Prakrit, also derived from Indo-Aryan. This had local variations: the western variety was called Shauraseni and the eastern variety Magadhi, after the regions where they were spoken. The Buddha, wishing to reach a wider audience, taught in a variety of Magadhi. The Buddhist Canon in the subsequent period was composed in Pali, an associated Indo-Aryan language. Urban centres were host to a variety of languages, so inevitably there would have been changes in the structure and vocabulary of these.

These features of social and economic life were closely linked with alterations in other spheres. It was doubtless this new situation that from the brahmanical perspective required regulations relating to social norms. Hence the composition of the *Dharmasutras*, setting out the social codes, social obligations and duties, and the correct behaviour for each *varna*. Creating social norms involved the adjusting of various practices prevalent among the societies now juxtaposed. This is demonstrated, for instance, in the listing of the legitimate forms of marriage that include the patriarchal practice of the father gifting his daughter to her husband-to-be as the best form, marriage involving bride-price as tolerable, with the lowest form being the kidnapping of the bride. That all these many forms were regarded as legitimate, although some received more approval than others, must have posed serious problems for the authors of the *Dharmasutras* in juxtaposing and accepting variant practices. An attempt was made to give some uniformity and homogeneity to the social regulations for the upper castes, whereas the variations in social custom of the lower castes were difficult to regulate. There was an underlining of upper-caste privileges with their counterweight of lower-caste disabilities. Lower castes and women are frequently bracketed in these texts and the subordination of both is exemplified.

Religions and Ideologies: Questions and Responses

The contestation or accommodation between the established orthodoxy and the aspirations of newly rising groups intensified changes in religious belief and practice and in philosophical speculation, resulting in a remarkable richness and vigour in thought, rarely surpassed in the centuries to come. The ascetics and the wandering sophists of the earlier age maintained a tradition of unorthodox thinking, and, in general, philosophical speculation ranged from controlled determinism to free-ranging materialism. Rivalries and debates were rife. Audiences gathered around the new philosophers in the *kutuhala-shalas* – literally, the place for creating curiosity – the parks and groves on the outskirts of the towns. This was a different ambience from that of Vedic thought where teachings or disputations were not held in public. The presence of multiple, competing ideologies was a feature of urban living.

Some of those expounding different ideas were identified as sects. This meant that they were small groups, usually supporting a single doctrine or belief, who had voluntarily come together. There were, therefore, a large range of sects. Their recruitment was not bound by caste, although they tended to use a language common to all their members and their aspirations were most likely similar. Much of our information on these comes from texts of the subsequent period, reflecting on the beginnings of philosophical thought. Some of these sects grew in number in the subsequent period through a following or incorporation and, where they were successful in finding support and patronage, they emerged as an Order, being referred to as various Sanghas or assemblies. These were characterized by a broader identity than the narrow conformity of the sect and could result in the breaking away of groups that then became the nuclei of new sects.

The Ajivikas were followers of a philosophy of predetermination – that destiny controlled even the most insignificant action of each human being and nothing could change this. They had a body of monks – those becoming monks believing that this was predetermined – and their occupation was asceticism. There were various other sects, some supporting atheism, such as the Charvakas whose philosophy derived from materialism and challenged the ideology of Vedic Brahmanism. Man was made of dust and returned to dust, as described in the teaching of the influential Ajita Keshakambalin:

Man is formed of the four elements. When he dies, earth returns to the aggregate of earth, water to water, fire to fire, and air to air, while his senses vanish into space. Four men with the bier take up the corpse: they gossip as far as the burning-ground, where his bones turn the colour of a dove's wing and his sacrifices end in ashes. They are fools who preach almsgiving, and those who maintain the existence [of immaterial categories] speak vain and lying nonsense. When the body dies both fool and wise alike are cut off and perish. They do not survive after death.

Digha Nikaya, 1.55, tr. A. L. Basham, *The Wonder That Was India*, p. 296

The Buddha described such sects as 'eel-wrigglers', inconsistent in their teaching. Those who regarded them with scorn, such as those with orthodox views, accused them of immoral practices as is usual among confrontational groups. Brahman attitudes to them were particularly harsh, since the materialists objected to what they perceived as the senseless ritual and ceremonial on which the priests insisted, largely because it was their livelihood. References to materialist schools of thought were blurred in the priestly writings that have survived and, until recently, it was generally thought that Indian philosophy had more or less bypassed materialism. The participation of the Charvaka and the Lokayata groups in discussions on knowledge is now seen as more significant than was thought before.

But, of all these sects, the two that came to stay were Jainism and Buddhism, both of which were to become independent religions. Part of the reason for this may have been that theirs was a more holistic understanding of contemporary changes than that of other sects, and, in the break-away from the earlier systems of thought and ethics, they reflected a more sensitive response to the pressures of the changes. Jaina ideas, thought to have been in circulation earlier, posited previous teachers – the *tirthankaras* or makers of fords – with the claims to an ancestry of the ongoing teaching. Claims to an earlier succession of teachers were also made by some other sects. Mahavira gave shape to these ideas in the sixth century, and this led to the organization and spread of the Jaina sect which was initially called Nirgrantha. Jaina is a secondary formation from Jina, 'the Conqueror', which refers to Mahavira. He is said to have renounced his family at a young age to become an ascetic. For twelve years he wandered, seeking the truth, and eventually gained enlightenment. Mahavira's teaching was confined to the Ganges Plain, though in later centuries the larger following of Jainism was in other parts of the subcontinent, particularly Karnataka and western India.

Jaina teaching was at first preserved as an oral tradition, but later it was collated and recorded. Some Jaina sects take their cue from the final version of the Canon, edited at the Council of Valabhi a millennium later. Compilations such as the *Acharanga-sutra*, *Sutrakritanga* and the *Kalpasutra* are regarded as the early texts. The conversion, at a later date, of oral traditions to written forms is often a pattern with religious sects. This makes it problematic to ascertain the original teaching and separate it from interpolations. Jainism later split into two major sects, the monks of which were either the Digambara/Sky-clad or naked, or the Shvetambara/Clad in White. Jaina history continued to be written, and was prolific in the eleventh to fourteenth centuries AD when Jainism was virtually hegemonic in western India.

Vedic authority was not accepted by the Jainas; nor was the claim that knowledge was revealed only to the brahman. The existence of deity was not central to early Jaina doctrine, which taught that the universe functions according to an eternal law and is continually passing through a series of cosmic waves of progress and decline. The purification of the soul is the goal of living, for the pure soul is released from the body and then resides in bliss. Purification is not achieved through knowledge, as some of the

Upanishadic teachers taught, knowledge being a relative quality. This is explained by the famous story of the six blind men, each touching a different part of an elephant and insisting that what they had touched was a rope, a snake, a tree trunk, and so on. Each man sees only a fraction of true knowledge, which makes knowledge unreliable for salvation. The purification of the soul required living what the Jainas regarded as a balanced life, but this, as described by Mahavira, was only possible for a monk. Yet, despite the vow of renunciation, the monk or nun was dependent on the lay community. The monk's vow of begging for alms had as its counterpart the commitment of the lay follower to the giving of alms.

The vow of non-violence became almost obsessive: even the unconscious killing of an ant while walking was regarded as sinful. The more orthodox wore a muslin mask covering the mouth and nose in order to prevent the involuntary inhalation of even the tiniest of insects. No breathing, existing, living, sentient creatures should be slain, or treated with violence, or abused, or tormented, or driven away, according to the *Acharanga-sutra*. The emphasis on *ahimsa*, non-violence, prevented Jainas from being agriculturalists, since cultivation involved killing insects and pests. Crafts endangering the life of other creatures also had to be avoided. Trade and commerce were possible occupations and Jainism spread among the trading communities. The encouragement of frugality in Jainism became an ethic and coincided with a similar sentiment upheld in commercial activity. The Jainas specialized in conducting the exchange of manufactured goods, acting as middlemen, with a preference for financial transactions. Thus Jainism came to be associated with the spread of urban culture.

Of the two near contemporaries, Mahavira and Gautama Buddha, the latter is the more famous since he founded a religion that was to prevail in Asia. The Buddha (or the Enlightened One), as he was called, belonged to the Shakya clan, and his father was the *kshatriya* raja of the Shakya *gana-sangha*. The legend of the Buddha's life has curious similarities with the legendary episodes in Christ's life such as the idea of the immaculate conception, and the temptation by the Devil. He was born in the sixth century BC and lived the life of a young aristocrat, but with increasing dissatisfaction after he came into contact with the sick, the suffering and the dead. Finally, he left his family and his home one night and went away to become an ascetic. After an austere period of ascetic practice he decided that this was not the way to achieve freedom from rebirth. He then resolved to discover the path towards liberation through meditation and, eventually, on the forty-ninth day of his meditation, is said to have received enlightenment and understood the cause of suffering in this world. He gave his first discourse at the Deer Park at Sarnath, in the vicinity of Varanasi, where he gathered his first five disciples.

This has been called the 'Discourse on the Turning of the Wheel of Law', which was the nucleus of the Buddha's teaching. It incorporated the Four Noble Truths: the world is full of suffering; suffering is caused by human desires; the renunciation of desire is the path to *nirvana* or liberation from rebirth; and this can be achieved through the Eightfold Path. The latter consisted of eight principles of action, leading to a balanced, moderate life: right views, resolves, speech, conduct, livelihood, effort, recollection, and meditation, the combination of which was described as the Middle Way.

 To understand this discourse did not call for complicated metaphysical thinking, nor did it require complex rituals. It required a commitment to ethical behaviour, a central feature of which was that it was not based on the privileges and disabilities of caste identity but on a concern for the welfare of humanity. Such an approach suggests a degree of sensitivity to the social mores becoming current in urban living. The rational undertone of the argument was characteristic of the Buddhist emphasis on causality and logic as the basis of analysis, particularly in a system where little is left either to divine intervention or else to the kind of metaphysics that the Buddha described as splitting hairs. The Buddha did not see his teaching as a divine revelation, but rather as an attempt to reveal the truths that were apparent to him and required to be stated.

To the extent that a deity was not essential to the creation and preservation of the universe, Buddhism was atheistic, arguing for a natural cosmic rise and decline. Originally a place of bliss, the world had been reduced to a place of suffering by human capitulation to desire. The authority of the *Vedas* was questioned, particularly as revealed texts associated with deity, and this was not specific only to Buddhism. Brahmanical ritual, especially the sacrificing of animals, was unacceptable. There was a closer association with popular, more unassertive forms of worship at funerary tumuli and sacred enclosures. Doubtless this relieved the austerity of an otherwise rather abstract system of thought. Independence from deities was also evident in Buddhist ideas about the origin of government and the state. Whereas Vedic Brahmanism invoked the gods in association with the origin of government, Buddhism described it as a process of gradual social change in which the instituting of the family and the ownership of fields led to civil strife. Such strife could only be controlled by people electing a person to govern them and to establish laws for their protection: an eminently logical way of explaining the origins of civil strife and the need for law.

In underlining elements of logic and rationality, the Buddha was reflecting some of the philosophical interests of his day. Freedom from the cycle of rebirth led to *nirvana*, interpreted either as bliss through enlightenment, or extinction. Thus the doctrine of *karma* and *samsara*, linking action and rebirth, was essential to the Buddhist system even if the Buddha denied the existence of the *atman* or soul. What continued was consciousness and this was modulated by actions. The denial of the soul gave a different edge to the Buddhist doctrine of action and rebirth. Implicit in the Four Noble Truths is the concept of *karma*, causally connected to desire and suffering. The Buddha's teaching was partially a response to the discourse of the early *Upanishads*, agreeing with some ideas and disagreeing with others. The disagreements were not insubstantial. But the teaching was a departure from that of the Vedic corpus and also a response to the historical changes of the time, among which were the emergence of the state and the growth of urban centres, posing questions that could not be answered by existing ideologies. The institutions that they generated were still in flux. The individual was involved in a struggle for status in the current defining of social hierarchies. The wish to opt out of social obligations was in part determined by these changes, and also by the search for answers to questions that troubled a changing society.

Unlike the brahmanical idea, the Buddhist notion of *karma* was not tied to the regulations of *varna* society, nor were social ethics measured by the rules of *varna*. The improvement of one's *karma* to ensure a better life was dependent on observing a code of social ethics based on the Eightfold Path and not merely the norms of sacred duties drawn up by brahmanical authors. The Buddha did not envisage the elimination of caste, as that would have required a radical re-ordering of society. Caste – whether *varna* or *jati* – registered social status, and *jati* was important to determining marriage circles and occupations. The norms of ethical behaviour were distinctive and were irrespective of caste status. The curiosity about the dual division of master and slave among the Yonas of the west was in its own way a questioning of the universality that was claimed for caste.

A subtle questioning of caste also lay in the freedom given to women to function in ways other than subjugation to rules of marriage. Despite the Buddha's hesitations, he was persuaded to permit the ordaining of women as nuns. This held at least an option for an alternative way of life, if only a limited one. The general hesitation in admitting women as nuns came from the notion that this would weaken marriage and family. The poems and hymns composed by the nuns that were later compiled as the *Therigatha* provide statements of considerable sensitivity on perceptions by women. That women could be lay followers and patrons allowed them a more assertive role. For example, cities of the Ganges Plain boasted of wealthy and accomplished courtesans, some of whom gave munificent gifts to the Buddhist Sangha/Order. Such women were respected for their attainments and were acceptable to the Order. A distinction was maintained between prostitutes and courtesans, both symptomatic of urban life, but the courtesan was admired for her accomplishments. Making donations was an expression of self-confidence, as it permitted women some control over wealth and the right to donate it where they thought fit. Again, this was a contrast to Vedic Brahmanism where women, although associated as wives with the patrons of the sacrifice, are hard to trace as patrons in their own right. The founding of an Order for nuns was a striking innovation, as there were increasing limitations being placed on the activities of women in the *Dharmasutras*.

The Buddha travelled in the towns of the middle Ganges Plain and later resided at the Buddhist monasteries that were established, teaching the monks and those who came to be taught. The Sangha was not initially encouraged to own property, but some provision was needed for a residence for monks during the long season of monsoon rains. The religion was congregational for most, but did not preclude those who wished to meditate in isolation. Monastic orders were introduced, the assembly of monks constituting the authoritative body, the Buddhist Sangha or the Buddhist Order. Monks wandered from place to place, preaching and seeking alms, and this gave the religion a missionary flavour. The Buddha's teaching came to be compared to a raft, enabling a person to cross the water of life, and it was suggested that the raft should be left at the shore so that it could assist another person to do the same. Later, when monks and nuns acquired residences, their monasteries and nunneries were built near towns, thereby facilitating the support expected from the lay community.

The establishment of Buddhist monasteries accelerated education, since they became a source of teaching, additional to the brahmans; even more important was the fact that education was not restricted to the upper castes. Brahman monks symbolized an ideological conversion. However, initiation seemed to focus on members of the upper castes to begin with, thus ensuring that people of status were entering the monasteries. The *kshatriyas* of the *gana-sanghas* who were not patrons of Vedic sacrifices were potential supporters of Buddhism and Jainism. Wealthy merchants, given a lesser status in the *varna* hierarchy, were respected by the Sangha and included among the patrons of the new religions. The inclusion of other castes as monks was a gradual process.

The organization of the monasteries was modelled on the procedures adopted for the functioning of the *gana-sanghas*. Regular fortnightly meetings were held, the views of monks were heard and decisions arrived at in accordance with the regulations of the Sangha. Dissident opinion, if it was weighty enough, could lead to a breaking away from the dominant sect and the founding of a new sect. The directive in the functioning of the monastery was that opinions were to be democratically discussed, with decisions arrived at through this process. This is likely to have been the prevalent mood in the early history of the Sangha, but by the third century BC mention is made of the expulsion of dissidents.

The Buddhist Canon, the *Tripitaka*, was recited and collected after the Buddha's death, but was probably not written until a couple of centuries later. It is difficult to separate the original teaching from the additions and changes made by his followers, or to give a precise date to the texts included in the Canon. Periodic councils were held, the first at Rajagriha, the second at Vaishali and the third at Pataliputra. These meetings would have introduced their own interpolations. The intention was to determine and define the original teaching and to record it. This also required decisions on regulations governing the Sangha if there was a difference of opinion. A major contention, for instance, was over whether monks could receive donations of money as alms. The question of accepting property as donation, as in the case of the parks gifted to the Sangha, would have required careful discussion and consideration since such donations were the thin end of the wedge, introducing the notion that it was legitimate for the Sangha to own property. The ownership was said to be communal, providing a residence for the monks, particularly in the period of the rains when they could not travel. Nevertheless, the ownership of property would have posed problems to a body of renouncers, as has been the case among monastic religious sects in every age.

Much of the Buddhist Canon was later translated into Chinese and other languages. This allows a comparative study of the Pali and the other versions that can assist a better understanding of the original intention. Buddhism was to undergo many sectarian breakaways, both in the country of its origin and in the course of its spread to other parts of Asia. Some forms claim an unbroken descent, but have in fact suffered historical vicissitudes that created breaks, in common with many sectarian religions. Theravada Buddhism is predominant in Sri Lanka and some south-east Asian countries. Elsewhere, the Sarvastivada has been more influential.

In recent times Buddhism and Jainism have often been included as a part of Hinduism, but the three were differentiated in contemporary texts. The prevalent elite religion at that time was Vedic Brahmanism, to which neither

Buddhism nor Jainism subscribed. In fact, they were opposed to many brahmanical theories and practices, and provided an alternative through their heterodox ideas. Unlike Vedic Brahmanism, or the later Puranic Hinduism, Buddhism and Jainism had specific historical teachers that have now come to be viewed almost as founders, had organized an order of monks and nuns and an ecclesiastical structure, were not concerned with a deity, did not perform rituals of sacrifice, emphasized the centrality of social ethics rather than caste distinctions and had a strong sense of the history of the religion with reference both to teachings and sects. The chronological focus in the case of Buddhism was provided by the date of the *mahaparinirvana* – the death of the Buddha. This was calculated as the equivalent of 486/483 BC and came to be used as an era. (Recently this date has been questioned and later dates have been suggested, but there is no consensus on an alternative date.)

Buddhist and Jaina sects and some of other persuasions had orders of monks (*bhikkhu* – literally, mendicants) and nuns (*bhikkhuni*). As a general category they were referred to as *shramanas* or *samanas* – those who labour towards freedom from rebirth. This led to a distinction between what has been called Brahamanism and Shramanism, the two parallel streams of religious articulation that prevailed for many centuries. They are referred to as distinct by many, even by Alberuni, writing as late as the eleventh century AD. Monks renounced social obligations to take on an alternative life when they joined the Order. They lived as equal members of the Order, denying caste distinctions. But they lived in monasteries near villages and towns so that they could draw on the support of the lay community, namely, those who were Buddhists or Jainas but were not initiated into renunciatory groups. Lay followers were referred to as *upasaka* and *upasika*. Renunciation also gave the monks greater freedom so that they could concentrate on their own *nirvana*, as well as attending to the well-being of the community. Renunciation was not necessarily identical with asceticism and a distinction between them might be useful. The ascetic ideally lived in isolation, discarding all social obligations and performing his death-rites before leaving home. The renouncer discarded the social obligations required through family and caste ties, but entered an alternative society – that of the Sangha, where new obligations were assumed relating to the life of renouncers.

With the increase in numbers of the lay community, the monks were called upon to perform life-cycle rituals linked to birth, puberty, marriage and death. This may well have been the beginning of a change, introducing a larger body of rituals than was originally intended. Places of worship such as the small *stupas*, or funereal tumuli, as they were at this stage, and the *chaityas*, or sacred enclosures, often at locations of sacred trees or local deities, were gradually incorporated into Buddhist worship and were later to take on impressive dimensions. The mounds at Lauriya Nandangarh in north Bihar are thought to be among the early places of worship and some have also provided small representations in gold of what might have been goddesses. The incorporation of popular religion was essential to any sect wishing to collect a following in an area.

Some persons became monks because they disapproved of the ways of society and expressed this by opting out. This was an act of individual choice and is to that extent expressive of individual freedom, although admittedly it was confined to joining an Order. Because these were renunciatory Orders a distinction was gradually made between the Sangha that consisted of the Orders, and the *upasakas* or lay followers, ranging from royalty to artisans, providing the support for the Sangha. The donations of the lay followers were not for a single, sacrificial ritual, but contributed to the permanent maintenance of the Sangha. When monasteries began to receive large donations and prospered, the life of the monk could become comfortable. This may have occasioned some persons, in search of a minimally comfortable life, to join the wealthier monasteries.

There was much in common between Buddhism and Jainism. Both were started by *kshatriyas* and were opposed to brahmanical orthodoxy. Although they did not call for the termination of the *varna* system, they were nevertheless opposed to it as set out in the *Dharmasutras*. But it took a while for them to build up a following of people other than those of the upper castes. When this did happen some of the practices underwent change. As with all historically evolved religions, the original teachings in new contexts were given new meanings, some of which contributed to changing the religion in varied ways. The readings of such histories of change requires a juxtaposition of the original teaching, together with contemporary texts as they came to be written in later times.

The historical transition from the sixth to the fourth century BC saw the expansion of agriculture, the evolution of towns and the beginning of commerce on a wider scale than before, and political authority in the form of the state and monarchy with some contestation between the two political systems of monarchy and chiefship. These changes were not unconnected with the new formulations in religion and ideology, distinctively different from what had gone before. Such formulations received a further and perhaps diverse assertion in the Mauryan period.

6

The Emergence of Empire:
Mauryan India

c. 321–185 BC

The Mauryas and their World

The concept of an empire becomes familiar to Indian historiography in the colonial period. There was an attempt to identify a few empires from the past and see the current one as part of an ongoing legacy. Empires were defined by extensive territory and their glory was said to lie in monumental architecture, grandiose public works and imperial proclamations. In these descriptions empires outside Europe were generally characterized by autocracy and backwardness, explicitly stated in concepts such as Oriental Despotism. The source of revenue was solely agrarian, as this was a system where land was entirely owned by the state. This was a historical justification for the claim to ownership of resources by nineteenth-century imperial systems.

When the term came to be used for large states in early times the focus of the definition had to shift. In relation to the early past an empire is recognized as a more evolved and complex form of state, and therefore embedded in the nature of the formation of states that preceded it. The change from non-state to state becomes central to understanding the context in which empires arise. A qualitative change is also significant. Empires, for instance, control a differentiated economy, unlike kingdoms, where the economic base tends to be relatively more uniform. A crucial question relates to whether the state attempts to restructure the economies – and if so, which economies – or is it content merely to cream off revenue from the resources. There was also an assumption of cultural uniformity, based largely on the symbols of imperial power. But there has been less investigation of the extent to which imperial cultural forms penetrated into distant areas. These investigations are necessary to the definition of an empire. Thus, monumental architecture was seen as important, but largely as a statement of power and presence. Another aspect of such a presence would have been uniformity in laws, perhaps mentioned indirectly in one of the edicts of the Emperor Ashoka, although the laws in question are not spelt out.

With the coming of the Mauryas in the latter part of the fourth century BC, the historical scene is illuminated by a relative abundance of evidence from a variety of sources. Not only do these provide information, but they also encourage tangential thoughts on the history of those times. The political picture is relatively clear, with the empire of the Mauryas covering a large part of the subcontinent, the focus being control by a single power. Attempts were made to give the political system a degree of uniformity, and historical generalization can be made with more confidence for this period than in earlier centuries. Inevitably, in an imperial system, there were attempts to draw together the ends of the empire, to encourage the movement of peoples and goods and to explore the possibilities of communication at various levels. These included the use of a script, of punch-marked coins in exchange transactions and the projection of a new ideology, intended to pursue new precepts.

In the typologies of states, kingdoms differ from empires. Kingdoms tend to draw the maximum profit from existing resources and therefore do not make too great an attempt at restructuring access to resources. The pressures on an empire and its requirements are of a different order, so meeting the financial needs of administering an empire requires considerable restructuring wherever there is a potential for obtaining revenue. An imperial system is not static and has continually to adjust to demands and resources. Although they rarely succeed, imperial systems attempt to erase variation in favour of homogeneity. The variations are cultural and economic. Cultural homogeneity is often sought by propagating a new ideology, in this case the *dhamma* of Ashoka. Not every part of the empire has the same resources, nor is their utilization identical, therefore some degree of economic restructuring also becomes necessary. The restructuring tends to be limited to those resources thought to have the maximum potential. The restructuring in the Mauryan Empire was attempted through both the extension of agriculture, together with mobility of labour in some instances, and the introduction of more wide-reaching commercial exchange. But imperial systems also exploit economic differences and restructure economies in order to suit new alignments. The differentiation is based on the manner in which resources are garnered through administration.

The empire was founded by Chandragupta Maurya, who succeeded to the Nanda throne in *c.* 321 BC. He was then a young man and is thought to have been the protégé of the brahman Kautilya, who was his guide and mentor both in acquiring a throne and in keeping it. This is suggested by a range of stories that relate his rise to power, particularly from Buddhist and Jaina texts, as well as by the play *Mudrarakshasa* by Vishakhadatta, which, although written many centuries later, still supports this tradition. The origins and caste status of the Maurya family vary from text to text. Thus Buddhist texts speak of them as a branch of the *kshatriya* Moriya clan associated with the Shakyas, presumably to give the family a higher status; but brahmanical sources imply that they were *shudras* and heretics, presumably because each king was patron to a heterodox sect. Predictably, the family has also been associated with the Nandas. The *Puranas* had described the Nandas as *shudras*, with the ambiguous statement that in contrast to the *kshatriya* heroes of the solar and lunar lineages the successor dynasties would be of *shudra* origin. This shift in the status of the ruling family is an aspect of the coming of the state, where political power was to be increasingly open – virtually accommodating any *varna*.

The young Maurya and his supporters were inferior in armed strength to the Nandas, and it was here that strategy came in useful. The acquisition of the throne of Magadha was, according to some accounts, the first step. Other stories suggest that Chandragupta began by harassing the outlying areas of the Nanda kingdom, gradually moving towards the centre: this strategy was based, we are told, on the moral drawn from the fact that the young Emperor-to-be saw a woman scolding her child for eating from the centre of a dish, since the centre was bound to be much hotter than the sides. Once the Ganges Plain was under his control, Chandragupta moved to the north-west to exploit the power vacuum created by Alexander's departure. These areas fell to him rapidly, until he reached the Indus. Here he paused, as the Greek Seleucus Nicator – the successor to Alexander – had fortified his hold on the area. Chandragupta moved to central India for a while and occupied the region north of the River Narmada. But 305 BC saw him back in the north-west, involved in a campaign against Seleucus, in which Chandragupta seems to have been successful, judging by the terms of the treaty of 303 BC.

Some Seleucid territories that today would cover eastern Afghanistan, Baluchistan and Makran were ceded to the Maurya. With this, the routes and nodal points of the north-west region shifted from Persian-Hellenistic to Mauryan control, a shift from one to the other of the major states of Iran and northern India becoming a pattern in the history of the region. Given this historical reality, the notion of some dynasties being 'foreign' would possibly have been unfamiliar to the people of the north-west, who were themselves of varying cultures. In return for the territory ceded, Seleucus obtained 500 elephants, a belief in their effectiveness in campaigns being axiomatic in Hellenistic military strategy. There was also an *epigammia* – a marriage agreement – which has been interpreted as a possible marriage alliance between the two royal families. But it could also have referred to the legalizing of marriages between Hellenistic Greeks and Indians living in the cities or as part of the garrison settlements in eastern Afghanistan. The territorial foundation of the Mauryan Empire had been laid, with Chandragupta controlling the Indus and Ganges Plains and the borderlands – a formidable empire by any standards.

Campaigns in the ancient world were not merely a mechanism for acquiring more territory. They were frequently enterprises motivated by considerable diplomatic play, as well as a search for economic advantage. Diplomacy took the form of relationships with neighbours, and was later to provide the basis of the theory of *mandala* – the circle of diplomacy involving allies and enemies. Economic advantage was more visible, not only in the nature and location of the territory to be conquered and its resources, but also in the nature of the campaign. Large-scale campaigns against wealthy neighbours were a source of booty, as well as the taking of prisoners-of-war who could be used as labour. Campaigns have therefore been more than matters of military concern. The campaign against the Seleucids was to wrest Gandhara from them, as it had yielded impressive revenues since the time it was part of the Achaemenid Empire. It was also linked to the land routes to west Asia. The acquisition of central India meant access to the peninsula, another area with resources as yet untapped by northern powers.

Despite the campaign, there was considerable contact of a friendly and inquisitive nature between the Mauryas and the Seleucids. Chandragupta is referred to as Sandrocottos in later accounts and is said to have met Alexander as a young man. In the eighteenth century William Jones identified Sandrocottos with Chandragupta, which provided a clue to Mauryan chronology. It is possible that as a result of the marriage alliance one of the daughters of Seleucus came to the Mauryan court at Pataliputra, in which case a number of Greek women would have accompanied her. An exchange of envoys between the Mauryas and the Seleucids, and with the Hellenistic states further west, was initiated, accompanied by an exchange of gifts (which included potent aphrodisiacs!). Pataliputra welcomed visitors and the city administration had a special committee to look after their welfare.

Seleucus's envoy, Megasthenes, is said to have spent time in India and left an account entitled *Indica*. Much of this account could have been gathered from conversations and travellers' tales, rather than from personal knowledge, and some of his contemporaries doubted that he spent time at Pataliputra. Unfortunately, the original account has been lost and what survive are paraphrases in the writings of later authors such as Diodorus, Strabo and Arrian. That these later authors were reformulating the original text is possible as there are some points of disagreement among the three. The Hellenistic states were all seeking historians to give them legitimacy and to describe their governance. Megasthenes was the choice of the Seleucids. His account of Mauryan India can be better appreciated if seen in the context of the discussion on Hellenistic states by other writers.

The Jaina tradition claims that towards the end of his life Chandragupta, by now an ardent Jaina, abdicated in favour of his son Bindusara and became an ascetic. Together with one of the better-known Jaina elders, Bhadrabahu, and other monks he went to south India, and there he ended his life by regulated slow starvation in the orthodox Jaina manner. A site close to the Jaina centre of Shravana Belgola in Karnataka is associated by local tradition with this story.

Bindusara succeeded in about 297 BC. To the Greeks, Bindusara was known as Amitrochates – perhaps a Greek transcription of the Sanskrit *amitraghata*, the destroyer of foes. Apparently he was a man of wide interests and tastes, and it is said that he asked the Greek King Antiochus I to send him some sweet wine, dried figs and a sophist. Buddhist tradition associates him with an interest in the Ajivika sect. A Tibetan history of Buddhism, written many centuries later, attributes to him the conquest of 'the land between the two seas' – presumably the Arabian Sea and the Bay of Bengal. This would suggest that Bindusara campaigned in the Deccan, extending Mauryan control as far south as Karnataka. The recent discovery of Ashokan edicts at Sannathi in Karnataka, similar to those found at Kalinga in Orissa and issued after the Kalinga campaign, raises the question of whether this region was conquered later by Ashoka, rather than by his father Bindusara; or were these edicts located at this site by mistake? Early Tamil poets of south India speak of Mauryan chariots thundering across the land, their white pennants brilliant in the sunshine. Yet there appeared to have been friendly relations with the chiefdoms of the far south. At the time of Bindusara's death in *c.* 272 BC, a large part of the subcontinent had come under Mauryan suzerainty. One area that was hostile, possibly interfering with Mauryan commerce to the peninsula and south India, was Kalinga on the east coast (Orissa). Its conquest was left to Bindusara's son Ashoka, whose campaign in Kalinga was more than just an event of military significance.

Until about a hundred years ago in India, Ashoka was merely one of the many kings mentioned in the Mauryan dynastic list included in the *Puranas*. Elsewhere in the Buddhist tradition he was referred to as a *chakravartin/*

cakkavatti, a universal monarch, but this tradition had become extinct in India after the decline of Buddhism. However, in 1837, James Prinsep deciphered an inscription written in the earliest Indian script since the Harappan, *brahmi*. There were many inscriptions in which the King referred to himself as Devanampiya Piyadassi (the beloved of the gods, Piyadassi). The name did not tally with any mentioned in the dynastic lists, although it was mentioned in the Buddhist chronicles of Sri Lanka. Slowly the clues were put together but the final confirmation came in 1915, with the discovery of yet another version of the edicts in which the King calls himself Devanampiya Ashoka.

The edicts of Ashoka, located as inscriptions in various parts of his empire, acquaint us not only with the personality of the King but also with the events of his reign and above all his policies as a ruler. As statements of his personal concerns they are remarkable documents, vividly capturing the ambience of his time. This allows glimpses of something other than the conventional limitations of official documents. The edicts do in fact 'speak' of his concerns, both as a human being and a statesman. Their almost conversational style brings to life the personality of the King.

The edicts of the earlier half of his reign were inscribed on rock surfaces wherever these were conveniently located, and are therefore referred to as the Minor and Major Rock Edicts. These were distributed widely throughout the empire especially in areas of permanent settlement and concentrations of people. In the latter part of his reign his edicts were inscribed on well-polished sandstone monolithic pillars, each surmounted with a finely sculpted animal capital, and these have come to be known as the Pillar Edicts. The stone was quarried from sites at Chunar near Varanasi and would have involved much technological expertise in cutting and engraving. The Pillar Edicts are confined to the Ganges Plain, probably because they were transported by river. The area coincides with the heartland of the empire.

Ashokan inscriptions continue to be found and there is always anticipation regarding information that a new edict may bring. Even where the text is the same as that of earlier ones, the significance of the location adds to our information on Mauryan history. Translations or versions in Greek or Aramaic of the Ashokan edicts, intended for the Greek- and Aramaic-speaking people on the north-western borders, have been helpful in clarifying the meaning of those Prakrit terms that are ambiguous or controversial. Thus *dhamma* was rendered by some scholars as the teaching of the Buddha and by others as a more general concern for ethical behaviour. Its translation into Greek as *eusebeia* would tend to support the second meaning. There is interestingly no reference to the teachings of the Buddha in the Greek and Aramaic versions. This might have been expected if their intention was to propagate Buddhism. What is equally fascinating is that some concepts in these edicts are drawn from the philosophical discourse in that language. Thus the edicts in Aramaic are better understood if read in the context of some Zoroastrian concepts. At a more mundane level, the Greek version of the Minor Rock Edict clarifies the date as being in expired regnal years, which is helpful to chronological reconstruction.

Ashoka's experience as an administrator began with his being the governor at Taxila and at Ujjain, both cities handling commercial activities. His sojourn in Taxila is described in texts associated with the later northern Buddhist tradition. These write of his bid for the throne on the death-bed of his father, a bid encouraged by some of the more powerful ministers. His stay at Ujjain is described in the Sri Lankan chronicles of the southern Buddhist tradition. They refer to his love for the beautiful daughter of a merchant, a devout Buddhist and the mother of his son Mahinda who is said to have introduced Buddhism to Sri Lanka.

There continues to be a controversy as to whether Ashoka succeeded his father immediately on the latter's death or whether there was a four-year interregnum involving a struggle for the throne among the brothers. Of the events of Ashoka's reign, the most frequently referred to by modern historians has been his conversion to Buddhism. This was linked to the famous campaign in Kalinga. In about 260 BC Ashoka campaigned against the Kalingans and routed them. Presumably the campaign was to obtain resources from Kalinga; to safeguard the routes of the profitable Mauryan trade with the peninsula that went past the eastern coast; or to chastize the Kalingans for having broken away from Magadhan control, if the canal built by the Nandas was a symbol of control. The destruction caused by the war filled the King with remorse. His earlier perfunctory interest in Buddhist teaching was rekindled and this time it became a central pursuit. It has been stated in the past that he was dramatically converted to Buddhism immediately after the battle, with its attendant horrors. But his was not an overnight conversion; he states in one of his inscriptions that only after a period of two and a half years did he become a zealous devotee of Buddhism. It eventually led him to endorse non-violence and consequently to forswear war as a means of conquest. Yet, curiously, he refrained from engraving his confession of remorse at any location in Kalinga. This was replaced by the Separate Edicts (as they have come to be called), which are instructions to his officers, emphasizing the need for good administration.

Nevertheless his statement on the campaign is indeed extraordinary, coming from a conqueror, setting him apart as a rare human being. He states:

When he had been consecrated eight years the Beloved of the Gods, the king Piyadassi, conquered Kalinga. A hundred and fifty thousand people were deported, a hundred thousand were killed and many times that number perished. Afterwards, now that Kalinga was annexed, the Beloved of the Gods very earnestly practised *Dhamma*, desired *Dhamma* and taught *Dhamma*. On conquering Kalinga the Beloved of the Gods felt remorse, for when an independent country is conquered the slaughter, death and deportation of the people is extremely grievous to the Beloved of the Gods and weighs heavily on his mind. What is even more deplorable to the Beloved of the Gods, is that those who dwell there, whether brahmans, shramans, or those of other sects, or householders who show obedience to their superiors, obedience to mother and father, obedience to their teachers and behave well and devotedly towards their friends, acquaintances, colleagues, relatives, slaves and servants – all suffer violence, murder and separation from their loved ones. Even those who are fortunate to have escaped and whose love is undiminished suffer from the misfortunes of their friends, acquaintances, colleagues and relatives. This participation of all men in suffering weighs heavily on the mind of the Beloved of the Gods.

Major Rock Edict XIII, tr. R. Thapar,
Ashoka and the Decline of the Mauryas, pp. 255–6

It was during Ashoka's reign that the Buddhist Sangha underwent further reorganization, with the meeting of the Third Buddhist Council at Pataliputra in *c.* 250 BC. The Theravada sect claimed that it represented the true teaching of the Buddha, a claim that enabled it to become a dominant sect in the southern tradition and allowed it to exclude those regarded as dissidents. Theravada Buddhist sources have naturally tried to associate Ashoka with this important event in order to give it greater legitimacy. Ashoka does not mention it directly in any of his inscriptions, but there is a possibly oblique reference in an inscription addressed to the Buddhist Sangha, stating that dissident monks and nuns are to be expelled. The exclusion of dissidents is a recognized pattern in sectarian contestations.

The decision to send missionaries to various parts of the subcontinent and even further, and to make Buddhism an actively proselytizing religion, appears to have been taken at this Council, leading eventually to the propagation of Buddhism all over Asia by the turn of the Christian era. This heightened sense of mission was in some ways more characteristic of Buddhism than of the other religions that evolved in India. Conversion as a religious act was partially determined by links between caste and religion.

Buddhism did not make caste a barrier to those who wished to be either Buddhist monks or lay followers. This was a contrast to Vedic Brahmanism where caste was crucial to participation in, and sometimes even defined, various forms of worship. Buddhism was unable to negate caste as a form of stratification, which in later times other non-caste religions such as Christianity and Islam also failed to do.

Communications with the world beyond the subcontinent were once again being developed. Most of the contacts were with countries to the west. The east was comparatively unexplored. Ashoka's missions to the Hellenistic kingdoms, and the enhancement of trade with these, familiarized the Hellenistic world with Indian life and provoked an interest in things Indian. Exchanges of envoys are on record. The closest of these kingdoms was that of the Seleucids whose border was contiguous with the Mauryan. The north-western provinces, having once been part of the Achaemenid empire, retained many Persian features. It is not surprising that the capitals of the Ashokan pillars bear a remarkable similarity to those at Persepolis, and the idea of engraving inscriptions on appropriately located rocks may have come to Ashoka after hearing about those of Darius. However, the content of the inscriptions and their locations are very different from those of the Achaemenids.

Ashoka mentions various contemporaries in the world to the west with whom he exchanged missions, diplomatic and other. A passage in one of his inscriptions reads, 'where reigns the Greek King named Amtiyoga and beyond the realm of that Amtiyoga in the lands of the four kings Tulamaya, Antekina, Maka, and Alikyashudala'. These have been identified as Antiochus II Theos of Syria (260–246 BC), the grandson of Seleucus Nicator; Ptolemy II Philadelphus of Egypt (285–247 BC); Antigonus Gonatus of Macedonia (276–239 BC); Magas of Cyrene; and Alexander of Epirus. This passage is the bedrock of the chronology of Indian history, interlocking the date of the Mauryas with Hellenistic kings. The choice of these kings was not arbitrary since each had some kinship connection with his neighbour.

The Ashokan inscriptions were generally in the local script. Other than the ones composed in Greek and Aramaic, they were in the Prakrit language. Thus, those found in the north-west, in the region near Peshawar, are in the *kharoshthi* script which was derived from Aramaic used in Iran. At the extreme north-west of the empire, near modern Kandahar, the inscriptions are in Greek and Aramaic. Elsewhere in India they are in the *brahmi* script. Whereas in the north-west a concession was made to both the local language and script, in the southern part of the peninsula where people did not yet speak Prakrit – the more widely used language being Tamil – such a concession was not made. Perhaps this was because Tamil did not have a script at that time, the earliest script being an adaptation of *brahmi*; or perhaps also because these were regions which were still chiefdoms and therefore were not given the same status as the kingdoms of the north-west. The extensive use of Prakrit would suggest that the edicts encouraged an element of cultural uniformity in the empire quite apart from the geographically limited use of other languages, but regional linguistic variants are common in the Prakrit of the inscriptions. The origin of the *brahmi* script remains a source of controversy. Some point to its similarities with the southern Semitic script and argue that trade connections led to its evolution; others maintain that it is indigenous and was invented to assist in the administration of a state. The close link between *kharoshthi* and *brahmi* could suggest that the former influenced the latter, since engravers with knowledge of *kharoshthi* were sometimes used to engrave the inscriptions in *brahmi* as far south as in Karnataka.

Tibetan sources maintain that the kingdom of Khotan in central Asia was jointly founded by Indian and Chinese political exiles, and that Ashoka actually visited Khotan. This sounds improbable in view of the hazardous terrain encountered in making such a journey. Contacts with China are difficult to determine with any precision at this date. The central Asian route may have been known but not used regularly. The mountains of the north-east were on the borders of areas that came to be part of the Chinese domain, but the alignment of these mountains in a north–south direction may have created an effective barrier to frequent communication. One of Ashoka's daughters is said to have married a nobleman from Nepal, thus setting up a connection. The eastern Ganges region was included in the location of Vanga (Bengal). Urban centres and ports in the delta such as Chandraketugarh and Tamralipti/Tamluk became centres of trade, and ships heading for the eastern coast and south India began their voyage from the ports of the delta. On the western coast the major ports were Bhrigukaccha (the Barygaza of Greek texts) and Sopara near Mumbai.

The Mauryan capital, Pataliputra, was linked to the northern route – the *uttarapatha* – of earlier times, which ran along the foothills of the Himalaya and then probably along the Gandak. The capital was also at a nodal point, facilitating control over the Ganges system. The Ganges Plain, apart from river routes, was connected with the main commercial centres. Pliny, writing in the post-Mauryan period, mentions a royal highway which followed the route from Taxila to Pataliputra, with a possible extension to Tamralipti. Routes through the peninsula are indicated by the location of the edicts at strategic points – Sahasram, Panguraria (near Hoshangabad), Sannathi. The sites of the inscriptions in southern Karnataka could also have been reached by sea along the eastern coast to the delta of the Krishna River and then inland.

The extent and influence of Mauryan power in the peninsula can be gauged from the location of Ashoka's inscriptions, which are not found beyond southern Karnataka. Ashoka mentions the people of the south with whom he was on friendly terms – the Cholas, Pandyas, Satiyaputras and Keralaputras, as far as Tamraparni (Sri Lanka), and there is no indication that he attempted to conquer them. The resources of the far south seem not to have been so visible as they were to become later. The chiefdoms, in turn, having had or heard of the experience of Mauryan arms from earlier campaigns, probably preferred to give pledges of friendship and remain at peace.

Mauryan relations with Sri Lanka are described as particularly close in the chronicles of the island – the *Dipavamsa* and the *Mahavamsa*. Not only was the first Buddhist missionary to the island said to be Ashoka's son Mahinda, but the then King, Tissa, appears to have modelled himself on Ashoka. There were frequent exchanges of gifts and envoys. The Indian Emperor gifted a branch of the original *bodhi* tree under which the Buddha had gained enlightenment and which, it is claimed, survived in Sri Lanka, although the parent tree in India was cut down in later centuries by an anti-Buddhist fanatic.

The reigns of the first three Mauryas – the first ninety years or so of the dynasty – were the most impressive. Their significance lay not merely in the administration of the rulers over a vast territory, but also in the fact that they were able to draw together the largely diverse elements of the subcontinent. They gave expression to a political vision that coloured subsequent centuries of Indian political life, even if few rulers succeeded in repeating the Mauryan pattern. How and why this imperial vision was possible in the third century BC was determined by a variety of factors.

The Political Economy of Empire

Among the sources used extensively to reconstruct the polity of the Mauryas is the *Arthashastra*, which provides a detailed blueprint of how a kingdom should be governed. The precise date of the text remains uncertain, this being the case with many major texts of the early Indian past. Its authorship is attributed to Kautilya, also identified by some with Chanakya and thought to be the chief minister of Chandragupta. The present form of the text is the work of Vishnugupta in about the third century AD. The main chronological controversy hinges on which parts of the texts are datable to the Mauryan period, or if at all, and which are later. Even if some sections are likely to be dated to the Mauryan period, such as Book II, they should not be taken as descriptive since, as a theoretical treatise, it is only a pointer to what were regarded as essential matters pertaining to governance and to a particular political economy. These ideas did derive from some existing features, but the precision of detailed functioning on the part of a centralized government was doubtless an ideal. It is more important to recognize that such an ideal was seen as a possibility. The text therefore is essentially an encouragement to a particular pattern of governance.

The revenue-producing economy of northern India was now predominantly agrarian, with large areas being brought under cultivation. Land revenue had become the accepted source of income for the government, and it was realized that regular assessments assured increased revenues. The predictability of revenue from these taxes would have created a sense of fiscal security. The administrative system was largely concerned with the efficient collection of taxes. Regarded by many as the theorist of such a system of administration, Kautilya refers at length to methods of tax collection and related problems and a control over potential sources of revenue. Thus forests could not be privately cleared, and clearance was supervised by the state, doubtless to collect the forest products as well as to prevent any arbitrary extension of agriculture. It is a moot point whether such a degree of control was actually exercised. Economic activities other than agrarian were neither unknown nor discouraged. Villages still maintained herds of animals and these were listed under items that were assessed and taxed. In theory, commercial enterprises, particularly in the coastal regions, came under government supervision, and taxes, tolls and customs dues were collected wherever and whenever possible, the techniques of taxation having evolved from the earlier tax on agricultural produce.

Apart from the activities of the state in agriculture, private owners, as farmers or landowners, cultivated the land or had it cultivated and paid the state a variety of taxes. The large landowners collected a rent from their tenants. The recognition of private property in land was gradually conceded, shown by the statement that priority over the sale of landed property would go to kinsmen and creditors before others. Kinship links in relation to land had not been entirely terminated. Extensive areas of wasteland and of *sita* or crown lands were cultivated under the supervision of the state. The latter could be directly cultivated by those appointed to do so, or could be cultivated by sharecroppers or tenant cultivators who paid the state a tax, or by wage labourers employed directly by the state. Greek writers, referring to the account by Megasthenes, unfortunately make contradictory statements about the relationship between the cultivator and the state, although they all agree that cultivators were the largest in number and maintain that the ownership of land was claimed by the ruling dynasty. The variations in tenancy mentioned in the *Arthashastra* are missing in these accounts. The text advocates that the state should organize the clearing of new areas or deserted lands and should settle on such lands large numbers of *shudra* cultivators, either deported from over-populated or sub-standard areas, or enticed from neighbouring kingdoms. Doubtless, the 150,000 people deported from Kalinga after the campaign of Ashoka were sent to clear wasteland and establish new settlements.

Shudras settling in new land were initially exempt from tax, but, once they were working the land, tax was imposed. They have in the past been described as helots, owned and employed by the state. But they were neither owned by the state nor by the ruling community, as in helotage. Other categories that were not necessarily peasants, but provided labour, are referred to in the compound phrase *dasa-karmakara* – slaves and hired labourers. The status of both allowed little freedom and permitted much oppression. Buddhist texts seem to be more sensitive to the condition of such people.

Megasthenes has commented on the absence of slavery in India, but this is contradicted by Indian sources. Perhaps he had the pattern of Athenian slavery in mind and the Indian pattern differed. He suggests a parallel with the Spartan system in Greece, which may have occurred to him because of the centrality of status through birth in both instances. Domestic slaves were a regular feature in prosperous households, where the slaves were of low-caste status, but were not untouchables or they would not have had entry into the homes of the upper castes. Slave labour was also used in the mines and by some craft associations. The conditions leading to slavery are listed in more than one text, and among them are: that a man could be a slave either by birth; by voluntarily selling himself; by being captured in war; or as a result of a judicial punishment. Slavery was a recognized institution and the legal relationship between master and slave was clearly defined. For example, if a female slave bore her master a son, not only was she legally free but the child was entitled to the legal status of a son of the master. Megasthenes may have confused caste status with stratification defined by degrees of freedom. Although Greek society in practice acknowledged degrees of unfreedom, in theory it made a distinction between the freeman and the slave, a distinction which was not so apparent in Indian society. A slave in India could buy back his freedom or be voluntarily released by his master; and, if previously he had the status of an *arya*, he could return to this status on the completion of his term as a slave, according to the *Arthashastra*. Possibly the function of *arya* and *dasa* had again undergone some change. What was immutable in Indian society was not freedom or slavery, but caste. In effect, however, the condition of freedom or slavery was implicit in caste, where, in the overall scheme, the lower castes were less free than the higher, and untouchability could coincide with slavery.

Land revenue was of at least two kinds. One was a tax on the area of land cultivated and the other on the assessment of the produce. Ashoka's inscription at Lumbini, commemorating the birthplace of the Buddha, speaks of *bali* and *bhaga* which may have been these two taxes. Interestingly, he exempts the people of Lumbini from the first, but continues to impose a tax on produce. The assessment varied from region to region and the sources mention a range from one-sixth to a quarter of the produce of the land. It was generally based on the land worked by each individual cultivator, and also on the quality of the land. A reference to *pindakara* – a heap of taxes – could suggest a tax collected jointly from a village. The treasury was entitled to tax the shepherds and livestock breeders on the number and the produce of the animals. Taxes on other activities, referred to by the general term *kara*, were also levied. A tax of a different kind, *vishti*, was paid in labour for the state and is therefore sometimes translated as corvée. It could be forced labour, although some historians regard it as a labour tax that provided labour in lieu of a tax. *Vishti* pertains more to the individual than the other taxes. At this period it is mentioned often in the context of craft production, where craftsmen provide a stipulated amount of free labour to the state.

Taxes for the provision of water for irrigation were regularly collected wherever the state was responsible for providing irrigation. One of Chandragupta's governors had a dam built across a river near Girnar in western India, thus constructing the Sudarshana lake to supply water for the region. An inscription in the neighbourhood mentions the continuous maintenance of this dam for 800 years, stating that it was built through local but official initiative. But where irrigation was privately managed – through wells, channels off rivers and pools, and systems for lifting water – there was either a reduction on the water levy or an exemption. The *Artha-shastra* had a preference for the private management of irrigation. Thus, although the construction and maintenance of reservoirs, tanks and canals were regarded as part of the functions of governing, there is no ground for holding that the control of irrigation was the key to the control of the economy and therefore the prevalence of despotism.

According to Megasthenes, the fertility of the land was such that two crops a year were normal. However, other sources mentioned famines. The Jaina tradition referred to a famine towards the end of the reign of Chandragupta Maurya. An inscription from Mahasthan in eastern India dated to the Mauryan or the immediately post-Mauryan period listed the measures to be taken by the local administration during times of famine. Twelve-year famines were referred to in the epics and texts associated with the Vedic corpus, but such references were more likely a rhetoric for disaster.

If the agrarian economy helped to build an empire, the latter in turn furthered another form of economic activity. The attempted political unification of the subcontinent, and the security provided by a stable government, encouraged the expansion of various craft associations, and consequently in trade. The state employed some artisans, such as armourers and ship-builders, and they were exempt from tax. Others who worked in state workshops, for example the spinning and weaving shops and the state mines, were liable to pay taxes. The rest worked either individually or, as was most often the case, as members of an association. These associations – *shreni* or *puga* – were to become increasingly large and complex in structure, and artisans found it advantageous to join them since this eliminated the expense of working alone and having to compete with the larger organization. From the perspective of the state, such associations facilitated the collection of taxes. They were in turn strengthened by the localization of occupation and the preference for hereditary occupations, and gradually acquired features suggesting the functions of a guild.

The sale of merchandise was, in theory, strictly supervised. Goods were required to be stamped so that consumers could distinguish between the old and the new. Before assessing the goods the superintendent of commerce was expected to inquire into their current price, supply and demand, and the expenses involved in production. A toll was fixed at one-fifth of the value of the commodity and, in addition, there was a trade tax of one-fifth of the toll. Tax evasion is on record and Megasthenes tells us that it was heavily punished. Prices were controlled to prevent too great a profit on the part of the merchant. The degree to which the Mauryan administration could collect revenue from commercial sources would have varied according to Mauryan control over an area or a route. There was no banking system but usury was customary. The recognized rate of interest on borrowed money was 15 per cent per annum. However, in less secure transactions that involved long sea voyages the rate could be as high as 60 per cent. How much of all this was actually in practice remains uncertain.

Mauryan levels from excavations of urban centres show an improvement in the standard of living compared to the previous period. Domestic housing was of brick, although what are thought to be the palace and the audience-hall at Pataliputra were of stone. The massive wooden palisade with its towers and gateways circumscribing the city, as described by Megasthenes, has been corroborated from excavations. A timber palisade was safer in the soft alluvial soil of the river bank. However, he does mention that many of the buildings were of timber and therefore fire was a major hazard. Pataliputra is the only Mauryan city of that period with monumental architecture. Such architecture is often seen as a statement of imperial power and presence. In the Mauryan case it is limited to the capital. Elsewhere, the imperial presence is encapsulated in the inscribing of the king's edicts. Unfortunately, the site of Pataliputra is now built over by the city of Patna, making extensive excavation virtually impossible. Characteristics associated with urban centres are met with at Mauryan levels, for example a frequency of ring wells and soakage pits. There is a quantitative increase in the use of iron, as well as a greater variety of iron artefacts. The distribution of Northern Black Polished Ware as far as south India is an indication of the reach of trade.

Major towns tend to be distantly located in relation to each other, barring those in the Ganges Plain. Mahasthan (Bogra Dt. of Bangla Desh), Shishupalgarh (Orissa), Amaravati (in the Krishna delta), Sopara (near Mumbai) and Kandahar (in Afghanistan) are unlikely to have been in close contact. Some of these were larger than the cities of the earlier period but none could compare in size to Pataliputra. Shishupalgarh is identified by some with Tosali, an important administrative centre mentioned in an edict of Ashoka, not far from the location of the edict at Dhauli. The conquest of Kalinga and the location of Amaravati would have occasioned some activity along the east coast. In the post-Mauryan period this takes the form of a series of Buddhist sites along the coast.

Punch-marked coins and some uninscribed cast copper coins continue to be associated with these levels. The more commonly found punch-marked coins carry familiar symbols such as the crescent-on-arches or hills, the tree-in-railing, the sun symbol and the circle with six arrow-like extensions. An attempt was made to arrange all the coins from a hoard by weight and then relate them to the symbols in order to ascertain a chronological sequence, arguing that the older coins would have less weight because of greater wear and tear. But it did not provide conclusive results.

Terracotta figures, both human and animal, appear to have been popular and can be contrasted stylistically with the far more sophisticated pillar capitals of stone. Whereas the terracottas were made for use by ordinary people, the stone pillars and capitals were artistic statements of the royal court that drew attention to the message engraved on the pillars. Terracotta moulds have been found in large numbers and the repertoire included forms that are linked to fertility cults. Stone-cutting and carving acquired significant dimensions, both in the assertion of a distinct aesthetic and in the techniques of polishing the stone after it had been carved. What has come to be called the Mauryan polish or gloss is easily recognized and gives a special quality to the stone. Stone was the medium for the large figures of *yakshas* and *yakshis*, demi-gods and spirits (such as the now famous one from Didarganj), possibly Mauryan and displaying the same perfection in polish as the pillar capitals. The stone elephant emerging out of the rock at Dhauli is of rougher workmanship. Stone sculpture was evidently the preferred medium of the wealthy and powerful, and is a contrast to the more humble terracotta images.

Welding a Subcontinental Society

Megasthenes speaks of Mauryan society as having seven divisions – philosophers, farmers, soldiers, herdsman, artisans, magistrates and councillors. These have been interpreted as castes because he states that no one is allowed to marry outside his own division or change one profession for another. Only the philosopher is permitted this privilege. All the seven divisions did not follow identical rules. It is thought that he was confusing caste with occupation and by the seven divisions he meant *varnas*. But these were only four, and seven was a fairly common number for classifications of various kinds. It is more likely that he was describing the principle of *jati*, where the social group one was born into was perhaps a closer determinant of marriage rules and occupation than *varna*. Curiously, he makes no mention of the notion of social pollution or of the category of untouchables. Was this too complicated a system for a visitor to understand or was its practice not as widespread as it was to become later? His description is of interest, not because it is accurate but because it is based on the observations of a visitor and reflects hearsay as well as current notions.

The category of philosophers consisted of the dual division of the Brachmanes and the Sarmanes – brahmans and *shramanas* – referring to what we would call the religious identities of Vedic Brahmanism and

Shramanism. These were blanket terms which were also used in later times. The *shramanas* included a variety of ascetics, as well as the monks and lay followers of various sects – Buddhist, Jaina, Ajivika and others. They were large and influential enough to constitute a separate category. The philosophers were exempt from taxation, as corroborated by Indian sources when referring to brahmans and to monks.

The category of farmers, apart from the owners of land, would have included the *shudra* cultivators and the labourers working on the land. The cultivators, listed as the largest category, underline the centrality of agriculture and its requirement to maintain the Mauryan infrastructure, both civil and military. Cultivators were kept unarmed, thus reducing the likelihood of peasant revolts. When Buddhist sources speak of peasants being oppressed by a king they very occasionally refer to the exiling of the king. More often such peasants are said to migrate to neighbouring kingdoms. Migration was doubtless an easier solution than revolt, and although revolts occur in a much later period even then they were infrequent.

For Megasthenes to mention soldiers as one of the seven divisions emphasizes the importance of the army. The Mauryan standing army was larger than that of the Nandas, according to Roman sources. Pliny, writing in post-Mauryan times, quotes the figures at 700 elephants, 1,000 horses and 80,000 infantry, which figures are inflated by Plutarch to 600,000 for the foot soldiers. These enormous figures are obviously exaggerated, as were those quoted earlier for the armed opposition met with by Alexander. In peacetime such a vast army would have been an economic liability. Megasthenes writes, 'when they are not in service they spend their time in idleness and drinking bouts, being maintained at the expense of the royal treasury.' In the circumstances it is not surprising that the treasury had to be kept replenished at any cost, whether it meant taxing every possible taxable commodity or deporting whole communities to establish new settlements. The curtailing of military campaigns might have been encouraged by financial constraints as well. Membership of the armed forces was not restricted to *kshatriyas*, for foot soldiers, charioteers and attendants would have been of the lower castes. Kautilya requires that soldiers should return their weapons to the armoury.

Of the other categories a different term is used for the herdsmen, who are listed as tribes, presumably pastoralists still adhering to clan identities. Pastoralists were sufficiently visible to constitute a distinct social group. They may well have included some hunter-gatherers and shifting cultivators, apart from horticulturalists who had come within the purview of the administration. These could be the people of the forest referred to as *atavikas* in Indian texts, since pastoralists frequently grazed their animals in forests and doubtless were familiar with the people who lived there.

The status of the artisan would depend on his particular craft. Metalworkers, for instance, making armour and other expensive items, were accorded a higher status than weavers and potters; itinerant smiths, catering to the needs of households, had a low status despite the importance of their work. Wealthy artisans were counted among the *gahapatis*, householders, in Buddhist texts. Those with small incomes would have been among the *shudras*. Curiously, there is no mention of merchants, except that one of the Greek terms used for artisans suggests townsmen who could have been petty traders. Magistrates and councillors were obviously part of the administrative system and would tend to be either brahmans or *kshatriyas*, although exceptions are on record.

The picture of Indian society presented by Megasthenes would suggest a more flexible society than has been assumed by modern scholars, and the differentiation between the upper and lower castes was derived from both economic and social status. A useful aspect of the description given by Megasthenes is that it depicts the range of societies that the Mauryan system was attempting to integrate. The distinctive characteristics of these probably changed only in areas where agriculture and commerce enveloped more simple and localized economies.

Caste society need not have worked in the smooth manner envisaged by the brahman theoreticians. It assumed the validity of the principle of social inequality. The first three castes, the *dvija* or twice-born, were theoretically more privileged than the *shudras* and the outcastes. But *vaishyas*, though technically *dvijas* or twice-born, did not benefit recognizably from their privileged position, since they had an ambiguous relationship with the first two. Yet traders and merchants were by now economically powerful, because of the opening up of commerce. Confrontations between them and the socially superior castes would have been inevitable. Guild leaders in urban centres had a significant role in urban institutions, yet the social code denied them a position of prestige. However, narratives of urban life in Buddhist texts are not too troubled by brahmanical norms, although if taken literally the norms of the *Dharmasutras* would have been resented by the less privileged groups. A partial expression of such resentment would have been their support for the heterodox sects, Buddhism in particular. Buddhist texts, unlike the brahmanical, are respectful towards the *setthis* – the financiers and the merchants – who were often their patrons, as they also were of the other sects. This may well have caused friction between the brahmans and the heterodox sects. Ashoka's emphatic plea for social harmony and repeated calls for equal respect towards brahmans and *shramanas* would suggest that there were social tensions.

Activity related to women takes a variety of forms. There is a curious reference to the king's bodyguard consisting of women archers who also accompanied him on hunts. This statement echoes some from other societies with similar royal bodyguards, presumably regarded as impeccably reliable. In addition, women were liable to be employed by the state as spies and performers. Women of the upper castes who had become impoverished or widowed, wives who had been deserted, or ageing prostitutes could get work from the state, such as spinning yarn, but their movements had to be circumspect. Should a peasant fall into debt his wife was required to continue farming his land if he still held it, so that the debt could be cleared. This was not required of women of the upper class. Yet, if a slave woman gave birth to her master's child, both she and the child were immediately manumitted. Female ascetics were known, but were few and far between, and more frequently were found moving around as part of the palace scene in literary works. Kautilya has no qualms about insisting that prostitutes also be taxed on their takings. This would suggest that they were of a sufficient number to bring in a worthwhile amount in tax. That the state should be concerned about their welfare is evident from the punishments to be imposed on those who harmed them. Women camp-followers probably came from the same profession. As in many texts the discussion on women assumes that, other than these few groups, the majority of women followed the wishes of the men in their family.

Surprisingly, there is no mention of either *varna* or *jati* in the Ashokan edicts, which may suggest that they were not yet so prominent as social categories. Social distinctions were, however, evident, and among the markers are the ways in which sculptural representations are used. The capitals surmounting the stone pillars that carried the edicts of Ashoka had animal motifs, and their representation seems to combine both a Buddhist and an imperial ideology. As a contrast to these, the small but extensive terracotta figures of animals and humans were more suggestive of a popular form drawing on religious ideas and decorative functions.

Administration and Empire

The economic conditions of the time and the requirements of the Mauryan period have tended to give the form of a centralized bureaucracy to the Mauryan administration, which has been imprinted with the structure envisaged in the *Arthashastra*. If this text can be presumed to reflect the changes of this period, then it can be argued that it was projecting the potentialities of a centralized administration. But the degree to which it was actually so, and the manner in which this administration was practised, may require a closer look at other texts claiming to be descriptive. The earlier assumption of a uniform and centralized administration needs modification. Nevertheless, some degree of centralization is suggested from other sources and this would have provided leads to the system as constructed in the *Arthashastra*. It might be more useful, therefore, to look at the variations within the system.

The nucleus of the Mauryan system was the king, whose powers had by now increased tremendously. Ashoka interpreted these as paternal kingship, whose rallying call was 'All men are my children'. He travelled extensively throughout the empire to be in touch with his subjects. Legislation was largely a matter of confirming social usage and in this the king had a fairly free hand, but was expected to consult with his ministers. The ministerial council had no well-defined political status, its power depending on the personality of the king. Ashoka's edicts mention frequent consultations between him and his ministers, the latter being free to advise him on his regulations. However, the final decision lay with the monarch.

If the *Arthashastra* can be taken as a guide to the kind of administration adopted by the Mauryas, then the two key offices controlled by the central administration were those of the treasurer and the chief collector. The treasurer was responsible for keeping an account of the income in cash and for storing the income in kind. The chief collector, assisted by a body of clerks, kept records of the taxes that came in from various parts of the empire. The accounts of every administrative department, properly kept, were to be presented jointly by all the ministers to the king, perhaps to avoid fraud and embezzlement. Each department had a large staff of superintendents and subordinate officers, linked to local administration and the central government. Those specifically listed in the *Arthashastra* are the superintendents of gold and goldsmiths, and of the storehouse, commerce, forest produce, the armoury, weights and measures, tolls, weaving, agriculture, liquor, slaughterhouses, prostitutes, ships, cows, horses, elephants, chariots, infantry, passports and the city.

Salaries of officials and expenditure on public works constituted a sizeable portion of public expenses, one-quarter of the total revenue being reserved for these. The figures given for the salaries of those running the administration come from a section of the text that is believed to be post-Mauryan. The hierarchy that emerges is of some interest in explaining where the emphasis lay in administration. The higher officials were extremely well paid according to this scheme and such salaries could have been a drain on the treasury. The chief minister, the *purohita*, and the army commander received 48,000 *panas*, the treasurer and the chief collector 24,000; the accountants, clerks and soldiers received 500 *panas*, whereas the ministers were paid 12,000; and artisans received 120 *panas*. The value of the *pana* is not indicated, nor the interval at which salaries were paid, assuming that they were paid in money. Some comparison can be made with other sources, mentioning that a pair of oxen cost 24 *panas* and a slave could be bought for 100 *panas*. These may not have been the actual salaries but the implicit ratios in these amounts are of interest. Thus, the ratio of the clerk's salary to that of the chief minister or of the soldier to that of the commander of the army works out at 1: 96.

The upper levels of the bureaucracy would have been extraordinarily well paid if these ratios are even reasonably correct. Public works covered a wide range of activity: building and maintaining roads, wells and rest-houses, and planting orchards, as stated by Ashoka in his edicts; irrigation projects such as the Sudarshana lake; maintaining the army; running the mines; financing certain kinds of items in which the state had a monopoly, such as armour; the grants of the royal family to religious institutions and individuals, for example where Ashoka refers to the gifts made by his queen; and the maintenance of the royal family itself.

Administration doubtless attempted to follow some of the prevailing precepts, but also had to adjust to the political and economic reality. The *Arthashastra* endorsed a highly centralized system where the king's control over the entire exercise remained taut. This would have been difficult for an area as vast as that of the Mauryan Empire, economically and culturally so diverse, although it could have been possible in a smaller area such as Magadha, the governance of which seems closer to what Kautilya envisaged. It may be more realistic to suggest that the administration was adjusted to the socio-economic patterns and differentiations. Seen from this perspective, three variants in the administrative pattern can be suggested which would be appropriate for distinctly different conditions, but which would all the same underlie the emphasis on revenue collection and redistribution.

At the hub was the metropolitan state of Magadha, an area with long experience of functioning as a state. The Ganges Plain was doubtless part of the same system. This is broadly the area of the distribution of the Pillar Edicts of Ashoka, many of which are his retrospective on his reign. Although the location of the pillars doubtless had to do with access to transportation by river, it would have been an interesting coincidence if this was the area of maximum centralized administration which probably functioned more closely to the Kautilyan system than elsewhere. The metropolitan state was the pivot of the empire, controlling the income and its redistribution. It extended its hegemony by conquering areas of strategic importance and of agrarian and commercial potential, the revenue from which would enrich it. Such areas could be regarded as core areas, scattered throughout the subcontinent and constituting a second category that was distinct from the metropolitan state.

The core areas were less directly under central control and more effectively under the control of governors and senior officials. As areas brought into the ambit of the Mauryan system they experienced state formation at second remove. The state was foisted on them through conquest and they subsequently accommodated themselves to the new situation, being incorporated into the state system. The imperial administration would have attempted to restructure the economy of these areas to bring them into some conformity with the metropolitan state. Core areas seem to coincide with closer clusters of Ashokan edicts and the Major Rock Edicts, such as those in Gandhara, in the Raichur *doab* and southern Karnataka, in Kalinga and in Saurashtra. The importance of Gandhara was that it controlled access to the Hellenistic kingdoms of west Asia and was an obvious area for commercial exchange. In Karnataka the locations of the inscriptions seem to have been determined by the potential for mining gold and the activities of chalcolithic and megalithic people. Urban centres were probably initially limited to Mauryan administrative centres, such as Suvarnagiri, perhaps so named because of its proximity to gold-mining areas. Mining was an important source of wealth and, apart from the availability of gold in Karnataka, there was copper in Rajasthan and iron in south Bihar. Some of the core areas would have included the peoples mentioned in the edicts, such as the Kambojas, Yonas, Bhojas, Pitinikas and Andhras, all of which were located in the imperial domain.

The third form was that of the peripheral areas, which have been called areas of relative isolation rather than attraction, and where extensive settlements were more limited. The imperial administration did not attempt to restructure the economy of these areas but limited its activities to tapping the existing resources. Peripheral areas were probably controlled more by fiat than by conquest and direct administration. Such territories were often viewed as buffer zones. These were generally forested areas providing a wealth of resources in timber, elephants and semi-precious stones. It would not be surprising if the people living in the forests tapped these resources more effectively than the Mauryan administration, and the administration would have had working relations with them in order to obtain the resources. Some who were brought within the ambit of the Mauryan administration, the *atavikas* or forest-dwellers, were referred to in the Ashokan edicts.

These references to the forest-people are in a tone that is both cajoling and threatening. The threat may have resulted from a resistance by forest-dwellers to encroachments. These were not always related to a control over the area by the army or the administration, but could also arise from hermitages or settlements of graziers and cultivators that often acted as the vanguard of a more determined intrusion. To the forest-dwellers they were alien and invasive, since the norms of the forest-dwellers were different from those of the settlers. For the latter, the former were without norms and unpredictable, and therefore often mythologized into the demons of the forest.

In the peninsula the societies of the megalithic settlements, cultivating rice, using iron artefacts and with elaborate burials, were more complex compared to the forest-dwellers who coexisted with them. A Mauryan presence is not registered in any striking way among the artefacts in the megalithic remains, although Ashokan inscriptions are located in these areas and refer to Mauryan administration. Possibly, resources were tapped by the administration through local channels without any extensive restructuring of the economy in these areas. There is a cluster of Ashokan inscriptions in the gold-bearing region of Karnataka and it is likely that the ore was mined. It is otherwise difficult to explain why there should have been so much administrative activity in the area, even though gold objects from Mauryan levels are rare.

The suggestion that Mauryan administration and economy be viewed in terms of the metropolitan state, together with core and peripheral areas, should not be confused with what has been described as the segmentary state. Terms such as centre, core and periphery have been used in historical models other than the segmentary state, for example in the analyses of commerce relating to the function of markets and production. The Mauryan system suggested here had little to do with ritual status, ritual hierarchies or the separation of the political from the ritual. Mauryan control over administration and revenue collection did not vary, but rather there were variant mechanisms and forms in this control. Thus, it is possible that the chiefs among the forest-dwellers collected the forest produce demanded by the Mauryan administration and were the channels by which the administration obtained this tax in kind. Ashoka's admonition to the people of the forests does not suggest a dilution of Mauryan control.

The edicts make it evident that the empire was not viewed as consisting of uniform units of administration and they acknowledge the presence of diverse peoples. The variants suggested here accommodated these diversities without detracting from the general, overall control exercised by the imperial administration, or from the recognition that the metropolitan state was at the heart of the Mauryan system however uniform it was. This is made clear by the King's statement to the forest-dwellers which was conciliatory but accompanied by the threat that the state could be severe. The *Arthashastra* also warns that the forest-dwellers, although at some levels marginal, can be a danger when kings are campaigning in the area and should therefore be treated with suspicion and, if possible, appeased. They are a political reality and have to be treated tactfully. Mention is also made of the presence of pastoralists, in addition to cultivators, and the archaeology of this period points to a variety of settlements. The coexistence of such diversity required a focus, but also required diverse ways of administrative handling. Acknowledging diversity requires more than a single pattern of administration, and these patterns have to be flexible since the diversities were to be found in various parts of the empire.

Apart from the metropolitan area, which was directly governed, the empire was divided into provinces, each one apparently under a prince or member of the royal family. Centres of provincial administration were located at Taxila, Ujjain, Dhauli, Suvarnagiri and possibly Girnar. Governors administering smaller units were selected from among the local people, such as the Iranian Tushaspa associated with Saurashtra, or Romodote at Taxila. Senior officers – *pradeshikas* – toured every five years for an additional audit and check on provincial administration. There were specially appointed judicial officers – *rajukas* – both in the cities and rural areas, and they combined their judicial functions with assessment work. Among the duties of the *yukta* was the recording of information from varied sources. Fines served as punishments in most cases. But certain crimes were considered too serious to be punished by fines alone and Ashoka, despite his propagation of non-violence, retained capital punishment.

According to the blueprint of the *Arthashastra*, provinces should be subdivided into districts, each of these into groups of villages, the final unit of administration being the village: a system which has been implemented from time to time and has remained approximately unchanged. The group of villages was to be staffed with an accountant, who maintained boundaries, registered land and deeds, kept a census of the population and a record of the livestock; and the tax collector, who was concerned with the various types of revenue. The most frequently mentioned person in the village, the headman, functioned in some official capacity and was responsible to the accountant and the tax collector. Administrative divisions are referred to in the edicts, one of which was called *ahara* – a term with an intrinsic interest since it is derived from collecting and eating.

Urban administration had its own hierarchy of officers. The city superintendent maintained law and order and the general cleanliness of the city. He was assisted by an accountant and a tax collector, with functions similar to those of their village counterparts. Megasthenes' description of the administration of Pataliputra states that the city was administered by thirty officials, divided into six committees of five members. Each committee supervised one of the following functions: questions relating to industrial arts; the welfare of visitors coming from distant places; the registering of births and deaths; matters relating to trade and commerce; supervision of the public sale of manufactured goods; and, finally, collection of the tax on articles sold (this being one-tenth of the purchase price). A similar administration is proposed by the *Arthashastra*, supporting supervision of production and exchange in urban centres, presumably to control revenues. If it was literally so, could it have acted as an inhibiting factor in exchange activities?

Whether the administration was quite as effective as suggested by these statements remains uncertain. There is for instance much emphasis on the keeping of records, but unfortunately such records have not survived, nor for that matter have records from later times. The communication between the province and the centre, which would be crucial to the kind of administration suggested, might have been difficult given the distances and the time taken for orders to be carried from Pataliputra to the other cities. Decisions on lesser activities were doubtless taken at the local level.

For the Mauryan administration espionage was a recognized official activity, one which was common to many other imperial systems. The *Arthashastra* advocates the frequent use of spies, and recommends that they should work in the guise of recluses, householders, merchants, ascetics, students, mendicant women and prostitutes. Ashoka also refers to agents who bring him news and generally keep him informed about public opinion. This was one of the means through which contact was maintained with even the more remote parts of the empire.

Ashoka's *Dhamma*

It was against this background that Ashoka expounded an idea which was new to Indian political and social theory, which has also received much attention in recent years, enhancing the curiosity about Ashoka. It is based on his interpretation of the 'philosophy' or idea of *Dhamma*, a term he used frequently. *Dhamma* is the Prakrit form of the Sanskrit word *Dharma*, meaning, according to the context, the universal law or righteousness or, by extension, the social and religious order found in a society where Brahmanism was the norm. In the Buddhist Canon it was used for the teaching of the Buddha. However, the word had a much more general connotation at the time and, judging by the way in which he used it in his edicts, Ashoka gave it a wider meaning.

Early studies of Ashoka drew on the evidence from the Buddhist chronicles of Sri Lanka in conjunction with the King's own edicts, and this naturally emphasized a Buddhist reading of the edicts. His supposedly sudden conversion to Buddhism after the battle of Kalinga was dramatized and he was depicted as a paragon of Buddhist piety following his conversion – one historian suggesting that he may have been both a monk and a monarch at the same time. Ashoka was certainly attracted to Buddhism and became a practising Buddhist. But the Buddhism of his age was not merely a religious belief; it was in addition a social and intellectual movement at many levels, influencing many aspects of social life. Obviously, any responsible and sensitive statesman would have had to locate himself in the context of the Buddha's teaching, among others, and be aware of its impact on the society of that time. Ashoka's edicts reflect this sensitivity, as also do his concerns for the ethics of those whom he was governing.

Ashoka, it would seem, made a distinction between his personal belief in and support for Buddhism and his obligation as a king and a statesman to insist that all religions must be respected. His inscriptions are therefore of two kinds. The smaller group consists of declarations of the King as a lay Buddhist, addressed to the Buddhist Sangha. These edicts describe his adherence to Buddhism and his relationship with the Sangha. Here the voice is that of a confirmed believer with some degree of intolerance of differing opinion, as for instance in a passage where he proclaims in no uncertain terms that dissident monks and nuns should be expelled from the Sangha. Another inscription mentions the various teachings of the Buddha with which Buddhists, and in particular Buddhist monks, should be familiar.

Far more important, however, is the larger group of inscriptions on rock surfaces known as the Major and Minor Rock Edicts, and the Pillar Edicts inscribed on specially erected pillars, all of which were located in places where people were likely to gather. Given that literacy would not have been widespread, these were presumably locations where the edicts would be read out to the gathered people. This was part of the propagation of ideas through the oral tradition. These may be described as exhortations to his subjects.

The versions of the Minor Rock Edicts reiterate the fact of his being a Buddhist and these, together with the Major Rock Edicts and the Pillar Edicts, define what he understands by *Dhamma*. The achievement of Ashoka lay in his exposition of this idea in the context of Mauryan India. He did not see *Dhamma* as piety, resulting from good deeds that were inspired by formal religious beliefs, but as conformity to a social ethic. Some historians have interpreted Ashoka's *Dhamma* as a synonym for Buddhism, arguing that Ashoka's intention was the propagation of Buddhism to make it virtually the religion of the Mauryan state. The edicts would belie such an intention. He appears to have been concerned with using a broader ethic to explore ways of governance and to reduce social conflict and intolerance. *Dhamma* was aimed at creating an attitude of mind in which the ethical behaviour of one person towards another was primary, and was based on a recognition of the dignity of human beings. It was couched in a language that was familiar to the discourse of that time. The ideas on which he focused, which do have some parallels in Buddhist teaching, were nevertheless central to contemporary debates on matters beyond the concerns of religious organizations.

This concept of *Dhamma* can perhaps be better understood by analysing it as a response to contemporary conditions. It was in part a policy that was nurtured in the mind of Ashoka, but, since he also saw it in relation to existing problems, it is in the light of these that its nature can be assessed. As a family, the Mauryas tended to be eclectic and favoured the heterodox sects – the Jainas, the Ajivikas and the Buddhists – although they were not hostile to Brahmanism. These dissident sects questioned brahmanical ideas and suggested alternative ways of life and thought. The strength of, and the support for, ideologies alternative to Vedic Brahmanism was apparent, and this would have made them all the more competitive. That the competition was sometimes expressed in contestation was unavoidable. There were other tensions, involving the status of newly emerging communities, such as the mercantile community, the assertion of craft associations in urban centres, the strain of an administrative system more complex than before and the sheer size of the empire.

It would seem that with such divergent forces a focus or common perspective was required. The empire included multiple cultural and social systems. In the north-west, Hellenistic society was characterized by two divisions, the master and the slave; in the Ganges Plain and the core areas four *varnas* were more common, as well as innumerable *jatis*; among the *atavikas* or forest-people, scattered in many parts of the empire, there were no *varnas*. Such plurality could be juxtaposed or even minimally welded either by force or by persuasion. Ashoka chose the latter. Given the structure of Mauryan society and politics, in order to be successful such a focus had to derive from a central authority. He sought a group of unifying principles, influenced by the intellectual and religious currents of the time. Ashoka mutated *Dhamma* to his needs and explained it through a personal definition.

The principles of *Dhamma* were such that they would have been acceptable to people belonging to any religious sect. *Dhamma* was not defined in terms of caste duties and regulations and was left vague in details, referring itself to the requirements of social ethics. Of the basic principles, Ashoka emphasized tolerance. This, according to him, extended to tolerance towards people and towards their beliefs and ideas. He defined it repeatedly as consideration towards slaves and servants, respect for teachers, obedience to mother and father, generosity towards friends, acquaintances and relatives, regard for and donations to brahmans and *shramanas*, a concern for all living beings and an abstention from taking life. He went on to say:

But the Beloved of the Gods does not consider gifts of honour to be as important as the essential advancement of all sects. Its basis is the control of one's speech, so as not to extol one's own sect or disparage that of another on unsuitable occasions . . . On each occasion one should honour the sect of another, for by doing so one increases the influence of one's own sect and benefits that of the other, while, by doing otherwise, one diminishes the influence of one's own sect and harms the other . . . therefore concord is to be commended so that men may hear one another's principles.

Major Rock Edict XII, tr. R. Thapar,
Ashoka and the Decline of the Mauryas, p. 255

This was a plea to accommodate differences in the interests of harmonious living. Differences can be openly expressed and admitted, while at the same time being tolerated. There was a concern that differences should not lead to disharmony. Occasions that might encourage disharmony or become the starting point for opposition, such as assemblies and gatherings, were discouraged.

Refraining from violence was another principle of *Dhamma*, which included the renunciation of war and conquest by violence, as well as a restraint on the killing of animals. But Ashoka was not adamant in his insistence on non-violence. He recognized that there were occasions when violence might be unavoidable, for instance when the forest-dwellers were troublesome. In a moving passage on the suffering caused by war, he declares that by adhering to *Dhamma* he will refrain from using force in the future. He also states that he would prefer his descendants not to conquer by force, but should it be necessary he hopes they will conduct this conquest with a maximum of mercy and clemency. He pared down the cooking of meat in the royal kitchen, allowing for only a little venison and peacock meat – evidently his personal preferences. He also lists a number of birds, animals and fish of a curiously mixed kind that he declares inviolable. The inviolability of some is linked to particular days of the calendar. This is frequently quoted today as an early example of the conservation of wildlife, but a more likely explanation of their preservation points to a ritual or medicinal connection. In another edict he refers to the planting of medicinal herbs to help both men and animals.

The policy of *Dhamma* included the state's concern for the welfare of its people. The Emperor claims that:

On the roads I have had banyan trees planted, which will give shade to beasts and men. I have had mango groves planted and I have had wells dug and rest houses built every nine miles ... And I have had many watering places made everywhere for the use of beasts and men. But this benefit is important, and indeed the world has enjoyed attention in many ways from former kings as well as from me. But I have done these things in order that my people might conform to *Dhamma*.

Pillar Edict VII, tr. R. Thapar, *Ashoka and the Decline of the Mauryas*, p. 265

He criticized in no uncertain terms what he described as 'useless ceremonies and sacrifices', held as a result of superstitious beliefs, for example those meant to ensure a safe journey or a quick recovery from an illness. These were the stock-in-trade of the lower order of priests, who depended on such ceremonies for their livelihood. Yet he has no objection to spectacles and displays conjuring up divine forms as a means of attracting an audience to create an interest in *Dhamma*. This was propaganda of an obvious kind.

To implement the policy of *Dhamma* and publicize it, Ashoka instituted a special category of officers – the *dhamma-mahamattas*. Their concern was with the well-being of his subjects. As can often happen with such categories of officers, although the intention was worthy they may have interfered more than was necessary in the lives of people, thus to some extent nullifying their very purpose. Had his interest been only to propagate Buddhism, then his support to the Sangha would have sufficed; but the appointing of the *dhamma-mahamattas* points to wider concerns.

Yet the policy of *Dhamma* did not succeed. It may have been due to Ashoka's over-anxiety for its acceptance, or to his own weakness when he became obsessed with *Dhamma* in the latter part of his reign. The social tensions and sectarian conflicts continued, or else were adjusted but remained. Nevertheless, Ashoka deserves admiration, not only for recognizing the need for a social ethic, but for attempting to both define and implement such an ethic in his capacity as emperor. Buddhist tradition depicts him as the *chakkavatti* – the universal monarch who ensures that the turning of the wheel of law is the essence of his rule. Universal monarchy was a concept rather than a reference to reality. Ashoka does not describe himself as a *chakkavatti*, possibly because this was not his intention.

Imperial Decline

Ashoka ruled for thirty-seven years and died in about 232 BC. Subsequently, a political decline set in and the empire began to break up. The last of the Mauryas, Brihadratha, was assassinated during an inspection of the troops by the brahman Pushyamitra, the commander of the army. Pushyamitra founded the successor Shunga dynasty. However, military coups were rare in the early history of India. This incident is frequently quoted as a case of the ineptitude of the ruler allowing himself to be removed.

The pattern of the break-up of the empire has its own interest in terms of the continuance of the metropolitan area and the evolving of the core regions into independent states. The Ganges Plain remained under the Mauryas, becoming the nucleus of the kingdom of their successors. The north-western areas were lost to the rising ambitions of the Bactrian Greeks, and remained vulnerable to the politics from across the borderlands. Interestingly, some of the *gana-sanghas* of the Punjab and Rajasthan seem to have survived and were able to reassert themselves. However, the *gana-sanghas* of the middle Ganges Plain had succumbed to monarchical rule. This is to some degree a commentary on the nature of the imperial administration. Other parts of the empire, erstwhile core areas, such as Gandhara, Kalinga and parts of the western Deccan, broke away into smaller states, some with occasional evidence of dynasties and others with more continuous dynastic control. The forest-dwellers continued to inhabit various parts of the subcontinent. It was not the ambition of the Mauryas to uproot local societies, nor did these become part of a single, uniform culture.

It has been asserted in the past that the decline of the Mauryan Empire can be attributed largely to the policies of Ashoka. He has been accused of causing a revolt of the brahmans because of his pro-Buddhist policy. But his general policy was not an active proselytizing in favour of Buddhism at the expense of Brahmanism. It was open to acceptance or rejection by all or any. He repeatedly states that respect is to be shown to both brahmans and *shramanas*. There is little evidence to suggest that Vedic Brahmanism was the prevalent religion in the Indian subcontinent at that time. It was still the religion of a small minority, although gradually becoming powerful. To the extent that Ashoka patronized Buddhism it came to be established in some parts of the empire. But the more extensive spread and enhancement of Buddhism came from its new patrons in the mercantile community in the post-Mauryan period. It has also been said that his obsession with non-violence led to the emasculation of the army, thus laying the country open to invasion. Yet his propagation of non-violence did not override other considerations, as is evident from his advice to his sons and grandsons on the use of violence; nor do the edicts imply that he deliberately weakened the military strength of the state by pursuing a policy of non-violence.

More probable reasons are to be found elsewhere. The suggestion that the Mauryan economy was under considerable pressure seems a more likely cause, although this requires further investigation. The need for vast revenues to maintain the army, and to finance the salaries of the upper levels of the bureaucracy, not to mention the cost of establishing settlements on newly cleared land, could have strained the treasury. Although excavation of the Mauryan urban sites points to an expanding economy in the early stages, the view that there was a debasement of silver coins in the later Mauryan period would suggest a different picture. This has been interpreted as a severe pressure on the economy where the normal channels of revenue were not sufficient for the Mauryan state. However, the chronology of the coins remains uncertain and debased coins alone are not conclusive proof of a fiscal crisis. Kautilya suggested that double-cropping should be undertaken during times of financial need, but this was practised in some areas even before the Mauryan period.

Other economic factors had a more direct bearing on the question. Kautilya's advice that virtually every human activity should be taxed has also led to the suggestion that there was a fiscal crisis. Although an agrarian economy prevailed in the Ganges Plain, there was still a great variation in economic patterns throughout the empire. Significantly, despite increasing the land under cultivation, there is a record of famine in eastern India, which suggests that the lines of supply were not adequate. This variation may well have prevented an economic equilibrium in the state, with the revenue from agrarian areas not being sufficient to maintain the entire empire. Possibly the Mauryan administration was content to cream off the revenue as and when it could, and did not restructure the economy sufficiently to provide longer-term support for an imperial system. The economic development of the core areas of the empire, such as Gandhara and Kalinga, led to the emergence of new states that coincided with the decline of the empire. It has therefore been argued that, although Mauryan control may have declined, this was nevertheless a period of local economic development.

As an imperial system it was short-lived when compared to those of other parts of the world, and perhaps features at the root of the system were not conducive to long-lasting empires. An imperial structure requires a well-organized administration with built-in factors to ensure its continuity. The Mauryan bureaucracy was centralized, with the ruler – or king – as the key figure towards whom loyalty was directed. A change of king meant a re-alignment of loyalty or, worse, even a change of officials. The system of recruitment was arbitrary, with local governors choosing their officers, and the same pattern is likely to have been repeated throughout the hierarchy of office. This might have been avoided if some form of recruitment had been adopted to eliminate the possibility of particular social groups and local cliques monopolizing administrative control. The building of institutions requires some distancing from personal concerns and choices, with the replacement of these by social and civic concerns.

The lack of any representative institutions to stabilize public opinion would have added to the problem. The system used by the Mauryas, as also by other ancient imperial systems, was espionage. This must have created manifold tensions in both political and administrative activity. The mood of the *Arthashastra* is hostile to notions of representation – however limited – and the participation of larger numbers in decision-making. This can be seen in the section where various methods are suggested for sowing dissension and terminating the existence of the *gana-sanghas*. They are not merely to be conquered and incorporated into the kingdom, but are to be rooted out as a system. Even if the *gana-sangha* system was not exactly one of representation, nevertheless it did endorse a wider distribution of authority than in kingship.

Among its essentials, the factor of political loyalty implies loyalty to the state, the state being a concept that is over and above that of the king and the government. The monarchical system, which increasingly leaned on religious orthodoxy, tended to blur the concept of the state, and instead loyalty was directed to the social order. The interdependence of caste and politics had gradually led to caste being accorded higher status than political institutions. This is partly seen in the changing attitude towards kingship and the functions of the king. To begin with, the divinity of the king had been emphasized in brahmanical sources, but the Buddhists and Jainas had introduced a contractual concept for the origin of the state. In order to lay stress on the necessity for a controlling authority, brahmanical sources also introduced the idea of a contract. Not only was the king invested with divinity, but his status and power resulted from a contract between the people and the gods. The earlier theory of *matsyanyaya* had reflected a fear of anarchy, which was believed to be inevitable in a society without kingship.

The essential constituents of a state are discussed in the *Arthashastra* in its reference to the *saptanga*, the seven limbs of the state. These were the king, the territory, the administration, the treasury, the capital, coercive powers (as invested in the army and in punishments) and allies. Two factors were gradually being emphasized in brahmanical texts as essential to the existence of the state. One was *danda* (coercion), which gave the state the power to coerce and to enforce laws even if this involved punishment, the other, which became more important, was *varna-ashrama-dharma* (social and ritual obligations in accordance with *varna*). Gradually the latter took precedence over the state. This was rooted in the idea that the king was required to protect his subjects and to ensure the preservation of the *varna-ashrama-dharma*, which encapsulates the acceptance of social duties and obligations set out in the *Dharma-shastras*. The Buddhist requirement had a different emphasis in that the universal monarch or *chakravartin/chakkavatti* should rule righteously, which also meant ensuring the welfare of all his subjects irrespective of upholding *varna*. If he did so the wheel of law would roll through his kingdom. An unrighteous act would stop the wheel and lead to its sinking into the ground. In political theory from brahmanical sources, the highest authority on the empirical plane was accorded to the king and, on the abstract plane, *dharma*. The latter changed by slow degrees and the change was consequently hardly noticed, which ensured continued and unabated loyalty. *Dharma* obtained its sanction from divine sources, which made it imperative to defend it as a sacred duty.

There are multiple aspects of the Mauryan period that make it a time of great historical interest. The state controlled many activities and was sustained by systems of revenue collection. The focus therefore was on the state as an agency of control, largely through administrative functionaries concerned with assessing sources of revenue and collecting taxes. The relationship between the state and the peasant or the artisan was without effective intermediaries, other than the bureaucracy. The peasant was largely free, except where he worked on land under the control of the state, and even in the latter case a variety of tenures could apply. The state, however, appears to have taken the initiative in extending agriculture. Peasant discontent was articulated largely in the form of migration, but nevertheless the state was being advised to open up new areas to settlement. Systems of exchange were varied, but coined money played a visible role and the potentialities of commerce were beginning to be tapped. The absence of reference to *varna* in the edicts of Ashoka suggests that other social categories were more significant, such as family, clan and sect. *Varna* categories would have been observed, for instance, in the reference to brahmans, but possibly *jatis* were more prominent in the social landscape. This could have been closely related to the prevalence of, and patronage to, the heterodox sects. These aspects gradually changed in the post-Mauryan period and by the mid-first millennium AD were superseded by other forms that gave a new direction to historical activity.

By the early second century BC the first experiment in imperial government in India had ended. Other experiments were to be made in later centuries but the conditions were never quite the same. The degree of central control attempted in the Mauryan polity, particularly in the metropolitan area, became increasingly difficult in later periods when officials and landowners, to whom the king delegated much of his power, became the intermediaries between king and subject. The desire for empire did not disappear, but there was no longer the same compulsion and intensity which accompanied the first of the empires. And beyond that there remains the solitary figure of Ashoka as a ruler with a commitment to a social ethic. This was unique in Indian history and rare in the histories of other societies.

7

Of Politics and Trade

c. 200 BC – AD 300

Shungas, Kharavela, Oligarchies

Political events in India became diffuse after the Mauryan period, involving a variety of kings, eras and people. Evidence is gleaned from yet more diverse sources than in earlier times, and texts are consulted from as far afield as the history of contemporary China by Ssu-ma-chien/Sima Qian. Whereas the people of the peninsula and south India were seeking to define their polities and experiencing the reach of maritime trade, northern India was caught up in the turmoil of happenings in central Asia. The Mauryas had begun to explore the potential for activities, not only in various parts of the subcontinent but also in areas beyond, particularly looking westwards. The need to extend the horizon and consider participation in new ventures was recognized by the successor states. The many new states with their growth and interrelations can be confusing, unlike the relatively uncomplicated picture of the Mauryan period.

There is a tendency to give primacy to events of the north-west since there is a range of evidence, including much from Hellenistic and Roman sources, but events in other parts of the subcontinent were equally consequential. The focus of politics did not shift to the north-west, as there were multiple centres of political ambition. This was a recurring pattern with the disintegration of large kingdoms. That which followed the break-up of the Mauryan Empire anticipated and shaped the emergence of regional states in the next few centuries. From a superficial view, there appears to have been no connecting theme in the post-Mauryan period. Yet there was a theme, even though it was less immediately apparent in political events.

Coins and inscriptions provide primary evidence but both are different in form from their predecessors, the punch-marked coins and the Ashokan edicts. Indo-Greek coins in particular are miniatures of aesthetic excellence, of precise economic value, providing information on centres of exchange and on emerging religious sects and cults that were prominent in north-western India and its vicinity. Inscriptions from this time on tended to record donations and grants, or else were royal eulogies and annals. The King's attempt to 'speak' to his subjects through inscriptions, as was Ashoka's intention, was not to be repeated. Either the problems were less pressing than affairs of state, or, as is more likely, kings were not inspired to do so.

The immediate heirs of what remained of the Mauryan Empire were the Shungas, a brahman family, who were officials under the Mauryas. The founder of the dynasty, Pushyamitra, assassinated the last of the Mauryas while commanding the Mauryan army, and usurped the throne. Kalidasa's romantic play, *Malavika-agnimitram*, presents an image of Shunga rule which differs from that of the Buddhist narrative text, the *Divyavadana*. Buddhist sources claim that they persecuted the Buddhists and destroyed their monasteries and places of worship. This could have been an exaggeration, but archaeological evidence reveals that Buddhist monuments in the Shunga domain were at this time in disrepair and being renovated. However, if the chronology of these monuments shifts forward as is now being suggested, then this would make them post-Shunga renovations. Nevertheless, even if some renovations were of a later date, the damage to the *stupa* at Sanchi and to the monastery at Kaushambi dates to Shunga times. Added emphasis is given to this from Pushyamitra having performed *ashvamedhas*, or horse sacrifices. This is sometimes viewed as indicating support of Vedic Brahmanism and a disapproval of the heterodox sects. The sacrifices are also linked to his having held back Yavana forays from the north-west.

The Shungas were occupied with wars: they campaigned against their southern neighbours in the Deccan, against the Hellenistic Greek inroads from the north-west and against Kalinga to the south-east. Intense competition in the creation of kingdoms followed the decline of the Mauryan Empire. The Shunga kingdom may have originally comprised a large part of the Ganges Plain, although some of the more distant regions were probably not directly under their control and merely owed them political allegiance. Within a hundred years, however, the kingdom had dwindled to the boundaries of Magadha and its fringes, and even here the Shunga hold was precarious: a situation that continued for a half-century under another brahman dynasty, the Kanvas, whose founder usurped the Shunga throne, and its kings reigned uneventfully until the late first century BC.

One striking feature of this period is the reappearance of what are sometimes called the tribal or the clan-based polities in Punjab and Haryana – especially clustered around the watershed – and in Rajasthan. Their presence is established largely through their coins and we know of the Arjunayanas, Kunindas, Audambaras, Trigartas, Agastyas, Shibis and Yaudheyas. Some among them migrated to adjoining areas, as and when local politics required it. Thus the Abhiras are found in the northern Deccan. The Malavas moved to southern Rajasthan and may have been later associated with the era of 58–57 BC, perhaps because of their connection with Ujjain.

Many of these clans claimed *kshatriya* status; implicit in this claim was descent from the *kshatriya* heroes of epic and legend. Some of their rajas took titles that implied an approximation to kingship, but their coins were more often minted in the name of the *gana* or the *janapada*, revealing a structure similar to the *gana-sangha* as in the case of the Yaudheyas. The repeated reference to kings attacking the *kshatriyas* was possibly a reference to such polities, which would indirectly underline their continuing political significance as an alternative to kingship.

Monarchical systems, however, were more widespread by now. Kalinga in Orissa was an independent kingdom in the mid-first century BC under Kharavela. This was an example of secondary-state formation, as it had been a core area in the Mauryan system and had been imprinted with the structure of a state through being under Mauryan administration. The Mauryan centre at Tosali developed into a Buddhist site, but Kalinga was also associated with Jaina monasteries, encouraged no doubt by the initial patronage of Kharavela. A long inscription that includes an almost year-by-year biographical sketch of Kharavela survives at Hathigumpha – the Elephant's Cave. The inscription is tantalizing as it is damaged, and permits of alternative readings. Kharavela was of the Meghavahana lineage associated with the Chedis. (Curiously, Ravana is said to be of the same lineage in the *Paumachariyam*, a Jaina version of the *Ramayana* that was probably composed in the third century AD.) Despite his support for Jainism, Kharavela protected the independence of Kalinga through raids against neighbours. Kharavela refers to irrigation canals built by the Nandas, but proudly mentions his own efforts in this direction. There is no reference to the Mauryas, unless it was included in the sections of the inscription that are now illegible, yet there are a few hints of ideas that seem to echo those of Ashoka, such as his veneration for all sects. He also lays claim to investing much wealth in the welfare of his subjects, although this could be the predictable rhetoric of royalty.

The inscription is among the early biographical sketches of a king and deserves a more detailed summary as it represents the beginnings of a style of royal eulogy. An adaptation of the lengthy inscription would read:

Salutation to the Arhats (Jinas) . . . by illustrious Kharavela, the Aira, the great king, the descendant of Mahameghavahana, increasing the glory of the Chedi dynasty, endowed with excellent and auspicious marks and features, possessed of virtues that have reached the four quarters, overlord of Kalinga.

Fifteen years were spent in youthful sports with a body ruddy and handsome.

Administration as an heir apparent lasted for nine years and he mastered correspondence, currency, finance, civil and religious law and was well-versed in all branches of learning.

On attaining manhood he was crowned king in the dynasty of Kalinga. In his first year he repaired the gates, walls and buildings of the city damaged in a storm; built embankments on the lake, and tanks and cisterns in the city; and restored the gardens.

This was done at the cost of thirty-five thousand and pleased the people.

In the second year his strong army of the four-fold units of cavalry, elephants, infantry and chariots was sent against the western regions controlled by Satakarni [the Satavahana king], and also threatened the city of the Mushika peoples.

The third year was given to dance performances and music at festivals and assemblies.

In the fourth year the Rathikas and Bhojakas were attacked and they submitted to him.

In the fifth year he extended the canal originally built by the Nanda king.

Since he was performing the *rajasuya* sacrifice he remitted taxes and cesses and bestowed many hundreds of thousands on the institutions of the city and the realm.

In the seventh year his wife became a mother.

In the eighth year he threatened the capital of Magadha which led to the king Dimita [Demetrius, the Indo-Greek king], retreating to Mathura.

More gifts follow – golden trees, elephants, chariots, residences and rest-houses as well as the declaration that brahmans were exempt from tax.

A royal residence was built at the cost of thiry-eight hundred thousand.

In the tenth year he sent an expedition to conquer Bharatavarsha.

Another expedition went south towards the Krishna river and attacked the town of Pithunda which was ploughed with a plough yoked to asses. He broke up the confederacy of the Tramira [Tamil countries] which had been a threat to Kalinga.

In the twelfth year his armies turned northwards causing panic among the people of Magadha. He retrieved the image of the Jina which had been taken away from Kalinga by the Nandas and brought back the riches of Magadha and Anga.

He settled a hundred builders, giving them exemption from land revenue, to build towers and carved interiors and stockades for elephants and horses.

Precious stones were brought to his court and pearls from the Pandya realm in the south.

In the thirteenth year he offered maintenance and gifts to the monks of a Jaina monastery.

An assembly was held of ascetics and sages and monks and the depository of the relic of the Arhat was embellished. He caused Jaina texts to be compiled.

He is the king of peace, of prosperity, of the monks and of the teaching.

He is accomplished in extraordinary virtues, respects every sect and repairs all shrines. His armies cannot be vanquished and he protects the realm. He is descended from the family of the royal sage, Vasu.

Adapted from *Epigraphia Indica*, XX, pp. 71–89,
K. P. Jayaswal and R. D. Banerji, 'The Hathigumpha Inscription of Kharavela'

The attributes of royalty such as conquest, patronage and the welfare of subjects are accentuated, with royalty being emphasized in the sculptures and reliefs in the surrounding caves. Such an assertion would have been necessary if Kalinga was still supporting some chiefdoms. The Rathika and Bhojaka peoples are mentioned in the Ashokan inscriptions and in later Satavahana inscriptions they refer to designations – Maharathi and Maha-bhoja – implying they were chiefs who had been given administrative functions. Shishupalgarh, a Mauryan administrative centre, was also an exchange centre. But Kharavela did not issue coins and the use of punch-marked coins continued. It is possible that, despite the vast sums mentioned in connection with the development of the town, the Kalingan economy was not yet ready for its own coinage. Descent from Vasu refers to the Vasu who was the raja of the Chedis, believed to be the recipient of a gift from the gods – a chariot that could fly. The claim to a connection with Vasu links Kharavela to epic and Puranic genealogies, and the flying chariot would have linked him to Ravana in the *Ramayana*. On Kharavela's death, Kalinga relapsed into quiescence.

Indo-Greeks and Shakas

The end of Achaemenid rule in Iran and the death of Alexander gave rise to kingdoms ruled by Alexander's erstwhile generals, for instance the Seleucid kingdom that was contiguous with the Mauryan. The mingling of Hellenistic Greeks and Indians in the second century BC came about through the Hellenistic kings, who ruled in the north-west as successors to those who had succeeded Alexander. Some differentiate between the Greco-Bactrians who ruled over Bactria and the Indo-Greeks who included north-west India in their domain; others refer to them as Indo-Bactrian Greeks or use Indo-Greek in a more general sense. Indian sources refer to them as Yavanas. This term makes no distinction between what some would call the Hellenic Greeks, living on the mainland of the peninsula of Greece, and the Hellenistic Greeks. The latter were those of Greek descent or of mixed descent, but broadly conforming to Greek culture and living in the eastern Mediterranean and west Asia. Hellenistic Greek culture drew on Greco-Roman culture of the eastern Mediterranean, as well as Iranian sources and some central Asian influences, and can be regarded initially as Greco-Roman colonial culture. The political ambitions of these Hellenistic kings, who ruled between the third and first centuries BC, were torn between asserting themselves in the eastern Mediterranean and intensifying their hold on the gainful trading activities in west and central Asia. Indians would have been more familiar with Hellenistic Greeks than with the Greeks of the peninsula. The term Yavana continued to be used in later times for all those who came from west Asia.

The rulers of Bactria and of Parthia made the most of the decline of Seleucid power by breaking away from Seleucid control, acting as virtually independent kingdoms by the second century BC. At first, Bactria was the more forceful of the two. It lay between the Hindu Kush and the Oxus, a fertile region well provided with natural resources and controlling the main northern routes from Gandhara to the Black Sea, to central Asia and to the eastern Mediterranean. The Greek settlements in Bactria traced their origin to the Achaemenid period (*c.* fifth century BC) when the Persian kings settled Greek exiles in the region. These were reinforced by Greek artisans settling in the cities of Bactria.

Diodotus, the governor of Bactria, rebelled against Antiochus, the Seleucid King. Antiochus was unable to suppress the revolt because his primary interest lay in the eastern Mediterranean, and consequently Diodotus achieved independent rule. Nevertheless, in 206 BC Antiochus made an alliance with Subhagasena, an obscure Indian king, largely to replenish his supply of elephants. The alliance revealed that the north-west of India was vulnerable to annexation. Demetrius, the son of Euthydemus (who had also defeated the Seleucid king), took his armies to the south-east of the Hindu Kush where he successfully acquired territory. Eventually, a Demetrius who was probably the second king of this name, came to rule a large area in southern Afghanistan, the Punjab and the Indus Valley, thus establishing Indo-Greek power in north-western India. Forays were made into the Ganges heartland, but the power base remained the north-west and possibly the Punjab. This is corroborated in an indirect manner in Patanjali's grammar, the *Mahabhashya*, dating to the second century BC. In giving examples of the use of a particular grammatical form he refers to Yavana raids in the western Ganges Plain and in Rajasthan.

The best remembered of the Indo-Greek kings was undoubtedly Menander, who, as Milinda, attained fame in the Buddhist text *Milinda-panha* – the Questions of King Milinda – a catechismal discussion on Buddhism. Supposedly conducted by Menander and the Buddhist philosopher Nagasena, it is claimed to have resulted in Menander's conversion to Buddhism. This was a period when Greeks were interested in Buddhism, so such a manual would have been extremely useful to the propagation of the religion. Menander, ruling from *c.* 150 to 135 BC, stabilized Indo-Greek power, in addition to extending its frontiers in India. He is known to have held the Swat Valley and the Hazara district in the north-west, as well as the Punjab. His coins have been found as far north as Kabul, and to the south in the Mathura region. He is thought to have conquered territory in the Ganges Plain, but failed to retain it. He may well have attacked the Shungas in the Yamuna region, if not closer to Pataliputra itself. His popularity gave rise to a legend that various cities of the north-west vied with each other for his ashes after his cremation, then built monuments over the relics. But perhaps the Roman writer Plutarch, who narrates this story, was confusing the legend of the Buddha's death with that of Menander.

Following Menander, there appears to have been a regency, after which came the reign of Strato. Meanwhile, Bactria was ruled by the line of Eucratides, which had broken away from that of Euthydemus and from which the first Demetrius seems to have split off. The Bactrian king cast longing eyes at Gandhara and, advancing beyond Kabul, he annexed the kingdom of Taxila. But the Bactrians did not hold Taxila for long.

The Hellenistic Greeks marked their presence by monumental buildings and by small, finely crafted objects. Excavation of the cities of Ai-Khanoum, on the confluence of the Oxus and the Kokcha, of Bactra (modern Balkh), of Antioch in Margiana and of Sirkap at Taxila, reveals a characteristic talent for urban planning. Ai-Khanoum was built on the usual city-plan, the citadel differentiated from the lower city with predictable features such as temples, theatres, buildings embellished with pillars and patterned mosaic floors, and promenades. Its location and its function as an evolved Hellenistic city indicate it was a successor to the Achaemenid presence in central Asia. Scattered throughout the area of Hellenistic activities are their coins – excellent examples of minting, with portraiture of a high aesthetic quality. Curiously, portraits on coins never became fashionable in India.

The history of the Indo-Greeks has been reconstructed mainly on the evidence of their coins. Some of the coinage of Bactria was based on the Attic standard and comparable to the Athenian 'owl' coins, suggesting close ties with the eastern Mediterranean. The silver Athenian owl coin, so called because it had the head of Athena – the goddess associated with Athens – on one side, and the bird associated with her – the owl – on the other, was legal tender virtually throughout the Mediterranean. Indo-Greek coins, based on the Attic standard with legends in Greek, circulated in Bactria. Coins with a reduced weight of silver often had bilingual legends in Greek and *kharoshthi* or *brahmi*, and these circulated in the north-west of India. Coinage was therefore adjusted to region and requirement.

Indo-Greek coins introduced innovations in Indian numismatics, such as die-striking, the use of legends, portraits of rulers, monograms and the representation of deities. These features help in identifying coins, and some sequence of rulers can be reconstructed even where they carry identical names. Portraits did not become the norm in coinage elsewhere in India. Even where kings are depicted in some specific activity, these depictions are not portraits. The rejection of portraiture on coins is curious, considering that there are sculptures with a limited depiction of kings and literary portraiture in the form of biographies occurs in inscriptions. Deities could be depicted iconographically or as symbols and were generally of the Shaiva or Bhagavata sects, or Buddhist, Jaina or Zoroastrian, or of the cults of Greco-Roman origin that were worshipped in the area at that time. This is another indication of the need for rulers of south Asian regions to be patrons of multiple religions. The depiction of deities familiar to the local people doubtless strengthened the acceptance of this coinage in diverse places linked by trade. Such depictions help to date the rise of sects, such as the worship of Krishna Vasudeva and Balarama, both depicted on Indo-Greek coins. In the choice of motifs, those on the more widely used copper coins were generally more eclectic and specific to the region.

The coins are symbolic of an intermingling of Hellenistic with Indian or Iranian cultures. Depictions of *yakshi* figures and Indian goddesses some-times replace the Hellenistic deities, although Herakles remained popular. At Takht-i-Sangin in southern Tajikistan the Iranian fire-temple carries the imprint of Greek decoration. A striking instance of this mingling is the inscription at Besnagar in western India, on a pillar erected by a certain Heliodorus, envoy of King Antialkidas of Taxila to the King of Besnagar, perhaps one of the later Shungas. Heliodorus professes to be a follower of Vasudeva (the incarnation of Vishnu as Krishna), and obviously, though Greek, had become a Vaishnava. The remains of what might be the earliest temple dedicated to Hindu worship have been located through excavations at Besnagar. It is thought to have been associated with the newly emerging Bhagavata sect, whose beliefs and practices facilitated the process of acculturation. These trends isolated Vedic Brahmanism as a recipient of royal patronage, all the more so because it had no use for those who worshipped images.

As a contrast to the Heliodorus inscription, the brahman author of the Yugapurana section of the *Gargi Samhita* was hostile to the Yavanas, who were said to behave in a brutal and inhuman manner. This demonizing of the Yavanas is curious, since they were familiar from Mauryan times. Possibly the source of irritation was that much of the patronage of these rulers went to the Buddhists and less to the brahmans, even if the newly emerging Shaiva and Bhagavata sects were also receiving patronage. But this was not the same as patronage to Vedic Brahmanism which, by the very nature of its belief and practice, would have been closed to the Yavanas and the *mlechchhas*, who were regarded as outside the boundaries of caste. The Bhagavata sect was open to accepting persons who came from societies without caste, such as the Hellenistic Greeks, and sometimes even allotted them a caste status. These cults flourished in the growing urban ambience, but the city was not a site conducive to the practices of Vedic Brahmanism.

Shakas, Parthians, Kushanas and Kshatrapas

The decline of the Greek kingdoms in the north-west coincided with an attack on Bactria itself by nomadic peoples from central Asia. From this point on the complicated migrations and movements of peoples in central Asia became a backdrop to events in northern India. Those who initially attacked Bactria in the late second century BC included the Parthians and the Scythians – referred to as the Pahlavas and Shakas in Indian sources – and were primarily responsible for weakening Bactrian power. Scytho-Parthian rule was established in north-western India around the Christian era. The Scythians inhabited the region around Lake Issykkul and the river Jaxartes in central Asia. They were attacked by the Yueh-chih/Yuezhi and forced to migrate, some going south and some west. The Yueh-chih were originally pastoralists whose herds were pastured in the plains to the west of China.

Such nomadic pastoralists were unlikely people to found large kingdoms, but in the interaction with existing kingdoms a pattern evolved in which the nomads came to dominate sedentary societies, and this eventually gave rise to kingdoms. In the process, the pastoralists themselves underwent mutations that permitted them to emerge as competent rulers. Raids, once the normal practice among nomads to obtain livestock – sheep and horses – as well as control over grazing grounds, changed to control over and administration of resources. The origins of such a change frequently lay in the pastoralists obtaining tribute from the sedentary society in return for protection. The extraction of tribute strengthened the heads of clans among the pastoralists and they came to form an aristocracy. Pastoralists could become cultivators but more often they preferred to rule over cultivators. Because of their circuits of herding, and the possibility of using the animals to transport goods, they emerged as important to transactions involving the exchange of produce and became effective as mediators between sedentary societies. Horses were traded eastwards, while in exchange silk travelled westwards to be sold in the markets of central Asia and further.

Although essentially pastoralists, the Shakas of central Asia acquired a sophistication that was reflected in their burial chambers. These vast graves constructed of timber have an almost architectural quality, with the variations of size and content reflecting a society conscious of social differentiation. Alongside the chiefs and the horses buried with them, grave goods consisted of weaponry, horse trappings and items of common use that were heavily decorated, often using gold. The horse was central to the activities of the Shakas, providing them with rapid mobility and enabling them to use various equestrian improvements in the shape of saddles and bridles, and the compound bow, to improve their military technology. It is thought that a primitive stirrup was also in use.

The geography of central Asia assisted them in their role of expanding pastoralism and as intermediaries of trade. Scattered across the deserts were fertile oases, some of which became the nucleus of towns and of states, especially those settled as a result of both the earlier Achaemenid enterprise to irrigate the oases and Hellenistic encouragement to trade. The Tarim Basin was a meeting point of Indian and Chinese commerce. Dunhuang had earlier been a garrison town but gradually incorporated commercial activities. Therefore the pastoralists also had to negotiate the nature of their relations with the oases, if they wished to exert power.

Gradually, as their pastures began to dry up, the pastoralists made intermittent raids into Chinese territory searching not only for new pastures, but also for the wealth of those Chinese who were sedentary. The later movement of these tribes westwards can be traced back to the activities of the

Chinese Emperor Shi Huang Ti, who built the Great Wall in the last half of the third century BC to defend China's frontiers against the nomadic Hsiung-nu/Xiongnu, Wu-sun and Yueh-chih. The Hsiung-nu suffered famines in the first century BC, brought about by excessive snow and the continuing raids of their neighbours. This led to their migrating and displacing the Yueh-chih, which started a chain reaction of population movements in central Asia. These in turn had an impact on northern India.

The Yueh-chih were driven from the best lands and had to migrate to distant places. They split into two hordes – the Little Yueh-chih, who settled in northern Tibet, and the Great Yueh-chih, who wandered further west to the shores of the Aral Sea. Here they stopped for a while, displacing the inhabitants of the region, the Scythians, or the Shakas, as they were called in Iranian and Indian sources. The Shakas advanced into Bactria and Parthia. A Chinese visitor in about 128 BC records that the land surrounding the Aral Sea had been cleared of the Scythians, and instead he had found the Yueh-chih settled there. Parthia failed to hold back the Shakas, except for a brief period, and was overrun. The Shakas however did not pause there, but swept down into the Indus Plain, eventually becoming established in western India, with their control reaching as far as Mathura. To the west their base was in Seistan in Iran. Horsemen herders had the potential of becoming a good cavalry and this was used to advantage in campaigns.

The Parthians, the Shakas and the Yueh-chih arrived in India turn by turn. This maelstrom of peoples was yet another occasion when the aridity of the deserts of central Asia transmuted the history of China and India. Pastoral nomadism also acted as an avenue for the intermittent exchange of goods, some exchanged directly for profit and some as gifts. Chinese silk, for example, found its way via central Asia to India and the eastern Mediterranean, some of it moving through a series of gift exchanges in the first area and some as an item of trade in the latter area. The people who came from central Asia were familiar with the rough passage of high mountains and deserts, relieved only by intermittent oases. The passes of the north-west mountains of India may have been inhospitable in themselves, but the fertility and wealth of the Indian plains were glimpses of a richer future. The attraction of India lay not just in the fertility of the land, but also in the profits of trade from the items it produced. The nexus between Roman trade and central Asia was seen as an avenue to prosperity and the same image was taking shape in the trade between the eastern Mediterranean, as part of the Roman Empire and western India. If itinerant trade was a subsidiary activity of the pastoralists, this was gradually overtaking other activities.

The pastoralists were emerging as traders and, with the backing of their herding horses, became newly converted to cavalry.

With the entry of the Shakas on the Indian historical scene, Chinese texts referring to events in central Asia become relevant to Indian history as well, apart from Shaka coins and inscriptions. The Shaka King Maues or Moga (c. 80 BC) established Shaka power in Gandhara. A successor, Azes, annexed the territory of the last of the Indo-Greek kings in northern India, Hippostratos. Azes is now being associated with the creation of the era of 58 BC that was to be known through the centuries as the Krita, Malava or Vikramaditya, *samvat*, era. Possibly the era was also calculated for use in astronomy as the term *krita*, created, would suggest, but was given status by association with royalty. The link with Vikramditya is later, and evidently mythological, since a ruler by this name important enough to start an era is not known in the first century BC.

Mithradates II established a Parthian presence in India, also in the first century BC, as did Vonones a little later. Gondophares, or Gundophernes, achieved fame through the association of his name with that of St Thomas – doubting Thomas – the disciple of Christ. Tradition maintains that St Thomas travelled from the eastern Mediterranean to the court of Gondophares, and the mission eventually took him to south India. This would place Gondophares in the first half of the first century AD. Historical evidence of the arrival of Christianity in south India is, however, of a later period.

Shaka administration continued largely along the lines of the Achaemenid and Seleucid systems in Iran. The kingdom was divided into provinces, each under a military governor called *mahakshatrapa* (great satrap). Each of these provinces was further subdivided into units under the control of lesser governors or *satraps*, who not only issued their own inscriptions in whatever era they wished to observe, but were also permitted to mint their own coins, thereby indicating a more independent status than was normal for an administrative governor. They carry a mixture of Indian and non-Indian names and some were local people of status. Another official title was that of *meridarch*, used for an officer in charge of a designated area. The minting of some coins in the joint names of two rulers has been interpreted to mean that the king associated himself with a ruler of lesser status. This marks a curious contrast to those Shaka kings who took exalted titles, such as 'great king' or 'king of kings', derived from Hellenistic and Achaemenid usage. This attempt to take on the nomenclature of an imperial structure must nevertheless have been bewildering to the recently nomadic Shakas.

The Shakas were driven southwards by the Yueh-chih. A Chinese source records that one of their chiefs, Kujula Kadphises, united the five tribes of the Yueh-chih and led them over the northern mountains into north-western India, establishing himself in Bactria and extending his control to Kabul and Kashmir, thus initiating the Kushana kingdom. This is confirmed by Greek and Latin sources complaining of attacks on Bactria from northern nomads. Indian sources do not refer to the Kushanas as such, but references to the Tukhara, or Tushara, are thought to refer to them. The Begram-Kabul area, a core area of this kingdom, was once the hub of the Paropamisadae under the Seleucids and Mauryas. The Indo-Iranian borderlands again became a contested region between northern India and powers further west. On his death, in the mid-first century AD, Kujula was succeeded by Wema Kadphises. Kushana coinage included some issues in gold that appear to be imitations of the Roman *denarius aureus* coins that were circulating in central Asia in the wake of Roman trade. A copper series of *tetradrachms* were also issued with an image of Shiva.

The Kushana dynasty was in the ascendant in central Asia under Kanishka, whose relationship to the earlier kings has been confirmed by the recent discovery of an inscription in Afghanistan. In this he claims that he conquered *hindo*/India, i.e., the better-known north-west of India, and proclaimed his conquest in all the cities as far as Champa (in the middle Ganges Plain). He also says that he issued an edict in Greek and then put it into Aryan – incidentally, a correct use of the term to indicate a language, in this case most likely Prakrit. His central Asian identity is imprinted on a statue, unfortunately headless, found near Mathura but identified by an inscription and representing the king as an impressive figure in boots and coat. The accession of Kanishka has been dated anywhere between AD 78 and 144. An era based on AD 78 has come to be called the Shaka era, but is also thought by some to be linked to the accession of Kanishka. The Kushana kingdom may have reached to the middle Ganges Plain, where Kushana inscriptions have been found. However, their most important cities were Purushapura, near modern Peshawar, and Mathura. Kushana artefacts are found at places such as Chirand, but this does not necessarily indicate the conquest of the area by the Kushanas. Artefacts and coins can travel with trade and are not necessarily proof of conquest or control.

The inclusion of parts of central Asia in the Kushana kingdom, as far as Kashgar, converted it into an extensive state that had the makings of an empire. India and China were brought closer through the interlinking oases and through Kushana territory bordering on both. Recently found inscriptions and coins along these frontiers indicate many interconnections within the region. The larger part of the empire was in central Asia, with its hub in

Bactria, hence the frequency of Kushana Bactrian inscriptions. There are inscriptions in Prakrit in Bactria, but none in Bactrian in the Indian north-west. An early Kushana settlement at Khalchayan in central Asia has coins with legends inscribed in *brahmi*, although *kharoshthi* was also used. This might have a bearing on cultural and commercial emphases and point to Prakrit-speaking groups beyond the subcontinent.

The construction of a road – the Karakorum Highway – a few years back, linking the north-west to central Asia, and connecting the upper Indus route with Gilgit, Chitral and Skardu, revealed the existence of a much earlier route following approximately similar directions. Going along the Indus and into the Hunza Valley, it eventually branched off towards Samarkand, Tashkurgan and Yarkand, and was evidently a branch of the Silk Route. The location of the Ashokan edicts at Mansehra and Shahbazgarhi in the north-west marked a logical area for the start of such a route. Inscriptions in *kharoshthi*, *brahmi* and Bactrian, and engravings of Buddhist images and themes along the way, date the earlier route to the start of the Christian era. Inscriptions in an early form of *sharada* (a script used later in northern India), in Sogdian and in Chinese indicate its continued use into later times. The occasional depiction of horses would suggest an early horse trade with central Asia, the horses of that area being highly prized. The route seems to have been used extensively and possibly also became another entry-point into India for central Asian armies. The proximity to central Asia through such routes encouraged exchange. It also influenced aspects of Indian technology, such as an improvement in horse trappings and equipment, already familiar to central Asia and now improving the efficiency of the cavalry in India.

Given the territorial span of the contact, and the intermingling of peoples, royal patronage had to be extended to a variety of religions – Buddhism, Jainism, the Bhagavata and Shaiva sects, Zoroastrianism and the Hellenistic cults. The northern Buddhists claimed Kanishka as a royal patron, associating him with the Fourth Buddhist Council held to clarify Buddhist doctrine. This was a parallel to the claim of the Theravada Buddhists that Ashoka presided over the Third Council at Pataliputra. The most significant outcome of the Fourth Council was the recognition of various new Buddhist sects and their attempts at missionary activity in central Asia. For the Kushanas, an overt association with divinity may be seen as part of the propaganda of royalty. The Kushana title of *daivaputra* – son of heaven – may have been derived from Chinese usage, although it could also have been influenced by the claims to divine status among Roman emperors and their cult, who also took a similar title, *diva filius*. Even stronger associations with divinity lay in the sanctuaries built to deify the king after his death – the *devakula*. These are rare in India, and the Kushanas may have thought this an appropriate form of acquiring respect as rulers in an area where they were migrants.

The Indo-Greek kings and the Kushanas took exalted titles. The Indo-Greeks used *basileos basilei* (king of kings) and the Kushanas borrowed titles from the Persians, Chinese and Romans, rendering them as *maharajati-raja* (king of kings), *daivaputra* (son of heaven), *soter* (Saviour) and *kaisara* (Caesar). The halo that occasionally adorns a Kushana ruler may well have been derived from the Mediterranean practice. Such titles nourished notions of empire. The stature of the ruler was enhanced by past kings being raised to the status of gods, with temples dedicated to them. The Kushana portrait galleries of their kings, at Surkh Kotal and Mat in Mathura, parallel temples to deities. This was ironic in a way, since despite their extensive territories they were not governing as an imperial system. The nature of control varied from region to region. Some areas were directly administered, in others greater power lay with the local satraps, and in still others control was exercised through existing rulers who had accepted Kushana suzerainty. The office of *mahakshatrapa* was frequently the precursor to independent kingship.

Kushana governance gradually diminished, weakened by the confrontations with the rising power of the Iranian Sassanids, and nibbled at by the assertive *gana-sanghas* of the Punjab and Rajasthan. The distinctiveness of the Kushana presence was slowly being eroded as is symbolized in the name of a late ruler, Vasudeva, reminiscent of the association of Heliodorus with the Bhagavata cult. At the same time, events in Iran were to intervene again in the history of north-western India. In AD 226 Ardashir overthrew the Parthians and established Sassanian ascendancy. His successor conquered Peshawar and Taxila in the mid-third century, and the Kushana kings were subordinated to the Sassanians.

The turn of the millennium had been a period of central Asian intervention in the history of northern India that took the form of conquests, migrations and commerce. Those who came were initially alien in custom and belief, but the mutations that had occurred among them and among the host societies expanded the cultural experience of both. If Greeks were converted to Vaishnavism or came to accept the presence of Bhagavata and Shaiva deities, Indians began to worship deities from across the borders, some of which entered the Indian pantheon, such as the goddess Ardochsho in the form of Shri. Kushana coins sometimes carried images of Zoroastrian deities.

The coming of the Kushanas had pushed the Shakas south into the region of Kutch, Kathiawar and Malwa in western India. Here they were to remain and to rule until the late fourth century AD. The rule of Rudradaman the Kshatrapa in the mid-second century stands out largely for the cultural change that he patronized. At Junagarh, in Saurashtra, a lengthy inscription – the earliest of any importance in Sanskrit – provides evidence of his activities. The language is the commonly used Sanskrit that had formed the basis of Panini's grammar. He may have chosen it in preference to the currently used Prakrits of inscriptions in order to project himself as supported by the conventions of the orthodox, despite their grading such rulers technically as low-status *kshatriyas*. Was Rudradaman deliberately aligning himself with Brahmanism as a stand against the prevailing patronage of Buddhism, Bhagavatism and other new sects in the north-west? This was not merely an act of patronage towards a religion, but also identification with an ideology. It is ironic that the use of Sanskrit in inscriptions should have begun with a person whose *varna* status could be questioned. Was he attempting to win the support of the orthodox in establishing his legitimacy as a ruler? Or was he reflecting the parallel patronage and language that was gradually to become predominant in court circles? Apart from listing conquests, as is common in such inscriptions, he is described as a man of literary sensibilities well able to use Sanskrit in the cultural idioms of the time. This was to become a regular accomplishment associated with kings in the eulogies and became increasingly popular, as did the issuing of inscriptions in Sanskrit.

Dated to AD 150, the inscription is engraved on the same rock as a set of the Major Rock Edicts of Ashoka. The Sanskrit text of Rudradaman is a contrast to the Prakrit text of Ashoka, effectively conveying the spirit of the historical change. It is primarily a record of the repairing of the Mauryan period dam on the Sudarshana lake, still in use but having been badly breached by a violent storm. The minister who carried out the repair is described as able, patient, not arrogant, upright and not to be bribed! The inscription also refers in eulogistic terms to Rudradaman's conquest in the Narmada valley, his campaigns against the Satavahana king (south of the Narmada) and his victory over the Yaudheya *gana-sangha* in Rajasthan. Rudradaman is described thus in the inscription:

(He) who by the right raising of his hand has caused the strong attachment of *Dharma*, who has attained wide fame by studying and remembering, by the knowledge and practice of grammar, music, logic, and other great sciences, who (is proficient in) the management of horses, elephants, and chariots, the wielding of sword and shield, pugilistic combat, . . . in acts of quickness and skill in opposing forces, who day by day is in the habit of bestowing presents and honours and eschewing disrespectful treatment, who is bountiful, whose treasury by the tribute, tolls, and shares rightfully obtained overflows with an accumulation of gold, silver, diamonds, beryl stones, and precious things; who (composes) prose and verse which are clear, agreeable, sweet, charming, beautiful, excelling by the proper use of words, and adorned; whose beautiful frame owns the most excellent marks and signs, such as auspicious height and dimension, voice, gait, colour, vigour, and strength, who himself has acquired the name of *mahakshatrapa*, who has been wreathed with many garlands at the *svayamvara* [the ceremony of a princess chosing her husband among assembled suitors] of the daughters of kings.

> *Epigraphia Indica* VIII, pp. 36 ff., tr. F. Kielhorn,
> 'Junagadh Rock Inscription of Rudradaman'

The inscription is an early example of what was to become the *prashasti* – eulogy – a style characteristic of royal biographies, not only in its use of Sanskrit but also in its adhering to the description of a conventional *kshatriya* king. The *prashasti* as a literary style was evolving, as can be seen in these inscriptions that eulogize rulers. It is even more apparent in Ashvaghosha's famous biography of the Buddha, the *Buddhacharita*. This style marks the entrenching of monarchy in areas where it had been less familiar and sets the tone for describing the ideal king. As a form of legitimation the *prashasti* could project even chiefs and governors as ideal *kshatriya* rulers, irrespective of their origins.

The compositions of such eulogistic inscriptions were also seminal to the later royal biographies written as part of courtly literature. Comparisons with deities had begun, but not in an excessive manner. The association with divinity became more outspoken, ironically, when the power of the ruler was not so exalted, except in the case of the Kushana title of *daivaputra*. Dynasties of central Asian origin had a choice of investment in local identities and ideologies – Buddhist, Jaina, Bhagavata – and it is of interest to see who chose what. Legitimation was also being sought by grants of land to Buddhist monasteries and to brahmans. This was as yet a marginal activity, but was later to take on a dimension that affected the structure of the political economy.

Satavahanas

In the first century BC the Satavahana dynasty was established in the western Deccan. The Satavahanas were also sometimes called the Andhra dynasty. This led to the assumption that they originated in the Andhra region, the deltas of the Krishna and Godavari Rivers on the east coast, from where they moved westwards up the Godavari River, finally establishing their power in the western Deccan. The break-up of the Mauryan Empire was thought to have assisted in this process. Ashoka specifically mentions the Andhras among the peoples in his domain, and not as a conquered kingdom. The generally held opinion now is that the family originated in the west and later extended its control to the eastern coast, associated with the name Andhra.

The rise of the Satavahanas follows the pattern of the transition from chiefdom to kingdom, with the newly established kings performing Vedic sacrifices as an act of legitimation. Their administration can also be seen as reflecting some continuation from chiefdoms in the designations of administrators. It is thought that they developed political ambitions because they held administrative positions under the Mauryas and, like many others, saw the potentialities of independent kingship on the disintegration of the empire.

The earliest of the Satavahana kings to receive wide recognition was Satakarni, because of his policy of military expansion. He was described as ruling in the west and being the king against whom Kharavela of Kalinga campaigned. He was also said to be the 'Lord of Pratishthana' (modern Paithan in the Deccan), the capital of the Satavahanas. Numismatic evidence suggests that he ruled around 50 BC. His conquests took him north of the Narmada into eastern Malwa, which at the time was being threatened by the Shakas. An inscription at Sanchi in central India refers to him as *Rajan Shri Shatakarni*. This is a surprisingly simple title for an aspirant to kingship over a large domain. His next move was in the southerly direction and, on conquering the Godavari Valley, he felt entitled to call himself 'Lord of the Southern Regions'. Satakarni performed the ritual of a horse sacrifice to put a stamp on his rulership. He also claimed to have destroyed the *khatiyas*, often interpreted as the Khatriaioi peoples mentioned by Ptolemy, but it could also be a reference to the *kshatriya* ruling clans of the oligarchic polities of western and central India. The continuing presence of these polities and their resilience in the face of opposition from monarchical polities has not received the attention it deserves.

The western possessions of the Satavahanas were, however, annexed by the very people whom Satakarni had feared – the Shakas – who were by now powerful in western India, north of the River Narmada. Coins struck by the Shaka satrap, Nahapana, have been found in the Nasik area, which could mean that by the first century AD the Shakas controlled this region. But the Satavahanas appear to have regained their western possessions soon after this, for the coins of Nahapana are often found overstruck by the name Gautamiputra Satakarni, who was responsible for re-establishing Satavahana power in western India. Judging by the references to ports and politics in the *Periplus*, the west coast was becoming a contested area, the contest being aggravated by the trade from Roman Egypt.

Vasishthiputra, the son of Gautamiputra, ruling in the early second century, had the additional name of Shri Pulumavi which led to his being identified with the Siro Polemaios ruling at Baithana (Paithan), mentioned by Ptolemy in his geography of India written in the second century AD. The Deccan was now the connecting link between north and south, not only in terms of politics, but more significantly in trade and in the spread of Buddhism and Jainism. Vasishthiputra states that Gautamiputra had uprooted the Shakas and had destroyed the pride of the *kshatriyas*: that he had stopped the contamination of the four *varnas*, and had furthered the interests of the twice-born. In brahmanical social codes the Shakas were ranked as being of low caste, and the Yavanas as degenerate *kshatriyas*, the same terms being used for the Shakas, Yavanas and Parthians in a royal Satavahana inscription.

In an effort to ease the relations between the Satavahanas and the Shakas, a matrimonial alliance brought together the daughter of Rudradaman and the Satavahana king. It is interesting that the Satavahanas, who boasted of having stopped the contamination of the four *varnas*, were nevertheless anxious to take a bride from a Shaka family. The discrepancy between theory and practice was subordinated to the primacy of political expediency. That this effort at an alliance was not entirely successful is clear from Rudradaman's statement that he twice defeated the Satavahana king in battle, but refrained from annihilating him because of a close relationship. After the death of Rudradaman, the Satavahanas were more successful in their attacks on Shaka territory. Towards the end of the second century the Satavahana domain stretched from western India to the Krishna delta and northern Tamil-nadu, but this extensive domain was not to survive long. The next century saw the weakening of the Satavahanas, with a corresponding increase in the power of local governors claiming independent status.

The Satavahanas refrained from taking imperial titles, perhaps because they recognized that their control over local chiefs and kings was not of a nature to justify such titles. This fact was conceded even in their administrative system, where power was distributed throughout the hierarchy of officials and not concentrated at the centre. Satavahana territory was divided into small provinces, each under civil and military officers (*amatya, mahabhoja, mahasenapati, mahatalavara, maharathi*). Some were permitted to marry into the royal family, suggestive of their being chiefs of the area, presumably in the hope that this would fortify their loyalty to the dynasty. Some were even allowed to mint their own coins. When the Satavahana power collapsed these governors followed the usual pattern of setting themselves up as independent rulers. Administration was left largely in local hands, though subject to the general control of royal officers, with the village remaining the administrative unit. There was some continuity from Mauryan times, as in the use of terms such as *mahamatra* for an officer or *ahara* for an administrative division. This was unchanged while the village was the source of taxes. There might also have been some obligation to provide soldiers in case of a war and this would tie down the village still further. Changes in political relationships were restricted to the higher level among provincial governors and their officers.

Some Satavahana kings use matronymics, which has led to the controversy as to whether this was a method of identifying the ruler more precisely or the influence of a local matrilineal custom. The adoption of caste society in new areas would not have required the discarding of all local practices. Even practices that were alien to the *Dharma-shastras* would have been permitted if they were necessary to local custom. Such texts may not have been quite as authoritative as is thought.

The Abhiras and the Traikutakas of western India made the declining Satavahana power their target. The Vakatakas were the next to dominate the northern Deccan. The Kalachuri-Chedi dynasty asserted control over the northern part of the peninsula. They were among the earlier dynasties to establish an era, in AD 248–49, no doubt as one aspect of staking a claim to power. A number of small kingdoms came alive in the Ganges Plain. Their most important role was to restrain the powers of the north-west from overrunning the plain, but they have left few traces. Some kings have been identified as belonging to the dynasties of the Maghas, Bodhis and Nagas, while others have names ending in the suffix 'mitra', although this does not link them to the Shungas.

Further south in the peninsula the kingdoms of the Shalankayanas, Brihatpalayanas and Ikshvakus arose in about the third–fourth centuries AD. The first two ruled in the west Godavari district and in the Masulipatam area. The Ikshvakus were located further south in the Krishna valley and were doubtless a local clan who took a lineage name from the Suryavamsha, the solar line, on coming to power. They built the magnificent city of Nagarjunakonda and are also remembered for their gender division of patronage: the kings performed Vedic sacrifices, while the women of the royal family were generous donors to the Buddhist Sangha. The two kinds of patronage would have had different functions. Setting apart the belief in either or both religions, the Vedic rituals were new to the area and were performed to claim legitimation as kings superseding earlier chiefships, whereas the Buddhist Sangha had a wide network that could perhaps be a more effective support to its royal patrons. The adoption of Vedic rituals sharply separated the chiefly families from the clansmen and others in an erstwhile clan society. On the conversion of the first generation to *kshatriya* status, other chiefs, such as the *mahatalavara*, also claimed *gotra* identity.

South India

Towards the end of the first millennium BC south India moved from pre-history into history, and literary records reflecting contemporary events are available. Ashoka in his inscriptions refers to the peoples of south India as the Cholas, Cheras, Pandyas and Satiyaputras – the crucible of the culture of Tamilakam – called thus from the predominant language of the Dravidian group at the time, Tamil. The use of the suffix *putra* in some of these names would suggest a system of clans and chiefs. The first three chiefdoms became almost generic to societies based on clans and lineages in the area and acquired the status of kingdoms in a later period. The Cholas and the Pandyas were located in the eastern area, with a Chola concentration in the lower Kaveri. Korkai and Alagankulam are recently excavated sites, thought to have been exchange centres in Pandyan territory. The first is linked to pearl fisheries and the second developed as a port. Karur on the banks of the Kaveri was an important inland centre, as was Kodumanal, with excavated evidence of working semi-precious stones. Gradually, over time, the Cheras were associated with the western coast. The Satiyaputras, with a more limited history, have been identified through being mentioned in a local inscription in Tamil-nadu.

The history of this area of south India has been reconstructed from diverse sources: megalithic burials, inscriptions in Tamil *brahmi* (where the *brahmi* script was the earliest script used for writing Tamil) and the Tamil poems of the *Shangam* literature. Some comparative data comes from sources in Greek – the *Periplus Maris Erythraei/The Periplus of the Erythrean Sea*, and Ptolemy's *Geography* (in both of which, parts of south India are described) – as well as in Pliny's *Natural History* in Latin. Megalithic burials are scattered across the peninsula as far north as the Vindhyas, with variations of frequency and form. Those of Tamilakam include menhirs, dolmens, urn burials and stone circles, while Kerala also has rock-cut chambers. A stone chamber, constructed from slabs of stone in a pit in the ground, was used for placing relics and grave goods; the chamber was then covered with earth and the small area demarcated by a circle of stones. Terracotta urns and legged sarcophagi also occur in the burials. Rock-cut chambers or passages occur in the hilly areas and urn burials in riverine areas. Societies using these forms of burials were not identical and were culturally heterogeneous. Yet there are some strands in their cultures, such as demarcating burial locations, that link them and make the cultures of the peninsula distinctive.

Burials accompanied by grave goods point not only to respect for ancestors, but also to beliefs in life after death. The burials include complete or partial skeleton remains; some horse and cattle bones; metal objects, largely of iron, but some of copper, gold and silver; ornaments of chank and ivory; beads; charred rice or millet; and Black-and-Red pottery. It is likely that these were the burials of chiefly families.

These burials date to the first millennium BC and, in a few cases, their terminal levels contain artefacts that date to the turn of the millennium, for example Roman Imperial coins. The structures are not arbitrary and required the quarrying of large blocks of stone laid in specific patterns. In all probability these were societies capable of organizing kinsmen as labour. Pottery placed in the burials is mainly the Black-and-Red Ware, which could have been made locally, suggesting craft specialization. Some of the potsherds have graffiti designs scratched on them, a few of which resemble the signs on Harappan seals. Iron artefacts – hoes, horse-trappings and implements – could have been obtained either from itinerant smiths working at the sites or through a network of exchange. A furnace for smelting metal has been excavated in the Deccan, and the site of Kodumanal in the south was a centre for the production of iron artefacts. Beads would also have been part of such an exchange. If these objects were not produced locally by craftsmen the networks of exchange must have been extensive.

Despite the diversity in burial forms, grave goods tend to be fairly uniform. Few settlement sites have been found in the vicinity of the burials, one theory being that this was due to the nomadic lifestyle of the society, but this explanation seems inadequate. Agricultural implements, such as hoes, could have been used either in shifting cultivation or in settled agriculture. However, a burial site is sacred and needs to be tended, so it is unlikely that a group identified with such a site would wander far from it. Memorial menhirs, constituting what is called a *sarna* among certain central Indian tribes today, frequently form the focus of community and religious activities, as a symbol of identity.

Other than the evidence of the megaliths, the earliest reasonably accurate sources for the history of this region are the short dedicatory inscriptions, dating to the period from about the second century BC to the mid-first millennium AD. The dedication is often a votive inscription to record the donation of a cave by a chief, or later by an artisan or merchant or even a Buddhist or Jaina monk. References to brahman settlements begin around the middle of the millennium. The language of the inscriptions is Tamil, although some Prakrit words are included. This provides clues to the process of the adaptation of the Ashokan *brahmi* script that was increasingly used, with emendations for Tamil. It is likely that the influence of Mauryan administration, together with the arrival in the south of itinerant Buddhist and Jaina monks, led to this adaptation. Such label inscriptions also occur as graffiti on potsherds, where names were inscribed on large pots. Where they are votive inscriptions, the later ones mention the occupations of the donors, many of whom were merchants dealing in cloth, toddy, grain and salt, or else craftsmen such as goldsmiths and lapidaries. The locations of the inscriptions provide evidence on links between routes. The inscriptions are invaluable, both in themselves for purposes of establishing chronology, and for providing cross-references to names of chiefs and clans mentioned in the *Shangam* literature, the earliest literary source.

The *Shangam* corpus is a collection of anthologies of poetry on themes popular among these early societies. Tradition has it that many centuries ago three successive assemblies (*shangams*) were held, the last at Madurai, and the compositions of the poets and bards are included in the anthologies of the *Shangam* literature. The latter mainly consist of the earliest stratum, the Ettutogai, and the somewhat later Pattupattu dating to between 200 BC and AD 300. To these are added the Tamil grammar, the *Tolkappiyam*, and the somewhat later didactic text, the *Tirukkural*. The precise dating of these compositions is problematic, which complicates their use as historical sources.

Many of the poems narrate episodes relating to raids and plunder. Some describe the capturing of brides. These are themes common to all heroic literature and there are close parallels with epic literature in other Indian languages. What is particularly remarkable in these poems is the awareness of the environment and the correlation of activities to ecological perceptions. Five ecological zones are listed, referred to as *tinai*, each supporting in turn hunter-gatherers, pastoralists, marauders, fishermen and rice cultivators. Because these were not sharply demarcated there were some overlaps. The gradual spread of agriculture can be observed through the association of wealth with cultivated land.

Among the clans the heads of households were important, but a higher status was given to the *velir*, the chiefs, who might have been associated with the megalithic burials. A still higher status was that of the powerful chiefdoms of the *ventar*, a term used for the Cholas, Cheras and Pandyas. Exchange and the redistribution of produce would have interlocked the three levels. Some elements are similar to the earlier *janapadas* of the north, many of which retained a *gana-sangha* polity, although others evolved into kingdoms. The change from chiefdoms to kingdoms takes place in the subsequent period.

The evolving of kingdoms may have been slower because the minimal craftsmanship did not require a concentration of craftsmen in towns, therefore the demand for agricultural produce to sustain such groups was limited. This in turn could have been related to items of exchange, probably raw materials and the produce from horticulture, with the exchange being carried out by itinerant traders. Initially, the major item bringing in wealth was pepper, a horticultural product intended for exchange. The exchange of pepper for items brought by the Roman trade – gold and silver coins, coral and wine – first took place in centres that only gradually developed into commercial towns. The cultivation of rice was sufficient for the society of the chiefdoms and the motivation to extend this cultivation is not apparent. Iron technology in the megalithic settlements was not the marker of full-fledged sedentary peasant farming, as has been argued for north India. Neither was the iron ploughshare necessary for a substantially increased yield, given that the lighter soil conditions of much of the south were different from the Ganges Plain. In this situation, the initial thrust towards urbanization and the formation of states may have resulted from the increasing demands of trade. The emergence of kingdoms was a gradual process.

As in all heroic societies, the poet or bard was held in high esteem even if his authority was not tangible. He composed and communicated the poems in praise of the hero, thus bestowing on him fame and immortality. Depending on the wealth of his patron his reward could be anything from a meal to a golden lotus. Gift-giving was taken for granted in such societies and the economy was tied into kinship. Lesser kinsmen provided for the chiefs who carried out raids, and the booty from these was distributed to the kinsmen as reward. The use of non-kin labour is again a later development. Where labour is regulated by kinship, customary practices tend to be observed. On the other hand, non-kin labour, the source of which is frequently coercion based on enslavement or impoverishment, is more impersonal. The *Shangam* poems refer to various occupations, but not directly to the social ordering of *varna*.

The settlement of the chief as the hub of the redistribution of wealth would gradually grow into an administrative centre and this, together with the coming of trade, prepared it for a move towards urbanism, as was the case in Uraiyur, Madurai and Karur. Items of daily necessity, such as salt and paddy, would have been available at more local levels and subject to barter. The shift to luxuries, as with the Roman trade, where pepper, semi-precious stones (particularly beryl) and textiles were exchanged for gold and silver coins, wine and coral, could take place at port settlements where the traders gathered: hence the importance of Muziris, Arikamedu and Puhar (Kaveripattinam). Puhar was later to become the focus of trade from many directions.

The Roman conquest of Egypt linked Alexandria to Rome and this probably spurred Egyptian interest into exploration of the Arabian Sea, their former interest having been hesitant. The range of ports increased from those linked to the Indus delta, and began to include ports further south. By the time that the Yavana traders became active in south India, at the turn of the Christian era, the votive inscriptions mention various craft specialists and merchants such as those handling gold, semi-precious stones, textiles, iron and suchlike. This would have marked a change in the chiefdoms.

There was frequent conflict between the Cheras, Cholas and Pandyas, which gave ample scope for compositions on war and love by the poets. Some chiefs are even said to have participated in the battle at Kurukshetra, described in the *Mahabharata*, an obvious attempt to give them antiquity and underline their claims to the status of heroes. The Tamils, under Elara, attacked and occupied a part of northern Sri Lanka, but only for a short while. They were expelled by King Dutthugamini, which has made of the latter something of a Sinhala hero in later times. Pottery pieces with graffiti in Sinhala *brahmi*, surfacing at subcontinental coastal sites, point to early contacts. The Chera chief, Neduncheral Adan, is said to have conquered all the land as far as the Himalaya, clearly a poetic conceit. He is also said to have defeated a Yavana fleet, which may have been an attack on Roman trading ships since Yavana initially referred to those coming with the maritime trade from the west. Among the early Chola heroes Karikala, the 'man with the charred leg', is credited with having fought and defeated the combined forces of the Pandyas, the Cheras and eleven minor chieftains.

For the far south, this was the period of transition from chiefdoms to kingdoms, with the formation of states. The catalysts in this region were not the same as those of the Ganges Plain. There is little evidence of the clearing of forests for cultivation although the cultivation of wet rice associated with the megalithic settlements would have provided some surplus. The use of iron extends over a long period yet it does not seem to have been a crucial factor in the change to urbanism. The ending of the chiefdoms is attributed to hostilities with the Kalabhras, who had upset the existing system. But other changes may have been more effective.

Migrants such as Buddhist and Jaina monks used the avenues opened by Mauryan administration. Somewhat later, further pointers to trade and the introduction of new agricultural settlements are provided by the brahman settlers, who probably came from the Deccan. The monks would have sought the patronage of the chiefs to establish monasteries, and later the patronage of merchants and wealthy craftsmen when towns were established. Some megalithic networks of exchange were doubtless extended by involvement in the trade with the eastern Mediterranean, which stimulated the accumulation of wealth. There were many likely reasons for change: the mutation of barter into trade; or clan-based agriculture becoming peasant cultivation, which was taxed; the use of non-kin labour organized by the chiefs; and the chiefs acquiring wealth through means other than raids.

The establishment of brahman settlements in the south, probably coinciding with the rise of kingdoms, gradually introduced Sanskrit into the local language. But it also meant that Sanskrit speakers had to learn Tamil and use it professionally, which some did. That it was a two-way process is seldom commented upon, yet this is central to analysing acculturation. More was involved than language change and the incorporation of deities and rituals, and it should therefore be seen as an ongoing process, similar to that occurring in many other parts of the subcontinent.

Networks of Routes and Trading Centres

The subcontinent presents a mosaic of political identities during this period. Each mosaic varies in size. Some are small but the patterns of others give an impression of large states, however loosely they might have been pulled together. The pattern is further variegated by the inclusion of distinct kinds of political systems – kingdoms, oligarchies and chiefships. It is therefore rather difficult to make historical generalizations about the subcontinent as a whole. But the one feature that threaded its way through all this variation was exchange and trade. Again this was not of a uniform pattern, but nevertheless it is striking how activities and political identities in many parts of the subcontinent were involved. This was done through the evolving of trading centres of various kinds, linked by far-reaching routes.

Earlier, items had been manufactured close to the sources of raw material or where a tradition of a particular craft existed, and artisans would gather there from surrounding areas. Now there was a greater dispersal of crafts-men, with many gathering in centres where there were markets. The proxim-ity of sources or of distribution possibilities often determined the location of smaller exchange centres, whereas the larger markets were in towns. The dispersal was also occasioned by the raw material having to be transported long distances. The spinning and weaving of cotton and silk involved various regional techniques. It was said that cotton had to be as fine as the slough of a snake, so that the yarn could not be seen. The use of the cotton carder's bow – an implement which is still in use in many places – improved the quality of cotton. Iron was available in mines scattered in various places, or from the iron-bearing soils of some areas. Copper was mined in Rajasthan, the Deccan and the foothills of the Himalaya. Semi-precious stones were available in many hilly and forested regions of the peninsula. The Himalayan slopes provided the much-used musk and saffron. The Salt Range of the Punjab remained the major source of salt. South India provided spices, gold, precious stones and pearls, together with sandalwood and ebony.

Numerous routes now traversed the subcontinent, some continuing further into central and western Asia. The political control of the Shakas and Kushanas linked central Asia to India. Once the connections had been made trade would continue, provided there were goods to exchange. Chinese traders imported fur and horses, and the horse trade was also of interest to Indian traders. The decline of the Kushanas was contemporary with the decrease in Roman commercial interests in central Asia. This affected com-mercial interests in north-western India, but not for an extensive period. Elsewhere, for example along the coasts of the peninsula, the trade with the eastern Mediterranean flourished, the eastern trade with south-east Asia becoming more profitable.

Routes tended to follow the highways and the river valleys. Rivers were not bridged, but ferries were common. Travel was restricted to the dry summers and winters, the rainy season being a period of rest. Caravans were large, and often several banded together for greater safety. Oxen and mules were the caravan animals, although in the desert camels were used. More nimble-footed asses were the pack animal in rough hill terrain. Kauti-lya advised that in the south roads running through the mining areas should be taken, as these traversed the heavily populated regions and were therefore safer than the more isolated routes. Mining activities seem to have expanded, especially the mining of gold and semi-precious stones. Buddhist sources refer to long-distance routes being regularly frequented, such as the north to south-west route from Shravasti to Pratishthana, and those that followed the river valleys of the north. Deserts tended to be avoided where possible except for short distances.

Coastal shipping was common, water routes being many times cheaper than land routes. But the former were not without drawbacks. There is an interesting passage in the *Arthashastra* comparing the advantages of land and water routes. At one point it says that although sea travel is cheaper the danger of pirates and the cost of losing ships to them makes it expensive. Pirates, throughout history, were to be the bane of coastal areas involved in maritime trade, and were no less of a nuisance than brigands on land. A coastal route is obviously safer than a mid-ocean route and it also affords greater opportunities for local trade. But where profits were guaranteed and time was of the essence, mid-ocean routes were faster. Goods were transported by light coastal vessels, larger ships constructed from single logs tied together, and yet larger ones for long-distance voyages to the Red Sea or to south-east Asia. According to Pliny, the largest Indian ship was 75 tons but other sources estimate ships that could hold up to 700 passengers.

Among ports, Barbaricum on the Indus Delta served as a port for the north-west, but the silting up of the estuary led to a relocating of its ports and its eventual decline. Its hinterland went as far north as Gandhara. Bhrigukachchha/Bharukachchha or Barygaza in Greek sources, the modern Bharuch, continued to be a major port for the western sea trade, as in earlier centuries, with its hinterland reaching the Ganges Plain. Ships arriving at Bhrigukachchha were conducted to their berths by pilot boats. At least one *Jataka* story refers to communication with Baveru (Babylon). The Gulf of Cambay remained the destination for much shipping from the Arabian Gulf, even up to recent times. But a large amount of trade was handled by other ports further down the western coast, such as Sopara and Kalyana, serving the western Deccan, and Muziris, linked to the centres in the south. Ports along the east coast were initially close to river estuaries, with the largest being in the Ganges Delta, for example, Tamralipti/Tamluk. The latter had access to the river trade along the Ganges, as well as the trade routes coming from the north-west through the Ganges Plain. Sherds with *kharoshthi* inscriptions which surface at sites in the Ganges Delta are an indication of these connections, as well as those with graffiti in Sinhala *brahmi*, found both here and as far afield as the island of Bali.

The Mauryas had built a Royal Highway from Taxila to Pataliputra, a road that was almost continuously rebuilt in some approximation to the original during the period of Sher Shah, the Mughals and the British. The

British referred to it as the Grand Trunk Road and its current revival is in the National Highway No. 1. Pataliputra was connected by both road and river with Tamluk, which was also linked by sea to Sri Lanka and Myanmar. Routes to the south developed rapidly in post-Mauryan times due to intensified trade demands. Land routes followed river valleys where possible, the elevations in the Deccan plateau discouraging direct north–south communication, but allowing for some east–west routes along valleys such as those of the Godavari and the Krishna. As with the Ganges Plain, the plateau was thickly wooded and therefore unsafe compared with the clearings and settlements along the valleys.

Nevertheless the Deccan was a hive of market centres, production centres and Buddhist monasteries at places such as Ter, Bhokardan, Karad, Kondapur, Dharanikota and Amaravati, not to mention the more northerly centres in Vidarbha and the north-western Deccan. Ujjain was linked via Bhokardan, Kotalingala, Dhulikatta and Peddabunkur to Amaravati, some of which had megaliths or *stupas* or were fortified settlements. Buddhist sites were sometimes close to megalithic sites. The arrival of Buddhist monks in these areas would have required the support of settlements that could provide alms. The sanctity of a megalithic burial site would bestow sanctity on a *stupa* as well – both being essentially burials or symbolic of burials, even if of a different kind. Another route linked Bhrigukachchha, Nasik, Kondapur, Nagarjunakonda and Amaravati. The archaeology of such sites suggests that they were not isolated staging-points along a route but had connections with cultivators, pastoralists and hunter-gatherers in the neighbourhood. This encouraged their function as markets.

Gaps and breaks in mountains were always utilized, as in the peninsula where a major line of communication was the route from the Malabar coast on the west, through the Palghat Gap, along the Kaveri Valley to the east-coast settlements, traversing sites such as Kodumanal and Karur, before arriving at Arikamedu, Korkai or Alagankulam. Sites on the east coast had contact with settlements in Sri Lanka. Coastal routes developed faster and became the basis of north–south links along each coast, sometimes preferred over land routes. It was earlier thought that the cargo from Roman ships was offloaded at the western ports to be transported overland to the east coast, where places such as Arikamedu became trading stations. Incoming cargo was received for further distribution and exports were specially packed for transmission to Red Sea ports. It is now thought that perhaps ships sailed to the ports of the east coast despite the dangers of the seas between south India and Sri Lanka.

Routes within India were actively used, and this activity increased through contacts with more distant places in west and central Asia that were linked to the Hellenistic world. In the north the most widely used highway westwards was from Taxila to Begram, where roads branched off in various directions. The northern route was via Bactria, the Oxus, the Caspian Sea and the Caucasus to the Black Sea. A more southerly route went from Kandahar and Herat to Ecbatana, after which it was linked to the ports on the eastern Mediterranean. Another important highway connected Kandahar with Persepolis and Susa. These routes brought a vast variety of goods to towns such as Begram, where the merchandise included delicately carved ivory from India and Chinese silk. Margiana, adjoining Bactria, was a transit point for silk coming from the east that was intended for the Mediterranean. Not unexpectedly, it has a number of Buddhist monasteries. Gandhara also became a nodal point for overland trade tapping the Silk Route and the eastern Byzantine trading centres. Its links to the Ganges Plain extended its hinterland to the delta. Gandhara was an old hand at surviving empires – that of the Achaemenids and the Mauryans, and even as part of the many diverse kingdoms of the north-west – yet it retained its cultural presence. Its array of items included some from India such as pepper, textiles of various kinds, metals, rhinoceroses and elephants, and some such as tortoise-shell from the west.

Although activity in central Asia was politically directed by the raids and migrations of the nomads, this was paralleled in the historically more significant emergence of the Silk Route and the trade that it carried. The Taklamakan desert was ringed round with oases which became stagingpoints on the route. From Loyang and Chang'an in China the route came to Dunhuang, where it bifurcated: the northern route went through Turfan, Qarashahr, Kucha to Kashgar; and the southern route through Niya and Khotan to Kashgar. From Kashgar it went to the town of Bactra/Balkh and from there either to Iran and the eastern Mediterranean or southwards to India.

This was not a single linear route for it incorporated a number of branches that led off from oasis towns. The politics of the Silk Route were determined by those who controlled its various segments. The oases were the places where animals for the caravans could be replaced or replenished, and armed escorts recruited. The roads were rough, traversing mountains and deserts, and travelling in the area involved having to face bandits as well as severe climatic conditions.

Indian traders were establishing trading stations and merchant colonies in places such as Kashgar, Yarkand, Khotan, Miran, Kuchi, Qarashahr and Turfan, remote regions which were soon to be opened up not only by Indian merchants but also by Buddhist missionaries. The attraction of profits kept the traders going, while the propagation of Buddhism galvanized the monks. As a result of this activity in central Asia communication with China further improved. In a sense Kushana rule was a link between India and China, and Buddhist missionary activities made the connections even closer. Traders from Roman territories occasionally ventured as far as the Gobi Desert, but Indian traders were quick to see the advantage of being middlemen in a luxury trade between the Chinese and the centres of the eastern Mediterranean and Byzantium.

Because of the Roman conflict with the Parthians, Chinese merchandise was sometimes diverted to Taxila and Bhrigukachchha, thus adding to the prosperity of north-western India. Overland trade with the Yavanas and central Asia went through the mountain passes of the north, with the cities involved in this trade, such as Taxila or Ai-Khanoum, acquiring enormous wealth, as is evident from the high standard of living revealed by their excavation.

A southerly route to west Asia went through the Persian Gulf to Seleucia, with ships travelling up the coast towards Babylon and the Tigris-Euphrates Delta. The inland towns of Palmyra in Syria and Petra in Jordan linked the west Asian routes with the ports of the eastern Mediterranean. Alternatively ships could cross the Arabian Sea to Aden or to Dioscurides – the island of Socotra – and from there the voyage was continued up the Red Sea. Indian vessels brought rice, wheat and textiles to Socotra and carried back tortoise-shell, among other items. There appears to have been an embargo on their going to the Red Sea ports. Goods brought back from India by Alexandrian sea-captains were offloaded at ports on the Egyptian side of the Red Sea, such as Berenice or Myos Hormus, then sent overland to the Nile where they were taken downstream to Alexandria, which was an entrepôt of the Mediterranean world.

The southern areas of Arabia boasted of agricultural wealth due to careful irrigation, as well as gaining an income from trade. The Indian merchandise was copper, sandalwood, teak and ebony, and exports to India included pearls, dyes, wine, dates, gold and specially trained slaves. Some of these ports may well have been used prior to this period. On the Indian side Barbaricum was much frequented, importing linen, topaz, coral, storax (a fragrant gum resin used for incense), frankincense, glass, silver, gold-plate and wine; and exporting a variety of spices, turquoise, lapis-lazuli, muslin, silk yarn and indigo. The Barygaza of Greek sources – Bhrigukachchha – was among the largest entrepôts on the western coast and handled the bulk of the maritime trade with west Asia. It imported an assortment of cargo, including wine, tin, lead, coral, topaz, gauze, storax, sweet clover, glass, realgar (red arsenic), antimony, medicinal ointments and gold and silver coin. Presents received by local rulers included gold and silver trinkets, singing boys, maidens, wines and textiles of a superior quality. Exports from Barygaza consisted of the usual variety of spices, spikenard, mala-bathrum (used in preparing ointments), diamonds, sapphires and precious stones. It appears from these items that there was a regular exchange of medical information.

The coastal route from India to western Asia was tedious and was retained for a looping trade in essential commodities. Mid-ocean routes across the Arabian Sea were facilitated by the use of the monsoon winds that blew from the south-west across the Arabian Sea in summer. These winds made mid-ocean travelling speedier than the coastal route. The Arabs were prob-ably the first to use the winds for this purpose. In the mid-first century BC other traders from the Mediterranean world realized their usefulness. Greek sources mention that the discovery of Hippalus introduced a radical change in navigation as ships could use the monsoon winds for a mid-ocean crossing. Hippalus was thought to be the person who discovered the winds, but it is now being suggested that Hippalus was actually the name given to the wind. Ships sailing from the southern end of the Red Sea would wait for the south-west monsoon to pass its peak before they set sail, using the now less ferocious wind. The returning north-east monsoon from across India in the winter would bring the ships back. The use of the winds for navigation may have made it necessary for seamen and traders from Egypt to stay a short while on the Indian coast before returning to their Red Sea ports, increasing contact between local Indians and the visiting Yavanas.

It was once argued that the initiative for the Roman trade with India came from the west and that this continued. At the time when the trade was first noticed the sources referring to it were in Greek and Latin, which gave the impression of an overly major participation by the Roman Empire. Since then the economic map of peninsular India, particularly the evidence on trade, has been filled in. The earlier statement has now been replaced by evidence of a substantial Indian participation. Given the pre-existing exchange networks in the peninsula, trade with west Asia and Egypt would not have been a radical innovation. Potsherds with the names of Indians inscribed on them, some in Tamil *brahmi* and some in Prakrit, have been found in recent excavations of the ports on the Red Sea, providing evidence of their activity in the trade. The discovery of hoards of Roman Imperial coins, the evidence of Indian products and their exchange, and of Yavana donors at some of the Buddhist sites in the Deccan, all go towards underlining a qualitative difference in the Indian presence in this trade. The centres and peripheries of trading circuits are not permanent. If initially the thrust towards an eastward trade came from the markets of Alexandria, the Indian networks were not slow to take advantage of these interests and control the Indian side of the trade.

A Greek maritime geography of the mid-first century AD, the *Periplus*, is a compendium of ports and routes along the Red Sea and the Indian coast, their hinterlands and the commodities exchanged in trade. There is some indirect reference to political conditions as well. Of the items traded, textiles, pepper, semi-precious stones and ivory were exchanged in the peninsula for high-value Roman coins, as the main import, together with coral and wine. Sherds of amphorae bases with wine sedimentation have been found in excavations. Elsewhere, the discovery of a distilling mechanism points to the consumption of wine and alcohol by both the local people and the vistors. Early Tamil literature describes Yavana ships arriving with their cargoes at ports such as Muziris, and is enthusiastic about the quality of the wine that they bring, not to mention the profitable exchange of the local black pepper for Roman gold coin.

Inland in the Deccan there were not only the capitals of kingdoms but also centres of production involved in this trade, such as Ter, Nevasa, Bhokardan, Kondapur, Sattanikota and Sannathi. Some, such as Pauni, Paunar and Sannathi, were also the location of Buddhist monasteries. The eastern Deccan saw the growth of trade, together with the establishing of Buddhist centres at Thotlakonda, Bhattiprolu, Dharanikota, Amaravati and Nagarjunakonda, among others. The towns along the east coast were linked to places further inland, such as Kondapur and Peddabankur, which were in turn linked to routes going to northern and western India. Some centres were situated in the proximity of gold-mining areas further along the Krishna Valley. These were important foci for Buddhist and Jaina monks migrating south from the cities of the Ganges Plain and central India.

Muchiri or Muziris, located perhaps in the vicinity of Kodangallur/Cranganore (near Kochi), was linked to the trade in pepper, spices and beryl. A recently discovered Greek papyrus of the second century AD, documents a contract involving an Alexandrian merchant importer and a financier that concerns cargoes, especially of pepper and spices from Muziris, which provides evidence of the large volume of this trade. References to the rich pepper trade with Malabar continue for centuries, up to the time of the Portuguese. Locations of coin hoards suggest a link from Muziris via the Palghat Gap – tapping the beryl mines – and along the Kaveri Valley to the east coast.

The route in the *Periplus* proceeds round the southern tip of the peninsula and up the eastern coast, where of all the ports mentioned there is fairly detailed knowledge of one – Arikamedu (known to the *Periplus* as Padouke). Excavations at this site have uncovered a large settlement that provides evidence of contact with traders from the eastern Mediterranean. Arikamedu was more than just a port of call in south-eastern India: not only were locally available goods shipped from here, but certain kinds of textiles are thought to have been locally manufactured, presumably to Roman specification, and shipped west to eventually reach Rome. Judging from the characteristic Roman pottery, such as *terra sigillata*, Arretine ware and amphorae sherds, as well as beads, glass and terracotta finds, it would seem that the settlement was active from at least the first century BC. It was initially tied into the local exchange networks and later into the more extensive maritime trade. A black pottery with a rouletted design became popular and its imitations had a wide distribution. Amphorae sherds have provided evidence not only of the import of wine in some quantity but of other items more specific to Yavana consumption, such as olive oil and garum (a fish sauce). Such sherds often carry the stamp of Mediterranean manufacturers and the wine seems to have been that from southern Italy and the Greek islands. Coastal sites such as Korkai and Alangankulam, and the inland site of Kodumanal, suggest similar contacts.

Imitations were made of Roman objects in bronze and clay. Bronze statuettes, such as the ones of Neptune and Poseidon, have been found in excavations in the peninsula. They would tend to authenticate the argument that Yavana traders were resident in India, although such objects could also be souvenirs brought back by Indian traders. Clay bullae with impressions of Roman coins are commonly found. In recent years a few coins have surfaced that have been labelled as Shangam Pandya, Chera and Chola coins, carrying symbols possibly derived from punch-marked coins. But more striking is the attempt on some to imitate the portraiture of Roman coins with substandard portraits of local rulers. The minting of these points to a more sophisticated form of exchange than simple barter.

Products that were in demand in Roman markets were exchanged mainly for Roman coins. The frequency of hoards of such coins in the Deccan and south India point to its being a trade of some substance. Most of the coins are of the earlier Roman Emperors, such as Augustus and Tiberius, the debased coins of Nero not being thought worthy of hoarding. Some coins are struck with a bar or nicked, which perhaps prevented their being put into circulation. The Roman historian Pliny complained of the trade with the east being a serious drain on the income of Rome, to the extent of 550 million sesterces each year, of which at least a fifth went to India. Imports from India were largely luxury articles – spices, jewels, textiles, ivories and animals (apes, parrots and peacocks) for the amusement of the Roman patrician and his family. It was therefore thought that the balance of trade was in favour of India. But recently it has been argued that even if Pliny's figure is correct, customs dues and taxes on the imports from the east into Roman Egypt were high enough to compensate for the drain of money in the initial outlay for this trade. It has also been argued that Tiberius and later Pliny, both of whom complained about the drain of Roman wealth to India, may have been more concerned about making a moral judgement on Roman patrician society with its display of wealth, and therefore used the trade to underline the point. Nevertheless, it was a profitable trade for the merchants and chiefs of the Indian peninsula. The profits from pepper were to be unceasing, even in later times, as it was used in Europe both as a preservative and in medicines. There is greater interest now in the varying nature of contacts between Indian and Yavana merchants, as well as in the existing networks of exchange in India and how these were drawn into the larger trade. The discussion of centres and peripheries in trading networks with their changing status provides yet another dimension to the understanding of this trade.

Yavana merchants from the eastern Mediterranean traded in both the Satavahana kingdom and further south, their presence being registered in the votive inscriptions at Buddhist centres in the Deccan. Traders from the west were not Romans from Rome, but were Egyptian Jews and Greeks from Alexandria and the eastern Mediterranean, as well as some from north Africa – all part of the Roman Empire. These connections may have fostered the legend in later centuries of the coming of St Thomas, the disciple of Christ, to India. Some may also have been descendants of the Indo-Greeks and Shakas of the north-west.

The tapping of south-east Asia by Indian traders for items of exchange was in part spurred by the Roman trade. The items sought were largely spices, especially those not easily available in India. Although the easiest route was by sea the risks were great, evidenced by stories found in anthologies of tales relating to the adventures of merchants in Suvarnadvipa, the Golden Isles (Java, Sumatra and Bali). But the immense profits on the spices sold to the Alexandrian merchants compensated for the hazards, and when the Roman trade took a downward turn the Indian trade with south-east Asia expanded, becoming independent of the western connection.

South-east Asian contacts with China and India date to the early centuries AD. Items such as an ivory comb, carnelian ring stones and a seal with *brahmi* letters all suggest the presence of Indian merchants. The presence was even stronger in places closer to India such as Shrikshetra (near Prome), in Myanmar, and at ports such as Oc-eo, situated between India and China near the Gulf of Siam. Recent excavations in south-east Asia indicate impressive pre-existing cultures with which Indian traders would have interacted. At Ban Chiang, there is evidence of the cultivation of rice with livestock such as water buffalo supplementing agriculture, while in some places there are mortuary complexes with burial urns and, in others, mega-liths. The Dong Son culture of decorated bronze drums and other bronze artefacts points to sophisticated chalcolithic societies. The distribution of small settlements around a large one has been interpreted as the existence of chiefdoms, with some degree of exchange prevailing among them. This would have encouraged the initial exchange with visiting traders and poss-ibly also drew upon inland networks, at least in mainland south-east Asia. The pattern has some similarities with that of south India, with exchange evolving into trade and incipient urbanism.

Perhaps the most striking feature of all these connections is that there is no single strand responsible for the creation of cultures. Each is dependent on another and the other can spread great distances. Nor can any of these cultures be isolated since the connectivity is essential to what they are. The connotation of the region also gets broadened with all this activity. Where one speaks of north-western India, there is inevitably the inclusion of the horizon towards Afghanistan and central Asia. The two coastal areas to the west and the east of the peninsula were also beginning to actively participate in trade with the Mediterranean and south-eastern Asia. It could be said that India, both because of its geographical position and because of its economic enterprise, participated effectively in what was probably viewed in those times as almost a global trade of the early first millennium AD.

8

The Rise of the Mercantile Community

c. 200 BC – AD 300

Economies of Exchange

The dynasties of this period had a relatively quick turnover, yet beneath these changes the most stable factor was trade. Through all the political vicissitudes of the Shungas, Kanvas, Indo-Greeks, Shakas, Kushanas, Satavahanas, Ikshvakus, Cheras, Cholas and Pandyas there was the increasing visibility of the merchant and the artisan, although with regional variations in its presence. Its associations range across kings, chiefs and monastic centres, whose roles differ from place to place. Perhaps the most striking feature of this period is the predominance of urban culture that brought better living conditions in the towns.

The Mauryan administration had opened up the subcontinent by building roads and attempting to make contact with relatively remote areas. The later annexation of north-western India by non-local rulers, with the ensuing migrations of people, was advantageous to the merchant, who ventured into places as yet untapped. The Indo-Greek kings strengthened the contact with western Asia and the eastern Mediterranean which had started in the Mauryan period. The Shakas, Parthians and Kushanas brought central Asia into the orbit of the Indian merchant, which in turn encouraged commerce with China. The Roman demand for spices, textiles, semi-precious stones and other luxuries led Yavana traders from the eastern Mediterranean to southern and western India, and also motivated Indian traders to visit south-east Asia as entrepreneurs. The prosperity of the merchant community is evident from their donations to religious institutions, and from descriptions of wealthy merchants in the literature of the time. Not surprisingly, the religions supported by the merchants, pre-eminently Buddhism and Jainism, saw their heyday during these centuries. However, this is not to suggest that economic activity was limited to trade, or that agriculture had decreased; the latter continued to yield revenue. But the more dramatic rise was in mercantile activity.

Agricultural enterprise was not only ongoing in areas already under cultivation, but more forest and wasteland was being ploughed. Even stray statements such as that in the *Dharma-shastra* of Manu, that the land belongs to him who first cultivates it, are pointers to this. Such a comment also reflects on the question of ownership that became important with an increase in privately owned lands. Tenures varied with agricultural practices and needs, so there is a frequent mention of taxes. *Gahapatis*, generally the larger landowners, are met with in votive inscriptions as donors to the Sangha. Donations can be the context to transactions involving land. Land was granted to Buddhist monasteries and to brahmans, although as yet on a relatively small scale. It is a hint of what was to come. However, state-supervised agriculture as suggested in the *Arthashastra* finds less reflection in the sources, which tend to reiterate the private ownership of land. Even if the more impressive finds from archaeology relate to trade, agriculture was obviously a substantial source of revenue.

The importance of land revenue is also partly determined by the varieties of irrigation systems. States continued to maintain earlier canals and dams: the dam on the Sudarshana lake was repaired; and the canal built by the Nandas in Kalinga is noteworthy. There is a suggestion that Karikala dredged part of the Kaveri River to provide irrigation. Among the more impressive hydraulic water-lifts was one excavated at Sringaverapura, near Allahabad. This may not have been used for irrigation, but the technology of using varying water levels to draw water may have derived from irrigation systems or even influenced them. Another method of drawing water was the wheel attached to a well, but initially without a gearing mechanism. Professionals involved in the making of 'water machines' were presumably developing small irrigation works, among other things. Nevertheless, much of the irrigation remained in the hands of wealthy landowners or was constructed through the joint effort of the village. Tanks, wells and embankments are referred to, with mention made of wells and tanks being gifted to the Buddhist monastic community by individual donors.

As a resource, therefore, land continued to be used in various ways, most of which were familiar from the past although some were innovatory. Exchange and trade, however, were activities that developed in many areas to provide revenue from new resources. Areas where there was a potential for trade made this their predominant economy. Variant forms of exchange were linked to specific kinds of societies. Older forms of barter and direct exchange often persisted, but were accompanied by innovations related to commercial exchange. Gift-exchange, involving status rather than profit, was prevalent in societies where clan chiefs were still dominant and where reciprocity was the norm, but nevertheless had an economic function as well.

Something material could even be exchanged for something intangible, the latter having ceremonial value. Bolts of silk changed hands among chiefly families in central Asia through a system of gift-exchange, until they finally reached the markets where they were converted into commercial commodities. In the ritual of sacrifice, or in a donation to the Sangha, the gaining of status by the patron of the sacrifice, or merit by the donor, was intangible but the gift made to the priest or to the Sangha was material. Earlier a gift was intended for the performance of a Vedic or other ritual. Now it could be a donation to the Sangha. But the relationship between the donor and the donee remained that of the worshipper and his/her object of worship. An extension of this practice took the form of donations in the names of others, for example one's parents, so that the merit thus acquired was transferred to them.

A more complicated exchange, determined largely by economic considerations, involved systems of redistribution. The germ of this already lay in societies where wealth was acquired through raids, the plunder being brought back for distribution among the clansmen. Even when raids were discontinued, the obtaining of loot remained a motive for going to war. Exchange was a more peaceful way to dispose of surplus while acquiring wealth. If substantial, income from trade could introduce urbanism and a state system. The evolving of the state, with a treasury and public expenditure, was a further form of redistribution. Wealth was gathered at a single point from which it was distributed and, where the state was involved, this often became the treasury of the kingdom. Both forms of exchange can coexist at different social levels in the same time period. They precede trade controlled through markets and are based on supply and demand. The linking of money with markets and a monetary economy are terms perhaps best left to later times, when such features can be gauged more accurately. For early periods the introduction of money and of markets intensified commercial trade and, although earlier forms of exchange were not discontinued, they would have been weakened.

The excavation of many urban centres of that period provide evidence of a rise in the standard of living. The Indo-Greek city of Sirkap at Taxila has been excavated to reveal its urban form, with the acropolis being distinct from the residential city. One can now walk through the streets of the latter, observe its well-demarcated quarters and almost reconstruct the city of that time. Bactria exploited its role as an intermediary of trade routes, and the layout of Bactrian cities was predictable – a fortified citadel for the ruling elite, with a larger residential city adjoining it. Houses, craft centres and monasteries were crowded into the latter, but suburbs were further away. The city of Bactra (modern Balkh) is believed to have had a population of about 100,000. The prominence of craft centres is characteristic of both these cities and others in parts of the subcontinent during this period. Mathura, like Bactra, was at the intersection of migrating groups, of artistic styles and of patronage for religious buildings. Kushana patronage maintained the importance of Mathura, even though it did not exceed Kushana patronage to towns in Gandhara. Mathura's political importance was emphasized by the location of the Kushana royal portrait gallery in its vicinity at Mat.

Production and exchange were facilitated through the institution of the *shreni*. This word has been translated as 'guild', which is its nearest equivalent, but the *shreni* was not identical with the European guild. The *shreni* was more in the nature of a group of professionals, merchants or artisans who worked in association, although it had some characteristics similar to the guild. Given this caveat, *shreni* can be translated as 'guild'. These organizations enhanced production essential to commerce and became an important factor in urban life. Many artisans joined *shrenis* since it was difficult for individuals to compete with professional organizations, and the *shrenis* also offered status and a degree of security. Buddhist texts such as the *Milinda-panha* and the *Mahavastu* mention seventy-five or more different occupations, not many of which could have been organized as guilds, even if there were that many. If efficiency in production and a profitable sale were the aims, guilds were probably limited to those that produced goods for which there was a commercial demand. When the demand increased some guilds began to employ hired labour and slaves. Such organizations were encouraged by the state as they facilitated collection of revenue on commercial production and sale.

According to the *Arthashastra*, although guilds had to be registered in the locality where they functioned and required permission to change location, this may not have been strictly adhered to. Artisans of any craft could constitute a guild, and those of importance included guilds of potters, metal-workers, weavers, goldsmiths, bead and glass makers, ivory carvers and carpenters. However, this did not preclude private entrepreneurship, and one wealthy potter named Saddalaputta who owned 500 pottery workshops also organized the distribution of his products, with a large number of boats taking the pottery from the workshops to the various ports of the Ganges River system.

The *shrenis* fixed rules of work, as well as the quality of the finished product and its price, in order to safeguard both the artisan and the customer. Prices of manufactured articles depended on their quality or were calculated according to a fixed scale. The behaviour of members was monitored through a court that ensured the customary usage of the guild, the *shreni-dharma*. This was on a par with the customary laws of the *jati* as an occupational group and had to be honoured by the king. Institutions such as the *shreni* and the *jati* had some elements of representative functioning, even if their reference was only to their own group. Sometimes there could be an overlap between the two and the *shreni* took on the functions of a caste. Among these was the possibility of its becoming an endogamous unit for arranging marriages. The *shreni* was presided over by the head, the *jyeshtha*, who would probably have negotiated with other institutions when required. To some extent the functioning of the *shreni* echoes that of the *gana-sanghas*. That the guild also intervened in the private lives of its members is clear from the regulation that, if a married woman wished to join the Buddhist Order as a nun, she had to obtain permission not only from her husband but also from the *shreni* to which he belonged. Recruitment was connected to its association with caste: the children of a particular *jati* tended to follow their father's trade, thus providing the *shreni* with regular numbers. Artisans who took on apprentices could supplement the hereditary recruitment. The threat to the guild came in periods of transition when the occupation followed by a *jati* underwent economic change, or when the demand for a particular product declined.

The goods produced by the artisan, whether individually or through a guild, were bought by merchants – *vanij*, a term that survives in the modern profession of the *bania*. Long-distance transportation of merchandise was organized by the *sarthavahas*, with a number of caravans travelling together for protection against brigands. Associated organizations assisting commercial activities, but less powerful than the guilds, were the *puga, goshthi* and *nigama* – corporations, committees and locations where exchanges were conducted. Towns such as Taxila, Kaushambi and Bhattiprolu are associated with *nigamas*.

Excavations have led to the discovery of a number of seals with the emblems of guilds and corporations. The banners and insignia of the guilds which were carried in procession on festive occasions have been depicted on sculptured panels associated with some Buddhist *stupas*. Insignia were also a means of advertising the guild, as were the donations many guilds made to religious institutions that were recorded as votive inscriptions. Examples of this were the prolific donations of the corn-dealers, and the

gold and silversmiths, towards the sculptured reliefs surrounding the Buddhist *stupas* at Bharhut and Sanchi. The ivory carvers' guild at Vidisha also
worked on some bas-reliefs at Sanchi. Donors at such places were not just
from nearby towns but also came from distant places in the Deccan.

An inscription issued by Shaka royalty in a cave at Nasik, in western
India, records an endowment to the Sangha provided by the interest on a
large sum of money invested with a guild of weavers. The inscription reads:

In the year 42, in the month Vesakha, Ushavadata son of Dinika and son-in-law of
king Nahapana, the Kshaharata Kshatrapa, has bestowed this cave on the Sangha
generally; he has also given a perpetual endowment, three thousand – 3,000 *kahapanas* which, for the members of the Sangha of any sect and any origin dwelling in
this cave, will serve as cloth money and money for outside life; and those *kahapanas*
have been invested in guilds dwelling in Govardhana 2,000 in a weavers guild,
interest one *pratika* (monthly) for the hundred and 1,000 in another weavers guild,
interest 3/4 of a *pratika* (monthly) for the hundred, and those *kahapanas* are not to
be repaid, their interest only to be enjoyed.

Out of them, the two thousand, 2,000 at one *pratika* per cent are the cloth money;
out of them to every one of the twenty monks who keep the *vassa* [the rainy season
when monks remained at the monastery] in my cave, a cloth money of twelve
kahapanas. As to the thousand which has been invested at an interest of 3/4 of a
pratika per cent, out of them the money for *kushana* [a monthly stipend?]. And at
the village of Chikhalapadra in the Kapura district have been given eight thousand
– 8,000 – stems of coconut trees, and all this has been proclaimed and registered at
the town hall, at the record office, according to custom.

Epigraphia Indica, VII, p. 82, tr. E. Senart, 'Nasik Cave Inscriptions',
Inscription No. 12

Such inscriptions provide an indirect comment on the political importance
of guilds. Although guilds were powerful in urban life, it seems their heads
did not seek direct political influence or office, presumably because politics
was regarded as the prerogative of the king – at least in theory. Undoubtedly,
the nexus with royalty did provide a political edge to their activities, but
their political ambitions seem to have remained subdued. A possible explanation for this is that in some cases the royal family appears to have had
financial interests in the guilds. Investments in a commercial enterprise
brought large returns, larger perhaps than the revenue from a piece of land
of comparable value. Royalty invested its money in commercial activities
and therefore had an interest in ensuring the well-being of the guild. Royal
support in a tangible form and the lack of opposition from the king may have

dulled the edge of political ambition among the guild leaders. Furthermore, access to political power on the part of a given guild would require that it first ally itself with other guilds in order to obtain their loyalty, without which no political ambitions could be achieved. Such co-operation may have been effectively prevented by caste rules, such as forbidding eating together – an effective barrier between guilds of different castes. But if such rules were not being observed, the inability to co-operate politically was for other reasons. The endowment created a nexus between royalty, the *shrenis* and the Sangha, and this nexus tended to keep their relations on a relatively even keel. The emergence of the *shreni* was essentially an urban phenomenon and, as a characteristic social institution, it also reflected the increasing significance of urban life.

Inscriptions such as the one above refer to investments in guilds of weavers, potters and suchlike. Clearly, these were occupations that were profitable and socially acceptable, otherwise they would not have attracted investments from the royal family and upper castes. Yet these are also the occupations of those listed as the lower social orders in the normative texts, where the *Dharma-shastras* dismiss them as *shudras*, explaining that some among them are born of *sankirna jatis*, or mixed castes, just a notch above the more polluting groups. They are called mixed castes as they are said to be the progeny of marriages across castes and occupations. These castes are ranked and reference is made to *anuloma*, hypergamy, literally in the direction of the body hair, indicating the father was of a higher caste than the mother, and *pratiloma*, hypogamy, which is the reverse. That the combinations and permutations were different in each text points to its not being taken literally, but being a theory intended to deny status to certain castes. Like much in the *Dharma-shastras* that seeks to explain a social condition, this is a fiction invented to prevent the upward mobility of those ranked as low. By the same token it may provide an oblique indication of an improvement in the status of certain *shudra jatis*.

There is a lack of fit between the vision of the normative texts and social reality. The former can be taken as the social norms endorsed by a small privileged group, but it cannot be taken as a description of the way in which the larger society actually functioned. These disdainful theories of the *Dharma-shastras* may have encouraged groups in so-called low occupations to prefer the social flexibility of Buddhism and the emergent Bhagavata sects. Despite some exaggeration, inscriptional depictions were more realistic, as were those in certain Buddhist texts. There is no uniformly better status for those ranked as *shudras* although a few among them could be reasonably well off, such as the potter-entrepreneur Saddalaputta with his large production and distribution of pots. And in most texts, including the *Dharma-shastras*, some among the *shudras* are described as poor. Judging by references to the impoverished, poverty was no stranger to these early societies.

Another aspect emerging from inscriptions is that the guild could also act as a banker, financier and trustee. Generally, however, these functions were carried out by a different category, that of merchants, the *shreshthins/setthis* or financiers, the designations of which continue to the present in the *sethis* and the *chettiars*. The use of the term *setthi-gahapati* would suggest that families of rich landowners, with surplus wealth to invest in trade, initially provided members to the profession of merchant. Banking was not a full-time occupation and the *setthi* often had other interests as well. As a profession, lending money became more widespread with the greater use of coined metallic money and the extension of the market for trade, since cowri-shells or the barter system were hardly conducive to investment.

Usury was an accepted part of banking and the general rate of interest continued to be between 12 and 15 per cent. Money lent for sea trade often called for a higher rate of interest. An authoritative writer suggested that the rate of interest should vary according to the caste of the person to whom money is lent, with the upper castes paying a smaller rate than the lower. This would have made it more difficult for the lower and economically poorer castes to pay off debts or to finance commercial ventures, and it would be far easier for the upper castes to invest in trade.

The post-Mauryan centuries saw a great spurt in the minting of coins. The kings of the north-west imitated Greek, Roman and Iranian coin-types, while others issued local coins that were superior to the punch-marked coins of the Mauryan period. Currencies minted elsewhere, such as the *denarii* of the Roman Empire, circulated freely. Coinage also allowed the possibility of forward speculation in goods and capital. However, the increasing use of money did not drive out the barter systems, particularly in rural areas where agricultural products, such as paddy, provided the unit of exchange. The diverse use of coins, even along the west coast from Barygaza to Muziris, indicates the variant trading economies, such variations being amply described in the *Periplus*. A large variety of coins were used in towns; these were of gold (*nishka*, *suvarna* and *pala*), silver (*shatamana*), copper (*kakini*) and lead. The most commonly used coin was the *karshapana* or *pana*. With the expansion of commercial enterprise, weights and measures became increasingly detailed and complex.

Roman gold and silver coins found in south India – literally in hoards – are thought to have been used in large number as bullion, or alternatively as high-value currency, given the absence of local gold coins in this area. This may explain the hoarding of gold and silver coins. These were also areas where local currency was marginal, unlike northern and western India. That there was a familiarity with coinage is evident from the presence of punch-marked coins, as well as sparse low-value local coins in imitation of the Roman. Coins of the Roman Republic have been found, but the immensely large numbers are of early Imperial issues that span the turn of the Christian era. The latter were valued for the high quality of their metal content and may have been hoarded as an item of gift-exchange among local chiefs, or as potential capital for further exchange.

There is a comparative paucity of high-value Roman coins in north India, less than a quarter of the number found in the south. This has suggested that in the north the coins were melted and re-issued even though there was metal available for coins. Had this been done on a scale to make it worthwhile, Greek and Latin sources would surely have commented on it, since they refer to the coinage in circulation at various places. The gold coins of the Kushanas followed the Roman weight standard, partly to ensure that they would be used as legal tender in areas familiar with Roman trade. The imitation of particular coins probably had more to do with the continuity of a medium of exchange than with fashion.

Cultural Interactions

Although coin hoards from the Roman maritime trade were more evident in southern India, the impact of Greco-Roman ideas and artefacts was obvious in the north. This was doubtless due to the longer association of north-western India as a neigbour of Hellenistic culture. Exchange of merchandise led inevitably to an exchange of ideas. At one level, words, largely of a technical kind, were borrowed. At another level the aesthetic impact is seen, particularly in Buddhist art. Buddhism may have been more popular with the Hellenistic Greeks because it provided easier access to Indian society than Brahmanism. Coin legends in Greek point to the continued use of the language in addition to Prakrit and Sanskrit. Indian folk-tales and fables travelled westwards and collections such as the *Panchatantra* were subsequently translated into neighbouring languages, appearing in European literature under various guises that perhaps included some versions of Aesop's fables. *Chaturanga*, a game named after the four traditional wings of the Indian army and played by four players, became popular in west Asia and evolved into chess.

One of the enduring results of this contact was the fairly detailed references to India in the various works of the Mediterranean world, such as Diodorus's *Library of History*, Strabo's *Geography*, Arrian's *Indika*, Pliny the Elder's *Natural History*, the *Periplus Maris Erythraei*, and Ptolemy's *Geography*. The first three claimed to be quoting at length from earlier but lost writings on India, such as the *Indica* of Megasthenes. That the supposed quotations from Megasthenes were paraphrases becomes clear from the variations in specific statements from the first three texts. The others were writing afresh. These works began to supersede the accounts associated with Alexander's campaign. India was now visible in the Greco-Roman world not merely as a land of the fabulous, but more realistically as a place with potential for trade and with traditions of knowledge that interested Mediterranean scholars. But despite this the image of its being 'the Other' was continually reinforced. Little attempt was made to correct the errors in the *Indica* of Megasthenes, although there was now far more familiarity with things Indian. The seven divisions of Indian society became axiomatic for these authors.

The most direct and visible interface was in the realm of art, with the emergence of Gandhara art in Afghanistan and north-west India. Gandhara art evolved as a mixture of styles, one of which was the Greco-Roman style of Alexandria, from where sculpture in bronze and stucco travelled along the west Asian trade routes to influence Hellenistic and Indian models nearer home. The emergence of Gandhara art coincided with the introduction of multiple celestial beings and heavens in Buddhist theology, which lent themselves ideally to manifestations in sculpture and painting. The diverse influences affecting Gandhara art suggest that it should not be taken as a uniform style and should be subdivided according to its diversity.

Indian ideas can also be traced in some west Asian belief systems and particularly in the doctrines of the Manichaeans, Gnostics and Neo-Platonists. The last of these had a long and eventful history in Europe as an alternative philosophy to the Judaeo-Christian tradition, and associated some of its ideas with what was believed to be Asian thought and practice. Certain aspects of the life of Christ (the immaculate conception or the temptation by the Devil) are so closely parallel to events in the legends of the life of the Buddha that – despite the archetypal qualities – there can be a suspicion of some indirect borrowing. The observances of the Essenes (to which sect Christ is said to have originally belonged) also point to some knowledge of Indian religious belief and practice. Certain other aspects of Indian practice find parallels in the eastern Mediterranean at this time, among them asceticism (associated with Paul of Alexandria and St Anthony), relic-worship and the use of the rosary.

Connections through embassies were even more direct: the best known of those sent by Indian kingdoms to Rome was the one that sailed from Barygaza in about 25 BC. It included a strange assortment of men and animals – tigers, pheasants, snakes, tortoises, a monk and an armless boy who could shoot arrows with his toes – all regarded as appropriate for the Roman Emperor. It took the mission four years to reach Rome. Such embassies would have reiterated the image of India as the land of the magical and the marvellous.

Communication with the west was not the only exciting possibility, for these centuries also saw the beginnings of Indian contacts with China and the introduction of Indian culture to south-east Asia, all of which commenced through trade. During the second and third centuries BC some goods of Chinese origin were in use in India with names derived from Chinese: for example, *china patta*, Chinese cloth; and *kichaka*, bamboo, which could be related to the Chinese *ki-chok*. When the first Buddhist missionaries arrived in the first century AD to establish themselves at the famous White Horse Monastery at Loyang in China the contact was of a different kind, but the mission was slow to take off. The central Asian oases at Yarkand, Khotan, Kashgar, Tashkend, Turfan, Miran, Kucha, Qarashahr and Dunhuang became useful staging-points when they developed into towns and later also became the sites of monasteries and *stupas*. The embellishment of these required semi-precious stones from India and banners of silk from China, all of which enhanced commerce. Manuscripts, paintings and ritual objects were also brought from India, and for many centuries these monasteries maintained a close and lively interest in the development of Buddhism both in China and in India. A considerable knowledge of the history of northern Buddhism has come from Chinese and central Asian translations of Buddhist texts, and is now increasingly available at these sites. Chinese Buddhists travelled to central Asia to learn about Buddhism, while the more courageous undertook the difficult journey to India, to study the texts at various monasteries.

Among the more valuable sources on Buddhism in recent times is the unravelling of the Buddhist scrolls from Gandhara, now placed in the British Library. These birch-bark rolls that had been packed into earthen pots are being unrolled, read and conserved, a process requiring the most delicate handling and careful study. The texts are composed in the Gandhari version of Prakrit and written in *kharoshthi*, expressive of a strong regional tra-dition. They form an interesting counterpart both to the northern Buddhist texts written in a hybrid Sanskrit and to the Buddhist Canon as recorded by the southern Theravada tradition in Pali. Dating to about the first century AD, they were in the library of a monastery in Gandhara, probably Hadda. The texts are parts of the Buddhist Canon and of some anthologies of stories linked to Buddhism, and are associated with the Dharmaguptaka sect of Buddhism. Although not conforming to the Mahayana school, the Dharmaguptakas accepted some of its teaching, for example anticipating the coming of Maitreya. Packing the scrolls tightly in pots could indicate they were no longer required, perhaps having been copied on to fresh birch-bark, and being stored because such texts could not be thrown away. These were the texts and forms of Buddhism that travelled to central Asia where Gandhari Prakrit was used in Buddhist circles.

Voyages to south-east Asian ports were encouraged by the search for spices. Graffiti in *brahmi* on sherds, carnelian beads and rouletted ware surface in south-east Asia at places accessible to ships from the Bay of Bengal: the Irrawady Delta; the Malay peninsula; and even as far as Oc-eo in the Mekong Delta, and the island of Bali. The prosperity of towns such as Mahasthan and Chandraketugarh near the Ganges Delta, and those of the eastern coast, may have been linked to these new connections. Legends about the origin of kingdoms in south-east Asia often trace the story back to Indian princes and merchants. An Indian brahman, Kaundinya, who is said to have married a Cambodian princess, is remembered as having introduced Indian culture to Cambodia. The story was an attempt to explain cultural practices. The Kalingans who came as traders are said to have settled in the Irrawady Delta of Myanmar. Indian literature narrates the adventures, some weird and fantastic, of Indian travellers in these parts. In local narratives the formation of states in south-east Asia is sometimes linked to the arrival of Indians as traders and as ritual specialists, and there has been much discussion related to identifying the catalyst in this process. The transition was from chiefdoms to states and, perhaps because of the presence of Indians, appropriate Indian practices and beliefs were adapted. The epithet of *suvarna*, gold, with place-names in south-east Asia suggests that the Indian perception of south-east Asia was initially probably linked to profits from trade.

Education, Literature and Systems of Knowledge

Apart from their role in the economy, the guilds provided education, although 'formal' education remained largely in the hands of the brahmans and the monks of the Buddhist and other monasteries. By restricting membership to artisans of a particular craft, the guilds became centres for technical education. Knowledge of mining, metallurgy, weaving, dyeing, carpentry and suchlike would have been maintained by the relevant guild. The spectacular progress achieved in this way is visible even in the minting of coins, or in the near perfection reached in stone-cutting, polishing and carving. Engineering skill in the building of dams and irrigation tanks is evident from their remains. Geometry, which had first been recorded as an aid in the building of altars and sacrificial structures, was later applied to more complex architecture. Building initially followed the constructional methods of wooden buildings, but gradually shifted to stone structures that necessitated new formulations in engineering and architecture. Religious edifices at this stage did not provide much occasion for exploring constructional skill and variation, since the Buddhists contented themselves with tumuli surrounded by gateways and railings, or else caves of a simple kind cut into hillsides. The architecture of free-standing monasteries was an extension of domestic architecture.

Knowledge benefiting from familiarity with developments in other parts of the world was applied to astronomy, mathematics and medicine. Mid-ocean navigation required a reliable study of the stars, and no doubt mercantile patronage was forthcoming for this study. But astronomy was also linked to mathematical knowledge and to astrology. Communication with western Asia led to an exchange of knowledge on astronomy and astrology, with some texts from Alexandria, such as the *Sphujidhvaja*, being translated from Greek into Sanskrit. Hellenistic ideas on astrology were of interest to Indians and in astronomy earlier systems used in India were being augmented by those based on the zodiac. This was also the period when astronomers and cosmologists began a dialogue that enriched theories of time. Cyclical notions from cosmology interacted with the more linear forms of historical time. A sharpened sense of time in relation to past events associated with human activities took shape as linear time, implicit in literature of a historical kind, and in a multiplicity of eras.

A gradual distancing from the *bhishaja*, the healer or shaman, was registered by a move towards the formal study and systemization of medical knowledge. Texts written in Sanskrit generally endorsed the latter. However, the tradition of the shaman did not disappear: it had its own clients and there was still a place for it within the formal tradition. The shift was from knowledge based on experience alone to an inclusion of experiment and analyses, derived from practice and from formal knowledge. The Indian medical system was based on the theory of the three humours – air, bile and mucus – the correct balance of these resulting in a healthy body. The processes involved in the functioning of the body drew from the five *vayus*, winds, and their interaction. Medical pharmacopœias and discussions on medical practices were composed at this time, the most famous being that of Charaka. Another study was that of Sushruta, focusing on surgery. Some of the earliest medical texts have been found in central Asia, where the dry climate of the desert oases preserved birch-bark manuscripts. It is evident that Indian herbal knowledge reached the western world, since the Greek botanist Theophrastus gave details of the medicinal use of various Indian plants and herbs in his *History of Plants*.

The texts were obviously written by those who had received a formal education. Yet brahmanical rules placed the practitioners of medicine low on the social scale, although those who wrote on medical matters pertaining to humans, horses and elephants were often accorded brahman status. Because of its study of the human body, and its utility in veterinary sciences, medical knowledge became independent of orthodoxy. This was to become an underlying contradiction in Indian society. Some professions were theoretically rated as low, but when their utility was valued socially technical treatises were written in Sanskrit which gave status to the profession. These were naturally written by authors with a formal education, generally brahmans or those associated with them. Presumably some of them were practitioners of that profession.

Linguistic analyses had resulted in Panini's grammar of Sanskrit, which became the bedrock of the language. The grammarian of this period was Patanjali whose *Mahabhashya*, a commentary on the earlier grammar, is an impressive study of syntax and the evolution of words which teases out the more abstruse rules. In addition, it provides some historical material through references in its grammatical examples. Patanjali was doubtless also aware of the usefulness of a grammar to the *mlechchhas*, those who did not know Sanskrit but wished to learn it. Analysis of language through grammar was to remain a monumental contribution of early Indian thought. It is curious, though, that with all the interest in Greek writings, no Indian grammarian stumbled on the parallels in Sanskrit and Greek.

Literary output was not restricted to *Dharma-shastras* and grammars, for poetry and drama were popular. The short poems in Prakrit by Hala, the *Gathasaptashati*, touched on love, some being sentimental and others rather bawdy but enjoyably witty. Among works in Sanskrit, the *Vajrasuchi*, ascribed to Ashvaghosha, is a Buddhist tract critical of both brahmans and the social system which they upheld. He is better known for his long poem on the life of the Buddha, the *Buddhacharita*, which was also seminal to the evolution of historical biographies. Ashvaghosha handled Sanskrit with dexterity. It became the preferred language for reflecting on Buddhism. Sanskrit developed into the language of the literati and of philosophical debate in all but peripheral areas. The philosopher Nagarjuna, possibly the most influential mind of this period, chose to write in Sanskrit, using it extensively in Buddhist discourse and in response to brahmanical and other philosophies. This did not however lead to the abandoning of the local languages or the local Prakrits. The tendency to demarcate the culture of the elite and the formally educated – what is said to be high culture – from popular culture, became more marked.

Fragments of Ashvaghosha's plays were found in a distant monastery in Turfan in central Asia. The interest of the audience would have been as much in the Buddhist themes as in a relatively new genre of literature. A more accomplished playwright, Bhasa, whose cycle of plays included the now famous *Svapnavasavadattam*, sought to capture the courtly mood. The dates for Bhasa are controversial but it is thought that he preceded Kalidasa in the early Christian era. His themes concerned incidents from the epics or historical romances, and court audiences enjoyed the amorous exploits of Kings. Bhasa wrote for the limited audience of the court circle, whereas Ashvaghosha's plays could have been performed for a wider audience at religious assemblies.

Unlike earlier periods, much of the literature drew on an urban background in its authorship, content and style. City life was by now distinctive, as evidenced by references to major cities such as Taxila, Mathura, Shishupalgarh, Mahasthan, Nagarjunakonda and Kaveripattinam. Brahmanical sources remained dubious about or even hostile to urban life, particularly where it was a commercial centre, and viewed the city as acceptable primarily as the location of the court.

Social Forms

The increase in trade and the coming of people from western and central Asia resulted in a visible, new population which included former ruling families with their own ancestral identities. The assimilation of those not born into a caste-based society would have posed a problem for brahman theorists who either ignored or downgraded such people – not that their caste-ranking made much difference to their activities. Social laws continued to be projected as rigid and the patriarchal theories of the Manu *Dharma-shastra* regarded as authoritative.

The sharpening of stratification at the theoretical level may have been a brahmanical response to the more flexible attitudes reflected, for example, in Buddhist texts. These resulted both from trading with non-Indians and from the opening up of new lands within the subcontinent, necessitating relations with people of different customs and cultures. One of the basic requirements of a stable *varna* identity, other than birth and occupation, was continuity in a particular place which established locational identity. But with the emphasis on new occupations, migration and identities from distant lands, it was difficult to insist on *varna*, other than in the category of the brahmans. The fluidity of an urban population was doubtless one reason for urban life being downplayed in the *Dharma-shastras*. Theoretically, the four *varnas* were precisely and clearly defined, with rules pertaining to their lawful activities and functions set out in the *Dharma-shastras*. Yet in practice there were many discrepancies.

Conversion to Vaishnava or Shaiva sects was theoretically not so easy because of the interdependence of birth, caste and sectarian practice, although these sects did find ways around this problem. A large non-Hindu group could be gradually assimilated through its becoming a *jati*, but the conversion of a single individual would raise the problem of appropriate caste-ranking which depended on birth. It was therefore easier for the incoming individual to become a Buddhist, although some also joined a Bhagavata sect. Votive inscriptions from Buddhist sites in the Deccan register the adoption of Buddhism by Yavanas. Mention is made of a Theodorus Datiaputta making a donation, and also a Yavana Indragnidatta, the son of the northerner Dhamadeva who came from Dattamiti (thought to be the town of Demetrius in Arachosia). As Buddhism was in the ascendant at that time, its prestige made the adjustment of the newly converted much easier.

While brahman orthodoxy maintained a distance from lower ranks it also had to come to terms with the new ruling elite, since those with political power could not be treated as outcastes. The 'fallen *kshatriya*' status was a strategic concession to the new ruling dynasties, although the qualifier *vratya*, degenerate or fallen, would hardly have been appreciated by those to whom it was applied. The presence in India of such people, prominent in political and economic spheres, must have challenged the theoretical structure of *varna*, even though the political arena and particularly kingship had earlier been relatively open, irrespective of *varna* status. Doubtless those in an inferior caste would have attempted to move up the scale by associating with the newcomers. Expansion in trade and commerce also meant an increase in guilds, with employment of many more artisans and greater access to wealth. The latter were largely drawn from the *shudra* caste, some of whom aimed to improve their caste status by changing their occupation and location. The category of *sankirna jati*, mixed caste, was also intended to keep such groups in check. The lower castes were theoretically to be located in the particular areas where they carried out their occupations, often on the margins of the city, and the untouchables were expected to remain outside city limits.

Some *jatis*, normally ranked in the lower half of the social scale, may have exploited the demands of urban life by attempting an improvement of their status, causing concern to the upholders of orthodox social law and usage. This may explain the reiteration in the *Dharma-shastras* of the inherent superiority of the brahman compared to other members of society, stressing he should be shown the utmost respect. The texts read as if the status of the brahman was being challenged. There seems to be a counterpoint between the rigidity of social laws within normative texts, and greater flexibility in the functioning of society. The earlier *Dharmasutras* were written when urbanization in the Ganges Plain was upsetting the mores of the *Vedas*, and the 'heterodox' sects were questioning brahmanical norms. The Manu *Dharma-shastra*, perhaps the most conservative of these texts, dates to the period of the rule of the 'degenerate *kshatriyas*' with the opening up of the subcontinent to trade and new ideas. The post-Gupta period saw the rapid emergence of new *jatis*, cults and states, challenging set ideas, which again produced a crop of normative texts and commentaries.

Votive inscriptions recording donations at *stupa* sites such as Sanchi and Bharhut complement the bâs-relief panels in presenting a picture of the reasonably well-off. With few exceptions, these inscriptions record donations from guilds, artisans, small landowners, monks and nuns. Donors identified themselves by occupation and place of residence, and not necessarily by *varna* or *jati*. The geographical spread covers the Deccan and its fringes. Many came from big towns such as Ujjain and Bhogavardhana, but the smaller places are now often unidentifiable. Almost half the donations at the Deccan sites are from monks and nuns, which raises the question of the source of this wealth. Were the donations made at the time of their ordination? Or did they still have shares in family property, and if so were they permitted to inherit wealth? Or did they invest their initial wealth in trade and donate the profits to the Sangha? Categories of donors varied according to location: at Mathura there were larger numbers of Jaina women donors than Buddhist, and this pattern was different from Buddhist sites in central India.

The presence of nuns, recorded in Jaina and Buddhist centres, is striking both in terms of their numbers and the fact of personal wealth which enabled them to make grants. Life as a monk or a nun was a possible alternative life offered by the Sangha, and as the Sangha became prosperous it was not so far removed from the working of other institutions. Although the Sangha ranked nuns lower than monks, this did not prevent women joining the Order. For women, it was attractive inasmuch as it offered security within a socially approved institution. In a seemingly contradictory way, entering the Order enabled them to play a socially useful role of a kind different from the usual. Jaina nuns, for example, were quite assertive as members of society. It also released women from the chores of household duties, as stated in one of the hymns which glories in the release from the quern, the mortar and the husband, adding that becoming a nun is also a release from rebirth. Women donors identified themselves in kinship terms as sisters, daughters, mothers and wives, and the latter two are frequent.

Where the donation is by a nun the source of the wealth is unclear. Was the wealth of the women their *stri-dhana* – the wealth given to a woman by her mother, a kinswoman or a relative and over which, in theory, she alone had control? The right to *stri-dhana* was partially to balance the exclusion of women as heirs to patrimonial property, except in the absence of male heirs when the patrimony might be allocated to the daughter. The *Dharma-shastras* carry discussions on what constituted *stri-dhana* and the right of the woman to dispose of it as she wished. It rarely made a difference to the general status of the woman, since it was not consolidated wealth but more frequently scattered, movable wealth, variously collected. These donations to Buddhist *stupas* contradict the statements about women and their rights to property, as formulated in the *Dharma-shastras*. It would be incorrect to take the latter as the normal practice and the social code for these times. It is not that women are depicted as relatively free in the inscriptions, but that there is a difference in the perceived activities open to women and their role in the family compared to the more rigid stance of the *Dharma-shastras*. This emphasizes the point that knowing the authorship, intention and audience of texts is essential to understanding what they say.

Architecture and Visual Expression

Artistic and visual aesthetics in both architecture and sculpture generally arose from the requirements of Buddhism, and many of these were made possible through the patronage of wealthy merchants, guilds and some royal donations. Buddhist religious architecture consisted of *viharas*, monasteries, *stupa*s and *chaitya* halls, some free-standing and some cut into rock at hillsides. The idea of a distinctive building to identify a religious location was relatively new. The earlier worship at *stupa*s and *chaitya*s had been on a small scale and Vedic *yajnas* left few traces. The new architecture would have been determined in part by religious requirements and the need to distinguish these buildings from domestic architecture. Votive inscriptions also had to be clearly displayed, narratives in the life of the Buddha made accessible together with the message they carried, and the occasional congregations for worship on particular days had to be accommodated, all of which required the structure to be impressively large. Size was also a pointer to power and prestige and this is demonstrated in the increasing size of the *stupa*.

The free-standing complex had early beginnings at Kaushambi, Sanchi and Bharhut, but with the spread of Buddhism monastic complexes gradually became more elaborate, as with the magnificent monastery at Takht-i-Bahi near Peshawar. Cave monasteries probably grew out of the initial attempt at seeking isolation, an attempt that the system soon outgrew. Where the location of a monastery was on a trade route in a hilly area, the rock-cut complex was natural, particularly in the western Deccan with its layered volcanic rock, relatively easier to excavate. The ground-plan of the *vihara*, monastery, was based on its being the residence for a group of monks and therefore evolved from domestic architecture. A large courtyard space was surrounded by rows of small rooms – the cells for the monks. The courtyard sometimes had a votive *stupa* which was used for the convocation of monks. It could also be used for community meals.

The origin of the Buddhist *stupa*, traced to pre-Buddhist burial mounds, was a hemispherical mound built over a sacred relic either of the Buddha himself or of a sanctified monk or saint. The relic was generally kept in a

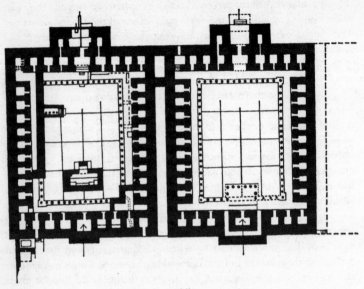

1. *Plan of a Buddhist monastery*

casket that was placed in a smaller chamber in the centre of the *stupa*. A circular platform provided the base for the semi-spherical drum or tumulus. This was flattened at the top to accommodate a small square platform from which a shaft ran down for the relic casket. At the centre of the square was a post with a series of superimposed umbrellas. Encircling the drum was a fenced path symbolically separating the sacred from the profane. The interplay of all these features has been read as a cosmic pattern linking the terrestrial to the celestial, but this reading could be subsequent to the original intention of venerating relics and embedding the sacred. It was in many ways the antithesis of a Vedic sacred enclosure. Unlike the temporary sanctification of the location of an area for the sacrifice, the *stupa* was a permanently demarcated sacred place. The burial and the worship of bodily relics were incompatible with the pollution rules of Brahmanism that preferred to dispose of the cremated remains. The relics symbolized the presence of the Buddha or the person being venerated, and the *stupa* became an object of worship.

Underlining the separation of the sacred and the profane areas was the spilling out of daily life, as depicted in the bâs-reliefs carved on the railings and gateways. Townspeople are shown standing on balconies, curious about

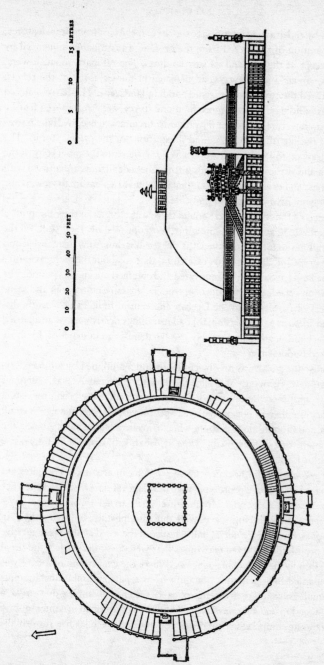

2. *Great Stupa, Sanchi: ground plan and elevation*

passers-by and drawing attention to the cityscape. Apart from ritual features, the separation of the sacred from the profane was probably influenced by the concept of the city and its surroundings. The rampart, moat, towers, palaces, streets and gateways, all depicted in the cityscape of the reliefs, demarcated the town from the surrounding landscape. The barrel-vaulted roofs of buildings, some of more than one storey, are a recognized feature of this architecture. Buddhist narrative art became a genre, with the narratives of the life of the Buddha and illustrations of the *Jataka* stories. The latter drew on folk-tales that were cleverly woven into the biography of the Buddha and stories of his previous births. These depictions are infused with a liveliness and occasional humour that make them a pleasure to view, while providing incisive vignettes of daily life.

At each of the four cardinal points there was a break in the railing for a large gateway, giving the sculptors further scope to show their skill. Of the *stupa* railings that have survived, the ones at Bharhut (now dismantled and lodged in the Indian Museum at Calcutta) date to about the second century BC. The *stupa* at Sanchi was renovated and enlarged during this period. The renovation was due to the efforts of traders, artisans, cultivators and some members of royalty from the Deccan and central India. The recently discovered *stupa* at Sanghol (Punjab) had its railings neatly packed and buried in the ground nearby, presumably to save them from destruction by those hostile to Buddhism.

Because the *stupa* was an object of worship maintained by a monastery, its location was generally at places where people collected. As was sometimes the case with sacred monuments, the location could have been an existing sacred site, a place of pilgrimage where people would congregate; or it could be at a nodal point along a route where travellers would stop. Among the more interesting of these is the *stupa* at Amaravati, close to an impressive megalithic burial.

The *stupa* itself did not offer much scope to an architect. The gateways were based on wooden prototypes used in villages and towns. The adherence to the themes of wooden architecture was carried through into cave-architecture as well. Huge caves were dug into hillsides, following the plan of a monastery or of a *chaitya*, hall. The use of the word *chaitya* is suggestive of the pre-Buddhist sacred enclosures that were a regular part of the ritual of worship in the early *gana-sanghas*. Where the excavation of a cave was accompanied by a generous donation from a patron, ambitious attempts were made to simulate in a series of caves the entire complex of a *stupa*, a hall of worship and a monastery, as it had been established in contemporary free-standing complexes. Thus the more elaborate caves, such as those in the

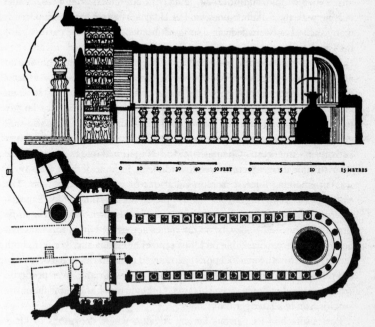

3. Chaitya hall at Karle: plan and elevation

western Deccan, especially at Karle and Bedsa, consist of fairly complicated structures all cut into the rock. Where rock formations permitted such excavations of caves, they occur in large number, for example at Barabar in Bihar, in Orissa and in the western Deccan. Interestingly, megalithic rock-cut caves containing burials and grave furnishings are found south of the Deccan in Kerala.

At Karle, the cave is entered through a small entrance area, which leads into the hall of worship, rectangular but with an apse at one end to accommodate a votive *stupa*. The apsidal form is often associated with *chaitya* halls. A row of pillars on each side separates the nave from the aisle. The ceiling of the Karle hall is in imitation of a barrel vault with wooden ribs, although the representation of ribs here is probably architecturally irrelevant. Cells for monks, in the form of caves, are cut into the hill on both sides of the *chaitya*. Buddhist rock-cut structures of the subsequent period, at Ellora and Ajanta, are more elaborate in plan and richer in sculpture than the early ones. At the former site, the tradition later extended to Jaina, Vaishnava and Shaiva temples cut into rock. Jaina rock-cut monasteries were parallel in time with the Buddhist ones, and at Udayagiri and Khandagiri (Orissa) many such caves were dedicated to Jaina monks, carrying the patronage of the Chedi rulers.

Rock-cut monasteries and *chaityas* did not permit much evolution in architectural style. But they occur with remarkable consistency at sites controlling the trade routes and the passes of the Deccan, such as at Bagh, Nasik, Junnar, Kanheri, Bhaja, Kondane and Karle. A chain of largely free-standing *stupa* sites and monasteries along the eastern coast also suggests a route. The early centuries of the Christian era saw much artistic activity at Amaravati, Ghantashala and Nagarjunakonda. Although the most striking images were related to Buddhism, in some of these areas there was an emerging interest in representations of other religious sects. The *ekamukhalingam*, the *lingam* incorporating anthropomorphic elements, emerged here at this time. Equally impressive in the north-west are the *stupa* sites along the Swat Valley, or on the routes across the Hindu Kush at what became the once remarkable Buddhist centres of Hadda and Bamiyan, both recently destroyed. Such locations encouraged monasteries to participate in the trade. Those with endowments of land claimed rights over property, which required maintenance. This was a prelude to what became monastic landlordism in a later period.

Portraiture had its patrons among royalty, where depictions of kings moved from the coins of the Indo-Greeks to the life-size statues of the Kushanas. Devotees of Jainism patronized a school of free-standing sculpture in which the craftsmen of Mathura were particularly adept. Mathura was also a centre for images of the Buddha, perhaps a parallel to Jaina icons, or, as others would argue, deriving from the Hellenistic fashion for representing deities. In the earlier *stupa* sculptures there is no image of the Buddha, his presence being indicated by symbols such as a horse to represent renunciation, a tree (*ficus religiosa*) to suggest his enlightenment, a wheel indicating the first sermon that he preached, and a *stupa* to evoke his death and *nirvana*. When the image came to be established as a part of worship, it took on local styles, such as in the portrait statues of the Buddha from Gandhara, Mathura and Amaravati.

Sculpture during this period began as an adjunct of architecture, being essentially ornamental on gateways, railings and entrances, where deep relief was mixed with some free-standing sculpture. Among the latter were figures of *yakshas* and *yakshis* – earth spirits of the status of demi-gods and widely worshipped. These also encouraged an increase in the worship of images. Donations of such images were common among religious sects.

Icons crafted at established centres such as Mathura were taken to other places, but very soon each region developed its own style. The earlier sculptors were less familiar with working in stone, being used to the softer media of wood and ivory. But by the early Christian era the sculptures of the Deccan show a mastery over stone. In the north-west, at Jalalabad, Begram, Taxila and the Swat Valley, the preferred stone was schist. In the Mathura region red sandstone found its connoisseurs in the images of *bodhisattvas* and Jaina *tirthankaras*. These were the precursors to Gupta sculpture. At clusters of sites in the Krishna Valley, such as Amaravati, Nagarjunakonda, Ghantashala and Jaggeyapeta, both the stone and style change to incorporate the local material and aesthetic.

Stone was not the only medium for artistic expression, with the use of ivory continuing for combs, the backs of mirrors or inlays in furniture. The exquisite and delicate workmanship in ivory is of a different genre from stone sculpture, closer to the making of beads and fine jewellery that had a head-start in India. The art of the goldsmith, similar in some ways to ivory carving, has few spectacular representations although it is a regularly mentioned activity in the texts. More extensive excavation may help in uncovering the best examples. But doubtless they will still be small in number compared with the wealth of gold in the Shaka tombs of central Asia.

The art of Gandhara reflected a Buddhist patronage, although other deities and themes were not ignored. The mother of the Buddha resembled an Athenian matron and an Apollo-like face went into the making of portraits of the Buddha. Greek gods were depicted paying obeisance to the Buddha. The range of ordinary people shown in various scenes bore the imprint of a distinct Greco-Roman style, although further afield in India and central Asia stylistic identities became more diffuse. Stucco was a popular technique melting into the architectural form. At Hadda, and later at Bamiyan in Afghanistan, monasteries were decorated with an abundance of stucco images of the Buddha and of *bodhisattvas*, or statues were cut from the local stone. The magnificence of stucco art at Hadda was a high point of the achievement of local artists. Striking figures of immense size, commanding the landscape, were located in a cliff at Bamiyan. Mother-goddess images were abundant, their worship continuing to be popular both in themselves and as part of fertility cults. Buddhist practice incorporated some aspects of popular religion, evident from the symbolic importance of the *stupa* and the brackets with female figures sculpted on the gateways at Sanchi and elsewhere. Terracotta figures were plentiful, some being toys, others decorative objects or figures used in ritual. Patronized by a different social category from royalty, they provide a fascinating glimpse of the popular fashions of the time.

This was also the seminal period for the evolution of the temple which housed images that the Vaishnavas and Shaivas were beginning to worship. Early locations can be traced to Besnagar, Nagarjunakonda, Sanchi and the temple at Jandial near Taxila. The last of these may have been heavily influenced by nearby Hellenistic temples, or may have been a temple that was converted to a fire temple by a local sect. Kushana cult shrines built for divinized kings may also have influenced the initial idea of the temple. Temples tended to be small and inconspicuous compared to Buddhist monuments during this period, focusing on a room to house the image, but they come into their own in the subsequent periods.

The Intermingling of Religious Beliefs and Practice

Buddhism hovered in the background of most activities at this time, also supported by the rich and the powerful. Buddhist texts such as the *Milinda-panha*, *Mahavastu* and *Saddharma-pundarika* were supportive of the ethos created by the mercantile community. It is therefore not surprising that monasteries were well endowed, with huge *stupas* being built or small ones renovated, and that the Buddhist Sangha became affluent and respected. Some monasteries had large endowments, employing slaves and hired labourers to work the land and labour on other enterprises. The excavating of these structures into hillsides, or the building of free-standing ones, would have required the monks to be proficient in various kinds of management skills: collecting donations, gauging technical expertise, controlling labour, maintaining accounts, supervising construction, to say the least. Some were given special designations to carry out this work, but most, being untrained, would have merely supervised the labour. They would doubtless have been assisted by lay followers in these professions. The days when the Buddhist monks lived entirely on alms collected in the morning hours became a distant memory for those in the bigger and richer monasteries who ate regular meals in monastic refectories.

Monasteries were built adjoining a town or on a route frequented by merchants and caravans or pilgrims, or – very occasionally – on some beautiful and secluded location far removed from busy cities. Secluded monasteries were sufficiently well endowed to enable the monks to live in reasonable comfort. In these cases the Sangha was moving away from the common people, which may have diminished its strength as an ideology endorsing social ethics, a development one suspects the Buddha would have resisted.

Another side to the popularity of Buddhism was its readiness to assimilate local cults. A late Kushana monastery in the Mathura area carried some donations from those propitiating a fertility deity associated with the popular cult of the area, the Naga cult associated with snake worship. This raises the question of whether a site originally of Naga worship had been appropriated by the Buddhist monastery through assimilating the cult. At the same time, places such as Mathura were not only sacred to virtually all the religious sects, but were also cities of political importance and boasted of commercial wealth. All these factors appear to have influenced the choice of a site, although their social functioning could have varied. Whereas the Buddhists tended to bring diverse groups together, the regulations of *varna*, if observed, would have set them apart.

The deification of the Buddha and the worship of his image, the concept of the *bodhisattva* and the notion of transferring merit were not part of the original tenets of Buddhist teaching, although after much debate their importance was conceded among many sects of Buddhism. The Buddha had opposed deification, yet, by the first century AD, his image was carved in stone, engraved on rock or painted, and worshipped. The *bodhisattva* was another new idea, defined as one who works for the good of humankind in an unselfish manner and is willing to forego *nirvana* until such time as his work is completed. Alternatively it was interpreted as the *bodhisattva* being a previous incarnation of the Buddha, working towards *nirvana* and accumulating merit through successive births. Such merit was intended for humanity and not just for the individual *bodhisattva*. Furthermore, merit could also be transferred from one person to another by a pious act in the name of the person to whom this transference was made. Thus, the wealthy could acquire merit by donating caves to the Sangha or else a stock of merit could be built up through the donations of others. The analogy with the common mercantile practice of the accumulation and transference of capital is striking.

These changes altered the interdependence of the Buddhist monk and the *upasaka*, lay follower. The latter became significant to the establishment and well-being of the Sangha. In order to be socially acceptable as an institution the Sangha needed the support of both the pious and the wealthy. The greater the respectability of the Sangha, the higher the respectability of those who supported it, even if they were from the lower castes. This was a mutual underpinning of strength, and was common to many religious sects.

However, Buddhism and Jainism differed in this matter from the Vaishnava and Shaiva sects. This was partly due to the absence of institutionalized renunciation in the form of monasteries and convents among the latter, the closest being ascetic hermitages, and partly because they were often rooted in *jati* identities and the concerned *jatis* tended to become a substitute for a laity. Alternatively the religious sect itself became a *jati*. The Sangha remained dependent on the laity and the laity responded well. Donations and the giving of gifts came to be linked to the acquiring of merit – the pre-eminent reward for any action.

Gift-giving or *dana* originated in the practice of a patron making a gift to the priests for a Vedic sacrifice. But the performance of Vedic sacrifices was beginning to decrease and the recipients of gifts preferred a donation of land. Land was becoming the most tangible form of permanent wealth as well as indicating a change in economic value. As landowners brahmans had greater flexibility of power than as performers of rituals, receiving gifts of objects.

Among the Buddhists and Jainas the act of giving was not restricted to the *kshatriya*. Anyone who wished to make a gift, be they *gahapatis*, landowners, *setthis*, financiers, or artisans, could do so and donations were welcome. The donation became an investment, with merit acquired by the donor, as well as tangible wealth for the donee. The act of giving was essentially the action of an individual, although sometimes in association with a few kinsmen: it was not a function of a clan or even the extended kin group. Some donors to the Sangha were in occupations classified in the *Dharma-shastras* as appropriate only for *shudras*. But they were in a position to make a donation. A concession was therefore made in some brahmanical texts allowing brahmans to receive gifts from *shudras*, although such brahmans were to be excluded from the annual rites commemorating ancestors, the *shraddha*.

Improved communications led to an increase in pilgrimages that opened up new places and new practices. Sending missions to various parts of the subcontinent and beyond, and proselytizing, resulted in fresh ideas filtering into Buddhism. The original doctrine was reinterpreted, a process that led to its split into two schools – the Hinayana or the Lesser Vehicle and the Mahayana or the Greater Vehicle. This was a schism more major than the sectarian splits. Apart from the doctrinal differences, the conflicting needs of the affluent and the impoverished could not be easily accommodated. These changes were likely to weaken the structure of Buddhism that had been inherited from earlier times.

Sectarian splitting-off was more common with religions tracing their origins to historical founders and institutions than among religions that grew around mythology and rituals. Arguments over the real meaning of the original teaching of the Buddha began, as often happens, soon after the death of the founder. Attempts were made to eliminate or modify these differences by a series of councils discussing diverse interpretations. The Theravada sect, which had its centre at Kaushambi, had collected the teachings of the Buddha into the Pali Canon. It was the oldest sect and claimed closeness to the original teaching. The Sarvastivada sect, originating at Mathura, spread northwards to Gandhara, central Asia and further. They collated material in Sanskrit, or what has come to be called hybrid Sanskrit. The Canon was also written in Gandhari Prakrit. The nuances of the earlier teaching could have been inadvertently changed in the process of translation, or by composing the text in a language different from that of the original. Added to this was the changing historical context of societies identified with Buddhism and the mutations they introduced into the teaching.

According to some Buddhist traditions, the schism between the Hinayana and the Mahayana was given recognition at the Fourth Buddhist Council, held in Kashmir in the early second century AD, which is often associated with Kanishka. The authenticity of this Council has been doubted, but it may have been an attempt to give status to the local Buddhist tradition that became the accepted form in the north-west and central Asia. The emergence of the Theravada after the Third Council held at Pataliputra, which was associated with Ashoka, may have provided the model. The more orthodox Buddhists maintained that the Hinayana preserved the original teaching of the Buddha, and that the Mahayana had incorporated new ideas not consistent with the original teaching. Eventually, there was an approximate geographical division, but with some overlap. Hinayana Buddhism found its strongholds in Sri Lanka, Myanmar and the countries of south-east Asia, whereas Mahayana Buddhism had its major following in central Asia, Tibet, China and Japan.

The Mahayana doctrine was also influenced by the formulations of some contemporary Buddhist philosophers. Among these the most outstanding was Nagarjuna, a convert to Buddhism from a brahman family of the northern Deccan. He is associated with the doctrine of the Void (*Shunyata*), which is sometimes read as saying that we are surrounded by emptiness and that whatever we see is an illusion. The Void however was *nirvana*, or the end to the cycle of rebirth, that every Buddhist was seeking. These ideas were further developed into a variety of sometimes opposing philosophical speculations, largely idealistic but with strands of rationalism and logic.

There might even have been parallels to the mathematical concept of zero that was more widely used in the subsequent period.

Other aspects of Mahayana Buddhism, although germinating from the earlier teaching, were further encouraged through its interaction with various religions – Christianity, Zoroastrianism and Manichaeism in particular – especially in the part of Asia stretching from northern India to the eastern Mediterranean and central Asia. Among these, prominence was given to the coming of the Buddha Maitreya to save the true doctrine. With this was connected the concept of 'the suffering saviour' – sometimes thought of as the *bodhisattva* who redeems humanity through his own suffering. Evidently the new beliefs current in the eastern Mediterranean were as familiar to the Buddhists as they were to the Zoroastrians, for whom the saviour to come was Saoshyant. Mahayana Buddhism also introduced cosmologies and eschatologies involving a complicated system of heavens, superimposed one upon the other, in which dwelt innumerable *bodhisattvas*, who became venerated virtually as deities. Common to most religions of this period was the attempt to attract greater support by incorporating popular cults, especially fertility cults. Numerous *yakshas*, *yakshis*, *nagas* and suchlike entered the mythology and cosmology of the major religions. There was also a noticeable focus on goddesses, sometimes imported from other areas such as west Asia.

The association of prosperity and power with a religion can sometimes lead to schisms. Jainism achieved popularity, particularly among the merchant families of the cities. It too suffered a schism, the Jaina monks being divided into the Digambara, 'Sky-clad', the naked or orthodox sect; and the Shvetambara, 'White-clad' or more liberal sect. They moved from Magadha westwards, settling in Mathura, Rajasthan, Ujjain, Saurashtra and along the west coast to Sopara, at all of which places they prospered. Their presence was particularly evident in Mathura and in central India, the former being a political and commercial centre and the latter being traversed by routes. Jainism became a noticeable presence in Rajasthan and Gujarat. Another group moved to Kalinga, where they enjoyed royal patronage under Kharavela. Moving further south, their main concentration was in Karnataka and the Tamil country. Sites such as Sittanavsal, with its beautiful mural, were monastic centres; but Shravana Belgola later developed into a considerable place of pilgrimage, with its immense statue ritually bathed at regular intervals. By and large Jainism, supported by a similar section of society as Buddhism, underwent crises much the same as those of Buddhism. However, it managed to maintain itself with more determination than Buddhism as a kind of 'parish religion', closely tied to the community.

Hence the number of its adherents has remained small but fairly constant. Unlike Buddhism, it did not become a pan-Asian religion, possibly because its ritual observances were difficult to follow in the midst of other cultures.

Vedic Brahmanism had a clientele that was initially smaller but influential, drawing on royalty and court circles such as the ruling families of the Shungas, Satavahanas and Ikshvakus. Vedic sacrifices played an important role in the coronation of kings, legitimizing claims through ritual. But the Vedic tradition remained the preserve of brahmans. At this stage there were only marginal overlaps with the recently evolving Bhagavata and Shaiva sects. There was some rivalry with Buddhism and Jainism, largely arising from competition for patronage and a divergent following. Some of the Vedic gods had quietly passed into oblivion, for example Varuna and Mitra; some lost their pre-eminence, such as Indra and Agni; and others were emerging as new gods with additional attributes. At this time Vedic Brahmanism became differentiated from sects such as the Bhagavata and Shaiva – now referred to as Puranic Hinduism – and which took form towards the latter part of the period.

To use the general term Hinduism at this stage is historically something of an anachronism. The term 'Hindu' was not in use in the early first millennium AD, and those who were supporters of what today we call 'Hindu' sects used their sectarian labels to identify their religion. Therefore they identified themselves by the broader labels of Vaishnava and Shaiva or, within these, by the narrower labels of Bhagavatas, Pashupatas and so on. The consciousness of a religious identity was that of the sect and not of an all-inclusive religion incorporating every sect. This makes a significant difference to understanding the nature of what today is called Hinduism.

The wider application of the term 'Hindu' originated with the Arabs after the eighth century AD, when it referred to all those who lived beyond the Indus. At a later date its meaning came to include those who followed the prevailing indigenous religions of India. Differentiation from Vedic Brahmanism has required that sects be described by another label, and Puranic Hinduism has come into use. It derives from the encapsulation of the change contained in the writing of the *Puranas*. The composition of these began in the early centuries AD. Each *Purana* is a manual on the worship of a specific deity and a guide for the worshipper. As a genre, it later gave rise to other categories of texts on mythology, legends about deities, the ritual of worship and the presumed histories of places sacred to the deities. Among these texts, the best known were to be the *Agamas* and the *Mahatmya*s. In the process, popular belief and worship were appropriated as necessary by upper-caste authors. Unlike Vedic Brahmanism, the mediation of a priest was optional and in later times was sometimes resisted by those for whom religion was essentially devotion to a deity.

As with Vedic Brahmanism, the Vaishnava and Shaiva sects were not founded by historical personages. They did not constitute a revealed religion but grew and evolved from a variety of cults, beliefs and rituals, some of which had filtered down from brahmanical practices. Others, which came from entirely different sources such as folk cults, could even be anathema to Vedic Brahmanism. Popular cults often became associated with the mainstream religion, a concession that the priests had to make to popular worship.

The origins of such sects were frequently tied to their earlier social identity, namely, as sects they incorporated their earlier beliefs from the time when their societies were organized as clans and on the basis of lineage. These identities would have changed when clans were converted into *jatis*, but some degree of belief and ritual would have continued out of habit and as a religious investment. The moorings of clan or kinship were replaced by membership of, and identity with, a *jati*, while the rituals of the clan priests would have been overlaid by rituals emerging from the consciousness of being a *jati*. A new form of worship evolved where the relationship between the worshipper and the deity did not require the intervention of priests. This process is more visible in the subsequent period but indications of change can be seen earlier. However, the intervention of the priest did not end and, after a brief period of distancing, the priests began to appropriate this new form of worship.

The form of worship was distinct from the Vedic sacrifice and evolved as the ritual of *puja*. As an offering to a deity it was a continuation of the sacrifice, except that the sacrifice of a living animal was optional and the deity was no longer an abstract notion but was represented by an icon housed in a temple. Both these changes were of substantial importance. The object of worship could be aniconic and of no recognizable form, such as a rock. Or it could be the representation of a concept, as was the case with the Shaiva worship of the phallic form, the *lingam*. A number of popular fertility cults were subsumed in this form. Even when images became anthropomorphic some were modified to include many arms, for instance, in order to accommodate a range of attributes associated with the deity so represented.

The worship of images was common to the Hellenistic world, but may have evolved in India through the focus on the worship of a single deity. Unlike the exclusion of other religious forms, which some claim was inherent to Vedic Brahmanism, these sects adapted their earlier religious practices to new forms and assimilated other cults into their mythology. This led to incorporating a variety of beliefs, such as the numerous incarnations of Vishnu. Viewed in the past as a form of willing co-opting and being co-opted, it is now also seen as a strategy for inducting those outside the boundaries of *varna* society, giving them a *varna* status and incorporating their beliefs in the form of additional mythology and iconography. Barring a few ritual specialists and clan chiefs, the status of such incorporated groups would inevitably be low, generally *shudra*. The incorporation may therefore not have been uncontested by those used to being equal members of a clan.

Although the worship of many deities continued, there was also the tendency to focus on a few. This may have encouraged some monotheistic thinking among the sects. Nevertheless the notion of a trinity of gods was encouraged, with Brahma as the Creator, Vishnu as the Preserver and Shiva as the god who eventually destroys the universe. Of the three gods, Vishnu and Shiva gained a vast following, and through ensuing centuries the Vaishnavas and the Shaivas remained major sects of Hindu belief. Brahma receded into the background.

Vishnu is said to observe the universe and, at times, when evil is rampant, to assume various incarnations in order to remove the evil from the world. He is believed to have been manifested in numerous incarnations, of which nine are popularly agreed upon. Some are animals and some humans. Epic heroes, such as Rama and Krishna, were projected as incarnations, and the epics, originally bardic poetry relating to rajas as clan chiefs and kings, acquired the status of sacred texts. They were revised for use as religious literature. In the course of redacting these epics many interpolations were included, the most famous being the addition of the *Bhagavadgita* to the *Mahabharata*. Texts such as these are multi-layered and where the history of interpolations can be observed it provides pointers to the role of the text. The tenth and final incarnation of Vishnu has yet to come, when Vishnu will take the form of the brahman Kalkin. He will set right the ways of the world, end oppression and reverse the attempts of those who have turned the world upside down by acting contrary to brahmanical norms, among which was the lower-caste appropriation of high status.

The idea of incarnations is a reminder of the theory of the previous births of the Buddha and the *bodhisattvas*. Kalkin echoes the Buddha Maitreya, the Buddha yet to come who will reinstate the norms of Buddhist belief and behaviour. Maitreya, although known from earlier texts, gained in popularity at this time when it was feared that Buddhism might decline unless a saviour appeared. From being the historical founder of a new way of life the Buddha became projected as a messianic, millenarian deity. These concepts of incarnations and saviours were not the result of one religion influencing another, but rather the existence of a universe of discourse among those who travelled, mixed and spoke with one another. This discourse is reflected in parallels of thought and belief among many religious ideologies of the time, particularly in the area including India, central Asia and west Asia.

Goddesses of various categories, often the focus of fertility rites, came to the forefront in the mythologies of Puranic Hinduism and were worshipped as primary and pre-eminent deities. This was in part the crucible of what later evolved into the Tantric deities. Nature and animals were treated as sacred metaphors of deity, with a focus on trees, groves, rivers and mountains, as well as bulls and snakes. Together with these cults were a myriad of demi-gods and celestial beings of various ranks.

The concern with escaping rebirth brought certain concepts to the forefront, such as the seminal idea of *karma* and *samsara*, often referred to by the term 'transmigration'. The idea had been mooted in the *Upanishads*, elaborated upon in Buddhist and Jaina teaching and now gained currency. The worship of an image, a departure from Vedic Brahmanism, focused attention on the individual deity and worshipper. The intention of the worship is attainment of *moksha* – freedom from rebirth for the individual soul. The centrality of the individual's liberation, as it developed in the Shramanic religions, made an emphatic contribution to its popularity.

Actions in the present life determine the condition of the next birth. This is not fatalism, since one can modify one's destiny by consciously performing good actions. What is fatalistic, however, is that the morality of an action depends on whether or not it is in conformity with *Dharma*. In Vedic Brahmanism, and to some degree in Puranic Hinduism, the arbiters of *Dharma* were the brahmans and their normative texts, the *Dharma-shastras*, justifying the ethics of *varna*. Buddhists and Jainas emphasized a different concept of social ethics, for example the Middle Way, that was not rooted in *varna*. The *Gita* proclaims that each man must do his duty according to the *Dharma* and not look towards the results of his actions. When Arjuna is disinclined to kill his kinsmen at the start of the battle at Kurukshetra his charioteer, Krishna, explains to him that he would be exempt from the sin of killing since this is the demand of war; and that Arjuna, the *kshatriya* hero, was upholding a righteous cause. Had the Buddha been the charioteer the message would have been different.

Another religion – Christianity – entered India by way of the trading ships from the west, although the date of its arrival remains controversial. The coming of Christianity is associated with the legend of St Thomas, who, according to the Catholic Church of Edessa, came twice on missions to India. The first took him to the north-west, to the Parthian King Gondophares. On the second occasion St Thomas is said to have arrived in Malabar in about AD 52, the assumption being that he was the disciple of Jesus Christ. Tradition has it that he was martyred at Mylapore near Madras, but historical evidence to back this claim is unavailable. Other versions from eastern Mediterranean traditions have him coming from Socotra to Muziris. Given the amount of travel between the two places because of the Indo-Roman trade, this is a plausible story. Interestingly, these traditions connect him with the most active areas in the trade, the north-west and south India. However, historical links that date to the mid-first millenium AD seem stronger with Edessa and the Persian Church. A group of Persian Christians led by Thomas Cana migrated to Kerala, where they were given a grant of land by the local king. The first coming of Christianity to India is more likely linked to the establishing of the Syrian Christian Church.

The picture of this period is that of many people moving in many directions. There were not only Yavanas trading with the subcontinent, but traders from various parts of India finding their way to central Asia, to west Asia, to the ports of the Red Sea and to south-east Asia. The wide distribution of pottery, artefacts and scripts are also indicators of this movement within the subcontinent and beyond. In many areas there were multiple communities with varying identities that drew upon occupation and caste status, religious sectarian affiliation and the use of a particular language. These were the identities that were to dominate in subsequent centuries. This variation would have been difficult for the *Dharma-shastras* to map, let alone attempt to control. These texts could apply strong biases to theoretical arguments when the opportunity arose. References to *varnas* occurred, but more often with reference to the upper castes; and the lower castes, often described as mixed castes, were more frequently identified by occupations. The severity of the *Dharma-shastras* was doubtless a commentary arising from the insecurity of the orthodox in an age of flux.

9

Threshold Times

c. AD 300–700

Classicism

In the days when historians wrote of 'Golden Ages', the Gupta period was described as such. Civilizations were said to have a Golden Age when virtually every manifestation of life reached a peak of excellence. The Gupta period was selected largely because of impressive literary works in Sanskrit and the high quality of art, which coincided with what was viewed as a brahmanical 'renaissance'. Since Indian civilization had earlier been characterized as Hindu and Sanskritic, the initial spread of brahmanical culture as 'high' culture on an unprecedented scale was described as a golden period. High culture was associated with the elites at various courts and focused on the aesthetics expressed in creative literature, sculpture, architecture and philosophy, together with their style of life. Quite apart from the elite, it was also assumed that ordinary people were materially well off, with little to complain about.

A Golden Age invariably had to be utopian, but set in the distant past, and the period chosen by those working on the early history of India was a time when Hindu culture was more firmly established than ever before. The distant past had an advantage, for it allowed greater recourse to imagination in recreating that past. Now that historians are commenting on all aspects of society, the notion of a uniformly Golden Age that encompasses an entire society has been questioned. This questioning applies to Periclean Athens, Elizabethan England, or any other culture. Most societies of the pre-modern world were divided into the better off and the not so well off, the former having little concern for the living conditions of the latter. The description of a Golden Age reflected the life of the wealthy and their activities alone characterized such an age.

There was previously some overlap between the notion of a Golden Age and that of a Classical Age, whereas now the two are treated as distinct.

The label 'classical' has a different connotation – it sets the standards for assessing forms. The criteria are enduring excellence and an exemplary standard. Innovatory attempts mature into formal styles and the classical form precedes the tendency to create over-decorative forms. Even this notion is now thought inadequate by many historians since formal expression varies according to place, time and object. The predisposition to artistic and literary expression in the idea of classicism may have been due to these being viewed in isolation from the larger process of historical evolution. The existence of more than one classical period must also be conceded, since standards of excellence change in accordance with the expression of language, art, philosophy, knowledge and even material culture; nor has the obvious been stated, that classicism has a long gestation period.

There are at least three epochs when artistic and literary expression achieved impressive standards – the post-Mauryan and Gupta period; the Cholas; and the Mughals. The precursor to the culture of the Gupta period was not restricted to northern India, since the Deccan shows a striking evolution of cultures. It could also be argued that every regional culture in the Indian subcontinent has its classical period and classical periods should be viewed as such. They are not periods when the entire subcontinent subscribed to a single, universal, cultural form. The definition is therefore not one of widespread excellence but of a limited excellence, one that can be treated as a point of evaluation. The preference for using the concept of a Sanskritic culture is an attempt at introducing a historical focus, while directing attention to the more striking changes. It refers to the obvious and extensive use of Sanskrit as the language of intellectual discourse and as an idiom of various activities, even if these were limited to the culture of the court and the learned. The wider dimensions of historical change ranging from land relations to philosophical discourse, of which this was a signature, have also to be incorporated.

There has been a tendency to treat the Sanskritic culture of this period as rooted entirely in brahmanic norms. Hence the reference to its being a period of brahmanical renaissance. Yet there is much in the articulation of these times that evolved from an idiom drawing on the Shramanic tradition, particularly Buddhism. Images of the Buddha were the more impressive icons, Buddhist Sanskrit literature encouraged creative literature, and the philosophic discussions often developed from earlier Buddhist and Shramanic questioning of existing thought.

The classicism of the Gupta period is not an innovation emanating from Gupta rule but the culmination of a process that began earlier. New artistic forms were initiated during the pre-Gupta period in north India, such as those associated with Buddhism and which also found parallels in other religious sects, with the writing of texts on technical subjects and creative literature of various kinds. Much of the articulation is in Sanskrit, but it is not the language alone that gives the period a particular quality. The spread of Sanskritic culture assumes certain kinds of social and cultural exclusivity and demarcates social groups. Classicism emerges out of the interface of many styles, forms and aspirations and is therefore an evolving continuum. It attempts a transition towards a uniform, elite culture, but in the process becomes a catalyst for many others. The Gupta period is therefore the threshold to a marked mutation of north Indian society during the late-first millennium AD, rather than a revival or a renaissance.

The description of the Gupta period as one of classicism is relatively correct regarding the upper classes, who lived well according to descriptions in their literature and representations in their art. The more accurate, literal evidence that comes from archaeology suggests a less glowing life-style for the majority. Materially, excavated sites suggest that the average standard of living may have been higher in the preceding period. This can be firmly established only by horizontal excavations of urban sites and rural settlements, involving comparative analysis with the remains of the preceding period. The existing discrepancy between the level of material culture shown by excavations and that reflected in literature and the arts is in itself a commentary on the social context of classicism.

The Guptas and their Successors

Evidence on the origin and antecedents of the Gupta family is limited, as it seems to have emerged from obscure beginnings. It was thought that the family ruled a small principality in Magadha, but recent opinion supports the western Ganges Plain as a base. The name could indicate that they were of the *vaishya* caste, but some historians accord them brahman status. The eulogy on a later king of the dynasty envisages many small states subsequent to the decline of the Kushanas, and theirs may have been one such. The dynasty came into its own with the accession of Chandra Gupta I, who made his kingdom more than a mere principality. Chandra Gupta married into the Lichchhavi family, once an old, established *gana-sangha* of north Bihar, now associated with a kingdom in Nepal. The marriage set a stamp of acceptability on the family and was politically advantageous for them, since Chandra Gupta I made much of it in his coins. His rule extended over the Ganges heartland (Magadha, Saketa and Prayaga) and he took the title of *maharaja-adhiraja* (great king of kings), although this ceased to have much significance since it was now used by many rulers, major and minor. The Gupta era of AD 319–20 is thought to commemorate his accession.

Samudra Gupta claimed that he was appointed by his father to succeed him in about AD 335. A lengthy eulogy on him was inscribed on an Ashokan pillar, now at Allahabad, which provides the basic information on his reign. It is curious that he should have chosen this pillar, carrying the Pillar Edicts of Ashoka, suggesting either that he was claiming some historical continuity or, if the earlier inscriptions could still be read, that he was taking a contrary stand to the views of Ashoka. This pillar with inscriptions of even later rulers has become something of a historical palimpsest.

Trouble over the successor to Chandra Gupta I, and the coins of an obscure Prince, Kacha, suggest that Samudra Gupta had a rival whom he finally overcame. It would seem that Samudra Gupta's ambition was to establish an extensive empire, controlled centrally from the capital by the king. Shades of the Mauryas were re-emerging. The eulogy, if it is to be taken literally, provides an impressive list of kings and regions that succumbed to Samudra Gupta's triumphal march across various parts of the subcontinent. In the subsequent period such lists of conquests were often part of the courtly rhetoric, but in this case the exaggeration of a court poet may have been more limited. The emphasis seems to be on the paying of tribute rather than the annexing of territory. Four northern kings were conquered, mainly in the area around Delhi and the western Ganges Plain. Kings of the south and the east were forced to pay homage, were captured and released. From the places mentioned, it appears Samudra Gupta campaigned down the east coast as far as Kanchipuram (near modern Chennai). Nine kings of Aryavarta, in northern India, were violently uprooted; the rajas of the forest-peoples of central India and the Deccan were forced into servitude. In a sixth-century inscription eighteen forest kingdoms of central India are said to have been inherited by a local ruler, which suggests that the conquest of these areas began earlier. Kings in eastern India, as well as small kingdoms in Nepal and the Punjab are said to have paid tribute. Nine of what were earlier *gana-sanghas* in Rajasthan, including the age-old Malavas and Yaudheyas, were forced to accept Gupta suzerainty. In addition, more distant rulers such as the Daivaputra Shahanushahi ('The Son of Heaven, King of Kings', clearly a Kushana title), the Shakas, and the King of Sinhala (Sri Lanka) also paid tribute, as did the inhabitants of all the islands.

The *prashasti*, eulogy, is a continuation of the earlier style of courtly eulogies on kings and becomes a model for later ones. Coming as it does from a recognized genre with an obvious intention, one hesitates to take it literally. Nevertheless, it carries a core of historical information and the list of Samudragupta's conquests is impressive. The kings of the south and of the Deccan were not under the suzerainty of Samudra Gupta but merely paid him homage, as did a number of the northern rulers. His conquests allowed him to annex territory in northern India as he originally intended, exacting tribute from defeated rulers whose territory he could not annex. He probably met with stronger opposition than he had anticipated. His direct political control was confined to the Ganges Plain, since the Shakas remained unconquered in western India; and his control over the north-west may have wavered.

This inscription makes a striking contrast to those of Ashoka. The Mauryan king controlled far more territory yet was modest in his claims to power. Whereas Ashoka came close to renouncing conquest, Samudra Gupta revelled in it. An interesting feature of the conquests is their variety and number, from chiefdoms to kingdoms. Samudra Gupta broke the power of the chiefdoms in the watershed and northern Rajasthan, which led to an unfortunate consequence for the later Guptas when the Huns invaded north-western India. The watershed, the frontier to the Ganges Plain, could no longer act as a buffer. Apart from this the termination of these chiefdoms was the death-knell of the *gana-sangha* polity, which had held its own for a millennium as an alternative to monarchy. Those of the middle Ganges Plain had earlier succumbed to monarchy under the Nandas and Mauryas. It would seem that the antecedents of the Lichchavis as a *gana-sangha* were forgotten, for the Guptas made no mention of the earlier form, despite their pride in this connection. In the competition between caste and clan, and their role in creating state systems, the former had superseded the latter. It is interesting, however, that the non-monarchical states survived for so many centuries despite being repeatedly attacked.

The validity of the wider claims is questionable. Samudra Gupta's relationship with the declining Kushanas remains uncertain. Regarding Sri Lanka, a later Chinese source provides evidence that a Sinhala king sent presents and requested the Gupta king's permission to build a Buddhist monastery at Gaya. Such a request can hardly be termed tribute and it is probable that his relationship with other distant kings was similar. Who the 'inhabitants of the islands' were remains unclear and possibly refers to parts of south-east Asia hosting Indian settlements, with which contacts had increased.

Samudra Gupta had more cause than other kings to perform the horse sacrifice when proclaiming his conquests. It is said that it had been suspended for a while, which presumably is a reference to kings supporting non-brahmanical religions. A statement claiming the king's protection of brahmans and cows became formulaic in later inscriptions. However, he was not merely thirsting for conquest and battle. His more cultured side as a lover of poetry and music was mentioned, complemented by some of his coins showing him playing the *vina* (lute), although these accomplishments had also become part of the signature of kingship.

Of all the Gupta kings, Chandra Gupta II, the son of Samudra Gupta, is reputed to have shown exceptional chivalrous and heroic qualities. His long reign of about forty years from *c.* AD 375 to 415 had a rather mysterious beginning. A play written some two centuries later, *Devi-chandra-gupta*, supposedly dealing with events on the death of Samudra Gupta, introduced Rama Gupta as the son who succeeded Samudra Gupta. The story goes that Rama Gupta was defeated in battle by the Shakas, to whom he then agreed to surrender his wife, Dhruvadevi. His younger brother Chandra was incensed by this, disguised himself as the Queen and, getting access to the Shaka king's apartments, he killed him. This action gained him the affection of the people but created enmity between him and his brother Rama. Chandra finally killed Rama and married Dhruvadevi. The discovery of the coins of Rama Gupta, and of inscriptions mentioning Dhruvadevi as Chandra Gupta's wife, lend some authenticity to this story. Furthermore, Chandra Gupta's major campaign was fought against the Shakas. However, the heroic tenor of the story may have been an attempt to hide an unsavoury event, often the case in courtly literature. The play subscribed to a theme frequent in historical biographies where the usurpation of the throne by a younger brother is justified.

This campaign led to the annexation of western India, commemorated by the issuing of special silver coins. Its significance lay not only in the western border of India being secure, but also in its giving access to the western trade since the ports were now in Gupta hands. The western Deccan, earlier held by the Satavahanas, was ruled by the Vakataka dynasty which emerged as a dominant power in the Deccan. One branch which had close relations with the Guptas was associated with Ramtek, where they built a number of temples, and the other with Vatsgulma. The available inscriptions recording their grants of land reveal some in relatively remote areas, which they probably opened up to settlement, and the names of some donees hint at possible tribal origins. A marriage between Chandra Gupta's daughter and the Vakataka King Rudrasena II strengthened Gupta access to the Deccan, although the Vakatakas remained an independent power. As it happened, Rudrasena II died five years after coming to the throne and his widow Prabhavati Gupta, the daughter of Chandra Gupta II, acted as regent from *c.* 390–410 because his sons were minors. This brought the Vakataka kingdom closer to the Guptas. Chandra Gupta II took the title of *Vikram-aditya*/'sun of prowess', and has therefore been linked with the legendary king of that name, associated with a strong sense of justice. The Gupta King is remembered for his patronage of literature and the arts.

It was during the reign of Chandra Gupta II's son and successor Kumara Gupta (*c.* AD 415–54) that the first hints arose of a new invasion from the north-west, but these remained a distant threat during the first half of the fifth century. A branch of the White Huns, the Hephthalites from central Asia, known as Hunas to Indian sources, had occupied Bactria in the previous century and were threatening to cross the Hindu Kush mountains. The Hun threat on the Indian frontier continued for the next hundred years, with the Guptas and their successors being hard pressed to keep them back. Yet they succeeded up to a point, for when the Huns finally broke through they had been sufficiently weakened to prevent India from meeting the fate of the Roman Empire. It has been plausibly suggested that the resistance offered by the Chinese and Indians to the central Asian nomads was partially responsible for the fury with which they fell upon Europe. The coming of the Huns was another intervention by central Asia in the politics of northern India. The pattern followed that of the Shakas and the Kushanas, to be repeated later by the Turks, a possible difference being that for the Shakas and Kushanas it was an extension of their rule from central Asia to northern India, whereas for the Huns and Turks it was initially only an interest in acquiring loot.

But the successors of Kumara Gupta could not defend their kingdom as he had done, each repeated wave of the Hun invasions making the Guptas weaker. Skanda Gupta battled against the *mlechchhas* – the barbarians – also but he faced domestic problems, involving court rivalries and the breaking away of feudatories whose political integration into the metropolitan area of the Gupta state was tenuous. A fiscal crisis is suggested when some issues of the erstwhile high-value Gupta coins, which had changed from a Roman standard to an Indian standard, were debased. By *c.* 460 he had managed to rally the Gupta forces, but 467 is the last known date of Skanda Gupta. After his death, the central authority of the Guptas declined at an increasing pace. The succession of the various kings who followed is uncertain. A number of seals of administrative office have been discovered with the names of these kings, but the varied order of succession points to a confused close to the dynasty. A major blow came at the end of the fifth century when the Huns successfully broke through into northern India. Gupta power was eroded over the next fifty years, after which it gave way to a number of smaller kingdoms.

The wider Hun dominion extended from Persia to Khotan, with a capital at Bamiyan in Afghanistan. The first Hun king of any importance in India was Toramana, who claimed conquest over northern India as far as Eran in central India. Toramana's son Mihirakula (AD 520) conformed to the conventional image of the Hun. A Chinese pilgrim travelling in northern India at the time described him as uncouth in manner and an iconoclast, and especially hostile to Buddhism, a hostility expressed in the killing of monks and destruction of monasteries. According to the twelfth century historian, Kalhana, the hostility to Buddhism was apparently shared by the Shaiva brahmans. He comments in the *Rajatarangini* on the greed of the brahmans who eagerly accepted grants of land from the Hun rulers. Inscriptions from central India suggest that the Guptas were still making belated attempts to organize resistance to the Huns. Mihirakula was finally driven out of the plains and into Kashmir, where he died in about 542, after which the political impact of the Huns subsided. But the threat of the Huns continued for another century, even if it was largely ineffective. Gupta power was gradually weakening and the Huns accelerated the process of decline.

But this was not the sole effect of the Huns. In the wake of the Hun armies came migrants from central Asia who settled in India, some continuing to be pastoralists in hill areas and others following a variety of professions. At a less visible level, the potential for the creation of an imperial structure in northern India was now demolished, because political energy was directed towards keeping back the Huns to conserve what remained of the small kingdoms. Defence was conceived in local terms with occasional combinations of the smaller kingdoms, which sometimes led to consolidation under capable protectors whose military acumen rather than concern for their royal antecedents was a deciding factor. As elsewhere, the Huns had disrupted the tenor of north Indian life. The tide of Hun invasions did not recede until the end of the sixth century, when the Turks and the Sassanian Persians attacked them in Bactria. Subsequently, the Turks attacked the Persians but retained Bactria. Northern India was later to experience the Turks at close quarters.

Harsha

From the decline of the Guptas until the rise of Harsha in the early seventh century four kingdoms effectively held power in northern India: the Guptas of Magadha; the Maukharis of Kanauj; the Pushyabhutis of Thanesar; and the Maitrakas of Valabhi. The Guptas of Magadha were not part of the main Gupta dynasty, but were a minor line bearing the same name. At first the Maukharis held the region of the western Ganges Plain around Kanauj, gradually ousting the Magadhan Guptas from their kingdom. Originally, they were tributary rulers who established an independent kingdom, changing their title from *maharaja* to *maharaja-adhiraja*, doubtless in imitation of the earlier Guptas. The Pushyabhutis ruled in Thanesar, north of Delhi. A marriage alliance with the Maukharis led, on the death of the last Maukhari king, to the unification of the two kingdoms, which were eventually ruled by Harsha of the Pushyabhuti family. The Maitrakas, who had held administrative office under the Guptas, ruled in Saurashtra in Gujarat and developed Valabhi, their capital, into an important centre of commerce and of learning. On the periphery of these four were a number of lesser dynasties – the Manas and the Shailodbhavas in Orissa, the Varmans in Assam and the Aulikaras, with various others, recorded in inscriptions for their grants of land. Of the four main kingdoms, the Maitrakas survived the longest, ruling until the middle of the eighth century when they were weakened by attacks from the Arabs.

The Pushyabhuti family became influential on the accession of Prabhakara-vardhana, who has been described as:

a lion to the Huna deer, a burning fever to the king of the Indus land, a troubler of the sleep of Gujarat, a bilious plague to that scent elephant the Lord of Gandhara, a looter to the lawlessness of the Latas, an axe to the creeper of Malwa's glory.

Banabhatta, *Harshacharita*, tr. E. B. Cowell, p. 101

Prabhakara-vardhana's desire for conquest was eventually fulfilled by his younger son, Harsha-vardhana, generally known as Harsha.

Harsha began his reign in AD 606. A lively narrative of his early life comes from a biography, the *Harshacharita* (*The Life of Harsha*), written by his learned and bohemian friend, Banabhatta. This was the first formal *charita*, biography, of a king and inaugurated a genre of literature that became common in the subsequent period. Despite the eulogistic style these biographies focus on some salient events, although these have to be sifted from the formulaic. They provide contemporary perceptions of what was significant in the events of a reign, and have to be understood from the historical perspective of that time, apart from being assessed by modern standards of historical writing. One immediate reason for writing a biography (as in this case) was the legitimizing of the reign of the younger brother who might have been a rival of the elder, an act that challenged the sanctity of primogeniture.

As a contrast to the biography, the Chinese Buddhist monk Hsüan Tsang/ Xuan Zhuang, who was in India during Harsha's reign, left a much fuller account of his travels than that of the earlier Chinese monk, Fa Hsien/Fah Hian. Hsüan Tsang, originally a Confucian who became a zealous Buddhist, came from a mandarin family, hence the meticulous detail of his observations. His account is largely read as descriptive, a reading that omits the many nuances of his perceptions.

In the course of the forty-one years that he ruled, Harsha included among his tributary rulers those of Jalandhar (in the Punjab), Kashmir, Nepal and Valabhi. Shashanka, ruling in the east, was hostile to him and Harsha was unable to extend his power into the Deccan. He suffered his one major defeat at the hands of Pulakeshin II, a Chalukya king of the western Deccan. He shifted his capital from Thanesar, in the watershed region, to Kanauj. The first was perhaps too close to the threats from the north-west, while the second was located in the rich agricultural region of the western Ganges Plain, giving him control over the plain which linked him more directly to western India, as well as to routes to the south and east. Harsha was energetic and travelled frequently to ensure familiarity with his domain, to be accessible to his subjects and to keep a closer watch on his tributary rulers.

Despite his duties as king and administrator, Harsha is said to have written three plays, of which two are comedies in the classical style and the third has a contemplative theme influenced by Buddhist thought. There is some uncertainty whether he was the actual author or whether the plays should only be attributed to him. What is significant is that not only literary accomplishment but specific authorship had become associated with kings.

Events towards the end of Harsha's reign are described in Chinese sources. His contemporary, the T'ang Emperor Tai Tsung, sent an embassy to his court in 643 and again in 647. On the second occasion the Chinese ambassador found that Harsha had recently died, with the throne usurped by an undeserving king. The Chinese ambassador rushed to Nepal and Assam to raise a force with which the allies of Harsha defeated the usurper, who was taken to China as a prisoner. His name is recorded on the pedestal of Tai Tsung's tomb. The kingdom of Harsha disintegrated rapidly into small states. Some of his successors tangled with the ambitions of the Karkota dynasty ruling in Kashmir, and in the eighth century Lalitaditya attacked Yashovarman of Kanauj. Harsha realized the weakness of a cluster of small kingdoms and had conquered his neighbours to weld them into a larger structure. However, this did not survive owing to the particular political and economic conditions of the time.

Indicators of a Changing Political Economy

The Gupta kings took exalted imperial titles, such as *maharaja-adhiraja*, 'the great king of kings', *parameshvara*, 'the supreme lord', yet in the case of later rulers these titles were exaggerated since their claimants possessed limited political power when compared with the 'great kings' of earlier centuries. Such grand titles echo those of the rulers of the north-west and beyond and like them carry the flavour of divinity. The fashion for such titles extends even to those who patronized Buddhism, for example the Bhaumakara dynasty of Orissa, where the kings referred to themselves as *paramopasaka*, 'the most devout lay-follower'. Statements on royal power drew increasingly on rhetoric, some going back to the sacrificial rituals of kingship in Vedic Brahmanism and some being currently invented. Among the latter were the *mahadanas*, the great gifts, the great gift frequently referring to those who performed the rituals and bestowed status on the ruler.

In the Ganges Plain, under the direct control of the Guptas, the king was the focus of administration, assisted by the princes, ministers and advisers. Princes also held positions rather like viceroys of provinces. The province (*desha*, *rashtra* or *bhukti*) was divided into a number of districts (*pradesha* or *vishaya*), each district having its own administrative offices. But for all practical purposes local administration was distant from the centre. Decisions, whether of policy or in relation to individual situations, were generally taken locally, unless they had a specific bearing on the policy or orders of central authority. The officers in charge of the districts (*ayuktaka*, *vishayapati*) and a yet higher provincial official (with the title of *kumarama-tya*) were the link between local administration and the centre. In some cases the office became hereditary, further underlining its local importance. Lower down in the bureaucratic hierarchy were the *ashtakula-adhikaranas*, members of the village assembly, *mahattara*s, elders of the community, and *grama-adhyaksha*s, headmen of villages. The terms used for administrative units carried their own symbolic meaning, incorporating the notion of that which nourishes – *ahara*, *bhoga*, *bhukti*, etc.

This was significantly different from the Mauryan administration. Whereas Ashoka insisted that he be kept informed of what was happening, the Guptas seemed satisfied with leaving it to the *kumaramatyas* and the *ayuktakas*. Admittedly, a taut administration is described in the *Artha-shastra*, but this was a normative text and the evidence from inscriptions and seals suggests that the Gupta administration was more decentralized, with officials holding more than one office. Harsha's tours were similar to those of a royal inspector since he looked into the general working of administration and tax collection, listened to complaints and made charitable donations.

Villages were of various categories: *grama, palli*, hamlet; *gulma*, a military settlement in origin; *khetaka*, also a hamlet; and so on. They came under the control of rural bodies consisting of the headman and the village elders, some of whom held the office of the *grama-adhyaksha* or the *kutumbi*. In urban administration each city had a council consisting of the *nagarashreshthin*, the person who presided over the city corporation, the *sarthavaha*, the chief representative of the guild of merchants, the *prathama-kulika*, a representative of the artisans, and the *prathama-kayastha*, the chief scribe. A difference between this council and the committee described by Megasthenes and Kautilya is that the earlier government appointed the committees, whereas in the Gupta system the council consisted of local representatives, among whom commercial interests often predominated.

If the Mauryan state was primarily concerned with collecting revenue from an existing economy, or expanding peasant agriculture through the intervention of the state, the Gupta state and its contemporaries made initial attempts at restructuring the agrarian economy. This took the form of land grants to individuals, who were expected to act as catalysts in rural areas. There was more emphasis on converting existing communities into peasants than bringing in settlers. The system developed from the notion that granting land as a support to kingship could be more efficacious than the performance of a sacrifice, and that land was appropriate as a *mahadana* or 'great gift'. This investment by the king was also intended to improve the cultivation of fertile, irrigated lands and to encourage the settlement of wasteland. Peripheral areas could therefore be brought into the larger agrarian economy, and the initial grants tended not to be in the Ganges heartland but in the areas beyond. There was gradually less emphasis on the state in establishing agricultural settlements, with recipients of land grants being expected to take the initiative.

Grants of land were made to religious and ritual specialists or to officers. This did not produce revenue for the state, but it allowed some shuffling of revenue demands at the local level and created small centres of prosperity in rural areas that, if imitated, could lead to wider improvement. If the land granted to brahmans (whether as ritual specialists or as administrators) was wasteland or forest, the grantee took on the role of a pioneer in introducing agriculture. Brahmans became proficient in supervising agrarian activities, helped by manuals on agriculture, such as the *Krishiparashara*, which may date to this or the subsequent period. Some normative texts forbid agriculture to the brahmans, except in dire need, but this did not prevent brahmanical expertise in agricultural activity.

Commercial enterprise was encouraged through donations to guilds, even if the interest was to go to a religious institution, and by placing commercial entrepreneurs in city councils and in positions with a potential for investment and profit. The range of taxes coming to the state from commerce was expanded, which in turn required an expansion in the hierarchy of officials. Although the granting of land was at first marginal, by about the eighth century AD it had expanded, gradually resulting in a political economy that was recognizably different from pre-Gupta times.

Kings who conquered neighbouring kingdoms sometimes converted the defeated kings into tributary or subordinate rulers, often referred to in modern writing as feudatories. Agreements were also negotiated with such rulers. The term *samanta*, originally meaning neighbour, gradually changed its meaning to a tributary ruler. This implied more defined relationships between the king and local rulers, relationships that became crucial in later times with a tussle between royal demands and the aspirations of the *samantas*. Where the latter were strong the king's power weakened. But he needed the acquiescence of the *samantas* – the *samanta-chakra* or circle of *samantas* – to keep his prestige. *Samantas* were in the ambiguous position of being potential allies or enemies.

In addition to the tributary rulers, grants of land had created other categories of intermediaries. Grants to religious beneficiaries included some to temples, monasteries and brahmans. Such grants to temples empowered the sects that managed the temples. Villages could also be given as a grant to a temple for its maintenance. This added local administration to the role of the temple, in addition to being an area of sacred space. At a time when land grants were tokens of special favour the grant to the brahman must have underlined his privileged position. The *agrahara* grant of rent-free land or a village that could be made to a collectivity of brahmans, the *brahmadeya* grant to brahmans, and grants to temples and monasteries, were exempt from tax. The brahmans were often those proficient in the *Vedas*, or with specialized knowledge, particularly of astrology. Gifts to brahmans were expected to ward off the evils of the present Kali Age, and recourse to astrology appears to have been more common. Even if it was not a grant in perpetuity, the descendants of the grantee tended gradually to treat the land granted as an inheritance. But the king had the power to revoke the grant, unless categorically stated to the contrary by the original grantor. However, revoking a grant carried the danger of creating a nucleus of political opposition. Many of the inscriptions contained a formulaic sentence that the preservation of a grant is more meritorious than the making of a grant.

Grants of land began to supersede monetary donations to religious institutions. Land was more permanent, was heritable and the capital less liable to be tampered with. Such grants were more conducive to landlordism among brahman grantees, although the monasteries did not lag too far behind. Receiving revenue was easier to handle than pioneering agrarian settlements. Nevertheless, granting land was seen as accumulating merit by the donor and began to replace gifts of monetary or other wealth among Buddhists. Grants to Buddhist institutions tended to be concentrated in particular areas after the seventh century, when Buddhism was less widespread. The larger Buddhist monasteries often received villages, presumably because these were easier for monasteries to administer than the colonization of new lands. Nalanda is said to have received the revenue of a hundred, or possibly even two hundred, villages.

Another significant feature of this period was that officers were occasionally rewarded by revenue from grants of land, which were an alternative to cash salaries for military or administrative service. This is mentioned in some land-grant inscriptions from this period onwards, and also in the account of Hsüan Tsang. Such grants were fewer in number. Not all grants to brahmans were intended for religious purposes since there were many literate brahmans performing official functions. Vassalage, involving a warrior class with ties of obedience and protection, is not commonly met with.

The granting of land and villages could weaken the authority of the king, although initially the grants were moderate and only later became frequent or extensive. Such grants distanced the owners from the control of the central authority, thus predisposing administration to be more decentralized. Those with substantial grants of land providing revenue could together accumulate sufficient power and resources to challenge the ruling dynasty. If in addition they could mobilize support from peer groups and others such as the forest chiefs, or coerce the peasants into fighting for them, they could overthrow the existing authority and establish themselves as kings, at least on the fringes of the kingdom.

Brahmans as religious beneficiaries were granted land, ostensibly in return for legitimizing and validating the dynasty, or averting a misfortune through the correct performance of rituals or the king earning merit. Lineage links with heroes of earlier times were sought to enhance status through a presumed descent. If the grant was substantial enough the grantee could become the progenitor of a dynasty through appropriation of power and resources.

The grants were also part of a process of proselytizing where the grantee sought to propagate his religion. Many grants were made to brahmans proficient in the *Vedas*, but when they settled near forested areas, or in villages already observing their own beliefs and rituals, the very different observances of the brahmans may have created tensions requiring a negotiated adjustment on both sides. In this situation the Puranic sects were useful mediators between Vedic Brahmanism and the religions of the local peoples. Even if the brahman took over the ritual of the priest, he would have needed to incorporate local mythology and iconography into the flexible and ever-expanding Puranic sects.

This would also have required existing social organizations to give way to *jati* and *varna* status. Inscriptional evidence of the sixth century AD refers to the conquest of eighteen forest polities as the inheritance of those who called themselves *parivrajaka* rajas (*parivrajaka* normally refers to wandering religious mendicants). This may point to the ancestor having received a grant of forested land. Some such rajas were given a *brahma-kshatra* origin, suggesting a merging of ancestors claiming brahman and *kshatriya* status. The process of change would have involved the conversion of a forest tribe to a caste. Sometimes *mlechchha* tribes are said to be participants in the origin myths of dynasties, such as Pulindas in the Shailodbhava myths and Bhils in the Guhila myths. These were probably chiefs of forest-peoples who became allies of the grantees, perhaps intermarried and either founded kingdoms or were involved in the founding of a kingdom. Many of the early temples dedicated to Puranic deities are located in central India, possibly because of the proximity of forest settlements. Incarnations of deities, such as the *varaha*/boar incarnation of Vishnu, are also found in central India and may represent a compromise between a tribal cult and a sect of the Puranic religion.

The granting of land gradually changed the political economy through conversion to peasant cultivation in new areas. Wasteland, theoretically belonging to the state, included grassland and jungle, the intention being for the grantee to clear and settle it then introduce plough agriculture to yield a revenue. Arable land was already cultivated even if it was lying fallow at the time of the grant. Crop patterns continued broadly along the same lines. Hsüan Tsang stated that sugar-cane and wheat were grown in the north-west, and rice in Magadha and further east. He also mentioned a wide variety of fruit and vegetables.

Cultivated land was further classified according to whether or not there were facilities for irrigating the fields. In western India, apart from the donation of villages and fields, donations of stepwells are also recorded in inscriptions. Water wheels, built and maintained by cultivators, became a familiar part of the rural landscape and in one case such a wheel is described as a garland of pots. Smaller irrigation works, from water-lifts to tanks or small dams, were built through local initiative or by the grantee. Some inscriptions, referring to the latter, touchingly say that these are contributions towards the religious merit of the author's parents. There was a sense that the presence of the local community and its well were associated with the smaller grants. The dam on the Sudarshana lake, originally constructed by the Maurya governor and repaired by Rudradaman, was once again repaired and brought into use. It is specifically stated that the cost of the renovation was borne entirely by the administration, with no extra taxes or corvée being imposed. Presumably, such extra taxes and labour were normally demanded.

The grantee received rights over revenue, together with some administrative and judicial rights. These increased in later periods and were included in the terms of the grant. In the case of grants of villages and cultivated land, the peasants working the land were transferred together with the land. This created a category of tied peasantry whose numbers gradually grew larger. But this was not the equivalent of serfdom as the contractual relation between peasant and grantee was not identical with the generally accepted pattern of serfdom. Nor was the labour used parallel to that of serfs. The peasant so transferred was not necessarily required to cultivate the land of the grantee in addition to his own. His contribution was to pay the grantee the equivalent of what he had earlier paid to the state as tax. Demands of other kinds could be made by the grantee as stipulated in the terms of the grant. Major concessions to the grantee were exemption from billeting troops or provisioning officials, and the right to impose new taxes and *vishti*, corvée. What was emerging gradually was a juxtaposition of large-scale ownership of land with small-scale peasant production. The compulsions on the peasant were not always economic and the production of a surplus could be enforced. This was complemented by a hierarchical society in which caste differentiation was an additional form of control.

The inscription recording the grant was often engraved on copper plates, held together by a ring which carried the seal of the donor. Since this was the legal document registering the grant, it was necessary to keep it in the family and produce it when required to prove ownership or the claim to rights. Sometimes the grant was inscribed on a slab of stone that would be kept in a safe and prominent place, for instance, the local temple. An example of the standard formula is shown by the following grant, issued by Prabhavati Gupta, the Vakataka Queen:

Success. Victory has been attained by the Bhagavat. From Nandivardhana. There was the *maharaja* the illustrious Ghatotkachchha, the first Gupta king. His excellent son was the *maharaja* the illustrious Chandra Gupta [I]. His excellent son was the *maharaja-adhiraja*, the illustrious Samudra Gupta who was born of the Queen Kumaradevi; who was the daughter's son of the Lichchhavi; who performed several horse sacrifices. His excellent son is the *maharaja-adhiraja* Chandra Gupta II graciously favoured by him; who is a fervent devotee of the Bhagavat; who is a matchless warrior on the earth; who has exterminated all kings; whose fame has tasted the water of the four oceans; who has donated many thousands of crores of cows and gold. His daughter the illustrious Prabhavatigupta of the Dharana *gotra* born of the illustrious Queen Kuberanaga who was born in the Naga family; who is a fervent devotee of the Bhagavat; who was the chief Queen of the illustrious Rudrasena [II] the *maharaja* of the Vakatakas; who is the mother of the heir-apparent the illustrious Divakarasena; having announced her good health, commands the householders of the village, brahmans and others in the village of Danguna in the *ahara* of Supratishtha to the east of Vilavanaka, to the south of Shirshagrama, to the west of Kadapinjana, and to the north of Sidivivaraka, as follows: 'Be it known to you that on the twelfth lunar day of the bright fortnight of Karttika, we have, for augmenting our own religious merit, donated this village with the pouring out of water to the acharya Chanalasvamin who is a devotee of the Bhagavat as a gift not previously made, after having offered it to the footprints of the Bhagavat. Wherefore you should obey all his commands with proper respect.

And we confer here on him the following exemptions incidental to an *agrahara* granted to the *chaturvidya* brahmans as approved by former kings: this village is not to be entered by soldiers and policemen; it is exempt from providing grass, hides for seats and charcoal to touring officers; exempt from purchasing alcohol and digging salt; exempt from mines and *khadira* trees; exempt from supplying flowers and milk; it carries the right to hidden treasures and deposits and major and minor taxes.

Wherefore this grant should be maintained and augmented by future kings. Whoever disregarding our order will cause obstructions when complained against by the brahmans, we will inflict punishment together with a fine . . .'

The charter has been written in the thirteenth regnal year and engraved by Chakradasa.

> 'The Poona Plates of Prabhavatigupta', in V. V. Mirashi (ed.),
> *Inscriptions of the Vakatakas*, CII, V, p. 5 ff.

Land revenue was a substantial source of income for the state, which claimed one-sixth of the produce and sometimes raised it to a quarter. One-sixth was a conventional figure, applying even to the merit acquired by the king from the asceticism of the renouncers! Variations on this figure as a revenue demand occurred with other taxes, such as that on the area under cultivation, the provision of irrigation facilities and suchlike. The making of land grants, when they grew to a substantial size, would have meant a loss of some revenue to the state. But there were other compensations in the system, such as the grantees forming a network of support, even in far-flung areas, which provided legitimacy to the ruling dynasty; and in the granting of wasteland new areas were opened up to cultivation without state investment, such as land to the east of the lower Ganges.

As always, the measuring of land varied. A variety of terms were used, based on the length of the hand, the arm, the bow, the plough or, in a different system of measurement, the amount of land sown by using a specific quantity of seeds or ploughed by yoked oxen in a specific time (for example, *kulyavapa*, *dronavapa*, *nivartana*). A *nivartana* has been variously calculated as less than 1 acre or up to 4 acres. The former is more likely, since six *nivartanas* are said to suffice for a household. That some grants were of an enormous size can be gauged by one statement that a merchant bought half a village, then donated it to a brahman. If this statement is taken literally, it conjures up an immensity of complications for all concerned in terms of rights and obligations. The price of land inevitably varied. Cultivated land, especially if it had irrigation facilities, was more highly valued than wasteland. In one case a certain acreage in Bengal, probably of cultivated land, was valued at four *dinara* (gold coins), equivalent to sixty-four silver coins. It has been suggested that the area mentioned would be the equivalent of 12 to 16 acres, but estimates vary. The purchase of land for donation to religious beneficiaries is recorded in inscriptions, but the purchase of land as an investment is also referred to in texts.

Urban Life

State revenue was derived from a variety of taxes – from the land, and from trade. The maintenance of a powerful state extending patronage to various activities was expensive, and may have put pressure on the economy. The debasement of the later Gupta coinage has been interpreted as recording a fiscal crisis. If Harsha really did divide the income of the kingdom into four, as Hsüan Tsang maintained – a quarter for government expenses, another quarter for the salaries of public servants, a third quarter for the reward of intellectual attainments, and the last quarter for gifts – such a division, although idealistic in concept, may have been economically impractical.

It has been argued that there was a decay in urban centres at this time, pointing to the Gupta period economy having feudal characteristics. Towns not only declined, but many suffered a visible termination of commerce. Excavation levels of the Kushana period show a more prosperous condition. Maritime trade continued in the peninsula but with a smaller impact. The Hun invasion of the Roman Empire would have disturbed the commercial circuits, not only in the areas beyond north-western India but in the eastern Mediterranean. The insufficiency of agricultural produce to maintain towns has been attributed to climate change, with increasing desiccation and aridity of the environment, catastrophes of various kinds in the countryside and a fall in fertility. A decrease in rainfall and the ill-effects of deforestation would also have affected agricultural production. Such changes would have weakened the agrarian support necessary to towns. An urban decline can be suggested on the basis of these combined changes.

One difficulty in assessing urban life by counterposing textual and archaeological data is that the former reflects the norms of the wealthy and therefore projects a positive image, whereas the latter can present a different picture including that of more ordinary people. Textual data presents a range of social conditions and it may be necessary to wait for horizontal excavations in order to draw further inferences from archaeological data. It was earlier argued that the revival of urbanism did not take place until the twelfth century or thereabouts, but this time period has now been reduced by evidence of towns to the ninth or tenth centuries. A further problem relates to the question of whether this decline was subcontinental or restricted to certain regions. The evidence for some urban decline in the Ganges Plain has been discussed but noticeable decline in some other regions is not so apparent.

Some towns certainly declined, but it was not a subcontinental phenomenon and the reasons for decline varied. Apart from environmental changes the reasons would have been connected with economic change. If there was a tapping of new resources, with distribution from new centres of exchange, trade routes may have bypassed areas that were once important. New towns sprang up in the eastern Ganges Plain. Elsewhere Kanyakubja/Kanauj commanded an impressive agrarian hinterland, which remained necessary to the growth of a town, the exchange of agricultural produce being one avenue to a more broad-based exchange. Paunar in the Deccan flourished during the Vakataka period. Valabhi grew in commercial importance through being linked to the trade of the Arabian Sea. Arab traders, affluent in the Arabian peninsula, were picking up the trade across the Arabian Sea.

Meanwhile, Indian merchants had become more assertive in central Asia and south-east Asia. The establishment of Indian trading stations in both regions initially diverted income to these parts. This may have been responsible for a brief decline in the wealth of Indian cities, until the Indian middleman began to prosper in both regions. In some parts of the subcontinent the Gupta age was the concluding phase of the economic momentum that began in the preceding period. In other parts the sixth century saw commercial links involving new groups of people. Merchants along the west coast became active, while contacts with Arab traders probably initiated a new pattern of exchange.

Sources of commercial wealth consisted of the produce from mines, plants and animals, converted to items through craftsmanship. Gold was mined in Karnataka but panned in the mountain streams of the far north. The high quality of craftsmanship in gold is evident in the superbly designed and meticulously minted Gupta coins, each a miniature piece of sculpture. They tend to be found in hoards and some are in mint condition. This has led to the suggestion that they were used for presentation, rather than commercially. However, they initially followed the Kushana weight standard, so presumably they circulated in central Asian and north Indian trade. High-value coins were useful for trading in horses and silk, and a familiar weight standard facilitated commerce. Although the art of portraiture seems not to have attracted the designers of coins in India, Gupta coins carry aesthetically impressive depictions of the activities of the rulers. Some of these endorse the symbols of kingship from what were now ancient rituals. Seals are another source of information, both in themselves where they carry succession lists and as attached to copper plate inscriptions.

The mining of copper and iron continued, being used for household items, utensils, implements and weapons. The refining of iron led to a wider use of steel. Among the most impressive metal objects of this period is the pillar of iron, now located at Mehrauli in Delhi, reaching a height of just over 23 feet and made of a remarkably fine metal which has scarcely rusted. It carries an inscription referring to a King called Chandra, identified by some as Chandra Gupta II. Equally impressive is the life-size copper statue of the Buddha, cast in two parts, and now in the Birmingham Museum. Polished metal mirrors were also popular among the rich.

Ivory work remained at a premium, requiring as much delicacy and skill as the making of jewellery. The pearl fisheries of western India prospered when pearls were in demand in distant markets. The cutting, polishing and preparing of a variety of precious stones – jasper, agate, carnelian, quartz, lapis-lazuli – were also associated with more distant trade. Bead-making was linked to towns such as Ujjain and Bhokardan. Seals were cut from stone and ivory, some were engraved on copper, and a few terracotta impressions also survive. Pottery remained a basic craft though the elegant black polished ware was no longer used. Instead a red ware was common, some of it with an almost metallic finish.

The manufacture of various textiles had a vast domestic market, since textiles featured prominently in the north–south trade within India, and there was also considerable demand for Indian textiles in Asian markets. Silk, muslin, calico, linen, wool and cotton were produced in quantity, and western India was one of the centres of silk-weaving. Later in the Gupta period the production of silk may have declined, since many members of an important guild of silk-weavers in western India migrated inland to follow other occupations.

Guilds continued to be vital in the manufacture of goods and in commercial enterprise. In some matters they retained their autonomy, for instance in their internal organization, their laws being respected. The institutionalizing of a craft, ranging from architecture to oil-pressing, by forming a guild which included mercantile corporate organizations had advantages not limited only to commerce. The guilds provided socio-economic support in some ways parallel to that of a *jati*. Judging by the frequency of guild representatives and merchants being members of urban administrative bodies, it would seem that the authority of the *Dharma-shastras*, which gave some professions a low social ranking, did not hold for all situations. This is another example of the norms of the *Dharma-shastras* giving less attention to the alternative perspective on urban and commercial life arising from the actual functioning of social groups. The royal and corporate authorities governing urban life were not always in agreement with brahmanical statutes, and this had its roots in the pre-Gupta period. There is a continual interplay of status from text to real life, which disallows any simplistic generalization about the unchanging function of caste.

The rate of interest on loans varied according to the purpose for which money was required. The excessively high rates demanded in earlier times on loans for overseas trade were reduced to a reasonable 20 per cent, indicating a confidence in overseas trade. Interest could exceed the legal rate, provided both parties were agreeable, but it could seldom be permitted to exceed the principal in total amount. The lowering of the rate of interest also indicates the greater availability of goods and a possible decrease in rates of profit.

The campaigns of Samudra Gupta to the east and the south, and the repeated tours of Harsha, would have required efficient communication and the movement of goods. On the roads, ox-drawn carts were common, and where travel was over rougher terrain pack animals were used, or even elephants in heavily forested areas. The lower reaches of large rivers such as the Ganges, Narmada, Godavari, Krishna and Kaveri were the main waterways. The ports of the eastern coast, such as Tamralipti and Ghanta-shala, handled the northern Indian trade with the eastern coast and south-east Asia, and those of the west coast traded with the eastern Mediterranean and western Asia. The ports and production centres of peninsular India that were involved with maritime trade appear not to have declined at this time, but these were outside Gupta control.

The export of spices, pepper, sandalwood, pearls, precious stones, per-fumes, indigo and herbs continued, but the commodities that were imported differed from those of earlier times. There appears to have been an appreci-able rise in the import of horses, coming overland from Iran and Bactria to centres in north-west India, or from Arabia by sea to the western coast. India never bred sufficient horses of quality, perhaps because of adverse climatic conditions and inappropriate pasturage, so the best livestock was always imported. This may have had consequences for the cavalry of Indian armies, eventually making it less effective in comparison with central Asian horsemen.

Indian ships were now regularly traversing the Arabian Sea and the Indian Ocean, and venturing into the China Seas. The 'Island of the Black Yavanas' is mentioned, which may have been a reference to Madagascar or Zanzibar. Indian contacts with the east African coast are thought to date to the first millennium BC, and by now this contact had developed through trade. Despite this activity, the codifiers of custom and social laws were prohibiting an upper-caste person to travel by sea, to cross the black waters. The objection to travelling to distant lands was due to the risk of contamination by the *mlechchhas* (those outside the boundaries of caste and therefore ritually impure); it was also difficult to observe rituals and caste rules. The ban had the additional and indirect advantage for the brahman that, if insisted upon, it could theoretically curb the economic power of the trading community. But this did not curtail the entrepreneuring spirit of Indians who wished to trade, irrespective of whether they were brahman or non-brahman. Many were Buddhists and would not have paid much attention to brahmanical rules. The Jainas, however, did not venture out in large numbers, perhaps because their rigorous religious observances discouraged travel to distant places.

The plan of most cities had not changed radically from that of earlier cities, being laid out in broad areas following the intersection of the two arterial roads. Streets containing markets and shops were separated accord-ing to the commodity produced and sold. Houses often had a balcony giving a view over the street. Buildings were of brick in the richer sections of the city. Wood and wattled bamboo remained the usual building material in the less prosperous sections. Houses were orientated to cardinal points, and there were adequate drains and wells. Yet it was a culture showing a wide variation in living. The comfortably installed town-dweller would have had little to do with the areas outside the town limits, where the outcastes dwelt, in probably much the same way as the modern shantytown. However, villages probably showed less disparity in their standard of living.

The daily life of a comfortably well-off citizen as described in the *Kamasutra* – the book on the art of love – was a gentle existence devoted to the refinements of life for those who had both the leisure and the wherewithal for these. Comfortable if not luxurious surroundings were provided to harmonize with moods conducive to poetry, painting and recitals of music, in all of which the young city dilettante was expected to excel. The writing of a text on erotica is not altogether unexpected in a situation where urban living was held up as the model of civilized life. The young man had also to be trained in the art of love. The *Kamasutra* discusses this with lucidity and sometimes startling imagination, a parallel to modern writing on erotica. The courtesan was a normal feature of urban life, neither romanticized nor treated with contempt. Judging by the training given to a courtesan, it was among the more demanding professions, for, unlike the prostitute, she was a cultured and sociable companion similar to the geisha of Japan or the hetaera of Greece.

Social Mores

However pleasant life may have been for the well-to-do urbanite as depicted in the *Kamasutra*, life for most people was less so. Famines and poverty were explained away by resort to astrology and by the frequently made statement that one cannot expect better times in the Kaliyuga since it is the age of decline. A telling incident comes from Kalidasa's play on the story of Shakuntala. The fisherman who caught the fish that had swallowed the king's signet ring is brought before the officers and is roughed up, taunted about his low status and made ready for execution as a thief. But when the king sends him a purse of money as a reward, he shares it with his erstwhile tormentors to keep them happy (as he states in an aside), and the officer suggests a visit to the wine shop, which is gladly agreed to by the fisherman. An official drinking with a low-caste fisherman needs some reconciling with the rules of the *Dharma-shastras*. Or does this provide evidence of a social flexibility generally denied in the normative texts? Bana's *Harshacharita* refers to the poor people of villages garnering the grain left in the camp of the king after the soldiers have moved away; he also describes the king's elephants trampling on the hovels of the poor who are thereby left homeless, and all they can do is to pelt the soldiers with clods of earth.

Categories of slaves were drawn more commonly from the lower castes and untouchables. There is a fuller treatment of slaves in the *Dharmashastras* of this time than in the earlier ones, which suggests a greater use of slave labour although it still did not reach anywhere near the proportions of slave labour in some other parts of the ancient world. But there is a continuing mention of hired labour that seems to have been used on a larger scale than before. The sources of slaves were the usual – prisoners-of-war, debt bondsmen and slaves born to slave women – but also include the curious category of those who have revoked their vows of renunciation. The largest number of slaves seems to have been employed in domestic work. For labour in agriculture there were other categories such as bonded labour, hired labour and those required to perform stipulated jobs as a form of *vishti*, forced labour or labour tax. Caste regulations prevented the untouchables from being employed in domestic work. Forced to work in a caste society, untouchables constituted a permanent reservoir of landless labour, their permanence ensured by the disabilities of their birth.

Fa Hsien/Fah Hian, a Chinese Buddhist monk who was on pilgrimage to India in the years AD 405 to 411, collecting Buddhist manuscripts and studying at Buddhist monasteries, describes people as generally happy. Yet he also writes that the untouchables had to sound a clapper in the streets of the town so that people were warned of their presence; and that if an untouchable came into close range, the upper-caste person would have to perform a ritual ablution. All this may have become normal practice by now. Hsüan Tsang states that butchers, fishermen, theatrical performers, executioners and scavengers were forced to live outside the city and their houses were marked so that they could be avoided. Yet accounts by Buddhist monks from China tend on the whole to be complimentary, perhaps because for them India was the 'western heaven', the holy land of the Buddha, or perhaps because they were making subconscious comparisons with other places.

Another reflection of the structures in a society can be gauged from the social construction of gender relations. Women were idealized in literature and art and some of the images thus created are attractive to the reader or the viewer. But they conform to male ideals of the perfect woman and such ideals placed women in a subordinate position. Education of a limited kind was permitted to upper-caste women as a marginal qualification, but was certainly not intended to encourage their participation in discussion or provide professional expertise.

Women's access to property or inheritance was limited and varied according to caste, custom and region. Social practices were not uniform, however much the codes attempted to make them so. Matrilineal systems organized inheritance differently from the patriarchal. The prevalence of cross-cousin marriage among some social groups also had implications for the inheritance of property. There are hints of what might earlier have been cross-cousin marriage in elite circles in northern India, but since the normative texts supported patriarchy those wanting upward social mobility would have adopted the same pattern.

Characteristic of the status of upper-caste women in later centuries was that early marriages were advocated, often even pre-puberty marriages. A widow was expected to live in austerity, but if of the *kshatriya* caste should preferably immolate herself on the funeral pyre of her husband especially if he had died a hero's death. This would make her a *sati*. The earliest historical evidence for this practice dates from AD 510, when it was commemorated in an inscription at Eran. Subsequently, incidents of *sati* increased. This coincided with the current debate on whether or not a woman, particularly a widow, could remarry. Some argued that it should be permitted if her husband disappeared, died, became impotent, renounced society or was ostracized. Others were opposed to the idea. Encouraging a woman to become a *sati* could have been one solution. This also coincided with the forging of the culture of the new *kshatriya* and, as with many upstart groups, some rules were likely to have been taken rather literally. If the origin of the family lay in a society where widow remarriage was common, there the custom would have to be curbed.

A small number of women with some measure of freedom chose to opt out of the 'normal' householding activities required of a woman, and became nuns, or trained to be courtesans or joined troupes of performers. The world of the artisan, merchant and small-scale landowner was different from that of the court circles and the landed aristocracy. The difference is reflected in the former being more frequently the laity of the Shramanic religions, whereas the latter tended to support the *Dharma-shastra* norms – at least in theory. Conflict with these norms may have arisen where newly created castes continued with their pre-caste practices, and some would have supported a more open participation of women in society. The rulers of Uchchakalpa in central India were meticulous about naming the mother of each of the rulers in the genealogical section of the inscription. The concession to custom over norms as advised in the *Naradasmriti*, a contemporary *Dharma-shastra*, was a more significant statement than is often realized.

It is evident from the inscriptions of this period that some degree of mobility among *jatis* was accepted. The most interesting example is probably that of the guild of silk-weavers in western India. When they could no longer maintain themselves through the production of silk, the guild members moved from Lata in western India to Mandasor (Madhya Pradesh), some of them adopting professions of a higher-caste status than their original one, such as those of archers, soldiers, bards and scholars. Despite the change of profession, loyalty to the original guild seems to have remained, for at least one generation. Being sun-worshippers they financed the building of a temple to Surya, and gave the history of the guild in a lengthy inscription in the temple, dated to AD 436. The language of the inscription echoes the language of Kalidasa.

A number of *Dharma-shastras* were written and they were not uniform in all the views they propagated. While none supported a liberal position in relation to caste and gender, nevertheless the degrees of orthodoxy differed. The best known were those of Yajnavalkya, Brihaspati, Narada and Katyayana. The latter two describe the theoretical norms of the judicial process. The king appointed the judges. If necessary he could be present as the highest court of appeal, assisted by the judges, ministers, chief priest, brahmans and assessors, depending on the needs of the individual cases. Representatives of professions, especially merchants, could also advise the king. Judgement was based on the *Dharma-shastras*, social usage or the edict of the king, with usage often having priority. Evidence was based on any or all of three sources – documents, witnesses or the possession of incriminating objects. Ordeal as a means of proof was not only permitted but prescribed. Katyayana accepted the theory of punishments according to caste, with the highest receiving the lightest punishment. In some conditions, however, this could be reversed.

Contrary to Fa Hsien's statement that vegetarianism was customary in India, other sources indicate that meat was commonly eaten especially among the elite. The flesh of the ox was medically prescribed to enhance vigour. Wine, both the locally produced variety and that imported from the west, was popular as was the chewing of *pan*, betel leaf. Theatrical entertainment had a wide audience, some drawn from court circles and some from townspeople. Folk dance performances and recitals of music are mentioned, particularly on special occasions. Gambling continued to hold the attention of men, as did animal fights, particularly of the ram, the cock, and the quail, which were more common in rural areas.

Systems of Knowledge

Formal education was available in brahman *ashramas*, hermitages, and in Buddhist and Jaina monasteries. In the former it would have been restricted to the upper castes. Theoretically, the period of studentship at the former lasted over many years, but it is unlikely that most would spend long periods as students. Learning was a personalized experience involving teacher and pupil. The emphasis was on memorizing texts such as parts of the *Vedas*, and gaining familiarity with the contents of the *Dharma-shastras* and subjects such as grammar, rhetoric, prose and verse composition, logic and metaphysics. But much else was included in Sanskrit learning, such as astronomy, mathematics, medicine and astrology.

Tangential to medicine were works on veterinary science, relating mainly to horses and elephants, both important to the army. In some subjects Sanskrit texts reflected the theoretical view, as well as the practical application. Generally, however, the practice of a profession was maintained as a distinctive form of education, handled by the actual professionals. The writing of a manual in Sanskrit on a particular subject was an indicator of its importance. Varahamihira discussed aspects of agricultural practice that included the cultivation of new crops such as indigo, the effects of rainfall and methods of water-divining. These discussions were continued in works such as the *Manasara* and the *Krishiparashara*.

Buddhist monasteries took students for a shorter time of about ten years, but those wishing to be ordained as monks had to remain longer. Learning for novices began through an oral method but changed to literacy. Libraries in monasteries contained important manuscripts that were copied when they became frayed. Nalanda in south Bihar became the foremost Buddhist monastic and educational centre in the north, attracting students from places as distant as China and south-east Asia. This was possible because it had an income from a large number of villages granted to it for its upkeep. Excavations at Nalanda have revealed an extensive area of well-constructed monastic residences and halls of worship.

The early expositions of Indian astronomy, used in part to organize the large sacrifices, were recorded in the *Jyotishavedanga*. Contact with the Hellenistic world had introduced a variety of new systems, some of which were incorporated into Indian astronomy. There was also a shift from astronomy based on the lunar mansions and constellations, as discussed in early sources, to astronomy that placed greater emphasis on the planets. In part, this followed from the dialogue between Hellenistic and

Indian astronomers. The new astronomy marked a departure that gave direction to the new theories influencing astronomy and mathematics in the Eurasian world. Some of this information was included in larger texts of the later period, but some was discussed in texts specific to astronomy. Ujjain, which was on the Indian prime meridian, became a centre for studies in astronomy.

Aryabhata, in AD 499, was the first astronomer to tackle the more fundamental problems of the new studies. He calculated *pi* to 3.1416 and the length of the solar year to 365.3586805 days, both remarkably close to recent estimates. He believed that the earth was a sphere and rotated on its axis, and that the shadow of the earth falling on the moon caused eclipses. The explanation for the cause of eclipses was quite contentious as the orthodox theory described it as a demon swallowing the planet, a theory strongly refuted even in later times by the astronomer Lalla. Aryabhata and those who followed his line of thought are regarded as more scientific than other Indian astronomers of the time. Aryabhata's contribution to knowledge relating to astronomy was quite remarkable and was a departure from earlier theories of Vedic astronomy. The later objection to some of these ideas, for instance, by Brahmagupta, appear to have been motivated by a wish not to displease the orthodox.

In the work of a close contemporary, Varahamihira, the growing interest in horoscopy and astrology was included in the study of astronomy and mathematics. This was an addition that Aryabhata might have questioned, since Varahamihira's emphasis was on astrology rather than astronomy, and, although a sharp dichotomy between the two may not have been common, the emphasis did make a difference. Astrology denied the validity of Aryabhata's theories. Varahamihira's *Panchasiddhantika* (*Five Schools*), discussed the five currently known schools of astronomy, of which two reflected a close knowledge of Hellenistic astronomy. The exploration of all these systems had not been carried out in isolation: an increasing dialogue existed between Indian and Arab astronomers and mathematicians, similar to the earlier one between Hellenistic and Indian astronomers. Indian works on mathematics, astronomy and medicine in particular were much prized in the scholarly centres that arose under the Caliphate at Baghdad and where Indian scholars were resident. The interchange of ideas was a characteristic of these systems of knowledge, even though some of the breakthroughs came from Indian thinkers.

Technical knowledge remained largely with the guilds, where the sons of craftsmen were trained in hereditary trades. These centres had little general interaction with formal institutions of learning, but in specific categories of knowledge there appears to have been an exchange. The study of mathematics would have provided a bridge between the two types of education, and not surprisingly this was an intensely active period in the diffusion of mathematical knowledge. Arab scholars mention that mathematical knowledge from India was more advanced than what they had retrieved from Greek sources. Numerals had been in use for some time. They were later introduced to the European world as Arabic numerals, the Arabs having borrowed them from India, as is evident from the name they used for them – Hindasa. These were to replace Roman numerals. The decimal place-value system was in regular use among Indian mathematicians, and the earliest inscription using the zero dates to the seventh century, indicating that its use was familiar. The development of what came to be called algebra was also introduced to the Arabs.

Interest in medicine triggered off a tangential interest in alchemy. This became essential to a variety of experimental forms of knowledge, relating not only to the study of material substances, but to those with an influence on religious beliefs concerning the transmutation of mind and matter. Alchemy was examined in some detail by the Chinese and is an area where Indian information on the subject was valuable.

A notable feature of intellectual life had been the lively philosophical debates among various thinkers across the spectrum, from Buddhism to Brahmanism. Gradually, the debates focused on well-defined philosophical systems, of which six are generally counted. Although these had their origin in the philosophical thinking of a period earlier than that of the Guptas and continued into a later period, some of their cardinal principles were enunciated at this time. Nyaya/Analysis, based on logic, was often used in debates with Buddhist teachers who prided themselves on their advanced knowledge and use of logic. Vaisheshika/Particular Characteristics argued that the universe was created from a number of atoms, but these were distinct from the soul, therefore there were separate universes of matter and soul. Sankhya/Enumeration, essentially atheistic, drew on what were enumerated as the twenty-five principles which gave rise to creation. The dualism between matter and soul was recognized. Sankhya philosophers supported the theory that the three qualities of virtue, passion and dullness, correctly balanced, constituted normality. This was perhaps the influence of the theory of humours current in the medical knowledge of the time. Yoga/Application maintained that a perfect control over the body and the senses was a prelude to knowledge of the ultimate reality. Anatomical knowledge was necessary to the advancement of yoga and therefore those practising yoga had to keep in touch with medical knowledge. Mimamsa/

Inquiry, developed from the view that the source of brahmanical strength, the *Vedas*, was being neglected, and its supporters emphasized the ultimate law of the *Vedas* and refuted the challenge of post-Vedic thought. Vedanta/ End of the Vedas was decisive in refuting the theories of non-brahamanical schools, particularly in later centuries when it gained currency. Vedanta also claimed origin in the *Vedas* and posited the existence of the Absolute Soul in all things, the final purpose of existence being the union of the individual soul with the Universal Soul after physical death.

These were not schools of thought that developed in isolation, for they included discussions and refutations of each other's view and of other schools and sects. One of the methods required in any discussion was almost a simulation of the dialectical method. A proposition was stated with arguments supporting it, followed by a detailed rebuttal, or the negative formulation was stated first and then rebutted, and finally an assessment was made of both, although a consensus was optional. Not only was this a logical procedure, but the weight of philosophical perceptions seems to have favoured openness to ideas and debate, even where some of this discussion led to agnosticism, or possibly even atheism. Clearly, philosophical thinking was not isolated from the new systems of knowledge being debated. At this stage, only the last two schools were essentially metaphysical, the first four maintaining a strong link with empirical analysis. The focus on Nyaya was given prominence, in part because it had been central to many schools of Buddhist philosophy. The debates among philosophers of logic continued from century to century. Yet in modern times Vedanta was given maximum attention, to the point of being projected as the dominant philosophical school in pre-modern India. The period of the *Vedas* was now sufficiently remote for them to be routinely cited as the authority derived from divine origin, as the arbiters of priestly knowledge and sanction, even if this was largely formulaic. Invoking the *Vedas* did not require that the text conform to Vedic knowledge, for it could also be a way of seeking legitimation.

The new systems of knowledge that contributed to the label of classicism were not arbitrary activities. They arose from various preconditions, among which were the continuing confrontations between orthodoxies and hetero-doxies, and the articulation of philosophical scepticism. The strength of relying on careful observation is demonstrated by the accuracy of various theories in astronomy arrived at without the help of a telescope. In many such theories, for instance the discussion on the cause of eclipses, rationality was at a premium among scholars, even if others did not dismiss mythologi-cal explanations. The cultivation of astrology is not surprising, since it was a predictable response by those opposed to the logical foundations of knowledge. The world-view of Vedic Brahmanism was being superseded by new formulations, in some of which the imprint of debates with Buddhist and other philosophers was apparent. The counterpoint of orthodoxy and heterodoxy was not limited to religious belief, but pervaded many areas of knowledge.

Inevitably, astronomy and mathematics encouraged an interest in time and cosmology. Time, in a cosmological context, was viewed as cyclic and there were at least two views of cyclic time, both involving a leap of imagination. The more commonly known was the theory of the *mahayuga*, and the one used less frequently was that of the *manvantara*, although the two were sometimes merged. The cycle was called a *kalpa* and was equivalent to 4,320,000 human years. According to the second of these theories, the cycle has fourteen *manvantaras* separated by lengthy intervals and at the end of each the universe is recreated and ruled by Manu (primeval man). At the moment we are in the seventh of these fourteen periods of the present cycle. Each of these is divided into 71+ *mahayugas* (great cycles).

The other form of reckoning is numerically neater, where the great cycle, the *mahayuga*, is divided into four *yugas* or periods of time, each again a cycle and, barring the first, named after the throw of dice – Krita, Treta, Dvapara and Kali. The *yugas* contain respectively 4,800, 3,600, 2,400 and 1,200 divine years. Their equivalence to human years requires multiplication by 360. The decline is by arithmetic progression, and is accompanied by a similar decline in the quality of life. We are now in the fourth of these *yugas*, the Kaliyuga or 'the age of the losing throw', said to have begun at a date equivalent to 3102 BC, and this is a time when the world is full of evil and wickedness. Thus the end of the world is by comparison imminent, though there are several millennia yet before the end!

The latter part of the Kaliyuga is characterized by the absence of the social norms laid down in the *Dharma-shastras*, and by the lower castes usurping the status of the upper castes. The world turns upside down and this becomes an explanation for reversals of the norms at any point of time. The unexpected is explained as due to these reversals. Since the world is now in the Kaliyuga, its characteristics are repeated throughout the centuries and become a metaphor among those for whom the present is viewed as bad times. The world awaits the coming of Kalkin, the tenth incarnation of Vishnu who will reinstate the norms. Cyclic time was also a convenient context for the theory of rebirth.

Long spans of time were needed for theoretical calculations in astronomy and mathematics and long spans were more easily visualized as cyclic. But this was not the only form in which time was projected. The linear form was used in recounting the past or making historical claims related to the present. The *Puranas* gave importance to what they claimed were genealogies of heroes and dynasties from the past. The generations listed, whether actual or fictional, conformed to linear time. The term *vamsha*, used for genealogical descent, is the word for bamboo or cane, where each segment grows out of a node. It was an appropriate analogy for reckoning time in generations. The use of regnal years to begin with, and later of eras, was a further indication of linear time. It would seem therefore that cyclic and linear time were both used, with the first sometimes enveloping the second, but that the historical and social function of each differed.

Creative Literature

Much creative literature of this period became the source of studies of dramaturgy, poetry and literary theory in the subsequent period. Some would date the famous *Natya-shastra* of Bharata – a foundational treatise on dance, drama and poetry – to these times, suggesting its catalytic role. Literary criticism was soon to explore the interface between sound and meaning, mood and evocation, some of which were seminal to the discussion on the theory of *rasa*, where one of the arguments was that the quality of creativity can be related to the manner in which it evokes a reaction.

Poetry and prose in Sanskrit were largely the literature of the elite, the court, the aristocracy, the urban rich and those associated with such circles. Kalidasa was an extraordinary poet and dramatist whose work augmented the prestige of the language and was echoed in many later poetic forms. *Meghaduta* (*Cloud Messenger*) was his long lyrical poem, meshing landscape and emotion. His play *Abhijnana-shakuntala*, regarded as an exemplar in Sanskrit drama by literary critics, was to be widely discussed both in Sanskrit literary theory, and later throughout Europe, with its impact on German Romanticism. There was a blaze of creative literature in Sanskrit just after Kalidasa: Bharavi's *Kiratarjuniya*, Magha's *Shishupalavadha* and the *Bhatti-kavya*, among others, and somewhat later Bhavabhuti's *Malati-Madhava*. These drew on epic themes or familiar narratives that were treated in courtly style and subjected to literary virtuosity of many kinds. The more erotic poetry was that of Bhartrihari and Amaru. Plays continued to be romantic comedies in the main, tragic themes being avoided, since the purpose of the theatre was to entertain. The *Mrichchha-katika* (*The Little Clay Cart*) by Shudraka provides glimpses of urban life. Vishakhadatta chose to drama-tize past political events in his *Mudrarakshasha*, a play on the Mauryan overthrow of the Nanda King, and in *Devi-chandra-gupta*, on the bid for power by Chandra Gupta II. There are elements of court intrigue in both, but these are significantly different and suggest his sensitivity to changing historical contexts.

The fables of the *Panchatantra*, written to educate a young prince in the ways of the world, were elaborated in various versions and travelled west through translations. Subandhu's *Vasavadatta* claims renown for its literary quality. Bana's *Harshacharita* was quoted as a model of both biography and Sanskrit prose, and his fantasy narrative *Kadambari* has such an involved plot that one almost loses track of the narrative. Literary criticism came into its own in the writings of Bhamaha. A striking feature of this intense creativity in literary forms is that the essential concern is not with projecting religious ideas, as some modern commentators maintain, but with reflecting on human behaviour even if only of segments of society. The historical context is largely that of the royal court, although some would argue that the court is a metaphor.

Classical Sanskrit became popular as the language of the chancellery, through its being the language of the court and through inscriptions. It was therefore different from the language of ritual, and had earlier been recognized as such by grammarians. The dominance of Sanskrit, however, dates to the Gupta period and continued until about the early second millennium AD, after which the regional languages were widely used. In Turkish and Mughal times the court language was Persian. The hegemony of Sanskrit was political and cultural and enjoyed the patronage of the elite. But the local languages and cultures were not abandoned. They can be glimpsed in the use of Prakrit in various contexts, such as the elements of some inscriptions and in the languages of religious sects. The *Natya-shastra* lists a number of languages and dialects, even after setting aside those spoken by members of the lower castes and *chandalas*. Since the latter worked for the upper castes there must have been some degree of bilingualism. The upper castes, it is said, should avoid Prakrit because it is the language of the *mlechchha* and of the populace. The differentiation between high culture and popular local culture was recognized in the gradual adoption of distinctive terms for each – *marga*, literally the path, for the former, and *deshi*, literally the region, for the latter. Sanskrit also became the language of the scholastic tradition, and doubtless the patronage to brahmans and to Buddhist monasteries encouraged this.

In addition to Sanskrit, literature in Prakrit (more closely related to popular speech than Sanskrit) also had its patronage outside the court circle. Prakrit literature associated with Jaina texts tended to be more didactic in style. The *Paumacariyam* of Vimalasuri, a Jaina version of the Rama story, is remarkable not only for presenting different views from those of Valmiki, but also for reiterating the function of the epic form as popular literature. A notable feature in the Sanskrit plays of this period is that the high-status characters speak Sanskrit, whereas those of low or ambiguous social status, and all the women, speak Prakrit. Status and gender were linked to language.

Architecture, Art and Patronage

Only a few, small examples of temple architecture have survived from this period. The stock answer to temples being in ruins is that the iconoclasm of the Muslims five centuries later destroyed them. But the Gupta-period temples were unlikely to have attracted attention, the architecture still being in a formative stage. Apart from its religious affiliation, the temple was not yet perceived as a statement of political power or as a repository of wealth, and was therefore not a prime target for attack. Artistically and aesthetically, the most stunning achievements were the rock-cut Buddhist caves, particularly at Ajanta and Ellora. These were the inspiration for the later Vaishnava and Shaiva rock-cut temples at Ellora, Elephanta and Aurangabad. The latter were perhaps less statements of power than statements of faith, and they did not experience iconoclasm.

Some Buddhist *stupas* were newly built, as in Sind; others were renovated as at Sarnath. Activity in Orissa resulted in continued building of Buddhist *stupas* and monasteries, the most impressive being those at Lalitagiri, Ratnagiri and Udayagiri, which clearly reflected patronage by the rulers and merchants. Buddhist monasteries and *chaityas* at Ajanta and Ellora are cut into a ravine and a hillside. The caves at Ajanta were decorated with sculpture, and some contained mural paintings depicting the life of the Buddha, the *Jataka* stories and other familiar narratives, that in effect provide a visual representation of contemporary life. The cross-section of society seemingly stepping out from the walls is complementary to the scenes earlier sculpted in bâs-relief at *stupa* sites. The quality of realism in these murals evokes in a remarkable way the *joie de vivre* of daily activities, as well as reflections on the human condition, and yet they are enveloped in a style both elegant and aesthetically pleasing.

Literary references to painting are frequent, and it was widely appreciated as an accomplishment. The aesthetic quality emanating from these cave shrines leaves the early Shaiva and Vaishnava temples looking rather pale by comparison. The most impressive artistic achievements of this period lie in Buddhist art and the patronage that accompanies it. Ajanta epitomized its finest stylistic quality in painting and, although it might have been politically influenced by the Vakataka-Gupta sphere, it effectively represented Buddhist art rooted in the peninsula.

The earliest temples were single cells housing the image, as at Sanchi. Such temples form the nucleus at Aihole, Tigowa, Bhumara, Nachna Kothara, Ladh Khan and Deogarh, among others. In some cases the site was an existing sacred place, for example, at Aihole where there are megalithic burials in the vicinity. Early temples at Chezarla and Ter in the peninsula, with an apsidal plan and ambulatory path, are thought to have been Buddhist *chaityas* that were converted into temples. The use of existing sacred space by newly evolving religions is well known, and could be the result of a gradual conversion of the site or a forced change. When temples began to receive grants of land for their maintenance, this became a major source of finance for the temple. Worship in such temples was generally of Puranic deities – Vishnu, Shiva, Parvati, Durga and Varaha. The Dashavatara temple at Deogarh is, as the name implies, among the earliest dedicated to the incarnations of Vishnu.

The architecture of the Shaiva and Vaishnava temples was constructed around the sanctum cella, the *garbha-griha* – literally the womb-house, or the room in which the image of the deity was placed. In the small temples the entrance to this was through a porch. There is a certain correlation therefore between the image and where it is housed. The expansion of the temple required that the room housing the image be approached through a vestibule, which in turn was entered from a hall that opened on to a porch. This was surrounded by an enclosed courtyard, which later housed a further complex of shrines.

The Buddhists in the Deccan continued to excavate rock-cut *chaityas* and the Vaishnavas, Shaivas and Jainas imitated these in later centuries, often excavating temples adjacent to the Buddhist caves. Temples that were free-standing and not rock-cut were generally built in stone (although there is an early brick temple at Bhitargaon) and stone became the medium for the increasingly monumental style. The preference for free-standing temples was partly due to their being built in areas without convenient hillsides and appropriate rock to cut caves, but it was also because the expansion of the temple was inhibited when it was cut into rock. Gradually, the image came to be surrounded by a host of attendant deities and figures, leading to the rich sculptural ornamentation associated with later styles.

Classical sculpture reflecting a high aesthetic sensibility is visible, particularly in the Buddha images from Sarnath, Mathura, Kushinagara and Bodh

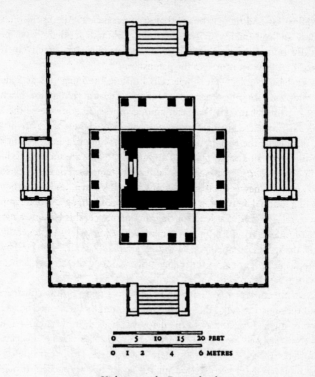

4. Vishnu temple, Deogarh: plan

Gaya. Doubtless this encouraged the portrayal of the more important Vaish-nava and Shaiva deities as impressive icons. These images were often more symbolic than representational: thus, although the deity was anthropomorphic and took a human form, it may have been given four, eight or more arms, each arm carrying a symbol of an attribute associated with the deity. Vaishnava representations were either of the deity or of an incarnation, which allowed a wider range of images. Shiva was most often represented as a *lingam*. This limited the scope for sculptural representation, except in the *mukha lingas* where a face or even a body was sculpted into the *lingam*, although other anthropomorphic forms were also evolving. The making of images was characteristic of the Puranic religion and was a departure from Vedic Brahmanism that had excluded icons.

A popular medium for images was terracotta, which was more accessible to people. If stone sculpture required the patronage of the rich, forms in

5. Nagara-style temple: elevation

terracotta were readily available to the ordinary person throughout history. They are now being taken seriously as an articulation of popular culture. Both deities and human figures were depicted, some forms indicating considerable efficiency in the technical handling of the medium. Terracotta figures have been found in great abundance, particularly in the Ganges Plain and eastern India. Many are mould-made and were therefore mass-produced. Some of the figures were used in religious ritual, but many were of a more general nature and used as toys or decorative pieces. Some of the larger forms were images of deities, among which are the striking representations of the river goddesses Ganga and Yamuna.

Religious Formulations

By this time the Indian subcontinent already hosted a range of religions. Theoretically, Buddhism was a rival to Vedic Brahmanism, but the rivalry more often took the form of confrontations with Shaivism. But in the ritual of worship and in practice the influence of the other religions was becoming more apparent. Buddhism had a following beyond the frontiers of India, in central Asia, China and south-east Asia. Religious practices current in these regions were accommodated in the practices of the newly established Buddhism. This sometimes required a reformulation of the pristine teachings.

Jainism moved towards support from the merchant communities of western India, and the patronage of local royalty in Karnataka and the south. In the early part of the sixth century the Second Jaina Council was held at Valabhi, and the Jaina Canon was defined substantially as it exists today. The use of Sanskrit was on the increase, since it was now the prestigious language of the elite in many areas. But it had the same effect on the religions that used it, isolating the religious teachers from a wide following. The Jainas had also evolved a series of icons. The straight-standing rather stiff figures of Mahavira and others, or the cross-legged seated figures, became the pattern for depicting Jaina teachers.

The mid-millennium saw the surfacing of cults that seem to have been substratum cults in many areas. These focused on the worship of female deities, associated with notions of fertility. Female deities became the nucleus of a number of rites, imbued with magical properties, which in a later form were foundational to Tantrism. The female deity was subsumed in the worship of the all-encompassing Devi. She was said to be the initiator of action, and of the power and energy – *shakti* – of Shiva. It was held that the male could only be activated through union with the female. That these ideas were influential can be seen from the temples dedicated to the *yoginis*, females endowed with magical power and sometimes linked to goddesses. The temples that have survived, mostly in central India, are somewhat later in time. They are circular in design, the circular wall lined with sculptures of various *yoginis* and open to the sky. Some of the mythology linked to the worship of the goddess was brought together in the text that acquired fame as the *Devi-mahatmya*.

The Shakti-Shakta cult became not only the underlying belief in many religious sects, but gradually attained a dominant status. The consorts of male deities were worshipped in their own right, such as Lakshmi the consort of Vishnu, or Parvati, Kali and Durga who were various consorts of Shiva. This cult drew on the continuing worship of the goddess, which has remained a predominant feature of Indian religion, possibly since Harappan times. Since this could not be suppressed, it was given a priestly blessing and incorporated into popular belief and ritual. Yet, over the centuries, worshipping the goddess could be seen at some social levels as the counterpoint to subordinating women in society.

Tantric beliefs and rites were also to influence Buddhism. A new school of Buddhism was to emerge, Vajrayana or the Thunderbolt Vehicle, with its centre in eastern India. Vajrayana Buddhists gave female counterparts to the existing male figures of the Buddhist pantheon. These counterparts were termed Taras and regarded as Saviouresses, and were especially popular in Nepal and Tibet. On a subcontinental scale Buddhism registered a decline in some areas in about the seventh century, and Hsüan Tsang noticed such a decline at Bodh Gaya, Sarnath and some other places. He mentioned the hostility of some rulers, such as Shashanka. That Harsha was a major patron points to its still having a substantial following, but Harsha was also a patron of its rival, Shaivism. If monasteries and monuments are an indication, its popularity in eastern India was on the rise.

Three important aspects of Vaishnavism and Shaivism that had their roots in the changes of this period led to a different religious ethos from that dominated either by Buddhism or Vedic Brahmanism. The image emerged as the focus of worship and this form of worship, centred on *puja*, superseded the Vedic sacrifice. However, an offering to the image – often food or in some cases an animal – remained a requirement of the ritual. Some would argue that *puja* had its closest parallel in the rituals of the Buddhists. The reduction of the emphasis on the priest compared to his role in the sacrificial ritual of Vedic Brahmanism gradually led to devotional worship – *bhakti* – becoming the most widespread form of the Puranic religion. Worship of a deity became the main concern of the individual, as it was through *bhakti* that the individual could aspire to liberation from rebirth. The Vedic religion had well-defined rituals and was exclusive to the upper castes. The Puranic religion had a far wider appeal. Its accessibility lay in performing acts that required little investment – the giving of gifts however small, the keeping of fasts and vows, travelling collectively to places of pilgrimage and subscribing to local mythologies. This underlined the individual's participation in the religion, as well as the cohesion of a sect while members were chosen not necessarily by birth but by faith, even if it tended to remain somewhat closed.

Its emphasis on the individual's relationship with a chosen deity was in part parallel to the heterodox religions that emphasized the individual rather than the clan or the caste. It would seem that although formal Buddhism was fading out in the post-Gupta period, it was nevertheless leaving an imprint on the Puranic sects as part of the Shramanic legacy. The centrality of the individual in the Shramanic religions was in a sense generic, inasmuch as these religions were historically rooted in urbanism within a society changing its social moorings. A similar but more complex paradigm had been witnessed in the early centuries AD, with the overarching state giving way to the insecurities of small kingdoms. Vaishnavism and Shaivism, even when assimilating a variety of cults and deities, strengthened the notion of *bhakti* as a form of worship focused on the individual.

A few of the *Puranas* were written at this time, although it is difficult to date these precisely. They read somewhat like sectarian tracts, informing the worshipper about the mythology, rituals of worship and observances associated with the particular deity to whom the *Purana* was dedicated. As texts of the Puranic religion, they tended to be critical of those whom they regarded as heretics – the followers of the Shramana religions – despite the fact that some new sects were imitating the organization and strategy of the Shramanas. At some levels they were attempts at propagating the religions of the sects through an oral tradition. Recitations were regular and intended for those who could not read the texts. Doubtless, even then the recitation would have required an explanation for many audiences.

Where they claimed to be repositories of the past, the *Puranas* began with the creation of the universe and continued with what they projected as the historical past – the ancient *kshatriya* lineages and the later dynasties. The succession of dynasties was recorded in the form of a prophecy in order to enhance the power of the text. The list stopped with the Guptas, suggesting that it was compiled at this time. The *Vishnu Purana* has a section on genealogies and dynasties of the past – the *vamsha-anu-charita*. It is claimed as a record of the past but little of it is acceptable as history. It was an attempt at creating a historical tradition. The past was viewed in a specific pattern, largely invented but perhaps with a scatter of remembered history. Even if fabricated, this form of remembering the past recognized linear time and that gives it a hint of history. The format of solar and lunar lineages, and the recital of dynasties, were accessible to those who wished to latch on to any of these connections. Placing this information in a religious text gave it a legitimacy, but also ensured that it would be known.

Thus, what began as popular memories of the past were revised and re-written as prophecy and became the brahmancial interpretation of the past. The *sutas* or bards, who had earlier immortalized their patrons in poems and narratives, were relegated to a low-caste status and their oral tradition was redrafted to serve other purposes. One of these was that the new dynasties emerging were given *kshatriya* status by the brahmans. This was done by linking them to the heroes of ancient times by stating that they were descended from the old, established *kshatriyas*. Dynasties therefore soon began describing themselves as being of either the Suryavamsha or the Chandravamsha lineage. The authors of the *Puranas* now had the power of legitimizing new dynasties as *kshatriyas*, irrespective of what the actual origin of the royal family may have been. Those who performed this function were handsomely rewarded. Using the past in this fashion for a political purpose, whether historically accurate or not, is common to many societies. This was similar in function to writing biographies of kings, and was parallel to the writing of chronicles in later times.

The Puranic religion easily lent itself to the assimilation of new deities, mythologies and rituals. This was particularly useful when marginal societies were being incorporated into caste society, and the slotting in of their deities facilitated the change. This period witnessed not only the uprooting of the *gana-sanghas*, but also the gradual process of inducting societies from the forest and other marginal areas into caste society. The forest as a symbol changed from being the untamed and unknown part of the wilderness, to being romanticized, with the establishment of ascetic hermitages in its midst, eventually becoming an area to be cleared for peasant cultivation. The latter process probably became more evident because the pressure on cultivated land was being felt in certain areas. Some inscriptions refer to the founders of dynasties overpowering forest rajas. The *Harshacharita* has a lengthy description of a village of Shabaras, pre-eminently a forest-people, now living as peasants.

The social observances of earlier times were being regarded as sacred law, with rigid rules of exclusion for those who were not allowed to participate in caste society. Fortunately, many saw the difficulty of enforcing rules that were largely theoretical. Some tried to define the Four Aims of Man as *Dharma* (religion and the social law), *Artha* (economic well-being), *Kama* (pleasure) and *Moksha* (the release of the soul from rebirth) – the correct balance of the first three leading to the fourth. The description of the balance was left to those who framed the social code, but the demands of earthly life were adequately met in practice.

India and Asia

Religion found an ally in commerce to carry the Indian way of life outside India. In this, Buddhism took the initiative by introducing Indian culture into various parts of Asia. Buddhism found support in central Asia, with monasteries endowed by local rulers and merchants in oases that became trade centres. The closeness of culture between Afghanistan and India continued, especially at the once magnificent sites of Hadda and Bamiyan. The adoption of Indian scripts and the use of Indian languages would have assisted Indian merchants, providing openings for these with literacy. Indians began to settle in central Asia, among them Kumarajiva, the Buddhist philosopher who lived at Kucha in the fourth century AD, where his father had married into a local family of rank. Nearer home, Tibetan interest in Buddhism was encouraged by its King Srong-tsam-gampo, ruling in the seventh century. He used Buddhism to strengthen the foundations of kingship, in a situation where powerful clans had not reconciled themselves to central rule. It also enabled him to make contact with the world beyond Tibet.

Indian Buddhists took missions further afield to China. By AD 379 Buddhism was an accepted religion in China, supported by the state, which swelled the following. However, it had its tribulations, since later centuries saw the persecution of Buddhists. Chinese Buddhist monks were interested in obtaining copies of the original Buddhist scriptures. Fa Hsien, Sung Yun, Hsüan Tsang, and later I Tsing/Yi Jing, all travelled and worked in India, the earlier ones braving the rigours and dangers of a central Asian journey. Judging by their descriptions, this was still an uninviting area apart from the oases. Indian elements began to be introduced into Chinese culture. The most visual was the initial use of Indian techniques in sculpture and painting in Buddhist monasteries. The most striking of these in range and aesthetic expression are at Dun Huang – a virtual historical museum of Chinese painting. Other monastery sites, such as Miran, Kucha and Turfan, have also provided an array of murals. Astronomy, alchemy and medical knowledge were enriched by this interaction. The expansion of the Indian maritime trade to south China increased Sino-Indian contacts. During the T'ang period (AD 618–907) Indian merchants resided at Canton, and T'ang coins from the seventh century have been found in south India. Buddhist missions went to Japan from China.

Commerce in central Asia also touched on trade with the eastern Mediterranean and this involved west Asia. The Arabian peninsula was tied into the Ethiopian–Byzantine trade, with Arab camel caravans as the carriers. The wealth and activities of this trade are linked to the rise of Islam.

The demands of trade with the eastern Mediterranean had encouraged Indian enterprise in south-east Asia, since it provided many of the essential commodities such as spices and semi-precious stones. Having once discovered the potentialities of south-east Asia, Indian traders – Buddhist and Hindu – developed these links. Trade led to settlements, and to closer interactions. Indian cultural forms entered the local pattern of life, particularly in the regions known today as Thailand, Cambodia and Java.

Chinese annals of the time, referring to Indian activities in south-east Asia, mention Funan (the Mekong Delta) as the first sphere of activity. Small settlements were also made in the Malay peninsula, since it was connected with east-coast maritime centres of India. Ships sailed from Tamralipti and Amaravati to Myanmar, Martaban and Indonesia. The ports of south India sent ships to Tenasserim, Trang, the Straits of Malacca and Java. The ports along the western coast also came to participate in this trade.

The nature of the Indian connection varied according to the region from where it came and the kind of relations it had with the host society. The process was probably similar to the mutation of peripheral societies in relation to the mainstream in the subcontinent. However, with the absence of a heavy overlay of caste much of the indigenous social form continued. Sanskrit influenced the languages of elite cultures, probably because it was the language of the formal rituals introduced by Indian functionaries. Some of the finest Sanskrit inscriptions come from these areas. Geographical place-names associated with the Indian cultural tradition were adopted: for example, Ayuthia, the ancient capital of Thailand, was named after Ayodhya, the capital of the kingdom of Rama, this being one among many instances of the popularity of the Indian epics. Indian iconographic norms were fused with local forms in the images. The particular style of intertwining Buddhism and the Puranic religion, so representative of sites in south-east Asia, evolved later in its most creative forms at Angkor Vat and the Bayon in Cambodia, and the stepped *stupa* at Borobudur and the Prambanam temple, both in Java.

Yet these societies retained much of their indigenous culture. The Indian impact is understandable in terms of certain advanced technologies arriving in the area and the local elite adopting new patterns. The presence of Indian traders also assisted the change, introducing an exchange economy that benefited them and allowed them to participate at various levels of power. However, to refer to south-east Asia during this period as 'Greater India' is a misnomer. The local culture was visible in all aspects of life. The Javanese version of the *Ramayana* retained only the bare bones of the Indian story, the rest being the incorporation of traditional Javanese legends. The conception of the god-king among the Khmer rulers of Cambodia drew from a pre-Indian source, although in a later period Indian concepts were also brought in.

The existence of Buddhism in south-east Asia, in about the seventh and eighth centuries AD, would have been contemporary with its adoption in Tibet. Local modifications in both cases were so strong that the forms of Buddhism in Cambodia and Java, for example, were distinctively different from those of Tibet. In court circles the imitation of things Indian or Chinese (in areas close to China) was recognizable, but the rest of society in these countries maintained its own identity despite its assimilation of certain imported customs.

The creation of Sanskritic cultures refers to more than just the extensive use of the language. It refers to the initial steps towards the legitimation of a new order – the culture and society of the landed intermediaries, of the new *kshatriyas* and the new religious sects. But beyond the horizon of these were the spectacular explorations of new systems of knowledge and creativity in literature. The former brought Indian learning into what was fast developing as the Asian interchange of knowledge, and the latter was marking a presence in many parts of Asia.

This period is a threshold period. It carries some items from earlier times, but announces others which take on a more definitive shape in later times. Oral traditions were converted into texts and interpolations added to these. Implicit in these was an underlining of the upper-caste perspective, strengthening its effectiveness and power. The granting of land to brahmans, which increased in the post-Gupta period, emphasized the pre-eminence of the brahman in society. The brahmans strengthened this position by asserting an inheritance of Vedic Brahmanism. This tended to marginalize the heterodox and those who had opposed Vedic Brahmanism with its claim to a monopoly over knowledge, a claim that had become an additional source of power. However, with the establishing of the Puranic sects yet another dimension was introduced to social and religious life, different from either Vedic Brahmanism or Shramanism.

Distinctions between courtly high culture and popular culture became more sharply defined. Such distinctions created separate areas of cultural engagement and the incorporation from one to the other required substantial social changes. Culture is therefore better understood not only by what became dominant, but also through what fell by the wayside. There are limitations to the historical sources for early Indian history which are mainly the writings of elite groups. For this reason, it is possible only to infer the process of negotiation between the courtly and the popular culture, which is essential to the creation of a dominant culture. Those identified by popular culture spoke other languages; their women were more liberated than those of the patriarchal elite; their rituals and customs were different. If the elite projected the *varna* stratification as frozen, one can only suspect that it was not so widely observed. For the majority, possibly, *jati* stratification was more real. If families of obscure social origin aspired to be kings then their genealogies had to be constructed. Brahmans, taking over the bardic data, could provide this legitimation. The spread of Sanskrit was legitimizing a new order.

A significant medium in this process was the issuing of inscriptions as orders of the court, king and other functionaries, and their observance in distant areas. Inscriptions now emerge as a major historical source, encapsulating social and economic information relating to grants of land, commerce, administrative arrangements, religious endowments and suchlike. They tend to increasingly parallel the texts as sources.

Politically, it was a period that registered the triumph of monarchy over the *gana-sanghas* and the forest-clans. Earlier, kings of non-*kshatriya* origin were not concerned with acquiring *kshatriya* status, but from the post-Gupta period this became common to monarchy. The newness of these *kshatriyas* was evident in more than one sense, since they set the style for the definition of the *kshatriya*. In seeking roots among the earlier *kshatriyas*, the assistance of the brahman was necessary and this assistance was not only recognized but rewarded.

In the ideology of kingship current at the time there was a glorying in successful campaigns and suzerainty over many kings. Was this a revival of the Vedic concept of the king being a *digvijayin*, conqueror, of the four quarters, or a *chakravartin*, universal monarch, or was it echoing the pattern set by earlier rulers of the north-west? The identification of the king with a deity could again have come from both Vedic sources and Kushana ideas of kingship. The Vedic *chakravartin* had been set aside by the Buddhists, whose definition of the *chakkavatti* was the king who ruled not by conquest but by setting in motion the wheel of law. In the post-Mauryan period Ashoka was being referred to as a *chakkavatti* in Buddhist texts, and he was certainly not the role model for the Gupta kings. Those Gupta kings who took the title of *paramabhattaraka* were Vaishnavas, and claimed to be protectors of the *dharma*. This was the *varnashrama-dharma* – the defence of the normative – rather than the *dharma* of the Buddhists and the Jainas.

The innovation of this period in the use of agencies to establish power lay in the notion of rewarding the legitimizers of kingship with grants of land. They were not the colonies of agriculturalists advocated by the *Arthashastra*. New settlements were to become the nuclei of support for the king. The extension of caste status implicit in these settlements was another agency of control, where the elite was given *varna* status and the rest constituted *jatis*.

Does this amount to a revival or renaissance of Vedic Brahmanism or does it point towards concessions that Vedic Brahmanism made to what has been called Puranic Hinduism? In the ideology of kingship the rituals of Vedic Brahmanism were encouraged and grants of land enabled its survival, although it eventually made way for Puranic Hinduism. But, as priests in Vaishnava and Shaiva worship, the brahmans had to make many concessions, for instance that brahmans could be temple priests although these were given a lower status than specialists in Vedic ritual. There was a certain attraction to the performance of rituals of sacrifice, which may no longer have been regarded as wholly efficacious but which evoked the power of the initial formulation of kingship emerging out of a system of chiefships. More evidently, kings now drew on the imagery of the epic and heroic tradition where the eulogies on them echoed the earlier eulogies of the heroes of the *Mahabharata*. Were the Guptas, as patrons of the Puranic religion, inducting some rituals of Vedic Brahmanism into Puranic Hinduism in order to employ more than a single source of legitimacy?

But there would have been other reasons. Dynasties whose origins are obscure often seek legitimacy by becoming the patrons of sects that may not be dominant but have potential. In choosing to be patrons of Puranic Hinduism and Vedic Brahmanism, these kings were seeking a different legitimacy from those who patronized Buddhism. If Ashoka can be viewed as a prototype Buddhist *chakkavatti*, then Samudra Gupta can be said to have approximated the brahmanical version of the *chakravartin*. It is from this point on that the grants of land became the outliers of the Puranic religions, forming networks of support for many new and obscure dynasties claiming *kshatriya* status.

10

The Peninsula: Emerging Regional Kingdoms

c. AD 500–900

Pallavas, Chalukyas, Rashtrakutas

With the passing of the Guptas and their immediate successors in northern India, historical interest shifts southwards to the Deccan and to the area referred to as Tamilaham. The more significant events of the period took place south of the Vindhyas in spheres other than the purely political. The institutions of south India were being established at this time and were to maintain a striking continuity. The polity of chiefships and small kingdoms from earlier times gave way to large kingdoms. There were some parallels with changes in northern India, but there were also significant differences. The courts of the peninsula reflected an interface between the assertion of local cultures and that of the expanding Sanskritic culture. The process can be seen in various spheres, but perhaps most clearly in the language of the inscriptions. The early inscriptions had been in Tamil. Later, Prakrit and Sanskrit were also used, but in the south Tamil soon predominated, until finally the main corpus was in Tamil and the more formulaic sections in Sanskrit. Similarly, inscriptions in other parts of the peninsula used Sanskrit and Kannada. Parallel to this in some ways was the juxtaposition of Vedic Brahmanism with what has come to be called the Tamil devotional movement. The kingdoms of the western Deccan maintained their historical role of bridging the north and the south, facilitating the transmission of ideas between the two. But it is clear from architectural history that this was not a passive role, as the Deccan style, or Vesara, provided forms and variants among what have come to be called the Nagara, or northern style, and the Dravida, or southern style.

The political history of the Deccan and further south focused on the long years of conflict between two geographical regions, the western Deccan and Tamilaham – the vast plateau areas enclosed by mountains along the coasts on the one hand, and the fertile plain south of Chennai on the other. Most of the rivers in the region rise in the west and flow into the Bay of Bengal. The division of the peninsula into the plateau kingdoms on the west and the coastal kingdoms on the east increased the desire of each to control the entire waterway, particularly the Godavari and Krishna Rivers. Vengi, lying between the Godavari and Krishna Deltas, was frequently a bone of contention, together with the fertile Raichur *doab* further inland. The conflict was as much political as economic, and consequently it continued through the centuries despite the fortunes of particular dynasties. What appears to be a complex interplay of the rise and fall of kingdoms is not so complex when viewed from a geopolitical perspective. The deltas were prime agricultural lands and the eastern coast, dotted with Buddhist centres by now, was active in trade networks. In the absence of vast areas of fertile plains, large agrarian-based kingdoms were less effective as polities, and the formation of smaller, regional kingdoms was an early and consistent feature. Thus, the kingdoms of the peninsula were probably oriented to regional loyalties earlier than in the north.

The Vakatakas in the western Deccan gave way to Chalukya power with a base in Vatapi/Badami. A series of kingdoms, south from the eastern Deccan, included those ruled by the Shalankayanas and later the eastern Chalukyas; the Ikshvakus in the Krishna-Guntur region, with Nagarjunakonda and Dharanikota as important centres, and with the Vishnukundins ruling close by. Control over Karnataka was divided between the Kadambas, Nolambas and Gangas. This was again an interplay between people of the hills and the forests with those settled in the plains. Granite hillocks were useful bases for fortresses. Kadamba control extended to the Konkan, and the Eastern Gangas ruled in Orissa. Other dynasties bordering on the eastern Deccan were the Sharabapuriyas and the Panduvamshis. Some dynasties had been founded by brahmans who had received grants of land and used these as nuclei which became small kingdoms. Hence the claim that some were of the *brahma-kshatra* caste – brahmans performing *kshatriya* functions or who could claim mixed brahman and *kshatriya* ancestry.

Further south in the Tamilaham area, the control of the Cheras, Cholas and Pandyas over their respective states was rocked by the rise of the Kalabhras. The origins of the latter are unknown and this is another example of a dynasty rising from obscurity, which became a trend in the subcontinent. The Kalabhras are said to have been hill tribes, but soon became sufficiently settled to extend patronage to Buddhists and Jainas. Possibly this is why they were reviled in later texts, some of which were of brahman authorship. The change encouraged the breaking down of the system of clan-based societies. This introduced a more impersonal rule through kingship, with the major dynasties of the Pallavas and the Pandyas in the east and the Cheras/Perumal in Kerala.

For 300 years after the mid-sixth century three major kingdoms were in conflict. These were the Chalukyas of Badami, the Pallavas of Kanchipuram and the Pandyas of Madurai, all seeking to control the fertile tracts. The Chalukyas first came into prominence as subordinate rulers of the Kadambas, from whom they broke away. The Chalukya base was in northern Karnataka at Vatapi/Badami and the adjacent Aihole, from where they moved northwards to annex the former kingdom of the Vakatakas, centred in the Upper Godavari. They also annexed some western coastal areas, presumably because these now hosted the traders from across the Arabian Sea. The power from the north was contained through the defeat of Harsha at the Narmada, by the Chalukya King Pulakeshin II, an event repeatedly referred to with pride in later Chalukya inscriptions. The eastern part of the Satavahana kingdom, the deltas of the Krishna and the Godavari, had been conquered by the Ikshvaku dynasty in the third century AD. Ikshvaku rule ended with the conquest of this region by the Pallavas. The latter were also responsible for the overthrow of the Kadamba rulers and the annexation of their kingdom, which lay to the south of the Chalukya kingdom.

The origin of the Pallavas remains a matter of debate. Some time ago it was suggested that Pallava is a variant of Pahlava (Parthian), and that the Pallavas were originally Parthians who moved from western India to the eastern coast of the peninsula during the wars between the Shakas and the Satavahanas in the second century AD. This seems unlikely, since there was no reference to Pallavas/Pahlavas travelling to the south. Another tradition weaves a romantic story round the name. A prince fell in love with a Naga princess of the netherworld. When he finally had to leave her, he told her that if she set their child adrift with a young creeper or twig tied to its body he would recognize the child on finding it and would bestow part of the kingdom on the child. The princess did so, and the child was duly recognized and installed as the founder of the Pallava – literally, a young twig – dynasty. The territory over which the Pallavas ruled was called Tondainadu and this name reiterates the association with a twig. Naga chiefs were symbols of local power, so the story may reflect the likelihood of initial Pallava rule involving ascendancy over many continuing chiefships. This legend is not unique to the Pallavas, for a similar story is told about the Khmer kings of Cambodia, though possibly it was borrowed from the Pallava legend. Ambiguity of status is met with fairly often in the origin myths of dynasties of the subcontinent. Rituals of a particular kind performed by ritual specialists were prescribed to clear the ambiguity, and genealogical connections were made in order to provide high status. The biography of a later king, encapsulated in an inscription, claimed a descent from the brahman Ashvatthama and a mother who was an *apsara*, a celestial woman.

It is also said that the original Pallava was the ancestor to the King, Ashoka-varman, presumably the Mauryan King, Ashoka. Buddhist tradition maintained that he built the *stupa* in the vicinity of Kanchipuram. He was also now being associated with the concept of the Buddhist *chakravartin* and was much revered. In making the connection with Pallava ancestry, it appears the intention was to draw on the Buddhist tradition that still had a presence in the area. The Buddha had been mentioned as an *avatara* of Vishnu in another inscription.

The earliest surviving records of the Pallavas are inscriptions issued when the Pallavas were still a local dynasty ruling at Kanchipuram. The later inscriptions were issued when the dynasty controlled Tamil-nadu. At that time it became the first dynasty of real consequence in the region, which led to earlier historians calling it the 'imperial Pallavas'. According to one of the early inscriptions the Pallava king performed various Vedic sacrifices, including the *ashvamedha*. These ceremonies, relatively new to the local population, were probably seen as largely symbolic, emphasizing the power associated with ritual in Sanskritic culture. The Ikshvaku kings are said to have distributed ox-ploughs in an effort to clear and settle wasteland. The early Pallavas may have encouraged a similar enterprise, the conversion to agriculture bringing in enhanced revenue. The Pallava kingdom was regarded as rich, and was therefore much targeted. Pallava sources refer to the subordinate rulers, Udayana and Prithvi-vyagraha, as chiefs of the Shabara and the Nishada. The latter were almost generic names for hunter-gatherers and shifting cultivators living in the forest, normally beyond the pale of caste society. This would again suggest that the Pallava state annexed forested areas and cleared them for cultivation, or as sources for forest produce such as timber, elephants and semi-precious stones. The adoption of Sanskritic names by these chiefs is a pointer to their acculturation.

Among the later group of Pallava rulers, Mahendra-varman I (600–630) was responsible for the growing political strength of the Pallavas. He also took on the role of arbiter and patron of early Tamil culture. He was a contemporary of the Chalukya ruler Pulakeshin II and of Harsha of Thanesar and, like the latter, was a dramatist and poet of some standing, being the author of a play, the comedy entitled *Mattavilasa-prahasana* (*The Delight of the Drunkards*). Associating kings with literary accomplishments became another gauge of Sanskritic learning, particularly when reflecting courtly culture. Some of the finest, even if small, rock-cut temples were hewn during his reign, including those at Mahabalipuram/Mamallapuram. Mahendra-varman is said to have begun life as a Jaina, but was converted to Shaivism by Appar, and the claim was that the conversion eroded the patronage to Jainism in Tamil-nadu.

But his accomplishments were not restricted to writing comedies and patronizing the building of temples, for wars had also to be fought. His northern contemporary Harsha was too far away for there to be conflict, but nearer home was the recently established Chalukya power, and Pulakeshin II was determined to confine the ambition of the Pallavas and prevent their control over Vengi. This was to start a long series of Chalukya–Pallava wars, which ceased for a while on the termination of the two dynasties but started again with the rise of their successors. Pulakeshin's ambition did not rest with the control of the western Deccan. He tested the strength of his army by defeating the Kadambas and the Gangas to the south, and this led him to an equally successful attack on Andhra. He also faced and defeated the army of Harsha on the banks of the Narmada, pressing on to receive the submission of Lata, Malwa and Gujarat in western India. On returning to Badami he conducted another successful campaign, this time against Mahendra-varman the Pallava, resulting in the Chalukya acquisition of some of the northern Pallava provinces. An inscription at Aihole recording the achievements of Pulakeshin II is among the finest literary documents in the category of archival texts.

The defeat of the Pallava was not to remain unavenged. Mahendra-varman had died, but his successor Narasimha-varman I was determined to reconquer lost territory, and this he succeeded in doing. Narasimha-varman swept into the Chalukya capital, and his occupation of the city justified his claim to the title of *Vatapikonda*, 'the Conqueror of Vatapi'. Mahabalipuram was further embellished with elegant temples. The next move was to be made by the Chalukyas, but a twelve-year interregnum in the Chalukya dynasty led to a respite from war. Meanwhile, the Pallavas had been involved in naval warfare to support their ally, the King of Sri Lanka, who was trying to regain his recently lost throne and in which he was eventually successful. The interaction between Tamil-nadu and Sri Lanka that began earlier with similarities in megalithic settlements was to continue through history, as would be expected from close neighbours.

The Chalukyas were trying to unite a divided kingdom and curb the ambitions of their subordinates. In 655 one of the sons of Pulakeshin succeeded in bringing about a semblance of unity, and the power of the Chalukyas was gradually restored with the regaining of the territory lost to the Pallavas. The Chalukya provinces north of the Narmada River were ruled by a prince of the main family whose descendants were later referred to as the Lata Chalukyas, named after the region they ruled and who were still loyal and as yet not troublesome. The Chalukya king was now free to give his attention to the Pallavas, who had been preparing for a renewal of the war. After a long-drawn-out campaign the Pallavas once more swept into Vatapi. The losses were heavy on both sides, according to a graphic description of the battle in a Pallava grant found in the vicinity of Kanchi. Doubtless this was generally the case, given that the armies of the Pallavas and the Chalukyas were equally matched and victory was usually achieved by a narrow margin. The inability of each to hold the other's territory after annexing it would point to a precarious balance in military strength and political authority.

Among the achievements of Narasimha-varman II, more frequently referred to as Rajasimha, was the building of the exquisite shore temple at Mahabalipuram and the temple now known as Kailasanatha at Kanchipuram. The latter marks a turning-point away from what was earlier a religious centre dominated by Buddhists. One of the by-products of major military campaigns was that famous icons were sometimes taken from royal temples as a trophy by the victors. Frequently, masons, builders and artisans were also taken back to work on the temples in the capital of the victor. Artistic styles therefore tended to merge on occasion.

But this seemingly halcyon period ended in 731, with the Chalukyas and the Gangas uniting in an attack on the Pallavas. The reigning king died and, there being no direct heir, the council of ministers in consultation with the college of priests appointed a member of the collateral branch of the family, who reigned as Nandi-varman II. The boy king was supported by the Bhagavata faction at the court, whereas earlier the Shaiva faction had been powerful. The Chalukyas had avenged their earlier defeat in the usual manner by occupying Kanchi. The Pallavas would now be expected to counter-attack, but at this point there was a change in the situation, with the southern neighbours of the Pallavas joining in the conflict. These were the Pandyas of Madurai, and they were not in sympathy with the Pallava cause although their enmity was less intense than that of the Chalukyas. The Pandyas had established their position in southern Tamil-nadu by the sixth century, and they were to remain in control of this region for many centuries. Their effectiveness varied according to their relations with the other powers. Despite the Pandyas harassing their northern neighbours they could never obliterate the power of the latter.

In Kerala, on the west coast, brahman settlement grew in various agriculturally rich areas, and these were a source of support to the Makotai kingdom in the Periyar Valley. But the wealth and standing of Kerala derived more from maritime trade. In Kerala, too, brahman migrants were later arrivals and had to function with cultures not altogether familiar. As usual, local recruitment into brahman ranks was inevitable, and adjustments also had to be made with local kinship systems. The adjustment to matrilineal societies, for instance, in the relationship between Nambudri brahmans and Nair landowners, took a different form from those recognizable in other parts of the subcontinent.

The earlier contacts between the east and west coasts of south India continued in the relations between the Pallavas and the Perumal dynasty of Kerala. The motive was largely trade with west Asia, a trade that others were also anxious to tap. Trade with the eastern Roman Empire had declined, but there continued to be a demand for pepper and spices in Europe. It had been kept going by Arab traders supplying items to the markets of Byzantium. The Malabar and Konkan coast had settlements of Arabs who were part of this trade. Unlike earlier traders linked to the Roman trade, the Arabs settled permanently in the coastal regions of the west and the south from about the eighth and ninth centuries. They were welcomed, given land for trading stations and left free to practise their religion, as had been the convention with Christians earlier in south India. However, they were scarcely regarded as new arrivals, for even in pre-Islamic times there had been traffic between the west coast and the Arabian peninsula. The present-day Mappilas or Malabar Muslims are descendants of these settlers, as are the Navayats who have emerged from those settled amid the Jaina trading communities of the Konkan.

Among the more interesting aspects of Arab settlements along the west coast is that each group adopted some of the customary law, and even some forms of worship, from the local community with whom they had the closest contact. Thus there is a difference in the Islam practised by the Khojas and Bohras of Gujarat, the Navayats of the Konkan and the Mappilas of Malabar. Matriliny and matrilocality, for example, were characteristic of the Mappilas but not of the others. These customs appear to have been borrowed from the local Nair practice, since they would otherwise seem unacceptable to conservative Islam. Being mainly traders, the Muslim Arabs settled along the western coast were not primarily concerned with acquiring political power or making large-scale conversions to Islam. Adjustments with local society were therefore not acrimonious. Arab authors describe the Arabs settled in India as *bayasirah*, which may suggest people from southern Arabia.

In the seventh century, Arab armies had invaded Persia. Some Zoroastrians were converted to Islam and some preferred to migrate to India, which they did from the early eighth century. They too came to western India where they already had trading contacts, and established large settlements to the north of Mumbai, such as the one at Sanjan. Their descendants founded a community later known as Parsi, reflecting the land of their origin and their language. Some settled in rural areas but close to centres of trade; others were more active in the trading circuits of the time. Arab officers working for the Rashtrakuta administration in the ninth century were appointed in the Sanjan area, which was important to commercial relations with west Asia. The settlement seems to have been peaceful. Since the Arabs were the people from whom the Zoroastrians are said to have fled, some of the migration to India may have been linked to pursuing commercial interests rather than solely to avoiding religious persecution.

The Arabs had however occupied Sind in the eighth century and established footholds in western India, both of which encouraged their advance towards Chalukya territory in an effort to control the ports of the west coast. The Lata Chalukyas managed to hold them back, thus allowing their southern neighbours time to arm themselves. The immediate danger from the Arabs passed, but the Chalukyas were faced with an even more formidable threat. Dantidurga, one of their subordinates, who was a high official in the administration, declared his independence, and by slow stages his family overthrew the Chalukyas to establish a new dynasty – the Rashtrakutas. The family was based in the Gulbarga region, with their centre of power located in what came to be called Manyakheta. Dantidurga was the father-in-law of Nandi-varman and helped him regain Kanchi, an act commemorated by the Pallava King in the building of the Vaikuntha Perumal temple, almost as a counterpoint to the Kailasanatha temple. The temple marked the end of the King's exile and his return to power. The Pallavas survived the Chalukyas by about a century, but with declining authority during the ninth century. The Pallava line was terminated by the last of the Pallavas being assassinated by a subordinate functionary.

The Rashtrakuta kingdom battened on the weakness of the other kingdoms. The Pallavas were in decline, and their successors, the Cholas, had not yet entered the fray. There was no power in northern India strong enough to interfere with the affairs of the Deccan. The geographical position of the Rashtrakutas led to their involvement in wars and alliances with both the northern and, more frequently, the southern kingdoms. The Rashtrakutas interfered effectively in the politics of Kanauj and this interference cost them many a campaign, though they did gain possession of Kanauj for a brief period in the early tenth century.

But the Rashtrakutas had the advantage of controlling a large part of the western seaboard and therefore the trade with west Asia, particularly with the Arabs. They referred to the Arabs as Tajiks, employing them as officers and even governors of their administrative districts in coastal areas. One of these governors, named Madhumati – thought to be a Sanskritization of the name Mohammad – granted land to a wealthy brahman *matha*. The inscription also states that he controlled many of the harbour officers on behalf of the Rashtrakutas.

Dantidurga established the kingdom in about 753, and was succeeded by Krishna I whose fame is associated with the remarkable rock-cut temple at Ellora, known as the Kailasa temple. Amoghavarsha is probably the best remembered of the Rashtrakuta kings. His long reign (814–80) was militarily not brilliant although he strengthened the core area at Manyakheta. His patronage of the Jaina religion and of Shaivism provided both with considerable support. He was the author of a work on poetics in Kannada, the *Kavirajamarga*, illustrating once again the interest taken by royalty in literature. The tenth-century ruler, Krishna III, was the last of the major Rashtrakuta rulers.

Amoghavarsha's persistent problem had been the threat of rebellion by subordinate rulers under his suzerainty and this was never eliminated. The Chalukyas, reduced to subordinate status, were once again asserting themselves. They were soon to overthrow the Rashtrakutas and install themselves as the rulers, bringing the wheel round full circle. The ambitions of another family, the Shilaharas, began to take shape although they too had been subordinates of the Rashtrakutas. Meanwhile, the rising power of the Cholas in Tamil-nadu was another threat to the independence of the Rashtrakuta kingdom. The first half of the tenth century saw the Rashtrakutas still in the ascendant, with one of their kings claiming the title 'conqueror of Kanchi'. But this was a short-lived claim. By the end of the tenth century, the new rulers of Kanchi and the Chalukyas had between them brought the Rashtrakuta dynasty to an end, and the second line of Chalukyas was ruling the kingdom of the Rashtrakutas.

Political Economies of the Peninsula

Dynasties tend to see-saw when they are equally matched, as in the peninsula. A relatively less obtrusive governmental system encouraged local autonomy in village and district administration, without too much interference from the capital. This autonomy did not divest the state of authority.

Instead it was effective in matters of administration and collection of revenue. It was preserved to a considerable degree in Tamil-nadu, where the tradition was actively maintained for many centuries.

Kings took high-sounding titles, some of which, such as *maharajadhiraja*, were familiar from northern usage. Others were of local invention, such as *dharma-maharaja*, great king ruling in accordance with the *dharma*. Kings were required to rescue and protect *dharma* since it was believed to be ebbing away in the Kali Age. The more unusual *aggitoma-vajapeya-assamedha-yaji*, he who has performed the *agnishtoma*, *vajapeya* and *ashvamedha* sacrifices, sounds like a self-conscious insistence on conformity with Vedic practices prescribed for kingship. Many inscriptions now carried *prashastis*, eulogies, of the king. This had a political purpose, for, with the strengthening of monarchy, the king had to be projected as extraordinary.

In theory, the king was the supreme arbiter of justice, but it is more likely that conflicts were settled at the local level. He was assisted by a group of ministers, and in the later Pallava period this ministerial council played a prominent part in state policy. Some of the ministers bore semi-royal titles, and may have been appointed from the tributary rulers, landed magnates and others who had access to power through administration and economic control over revenue. Among the latter, some may have begun as tenants with large holdings, gradually assuming positions of authority. The term 'feudatory', used for those who controlled power at the local level and who had a subordinate relationship with the king, covers a generally prevailing situation, but it has the disadvantage that in earlier historical writing it has often been taken as suggestive of a similarity with European feudalism. Irrespective of similarities, the nature of power held by such persons differs over space and time in the subcontinent. It might therefore be better to mention the specific categories.

The names given to some administrative units went back to the Mauryan period, such as *ahara*, *vishaya* and *rashtra*, and in Tamil-nadu the basic unit continued to be the *nadu*. There was a hierarchy of officials in charge of provincial administration who worked with local autonomous institutions, largely in an advisory capacity. These institutions appear to have been more common in the south than in northern India during this period. They were built on local relationships of caste, profession and religious sect. Frequent meetings or assemblies were essential to their functioning. Assemblies were of many varieties and at many levels, and could include those of merchant guilds, craftsmen and artisans – weavers, oil-mongers and suchlike – as well as students, ascetics and priests. The smaller groups were chosen by lot from among the eligible persons, and worked in a manner somewhat analogous to modern committees, each group having its specific function.

In the village the basic assembly was the *sabha*, which was concerned with all matters relating to the village: temple property and endowments of various kinds; irrigation; cultivated land; punishment of crime; the keeping of a census and other necessary records. The *sabha* was a formal institution but it worked closely with the *ur*, a gathering of the leaders of the area controlled by non-brahman cultivators. Beyond the *ur* was the *cheri*, the habitat of those regarded as outside the boundaries of caste. A council of landowners worked with the administration of the *nadu*. The *nagaram* was largely a collectivity of traders. Villages which were populated mainly by brahmans have sometimes preserved records of the functioning of assemblies and councils. Records of assemblies in other villages have not survived. This has led to the suggestion that these autonomous bodies were restricted to the former villages. But this does not necessarily follow. If village assemblies were found useful in a particular set of villages, it is likely they would become more common in other villages of that region. The link between the village assembly and the official administration was the headman of the village, who acted both as the leader of the village and the mediator with the government.

Further north in the Deccan there was less autonomy in administrative institutions. In the Chalukya domains government officers were more involved in routine administration, even at the village level. Village assemblies functioned under the paternalistic eye of the official, and the role of the headman as the leader of the village was of a more formal nature. From the eighth century onwards some of the Deccan rulers adopted administrative divisions where groups of ten or twelve villages were formed into larger units.

The expansion of political power was largely based on increased revenue from the introduction of agriculture in areas previously treated as wasteland. One mechanism for doing this was by making grants to brahmans and to temples. This differed from the earlier period. Initially brahmans from elsewhere were invited to settle locally and in the process to convert land to agriculture. The process also involved the conversion of local societies to peasant cultivators in areas where such cultivators had not existed before. The settlement of migrant cultivators is not recorded, although they probably came as and when it was feasible. They would have brought only their labour and not the ideological backing that the rulers received from brahman grantees. The latter included the performance of Vedic sacrifices, which carried echoes of the period of state formation in the first millennium BC. The transition from chiefship to kingship involved the performance of these elaborate rituals that also permitted some claim to association with divinity. In some ways this was both a replay of earlier times and the continuation of a historical tradition. Once the kingdoms were well established the rituals were performed less frequently, or else largely as statements of conformity.

There was a gradual shift from ruling through chiefs to ruling through landed intermediaries, and through temples performing a similar role. The economy was being restructured in areas where there were frequent grants of land. Brahmanical legitimation and the support of the temple networks were sought. *Varna* rules were introduced, but with limited success except among the brahmans. The support for orthodoxy among brahmans was probably related to their dependency on the *velalas*, the other landowners and peasants, who were culturally distinctive and whom the brahmans tried to subordinate by giving them the status of *shudras*. But those among the latter who were landowners also had power.

Other than the land privately owned, the remainder was mostly regarded as crown land. The king could make revenue grants to his officers and land grants to brahmans, or else continue to have the land cultivated by small-scale cultivators and landlords who paid taxes. Tenancies in the latter situation were by their nature not permanent. Private landowners could buy and sell land or gift it for religious purposes. Grants to officers of either land or revenue from land were largely in lieu of salaries, and did not stipulate that the grantee had to provision troops or give a percentage of the revenue to the state.

Grants were usually in perpetuity and their frequency increased over time. Although there is an impression that grants were the predominant form of organizing agriculture, this was not the case everywhere. As elsewhere in the subcontinent, cultivators had existed prior to their land becoming part of a grant. An agreement between the state and the peasant regarding assessment and taxes was either a continuation of the existing norm or required new arrangements. Such agreements were obviously more favourable to the state than to the cultivator. If such land became part of a royal grant then there would be more complex terms and conditions, given the intervention of an intermediary between the state and the peasant. The intermediary's right to alienate or inherit this land depended on the terms of the grant.

The status of the village and the tenures varied and eventually three kinds came to prevail. The most frequent was the village with an inter-caste population paying taxes to the king on the amount of land cultivated, together with its produce and taxes from other occupations. Another category included grants of various kinds to individuals or particular groups, generally brahmans, although the king could choose to make a grant to someone else. The *brahmadeya* villages were created when either the entire village or some lands of the village were donated to a single brahman or a group of brahmans. These grantees were prosperous because the brahmans normally did not pay tax and the holdings could be much larger than usual. The *agrahara* grant applied to a village consisting of a settlement of brahmans, the land being given to them as a grant and exempt from tax, but the brahmans could provide free education locally if they so wished. The third kind were the *devadana/devadeya*, donated to the god – lands or villages functioning in a similar manner to the first category, except that their cultivators were tenants of a temple. The revenue from these villages was donated to the temple, and was consequently received by the temple authorities rather than the state. The temple authorities assisted the village by providing employment for the villagers. This last category of villages gained greater significance in later centuries when the temples became the central institutions of rural life. During the Pallava period the first two types of villages were predominant.

The village included the homes of the villagers, gardens, irrigation works – mainly tanks or wells – cattle enclosures, wastelands, the village common, forests surrounding the village, streams passing through the village lands, the temple and the temple lands, the cremation ground, and the 'wet' (irrigated) and 'dry' lands under cultivation. Land owned in common and used for specific purposes, such as that kept for sifting paddy, was also included. Rice was the staple crop, used as both a unit of barter and a commercial crop when harvested in surplus. There were extensive coconut palm plantations, the produce of the tree being put to varied use. Both the palmyra and the areca palm were cultivated, the latter largely for the export of areca nuts. Groves of mangoes and plantains were a regular feature of the landscape. Oil extracted from the seeds of cotton and gingelly were much in demand.

A special category of land, *eripatti*, or tank land, is mentioned. Donated by individuals, the revenue from this land was set apart for the maintenance of the village tank. This indicates the dependence of the village on tank irrigation, although irrigation with water from wells was next in importance. Rainwater increased the volume stored in the tank so that land could be irrigated during the long, dry spell each year. The tank, lined with brick or stone, was built and maintained through the co-operative effort of the village, and its water shared by the cultivators. Inscriptions from the Pallava period pertaining to rural affairs refer to the upkeep of such tanks. Water was taken from the tank by water lifts to canals, and these were fitted with stone sluices to regulate the water level and prevent an overflow at the source. A special tank committee appointed by the village supervised the distribution of water for irrigation. Water taken in excess of the amount permitted to a particular cultivator was taxed.

Information on land tenures and taxation is available from the detailed records in the grants, which have survived mainly on copper plates. There were two categories of taxes levied in the village: the land revenue paid by the cultivator to the state varied from one-sixth to one-tenth of the produce of the land, and was collected by the village and paid to the state collector; the second category consisted of local taxes, also collected in the village but utilized for services in the village and its environs, ranging from the repair of irrigation works to the renovation or decoration of the temple. The state land tax was low and revenue was supplemented by additional taxes on draught cattle, toddy-drawers, marriage parties, potters, goldsmiths, washermen, textile-manufacturers, weavers, brokers, letter-carriers and the makers of *ghi* (clarified butter). Unfortunately, the percentage of tax was not always indicated and it doubtless varied according to the object taxed. Royal revenue came almost exclusively from rural sources, mercantile and urban institutions being as yet less intensively tapped.

An example of a land grant engraved and preserved on copper plate is quoted below. The eleven plates on which it is inscribed were found near a village in the vicinity of Pondicherry in 1879. The plates were strung on a ring of copper, the two ends of which were soldered and stamped with a royal seal depicting a bull and a *lingam* – the Pallava symbol. It records the grant of a village made in the twenty-second year of the King Nandi-varman (AD 753) and commences with a eulogy of the king in Sanskrit, followed by the details of the grant in Tamil and a concluding verse in Sanskrit. The grant appears to have been made to the preceptor of the king and the person who would have performed various rituals for him, including those pertaining to the Bhagavata sect. The temple built by the king would have been both a gesture honouring his preceptor, as well as a statement of his own political authority. The quotation below is from the Tamil section, and it is significant that the most relevant sections of these grants were in Tamil rather than Sanskrit.

The author of the above eulogy was Trivikrama. The above is an order of the king dated in the twenty-second year of his reign. Let the inhabitants of Urrukkattukottam see. Having seen the order which was issued after the king had been pleased to give

Kodukalli village of our country – having expropriated the former owners at the request of Brahmayuvaraja, having appointed Ghorasharman as the effector of the grant, having excluded previous grants to temples and grants to brahmans, having excluded the houses of the cultivators to the extent of altogether two *patti* [a measure of land] – as a *brahmadeya* (grant) to Shettiranga Somayajin [Shettiranga, who performs the Soma sacrifice], who belongs to the Bharadvaja *gotra* [a brahman exogamous sept], follows the Chhandogyasutra and resides at Puni, we, the inhabitants went to the boundaries which the headman of the *nadu* [district] pointed out, circumambulated the village from right to left, and planted milk-bushes and placed stones around it. The boundaries of this village are – the eastern boundary is to the west of the boundary of Palaiyur, the southern boundary is to the north of the boundary of Palaiyur, the western boundary is to the east of the boundary of Manarpakkam and of the boundary of Kollipakkam, and the northern boundary is to the south of the boundary of Velimanallur. The donee shall enjoy the wet land and the dry land included within these four boundaries, wherever the iguana runs and the tortoise crawls, and shall be permitted to dig river channels and inundation channels for conducting water from the Seyaru, the Vehka, and the tank of Tiraiyan . . . Those who take and use the water in these channels by pouring out baskets, by cutting branch channels, or by employing small levers shall pay a fine to be collected by the king. He (the donee) and his descendants shall enjoy the houses, house gardens, and so forth, and shall have the right to build houses and halls of burnt tiles. The land included within these boundaries we have endowed with all exemptions. He himself shall enjoy the exemptions obtaining in this village without paying for the oil-mills and looms, the hire of the well-diggers, the share of the brahmans of the king, the share of *shengodi* [a plant], the share of the *kallal* [a type of fig tree], the share of *kannittu*, the share of corn-ears, the share of the headman, the share of the potter, the sifting of paddy, the price of *ghi*, the price of cloth, the share of cloth, the hunters, messengers, dancing-girls, the grass, the best cow and the best bull, the share of the district, cotton-threads, servants, palmyra molasses, the fines to the accountant and the minister, the tax on planting water-lilies, the share of the water-lilies, the fourth part of the trunks of old trees of various kinds, including areca palms and coconut trees . . . The grant was made in the presence of the local authorities, of the ministers, and of the secretaries.

Kasakkudi Plates of Nandivarman, tr. E. Hultzsch, *South Indian Inscriptions*, II. 3, pp. 360 ff.

In this system, the function of the brahman was not restricted to the performance and the rhetoric of ritual. Beyond this the brahman grantees also had a role as settlers, colonizers and entrepreneurs, a role which is evident from the grant but is not always recognized. Up to a point the brahman settlements and the temples which developed alongside them acted as surrogates for the state, although they were required to work together with the officers of the state. They provided an administrative substructure in organizing the working of the lands and other resources gifted to them. To the extent that royal administration was concerned with integrating diverse economies into peasant economies this process was assisted by the nuclei of peasant economies that resulted from these grants. The grantees collected revenue and encouraged further extensions of agriculture, some of which would also provide revenue for the state. In addition they had responsibility for the effective management of irrigation, largely tanks, wells and channels that were maintained by the local village assemblies.

Ideologically, the underlining of Brahmanism and the role of the brahman helped to strengthen monarchy by investing the ruling dynasty with legitimacy, by conferring *kshatriya* status on the royal family in some instances and by converting existing social groups into castes, which were then slotted into a hierarchy to make them more functional. The frequency with which dynasties claimed *brahma-kshatra* descent reveals the close functioning of political power and brahmanical ideology in parts of the peninsula during this period. The emphasis on brahman and non-brahman status gradually became the foundational stratification in this area, drawing from the principles of *varna* organization to provide a framework for the juxtaposition of statuses, although it did not conform to the fourfold *varna* society. There were of course other ways of acquiring a high status. For example, the death of a hero in battle or in defending the village could be used by his kinsmen to claim status and land.

The expansion of agriculture did not terminate other activities such as pastoralism. That cattle-keeping remained important in particular areas is evident from the early *viragal*, literally hero-stones, depicting and thus memorializing the local hero defending cattle or fending off attacks by predators, both animal and human. Such depictions began as simple representations, but became elaborate by the end of the millennium. They underline the frequency of raids and suchlike, all of which had to be met through the efforts of the village. The need for the village to protect itself by its own resources emphasizes a decentralized administration. There is an impressive increase in the sheer numbers of such stones from the late first millennium AD.

Single memorial stones tend to occur in isolated areas and often depict a standing warrior or one with a horse. Where they occur in clusters it appears they were brought to the vicinity of the village, frequently in or near the temple used by the upper castes. Some memorials commemorate heroes who died in battle, but the heroic gradually became associated with all actions of defence. They occur in larger numbers in frontier zones or peripheral areas of forested land, presumably where state policing would be weak. Hero-stones are less common in agriculturally fertile areas. In the semi-arid zones of Maharashtra and Karnataka, fending off cattle-raids was a frequent theme. These raids may have reflected the dislocation of forest-peoples by agricultural settlements. In coastal areas such as Goa, representations of sea battles suggest attacks by pirates.

The embellishment of the hero-stone led to the single panel being replaced by three or four horizontal panels, sculpted in bâs-relief. The topmost panel indicated the symbols of the hero's sect, such as an image of Karttikeya, the son of Shiva; a *lingam* and *yoni* for a Shaiva; a small image of Mahavira for a Jaina; and invariably the sun and the moon, encapsulating eternity. The next panel depicted the fulfilment of the promise to the hero – carried to paradise by *apsaras*, celestial maidens. The lowest panels were representations of the event that had caused his death. Sometimes a brief inscription was included below the panels, providing information on the person and the occasion. In subsequent periods, when the wife of the hero was required to immolate herself on the funeral pyre of her husband, and thus become a *sati*, her death was also commemorated through a memorial. The sculpture on the slab was simple and generally depicted an open right forearm, with bangles still intact, symbolizing the continuation of the marriage. It was important to cultivate a heroic ethos in the defence of settlements not protected by the royal army.

Some of the royal revenue went to maintain an army. A system of levies was used in addition to the king's standing army. The army consisted mainly of foot soldiers, cavalry and a unit of elephants. Cavalry was the most expensive, since the availability of horses was limited and to import horses from north India or west Asia was costly. The Pallavas built dockyards at Nagapattinam and developed a navy, although this was inconsiderable compared to the naval strength that south India later acquired under the Cholas. The recent discovery of a possible wharf at Mahabalipuram also points to maritime activities.

The navy assisted in the maritime trade with south-east Asia, by now constituting many kingdoms: Kambuja and Funan (Cambodia); Champa (Vietnam); and Shrivijaya (the southern Malay peninsula, Java and Sumatra). All of these were in contact with India, as well as the trade routes travelled by south Indian merchants. On the western coast, commercial maritime initiative was gradually taken over by intermediary traders, mainly the Arabs. Indian traders gradually became suppliers, rather than carriers, of goods to countries westward. However, cultural contacts with south-east Asia not only continued but increased.

Continuing trade was one of the factors encouraging urbanization. In addition to maritime trade in coastal areas, trade was tied to internal networks traversing the peninsula. The cities of the Ganges Plain seem to have been in temporary decline, but in many other areas cities and commerce are evident. In the earlier period some items arriving at Indian ports were used as part of the ongoing gift-exchange necessary to chiefdoms. The emergence of kingdoms, with revenue from agriculture and commerce, probably reduced the role of gift-exchange. Growing wealth and stratification meant that exchanges took place through trade, rather than as gifts.

Earlier, there had been a difference between the two main regions of the peninsula, the Deccan and the south: votive inscriptions from the Deccan mentioned artisans, guilds, traders and landowners, whereas Tamil *brahmi* inscriptions recorded the donations of individual professionals and merchants with fewer mentions of landowners. This changed when land became a major segment of the economy.

A number of towns were mentioned in the Deccan inscriptions. Among them were Banavasi, Kolhapur, Vatapi, Aihole, Pattadakal and Shravana Belgola. Some, such as Puligere, were originally military camps that were gradually transmuted into administrative and commercial centres. Others were administrative centres to start with or else were the foci of local religious activity. Both categories acquired urban characteristics and were frequently the hub of exchange. Cash donations were recorded, although coins do not seem to have been minted in large amounts. Perhaps this was related to the greater expansion of agricultural interests at this time. Such an expansion would have encouraged the growth of exchange centres although the exchange may have been of local produce.

The centrality of the town can be seen in descriptions of urban life in the *Shilappadigaram* and the *Manimegalai*. Kaveripattinam, also known as Puhar or Pumpuhar, was the cynosure with its harbour and wharf, the houses of merchants and the special part of the city where the Yavanas lived. Paddy came in boats from rural areas to Puhar, where it was exchanged for other merchandise destined for inland market centres such as Kanchipuram, Uraiyur and Madurai. Commercial production at Puhar was also linked to resources from other places: beryl from Palghat; pearls from further south; timber such as sandalwood, teak and ebony from inland forests; and textiles from many centres. Puhar was a lively city with an affluent life-style.

Literary Culture

In the early part of this period, education was provided by Jainas and Buddhists whose teaching pervaded the urban ethos. Gradually, however, the brahmans superseded them. The Jainas had a tradition of religious literature in Sanskrit, such as the *Adipurana* and the *Yashatilaka*. They had also used Prakrit and now began to use Tamil. They developed a few centres for religious instruction, including advanced education, near Madurai and Kanchipuram, and at Shravana Belgola. Many Jaina monks tended to scatter, isolating themselves in small caves tucked away in the hills and forests. The most beautiful of these caves was at Sittannavasal in Pudukkottai, with its traces of what must once have been murals of elegant design. Monasteries were the nucleus of the Buddhist educational system and were located in the region of Kanchipuram and the valleys of the Krishna and the Godavari Rivers. Buddhist centres focused on the study of the religion, particularly as there was intense controversy between Buddhist sects and those adhering to Vaishnavism and Shaivism. Considerable time was spent in debating the finer points of theology. Royal patronage, which the Buddhists now often lacked, gave an advantageous position to the others. The popularity of Jainism was also eroded to some degree in competition with Shaivism when it received less patronage. When Mahendra-varman I, the Pallava king, lost interest in Jainism and took up the cause of Shaivism the Jainas were deprived of valuable royal patronage. Such swings in royal patronage were not common, since most rulers preferred to distribute their patronage tactfully. A change might be due to personal inclination, or to an assessment that a particular group was losing importance as a network of royal support or a provider of revenue.

Ghatikas, colleges and centres providing brahmanical learning, were generally attached to the temples. Entry to these colleges was at first open to any 'twice-born' caste. Although occasionally endowed by merchants, they were viewed as brahman institutions and concerned with advanced study. Extensive royal patronage allowed the potential for political activity, in that they were centres either of loyalty to the monarchy or – when supported by disaffected members of the royal family – of political opposition. Apart from the monasteries and colleges at Kanchipuram, which acquired fame almost equalling Nalanda, there were a number of other Sanskrit colleges. In about the eighth century, the *matha*, an institution supported by Brahmanism and Puranic Hinduism, emerged as a parallel institution to the Buddhist and Jaina monasteries. This was a combination of a rest-house, a feeding-centre, and an educational centre, which indirectly brought publicity to the particular sect with which it was associated. The *mathas* naturally served a more useful purpose in places where pilgrims gathered and where religious discussions could be more effective.

Sanskrit was now the recognized medium in these institutions and spread through its use in the *agrahara*, *ghatikas* and *mathas*. It was also the official language at the court, which encouraged its use in literary circles. Two outstanding works from this period were Bharavi's *Kiratarjuniya*, based on a theme from the *Mahabharata* which figures the hero Arjuna's contestation with Shiva, and Dandin's *Dashakumaracharita* (*The Tale of the Ten Princes*). Dandin's stories were located in various parts of the subcontinent and included a motley collection of characters from virtually every walk of life, while being narrated with wit and a conspicuous lack of sanctimoniousness. But conscious literary labouring was also fashionable, presumably as a virtuoso demonstration of proficiency in the language. Sometimes a poem was written with such skill that it could be read both forwards and in reverse, each reading narrating two different stories, such as the narrative of the *Ramayana* in one reading and of the *Mahabharata* in the other. Those who indulged in and acclaimed this degree of literary artifice ignored the languages of new literature – Tamil in the south, with Kannada, and later, Telugu, in the Deccan.

References were made to the existence of literature in Kannada at this time, but not too much has survived. A seventh-century inscription of a Chalukya king at Badami mentions Kannada as the local Prakrit or natural language, and Sanskrit as the language of culture, which neatly summarizes the relationship between the two languages. This relationship was later labelled that of the *deshi* or local, popular literature, and the *marga*, or mainstream literature in Sanskrit. An awareness of the social context of languages and literatures is implicit in this distinction. A century later, a Chalukya king had an inscription engraved in Kannada at Kanchipuram. The ninth-century *Kavirajamarga* is important to Kannada poetics.

Tamil could by now claim poetry of both the lyric and epic variety. Didactic poems of an earlier time frequently deriving from Jaina inspiration were known and recited, such as those of the *Kural* and the *Naladiyar*. The two Tamil epic poems, *Shilappadigaram* and *Manimegalai*, which laid the foundation for a mature and independent poetic style in Tamil, are often dated to the mid-first millennium AD. The author of the first, Ilango Adigal, a member of the royal family, was evidently partial to the Shramanas since the poem is suffused with an ethos highlighting *ahimsa* (non-violence) and *karma* (human action), although it also shows a certain religious eclecticism.

The sequel written by Cattan, who came from a merchant family, continues the story and the mood. These poems are departures from earlier stories and poems of sword-wielding heroes since the central figure of the first is the heroine Kannaki, whose heroic violence and reward take the unusual form of a curse on the city of Madurai, and her eventual ascension as the goddess Pattini. Although these poems are classified as epics, the themes are different from epic stereotypes. The didactic element is also evident in a series of Jaina *Ramayanas*, composed in diverse places, which are alternative texts to those inspired by a brahmanical ethos.

Both the long Tamil poems contain descriptions rich in imagery of the countryside as well as of the town of Kaveripattinam, and are particularly evocative of the activities of daily life. A passage from the *Shilappadigaram* reads:

> In the thicket
> Of fresh lotuses rising from the ponds
> Caressed by splendid paddy fields
> And sugarcane are heard, as on a battlefield
> Where two kings fight for victory,
> Various kinds of clamorous sounds
> Made by waterfowls, screaming cranes,
> Red-footed swans, green-footed herons,
> Wild fowls, cormorants, snipes,
> The *ural* water-birds, large herons
> And other birds. Buffaloes enter and immerse
> Themselves in the soft, unploughed mire.
> With the hair on their bodies unwashed, eyes
> Red, they come and rub
> Their itching backs against the unspoilt, straw bins,
> Thus loosening the twisted strands that hold them.
> The bins come apart spilling the rich grain
> Stored inside with sheaves of excellent paddy
> That resembles chowries.
> One heard the noise of the loud talk of labourers
> With strong arms and farmers standing
> In knots. One heard the sound
> Of songs in new styles by low born women
> Who turned on by strong wine worked in the fields.
> Eyes wide like red minnows,
> They bandied indecent words and looked

Singularly charming in their clothes splashed
With mud that also glazed their breasts and shoulders
Clasped by armlets. From their hair they picked
The fragrant flowers and thrust seedlings instead.
One heard the ploughmen's song of praise
As they stood by their ploughs and worshipped
With folded hands. They appeared to break open
The earth radiant with wreaths bound
With shining ears of rice, plaited
With blue lotuses and the thick, vine-like hariali grass

Ilango Adigal, *Shilappadigaram*, tr. R. Parthasarathy, *The
The Lay of an Anklet*, pp. 98–9

The description of the city comes from *Manimegalai* where Puhar is compared to a woman:

The moats filled with clear water, embellished with innumerable flowers, sounding
with the song of a thousand kinds of bird, form a ring round her ankle. The
surrounding walls, commanded by towers, are her diamond studded girdle. The
gates surmounted by staffs with flags flying, are her shoulders laden with many
necklaces. The temple of the tree of abundance (*kalpataru*) and the temple of the
thunderbolt (*vajra*) standing face to face, are her two superb and provocative breasts.
The vast palace, thousands of years old, of matchless splendour, commanding the
city, the residence of the Chola king who wears a necklace of orchid-tree leaves, is
her face. The full moon rising in the east and the sun setting in the west are her
earrings of silver and gold.

Cattan, *Manimekhalai*, tr. A. Danielou, p. 22

Classicism in Tamil includes many expressions invoking the emotion of
love, the seminal form of which can be found in earlier *Shangam* poetry. The
development of Tamil was furthered by a religious movement popularized by
groups of poets, hymnologists and preachers, who in modern studies are
often called the 'saints' of the Tamil devotional sects. Tamil was widely used
in these compositions, accelerating its evolution compared to other southern
languages. (The term 'saint' has been used extensively for those who were
teachers and poets of *bhakti*, where devotion was the primary religious
expression. The word should not be understood in the sense of a Christian
saint, but rather as a charismatic person gifted to teach the new doctrines and
to compose poems, and around whom large groups of followers gathered.)

Philosophical and Religious
Changes

The interaction of northern culture with that of the south, with the circuits of traders and regular routes of armies as well as brahman settlers, resulted in the assimilation of some of the patterns, ideas and institutions of the north, while others were rejected or modified. Some acted as catalysts and new forms were created. The brahmans settled in Tamilaham saw themselves as keepers of what they now regarded as sacrosanct Vedic tradition. The degree to which it was viewed as a contribution of the north is debatable, since sections of the *Vedas* had been composed or redacted at centres for Vedic study in the peninsula. More likely, the earlier process of Sanskrit becoming the hegemonic language through adoption and adaption was continued. However, in the peninsula its hegemony was not absolute, since the languages derived from Dravidian roots retained authority and were more widely used. Educated brahmans were becoming mobile and seeking new patrons since the *mlechchha* rulers of the north – the Shakas, Indo-Greeks, Kushanas and the Hunas – had been more supportive of Buddhism and Jainism, and of emergent Puranic religions. But the rulers of western India, the Kshatrapas, had been the first to use Sanskrit in their inscriptions, and others were patrons of brahmans.

As keepers of the Vedic tradition, they were venerated and gradually found supporters in the kings of the peninsula who, like rulers anywhere, sought respectability by conforming to conservative tradition – in this case, the tradition as interpreted by the brahmans. The performance of rituals by the kings was an avenue to high status. The brahmans' claim to be in communication with the gods, their supposed ability to manipulate unseen powers, and their conviction that they knew the correct *mantra* or formula to establish the well-being of the king, was probably more convincing to the kings than other claims. The belief that rituals bestow authority and power was widespread and an additional incentive was the promise of heavenly rewards. Frequently the rituals were from the *Agamas*, although Vedic practices continued. These would be the occasions that allowed some merging of both traditions.

The Vedic tradition was not confined to rituals. Commentaries on the Vedic corpus had encouraged the existing discussion of philosophical ideas. The evolution of philosophical schools was now recognized in many parts of the subcontinent. Some philosophers were anxious to revitalize Vedic thought and this would have been an accompaniment to establishing *mathas* and *ghatikas*. But revitalization involves making changes. One way of making philosophy based on the Vedic corpus more acceptable was by reducing its obscurities, thereby making it comprehensible to the educated. This was attempted by Shankaracharya, who accepted the challenge to Brahmanism from the Buddhists and the Jainas and the popular devotional sects, and attempted to meet it.

Coming from Kerala, he wrote and taught probably in the eighth–ninth century, although his dates remain controversial and could be of a later period. He achieved fame for his study of the Vedic system and as the new interpreter of Vedanta philosophy. He also rekindled a greater interest in the *Upanishads* through his commentaries elaborating on the relation between the *atman*, the individual soul, and the *brahman*, the universal soul, realized through *jnana*, appropriate knowledge.

Shankara argued in favour of a Monist position where reality is seen as *advaita*, non-dual; and that the world we see around us is *maya*, illusion, for the reality lies beyond and cannot be perceived through existing human senses. Asceticism alone enables one to control these senses and direct them in a manner that permits a glimpse of the ultimate reality. He was opposed to unnecessary and meaningless ritual and established his own *mathas*, where a simplified worship was practised and a systematized Vedanta was taught. These were visualized as parallel to monasteries and are said to have been located at Badrinath in the Himalayas, Puri in Orissa, Dvarka on the western coast, and the most important at Shringeri in the south. All these places collected large numbers of pilgrims and have been viewed as located at the four corners of the subcontinent. However, there is some chronological discrepancy since inscriptions relating to the Shankaracharya *mathas* are later. This has led to considerable debate over the chronology of the *mathas*. These institutions were richly endowed and soon had branches elsewhere, which became centres of Shankara's teaching. A hierarchy of control emerged in these institutions, taking the form of an ecclesiastical organization, but it did not become a parallel to the state, however influential it might have been in matters of administration.

Shankaracharya is said to have visited many centres of learning and debated with leading scholars, such as Madanamishra, Kumarila Bhatta and Prabhakara, as well as various Buddhist and Jaina scholars. He encouraged members of his ascetic order to propagate his teaching as part of a missionary enterprise. The philosophical forms and the institutional organization adopted by Shankara often paralleled or imitated those of the Buddhists. The latter were understandably indignant at a movement intended to undermine them by using their own methods. This is reflected, for instance, in the disparaging description of Shankara in a sixteenth-century Tibetan history of Buddhism by the Lama Taranatha. That Shankara saw Buddhism as a threat points to the continuing importance of Buddhist thought. The critique of some of Shankara's writing from non-Buddhist sources goes back to the comments of Ramanuja in the twelfth century.

Debates and discussions among scholars were common practice, and their public role derived from the earlier Shramanic tradition. It was also an age of commentaries and exegeses on what was regarded as established tradition, which was now being re-interpreted among new social groups. The commentaries and the glosses often carried new ideas. Where they were departures from earlier thinking they have a historical significance. The sources of law, for example, were changing and more emphasis was given to customary law of the family, the guild and the *jati*.

Shankara's enthusiasm in debating with his opponents and their reasoned responses contributed to a tradition that spurred philosophical centres into new speculative thinking, even if this sometimes encouraged conservative thought. Shankara's philosophy contained within it the possibilities of negative reactions as well. Among these was the argument that if the world around us is an illusion there is little incentive to understand how it functions or to derive empirical knowledge from it.

Vedic philosophy and practice was not the only culture that marked a presence in the south. Other groups, either anti-Vedic or non-Vedic in teaching, had also evolved and now had a presence. Apart from Jainism and Buddhism, there were Bhagavata and Pashupata sects, preaching devotion to Vishnu and Shiva respectively. Their rituals were described in the *Agamas* of each sect. The emphasis was on personal worship. The offerings as part of the ritual of *puja* were generally flowers, fruit and grain rather than the sacrifice of animals. The rituals drew on the believed efficacy of *mantras*, involving the worship of icons located in temples and the liturgies connected with this worship. This was a more comprehensible form of worship than the complicated Vedic and other rituals performed by kings under the guidance of their priests, and was to strike root in the populace.

Although orthodox brahmans initially dismissed the devotional movement, the latter eventually proved more popular than other religious trends in the south, and this was recognized even by royal patrons. The Tamil devotional movement was deeply affected by Vaishnavism and Shaivism in the choice of deity. Some sects were hostile to Buddhism and Jainism, but were nevertheless influenced by these religions. These sects were among the early expressions of what has been called the Bhakti movement.

This all-embracing label is used for various sectarian movements of the subcontinent at different times. Many of these had similarities, although they were by no means identical. There were many strands in the Bhakti tradition that need to be seen as distinct. As a broad-based tradition it registered forcefully a key characteristic of religion in India: that formalism was required of a small status-determined group, but for the majority religion remained an area of interplay, accommodation, contestation of a localized kind, and experimentation in seeking the emotional and psychological responses associated with religious belief and practice. The sectarian identity was the more recognizable identity. The essentials of religion lay in the articulation of these latter groups – in their compositions, their forms of worship and their places of worship. This tends to be overlooked by those who see religion unfold solely through a series of texts.

It could be argued that Vaishnavism and Shaivism were but a religious form given to movements that would have surfaced in any case. In this sense, they were an expression of local sentiment questioning the attempts at homogenization made by Vedic Brahmanism, with its insistence on orthodox practices and social inequality. Buddhists and Jainas were less popular in the devotional movement because they were said to mortify their bodies through ascetic practices as a form of worship. But this was not the sole reason for some of the more prominent teachers having converted from Jainism, and relations between Jainism and the Tamil devotional movement have not been adequately investigated. The appearance of this movement was not unexpected since it had a long gestation period, particularly if its origins are sought in the *Shangam* poems of love from which the poetry of love and devotion is said to have evolved. The deity as lover could sometimes inspire the most powerful poetry on the interface of the sacred and the erotic.

The devotional poetry focuses on the individual's search for liberation from rebirth, on devotion as a path to liberation, and on a preference for avoiding violence. Love was directed to a deity. The devotional aspect was formulated in a relationship between man or woman and their deity of choice, a relationship based on love, and on the grace which the deity bestowed on the worshipper. This formulation had not been so strongly emphasized in earlier religious thought. The worshipper, recognizing a feeling of inadequacy, would declare his love for his deity who was believed to permit a reciprocal relationship. This is described poignantly in one of the earliest Tamil poems of this tradition, dedicated to Murugan.

> When you see his face praise him with joy,
> worship him with joined palms, bow before him,
> so that his feet touch your head.
> Holy and mighty will be his form
> rising to heaven, but his sterner face
> will be hidden, and he will show you
> the form of a young man, fragrant and beautiful
> and his words will be loving and gracious –
> Don't be afraid – I knew you were coming.

> Pattupattu, 'Tirumuruganarrupadai', 285–90,
> in A. L. Basham, *The Wonder That Was*
> *India*, p. 330

Tamil devotionalism achieved a great wave of popularity in the hymns and poems of the Alvars and the Nayanars, the Vaishnava and Shaiva poets. The hymns dedicated to Shiva and Vishnu have been preserved in two separate collections, the *Tirumurai* and the *Nalayiradivya-prabandham*. Of the Shaiva poets the most popular were Appar – who is said to have converted King Mahendra-varman – Sambandar, Manikkavasagar and Sundaramurti, some of whom were apostate Jainas. The better-known Vaishnava Alvars were Nammalvar, Tirumankai Alvar and the much revered woman poet, Andal. Vedic gods were either denied or ignored, the emphasis being not on the object of worship but on the relationship involved in worship. Manikkavasagar explains it in his hymns:

> Indra or Vishnu or Brahma
> Their divine bliss crave not I
> I seek the love of thy saints
> Though my house perish thereby.
> To the worst hell will I go
> So but thy grace be with me
> Best of all, how could my heart
> Think of a God beside Thee? . . .
> I had no virtue, penance, knowledge, self-control
> A doll to turn
> At other's will I danced, whistled, fell.
> But me He filled in every limb
> With love's mad longing, and that I might climb
> There whence there is no return.

He shewed His beauty, made me His.
Ah me, when shall I go to Him . . . ?

P. Kingsbury and G. E. Phillips, *Hymns*
of the Tamil Saivite Saints, pp. 89, 127

Nammalvar's poems to Vishnu evoke an even stronger commitment to the
deity, with no concession to formal religion:

You believers in Linga mythologies
And you Jainas
you Buddhists
becoming all of you choppers of logic
becoming even your gods
he stands there
our lord:
Come see him in Kurukur
where rich ears of paddy
fan him like ceremonial yak tails.
In this place without lies
Come praise him.

Elsewhere he says:

I just said
'The grove and hill of my lord'
and he came down
and filled my heart . . .
My lord
who swept me away forever
into joy that day
made me over into himself
and sang in Tamil
his own songs through me:
what shall I say
to the first of things
flame
standing there,
what shall I say
to stop.

What her mother said:

> O women
> you too have daughters
> and have brought them up.
> How can I tell you
> about my poor girl?
> She talks of the conch shell,*
> she talks of the wheel,*
> and she talks night and day
> of the basil in his hair.
> what shall I do?

A. K. Ramanujam,
Hymns for the Drowning,
pp. 57, 78 ff., 35

* The conch shell and the wheel are symbols of Vishnu.

Appar says:

> Once he made me run about
> with the naked Jainas
> then made me sing sweet songs
> for his golden feet.
> Kurankatuturai's Lord
> saved me from *karma*
> and joined me with his true devotees.

Indira V. Peterson,
Poems to Shiva, p. 289

Although there were some brahmans among the singers of poems, many of the participants were of the lower castes, being artisans and cultivators. Not all were composers but they were nevertheless familiar with the compositions. They came from various parts of the Tamil country and travelled a great deal. Among the more radical features of these groups were the active participation of women poets and the presence of the *pulaiyar* or outcastes.

The poems of Andal, one of the best-known women poets, were frequently sung. She saw herself as the beloved of the god Vishnu and her verses encapsulated her love for the deity. These foreshadow the verses of Mirabai, who was to become equally famous as a Bhakti poet many centuries later in north India, celebrating her love for the Krishna incarnation of Vishnu. The evocations of Karaikkalamnaiyar were closer to asceticism. Women participants in the Tamil devotional movement renounced their social obligations, but did not join an alternative order or become nuns. They created alternative possibilities within society by their poetry, their activities and their sublimation of eroticism. Up to a point this was a challenge to patriarchy, but the challenge had to take the form of devotion to a deity. Nammalvar, in one of his poems, imagines himself as a woman in relationship with the deity who is a male. But the passionate love of a male poet for a goddess was not encouraged. Although goddesses were widely worshipped, they were rarely the focus of devotion in these poems.

The question still remains why the religion of the Alvars and Nayanars became so popular from the latter part of the first millennium AD. It may have been a reaction to the formalistic Sanskritic culture and religious practice introduced into elite circles, and a reluctance to be subordinated to this culture. The role of the Bhakti tradition in relation to Vedic Brahmanism was in many ways similar to that of the earlier Shramanic sects. The rituals and the claims of the brahmans to being close to the gods were unacceptable, as was the social exclusion of lower castes. But Tamil devotionalism was also ambivalent towards the Shramanic tradition and was hostile to the Shramanas. From the Vaishnava and Shaiva perspectives, Shramanic beliefs were heresy. The centrality of the deity, visualized in iconic form and housed in a temple, had become important facets of Puranic Hinduism with which the devotional movement had obvious links.

It has been suggested that the movement was parallel to changes in the polity. The king is seen as the focus of loyalty and demands devotion from the intermediaries and his subjects, while the deity receives similar sentiments from worshippers. This implicit overlap might have encouraged rulers to patronize the devotional sects, underlining the notion of loyalty. This was a more direct message than in religions that had no place for temples and the divinity of kings. But the equation of the state with the temple, and the king with the deity, was more complex. Although changes in polity of the kind that occurred in Tamil-nadu also occurred in other parts of the subcontinent at this time, the manifestation of what might be called Bhakti is a later phenomenon in other areas. A wide social range inspired the devotional movement, but the individual liberation suggested in these teachings may have resonated with historical changes. In Tamil-nadu it may also have related to the upward mobility of some groups of peasants and artisans, and with the freedom provided by cities to ideas and actions.

According to some traditions, Tamil society eventually rejected Buddhism and also reduced its patronage of Jainism. An incident frequently described is that of many Jaina monks, who agreed to a debate after attacking a Shaiva monastery, and, when they lost, further agreed to be impaled. The figure of those impaled is sometimes quoted as eight thousand. This sounds an unlikely story, particularly during a period when rulers were said to be converting from Jainism to Shaivism. In such traditions, the hostility is generally between the Shaivas and the Shramanic sects, as was the case in other parts of India. Gradually, the Jaina lay community in the peninsula was limited to Karnataka with small pockets elsewhere in the south. But the imprint of Buddhism and Jainism was evident in the Tamil devotional sects. They leaned towards rejecting the established order of society as stratified in the caste structure, but the rejection was on the ethical plane and not a prelude to a radical change of society.

The deity could be a folk-deity in origin promoted to a manifestation of a mainstream deity. The concept of a compassionate deity reflected Buddhist ideas, more specifically the notion of the compassionate *bodhisattva*, though the Christians of the south may also have made a contribution. The feeling of human inadequacy that became an important facet of the Bhakti devotional sects would have owed more to Buddhist ancestry than to Vedic. The decline of the heterodox sects coincided with the rise of the Bhakti sects, probably depriving them of much of their potential following.

At one level the Tamil devotional sects resisted Sanskritic culture. The brahmans enjoyed royal patronage, but the sects were widely supported by common people, although royal patronage was extended to the sects in later centuries when they had a substantial following, partly for reasons of political expediency apart from religious conviction. A constant awareness of the strength of popular movements was a necessary counterpart to royal power. Association with a popular movement brought a network of loyalty which, if the movement was widespread, could be territorially extensive. The Tamil devotional movement had roots in the area and was to that extent useful to political authority. Whereas Vedic Brahmanism propagated the use of Sanskrit through elaborate rituals, the devotional sects expressed themselves in easily understood forms using the commonly spoken language. The brahmans were obsessed with caste regulations, the Tamil poets excluded no one for reasons of caste alone and, on the contrary, welcomed lower castes.

Under the aegis of the brahmans, organized religion was well fortified with finance and patronage, both of which came from either royal families or wealthy landowners and merchants. The local temple, seen as the abode of the deity, was one location of religious activity. Some sought to integrate the two levels of religion – the brahmanical and the devotional movement – through rituals and functions, if only to a limited extent. The temple became a location for this attempt at integration. Temples had various categories of officiants. The most influential were the *smarta* brahmans proficient in Vedic and other Sanskrit learning. A large number of brahmans were locally recruited priests, with a smattering of Vedic and Puranic knowledge, who performed many of the routine rituals. Where the temple had emerged from a local cult centre the priests introduced the local mythology and ritual into the worship of deities. This was then given a stamp of authenticity by inclusion in the sectarian *Agama* texts, which provided the temple with a presumed history via the *sthala-puranas* and the *mahatmyas*, when these came to be written. The Tamil devotional poets addressed a specific deity and its icon. When their following grew, their compositions became part of devotional worship. Some tension between the different groups could have resulted from this divergence. At one level devotionalism focused on the local cult, forms of worship and language. At another level, by the worship of deities known to other areas of the subcontinent, it also acted as a way of partially homogenizing Puranic Hinduism.

The Role of the Temple

Temples were maintained from endowments that consisted either of villages and agricultural lands, or else came from the investment of capital. The donors could be members of the royal family, wealthy intermediaries or merchants or guilds. The smaller accessories of the temple, such as subsidiary images, lamps, oil, etc., were generally obtained through the individual donations of lesser members of the community. Temple attendants were of various categories. Brahmans alone could conduct the rituals in the *garbha-griha*, the holy of holies, whereas members of the other castes (generally the lower castes) played music for the ceremonies in the temple, lighted the lamps and attended to the flowers and garlands necessary for the worship of the images, as well as to the cleanliness of the temple. But castes of potters and tanners and the outcastes, regarded as ritually unclean castes, were not permitted to enter the temple since their presence was held to be polluting. A sizeable increase in the endowments and attendants of the temple usually led to the appointment of a formal managing committee to supervise their administration. Members of this committee included brahmans, *velalas* or landowners graded as ritually clean *shudras*, and some officers.

The Tamil poets popularized their hymns and music, which were slowly incorporated into temple ritual. In later times this inspired some deeply moving music. The *vina*, the lute, was probably the most frequently used instrument. Initially an instrument with a pear-shaped body, it later took the form in which it is found today – a long fingerboard with gourds at either end. Dancing and music were included in the temple ritual as forms of service to the deity. From the Pallava period onwards the more prosperous temples maintained trained dancers, singers and musicians. Originating in folk-dancing, the choreography of temple-dancing became the sophisticated and stylized renderings of religious themes apparent in its later forms. This gave rise to the system of employing *devadasis* – the women who served the deity – in many large temples, virtually all over India. The training was arduous and based on complex techniques and forms of dance, singing and music. Some among them became composers of devotional poems. In origin, the rituals they performed were related to the idea of the special power embedded in women, aspects of which were expressed in ritual and dance. But this was sometimes deflected to entertaining the more affluent temple functionaries and worshippers. Inevitably, where it degenerated it required the women to include activities that had little to do with homage to the deity.

The vogue established by the Buddhists for excavating cave temples continued. Patrons of brahmans and Buddhists vied with each other in having shrines and temples excavated in the Deccan hills and further south. The most impressive of these caves were at Ajanta and Ellora. At the latter site, the excavation of temples to Shiva and Vishnu, and of rock-cut Jaina temples, revealed that the earlier style of cutting cave shrines started by the Buddhists had continued.

Murals at some Buddhist cave shrines had illustrated Buddhist narratives. Such paintings depicted familiar themes from the narratives of Buddhist texts, but at the same time drew on a rich cross-section of contemporary life. To cover the walls of deep-cut caves with murals, or to sculpt into rock, was an achievement of no mean order, considering the difficulty of adequate lighting and working conditions in these vast caves. The technique of painting required the preparation of the ground before it could be painted. A paste consisting of powdered rock, clay or cow dung mixed with chaff and molasses was smeared on the wall as a base. This was carefully smoothed out and while still wet was overlaid with a coat of fine lime wash. Colour was applied when the base had dried, and the finished form was burnished.

The colours were made from minerals and plants, and a few still retain some of their original brilliance.

Murals were common not only in cave temples, but in the free-standing temples of the south as well. In the case of the former some of the murals may have been painted by the monks, although the professional excellence of those visible today almost certainly suggests the work of artists. Murals were not restricted to religious monuments alone, since, judging by literary descriptions, domestic architecture was also embellished with paintings, but unfortunately these have not survived.

In a rock-cut temple, sculpture cannot be added on, therefore every detail of positioning had to be planned in advance. The cutting of the rock required extremely careful control as a wrong move could ruin a sculpture or the architectural form. Rock-cut temples were introduced in the Pallava period, and these were akin to the Buddhist cave shrines, but much smaller and showing evidence of the preliminary stages of an artistic technique. The monolithic temples at Mahabalipuram, carved out of granite boulders, still carry the barrel-vault roofs and archways generally associated with the Buddhist cave shrines of the Deccan, as well as contemporary architectural styles. They range in style from what looks like a village hut to an elaborate house, and represent a transition from domestic architecture to more complex temple styles.

The rock-cut temples on the island of Elephanta near Bombay can claim an impressive style. But the most spectacular example is the Kailasanatha temple at Ellora, which is a transition from the rock-cut to the free-standing style on a massive scale. It was built, or rather hewn, under the patronage of a Rashtrakuta king in the eighth century. When finished, it was a free-standing temple open to the sky, wholly cut from the rock of the hillside. The plan of a free-standing temple was rigorously adhered to. The Kailasanatha temple at Ellora covered approximately the same area as the Parthenon at Athens, and was one-and-a-half times higher than the Greek structure. The number of stone-cutters and workmen employed and the expenses involved in cutting the temple must have been immense, perhaps the equivalent in cost to a major military campaign. It has been suggested that it was cheaper to cut the temple from the rock than to build a free-standing structure of the same dimensions. This supposition may partly account for the prolonged popularity of the rock-cut shrine and temple. Stone structural temples were built at Aihole in the late sixth century, at Mahabalipuram – the famous Shore temple – in the seventh century, and at Kanchipuram. But, as a form, examples of the rock-cut temple continued to the Chola period.

In Karnataka the temples at Aihole, Pattadakal and Badami range from the relatively simple to the more complex, and are examples of the developed Deccan style. The Chalukya temples evolved from the Gupta shrines, but in their period of maturity they had links with both the northern and southern styles of architecture – the Nagara and the Dravida. The Durga temple at Aihole is stylistically a continuation of the Buddhist *chaitya* plan, since it is an apsidal temple, but it does not have the barrel roof usual to apsidal temples. Aihole itself emerges as a temple town, possibly because it was regarded as an ancient sacred site. There were megalithic structures in the vicinity, as well as earlier Buddhist activity at the site. It was also an important trading centre, which bestowed its name on one of the foremost guilds of the peninsula.

The rapidity with which architectural styles changed is evident if one compares the plan and elevation of the Ladh Khan temple with the Virupaksha temple. Locations such as Aihole have temples of the post-Gupta style with elements of the Dravida style, and the meeting of styles is only too evident. Changing styles not only reflected contacts between the Deccan, south India and the Ganges Plain, but also reflected the evolution of political forms within a region. These moved from small to larger kingdoms, from reasonable to substantial revenue, with the conviction that the expense of building a temple complex was an act of enviable patronage likely to bring much merit. Temples now became more than places of worship, for they were recognized as statements of power and authority: as well they might, considering the enormous expense of building a temple. What is striking is that those commissioning and financing the temples were not only members of the royal family or ministers, but also well-placed merchants.

The free-standing temples at Aihole, Badami and Pattadakal in the Deccan, and at Kanchipuram and Mahabalipuram in the Tamil country, provided spaces for sculpture. The Deccan style in sculpture showed a close affinity to the Gupta. Pallava sculpture owed more to the Buddhist tradition especially of the Amaravati school, and on the whole remained both more monumental and linear in form, avoiding the tendency to ornamentation which occurred quite early in Deccan sculpture. Yet the sculpture and architecture of the Deccan and Tamil-nadu were not mere offshoots of the northern tradition. They were distinctly recognizable as different, with a character of their own: the basic form was taken from the older tradition, but the end result unmistakably reflected its local inspiration.

The Pallava royal temples carried assertions of royal authority in various ways. These could take the form of lengthy inscriptions narrating the history of the king, or could be sculptured panels such as the ones depicting the

6. Virupaksha Temple, Pattadakal: half-plan and section

king's biography, especially his consecration, in the Vaikuntha Perumal temples. These statements captured the counterpoint of the power of ritual and of political power, but did not indicate a separation of ritual and political sovereignty.

Other themes drew on the mythology of the deities and legends familiar from the *Puranas*, the *Mahabharata* and *Ramayana*. To some extent, they compare with the bâs-relief medallions and friezes at earlier Buddhist sites, carrying visual narrations of the life of the Buddha and of *Jataka* stories. Where the mythology was taken from a folk-cult and incorporated into the specific myth of a deity, its representation, even in a faintly recognizable form, on the walls of a royal temple would be an indication of its having been assimilated into the Puranic tradition. Depicting narratives from the epics on temple walls would have familiarized visitors with the mythology, which would then be recited by the professional reciters and story-tellers, the *pauranikas* and the *kathakaras*. The most impressive sculptures at Mahabalipuram were the large friezes, particularly one in deep relief showing a collection of numerous creatures in a scene variously ascribed either to the descent of the Ganges or to narratives from the epics. Apart from the placement of animals and their relative sizes, some of the scenes were imbued with a quiet sense of humour, such as the cat in the pose of an ascetic with an eye on the mice near by. Not only did the frieze illustrate myths, but there was also an attempt to contemporize the figures from mythology.

The nuclei of regional articulation were taking shape gradually, despite the overlay of a Sanskritic culture strongly supported by the elite. This became a recurring pattern in the evolution of regional cultures. Patterns of change, although not identical, were beginning to suggest some similarities, such as the grants of land, the diffusion of ideas, or popular teaching. Religious diversities were being expressed in variant ways. At one level there were debates among brahmans, and between brahmans and Shramans, frequently of a philosophical kind. At another level the Bhakti teachings were challenging Vedic Brahmanism, and focusing on a religious activity where the relationship of worshipper and deity could be kept discrete, but which evolved into icons, temples, sacred places and pilgrimages. Such changes were closely related to the more tangible changes of the time and were given expression in the re-ordering of social groups. This created a vibrant cultural activity.

11

The Peninsula: Establishing Authorities and Structures

c. AD 900–1300

The Politics of the Peninsula

The late first millennium AD saw a changed situation in the Indian subcontinent. Regional states, earlier seeking recognition, were now taking shape and the imprint of their identities was becoming clearer. Dynasties would change but successor kingdoms retained a relatively consistent core area. The trends that continued included some degree of political decentralization, an emphasis on extending agriculture, the induction of erstwhile marginal groups as castes, the interface between Vedic Brahmanism and the Puranic and Shamanic religions, and new cultural articulations drawing on these tendencies. Despite the appearance of similar patterns, each region retained its own strong identity. That this is not a contradiction lies in the nature of these regional forms.

The scene in the peninsula was dominated by the Tamil identity, forged under the Cholas. This period of south Indian history with its impressive corpus of inscriptions has been widely discussed in recent years. There have been diverse theories and many new interpretations about the nature of the Chola state. These enable one to speak of it as yet another classical period, should one choose to use the label. The classicism of the Chola period drew less on political authority and more on the institutions established at this time, together with the articulation of cultural forms. In many spheres of cultural life, whether of social institutions, religion, or the fine arts, the standards established during this period came to dominate the pattern of living in the south, and to partially influence the patterns existing elsewhere in the peninsula. There was also an active intervention in south-east Asia to a greater degree than before, in the commerce of the region and in its cultural forms.

In the ninth century the Pallavas succumbed to a combined attack from their southern neighbours, the Pandyas, and those tributary to them such as the Cholas. An agrarian foundation to kingdoms in Tamil-nadu had begun more systematically with Pallava land grants to brahmans. The subsequent expansion of newly cultivated areas encompassed pastoral regions and forests. Brahman settlements established Vedic Brahmanism, sometimes parallel to and sometimes intersecting with the religion of the Vaishnava and Shaiva sects.

The Cholas emerged as the dominant power in the south. The core region of their control – Cholamandalam – was the area around Tanjavur up to the eastern coast, the Coromandal of later times. Their early conflict was with the declining Rashtrakutas, whose place was then taken by a revived branch of the Chalukyas, now known as the Later Chalukyas, rising to power in the western Deccan. During this period the Deccan was divided into smaller kingdoms of similar status, with some of which the Cholas were occasionally at war. Political relations involved not only the Later Chalukyas, but also the Yadavas of Devagiri (northern Deccan in the region of Aurangabad) and the Kakatiyas of Warangal (in Andhra Pradesh). Further south there was competition with the Gangas (south Karnataka) and later the Hoysalas of Dorasamudra (in Karnataka), as well as with the Pandyas of Madurai and the Cheras in Kerala. In their last years the Cholas were weakened by the continued incursions of the Hoysalas and the Pandyas into Chola territory.

Mention of Chola chiefdoms goes back to the turn of the Christian era in the *Shangam* poems. Towards the middle of the ninth century, a chief claiming Chola ancestry conquered the region of Tanjavur, the heart of Tamilaham. He declared himself the ruler of an independent state, and sought to establish his status by claiming descent from the Suryavamsha or solar lineage. In AD 907 the first important ruler of the Chola dynasty, Parantaka I, came to power and ruled for almost half a century. He secured the southern frontier of the kingdom by campaigning against the Pandyas and capturing their capital, Madurai. This brought him into contact with Sri Lanka with which the Pandyas had had close relations. The ensuing hostilities lasted several decades. The later part of Parantaka's reign saw Chola defeat at the hands of the Rashtrakutas, who occupied some of the recently acquired northern districts of the Chola kingdom. There followed a period of thirty years in which a succession of weak kings brought about a decline in the power of the Cholas. However, this situation was eventually reversed. The Rashtrakutas in the Deccan were being harassed by the Chalukyas, who had once been subordinate to them and were to be their future overlords. In the confusion, Chola territory earlier lost to the Rashtrakutas was gradually recovered. Chola power was firmly established with the accession of Rajaraja I (985–1014) and of his son and successor, Rajendra, which allowed about half a century for the Chola kingdom to be consolidated and stabilized.

The reigns of both father and son were filled with extensive campaigns in almost every direction. Rajaraja began by attacking the alliance between the Cheras in Kerala, Sri Lanka, and the Pandyas, in order to break the monopoly of trade held by these kingdoms with west Asia. The Arabs had established themselves as traders on the west coast of India, and some had been integrated into local society in Malabar and the Konkan. The Cholas would have been aware of potential Arab competition in the south-east Asian trade, and they tried to strike at the root of this competition by bringing Malabar under their control. At a later date, Rajaraja conducted a naval attack on the Maldive Islands, a staging-point in the Arab trade. The Cholas, although unable to strike directly at the Arab trade, led a campaign in Sri Lanka devastating the existing capital, Anuradhapura, and moved to Pollonnaruva. At the same time campaigns against the rulers of the Deccan states continued apace. Echoes of the old Pallava–Chalukya conflict over the rich province of Vengi were heard now in wars between the Cholas and the Later Chalukyas over the same area.

Rajendra I ruled jointly with his father for two years, succeeding him in 1014. The policy of expansion continued with the annexation of the southern provinces of the Chalukyas, the rich Raichur *doab* and Vengi. Campaigns against Sri Lanka and Kerala were also renewed. But Rajendra's ambitions had turned northwards. An expedition set out, marching through Orissa to reach the banks of the Ganges. From there, it is said, holy water from the river was carried back to the Chola capital. Bringing back the water through conquest symbolized ascendancy over the north. But Rajendra did not hold the northern regions for long, a situation parallel to that of Samudra Gupta's campaign in the south almost 700 years earlier.

Even more ambitious was Rajendra's overseas campaign, involving both the army and navy against the kingdom of Shrivijaya in south-east Asia. It has been suggested that this major undertaking arose from a desire for an overseas empire. Had this been so, however, the campaign would have been followed by Indian colonization of the coastal areas and an attempt to conquer the hinterland. Since this did not happen, the cause of the war was more likely a desire to protect Indian commercial interests. By the tenth century merchants in China and south India had trading relationships. Ships passed through the seas held by the kingdom of Shrivijaya (the southern Malay peninsula and Sumatra) which controlled the Malacca and Sunda Straits. The rulers of Shrivijaya realized that it would be more lucrative for local traders if the China–India trade had to terminate in Shrivijaya, with local middlemen taking the goods to their eventual destinations. But when Indian merchants in Shrivijaya territory were threatened this raised the wrath of the Chola, who may have had his own investment in this trade, and the result was an attack on Shrivijaya. From the viewpoint of its own mercantile interests, Shrivijaya's interference in the China–India trade was justified, but in this case military power decided the issue. The campaign was successful in that a number of strategic places along the Straits of Malacca came under Chola control, and, for a while at least, Indian shipping and commerce were safe in their passage through Shrivijaya territory.

The successors of Rajendra I turned their attention to conflicts within the peninsula, primarily with the Chalukyas, reviving the competition to control the province of Vengi. The old pattern of lightning raids into each other's territory was repeated. A Chola raid into the heart of Chalukya territory saw the sacking of the capital at Kalyani. This was avenged in 1050 by the Chalukya king. Rivalry was less intense during the reign of the Chola King Kulottunga I (1070–1118), perhaps because of kinship links between the royal families, and this introduced a new element into the relationship. The old enemies of the far south, the Pandyas, Cheras and Sri Lanka, meanwhile remained hostile, but Shrivijaya was peaceful, although still smarting under its defeat by Rajendra. This permitted a steady improvement in the commerce of south India and better communications with the Chinese, to whom Kulottunga sent an embassy of seventy-two merchants in 1077.

Rajaraja I and Rajendra believed that their political status was higher than that of Amoghavarsha the Rashtrakuta ruler or Vishnuvardhana the Hoysala. The unobtrusive titles used by the early Chola kings were replaced with high-sounding ones, such as *chakravartigal* (emperor, the equivalent of the northern *chakravartin*). The cult of the god-king was encouraged through the worship of images of the deceased rulers, together with the building of temples as monuments to dead kings. This carries echoes of Kushana practices. The royal household was run on an elaborate scale and royal patronage was lavish. The political role of the *purohita* (priest) as known to northern Indian politics underwent a modification in the Chola system. The *raja-guru* (priest of the royal family) of the Cholas became a confidant and adviser in all matters temporal and sacred. In their support for Shaivism, the temple at Chidambaram was an important location, the Shiva-nataraja (Shiva as the lord of the cosmic dance) was the icon and the *Periya Puranam* was the revered text.

By the latter part of the twelfth century Chola ascendancy was waning.

Neighbours were annexing territories at the fringes of the kingdom. The power of the subordinate rulers in the Deccan increased as central control weakened. Frequent campaigns had exhausted Chola resources and, although they finally succeeded in establishing their supremacy, it was at the cost of their own stability. Furthermore, the eventual breaking of Chalukya power by the Cholas was to recoil on the Cholas themselves since it removed the controlling authority of the Chalukyas over their tributary rulers. The latter then set up independent kingdoms and made preparations to gnaw at the Chola kingdom, prior to more substantial attacks.

Among these the most powerful were the Yadavas, the Hoysalas and the Kakatiyas. The Yadavas kept mainly to the Deccan, and their contribution to the final disintegration of the Cholas was less significant. The Hoysalas and the Kakatiyas became active from the twelfth century onwards. The latter, having won their independence from the Chalukyas, retired to enjoy it, except for the periods when they were in action against the Cholas. Kakatiya power became visible when the Kakatiyas moved from the fortress of Hanamkonda to the plains in its vicinity, establishing their capital at Warangal. The city and the power that it encapsulated was largely the work of the thirteenth-century King Ganapatideva and his daughter, Rudramma-devi, who succeeded him. The city was enclosed in a series of circular fortifications. Its core, where the roads going in cardinal directions intersected, seems to have been the location of the palace and the royal temple. This would have conformed to the theoretical plan of a capital city. The Kakatiyas wished to annex Vengi, which would have given them a substantial seaboard, for they were well aware of the profits from the ports in the area.

The main attack on the Cholas from the west came from the Hoysalas, whom the Cholas were able to resist. But their older enemy, the Pandya kings of Madurai, saw this as an ideal opportunity to revive hostilities. The Chola strength therefore had to be diverted to two fronts, the western and the southern. The rise of the Hoysalas is in many ways representative of some dynasties of the Deccan from this period. The family began as hill chiefs whose main source of revenue was brigandage, an unfailing source in the higher regions of the plateau. Owing to the political confusion during changes of dynasty, the hill people were eager to gain protectors. Their support to the early Hoysalas enabled the latter to move down into the plains, from where an even more reliable source of revenue – tribute – was given by the people of the plains to buy off the attacks from the hill chiefs. The regular payment of tribute established the legitimacy and authority of the receivers. Tribute sometimes led to political loyalty, and the former hill chiefs gradually found themselves the possessors of small kingdoms, on the basis of which they established a dynasty. Not all such dynasties survived, the older kingdoms annexing the territories of some.

It was Vishnuvardhana who established a kingdom for the Hoysala family. He ruled during the first half of the twelfth century, when the Hoysalas were still in principle subject to the Chalukyas. The core of the kingdom was at Dorasamudra, near modern Mysore, and Vishnuvardhana prepared the way for political independence by consolidating his strength around his capital. Vishnuvardhana is also remembered for his interest in the teachings of the Vaishnava philosopher, Ramanuja, said to have persuaded the king to forsake Jainism for Vaishnavism. The consolidation of the Hoysala kingdom was continued by Ballala II, the grandson of Vishnuvardhana, and resulted in the domination of the southern Deccan by the Hoysalas.

Chola power weakened in the thirteenth century. A Hoysala king claimed to have rescued the Chola king who had been captured by his tributary raja. This raja had attacked the kingdom and destroyed the temples to Shiva and places sacred to Vishnu. According to another inscription, the Hoysala army attacked villages, cut down the forest, burnt the ports along the sea and seized the women. To the north, however, the Hoysalas met with opposition from the Yadavas of Devagiri, who had also expanded their kingdom at the expense of Chalukya territory. By the thirteenth century the Yadavas had laid claim to Gujarat, but they could not hold this for long. The Yadavas and the Hoysalas were to last until the fourteenth century, when new arrivals in the politics of northern India, the Turkish and Afghan sultans of Delhi, intervened in the affairs of the Deccan. The intervention led to other dynasties and different political alignments. Further south, the Pandyas had superseded the Cholas as the dominant power in the Tamil country, and might have maintained this position in the subsequent century had it not been for attacks from the rulers of the Deccan. The Pandyas remained local rulers and subject to the changing politics of the region. Marco Polo claimed to have visited the Pandyan kingdom in 1288 and 1293, and has left a vivid description of the richness of the land and the prosperity of its trade.

Political developments on the opposite coast, that of Kerala, were of a quieter nature. The Chera kingdom had alternating friendly or hostile relations with the Cholas, but the political ambitions of its rulers became apparent only during the reign of Ravivarman Kulashekhara at the end of the thirteenth century. Although unsuccessful, he set out to acquire a larger kingdom, building on the ruins of the existing southern kingdoms. But there was little economic pressure to encourage territorial conquest, the Malabar coast being naturally rich and obtaining an adequate income from trade with west Asia.

It was during this period that another group of people from the west came to India. Copper-plate charters of the Cheras, generally dated to the tenth and eleventh centuries, granted land to Jewish traders, such as Joseph Rabban – the earliest evidence of a Jewish community settling in India, although tradition has it that a previous settlement in Cochin dates to the early centuries AD. This parallels the chronological uncertainty of the arrival of the Syrian Christians. It is possible that this later group had links with the Jewish commercial community in Alexandria, or with the later trade between Aden and ports in the southern part of the west coast, such as Mangalore. The settlements in India were in pursuit of trade. The Cairo Geniza records contain many letters of a personal nature, as well as pertaining to business, written by Jewish traders active in commerce with India towards the end of the first millennium AD. Indians were partners, or representatives of Jewish merchants, and some of the latter spent time in India and married locally. The area associated with this group of traders was Kodungallur or Cranganore, identified by some scholars with the ancient site of Muziris, a port that had been active in the Roman trade. The frequency with which later traders from the west located their settlements in the vicinity of those used by earlier traders from the west is quite striking. Doubtless it was not coincidental, being connected with safe harbours and access to cargo. The arrival of new groups was part of the pattern of trade connections between the west coast and other commercially active parts of Asia. Subsequent to the persecution of the Jews in Europe in later centuries some Jews came to Kerala, already familiar from trading contacts, and made it a part of the Jewish diaspora.

Further north in the western Deccan, the Rashtrakutas were being gradually unseated by their *samantas*, the Shilaharas. The Shilaharas took the title of 'Lords of the West', presumably referring to their control over the trade with west Asia. So firm was this control that in one case an association of merchants was required to pay a regular and substantial sum to the royal family, from the revenue of a village donated to it. One inscription suggests that the commercial hinterland of the Konkan extended as far as Rajasthan. The Shilaharas, wanting a monopoly over trade, discontinued the employment of Arabs as part of their higher administration.

Apart from the families constituting the main dynasties, there were lesser rulers of smaller areas in the Deccan and some of these claimed descent from the lineages of the main dynasties. These often began as subordinate rulers of earlier kingdoms, or as landed magnates promoting the settling of new lands through clearing forests, extending agriculture and constructing irrigation tanks. Possibly some were chiefs of forest tribes, converted to cultivation and caste, and were claiming high status. The status sought was *kshatriya*, and the link was either with the Chandravamsha, or lunar line, or the Suryavamsha, or solar line. Land rights also had to be claimed and these required relationships with the ruling dynasty. The dynasty would bestow title and rank on those performing administrative functions. Taxes on a variety of produce were collected and some were transferred to the central administration. This inevitably meant that peasants were frequently under severe pressure to provide more wealth to the landholder.

Change in the agrarian system was noticeable throughout much of the peninsula in the late first millennium AD. The pattern of change carried some similarities with parts of the north, although the process in Tamilaham in south India had variations. This may be the result of the more detailed studies of this region. The economic backing given to political power in the south is apparent, and to that extent makes an interesting comparative study with other parts of the peninsula.

Structures of an Agrarian System

The Chola kingdom was initially described as a centralized bureaucratic state, the standard description of virtually every large kingdom in India. Recently, historians have been exploring the different ways in which states were formed and the social and economic links to changes in politics. The Chola state has been the subject of such attention. The most extensively discussed have been the concepts of the segmentary state and, on a broader level but with less intensive study, forms of feudalism for states of the peninsula. As pointed out in Chapter 1, the segmentary state model is untenable largely because of its insistence on a dual sovereignty – political and ritual. In the three zones envisaged – central, intermediate and peripheral – political control gradually fades out to be replaced by ritual sovereignty, moving from a smaller to a greater degree, from the first to the third. Inscriptions are described as expressions of ritual sovereignty rather than political sovereignty. Yet ritual encodes symbolism and ritual symbolism need not indicate a weakening of political sovereignty. The changes that led to the consolidation of power in the Chola state were reflected in ways not conforming to the segmentary state, such as in official titles especially at higher levels of administration, the tendency to reorganize administrative units territorially, standardization of taxation, and the gradual replacement of chiefs by high-status officers. The theory of a segmentary state also minimizes the impact of the merchant associations, some of which functioned across the administrative units, as well as the trade that developed in both the peninsula and south-east Asia to bring in a substantial commercial revenue. Although the spread of the Tamil devotional movement and the subsequent major changes in religion focused on the temple and sacred centres, temples were not a-political as is evident from their rivalries and competition for royal patronage when they functioned as major religio-political institutions. This would not have supported the concept of ritual sovereignty as distinct from political sovereignty.

Another theory argues that Chola wealth was acquired through campaigns that were essentially plunder raids. This also has not found support, in view of the impressive network of revenue collection from both agricultural and commercial activities. Virtually all campaigns at one level were plunder raids, but such raids could not have sustained a state as complex as the Chola kingdom.

The model of a feudal state has encouraged some forays into the social and economic history of south India, but it requires further investigation. The theories giving priority to agrarian change are those that emanate from various hypotheses originally relating to feudalism. Although in many respects they are closer to the evidence, the paradigm label of 'feudalism' for this period of Indian history is still being debated. However, these debates have led to a more precise understanding of social and economic change. Terms such as feudatory or feudal cannot be equated with their use in European history, where in any case the particular part of Europe under discussion would have to be specified. There are some similarities and some divergences. A clarification of the specific use of such terms in the context of the data is always helpful. The nature of the relative autonomy of local organizations, for example, is a theme receiving far more attention than it did when it was thought that the ruler alone exercised political control. In the currently emerging picture of agrarian and commercial structures, their relationship to hierarchies of authority is a central question.

Much of the argument hinges upon the changes introduced through the granting of land to religious beneficiaries or persons rewarded for their services to the king. The land granted was often 'wet land' which was already under cultivation and had irrigation facilities. Sometimes wasteland was also given in a grant. Wherever land had to be cleared before cultivation, and irrigation tanks constructed, this was done on a fairly substantial scale that would have changed the landscape. The density of population in the 'wet zone', for example the fertile and well-watered Kaveri Valley, indicates a preference. In the later Chola period, grants were made in the dry zone when presumably the extension of irrigation was more common. The ecology of an area was significant to its economic use. The two landowning groups were the brahmans and the *velalas*, the latter ranging from the wealthy to those less so. These two categories had superior rights over tenants and cultivators, although the range of tenurial rights complicates any easy descriptive label. In some cases tenants could even be dispossessed and earlier grants of land excluded. Artisans and cultivators formed yet another category at a lower level.

The *brahmadeya*, or the *agrahara*, introduced Sanskritic culture which included the norms of social organization as laid down in the *Dharmashastras*. The integration of the *brahmadeyas* and *agraharas* into existing agrarian communities led to some innovations. Negotiations were required between the existing peasants and the new landowners. Since the latter came with royal backing, and often with advanced knowledge of organizing agriculture and other technologies, they had a distinct edge over the existing peasants or those recently converted to peasant status.

Brahmadeya donations remained unchanged in pattern from those of Pallava times, as is evident from the Chola grants, such as the Anbil grant of Sundara Chola recording the donations of land to the brahman Anirudha Brahmadhiraja.

We marked [the boundaries of] the land thus defined by erecting mounds of earth and planting cactus. The several objects included in this land – such as fruit-yielding trees, water, lands, gardens, all upgrowing trees and down-going wells, open spaces, wastes in which calves graze, the village site, ant-hills, platforms [built around trees], canals, hollows, rivers and their alluvial deposits, tanks, granaries, fish-ponds, clefts with bee-hives, deep ponds included; and everything else on which the iguana runs and the tortoise crawls; and taxes such as the income from places of justice, the taxes on [betel] leaves, the cloths from looms, the *kanam* [of gold] on carriages, . . . the old tenants being evicted, everything that the king could take and enjoy – all these shall be made over to this man. He shall be at liberty to erect halls and upper storeys with burnt bricks; to dig wells, big and small; to plant southernwood and cactus; to dig channels in accordance with watering requirements: not to waste surplus water but to dam it for irrigation; no one shall employ small baskets [for lifting such water]. In this wise was the old order changed and the old name and old taxes removed, and an *ekabhoga brahmadeya* (land granted to a single brahman) under the name of Karunakaramangalam was constituted.

'The Anbil Plates of Sundara Chola', in K. A. Nilakanta Sastri,
The Colas (Madras, 1955), p. 577

Knowledge of agriculture included assessing irrigation. This involved tanks, reservoirs with sluices, canals and wells, which were built and maintained with local expertise available in the villages. The more impressive irrigation works of the Cholas, consisting of dams and anicuts on rivers, would have been directly controlled by the state. But whether under local or central control, irrigation involved organizing labour at both the village level and across villages. Landowners would have had enough control over the peasants under their jurisdiction to demand forced labour from them. Labour over longer periods would largely have been from the landless or from the lowest castes. Such subservient groups had existed for a long time in many parts of the subcontinent, and would be a short step from what some might call bonded labour or even slave labour, and slaves – *atimai* – are referred to. Even if not identical to forms of slavery in other societies, the terms of the bond were such that generally people were unable to regain their freedom. Bonded persons were liable to be transferred together with the transfer of land through a grant. The system would doubtless have been intensified in the later period of Chola rule when individual ownership of land became more frequent than the control of land by a village.

There are few instances of peasant revolts in Indian history. Sources of the earlier period suggest that discontented peasants migrated to a neighbouring kingdom or an area outside the jurisdiction of the current ruler, although such migration was not permitted. This would be a feasible protest causing a decline in the revenue of the ruler. But its feasibility was possible only while land was available. From the early second millennium there are sporadic instances of revolt, generally as objections to some aspect of administration. Possibly the availability of easily cultivable land had declined and the number of small kingdoms increased.

Village assemblies were crucial to Chola administration. Those living in the usual peasant villages met in an assembly called the *ur*, whereas those from the *brahmadeya* villages used the superior title of *sabha*. Royal officials were present at the meetings of the *sabha* but do not appear to have played a commanding role. Their participation in village affairs was more as observers and advisers. This permitted continuity in local growth and development without too much interference from political changes at the upper level, and the degree of apparent autonomy at village level deserves to be underlined.

Large villages could be divided into wards, each with a smaller assembly representing its households. Given the layout of the village and the tendency for people in similar occupations to be located in the same wards, the latter came to represent professional groups, such as carpenters, potters, smiths and so on. The assemblies controlled production through consultation with the heads of the peasant families, the *velalas*, who were their members. This necessitated discussion on a range of matters, including those of crucial importance, such as the setting up of irrigation facilities. Rights in land were insisted upon and among these were the *kani*, or hereditary rights.

Villages were grouped together within a *nadu*, a defined territory. Agrarian organizations of the *brahmadeyas*, temples, and the commercial associations linked to centres of exchange, such as the *nagaram*, functioned within the *nadu*, although some had connections traversing the *nadu*. Members of the associations of the *velala* handling agricultural products, such as the Chitrameli Periyanadu who were referred to from the twelfth century onwards, traversed the area more widely. The *nadu* was not an autonomous peripheral area but was under central control. This enabled the centre to regroup the *nadus* into units called the *valanadu* and the *mandalam*, especially as the *nadus* were not of a uniform size. Such a rearrangement was an indicator of control over the territories.

Agricultural expansion in the *valanadu* became associated with brahman settlers receiving grants of land, as in the Tamraparni Valley of the far south. Where the land was already under cultivation there had to be agreements between the cultivators and the grantees, obviously to the advantage of the latter. Other units such as *mandalams* could also be re-aligned to determine revenue demands, administrative controls and the needs of cities in the region. The population of the *mandalam* consisted of peasants, as well as the settlements of forest and hill peoples in their proximity.

If the *brahmadeya* and the temple were important players in the restructuring of the economy during the Chola period, it was not merely because of their ritual authority, but was also a result of their administrative and functional control over productivity. Ritual is important but does not exist in a social void and, more often than not, is also tied to social and economic realities and ambitions. The grantees themselves were beholden to the king for the grant, and the king's officers were required to allocate temple resources and audit temple accounts. As was the case with Buddhist monasteries, the temple complex could only survive where it had some control over resources from agriculture, or from revenue generated by the regular fairs and festivals which became surrogate markets. This necessitated temple control over agriculture and irrigation, together with some participation in commercial exchange.

The working of these assemblies differed according to local conditions. The *ur* was open to male adults of the village, but in effect the older members such as heads of households took a more prominent part, some of them forming a small executive body for routine matters. The *sabha* had the same system and, in addition, could constitute smaller committees of any size from among its members for specialized work. Election to the *sabha* sometimes appears to have been by lot from among those who were eligible, though amendments to the working of the *sabha* could be made whenever necessary. An inscription from the temple wall at Uttaramerur (a *brahmadeya* village) gives details of how the local *sabha* functioned. It dates to the tenth century and reads:

There shall be thirty wards. In these thirty wards those that live in each ward shall assemble and shall select each person possessing the following qualifications for inclusion for selection by lot:

He must own more than one quarter of the tax-paying land. He must live in a house built on his own site. His age must be below seventy and above thirty-five. He must know the *mantras* and *Brahmanas* [from the Vedic corpus].

Even if he owns only one-eighth of the land, his name shall be included provided he has learnt one *Veda* and one of the four *Bhashyas*.

Among those possessing these qualifications only such as are well conversant with business and are virtuous shall be taken, and one who possesses honest earnings whose mind is pure and who has not been on any of the committees for the last three years shall also be chosen. One who has been on any of the committees but has not submitted his accounts, and his relations specified below, cannot have their names written on the tickets:

The sons of the younger and elder sisters of his mother.

The sons of his paternal aunt and maternal uncle.

The uterine brother of his mother.

The uterine brother of his father.

His uterine brother.

His father-in-law.

The uterine brother of his wife.

The husband of his uterine sister.

The sons of his uterine sister.

His son-in-law.

His father.

His son.

One against whom incest or the first four of the five great sins are recorded. [The five great sins being killing a brahman, drinking alcohol, theft, adultery, and associating with criminals.] All his relations specified above shall not be eligible to be chosen by lot. One who has been outcaste for association with low people shall not have his name chosen until he performs the expiatory ceremonies.

One who is foolhardy . . .

One who has stolen the property of others . . .

One who has taken forbidden dishes . . .

One who has committed sins and has had to perform expiatory ceremonies of purification . . .

Excluding all these, names shall be written on tickets for thirty wards and each of the wards in these twelve streets shall prepare a separate covering ticket for thirty wards bundled separately. These packets shall be put into a pot. When the tickets have to be drawn a full meeting of the great assembly including the young and old members shall be convened. All the temple priests who happen to be in the village on that day, shall, without any exception whatever, be caused to be seated in the inner hall where the great assembly meets. In the midst of the temple priests, one of them who happens to be the eldest shall stand up and lift that pot, looking upwards so as to be seen by all people. One ward shall be taken out by any young boy standing close who does not know what is inside and shall be transferred to another empty pot and shaken loose. From this pot one ticket shall be drawn and made the arbitrator. While taking charge of the ticket thus given to him, the arbitrator shall receive it on the palm of his hand with the five fingers open. He shall read out the ticket thus received. The ticket shall be read by all the priests present in the inner hall. The name thus read shall be put down and accepted. Similarly one man shall be chosen for each of the thirty wards.

Of the thirty men thus chosen those who had previously been on the Garden Committee, and on the Tank Committee, those who are advanced in learning and those who are advanced in age shall be chosen for the Annual Committee. Of the rest, twelve shall be taken for the Garden Committee and the remaining six shall form the Tank Committee. The great men of these three committees shall hold office for full 360 days and then retire. Anyone on a Committee found guilty of an offence shall be removed at once. For appointing the committees after these have retired, the members of the Committee for Supervision of Justice in the twelve streets shall convene an assembly with the help of the arbitrator. The Committees shall be appointed by drawing pot-tickets . . .

For the Five-fold Committee and the Gold Committee, names shall be written for pot-tickets in the thirty wards (and the same procedure followed). One who has ridden an ass (i.e., been punished) or who has committed a forgery shall not be included.

Any arbitrator who possesses honest earnings shall write the accounts of the village. No accountant shall be appointed to that office again before he submits his accounts to the great men of the chief committee and is declared to have been honest. The accounts which he has been writing he shall submit himself, and no other accountant shall be chosen to close his accounts. Thus, from this year onwards as long as the moon and the sun endure, committees shall always be appointed by lot . . .

We, the assembly of Uttaramerur *chatur-vedi-mangalam* made this settlement for the prosperity of our village in order that wicked men may perish and the rest may prosper. At the order of the great men sitting in the assembly, I, the arbitrator Kadadipottan Shivakkuri Raja-malla-mangala-priyan, thus wrote the settlement.

Archaeological Survey of India Report (1904–5), pp. 138 ff.

Other inscriptions refer to similar general procedures, though there are variations in qualifications and requirements and in the sanction of expenditure. The making of rules through amendments from time to time, and the attempts to ensure that factions were kept at a minimum, are striking features of this inscription. The assembly was summoned by the beat of a drum and generally met in the precincts of the temple. Interchange and co-operation among village assemblies was not unknown.

The village assembly was responsible for collecting the assessment for the government and, where stipulated, the taxes on land and produce. In some cases it was collected as a joint assessment on the entire village. In addition, the assembly could make a levy for a particular purpose: for example, the construction of a water tank. Such local funds were kept separate from the taxes collected for the state. The activities of the assembly included the keeping of records, particularly those pertaining to charities and taxes, and the settling of agrarian disputes such as conflicts over tenure arrangements or irrigation rights. The larger assemblies kept a small staff of paid officers, but in the smaller assemblies most of the work was done on a voluntary basis. Professionals were appointed for special purposes at the *nadu* level as well. The higher officials were often drawn from among the better-off *velalas*, thus creating a link between state and local administration that enlarged the possibilities of upward mobility, incidentally providing a base for those with political ambitions. The latter part of the Chola period saw greater activity among revenue officials, with an increase in the number of taxes. The degree of autonomy at village level prevented shifting relations in the upper levels of the administrative and political structure from interfering to any large extent with the routine life of the village.

Property rights varied as did the method of paying taxes, depending on whether ownership was individual or whether a collective tax from the village was preferred. Sometimes dues were remitted, partially or totally, in return for some service, but this was generally on a very small scale, such as a remittance of tax to the temple in lieu of fetching the water for bathing the deity. In later centuries this tax included military service. Unlike temple service, involving proximity to the deity, military service could be performed by low-caste groups. The recipients of *brahmadeya* grants, as well as temples receiving grants, were treated as regular landowners where questions of rights were involved. There was a sharp distinction between those with land who paid tax, and those who did not, with the agricultural labourers working for a wage. The distinction was largely that the labourer was not included in the village assembly and could not hold a position of responsibility in local administration. Many were employed on temple estates, yet being of low caste they were not permitted entry into the temple. Reclamation of wasteland and the clearing of forests were regular work carried out by peasants and labourers, which was encouraged by the ruler since it increased the land under cultivation. Cattle-raising had by now become a subsidiary occupation except in the uplands.

Tax on land and its produce, whether in cash or kind, was a substantial source of income for the Chola state, although other taxes were also collected, such as those on mines, forests, salt, professional taxes, customs dues and tolls, judicial fines and the equivalent in forced labour (*vetti*). The assessment of land-tax was based on the quality of the land and the facilities to irrigate it. Two or even three crops of paddy per year were regarded as normal, though the yield varied. The tax could rise to one-third, which is high by any standards, though in exceptional circumstances remission or commutation was permitted by the king.

Permanent assessment of land for tax purposes was known, but was apparently not usual. Assessment required land surveys at frequent intervals. Land-tax, together with the local dues levied by the assembly or the temple, must have been a strain on the cultivator for whom there were few alternatives to paying the tax. He could in theory either appeal to the king for remission or reduction of the tax if conditions were difficult at a particular time, or else move away to a different area. The latter was an extreme step, since mobility among cultivators was restricted even if land was available. In the case of a village assessed as a unit, the return from the non-taxable land was deducted from the total revenue of the village. Non-taxable land consisted of the residential area, temples, tanks, irrigation channels, areas where the artisans and outcaste population lived, and the cremation ground.

In the Hoysala kingdom in Karnataka, the key figures in the rural areas were the landholders, the *gavunda/gauda*, and the *heggade*, mentioned in inscriptions referring to land transactions in villages, the maintenance of irrigation, the collection of taxes and the work of the village council.

References to them go back to Ganga inscriptions where they seem to have been the heads of the families of the original settlers. Their standing and status is indicated by their prefix. For example, the *praja-gavunda*, literally, the *gavunda* of the people, was economically and socially of a lesser status than the wealthy *prabhu-gavunda*, literally, of the lord. Their numbers varied and were sometimes determined by their dual role of being both representatives of the village and appointees of the state. Some judicial functions were also included, such as the raising of a militia when required. Initially the grants were made to brahmans and Jainas, whose activities included the clearing of forest land and the reclaiming of wasteland to extend cultivation. This also required the building and maintenance of tanks for irrigation. The increasing numbers of peasants were drawn both from the forest-peoples converted to cultivation and from migrations of peasants from the Tamil area after the campaigns of the tenth century.

The evolving of the status of landholders followed a fairly common pattern. Intermediary landholders and *samantas* changed the ecology of the neighbourhood through expanding agriculture, secured through the construction of irrigation tanks. Sometimes the grant of land was to the family of a hero who had died defending village property. The identity of the landholder was further emphasized by his establishing his family deity in the locality. This was also part of the two-way process of introducing new deities into Puranic Hinduism and superimposing existing Hindu deities on local ones. The installing of the new deity was not solely a religious act and should not be mistaken for ritual sovereignty. It accompanied the grant of land and was equally significant as an intervention of administrative rights and identity. With the coming of brahman settlements and the creation of *agraharas*, the picture changed further. Occasionally there were some confrontations between brahman settlers and existing cultivators and the terms of revenue collection had to be sorted out. Peasant protests in the peninsula are heard of from the thirteenth century, occasionally with religious undertones. The balance between state administration and the powers of local landowners, together with the requirements of cultivation as a support to royal power, became characteristic of kingdoms at this time.

In an area such as Warangal (Andhra Pradesh), with its less fertile tracts, major investments in clearing wasteland and building tanks and canals were required to establish agriculture. Deserted villages were reclaimed by order of the Kakatiya rulers and new villages were established, involving colonization or encroachments into forests. This was actively encouraged by the Kakatiyas and their tributary rulers through grants of land, especially to brahmans.

As a contrast to this, settlement in Kerala followed the fertile 'wet lands'. The earlier brahman settlements of the mid-first millennium AD, said to be thirty-two in number, expanded in this period. The alliance between rulers and brahmans was also related to a large number of temples being established, each of which controlled substantial land. Brahman control over temple management meant that they controlled land both as individual holders and as managers of temples. In some cases the two categories may have been distinct if the brahmans associated with the *Vedas* held land from earlier grants, whereas those who were only priests in the temples derived an income from their functions in the temple. The management of temples could have included wealthy non-brahmans, such as merchants and administrators. A hierarchy of tenants cultivated the lands of the temple and parallel to this were the artisans, also employed by the temple. Agricultural activities at various levels were controlled by a nexus between the brahmans and those claiming aristocratic status, pre-eminently the caste of Nairs. The wealth of the temple was such that many temples employed experts in the martial arts, who acted as a militia in times of trouble. Control over both the village assembly and the council managing the temple was tight, particularly when supervising tenants and craftsmen.

References to local militias were now more noticeable, but so too were increasing numbers of hero-stones. Some had a frame that suggested an imitation of a small shrine, and the sculptured panels became more professional. Their adornment underlined the status of the hero. There were also occasions when the memorialized hero either came from a family of landholders or else his kinsmen aspired to that status. In the former case, his kinsmen's aspirations to political power could be supported by both their landholding status and their relationship to a dead hero. The cult of the hero was further elaborated. It was believed that a hero's death would automatically lead him to heaven, and if his wife became a *sati* she was deified. The emphasis on what the individual gained by these acts also underlined the need for a village to be self-reliant in some situations. Memorials in coastal areas recorded defence against attacks from the sea or at sea. The depiction of ships on such hero-stones points incidentally to an improvement in shipping technology compared to their depiction in earlier sculpture. Hero-stones of this period could therefore be seen as comments on the structure of power at local levels, particularly where the state did not have a readily available presence or thought it unnecessary to mark such a presence.

The tendency to hoard wealth was not characteristic of village life. Apart from those in markedly rich villages, most village members had little wealth to hoard. The average holding yielded enough to feed and clothe a family with little surplus. Food was simple, rice and vegetables in the main. But diet could change with caste. Brahmans, who had once eaten meat, were now generally vegetarian. A non-vegetarian diet became customary among some higher castes, and meat of all kinds was eaten by others, provided it was affordable. Housing was relatively cheap, since the climate did not call for elaborate structures. Nevertheless, the wealthy lived in well-appointed houses. The richer members of rural society kept their wealth employed through economic advantages in schemes to reclaim land, improve irrigation or invest in trade. Equally, there was much religious merit to be acquired by donations towards the building of a temple or the endowing of a *matha*. Wealth was used in forms that would enhance the prestige of its owners.

Towns and Markets

The nuclei of urban centres were generally formed by exchange centres in rural areas where local produce was brought, administrative centres, places of pilgrimage where large numbers gathered and goods were regularly exchanged, or the locations of recurring festivals and fairs. Rural markets were recognized by chiefs and administrators as potentially important to generating revenue. The military camp, often set up as part of a regular tour of inspection, continued to be a precursor to a town, particularly if the location was repeated year after year. Towns that had existed prior to the tenth century often grew as a result of expanding trade during this period. In Karnataka and Tamil-nadu, towns referred to as *pattanam* began as commercial centres, often maritime. Sometimes the main occupation was specified in the name, for instance, Banajupattana, a town of traders. But prior to this they could have been focal points of local administration or places of pilgrimage. Shravana Belgola, for example, began as a pilgrimage centre in the seventh century and by the twelfth century was an important settlement of merchants that maintained a number of Jaina establishments. Trading associations and professional merchants often had their beginnings in rural centres of exchange or of administration.

Parallel processes occurred in the domain of the Later Chalukyas. Merchants and wealthy landowners wielded authority in the administration of cities. Elsewhere, weekly village markets sometimes developed into towns.

On occasion the *gavundas* and *heggades* were also associated with positions of urban authority. A designation of wider use familiar in many parts of the subcontinent was *mahajana*, literally, the big men, used sometimes for wealthy brahmans in their secular roles as landholders, and eventually for those involved in commerce that sometimes coincided with urban administration. Those who worked at the senior levels of urban administration were recompensed by permission to keep a percentage of the levies collected from householders. Towns went through periods of vicissitudes but from about the tenth century there was predictable growth.

The market centre, known as the *nagaram*, where traders gathered, was the focus for exchange of the produce of the region and also had links with the temple. Administered by the *nagarattar*, it was also taxed, particularly on its profits from overseas trade. Merchants and guilds paid tolls and customs duties. Inscriptions carry details of these taxes, and of the levels of tax collection which ranged from the local to the central. Inscriptions from Karnataka record customs taxes on the import of horses, on commodities made of gold, on textiles and perfume, and on produce such as black pepper, paddy, spices, betel-leaves, palm leaves, coconuts and sugar. This was produce that came from various parts of the peninsula and was more than just a regional trade. Corporate trading enterprise was particularly noticeable from the eleventh century onwards. Inevitably, the presence of a hierarchy in the bureaucracy was also recorded. In the transition from rural to urban, tax concessions were sometimes introduced by the local administration but were replaced with tolls, taxes and dues when commerce was profitable.

Overseas trade was among the strengths of the Chola merchants. Nagapattinam, Mahabalipuram, Kaveripattinam, Shaliyur and Korkai, on the east coast, had elaborate establishments controlling the south Indian trade eastwards. The port at Vishakhapattinam was named Kulottunga-chola-pattinam, after the King. Trade to the east received encouragement from a Cambodian mission to the Chola court in the early eleventh century. Maritime trade with China reached an unprecedented volume during these centuries. It became a state monopoly in China, the Chinese government not wishing to lose the income from it. Sung period sources from China refer to the presence of Indian merchants in the ports of southern China. Apart from trade, the earlier lively interest among Chinese savants in Indian astrology and alchemy continued, with some startlingly exaggerated stories in Chinese texts on the transmutation of stone and metal from worthless matter to valuable items by visiting Indians!

With the Mongols controlling central Asia, merchandise from China was transported by sea, particularly from southern China to western Asia and

Europe. South India exported textiles, spices, medicinal plants, jewels, ivory, horn, ebony and camphor to China. The same commodities were also exported to the west, to ports such as Dhofar and Aden and, in addition, Siraf received cargoes of aloe wood, perfumes, sandalwood and condiments. Persia, Arabia and Egypt were the destinations of those trading with the west, with Siraf on the Persian Gulf as an entrepôt, and Cairo as well as Alexandria involved in the trade across the Arabian Sea. Quilon, on the Malabar coast, channelled Chera overseas trade westwards.

Marco Polo, who like many others at the time claimed to have visited India, commented on the continuing and huge trade in horses which brought vast fortunes to both the Arabs and the merchants of south India, who between them had organized a monopoly of the import of horses. For a variety of reasons, India never took to breeding horses of quality, possibly because the climate, soil conditions and natural pasturage were not suitable. This extremely expensive commodity therefore always had to be imported. Marco Polo wrote:

Let me tell you next that this country does not breed horses. Hence all the annual revenue, or the greater part of it, is spent in the purchase of horses; and I will tell you how. You may take it for a fact that the merchants of Hormuz and Kais, of Dhofar and Shihr and Aden, all of which provinces produce large numbers of battle chargers and other horses, buy up the best horses and load them on ships and export them to this king and his four brother kings. Some of them are sold for as much as 500 *saggi* of gold, which are worth more than 100 *marks* of silver. And I assure you that this king buys 2,000 of them or more every year, and his brothers as many. And, by the end of the year, not a hundred of them survive. They all die through ill-usage, because they have no veterinaries and do not know how to treat them. You may take it from me that the merchants who export them do not send out any veterinaries or allow any to go, because they are only too glad for many of them to die in the king's charge.

Marco Polo, *Travels* (Pelican edition), p. 237

Allowing for Marco Polo's usual proneness to exaggeration, there is nevertheless some truth in these remarks. However, there were veterinaries familiar with the medical treatment of horses and elephants, both important to the cavalry and elephant wing of the army, and Sanskrit texts were written on the subject. If it is true that horses died in such large numbers, the reasons have to be sought elsewhere.

The continuing interference by coastal pirates was an impediment to maritime trade. *Shangam* poetry had referred to pirates attacking Yavana ships and similar references continue. On the west coast piracy was some-times organized by local chiefs to plunder the merchants active in the Rashtrakuta kingdom. Hero-stones from the Konkan carry graphic rep-resentations of the hero warding off the pirates. Such disturbances occurred in many coastal areas of the Arabian Sea, the Bay of Bengal and the South China Seas. In contrast, the less disturbed ports provided a rich potential for trade and merchant associations made large profits. The Kakatiya king issued a special charter in the thirteenth century to protect merchants trading at the port of Motupalli on the coast of Andhra. The inscription in Sanskrit and Telugu stated that only a fixed duty was to be taken from merchants and their safety was to be guaranteed. According to Marco Polo, the exports from Motupalli were diamonds and muslin, both of the finest quality. The larger associations maintained their own force to protect the goods and the traders, a tradition going back to earlier times.

Most production was for local consumption but trade, particularly over-seas, provided an additional incentive to an existing market. Elephants, horses, spices, perfumes, precious stones and superior quality textiles were the commodities involved in large-scale trade, with metalware, jewellery, pottery and salt (produced in salt pans from sea water) being of lesser importance. Merchant associations, often described as guilds, controlled much of the trade. They may not have traded collectively although they belonged to an association. The more frequently referred to were the Mani-gramam, Ayyavole, Nanadeshi, Nagarattar, Anjuvannam and Valanjiyar. They did not all deal in the same items or trade in the same regions. The Manigramam were smaller bodies than the Ayyavole, while the Anjuvannam was particularly active in Kerala. Long-distance contacts and activities are evident from the fact that the Ayyavole, originating in Aihole and constituted of brahmans and *mahajanas*, was active in the trade of the Deccan and the Chola centres. Such brahmans were sometimes from *agraharas* and had the wealth to speculate in trade, ignoring the prohibition on brahmans being traders except in dire necessity, or for that matter the prohibition on cross-ing the seas. Members of this association were known as the 500 *svamis* of Ayyavole and they claimed that they also protected the customary law of their members. Intervention in the trade within the peninsula would inevi-tably have meant some intervention in overseas trade as well. Such associ-ations are referred to in inscriptions in south-east Asia. The power of these associations in the economic life of the period is indicated by their access to any region irrespective of the boundaries of kingdoms, and by the fact that they could finance local projects, for example, the construction of a temple, or provide a loan to the king.

Local merchant associations, the *nagaram*, were probably affiliated with the larger ones that acquired goods at the place of manufacture to distribute through an elaborate network. State support was not a condition of their ventures into overseas trade, but if necessary and where the state felt that it could interfere effectively on their behalf, as in the case of Srivijaya, it came to their assistance. Even on such occasions, however, the purpose of interference was not to acquire centres of raw material or markets but to remove the obstructions placed on the trade. Kings and higher officers of state may have invested in this trade, or else were provided with exclusive presents by the guilds to ensure support where required.

Given the wealth and commercial ramifications of the large merchant associations, it is curious that they did not aspire to greater political power. The brahman element in these guilds was probably averse to challenging the political authority of the king, since they derived their financial capital from the land granted to them by the king, and the possibility of revoking the grant could have been a threat. Urban structures supporting the potential for an independent power-base, built on the ambitions of a range of professional organizations, seem not to have asserted greater independence. By now the concept of monarchy as the legitimate form of political authority was strongly rooted. Moreover, many guilds had overseas interests and were therefore dependent in the last resort on the military and naval strength of the Chola state. Those who bestowed legitimacy on the system would certainly have used every effort to curb the political power of the guilds. Merchant associations were more powerful, however, in the smaller maritime kingdoms which were largely dependent on mercantile prosperity.

Barter continued in rural areas as a means of exchange, the major items in these transactions being paddy, domestic animals and cloth. Copper coins continued to be in circulation and used in markets. Gold and silver coinage was naturally reserved for buying and selling goods of high value, for long-distance trade and occasionally for the paying of taxes. The Cholas minted some silver coins from time to time, but gold remained the metal of high-value currency. The gold *kalanju*, sometimes valued in terms of the *gadyana* of the Deccan, was used in expensive transactions and the *kashu* for lesser ones. One of the advantages of merchant guilds having bases in various parts of the country was that, as in earlier times, the use of promissory notes encouraged long-distance trade.

The circulation of gold coin was unrestricted, although some appear to have been debased from the eleventh century onwards. However, this is a debatable point since the gold content of coins varied from region to region. Differences in weights and standards compelled the gold committee of the assemblies, for instance, to constantly evaluate gold and gold currency. The use of coins encouraged an income from usury, by now a generally acceptable activity indulged in even by brahmans and the managers of temples. Presumably it was justified in these cases as helping in the propagation and prosperity of the religion.

The Temple as an Institution

There is a striking increase in the number of temples built at this time. This is unlikely to have been purely the result of a greater interest in worship. The temple would have performed other functions as well. Temples built from royal donations were not only closely connected to the court, but were also perceived almost as surrogate courts. As such, they could draw on resources from anywhere within the kingdom, for example, the Tanjavur temple which received revenue from villages in Sri Lanka. This encouraged a greater intervention of the court in local matters, although in many cases physical distance from the court and the immanence of local authority, required concessions to local opinion. The hymns of the Alvars and Nayanars underlined the parallels between the deity and kingship, and by endorsing the one they endorsed the other. Temples were visualized as palaces, and rituals marking the daily routine of the deity imitated those of the king. The temple received offerings and tribute and the service of the worshippers.

Temples built through royal donations could be located in the capital and intimately associated with the court, as was the case with the Rajarajeshvara temple at Tanjavur and the Rajendreshvara at Gangaikondacholapuram, both built in the eleventh century and celebrating the reigns of kings. The temple at Tanjavur had a commanding location and acquired the aura of the leading ceremonial centre. Sometimes worship came to focus on the king, thus helping to imprint divinity onto kingship. Ritual was another channel of authority, at times subtle and at other times obvious, particularly as it was not in itself sufficient and required reinforcing by more tangible sources of power. The rhetoric of ritual was not intended in a literal sense but as reflective of symbolic power. Puranic Hinduism did not require the king to be the patron of the Vedic sacrifice, but, being symbolic of the deity, he was thought to participate in the grace of the deity and this encouraged the devotion of the worshippers. The king, therefore, did not always have to proximate deity and in some situations it was sufficient if he was just the ideal *bhakta*, a devotee. Doubtless the king and the court, irrespective of religious conviction, were not unaware of the political edge of *bhakti*.

As in all such structures, the assumed presence of the deity converted the temple into a sacred space where a relationship between the deity and the devotee could be sought. But implicit in this space and in the rituals were questions relating to authority and the establishing of rights and duties. The temple of Puranic Hinduism provided social and political space for the working out of such concerns over a large social spectrum, although the lowest social groups were excluded. The managers of temples represented political and economic interests and religious concerns, as is apparent from a close reading of temple inscriptions. Royal grants were a form of distributing wealth and acquiring supporters, even if the ostensible purpose of donations was to please the deity. There was a continuous tradition of giving gifts and donations – *dana* – and, although the form of the gift changed, the intentions were similar.

Temples built from resources other than those gifted by the royal family had also evolved into complex institutions, related not only to religious requirements but also to fiscal, political and cultural needs. This can be seen more easily in the functioning of the larger temples in rural areas. Land owned by the elite was donated or, alternatively, land was purchased and then donated to the temple. The fiscal role of the temple became even clearer in later Chola times when both temples and merchants were the most frequent purchasers of land. As an institution, the temple became the location for many kinds of routine exchange, the focal point for many professions to whom the temple gave employment either directly or indirectly, a symbol of authority as a landlord who could intervene in the lives of rural people, a rural bank, a channel of various forms of legitimation and, not least, the focus of a particular sectarian religion. In rural areas, temples were the locations of the village assemblies and of formal education for upper-caste boys.

Whereas the *brahmadeyas* were often grants to brahmans who were specialists in Vedic studies, the temples were closely associated with the belief and practice of Puranic religions. The juxtaposition of the two brought the rituals into proximity, but at another level demarcated the difference between them. New rituals and deities, incorporated through the assimilation of local cults, could be given respectability if introduced into temple ritual and the creation of new myths. Cults that were refused such admission were generally those associated with the marginalized groups, such as untouchables and certain lower castes, and their places of worship were segregated.

The architecture, plan and embellishment of the temple marked a departure from the earlier monuments. Rock-cut temples gave way to free-standing temples, small to begin with but eventually reaching an immense size, as dictated by institutional functions. By the late Chola period, large temples were laid out in an extensive area with multiple courtyards, incorporating many lesser shrines within the parameters of the main temple. The presence of the *brahmadeyas* in the locality encouraged brahman control over temples even if the temple had been financed by an independent grant. The location was frequently at a nodal point of exchange or trade, or an administrative centre. Where it was the former it attracted merchants, some of whom were associated with the administration of the temple in addition to the brahman management. Small temples in the cities were built and maintained through the donations of guilds and merchants and would therefore be associated with a section of the city's residents. As in the case of Buddhist *stupa* complexes, the wealthier temples also had a wide geographical reach among their patrons and this was reflected in the donations that they received from merchants and landowners.

The income of the temple came from the wealth and land acquired as donation, from contributions by the village assemblies, from taxes that it was permitted to collect as part of the grant, from offerings of devotees and from its function as a banker in rural areas. The temple maintained the priests who performed the rituals, as well as the record-keepers, accountants and administrators who looked after its management. There were others who serviced the buildings and guarded them. Professional herdsmen took care of the animals owned by the temple. And those involved at a lesser level with the ritual and the entertainment were the cooks, garland-makers, musicians, dancers and *devadasis*. Many were encouraged to offer their services free as a form of devotion, but others were also dependent on the temple for their livelihood. Since temples had access to surplus resources they attracted traders and craftsmen, among whom were bronze-workers, stone-cutters and the makers of textiles.

The process of building a large temple, over many years, altered economic relationships within the area with the provision of building materials, labour, skilled artisans and those employed in its long-term maintenance. When this extensive patronage towards maintaining a temple ceased, the temple would fall into disrepair and even be deserted. Temples could be in ruins because of the collapse of the authority responsible for maintaining them, not necessarily only as a result of conquest and deliberate destruction. The decline of a temple, therefore, as of other large monumental structures, could be caused by a variety of changes.

The maintenance of temples compares with that of any large-scale institution. The temple at Tanjavur, which took almost a decade to build and was possibly the richest during this period, is said to have had an average income of 500 lb troy of gold, 250 lb troy of precious stones and 600 lb troy of silver, which was acquired through donations, income from taxes and the revenue from about 300 villages. It also maintained temple staff, consisting of about 600 employees, among which were the *devadasis*, 212 attendants – which included treasurers, accountants, record-keepers and watchmen, 57 musicians and readers of the texts, quite apart of course from the craftsmen of various categories (such as carpenters, braziers, goldsmiths, tailors) and the many hundreds of priests who also lived off the temple. A number of these were allotted land to live permanently in the vicinity, and inevitably an urban centre emerged alongside the temple. It became imperative for the temple authorities to keep the income flowing in. Temples did this in part through financing various commercial enterprises and through acting as banker and money-lender to village assemblies and similar bodies, loaning money at the generally accepted rate of 12 to 15 per cent per annum. In this the temples were now following the tradition of the wealthier Buddhist monasteries.

Caste and Sect

The *brahmadeya* also acted as an agency of political integration, the well-being of the elite being a primary concern. The system introduced the *varna* hierarchy into an area where it may have been new or may have become more dominant than before. Social distinctions of earlier times that drew on kinship connections were giving way to caste. Nevertheless, although caste was adopted as a form of social stratification there were adjustments of exclusion and inclusion of certain social categories that were related to regional forms and functions. The *velalas*, who in *varna* terms were often equated with *shudras*, were second in importance after the brahmans, but the *velalas* spanned a large economic range. The rest of society was gradually shuffled into a caste hierarchy.

Vedic Brahmanism had declined somewhat but was still the privileged practice of brahmans and kings. Its insistence on exclusivity confined it to the upper castes. The centrality of the temple grew with the growth of the Shaiva and Vaishnava sects. Those who managed the temple, especially in rural areas, were inevitably the brahmans and the wealthier *velalas*. These identities congealed into what had begun earlier as the brahman and the *shudra*, forming the two main social groups. Temples and Shaiva monasteries also followed the pattern of Buddhist and Jaina institutions and sought the patronage of merchants. This competition for patronage led to shifts and realignments among the sects, sometimes of a hostile and violent kind. The earlier rivalry between the Buddhists and Shaivas was extended to antagonism between the Jainas and the Shaivas. Compositions such as the twelfth-century *Periya Puranam*, with its hagiographies of Shaiva devotees, fuelled these rivalries, accompanied by attempts to convert Jaina temples to Shaiva use. It was said that kings achieved greater glory through association with Shiva, an idea also captured in painted and sculptured depictions of the king as a royal devotee of the god. Kings tended to give greater support to the more widespread religion, which in many areas was Shaivism. These changes also led to some confrontations with the Vaishnavas, who were attempting to reorient their rituals to bring in a wider range of worshippers and were also competing for patronage. The *Bhagavata Purana* projected a Vaishnava world-view. The *Agamas* provided information on the liturgies of the Puranic religions.

By the twelfth century the wealthier *velalas* were often the powerful functionaries of the temple. Caste consciousness was becoming a marked feature in social relationships, but the normative *varna* pattern does not seem to have been dominant in practice. The main distinction in the ordering of castes appears to have been the division of society into brahmans and non-brahmans. Compared to other regions, among the non-brahmans there was little mention of *kshatriyas* and *vaishyas*, but the *shudras* were prominent. The *shudras* were divided into the clean *shudras* – whose touch was not polluting – and the unclean *shudras*, who were debarred from entry into the temple. *Jatis* are referred to in association with artisans and craftsmen. Slavery was an established category and although some slaves were used in agriculture and craft production, most were employed in domestic work. Many such persons were sold to the temple, particularly those impoverished or without an income during a famine.

The temple could also act as a conduit of social mobility. In coastal Andhra, a large herd of cows was donated to the Draksharama temple. The herd was a considerable asset in terms of revenue from dairy produce, and was cared for by the local Boya tribal community. In the course of time, and because they were looking after temple property, these Boyas rose in status from outcastes to *shudras*. As *shudras* they entered the lower echelons of administration and gradually some attained high office.

The new activities had generated a range of items required for exchange. Inevitably those in the business of procuring raw materials, producing finished goods and distributing these, now acquired social importance. This affected the potential for social mobility in caste society. It took the form of the emergence of two new groups referred to as the Right- and Left-Hand groups – the *valangai* and the *idangai*. This was a social division among the non-brahman and the non-*velala* groups, which included those agricultural labourers who were performing services for the upper castes. The division began in the Chola period but became more evident from the thirteenth century onwards. Since the Right-Hand was considered superior to the Left, those anxious to attain a higher status made attempts to move from the Left- to the Right-Hand. It sometimes took the form of special organizations bestowing privileges on certain occupational groups, such as blacksmiths and carpenters. Some agricultural groups were also part of the scheme. Merchant associations were more concerned with the status of the artisans assisting in producing what was required for commerce. This was a new set of caste alignments arising out of a context in which the links between merchants and artisans were of mutual advantage. Inevitably the division into Left-Hand and Right-Hand, and the statuses associated with each, was to lead to caste rivalries.

Economic interests could overlook the norms of *varna*. Brahmans who were merchants readily crossed the seas, while special privileges were occasionally granted to those who worked for the court, like the engravers of the copperplate charters of King Rajendra, or the weavers of Kanchipuram who wove the textiles for the royal family, or the stone masons working on the royal temple or palace. All these were exempt from paying certain dues, and although some of them, such as the weavers, were of low status, they were regarded with greater respect than other members of their castes. References are occasionally made to mixed castes, which would suggest that although the rigidity of caste rules was being emphasized, in practice lapses were common.

Among the donations to the temples that were recorded, a fair number came from women devotees. These were larger in the ninth and tenth centuries, after which they declined and finally petered out after the thirteenth century. Presumably these were women who came from families that were financially comfortable, although donations from *devadasis* are also recorded.

The institution of *devadasis* attached to the better-endowed temples came to be seen as an additional source of income for the temple. Some *devadasis*, where they were reduced to being merely temple attendants, came to be regarded as women of easy virtue. Others, however, who were highly accomplished women, were treated with deference. Because of their accomplishments, such women had a certain freedom of movement in that they could distance themselves from social conventions to a greater degree than most other urban women. Part of the reason for this was that they were educated and professionally trained in the arts, particularly music and dance. Women of royal families were also often educated, which encouraged self-confidence.

One of the more notable features of royal patronage in the peninsula was the frequency with which queens were not only patrons but took an active interest in administration, for instance, among the Ikshvakus, Pallavas, Gangas, Cholas and Later Chalukyas. In the literature of the royal courts women are often projected as retiring, romantic and unconcerned with matters of state, as in the eleventh-century *Vikramanka-deva-charita* written by Bilhana at the Chalukya court. But contemporary Chalukya inscriptions sometimes referred to queens not only as patrons but as administrators overseeing specific areas. Such women participated in the activities of the court that related to governance. Their decisions carried weight and their governance was firm.

At the other end of the scale, peasant women had a limited access to movement being partners in the family occupation. The most liberated women were the poets and singers of hymns dedicated to the worship of Vishnu or Shiva, who rejected conventional restrictions. This rejection became part of their devotion, as in the poetry of Akkamahadevi writing in the twelfth century. But it is significant that this freedom was allowed them only because they were accepted as true worshippers who had taken on a degree of asceticism in their worship.

Language and Literature

The temple continued to function as a place for formal education in Sanskrit. Pupils were either taught by the temple priests, as in the smaller village temples, or else trained at a more advanced level in the *ghatikas* or colleges attached to the larger temples. Brahmans who were thus educated were absorbed either into the temples as priests or, being literate, into the administration of the region. Jaina and Buddhist monasteries also educated novice monks or even some lay persons, but as the number of monasteries decreased their impact lessened. Because the medium of instruction was Sanskrit, formal education became distanced from everyday life. Professional education was still maintained through the training given to apprentices in guilds and among groups of artisans. Where this was combined with a greater demand for technical expertise, with some training in Sanskrit, the status of professionalism rose. Oral instruction in the poetry of devotion serves as a reminder that audiences were not necessarily literate.

This period witnesses the more extensive use of regional languages and their consequent development for multiple purposes. The impetus towards this change came from the devotional movement that used these languages to express the ecstatic experience of closeness to the deity. At another level, the official archive used the regional language for recording locations and rights relating to grants of land. Books were written on palm leaves that were then tied together. Interpolations therefore required the untying of the book and the insertion of what was new. Books were stored in the libraries of the Jaina monasteries and the *mathas*.

Literary works in Sanskrit were largely grammars, lexicons, manuals, works on rhetoric, commentaries on the older texts, prose fiction, drama and poetry. These adhered to the classical conventions of composition, and experimenting with new forms was limited. This tended to place a premium on linguistic proficiency and a somewhat laboured description of mood. Kings continued to be described as authors of literary works and some may actually have been so. But the concept of learning had moved beyond creative literature. The *Manasollasa* of the Chalukya King Someshvara, for instance, takes on the character of an encyclopaedia.

A few works had their counterparts in Tamil, where the models of literary composition were sometimes taken from Sanskrit literature. Tamil literature of this period showed great liveliness and vigour, as in Kamban's version of the *Ramayana*. It was earlier thought that all the many *Ramayanas*, composed as part of the oral or literary tradition in various parts of India, by and large followed the Valmiki version. Further studies of these versions now reveal that the location and language of composition, the intended audience and the treatment of gender all point to noticeable variations. The narratives diverge according to the symbolic meaning intended by diverse authors for various audiences, which imbue the narratives with new events and sensitivities. For instance, the treatment of the personality of Ravana in the Kamban version is far more sympathetic to his predicament than in the Valmiki *Ramayana*.

The language of the inscriptions provides a perspective on wider historical change. Bilingual inscriptions increasingly became the norm in recording grants. The exclusive use of Prakrit for inscriptions had given way to Sanskrit by the fourth century. But the change to bilingual records dates to a few centuries later. The introduction of Sanskrit into a Tamil-speaking area is illustrated in the bilingual Sanskrit-Tamil inscriptions. The formulaic passages in these, stating the origin myths, genealogies, titles of the king and benedictions, tend to be in Sanskrit. The royal genealogies were sometimes fabricated, as they were in many kingdoms, in order to give legitimacy to the makers of the grant. But the actual terms of the grant were in Tamil, so that they were well understood in the locality. This covered information on the land or village granted, its boundaries, the participation of local authorities, the rights and obligations of the grantee, his taxes and dues, the witnesses to the grant and any other matter of local concern. The two languages had a purpose, the content of each being significantly different. Both sections were important to the legality of the document, but the description of the land in Tamil ensured that there was no ambiguity about the location of the land and the rights of the grantee.

The more extensive use of Sanskrit coincided with educated brahmans seeking employment and migrating to various parts of the subcontinent. Where they were successful they were given employment and a grant of land. This may on occasion have taken them into interior areas where Sanskrit would be a new language, requiring the grantee to become bilingual. The two languages of many inscriptions were Sanskrit and the regional language, such as Tamil or Kannada.

The Sanskrit section of the grant therefore had a political agenda, publicizing royal authority and legitimizing the titles and status of the king, along with his connections to ancient heroes and earlier rulers. The capturing of history became significant. By appropriating the compositions of the *suta* or bard – the traditional keepers of history – and editing these in a new format, the authors of the texts could control the use of the past and thereby the status of the rulers. The *Puranas*, claiming to record the past, were now authored by brahmans and written in Sanskrit, although there was often a pretence that they were still being recited by the bard who was placed formally in the role of the original composer.

The audience for this political agenda was the world of kings and courts. The forms in which the past was represented and their links with the present were not confined to a particular language or region. The genre of *charita* literature or historical biographies, inaugurated by Banabhatta's *Harsha-charita*, became fashionable in various courts. Bilhana travelled from Kashmir to various places seeking fortune and employment until he was given a position at the court of the Later Chalukyas, where he wrote the *Vikramanka-deva-charita*, the biography of Vikramaditya VI. This was again a defence of a king who had usurped the throne of his elder brother.

Apart from inscriptions that were virtually the annals of history at this time, attempts were also made to provide historical details of some dynasties in the form of *vamshavalis*, chronicles. That the notion of seeking historical legitimacy had filtered down fairly extensively would seem evident from some of the shorter chronicles on lesser dynasties, for example, the *Mushaka-*

vamsha-kavya, composed by Atula in the eleventh century on a little-known dynasty from Malabar. The structure of such chronicles remained similar irrespective of whether they were written in the state of Chamba in the Himalaya or in Malabar, and could take the form of a dynastic chronicle or the history of a region. Some of the myths were virtually identical. The chronicle moved from mythological beginnings to founding ancestors to more authentic genealogical history. A point of departure marked the establishing of a kingdom, which was accompanied by specific changes: more areas were opened to cultivation; a capital city was founded with a royal temple, and was connected to other places by a network of routes; the presence of an administrative hierarchy and an army were indicated; and inscriptions were issued to give the official version of royal activities. Subsequent to this, events of importance were recorded in the chronicle. Kalhana's history of Kashmir, the *Rajatarangini*, frequently described as unique, is actually rooted in the *vamshavali* form, although admittedly it is an extraordinarily fine example. The authors of these texts, allotting historical antecedents to dynasties, reiterated their hegemonic status in caste society. It underlined their role as the creators of a trans-regional Sanskritic network across the subcontinent, including even south-east Asia. Sanskrit inscriptions in south-east Asia date to approximately the same period. These gradually became bilingual, the second language being the local one.

Bilingualism, however, became less frequent from about the fourteenth century when records were written more often in the regional language. Reiterating the difference between the language of the court and that of local administration may have led to this. Where local administrators became rulers, they probably carried their language with them. This would be parallel to installing the family deity as a cult deity by a new dynasty. Adventurers establishing kingdoms would also tend to use the regional language, and if this sufficed to explain their change of status then Sanskrit might not have been required. The large element of rhetoric in the Sanskrit section of inscriptions would, if expressed in the local language, carry the same message. There are eleventh-century records of endowments of land given to those who recited the hymns of the Alvars and Nayanars. This was extending patronage to Tamil.

The performance of Vedic rituals was now mentioned less frequently. The growth of Vaishnavism and Shaivism required different rituals, as well as the use of the regional language, even if some of the literature of the religious sects was being written in Sanskrit. The latter bestowed prestige on the text and an elite readership. Brahmans who had taken to other professions, such as trade, would have been less proficient in the Sanskrit used in Vedic rituals.

The change may also suggest that regional authority was asserted with more confidence. Paradoxically, the ensuing regional diversity of identity and language created a condition common to the subcontinent.

Other regional languages such as Kannada and Telugu, also stemming from a Dravidian linguistic base, were widely used and bilingualism with Sanskrit led to some vocabulary being borrowed. But the memory of this derivation became distant as the languages came into current use. Telugu took shape and form in the Andhra region with texts from the eleventh century. The origins of Kannada in Karnataka go further back to the sixth century AD, with texts dating to the ninth century. Kannada had both royal patronage and support from the influential literate Jainas. It eventually became the language of the twelfth-century Virashaiva or Lingayat movement, which still had a significant religious and social identity. Many of the *vachanas* or verses composed in Kannada by the Lingayats had lower-caste authors, ensuring a popular appeal for both the language and the message. Malayalam as the language of Kerala evolved somewhat later, drawing on both Tamil and Sanskrit and with texts going back to the early second millennium AD.

Marathi, the language current in the western Deccan, had evolved from local Prakrits and retained closer links with Sanskrit. It received encouragement from the Yadava rulers. But its wider development grew from its becoming the language of a popular devotional movement, in some ways parallel to the Alvars and Nayanars, which soon became established in the western Deccan. This involved not only the composition of poems in Marathi but also the exposition of older religious texts, such as the *Gita*, in a language understood by common people. Such expositions naturally introduced innovations in interpreting these earlier texts and the religious concepts endorsed by them.

The literary forms of these languages were initially translations and adaptations from works in Sanskrit that were thought to encapsulate high culture. But the translations were infused with local variations in narrative and action and were not identical with the original. Adaptations gave way to new texts and forms in the regional languages, which helped establish these languages as the media of intellectual discourse. Meanwhile, Sanskrit was essentially the language of brahmanical activity, although it became more widely used by Buddhists and Jainas at this time. As a prestige language, Sanskrit also appealed to sectarian movements with social ambitions.

Religions and Ideologies

Buddhism had become less visible by the end of this period in all but eastern India, with the Buddha even being incorporated into Vaishnavism as an incarnation of Vishnu, an incarnation that never caught the popular imagination. Jainism survived with a following in Karnataka and western India. In Karnataka Jaina monks received handsome endowments, enabling them to have tenants cultivate their lands and even on occasion to make donations to other monasteries. Jaina merchants were prominent donors, as were Jaina officials, some of whom were military commanders. The Yapaniya sect of Jainas was popular as it was less austere than the well-established Digambara. The Yapaniyas supported the setting up of convents for nuns and even allowed senior nuns to tutor monks. The animosity between the Shaivas and the Jainas flared up on occasion.

The decline of Buddhism and Jainism is partly linked to the popularity of religious devotionalism. The hymns of the earlier poets were collated and the immense appeal of their theism inspired fresh compositions. The more philosophical treatises traced the origin of theism to Upanishadic sources, which in a sense attempted to bring Vedic Brahmanism and devotionalism closer, even if some of the differences were irreconcilable. Some of the Vaishnava *acharyas* and Shaiva *mathas* maintained the momentum of the Alvars and Nayanars. This also coincided with the rise of non-brahman castes in sectarian movements from the thirteenth century, a large number of which would be counted as members of the *shudra* castes. That they were specifically mentioned reflects the status that these castes had acquired. The untouchables, although not excluded, had a less visible presence.

The devotional movement had a form of worship and a concept of deity different from that of Vedic Brahmanism. The act of worship was open to a larger range of castes. Yet this change was almost conformist and conservative when compared with some of the more extreme sects that now had a concurrent following. Possibly the one was acting as a counterweight to the other. There were a variety of sects, such as the Tantric and Shakta, and those of the Kapalikas, Kalamukhas and Pashupatas, some more and some less esoteric than the others, which by this time had gathered supporters in various parts of the subcontinent. Some among them practised unusual rites, involving the remains from cremated bodies or ritualized sexual intercourse, which were evidently designed for those for whom non-conformity and the supposed power of magic was attractive, apart from its appeal for those who treated it as a statement of social confrontation. This disregard of even minimal social obligations among them became a necessity on certain ritual occasions. Such rites were also practised in other parts of the subcontinent, and had an underlying organization and message.

The deliberate deviation from accepted social norms was a form of protest, their extreme nonconformity providing the publicity that was desired; but these acts were also claimed as religious ritual possessing magical qualities. The Kalamukhas ate food out of a human skull, smeared their bodies with the ashes of a corpse, and were generally seen carrying a pot of wine and a club. Rumours had them behaving in strange ways and such rumours were associated with those of whom the orthodoxy disapproved. For some, nonconformity was also a genuine protest against the limitations placed on thought and knowledge by orthodoxy. The interest in magic, for instance, was not merely sensationalism, but could also result from a curiosity to experiment with objects and inquire further than was permitted by the custodians of knowledge. Experiments in alchemy, the attempt to change base metal to gold, or the concept of transmutation, are not unassociated with magic in its early stages. Yet for the most part, as it has been suggested, followers of these sects seem to have led a normal life, indulging in the cult rites only on certain occasions. For them, these rites were probably a catharsis.

There seem to have been three broad trends in religious belief and practice apart from the Shramanic that were becoming recognizable. Vedic Brahmanism, frequently enveloped in the theological discussions of philosophers, remained the religious concern of a minority – brahmans in the main, with some attention from Buddhist and Jaina scholars. It was influential in creating wealthy institutions of learning and writing theological discourses in Sanskrit, with only a limited influence on religion at a more popular level. The second and more popular trend was that of the Puranic religions, Vaishnavism and Shaivism, whose maximum appeal was through devotionalism. This drew a large number of people who were cultivators or craftsmen or in related professions. A variety of cults were assimilated from a range of sources, the assimilation being closely tied to the particular social groups observing the religion. The third trend was a scatter of cults of various kinds, some labelled as Tantric. These either continued to be observed independently or they became part of yet another set of religious beliefs and practices, formalized as the Shakta religion. This became an addition to the Puranic religions, and even influenced aspects of Buddhism. The three trends were not self-contained but were juxtaposed and therefore some elements were borrowed by one from another. There was an inherent and continuing flexibility in the belief and the practice of at least the second and third trends, which was characteristic of religion in India. The Alvars and Nayanars had echoed some of the social concerns earlier addressed by the Buddhists and Jainas, and this had won them much of the potential following of the latter.

Not all protests were expressed in aberrations of social norms. Other Shaiva sects were far more closely tied to social institutions. Among these was the Lingayat or Virashaiva sect that emerged in the twelfth century with some advocacy of social reforms, possibly influenced by other current religious thinking. The founder, Basavanna, an apostate Jaina, was associated with the Kalachuri court at Kalyani in the Deccan. He had, on occasion, a certain satirical strain in his statements that lent sharpness to the point he wished to make.

The lamb brought to the slaughter-house eats the leaf garland with which it is decorated . . . the frog caught in the mouth of the snake desires to swallow the fly flying near its mouth. So is our life. The man condemned to die drinks milk and *ghi* . . . When they see a serpent carved in stone they pour milk on it: if a real serpent comes they say, Kill. Kill. To the servant of the god who could eat if served they say, Go away. Go away; but to the image of the god which cannot eat they offer dishes of food.

Th. De Bary (ed.), *Sources of Indian Tradition*, p. 357

The Lingayats differed from the devotional cult in that they did not rest content with preaching devotion to a single deity, but actively attacked religious hypocrisy. Much of their early teaching questioned Brahmanism, the theory of rebirth and the norms of caste as maintained in brahmanical thought and practice. The idea of some groups being socially polluted was unacceptable. The Lingayats laid emphasis on the need for a social conscience and encouraged certain social practices disapproved of in *Dharma-shastra* norms, such as late post-puberty marriages and the remarriage of widows. Although advocating a better status for women, there was nevertheless a bar on women becoming priests. Brahman landlordism was seen as exerting excessive pressure on the cultivator to pay rent to the landlord, as well as tax to the state. Not surprisingly, the Lingayats came under attack from the brahmans. Such ideas had an appeal for non-brahman groups and reflect similarities with Shramanic thinking. Shiva was worshipped in the form of the *lingam* or phallic emblem, each member of the sect carrying a miniature *lingam*. They replaced cremation with the burial of their dead, the form generally adopted by ascetics, and this was again opposed to brahmanical ritual. Their more liberal social attitudes brought them the support of the lower castes. Eventually, however, the Lingayats themselves evolved into a caste.

Those who were excluded from worshipping at temples, such as some lower castes and the untouchables, had to find their own places and forms of worship, some of which could be incorporated into the ritual and mythology of a sect, presumably when the caste status of those who were low had improved. Sometimes this led to incorporating the worship of local deities not initially included in the Puranic pantheon. Among these was the cult of Panduranga or Vitthala at Pandharpur in western India, which came into prominence in the thirteenth century. Its origin may have been in the hero cults of the borderlands between Maharashtra and Karnataka, the image of Vitthala being similar to the local hero-stones. The god was identified with Vishnu on entering the Vaishnava pantheon. Pandharpur became one of the centres of the devotional movement in the Deccan, attracting in a later period preachers and hymn writers such as Namadeva, Janabai, Sena and Narahari (by profession tailor, maidservant, barber and goldsmith), who composed their hymns in Marathi and gathered around them the local people. These cult centres also became the foci of pilgrimage and exchange.

At a still more local level were the village deities. Among these a prominent deity in Tamil-nadu was Ayannar, whose shrine on the outskirts of the village was guarded by clay horses of varying sizes. The shrine may have been humble but the horses gave it a striking presence. They have now become characteristic features of the Tamil-nadu countryside and Ayannar is worshipped in many places as the son of Shiva and the Mohini incarnation of Vishnu. Variants occur in other parts of India where the worship of local deities and spirits prevails. This was sometimes parallel to Puranic Hinduism and sometimes overlapping with it, and where it overlapped it became an avenue of transaction between the religion of the elite and popular cults. This was the opposite end of the spectrum from the philosophical speculation current in many places.

Discussions on philosophy were largely the prerogative of the brahmans except in the few centres where Buddhists and Jainas joined the debates, in addition to focusing on their own philosophical schools, and in some Shaiva *mathas* where the non-brahman *velala* were prominent. Debates were held in the various *mathas* and colleges throughout the subcontinent, the link between them being the common language, Sanskrit. But their intellectual influence on the wider society was restricted. Unlike the early Buddhists who held open public debates in the parks close to towns, the Sanskrit discourse tended to include only recognized scholars, even if the debates and controversies involved scholars from various parts of the subcontinent. This resulted in some fine-tuned philosophical ideas among the rather exclusive groups of scholars. Shankaracharya's ideas continued to be developed and honed, and theories of other teachers were also discussed, some of which were opposed to the ideas of Shankara. Foremost among his critics was the eleventh-century Vaishnava philosopher, Ramanuja.

Ramanuja was a Tamil brahman who spent a considerable part of his life teaching at the famous temple at Shrirangam (Thiruchirapalli), eventually being regarded as the founder of the Shri Vaishnava movement. He disagreed with Shankara's theory that knowledge was the primary means of liberation from rebirth. According to Ramanuja, it was merely one of the means and was not nearly as effective or reliable as pure devotion, giving oneself up entirely to the deity, who was projected as loving and forgiving, as in the devotional cult. Although the relationship was expressed in philosophical terms it was viewed as essentially personal. Some of his followers argued that one must strive for this forgiveness, but others supported the notion that the deity selects those who are to be liberated – a concept curiously close to that of the Calvinists. Some of his ideas drew on the *Upanishads*, such as the need for the *atman*/the individual soul to unite with the *brahman*/ the universal soul for the attainment of liberation from rebirth. The emphasis on the individual in this relationship was not only a major feature of *bhakti*, but carried something of the flavour of Shramanic thought. Ramanuja thus was an effective bridge between the devotional movements and Brahmanical theology, attempting as he did to weave together the two divergent strands.

Madhva, a thirteenth-century theologian, made further attempts to synthesize the ideas of *bhakti* with brahmanical theology. He was also a Vaishnava and his concept of Vishnu was that the deity granted his grace to free the souls only of the pure, which implies selection. However, the selection was not quite as arbitrary as was believed by some of Ramanuja's followers. Some of Madhva's ideas suggest that he may have been familiar with the teachings of the Christian church of Malabar. Thus, Vishnu bestows his grace on a devotee through his son Vayu, the Wind-god, an idea that is alien to Brahmanical and Puranic belief but parallels that of the Holy Spirit in Christianity.

Ramanuja, while accepting special privileges for the higher castes, was nevertheless opposed to excluding certain categories of *shudras* from worship in the temple. He pleaded for the throwing open of temples to all *shudras*, though without much success. The growing strength of the devotional movement and the attempts at syntheses by theologians such as Ramanuja and Madhva did, however, force the orthodox to recognize the need for compromise. Although the temple was not opened to all *shudras*, the deities and rituals of a large number of subsidiary cults had crept in. This was an inevitable process if the temple was to retain its vitality as the centre of social and religious life, at least in caste society. The area of the temple was enlarged to accommodate new shrines and images. Economic prosperity led to larger and more ornate structures. Even the lesser dynasties invested in impressive religious monuments that would raise their status in the eyes of their peers and their subjects.

Religious monuments

Domestic buildings have unfortunately not survived from this period; only temples have remained. These tended to follow two main styles in the peninsula. The Deccan had temples built in what is generally referred to as the Vesara style, as in the Durga temple at Aihole or the Virupaksha temple at Pattadakal. In south India the Dravida style was more common but was regionally distinctive. In Kerala, for example, temple architecture takes a form specific to Kerala, the style changing because of building in wood rather than stone and because many temples were circular in form – the circular sanctum being surrounded by concentrically arranged areas. Despite many common features the imprint of regional architecture is apparent.

The early Chola temples were still relatively small, and superb in their simplicity. One example is the ninth-century temple at Narttamalai, free-standing, facing some earlier rock-cut caves, and from its perch on the hillside dominating a landscape of rice fields. From the eleventh century the Chola kings began to build their spectacular royal temples. The balanced proportions of the different components of the temple gave the structure its aesthetic quality. The central chamber of the shrine could be easily located, surmounted as it was by a tall *shikhara* or corbelled tower broadly pyramidal in shape. It was approached through one or more halls, the number depending on the size of the temple, and the surrounding courtyard was enclosed in a cloistered wall. The latter often had a colonnade of pillars on the inside, as at Tanjavur and Gangaikondacholapuram. The entrances, or *gopurams*, were elaborate gateways reflecting the style of the *shikhara*, and these were gradually given more and more emphasis until they overwhelmed the *shikhara*, as in the case of the later temples at Madurai and Shrirangam. In the temples of the Deccan the antechambers tended to be large, perhaps imitating Buddhist *chaitya* halls. Congregational worship was not a feature of Puranic Hinduism, but the increasing popularity of the recitations of the

Puranas, and of the epics now converted to sacred texts, would have drawn large audiences.

Stone sculpture was used in the temples largely as an adjunct to architecture, in niches or as a decorative motif in friezes and in the ornamentation of pillars and balustrades. It was, however, in bronze sculptures that the Chola craftsmen excelled, producing images rivalling the best anywhere. They were mainly images of deities, donors and the poets of the devotional movement. Made by the *cire perdu* or lost-wax process, they were kept in the inner shrine of the temple and some taken out in procession on special occasions. The Shiva Nataraja images were produced in fair number, yet the early examples of these are stunningly beautiful as are the icons of Shiva and Parvati with their son Skanda. Symbols of attributes were incorporated with incredible subtlety, given that by now a forest of symbols was sometimes required to represent what were thought of as the local, transregional and cosmic levels of a deity. These images, more than anything else, indicate the sculptural genius of the southern craftsmen.

To begin with, the temples of the Deccan preserved the earlier tradition of the Chalukya style. Gradually they became more ornate, a tendency which was accentuated by the extensive use of soapstone, a softer stone than the earlier sandstone. The temples built by the Later Chalukyas and Hoysalas changed the ground-plan and elevation from that common to both the northern or Nagara style and the southern or Dravida styles. The finest examples are the Hoysala temples at Halebid (the old Dorasamudra), Belur and Somnathapura. The ground-plan of some temples was no longer rectangular but was star-shaped or polygonal, the whole complex being built on a raised platform. Since there was not the same emphasis on towers and gateways as in the Chola temples, the elevation gave the impression of being more flat. This effect was emphasized by a series of narrow panels running horizontally right around the temple walls, carrying frieze decorations of animal and floral motifs, musicians, dancers, battle scenes and the depiction of well-known events from religious literature. The star-shaped plan provided more wall space for sculpture and bâs-relief than would a rectangular plan. Perhaps the most curious feature of these Hoysala temples are the wide, circular pillars which give the impression of having been lathe-turned. Obviously considerable skill went into their making.

Sculpture and architecture were on occasion identified with either the name of an individual *shilpin*/craftsman, or an association of sculptors and builders. This became a feature in many buildings in other parts of India as well. It is possible to link some builders with their patrons and their buildings. The notion that architects and artists remained anonymous is belied by the presence of apparently much respected architects and sculptors, for example, Kokasa. Both the demand for expertise and the high professionalism of what had earlier been regarded as a craft doubtless encouraged individuality in style and enterprise. The *sutradhara*, literally the one who holds the thread and therefore the one who superintends, had an exalted position as supervisor in the construction of a building. The *stapathi* was the master builder or the highly skilled craftsman. They were respected for their knowledge and expertise and sometimes described as belonging to the *Vishvakarma-kula*, literally the family of the deity of craftsmen, Vishvakarma. Some received grants of land and their descendants took to other professions. Among the manuals on constructing a building were the *vastu* texts that set out the requirements for the orientations of a building, some of which may have been based on technical understanding although others were quite arbitrary. There were other efficient manuals that described not only the methods to be used in constructing a building, but also the making of images. The information was so detailed that it gave the optimum size of the nail of the small finger in proportion to the hand and the figure. These *shilpa-shastra* texts were often written in Sanskrit, perhaps an indicator of the improving status of the profession.

The temples had a wider symbolism in that they were monuments to royal grandeur as well as to a deity. Moreover, the variation in style gave the architecture a regional character, as distinct as the language and literature of the region. Again, while the style was local, the plan and elevation had features recognizable throughout the subcontinent. The political ascendancy of the Cholas, although resented by the powers of the western and northern Deccan, serves to force home the fact that the centre of power in the subcontinent was not confined to one region: it could and did shift spatially. The classicism of the south saw the birth of new ideas and experiments. The evolution of local civic responsibility, the multiple roles of the temple as an institution, the philosophy of Shankaracharya and Ramanuja, and the new religious forms of the devotional movement, were all part of the changes of this time. Equally noticeable was the further growth of mercantile activity, involving a more extensive Indian participation in the commercial economy of Eurasia. At many levels, therefore, this was a period when the south was in the ascendant and set the pattern for cultural forms in the subcontinent.

12

The Politics of Northern India

c. AD 700–1200

The Struggle over the
Northern Plains

The emergence of states more firmly rooted in earlier core areas that gave them a regional coherence was characteristic of this period. But their distant boundaries tended to change frequently, despite the political ambition to build consolidated kingdoms. There was contestation therefore over prize areas among those who thought of themselves as significant powers. An example of this has been encapsulated in the phrase 'the tripartite struggle for Kanauj'. Another aspect of this complexity was that the changing frontiers blurred the demarcation between the north and south at the western and eastern ends of the peninsula. Notwithstanding similar characteristics within the regional states, generalizations about these states always have to be qualified by local conditions and ecologies.

The structure of the new kingdoms marked a departure from earlier forms: the tributary status of conquered kings had to be established, for this often had priority over the annexation of their territory; landed magnates had to be accommodated and ranked in the emerging hierarchy; and administrative changes involved reassessing the channels of revenue and income. An increase in the number and size of grants of land, among other things, evolved into a new political economy in many states. This change occurred in two phases: from the eighth to the tenth centuries, when some earlier forms were carried over, and then during the subsequent period, when the change is more noticeable. The terms and conditions of the grants resembled those of the peninsula, but were not identical. That many of the grants were permanent and could be inherited by descendants – or, to use the words of the inscriptions, were to last as long as the moon and sun endure – was assumed. But this was not invariable, since some grants could be revoked.

Some new kingdoms faced intervention from the Arabs, from the

Turkish and Chinese pressures in central Asia, and from Tibet. Arab writers comment at some length on these states, which they refer to as the Al-Ballhara or the Rashtrakuta rajas, the Al Jurz or Gurjara-Pratiharas and the Dharma or Pala kings. These were the major states battling to control the northern plains, a contest that eventually focused on capturing the city of Kanauj. The manoeuvres of these states can perhaps be better viewed as a form of political chess. But the game was circumscribed by the doctrine of *mandala* – the circle of friends and enemies – where the neighbour may be a natural enemy but the king beyond the neighbour a natural friend. The application of the doctrine was of course governed by political realities, but the theoretical exposition of the doctrine became quite elaborate. The concept was first set out in the *Arthashastra* of Kautilya, but continued to be discussed in a number of later texts such as the *Vishnudharmottara*.

The urban focus in the Ganges Plain had shifted from Pataliputra west-wards to Kanauj, now the hub of activity. It was closer to the north-west which was at the receiving end of interventions, and, as a distribution centre, Kanauj was linked to routes going eastwards into the Ganges Plain as well as to those going south. Its strategic importance to the politics of the post-Gupta period had been emphasized by Harsha and by Yashovarman, who established the city as a symbol of royal power in the northern plains. Subsequently, Lalitaditya from Kashmir sought to control Kanauj in the eighth century. Additionally, it was the focus of an agrarian concentration in the western Ganges Plain, which encouraged grants to brahmans in that area. For the next few centuries, brahmans who migrated from Kanauj to seek employment elsewhere were highly respected for their knowledge of ritual and their learning. As a prized city, the Rashtrakutas, Pratiharas and Palas directed their military activity towards its conquest from the eighth to the tenth centuries. The struggle over Kanauj was also an attempt to revive the notion of a single kingdom having primacy, and the choice of Kanauj was a concession to its earlier importance with its strategic location for purposes of contemporary politics. However, with the rise of many powerful regional kingdoms, the significance of Kanauj decreased. Subsequently, it was part of the Gahadavala kingdom during the eleventh and twelfth centuries, before its ultimate decline.

The 'tripartite struggle for Kanauj' has to be located in the context not only of south Asian politics, but also of the relations between Indian kingdoms and those beyond the subcontinent. Of the latter, the Chinese now had a presence in central Asia, and their interest in the power struggles of northern India was due to many reasons. One was their erroneous assumption that their occasional diplomatic interventions in the politics of northern India meant that Indian kingdoms were willing to pay tribute to the Chinese emperor. Having intervened after the death of Harsha, they also claimed that kings of Kashmir had asked for help from China on various occasions. Another reason was that the Chinese faced a threat from the Arab presence in central Asia and this was putting pressure on the Turks, setting off a movement of peoples in central Asia, an activity about which the Chinese were always apprehensive. The Chinese were also beginning to take an interest in the Indian Ocean, and maritime routes from south China were to touch trading centres along the Bay of Bengal, being extended to south India with stopping-points for trade going further west.

From another direction, Tibet was asserting its presence along the Hima-layan borders and claiming conquest of certain areas. Increasing references are made in Indian sources to the presence of the *bhauttas* or Tibetans along the Himalaya. Not only were the politics of other areas thus impinging on northern India, but there was a threat to the kingdoms as well. Yet the focus of political interest appears to have been directed to the north Indian heartland.

The Arab presence in western India was gradually increasing. Sind, con-quered in AD 712, was at the eastern extremity of the Arab expansion through Asia, Africa and Europe. The politics involved in the conquest of the lower Indus Plain were enmeshed in the conflict over the Caliphate and the internal politics of the Islamic world. Arab intentions in India seem to have preferred capturing trade routes rather than territory, judging by the places that they wished to control and their subsequent arrangements. Sind, for instance, was hardly an agriculturally rich region but had revenue from trade. Furthermore, Arab conquests were resisted by various rulers, although this resistance was not organized as an effort to permanently exclude the Arabs from the subcontinent. The Rashtrakutas employed Arabs at a senior level in their administration of the coastal areas, and recognized, as did the Gujarat Chaulukya kings of a subsequent period, that as traders the Arabs had the potential of bringing in impressive profits. The fact that an Arab empire was developing further west seemed to receive little attention from Indian rulers, perhaps because their predominant interest was com-merce. This concern with trade may have deflected the Rashtrakutas from concentrating on Kanauj, although they occupied it on two occasions, but like the others were unable to hold it for a substantial length of time.

The kingdoms involved in the struggle were the Rashtrakutas based in the Deccan, the Pratiharas in western India and the Palas who were their counterparts in eastern India. Since they were relatively equally matched, it became a war of attrition which was to exhaust all three. This encouraged their *samantas* to break away and found smaller kingdoms. With Kashmir, Gandhara and Punjab drawn into the vortex of the politics of the border-lands, Kanauj controlled the Ganges Plain, and the watershed was effectively becoming the northern frontier, rather than the passes of the Hindu Kush.

Kingdoms rising in the Deccan sometimes had the choice of participating in the politics of both or either the north or the south, or playing the role of a bridge. The Satavahanas were the initial transmitters of goods and ideas from one to the other. The Vakatakas preferred to opt for a closer alliance with the north through the Guptas. The Chalukyas held back northern incursion into the Deccan and were active in the politics of the peninsula. Had the Rashtrakutas restricted their ambition to the same end, they could have built a more powerful kingdom in the Deccan. But their ambition was domination over the north and the Deccan. By the time they came to power, communication between the two was well established, and therefore the political pull on the Rashtrakutas was equally strong in both directions, which to an extent dissipated their control. Arab sources, however, describe them as the most powerful of the three.

The participation of the Rashtrakutas in the politics of the peninsula has already been described. Dantidurga was a tributary raja of the Chalukyas, who declared his independence in the eighth century and took full imperial titles. Amoghavarsha in the ninth century, and Krishna III in the tenth, stabilized the kingdom despite internal problems and the additional ambition of capturing Kanauj. After defeating Arab incursions along the west coast, the Rashtrakutas converted a relationship of hostility to one of trade, to their mutual advantage. They therefore had the wealth to back their political ambitions. Shipments of teak and cotton textiles went west, while horses came to India to be sold at great profit to kingdoms further inland.

Historians have described the Pratiharas as being of an uncertain social origin and associated with the Hunas, or else descended from the Gurjara pastoralists of Rajasthan. Their enemies the Rashtrakutas claimed that they were literally *pratiharas*, door-keepers, in order to mark them with an insultingly low origin. They may have been officials who rose to power, a pattern known among rulers who had been administrators. Some credence, however, is given to the bardic tradition that the Pratiharas acquired Rajput status. The first important Pratihara King, Nagabhata, ruling in the eighth century, is said to have been a fierce enemy of the *mlechchhas*, those outside the pale of caste society, though who these *mlechchhas* were is not mentioned. Possibly this was a reference to the Arabs in Sind. Or it could have been the people not brought under any administration earlier and therefore regarded as unsettled. Jaina texts, such as the *Kuvalyamala*, supported the Pratihara kings and among them the ninth-century ruler, Bhoja, received the maximum coverage. The Pratihara court provided patronage to the poet Rajashekhara, who in turn endorsed their ancestry as descended from the Suryavamsha lineage and the line of the epic hero Rama. The Pratiharas ruled from Bhinmal near Mt Abu, and, significantly, the fire sacrifice, which embodies the myth of the four pre-eminent clans of Rajputs, was supposedly held at Mt Abu. Having successfully resisted the Arabs, the Pratiharas looked eastwards, and by the end of the millennium were not only ruling over a large part of Rajasthan and Malwa but had briefly held Kanauj.

The third power involved in the conflict over Kanauj was the Pala dynasty, which controlled much of the eastern Ganges Plain. The granting of land in this area had started in the Gupta period when land was sometimes bought with the intention of granting it to a religious beneficiary. This process was now accelerated through agricultural settlements in hitherto uncleared areas, the settlements being activated by brahman grantees. When cleared the land was low-lying and fertile, watered by the vast rivers of the east and the tributaries of the Ganges Delta, which suited the cultivation of rice. The new settlements hosted the more prestigious brahmans from Kanauj, but the process of settlement also led to local priests being recruited into the brahman fold. The grants were frequently recorded on copper plates, such legal and easily retrievable documents being necessary in areas newly settled.

In addition, the Palas derived an income from their substantial commercial interests in south-east Asia. This commerce was to be furthered by the circuit of Arab trade with south-east Asia and the arrival of Chinese trade on the way to east Africa, both using ports in the Bay of Bengal. Buddhism provided a link between eastern India and Java and Sumatra. Pala patronage towards the building of Buddhist monasteries, such as Vikramashila and Odantapuri in Bihar and Somapuri in modern Paharapura (Bangla Desh), together with their continuing patronage to Nalanda, was also related to commercial interests in Buddhist kingdoms further afield. The King of Shrivijaya in Sumatra participated effectively in an endowment to Nalanda. Centres such as Lalmai and Mainamati in the eastern part of Bengal were also important to Buddhist connections.

The earliest Pala ruler of importance who became king in the eighth century did so in an unusual way. Gopala attained renown because he was not the hereditary king, but was elected, and his son maintained that the election terminated the state of anarchy in the land. The sixteenth-century

Tibetan Buddhist monk Taranatha, referring to this event in his history of Buddhism, states that Bengal was without a king and suffered accordingly. Although the local leaders continually gathered to elect a king, on each occasion the person elected was killed by a demoness on the night following his election. Finally, when Gopala was elected, he was given a club by the goddess Chandi (a consort of Shiva) with which to protect himself. He used it to kill the demoness and survived. The story suggests that Gopala was elected because of his ability to protect, while it also endorses the Chandi cult which Gopala may have supported. This could imply that Gopala did not have royal antecedents but nevertheless succeeded in acquiring a kingdom – a pattern that was to become common in this period.

His successor, Dharmapala, made the Pala kingdom a force in north Indian politics. Despite the fact that he began with a severe setback – a defeat at the hands of the Rashtrakutas – by the end of his reign Pala power was dominant in eastern India. Towards the late eighth century Dharmapala led a successful campaign against Kanauj, resulting in the removal of the reigning king, a protégé of the Pratiharas, with Dharmapala claiming suzerainty. This affronted the Rashtrakutas and the Pratiharas, but Dharmapala stood his ground. Devapala later extended Pala control eastwards into Kamarupa (in Assam). Trade routes through Assam to the north-east and to the centres in Myanmar, as well as access to gold panned in the eastern rivers, is believed to have enriched the Palas, together with wealth from the south-east Asian trade. A still later king, Ramapala, faced the threat of the Kaivarta revolt aimed at preventing Pala expansion. This was barely put down through a combination of diplomacy in handling Ramapala's *samantas* and others with subordinate ruling powers, and a somewhat desperate military effort. Diplomacy required lavish gifts to the *samantas* and to the forest-chiefs to ensure their alliance, a procedure graphically described by Sandhyakara-nandin in his biography of Ramapala, the *Ramacharita*. The biographical highlighting of this event provided a wealth of detail on the subtleties of relations between the king and his tributary rajas. The Kaivarta revolt has also been seen as a peasant rebellion, since the Kaivartas were traditionally a low caste of cultivators and fishermen. However, the description seems more appropriate to a rebellion of lesser landowners, who would have mobilized the peasants.

Although threats from Tibet required constant vigilance from the Palas, friendly relations ensured the safety of their northern borders. The Palas and the subsequent dynasty of the Senas, ruling from the eleventh century, included, in their patronage to religious institutions, the Buddhists who had a visible presence in eastern India. Buddhism in eastern India, influenced by

Tantric belief and practice, was linked to Buddhism in Tibet. Patronage to Buddhism declined in the late Sena period, from the twelfth century, the boundaries between Buddhism and Tantric worship becoming faint.

Meanwhile the Pratiharas had consolidated their position and gained the initiative. The first step was obvious. Kanauj, which had been taken by the Rashtrakutas from the Palas, was now captured by the Pratiharas and the other two powers were driven back to their own borders. The Arab menace was firmly tackled by Bhoja, probably the most renowned of the Pratiharas. But his efforts to hold back the Arabs on the one side, and the Palas on the other, made it impossible for him to extend his control in the Deccan, which may have been his intention.

The Rashtrakutas waited for their opportunity and in 916 they struck for the last time, effectively attacking Kanauj. The rivalry between the Pratiharas and the Rashtrakutas was self-destructive. The Arab traveller, Masudi, visited Kanauj in the early tenth century and wrote that the King of Kanauj was the natural enemy of the King of the Deccan, that he kept a large army and was surrounded by smaller kings always ready to go to war. A hundred years later the Pratiharas were no longer a power in northern India. A Turkish army attacked Kanauj in 1018, which virtually ended Pratihara rule. In the western Deccan, the Rashtrakutas had been supplanted by the Later Chalukyas.

The decline of the Pratiharas gave the Palas an opportunity to participate more fully in north Indian affairs. In the early eleventh century Turkish raids into north-western India kept the local kings occupied. Soon the Palas reached Varanasi, but this expansion was checked by the advance of the Chola King, Rajendra, whose successful northern campaign threatened the independence of Bengal. The western campaign of the Palas was therefore abandoned and the King, Mahipala, hastily returned to defend Bengal against invasion by the Chola armies. Rajendra's impressive campaign was motivated both by a desire to obtain military glory and to assert a political presence. This was combined with an attempt to monopolize trade with south-east Asia, as well as the maritime trade with China, in which the Palas had been active. But the Pala dynasty declined soon after the death of Mahipala and gave way to the Sena dynasty.

The almost simultaneous decline of the three rival powers, the Pratiharas, Palas and Rashtrakutas, is not surprising. Their strengths were similar and they were dependent on well-organized armies. The rhetoric of conquest became a royal qualifier, with many inscriptions listing almost identical lesser kingdoms that are said to have been conquered. Such lists have a touch of the formulaic when they are repeated frequently. These claims can be taken seriously only when corroboratory evidence is available, to prove that they were more than a literary conceit. If the rhetoric has credence, then the constant campaigns would have required maintaining substantial armies with a subsequent pressure of taxes, particularly on the peasants. Because the sources of revenue to maintain these armies were similar, excessive pressure would produce the same damaging results in each kingdom. The continued conflict over the possession of Kanauj diverted attention from the *samantas*, and some of these local rajas succeeded in making themselves independent. Their insubordination destroyed the possibility of a single kingdom encompassing northern India with its centre at Kanauj, while invasions from the north-west and the south also contributed to prevent the creation of such a powerful state.

Kingdoms Beyond the Ganges Heartland

On the periphery of what had been the three major kingdoms there now arose smaller, independent kingdoms, some of which eventually established their power in regions more distant from the heartland. Among them were those of western India ruled by the Chaulukyas and the Vaghelas, and lesser ones by Arabs and others; the kingdoms in the mountains such as Kashmir, Nepal, and others that were smaller; Kamarupa in Assam in the north-east; the kingdoms centring on Utkala and Kalinga in the eastern part of the peninsula in Orissa; and the kingdoms ruled by Rajputs which emerged in Rajasthan, the western Ganges Plain and central India.

In the west of the subcontinent, the Arabs established small states after their advance beyond the lower Indus Plain was checked. Sind and the lower Punjab were held in the name of the Caliph through governors appointed by him. In the ninth century the Arab rulers of Multan and Mansura (in Sind) declared their independence and founded dynasties. Some aspects of the Arab conquest of Sind were described in the *Chachnama* and, apart from the political events, the most interesting comments relate to religious activities. The people of Sind at this time were said to be followers of either Brahmanism or Shramanism, and it would seem that the Buddhists and Jainas had a noticeable presence in the lower Indus Plain. Since the Arabs were anxious to encourage trade, they were open to accommodating non-Islamic religions and the latter seemed to have found them, by and large, acceptable. The practice of Buddhism continued, with *stupas* and cave monasteries attracting a lay-following in the area. Mansura and Multan also became influential centres of Shia'h and Isma'ili activity, not averse to involvements in commerce, but of course targeted by orthodox Sunni Muslims who were hostile to breakaway sects from conservative Islam. This arid area with patches of desert, now so different from the savanna forests of Harappan times, had a network of routes for camel caravans transporting merchandise. The temple to the sun in Multan is said to have been destroyed in the tenth century and converted into a mosque. But, not unexpectedly, there were confusing references to its continuing to function as a temple. Was the claim to destruction is some cases more rhetorical than real?

As a counterpart to these events, and the propagation of Islam in these areas, brahmanical sources raised the question of those with *varna* status having to live among the *mlechchhas* and participate in their practices. They particularly objected to practices that were normally prohibited, such as the ones pertaining to food, sexuality and rules of pollution, leading to the loss of *varna* status. This would of course apply more to the *dvija* or twice-born, upper castes. The *Devalasmriti* repeats what was said in earlier *Dharma-shastras*, that if a person is forced to act contrary to the norms of *varna* he could eventually reclaim his original *varna* status after performing certain expiatory rites. Concessions were obviously made in special circumstances.

The emergence of many of these kingdoms coincided with a general tendency at the time for erstwhile *samantas* to declare their independence and set themselves up as fully fledged monarchs. This tendency was also reflected in cultural life, with an increased attention to local culture in the regional and dynastic histories, and in the patronage to local cults. There was, however, also a consciousness of mainstream Sanskritic culture that was believed to provide the hallmark of quality. Courts vied with each other in attracting the best writers and poets, and invited talented craftsmen to build monumental temples. Some dynasties attained considerable prominence under particular rulers, for example, the much written about Chaulukya King, Kumarapala, ruling in Gujarat in the twelfth century. His minister was the renowned scholar, Hemachandra, said to have converted the King to Jainism by successfully performing the miracle of invoking the god Shiva to appear in person before the King. Kumarapala became something of a legend in Jaina scholarly circles, as did Hemachandra. *Samantas* that succeeded in establishing a successor dynasty sometimes sought lineage links with their erstwhile suzerains, as did the Vaghelas who succeeded the Chaulukyas.

The Himalayan foothills, with fertile valleys at lower elevations, lent themselves admirably to small kingdoms which were frequently founded by adventurers from the plains. These sites were well suited to agriculture and also had access to pastures in the uplands, with possibilities for trade in goods from Tibet and central Asia. Items for exchange were frequently carried by pastoral groups travelling with their animals as part of a circuit of transhumance. This involved a regular calendar of crossing through the passes and moving from a lower to a higher elevation in summer and back in winter. Such movement became part of what has elsewhere been called a vertical economy – trade between different elevations in mountainous areas. A number of hill states were founded in and about the ninth century. Some of these maintained their identity if not their independence until recent centuries, despite wars with each other and frequent raids by the men of the plains. States such as Champaka (Chamba), Durgara (Jammu), Kuluta (Kulu), Kumaon and Garhwal managed to remain largely outside the main areas of conflict in the northern plains. In the more distant and inhospitable mountainous terrain, the emergence of a state was narrated in the chronicles of the kingdom of Ladakh, again following the format of the *vamshavali* chronicle tradition. Ladakh was culturally close to both Tibet and Kashmir.

The creation of a state with the trappings of a kingdom was interestingly reflected in the local chronicles, for example that of Chamba. The earliest history was tied to mythology in which both local and Puranic myths feature, often interconnected. At the point when the kingdom was founded, a link was made with the ancient heroes of the Puranic genealogies and subsequent history became a narrative of the local dynasty. The transition to statehood can be recognized in a number of innovations. References were made to the opening up of adjoining valleys to agriculture through settlements and land grants to provide more resources; new castes were mentioned; a more complex administration was introduced; a centrally located capital city was established with royalty financing temples built of stone in the Nagara style, new to the hills but familiar from the plains; and there was significant patronage by the court to Puranic Hindu deities. This would have provided employment to migrant professionals such as learned brahmans and priests, artisans and masons, as well as to persons with administrative experience. These characteristics are also part of the process of states emerging in the plains, but the transition was perhaps more marked in hill areas.

Agriculture in the hills took the form of terraced fields irrigated typically by small channels that ran along the sides of the hills. But maintaining the terraces and keeping the channels clear were heavy on labour. Some amount of forced labour may have been necessary on land not owned by the cultivator, since the voluntary labour would not be forthcoming. The culture of the mountains and of the plains was initially juxtaposed but gradually, through filtration and overlap, new cultural ways were established in the mountains. However, marriage practices, rights of inheritance, rituals and myths tended to outlast other influences, often ignoring the norms of the *Dharma-shastras*. The practice of polyandry, for example, survived in some areas along the Himalayan border, due to the nature of landholdings and inheritance here.

Kashmir had come into prominence with Lalitaditya of the Karkota dynasty in the eighth century, and through gradual expansion and conquest it had come to control part of north-western India and the Punjab. Attempts to establish a foothold in the Ganges Plain were not successful, the base being too far away. The Punjab was not yet the bread basket it was to become later, but its attraction lay in its network of staging-points along routes linking the watershed and the Ganges Plain to the north-west and beyond. It continued to have close relations with Gandhara. The Shahya dynasty ruled in the north-west, acting as a bridge to central Asia and to the Turks (or the Turushkas, as they are called in Indian texts). Familiarity with the Turushka goes back to earlier times when Turkish mercenaries found employment in the armies of Kashmir. Lalitaditya, ruling Kashmir in the eighth century, took his armies briefly into the Ganges Plain, and also stopped Arab forces from overrunning the Punjab. In subsequent centuries the kings of Kashmir consolidated their position in the mountainous areas and the upper Jhelum Valley, leaving the Punjab to fend for itself. A sophisticated literary culture surfaced in Kashmir with work on Tantric Shaivism and on theories of aesthetics. Schools of philosophy continued the earlier tradition that had been founded in Buddhist centres.

Kalhana's impressive history of Kashmir, the *Rajatarangini*, was written in the twelfth century. It contains a striking description of the engineering works, supervised by the minister Suyya, that were carried out in the reign of Avantivarman of the successor dynasty to the Karkota. Landslides and soil degradation led to a great amount of rubble and stone being deposited in the Jhelum River, which impeded the flow of water. This was cleared, but to this day such impediments are a regular problem with rivers coming down from the mountains. Embankments were constructed to prevent landslides and, where possible, dams were built and the lakes that caused floods were drained. It is said that Suyya even managed to marginally divert the course of the Jhelum and Indus rivers, a shift that allowed the reclamation of land for cultivation. These were difficult engineering tasks since the rivers of Kashmir are the fast-flowing, unruly upper reaches of the rivers that come down to the plains. That Kalhana's was not an exaggerated description is evident from the subsequent economic prosperity of Kashmir. The large areas of the valley brought under cultivation were a stabilizing factor in Kashmir politics, as in other hill states, since the need to move to the fertile regions of the plains became less pressing. But it introduced problems of another nature.

The tenth century saw the regency of two famous queens who, in spite of much opposition, were determined to direct the affairs of state. In this they had to contend with a new phenomenon that was to dominate Kashmiri politics for a hundred years – the existence of bodies of troops with unshakeable political loyalties and ambitions. There were two rival groups, the Tantrins and the Ekangas, who between them made and unmade rulers in turn. Queen Sugandha used the Ekangas against the Tantrins effectively, but was unable to subordinate them and was deposed in 914. Her defeat meant almost unlimited power for the Tantrins, and none of the succeeding rulers could assert a position to counter this. Finally, the *damaras*, who were landowners of substance, were called in to destroy the power of the Tantrins. This they did with such success that the rulers of Kashmir were faced with the new problem of curbing the power of the landowners, evident from political events during the rule of Queen Didda. It was not unheard of for queens to participate as regents, as did Prabhavati Gupta in the Vakataka period, or to carry out administrative functions, as in the case of some Chalukya queens of the western Deccan. What differentiated Sugandha and Didda from the others was that their power came from their involvement in court intrigue and the politics of court factions.

The *damaras* were in origin agriculturists who, using the improvements in the valley, developed its agricultural potential and began accumulating a surplus each year that enabled them to change their status to landowners. This may explain Kalhana's advice that a king should never leave more than a year's produce in storage with the cultivators, and that whatever is produced over and above that should be taken by the state, otherwise the cultivators would use it as a base to become powerful. Kalhana was as scathing about the *damaras* as he was about the *kayastha* officers of the kingdom. He described the *damaras* as ill-mannered and uncultured. Once they had acquired some power they employed mercenaries and Rajputs from the plains to add to their strength. They also began to imitate the style of life of the *kshatriyas*, and Kalhana disapproved of some of these activities, such as their endorsing *sati*. The period from the eighth to the eleventh century in Kashmir saw the generation of considerable wealth, partly due to agricultural improvements but equally to trade connections with the north Indian Plains and with central Asia. Some of the wealth went into the building and maintaining of temples, such as the one dedicated to Martand – the sun. The accumulation of wealth, particularly in the temples, attracted the greed of Hindu kings in Kashmir during this period, some of whom looted the temples and removed the images made of precious metals. Kalhana adds that they oppressed the populace with additional taxes and the officials who carried out these orders were said to 'cause pain to the people'.

The Kabul Valley and Gandhara were ruled by a Turkish family, the Shahiyas, in the early ninth century. A brahman minister of the king usurped the throne and founded what has been called the Hindu Shahiya dynasty. He was pushed eastwards by pressure from other Afghan principalities and finally established his power in the region of Attock, near the confluence of the Indus and Kabul Rivers. The area supported a minimum of agriculture, its income coming from pastoralists traversing the area in their circuits, and from trading caravans. It was also an area that hosted a variety of religious beliefs – Buddhism, Zoroastrianism, Puranic Hinduism and, more recently, Islam, not to mention the various central Asian Shaman cults known to pervade religious activities of the region. The state became a buffer between northern India and Afghanistan. A later Hindu Shahiya ruler, Jayapala, consolidated the kingdom and made himself master of the Punjab Plain. However, this meant he had to face the armies of the ruler of Ghazni when the latter entered northern India in the eleventh century.

A kingdom in the Himalaya mountains that became an independent state was Nepal, which overthrew the hegemony of Tibet in the ninth century, commemorating it with the Nevar era equivalent to AD 878. This not only meant political freedom, but also resulted in substantial economic progress. Since Nepal was on the highway from India to Tibet, both Chinese and Tibetan trade with India passed through this area. New towns, such as Kathmandu and Patan, grew from the resulting commercial income. Lalitapura became a centre of Tantric Buddhist learning that attracted many scholars. Chronicles of the dynasties were maintained in the *vamshavali* tradition and written in Sanskrit, although the regional language was distinct. But the authority of the kings of Nepal was to be threatened by powerful landowners, more familiar from their later title of Ranas. The precarious balance between the position of the king and that of the landed magnates was a constant feature of politics in Nepal, as of many other states.

Further east, Kamarupa in Assam was a kingdom situated in the plains but in the proximity of mountains. The link it provided between eastern India and eastern Tibet and China encouraged commerce across the plains, as well as transhumance across the mountains. Rice cultivation was facilitated in the silt-laden plains of Assam that were watered by the Brahmaputra, although these were frequently subjected to extensive floods. The Varmans brought a part of the valley under their control. Harjaravarman attained eminence in the ninth century and took imperial titles, suggesting that he had become independent of the Palas. The building of embankments was a form of assistance from the state to encourage agricultural settlements, which also happened during the reign of the later Shalastambha kings. An inscription of 1205 records the killing of Turushkas, which may have been connected with Turkish attempts to annex the area. But at the same time in the thirteenth century much of Kamarupa was conquered by the Ahoms, a Shan people who came from the mountains to the south-east of Assam. It was they who finally gave the place its name, Assam being derived from Ahom. Their other contribution was the maintenance of lengthy genealogical records, the *Burunjis*, that help in the reconstruction of their history.

At the eastern end of the peninsula Orissa saw the rise of the Shailodbhava dynasty in the late eighth century, the origins of which were said to have been linked to the Pulinda people, who were generally regarded as outside caste society. That they were integrated into caste society is evident from a later king having performed an *ashvamedha* sacrifice. The Bhaumakaras, who were impressive patrons of Buddhism, were replaced through the conquest of the area by the Somavamshis in the tenth century. The subsequent conquest of Kalinga by the Gangas was an extension to their base in Andhra. The establishment of the Gajapati dynasty is associated with a high point in the regional culture of the east.

Rajputs

During the ninth and tenth centuries a number of Rajput clans became prominent as independent dynasties ruling over kingdoms. Their origins have been much debated, some arguing for their descent from central Asian migrants, perhaps the Hunas or possibly the Gurjaras, although this argument is now generally doubted.

Recent discussions of Rajput identity are related to processes of historical change characteristic of this period, particularly the widespread phenomenon of families from varied backgrounds rising to royal authority. Some traced themselves back to brahmans, presumably those who had received grants of land from existing kings. This enabled them to claim a *brahma-kshatra* status, a familiar term frequently linked to those who claimed a brahman and *kshatriya* ancestry, or who were brahmans performing *kshatriya* functions. Such dynasties had been known earlier in the peninsula. A high administrative office could also facilitate an upwardly moving status as had happened in earlier periods. Others could have been conquered forest clans, whose erstwhile chiefs managed to acquire *kshatriya* status, or at least assisted a clan to create a *kshatriya* status for itself. Yet others may have been descendants of clans that had earlier constituted the chiefdoms and oligarchies in Rajasthan, although the evidence for this remains uncertain. The association of some *kshatriyas* with groups regarded as outside caste society – what are sometimes termed 'tribal peoples' – such as the Pulindas, Bhillas, Shabaras, Meenas, Medas and Ahirs, suggests that these *kshatriyas* were helped by such groups in their rise to *kshatriya* status, or may even have had some kinship connections with them.

Subsequently their origin was linked to royal lineages that accorded them *kshatriya* status, upon which they have unfailingly insisted. In order to establish their claims to being *kshatriya* in keeping with the tradition of the *Puranas*, they were provided with genealogies that latched them on to either the Suryavamsha or solar line, or to the Chandravamsha or lunar line. They were among those who could be counted as the new *kshatriyas*, although they are not mentioned as such in the *Puranas*. These genealogical connections revived links with epic heroes as well. Thus, among the Suryavamsha or those claiming to be of the solar line, kings claimed descent from the lineage of Rama, and consequently some enemies, local or distant, were also referred to as Ravana. Dynasties in previous periods had ruled irrespective of their caste status, being accepted by virtue of their leadership qualities. But now those who ruled made a point of asserting that they were *kshatriyas*.

Bardic tradition holds that there were thirty-six Rajput founding clans, but the list varies from source to source. Among the Rajput clans, four claimed a special status. These four – the Pratiharas or Pariharas, the Chahamanas, more commonly called Chauhans, the Chaulukyas (distinct from the Deccan Chalukyas) also known as the Solankis, and the Paramaras or Pawars – claimed descent from a mythical figure who arose out of a sacrificial fire pit near Mt Abu in Rajasthan. The story – probably invented long after the rise of the Rajputs – maintained that the *rishi* Vasishtha had a *kamadhenu*, a cow that grants all one's wishes, which was stolen by another sage, Vishvamitra. Vasishtha therefore made an offering to the sacrificial fire at Mt Abu whereupon a hero sprang out of the fire, then brought the cow back to Vasishtha. In gratitude Vasishtha bestowed the name Paramara (explained as 'slayer of the enemy') on the hero, from whom the Paramara dynasty was descended. The other clans had variations on this story. Consequently these four were said to be of the *agnikula*, or descended from the fire.

Traditionally, the fire-rite had a purificatory symbolism and the insistence on the *agnikula* story is significant in view of the ambiguous origin of those involved. The rivalry of Vasishtha and Vishvamitra was a theme in many myths. In some versions, Vishvamitra was said to be a *kshatriya* attempting to become a *rishi* through asceticism, a practice more frequently associated with brahmans. Again, there was a hint of some connection between brahmans and *kshatriyas*, while to add interest to the myth Mt Abu later became important as a place sacred to the Jainas.

The four clans claiming *agnikula* origin dominated early Rajput activities. The kingdoms that they founded arose from the ruins of the older Pratihara kingdom. The new Pratiharas ruled in southern Rajasthan. The Chahamanas or Chauhans had their centre at Shakambari, south-east of Delhi, initially subject to the main Pratihara dynasty, but with branch lines arising later at Nadol, Ranthambhor, Jalor and Sanchor, all in Rajasthan. Chaulukya or Solanki power was concentrated in Gujarat and Kathiawar. The Paramaras established their control in Malwa with their capital at Dhar near Indore. They began by acknowledging the Rashtrakutas as suzerains, but broke away from them at the end of the tenth century and established their power during the reign of Bhoja Paramara in the next century.

Others, claiming to be Rajputs and descended from the solar and lunar lines, established themselves as local kings in various parts of western and central India. Among them were the Chandellas, prominent in the tenth century in Bundelkhand, with their centre at Khajuraho and their territory known as Jejakabhukti; the Guhilas of Mewar who participated in the early campaigns against the Arabs and who changed from an initial brahman identity to Suryavamsha *kshatriyas*; the Tomaras, also subject earlier to the Pratiharas, ruling in the Haryana region near Dhillika – modern Delhi – a city which they founded in 736, and who were overthrown by the Chauhans in the twelfth century. Another family, the Kalachuris of Tripuri near Jabalpur, also began as subject to the Pratiharas but acquired independence and prestige under their King, Karna, in the eleventh century.

The focus of each kingdom was the territory ruled directly by the dynasty. Branches of each dynasty, or clans claiming to be branches, proliferated in neighbouring areas. An explanation for this may lie in the distribution of land among kinsmen ruled over by branch lineages or clans, sometimes on behalf of the main dynasty. It provided a wider power base for dynastic control, but implicit in the system was also the threat of such lineages being replaced by others making the same claims. One way to consolidate clan relations was through marriage alliances, and this practice was common. From the ninth century onwards the territory was sometimes described as a notional unit of eighty-four villages, which may have been connected with tribute and tax, combined with the procedure of distribution. Fortified settlements in each unit functioned as both administrative centres and markets for local produce. The granting of land, or the acquiring of territory through a raid and its subsequent distribution, was seminal to the attaining of the required status.

The system of the branching of lineages had its own problems. Although they took the name of the main lineage, there was no certainty that they were in every case actual kinsmen. Segmentary lineage systems, as most of these were, can with some facility incorporate non-kinship-related families as a segment of the main line. The lineages do not necessarily have to be related by descent. But the main lineage and the subsidiary ones have to maintain a mutually agreed kinship. This is also suggested by the pattern that emerges on a mapping of the earlier segmentary lineages of the original Chandravamsha or lunar line, given in the *Mahabharata* and the *Vishnu Purana*. These descent lines fanned out to accommodate the many branch lines. They all claimed the same ancestry and kinship links, but the links were doubtful given the depth of the genealogy, the nature of the names and the stories told about them. Branch lines among Rajputs sometimes had variant origin myths and ancestral status, differing in location and time. The family of a high-ranking officer who had received a grant for service – preferably a grant in perpetuity – could also claim a lineage link with the ruling family, using this as an acceptable way of asserting power.

Not only was there a stronger insistence on being of the *kshatriya* caste, but an additional category of *kshatriya* status was thought necessary, that of the *rajaputra* or Rajput, claiming a filial kinship with kings. Some difference must obviously have been perceived between the two. The status was used widely, especially in areas and among people who did not have a long history of monarchy or of an agrarian economy, where claims to such status could have been awe-inspiring. Consequently, it was adopted in many parts of Rajasthan and central India. Initially, it appears that control over resources was not centralized in Rajput kingdoms. The heroic act in the *agnikula* story was not battling with demons to capture resources, but bringing back the wish-fulfilling cow for the sage. The procedures were known – grants of land, brahman settlements, agrarian revenue and trading networks, the court conforming to Sanskritic culture ways – and these had to be instituted. The pattern became especially apparent in areas which had been relatively isolated that now opened up to evolve into kingdoms.

The Creation of New Settlements

Creating new settlements or extending control over existing ones was crucial to retaining economic and political power. This included annexing territory, either of other kingdoms or of the *atavika rajas*, forest-chiefs. As always, wars and campaigns were necessary both to annex territory and to enhance income through collecting booty. Forest-chiefs were subjugated and their societies encouraged to imitate the society of the victors, supposedly through a process of osmosis but equally likely through some coercion. This involved induction into the caste system, the families of the chiefs being accorded *kshatriya* status or, if important enough, accorded a lineage connection through a marriage alliance. However, the rest of the clan generally fell into varying *shudra* statuses. Occupational changes could also have been involved if the erstwhile chiefs were drawn into administrative ranks, with the rest becoming peasants cultivating newly cleared areas, although a few became craftsmen. The identity of Rajput clans was also linked to their *kuladevis*, clan goddesses, whose origins often went back to the worship of aniconic deities. The interweaving of the many societies of a region can be observed in religious belief and practice as they evolved in relation to the forms adopted by various dynasties and centres, or as they were inducted into the Puranic religion.

The transition from *jana* to *jati* or from clan to caste, as this process has sometimes been termed, is evident from early times as a recognizable process in the creation of Indian society and culture. Given the availability of a variety of sources and the detailed information they contain, such processes become more apparent during this period. An earlier distinction differentiated the *grama* or *kshetra*, the settled area, from the *aranya* or *vana*, the unknown forest peopled by *rakshasas* or demons. When the forest became an area to be exploited, either through garnering its natural products such as timber and elephants, or by clearing and cultivation, the fear of the demon gradually diminished. This presumably brought state administration into closer contact with forest-peoples, who were or had been largely hunter-gatherers, shifting cultivators, pastoralists or horticulturalists. These were the groups that were subordinated or converted when settlers arrived searching for resources. The earlier tradition evident from inscriptions of the fifth and sixth century, where forest-chiefs – often appropriately called *vyaghraraja* or 'tiger chief' – became the founders of dynasties, continued. Some dynasties had also claimed that their founder was a brahman and that their power was established through conquering forest kingdoms. Now they had to build tanks and dam mountain streams for irrigation, maintain temples and use the services of brahmans before they could claim to be *kshatriyas*. The literature of the time occasionally showed vignettes of this change.

Setting up a royal line followed a familiar procedure. A *samanta* would rebel against his suzerain and successfully assert his independence. A *samanta* status emerged from one of various situations: conquest by a ruler who reinstalled the defeated king or chief in a tributary status; or a grant of land carrying governmental authority, which became a base for the recipient or his descendant to control a larger territory, proclaiming his new status by marrying into a family of established status; or the assertion of independence by a branch line which already had some administrative authority. Administrative office was a recognized channel to power. Tributary kings could not be shuffled, but appointment to administrative office indicated rank and this was a way of keeping the appointees within the hierarchy of the system. The feasibility of these procedures required a delicate control and adjustment over the functions of power. One aspect of this adjustment was the intricate connotation of manners and the coding of signs required by the royal court.

Large numbers of grants of land involved loss of revenue for the state. Some degree of administrative decentralization followed. Presumably compensation lay in the network of support from loyal grantees scattered across the countryside, at least until such time as the grantee broke away. In some areas grants of land meant an expansion of the agrarian base, either through intensifying agriculture in areas already under cultivation or else opening new areas to cultivation. Irrigation systems were built at the initiative of landowners and, where these were large and complex, the state could assist. It is ironic that state attention to the hydraulic machinery came together with a political control which was anything but despotic! An increase in production stimulated exchange centres and markets, which fostered trade. The grantees who settled in forested areas were often pioneers, and elsewhere they could act as the king's eye and ear. The larger temples built with a royal grant became another avenue for propagating royal authority.

The frequency of hero-stones may suggest a diffused administration where the initiative to defend a village or its cattle was left to the village. This would have varied from place to place. In Saurashtra/Kathiawar, for instance, there appears to have been a high dependence on the local hero. Where battles were fought there would of course be clusters of hero-stones commemorating dead warriors. Cattle-raids point to the continuance of pastoralism, possibly as an adjunct in areas otherwise said to be agricultural. Hero-stones and *sati* memorials became more common in parts of Rajasthan and Gujarat from the twelfth century, although many were also linked to battles. The stones were sculpted to depict the hero in a formal fashion or to depict the action in which he was killed. Stylistically, they were different from the hero-stones in the peninsula and were not always divided into panels. Some were in the shape of squat four-sided pillars, whereas others were upstanding slabs known as *paliyas* in Gujarat. The occasional camel may suggest an attack on a camel caravan of a trader. In Rajasthan, inscriptions on the stones sometimes mentioned names and some provided a date for the event. It has been suggested that such memorials may have evolved in various parts of the subcontinent from similar memorials used by people of the forest, and the same explanation is given for the menhirs, the upright stones, used by megalithic societies.

Associated with the hero-stone was the *sati* memorial. This was generally a slab containing the usual *sati* symbol of the right arm with bangles intact to indicate a continuing married state, a lime held in the palm to ward off evil and some small insignia. The sun and the moon signifying eternity were also depicted, as for the hero-stone. Intended originally as a ritual death for the *kshatriya* wife of the *kshatriya* hero dying in battle, the ritual of becoming a *sati* was later adopted by other castes as well, and received extensive sanction, ultimately leading to the deification of the *sati*. Such a deified *sati* has been worshipped since this period at a temple in Wadhwan in Saurashtra, set in a courtyard lined with *sati* memorials and hero-stones.

Hero-stones and *sati* stones were primarily memorials but they could also be symbols in aspirations for status and income, which was often the case in the peninsula. It was not unknown for families of the hero or *sati* to claim a higher *varna* status or some benefits from the ruler. The hero died in battle, or in defending the village or the herd, or in self-defence against brigands, but the *sati*'s death was a deliberate act. This of course was also a commentary on what was expected of upper-caste women in these societies. It is debatable whether such acts were always voluntary or whether they might have been encouraged because of the possibility of material gain for the surviving family. Most hero-stones have been left wherever they were set up. Some were reinstalled in the precincts of a temple, thus enhancing the status of those being memorialized, and some became the focus of worship. Temples and worship meant endowments, donations and offerings, apart from deification.

Central Asian Intervention

Northern India experienced a brief respite from aggression from across the north-western border. The impact of the Hunas had faded when they became a respectable caste in Indian society. The thrusts of the Arabs had been held back. For some time, the campaigns and battles of northern India were internal. Endless campaigns devoured the funds and energy of each dynasty, and victories were claims to status. Breaking away from a suzerain power also necessitated a demonstration of military power to maintain independence. Contact with the world outside became more limited as the obsession with local affairs increased. Politics increasingly emerged from local happenings and were chiselled by local concerns. This pattern was disturbed in the eleventh century. Of the campaigns within the subcontinent the most serious was that of Rajendra Chola along the east coast, his armies coming as far north as the Ganges. From outside the subcontinent, Mahmud of Ghazni began his raids into north-western India. Each was oblivious of the other, which is curious, given that there was far more communication of news now than there had been before, and the raids of Mahmud lasted for over two decades. Inscriptional references to places in south India, linked to trade, point to communication.

The conquest of Persia had taken the Arabs as far north as the Oxus region where, in an attempt to hold back the Turks, they established frontier posts. These settlements assisted in the conversion of the Turks to Islam, although Arab power in the area declined. Conversion was initially a slow process, since the Turks had supported Buddhism and a variety of central Asian Shamanist religions. Their conversion to Islam, and to Sunni Islam in particular, coincided with their attempts to create powerful states, legitimized by the strength of Islam in west Asia. The history of politics and religion in central Asia seems to have moved between Islam as an ideology of power among the Turks, and opposition to them from others for that reason. Gradually, the Turks succeeded in making their control dominant in what were then the eastern areas of the Islamic world. Further support for Islam came from the conversion of the trading elites in the oasis towns along the western part of the Silk Route. Islam was now playing a role similar to that of Buddhism in earlier times, although Buddhism remained a substratum religion in some areas. In addition, a few Zoroastrian communities that were exiled from Iran settled in central Asia and the borders of China, their occupation undoubtedly being trade. The arrival of Jewish traders in central Asia was also recorded. They had been pre-eminent in the

Mediterranean trade in the ninth century when they developed commercial connections with south India.

To begin with, a number of small kingdoms arose with rulers of Turkish origin. Among them was the kingdom ruled from Ghazni that acquired fame under Mahmud. A principality in Afghanistan, Ghazni became prominent in 977 when a Turkish nobleman annexed the trans-Indus region of the Shahiya kingdom, together with some territories adjoining central Asia. His son Mahmud decided to make Ghazni a formidable power in the politics of central Asia and in the Islamic world, especially in the world of eastern Islam. Mahmud's ambition was to be proclaimed the champion of Islam and in this he succeeded. For him, India was the proverbially wealthy land that had always appeared rich and attractive from the barren mountains of the Hindu Kush. Raids on Hindu temples provided him with quantities of wealth and also claims to being an iconoclast. His success in these activities needs some investigation.

Pastoral societies have frequently been significant to Indian history as adjuncts to agrarian societies, and the interaction between the two has promoted historical change. In Afghanistan, as in central Asia, political ambitions and the lure of profits from various kinds of exchange encouraged pastoralists to turn to trade, as well as transforming pastoral societies into military forces. This was a regular pattern in the central Asian intervention in northern India, which was repeated with the coming of the Turks. Centuries of trade had generated greater familiarity between the two areas and some of the earlier cultural forms shared between them, such as those associated with Buddhism, were gradually set aside with the conversion of the Turks to Islam. Nevertheless, they were not unfamiliar people.

Arab visitors to India wrote of the Pratiharas with their massive armies and the Rashtrakutas as among the great monarchs of the world. Such descriptions might have been provocative to those across the north-western borders. The politics of Afghanistan were at this time more closely allied with those of central Asia than with India, and from Mahmud's point of view incursions into India were essentially raids to gather wealth, but of little permanent significance. This made them different from the Arab campaigns that were more evidently a prelude to settlement in India, with participation in the local economy. Indian attitudes towards the Arabs and the Turks were somewhat different. The degree of hostility and accommodation were not identical. It would be worth examining the nature of the modifications that became necessary to various societies with settlements in their midst of people with different beliefs and customs, as well as the changes which the incoming migrants had to concede when they settled in various parts of India. The structures of each of these societies would have undergone some change, as they had also done with the migrants in earlier periods.

With the continuing trade between China and the Mediterranean, it was far more lucrative to hold political power in Khvarazm and Turkestan, as the Ghaznavids did for some years, than in northern India. The Ghaznavid kingdom therefore comprised parts of central Asia and Iran and was acknowledged as a power in eastern Islam. Mahmud turned with remarkable speed from raids in India to campaigns in central Asia. Apart from religious iconoclasm, the raids on Indian towns were largely for plunder aimed primarily at replenishing the Ghazni treasury.

These raids were almost an annual feature. In AD 1000 he defeated Jayapala, the Shahiya King. The following year he was campaigning in Seistan, south of Ghazni. The years 1004–6 saw repeated attacks on Multan, a town of strategic importance in the middle Indus Plain, with access to Sind. Multan was also a nodal point in the lucrative trade with the Persian Gulf and with western India. The renowned Sun temple maintained by the merchants was seen by Mahmud as a repository of wealth. For Mahmud, the mosque maintained by the wealthy Shia'h Muslims of the town was also a target for desecration, since, as an ardent Sunni Muslim, he regarded Shia'hs and Ismai'lis as heretics. Accounts of his destruction speak of the killing of 50,000 infidels and the same number of Muslim heretics, though the figures are formulaic and often repeated.

In 1008 Mahmud again attacked the Punjab and returned home with a vast amount of wealth. The following year he was involved in a conflict with the ruler of Ghur (the area between Ghazni and Herat in Afghanistan). Obviously his army was both mobile and effective, or these annual offensives in different areas would not have been successful. Careful planning of the campaigns led to the arrival of his armies in India during the harvest and well before the monsoon rains. This reduced the dependence on commissariat arrangements and enhanced the mobility of the army. Mahmud's targets were the richest temples, the looting of which would provide him with ample booty as well as making him a champion iconoclast. The destruction of temples even by Hindu rulers was not unknown, but Mahmud's was a regulated activity and inaugurated an increase in temple destruction compared to earlier times.

Temples built with royal grants, that were maintained through the income of estates and donations, served multiple functions as did religious monuments elsewhere, such as churches and mosques. The primary function of a temple was as a place for religious devotion, especially when built for a specific religious sect or deity. But frequently it performed other roles as well. It was a statement of the power of its patron, indicating the generosity of his patronage, and was intended to impress this on those who visited it. Conquest was therefore sometimes imprinted by the destruction of a temple. Thus when the Rashtrakuta King, Indra III, defeated the Pratiharas in the early tenth century, a Pratihara temple at Kalpa was torn up to establish the victory. On defeating the Chaulukyas, the Paramara King of Malwa, Subhatavarma, destroyed the temples that the Chaulukyas had built for the Jainas as well as the mosque for the Arabs. Both the Jainas and the Arabs were traders of some economic consequence, hence the royal patronage.

Temples controlled an income that included the revenue received from their lands and endowments, the wealth donated to them in gold and precious stones by wealthy donors, as well as the offerings of the many thousands of pilgrims. All this added up to a sizeable sum. Some temples invested in trade and the profits from this activity came to the temple treasury. Not surprisingly therefore they were targets for greedy kings. Kalhana writes of the kings of Kashmir of this period looting temples, and one among them, Harshadeva, even appointed a special officer to supervise this activity. Kalhana uses the epithet 'Turushka' for him! This would suggest that the destruction of temples by Hindu rulers was known and recorded, but such acts were viewed as more characteristic of the Turushkas. Mahmud's attacks would have been resented but may not have been an unfamiliar experience. This is demonstrated in the history of the Somanatha temple, subsequent to the raid by Mahmud.

Mahmud's greed for gold was insatiable, so his raids were directed to major temple towns such as Mathura, Thanesar, Kanauj and finally Somanatha. The concentration of wealth at Somanatha was renowned, so it was inevitable that Mahmud would have attacked it. Added to the desire for wealth was the religious motivation, iconoclasm being a meritorious activity among some followers of Islam. Somanatha had a large income from the taxes paid by pilgrims who visited the temple, money that was sometimes forcibly appropriated by unscrupulous local rajas, according to local inscriptions. Attempts to prevent this were a major headache to the Chaulukya administration. Arab sources refer to temples making profits on commercial investments, and Somanatha adjoined the commercially active port of Veraval. The most profitable item in this trade was the import of horses that enriched both those who imported them and those who bought them for further distribution to the hinterland. An additional reason for Mahmud's determination to attack Somanatha may have been to reduce the import of horses from Arab traders. This would have benefited the traders of Ghazni who imported horses into north-west India, a trade mentioned in inscriptional sources.

In 1026 Mahmud raided Somanatha, desecrated the temple and broke the idol. The event is described in Turko-Persian and Arab sources, some contemporary – the authors claiming to have accompanied Mahmud – and others of later times, the story being repeated continually in these histories up to the seventeenth century. The most accurate account appears to be that of Alberuni, who stated that the icon was a *lingam*, the temple was about a hundred years old and located within a fort on the edge of the sea, and that it was much venerated by sailors since Veraval had maritime connections with Zanzibar and China. But there is no unanimity about the idol in other accounts. The earlier descriptions of the event identify it with the idol of Manat, a pre-Islamic goddess of southern Arabia, whose shrine the prophet Mohammad had wanted destroyed and the idol broken; others write that it was a *lingam*; still others state that it was an anthropomorphic figure stuffed with jewels. Gradually a mythology was constructed around the temple and the idol, with alternative narratives. A thirteenth-century account from an Arab source gives yet another version, in which the temple and the icon are enveloped in further fantasy, presumably to make a greater impression on those who read the text:

Somnat – a celebrated city of India situated on the shore of the sea and washed by its waves. Among the wonders of that place was the temple in which was placed the idol called Somnat. This idol was in the middle of the temple without anything to support it from below, or to suspend it from above. It was held in the highest honour among the Hindus, and whoever beheld it floating in the air was struck with amazement, whether he was a Musulman or an infidel. The Hindus used to go on pilgrimage to it whenever there was an eclipse of the moon and would then assemble there to the number of more than a hundred thousand. They believed that the souls of men used to meet there after separation from the body and that the idol used to incorporate them at its pleasure in other bodies in accordance with their doctrine of transmigration. The ebb and flow of the tide was considered to be the worship paid to the idol by the sea. Everything most precious was brought there as offerings, and the temple was endowed with more than ten thousand villages. There is a river (the Ganges) which is held sacred, between which and Somnat the distance is two hundred *parasangs*. They used to bring the water of this river to Somnat every day and wash the temple with it. A thousand brahmans were employed in worshipping the idol and attending on the visitors, and five hundred damsels sung and danced at the door – all these were maintained upon the endowments of the temple. The edifice was built upon fifty-six pillars of teak covered with lead. The shrine of the idol was dark but was lighted by jewelled chandeliers of great value. Near it was a chain of gold weighing two hundred *maunds*. When a portion (watch) of the night closed, this chain used to be shaken like bells to rouse a fresh lot of brahmans to perform worship. When the Sultan went to wage religious war against India, he made great efforts to capture and destroy Somnat, in the hope that the Hindus would become Muhammadans. He arrived there in the middle of . . . [December AD 1025]. The Indians made a desperate resistance. They would go weeping and crying for help into the temple and then issue forth to battle and fight till all were killed. The number of slain exceeded 50,000. The king looked upon the idol with wonder and gave orders for the seizing of the spoil and the appropriation of the treasures. There were many idols of gold and silver and vessels set with jewels, all of which had been sent there by the greatest personages in India. The value of the things found in the temple and of the idols exceeded twenty thousand *dinars*. When the king asked his companions what they had to say about the marvel of the idol, and of its staying in the air without prop or support, several maintained that it was upheld by some hidden support. The king directed a person to go and feel all around and above and below it with a spear, which he did but met with no obstacle. One of the attendants then stated his opinion that the canopy was made of loadstone, and the idol of iron, and that the ingenious builder had skilfully contrived that the magnet should not exercise a greater force on any one side – hence the idol was suspended in the middle. Some coincided, others differed. Permission was obtained from the Sultan to remove some stones from the top of the canopy to settle the point. When two stones were removed from the summit the idol swerved on one side, when more were taken away it inclined still further, until at last it rested on the ground.

Al Kazwini, in H. M. Elliot and J. Dowson (eds),
The History of India as Told by its own Historians, vol. I., pp. 97 ff.

There is much fantasy in such accounts and they have to be seen in the historiographical context of the gradual change in the projection of Mahmud from an iconoclast and plunderer to the founder of Islamic rule in India – even if the latter is not quite what he was. The historiography of the raid on Somanatha has its own history. The popular view is that Mahmud's raid on Somanatha was such a trauma for the Hindus that it became seminal to the Hindu–Muslim antagonism of recent times. Yet there is no reference in contemporary or near contemporary local sources of the raid on Somanatha, barring a passing mention in a Jaina text, nor is there any discussion of what might have been a reaction, let alone a trauma among Hindus. Jaina sources describe the renovation of the temple by Kumarapala, the Chaulukya King, and the reasons for its falling into disrepair were said to be a lack of maintenance by negligent local officers and the natural decay of age.

Two centuries after the raid, in the thirteenth century, a wealthy ship-owning merchant from Hormuz in Persia, trading at Somanatha, was given permission by the Somanatha town authorities to build a mosque in the vicinity of the now renovated temple and to buy land and property for the maintenance of the mosque. He was warmly welcomed and received assistance from the Chaulukya-Vaghela administration, the local elite of *thakkuras* and *ranakas*, and the Shaiva temple priests. The latter would have been important participants in the deal since the estates of the temple were part of the transaction, together with properties from nearby temples. It would seem that Mahmud's raid on the Somanatha temple had not left a long-lasting impression and it was soon back to business as usual between temple priests, the local Vaghela administration and visiting Persian and Arab merchants. The silence about the raid in what would be called 'Hindu' texts remains unbroken, and has been commented upon by modern histori-ans. It remains an enigma as some comment would normally be expected. Interestingly, the earliest claim that the raid resulted in something akin to a trauma for the Hindus was made not in India but in Britain, during a debate in the House of Commons in 1843, when members of the British parliament stated that Mahmud's attack on Somanatha had created painful feelings and had been hurtful to the Hindus for nearly a thousand years. Subsequent to this, references began to be made to the Hindu trauma.

Mahmud's iconoclasm earned him a title from the Caliph of Baghdad and recognition as a champion of Islam. Alberuni's comment on Mahmud's raids was that they caused economic devastation in the area, quite apart from the looting of temples. Nevertheless, judging by the evidence of the history of Somanatha and its vicinity subsequent to the raid, there was an impressive bouncing back of the local authority and of the economy. Given the frequency of various campaigns, some degree of periodic destabilization was probably a familiar experience of these times.

Mahmud died in 1030 and this brought his raids to an end. He had used the loot from India to demonstrate his ability not only to establish power but also to indulge in cultural patronage, even if his activities involved acts of ruthlessness. A library was founded in central Asia with books of an impressive range, brought forcibly from other libraries in Persia, and a mosque was built at Ghazni incorporating the finest contemporary Islamic architecture. He recognized the strength of the Persian cultural tradition and wanted to nurture it at his court. The famous poet Firdausi, who wrote the *Shahnama*, an epic largely on the pre-Islamic heroes and kings of Persia, was invited to Ghazni but left because of Mahmud's niggardliness. From his campaign in Khvarazm, Mahmud brought back with him a scholar by the name of Al Beruni/Alberuni, perhaps the finest intellect of central Asia, who was ordered to spend ten years in India. His observations on Indian conditions, systems of knowledge, social norms and religion, discussed in his book, the *Tahqiq-i-Hind*, are probably the most incisive made by any visitor to India.

The importance given by historians to political events alone sometimes hides the longer-lasting activities of societies in communication with each other. Indian mathematicians, astronomers and specialists in medicine had been in residence at the court of the Caliph at Baghdad, introducing Indian numerals and the notion of the decimal, among other discoveries, to Arab science, and from there the usage travelled to Europe. Indian medical knowledge and the recovery of Greek medicine by Arab scholars gave rise to new schools of medicine. The context in which this information was exchanged was the wider philosophical discourse in various parts of the world. Raids and campaigns were therefore not only paralleled by an exchange of goods, but also by the fertilization of ideas and the communication of knowledge from one culture to another. The philosopher Ibn Sina/ Avicenna heard conversations in his family about Indian mathematics and philosophy in the early eleventh century, which stimulated his ideas in these areas. The power of the Caliphate and of orthodox Islam was challenged from time to time by the rise of dissident movements, and there was some familiarity with the intellectual discourse across continents. It has been plausibly argued that some strands of Sufi thought that arose in Persia at this time may reflect the proximity of Indian philosophical ideas.

Apart from iconoclasm and loot, another reason for Mahmud and his successors wishing to control north-western India was to capture the commerce between India and Afghanistan, Iran and central Asia. To this end, Mahmud was even willing to act contrary to some beliefs of Islam. His coins minted at Lahore sometimes carried a bilingual legend in Arabic and Sanskrit. This was the invocation at the beginning of the Qur'an, and the Sanskrit translation stated that there was only one God and Mohammad was his *avatara* – incarnation. This concept would have been unacceptable to Islamic orthodoxy that recognizes Mohammad only as the *paigambar*, messenger of Allah. Coins of his successors carried an image of Lakshmi in imitation of the coins of local rulers.

Apparently, the raids of Mahmud did not make Indian rulers sufficiently aware of the changing politics of west Asia and central Asia. The Turks in this period were viewed as part of a historical continuum, dating back to earlier times, at most a nuisance because of their raids. Confederacies were formed, drawing largely on the Rajput rulers who had been at the receiving end of the raids. Initially, some assistance was given to the Shahiya kingdom and, later, in 1043 an attempt was made to win back some of the territories lost to Ghazni. The Punjab had become the arena of claimants contesting the Ghaznavid succession and was treated as a base for raids into the Ganges Plain. The local rulers returned to their internal squabbles and a hundred years later were lulled by the strife between Ghazni and Ghur. When the second attack came at the end of the twelfth century in the form of an invasion led by Muhammad Ghuri, for all practical purposes the kingdoms of north-west India were as unprepared as they had been for meeting the raids of Mahmud of Ghazni.

Elsewhere in India local politics remained the primary concern. The Ganges Plain did not experience the disruption experienced by the Punjab, despite Mahmud's attack on Kanauj. The city was soon restored and eventually came under the control of the local Gahadavala dynasty. Bihar was ruled by the Karnatak-Kshatriya dynasty, the name suggesting a southern origin. A number of officers from various parts of the peninsula had found employment in eastern India, as evident from inscriptions of the time, and some eventually founded small kingdoms. Bengal experienced a brief efflorescence under the Senas, but eventually fell prey to the Turkish armies.

The Rajputs fought each other unceasingly in the eleventh and twelfth centuries. The possession of kingdoms was a precarious business and the competition for territory a perpetual activity. War became a part of the general code, aggravated by the public stance of male superiority characteristic of Rajput society. The Paramaras concentrated on their control over Malwa. The Chaulukyas/Solankis remained in Gujarat, centred on their capital at Anahilapattana. The Chandellas busied themselves in campaigns against the Paramaras and the Kalachuris, and the Chauhans attacked them in the twelfth century. The Guhilas were dominant in Mewar and southern Rajasthan. The Kachchhapaghatas ruled over Gwalior and the surrounding districts.

The power of the Chauhans, who had occupied the Tomara kingdom in the region of Delhi, remained reasonably constant despite severe reverses on occasion. The last of the Chauhan Kings, Prithviraja III, became a romantic hero because of the manner in which he wooed and won the daughter of the King of Kanauj. A long epic poem, the *Prithvirajaraso*, composed by the bard Chand Bardai a few centuries later narrates among other events the incidents of this Lochinvar-type story. The ingredients of the story are those typically employed in epic narrative. We are told that the daughter of the King of Kanauj was to marry. As was customary among princesses, a *svayamvara* was held, where the eligible suitors were assembled at her father's court and she was expected to choose her husband from among them. But she had set her heart on the gallant Prithviraja, who unfortunately was the enemy of her father. In order to insult Prithviraja, the King of Kanauj had not only denied him an invitation to the *svayamvara*, but had placed a statue of Prithviraja in the position of a doorkeeper at the entrance to his court. To the bewilderment of those present, the Princess of Kanauj rejected the assembled princes and instead placed a garland, indicating her choice, around the neck of the statue. Before the courtiers realized what had happened, Prithviraja, who had been hiding in the vicinity, rode away with the Princess and took her to his kingdom, where they were married. But they did not live happily ever after. Their happiness was marred by an invasion from the north-west – that of Muhammad Ghuri – for Prithviraja was defeated in battle and was later killed.

The Coming of Turkish Rule

Muhammad Ghuri entered the Indus Plain from the Gomal Pass, and was searching for a potential kingdom rather than indulging in plundering raids. By 1182 the rulers of Sind had acknowledge his suzerainty. The annexation of the upper Indus Plain and the Punjab brought revenue that could be accessed from Afghanistan.

This campaign saw Muhammad in control of Lahore and led to visions of further conquests in India. An attack was launched on the Rajput kingdoms controlling the watershed and the western Ganges Plain, now beginning to be viewed as the frontier. The Rajputs gathered together as best they could, not forgetting internal rivalries and jealousies. Prithviraja defeated Muhammad Ghuri at the first battle at Tarain, north of Delhi, in 1191. Muhammad sent for reinforcements and, in 1192, a second battle was fought at the same place. Prithviraja was defeated and the kingdom of Delhi fell to Muhammad, who pressed on and concentrated on capturing the capitals of Rajput kingdoms with the assistance of his General, Qutub-ud-din Aibak. Another General, Muhammad Bhaktiyar Khilji, moved to the east where he defeated the Sena King of Bengal. Although Muhammad was assassinated in 1206, this did not lead to the withdrawal of Turkish interests in India. Muhammad had been determined to retain his Indian possessions and his successors had equally ambitious visions of ruling in northern India.

There were many reasons for the success of the Ghuri armies. The earlier hit-and-run raids tended to act as irritants, rather than to reveal the political threat of what lay beyond the frontier. The intentions of the Ghuri conquest remained unclear for some time to Indian rulers and were probably viewed as a continuation of the earlier raids, rather than what they actually were, which was an assessment of the possibilities of establishing a Ghuri kingdom. The Ghuri armies on the Indian side of the border were in contact with troops and horse reinforcements across the border, their soldiers attracted by the possibilities of plunder. This did not give the impression of an ordered mobilization. The earlier rulers of what was eventually called the Delhi Sultanate and their followers, both aristocratic and others, were Afghans seeking a fortune and Turks from central Asia, some of whom had settled in Afghanistan. The armies with which they campaigned in India consisted of Turkish, Persian and Afghan soldiers, as well as mercenaries, some of whom were Indian. If the kings of Kashmir employed Turks as mercenaries, Mahmud of Ghazni had Indian soldiers and officers in his army, including one of his generals, and of whose fighting capabilities he thought well. Indian mercenaries in the Ghazni army were billeted in a special area of the capital and kept under constant training. The demand for mercenaries would have attracted soldiers from all over.

Reinforcements of good central Asian horses provided a better livestock for the Turkish cavalry, which was used to excellent effect in pitched battles. It is thought that Indian commanders were hesitant to exploit the tactics of a cavalry to the full, putting more faith in elephants, which were at a disadvantage when pitted against swift central Asian horses. Mounted archers were more effective when using metal stirrups that allowed the rider to comfortably stand up on them, facilitating and increasing his striking power. Indian riders knew of the use of stirrups and other equestrian technology, but perhaps the deployment of cavalry was more limited. Mounted archers could also carry a heavier mail that protected against the swords resorted to by Indian soldiers in preference to other weapons such as spears and arrows. The Turks used central Asian military tactics, emphasizing swiftness and carrying light equipment that allowed greater scope for manoeuvre. Indian armies tended to fight in solid phalanxes, relying on force to carry them through. The Turks attempted to capture forts with a strategic advantage that were often also the hub of local administration. Indian armies were therefore forced into defensive positions. Guerrilla warfare may have been one means of harassing the incoming armies, particularly when they were on the march, but this does not appear to have been used very effectively.

It is often said that the Ghaznavid and Ghurid soldiers regarded death in a war against infidels as martyrdom in the cause of Islam. But it is more likely that the real draw was the attraction of plunder, the likes of which they had not seen in campaigns in more arid lands. For Indian commanders, apart from plunder, battles incorporated the niceties of a sport with its own rules of play. Immortalizing the heroism of kings in battle, the poets and bards emphasized the rules of war and chivalry. To apply the chivalric code in minor campaigns may have relieved the tedium of war, but the campaigns against the Ghurids were of an entirely different nature and this may not have been realized initially. Notions of honour and devotion were often placed above expediency, and gradually the astrologically determined auspicious moment for attack took precedence over strategy and tactics. Inflated claims to valour, such as the hero who could defeat a thousand warriors simultaneously, began to enter the rhetoric of courtly literature.

The organization of Indian armies added to their weakness. Each army had as its permanent core the standing army, but many of the soldiers were local levies or soldiers supplied by *samantas* where this was part of the latter's obligation to the suzerain. In addition mercenaries were a visible section of the armies of these times. Such a collection of soldiers had not always been trained to fight as a consolidated army. It was possibly also the dispersed character of the army that gave it a licence to plunder indiscriminately. Villagers were harassed and looted by armies on the march, particularly if the campaign coincided with the harvesting of the crop, as it often did. For peasants and merchants, war was a nightmare that disrupted the routine of earning a livelihood. Laying waste vast tracts of inhabited and cultivated land, merely because it was part of the enemy's territory, was a proud boast attributed to Prithviraja Chauhan on defeating the Chandella ruler.

Historians have sometimes commented, perhaps more from hindsight, on why Indian rulers did not make a conjoint effort through the centuries to defend the north-western passes. Time and again invaders came through these passes, yet little was done to prevent this, the defence of the region lying arbitrarily in the hands of local rulers. It appears the construction of a series of fortifications along the passes was not thought feasible. Perhaps the need for defence was not given priority, the area being viewed as a natural frontier. Alternatively, given the mountainous terrain, the only routes for pastoralists and caravans were through the passes and it was therefore thought better to leave them open. The local kings and chiefs who controlled the passes derived an income from this trade. There would have been familiarity too with those coming across the passes and therefore a slow recognition that sometimes friendliness had turned into hostility. The effectiveness of mountains as a frontier was also thwarted by the many occasions when the Punjab was conquered from across the borders or was involved in the politics of Afghanistan and central Asia. This closeness militated against a properly focused perspective on political developments across the borderlands and in central Asia.

Invasions by outsiders are known in many parts of the world: the Huns attacking Rome, the Arabs invading Spain or the Spanish and Portuguese conquering Latin America. The potentialities of invasions were recognized only in hindsight. These invasions were mounted by alien peoples who were little known, if at all, to the societies they invaded. But the Turks had been a contiguous people, familiar from trade in horses and other commodities and from the Turkish mercenaries employed in some Indian armies. However, the historical scene in central Asia and west Asia had now changed, with new political ambitions after the rise of Islam. For the rulers of northern India to recognize this would have required an understanding of a wider range of politics beyond the areas enclosed by the immediate frontiers. This does not appear to have been an Indian concern. Indians who travelled to different parts of Asia on a variety of assignments wrote little about what they observed, remaining silent on the politics of other lands. It was almost as if the exterior landscape was irrelevant. Political interests therefore tended to be parochial. This marks a striking contrast to the world of the Chinese and the Arabs, both made aware of distant places through the detailed accounts of travellers and traders. The Arabs had a fascination for the geography of other lands and the Chinese were wary of happenings in their neighbourhood in central Asia.

Alberuni, in the opening chapter of his book, suggests other reasons for this lack of recording observations concerning the wider perception of the world, which one may or may not agree with:

The Hindus believe that there is no country but theirs, no nation like theirs, no king like theirs, no religion like theirs, no science like theirs ... They are by nature niggardly in communicating what they know, and they take the greatest possible care to withhold it from men of another caste from among their own people, still more of course from any foreigner.

E. C. Sachau (ed. and tr.), *Alberuni's India*, pp. 22–3

He has a more scathing assessment when he speaks of the ordering of knowledge:

They are in a state of utter confusion, devoid of any logical order, and in the last instance always mixed up with silly notions of the crowd ... I can only compare their mathematical and astronomical literature to a mixture of pearl shells and sour dates, or of pearls and dung, or of costly crystals and common pebbles. Both kinds of things are equal in their eyes since they cannot raise themselves to the methods of a strictly scientific deduction.

E. C. Sachau (ed. and tr.), *Alberuni's India*, p. 25

One suspects that he might have been referring here to the impressive advances in astronomy and mathematics, of which he was deeply appreciative, coupled with the travesty of this knowledge resulting from the patronage of astrology, divination and suchlike in the royal courts.

The Ghuri kingdom in Afghanistan did not long survive Muhammad's death, but the Indian part became the nucleus of a new political entity in India – the Delhi Sultanate ruled by Turkish and Afghan Sultans. Muhammad had left his Indian possessions in the care of Qutb-ud-din Aibak, who, on the death of his master, ruled the Indian provinces and founded the Mamluk or Slave Dynasty, since his career had begun as a slave. Qutb-ud-din established himself at Delhi by clearing the area of Chauhan control. He made frequent attempts to annex the neighbouring areas of Rajasthan, the importance of which was evident to him, but failed.

A Perspective of the New Politics

The coming of the Arabs, the Turks and the Afghans introduced further layers on the palimpsest of Indian ethnic identities. Today we speak of them as a collective entity, labelling them 'the Muslims', and label the hosts also collectively 'the Hindus'. But these labels are historically inaccurate, particularly for the initial centuries of Indian contact with Islam. It is historically more accurate to use the labels and terms that were current in those times. This would also convey a different impression from our perception of them today, namely, as monolithic religious communities that were uniformly identified by a single religion. Neither of these two communities had a homogeneous culture and religion. Even if defined by religious beliefs and practices, the sense of community was diverse within each category. People were more frequently identified by caste, occupation, language, region and religious sect, than by the religious labels we use today.

What we define as the Hindu community in religious terms actually consisted of a range of groups with clear internal identities as sects –

such as Vaishnava, Shaiva, Shakta or, more closely, Bhagavata, Pashupata, Kapalika and so on. The Buddhists and the Jainas were distinct even if some beliefs and practices overlapped. Hostility between the Shramanic sects and those of the Puranic religions were clear in the literature of the period, for example, in the biting satire meted out to various Shramanic sects in the famous play of Krishna Mishra, the *Prabodhachandrodaya*. Alberuni also stated unequivocally that:

Another circumstance which increased the already existing antagonism between Hindus and foreigners is that the so-called Shamaniyya [Shramanas] though they cordially hate the Brahmans, still are nearer akin to them than to others.

E. C. Sachau (ed. and tr.), *Alberuni's India*, p. 21

What we today call the Muslim community was equally differentiated between the Sunnis, Shia'hs, Ismai'lis, Sufis and Bohras, not to mention the Navayats and Mappilas of south India. The hostility of the Sunni towards the Shia'h is amply demonstrated as early as Mahmud of Ghazni's attacks on the Shia'hs. In India there were localized differences in belief and ritual, some of which continued after conversion. For well-placed individuals conversion may have been due to political ambition, but much of the large-scale conversion was through caste. A *jati* or part of it would convert, probably believing it to be a mechanism of social improvement. This meant some continuity of custom in marriage rules, inheritance and social ritual of the caste so converted. Such regulations were rooted in both the environment and traditional practice, so it took a while to adopt different normative rules after conversion to a new religion and even then there were reservations. Obviously there were some who converted out of a genuine conviction of belief, while others yielded to threats. But these were a smaller category. The larger numbers would have been the conversions of *jatis* or sections of a *jati*. The rhetoric of court chroniclers, of this or any other age, requires a careful historical assessment rather than a literal acceptance.

Reference to 'Hindu' was initially to a geographical identity and only much later did it take on a religious connotation. The clubbing together of all the castes, non-castes and sects under one label – Hindu – would have been strange to most people and even repugnant to some, since it would have made brahmans, *shudras* and untouchables equal members of a religious community of 'Hindus' who were treated on par in terms of their religious identity. This was alien to the existing religions in the subcontinent. It therefore took some time for the term 'Hindu' to enter current usage. Hindus did not use this name for themselves until about the fourteenth century, and then only sparingly.

Similarly, the Hindus did not refer to the incoming peoples invariably as 'the Muslims' or 'the Mussalmans' or 'the Mohammedans'. They were described by diverse terms that had varying origins. The Arabs were referred to in Sanskrit inscriptions as Tajiks and differentiated from the Turks who were called Turushka, a term used for people from central Asia. The choice of Tajik is not as curious as it seems since it was used earlier to differentiate Iranians from Turks and it appears that in India it was used to differentiate the Arabs from the Turks. Whereas the Arabs/Tajiks were more acceptable, perhaps because they had settled in India as traders and had held high administrative positions in some kingdoms such as that of the Rashtrakutas, the Turushkas were less so, possibly being seen largely as mercenaries and invaders to begin with. Later, Turushka and its variants became more widely used. The Turks and Afghans were also referred to as Shakas and Yavanas, the latter name being more frequent than the former. There was some confusion between Turushka and Kushana, and the Turkish Shahi rulers of the north-west claimed Kushana ancestry. This would suggest that they were viewed as representing a certain historical continuity and as linked to central Asia. Yavana, the term originally applied to the Greeks, was extended to mean those coming from the west and was used in this sense until recent times. The more generalized term *mlechchha* included a large variety of people regarded as culturally alien, and was a social marker pointing to those outside the pale of caste society. This would include kings and untouchables, irrespective of status. In a Sanskrit inscription issued by a merchant of Delhi, the Sultan was both eulogized and referred to as *mlechchha*. The term was clearly used as a social qualifier and did not imply disrespect or contempt. One is reminded of the reference to Hellenistic astronomers by Varahamihira, who stated that they were to be respected as sages, given their knowledge of astronomy, even though they were *mlechchhas*. The context of the term, therefore, is of the utmost importance in its specific uses.

The historical continuity of the labels used for those now settling in the subcontinent indicates that they were not perceived as altogether alien. The Arabs had been trading with the western coast of India since pre-Islamic times and the trade became more active in Islamic times. Over many centuries, the historical intervention of pastoralists, traders, armies and missionaries of Buddhism and later of Islam ensured continuous communication with those in the Indo-Iranian borderlands, in Afghanistan and central Asia. Hence the use of historically established names for those coming from these areas. That the Arabs, Turks and Afghans, and later the Mughals, settled in the subcontinent and married locally differentiates them from the people of later European colonial societies, who, having made their fortunes, retired to their own homelands and took their wealth with them.

The study of the subsequent period of Indian history has been conditioned by the theory of monolithic communities and a focus on the society of those in political authority. A wider study of society at the level of the majority of people suggests a different view and a more complex interweaving of social groups and their concerns. Towards the end of the first millennium AD, the fabric of Indian society was different from what it had been before: the texture of the political economy had changed, the warp and woof of religious belief and practice had been woven into varying patterns; and although the dominant culture of the Sanskritic tradition had come into its own, waiting in the wings there were forms of regional cultures.

13

Northern India: Distributive Political Economies and Regional Cultures

c. AD 800–1300

Theories of Historical Change

Historians writing a century ago recognized the post-Gupta period as different from the previous historical scene. From the perspective of colonial historiography this period was viewed as a Dark Age in contrast to the 'Golden Age' of earlier times. Thought to be characterized by small, unimportant kingdoms with much political confusion, it tended to be dismissed as something of a long hyphen between the Guptas and the Delhi Sultanate. The implicit assumption was that, in the absence of empires in India, there was political chaos. When work on regional history gained momentum it was discovered that the period was seminal to significant historical changes. Regional sources were read more avidly and the underlying similarities between the regions became noticed. The focus shifted from the dominance of the Ganges Plain to other parts of the subcontinent. Historical questions focused on the nature of these changes in form and in space.

In the last half-century this period has attracted the attention of many historians. Apart from the interest in regional history, this attention grew from the debate on whether or not the polity of these times constituted what has been called Indian feudalism. More recently there have been alternative theories seeking to explain the structure of emerging states and societies, such as the system incorporating an integrative polity or that of the segmentary state. The latter was proposed and discussed more fully in relation to south India, and initially elicited much discussion. This, however, revealed inadequacies of a kind that questioned its application, particularly to the wider history of this period.

It may be appropriate here to mention briefly the characteristics of the first two theories before proceeding with a description of the changes that occurred at this time. The counterposing of these theories has introduced varied and detailed explorations of the political economy, social changes and the historical role of religious institutions, all of which have contributed to enriching the historical investigation of this period. This has also been made possible because the range and quantity of textual and inscriptional sources are impressively larger than for pre-Gupta times.

Despite the many arguments supporting what is regarded as either a feudal society in India or a feudal mode of production, a summary may suffice. The extensive exploration of the term 'feudal' in the histories of other societies and its application to diverse contexts has resulted in variant meanings. There is generally agreement on the essentials among historians using the concept for interpreting this period of Indian history, but this does not negate degrees of difference.

The considerable evidence of royal grants of land reflects an alienation of rights to land revenue, with the more powerful political authorities investing these rights in those of lesser authority. Grants to brahmans and to officers created holdings of land or villages where the recipients had the right to collect revenue but were not required to pay tax. The grant could either be of the revenue from the land or, more commonly over time, of both the land and its revenue. In either case the grantee appropriated the surplus produced by the peasant through rent and labour taxes. The appropriation used the rights invested in the grantee and did not preclude coercion or the threat of force. The rights and obligations of the grantee in relation to those settled on the land were listed, together with the taxes and revenues which he could collect. In effect, the landed intermediary had immediate authority over the peasant. These changes are said to have coincided with a decline in urbanism and trade during this period and up to the tenth century, reflected in the excavation of urban sites. The decrease in profitable maritime trade is said to have accelerated a decline in urban centres, together with some environmental changes that may have led to a fall in agricultural production in some areas. This marginalization of trade was accompanied by a paucity of coins. It therefore became necessary to pay officials with grants of revenue from land instead of cash, which occurred more frequently after the seventh century. The number of feudatories, that is, holders of grants of land, increased, as did the hierarchy among them since they were not all of equal status. With differential access to political power there was decentralization and a parcelling of sovereignty.

It is also argued that the *Puranas* predicted a crisis in the Kali Age – the present and last cycle of time – when traditional rulers would lose their authority and be replaced by new *kshatriyas*. It was described as an age when righteous rule would be overthrown, with the lower castes taking over the functions of the upper castes, accompanied by the oppression of the people by those in authority. A general insecurity in relation to the existence of family and property was also predicted, such disorder being righted only with the coming of the last incarnation of Vishnu, the brahman Kalkin. This has been read as a reference to social changes of consequence in the centuries AD.

The argument in support of feudalism states that the movements of peasants were restricted and the grants converted the peasants who were paying tax to the state into peasants paying rent to the grantee. They were subjected to the requirements of *vishti* or forced labour/labour tax, as well as to non-customary taxes that the grantee had the right to impose. Grantees began to acquire fiscal and judicial rights that could aggravate the burden of labour, dues and demands on the peasant. There is some disagreement on whether this constituted serfdom. Villages tended to become self-sufficient and isolated from each other. There were a few instances of what have been interpreted as peasant uprisings, but the more widespread lack of these is partly attributed to the ideology of *bhakti* directing attention away from the impoverishment of material conditions. It is said these conditions roused little resentment because of the unflinching belief by many in the determinism of fate, reflected in part by the popularity of astrology.

Contractual relations in this model seem to have been limited to those between the king and the intermediary, referred to by historians as the feudatory. Underlying his loyalty to the king, the feudatory was expected to maintain armed levies, which he was in duty bound to furnish for the king's service. Disloyalty was regarded as a heinous offence. The feudatory might also be called upon to give his daughter in marriage to the king. He was expected to use the currency of his suzerain, whose name he dutifully mentioned in his inscriptions and charters. Attendance at court on certain occasions was obligatory. The use of a title and symbols of status were allowed, such as a throne, a fly-whisk, a palanquin, the riding of an elephant in state processions and being heralded by the sound of the five special musical instruments. The surplus wealth of the feudatories went into conspicuous consumption imitating the royal court, particularly in palatial homes, and in richly endowed temples.

Some of the more powerful intermediaries were permitted to grant land in their turn, without necessarily obtaining permission from the king, although a reference to the suzerain may have been made in the text of the grant. This is seen as an Indian parallel to sub-infeudation. Such feudatories often had their own sub-feudatories, thus building up a hierarchy. This had started in an earlier period where a Gupta king had Surashmichandra as his feudatory, who in turn had Matrivishnu as his sub-feudatory. It gradually became more frequent. The hierarchy was reflected in the titles taken by the feudatories, where the more exalted called themselves *mahasamanta*, *mahamandaleshvara*, and the lesser ones were the *raja*, *samanta*, *ranaka*, *thakkura* and so on. These titles were not an invention of this period as some go back to earlier centuries, but their connotations differed in a changed context. Thus *samanta*, which had earlier meant a neighbour, was now used as a general category to refer to a subordinate ruler, a chief or a grantee.

More recently there has been an attempt to analyse these changes from a different perspective and some historians have suggested what they call an integrative polity, rather than a feudal society. It is argued that the formation of states in the post-Gupta period was in itself a different process from the earlier one and therefore created a different kind of economy and society. This can be seen in various ways. Territories emerged under new names and ruling lineages were associated with territorial names rather than only with clan names. With more areas being brought under cultivation, settled societies stratified by caste were frequently in the proximity of forest societies that were not stratified by caste. Ruling groups attempted to bring the latter closer in structure to the former. In the process of mutual political dependency links were forged between the emerging kingdoms and the chiefdoms. Rather than see the change as a decentralization of power, as in feudalism, it is thought better to view it as the rise of smaller states drawing on local sources of power and emerging as centres of authority.

This may be seen as the horizontal spread of the state system where pre-state polities were transformed into states that transcended the bounds of local politics. Monarchy was established in what had been pre-state societies. The creation of centres of power involved the colonization of an area with settlements established by subordinate branch lineages of the main dynastic line, often with the entitlement of a *samanta*. The latter were ranked and therefore had varying access to the court. Their power was derived from the dynastic centre and there were rights and obligations between the two recorded in the grants. Rulers governed through an administration whose control was mitigated by the network of lineage connections and the influence these had over administrative functions.

Agriculture was expanded through the transformation of non-sedentary peoples into peasants, a change that occurred largely in peripheral areas. Networks of trade developed gradually, reflected in increased commercial taxes. The acceptance of caste society, largely determined by conversion to *jatis*, brought diverse groups into a defined system. Religious institutions also received grants and their network was parallel to that of the land assignments to the *samantas*. Sacred places played multiple roles. They were linked to political and economic interests with grants from royalty and the court, and where temples controlled the hinterland they could become the base for urban centres. Local cults were integrated into an overall structure of Hindu sects and the patrons of these included the ruling lineages. Temples that focused on these cults fulfilled a political as well as a religious function.

This theory has been applied in some detail to the creation of the status category of the Rajput and the Rajput state. Even where they claimed lineage links and created kinship networks, the Rajputs were not necessarily kin-related groups and may well have come from different backgrounds. They acquired political power over a defined territory and had access to economic resources through a shared control of land and trade. Their legitimation was assisted through grants of land to brahmans, temples and monasteries. Particular lineages became ruling elites through military resources and the support of other lineages. These retained power through ranked statuses such as *raja*, *ranaka* and *thakkura*.

This theory appears more suitable to the creation of the Rajput category and has yet to be applied more generally to the history of this period. The pattern of lineages and branch lineages was not universal. Regional variations occurred even in the granting of land: changes in terminology, in rights and obligations, with their implications, would be worth investigating both in time and space. The making of a grant could have been an attempt to maintain a balance between contesting factions. Hierarchies in ranks are likely to have been a source of disaffection. A realistic view of balancing *samantas* is evident in the theory of *mandala*, where, in a circle of kings, the one desirous of supremacy is surrounded by serried ranks of friends and enemies, and politics is connected with degrees of support and hostility within the widening circle. The concept of an integrative polity differs from that of feudalism but, like the latter, it has contributed to further exploration of the nature of societies during this period and has suggested alternative analyses.

Given the variations in organizing resources and in caste and custom, a uniform pattern of explanation presents problems. There are still many questions that require a fuller investigation. For example, the focus on agriculture would yield more specific data if differences of soil, crop patterns, agricultural technologies, types of irrigation and the nature and importance of landholdings could be introduced into the analysis of particular areas. There is little evidence, for instance, in the Punjab and the north-west generally, of a pattern of grants of land, and the dominant caste in the Punjab has been a trading caste: nor is there evidence for the creation of states based on systems of lineage connections. A comparative study with other areas would be revealing both for the north-west and for the granting of land as a system. If the pattern of caste hierarchy had regional variations, then the structure of service relationships, integral to the hierarchy, would also vary within the upper levels of society.

It has been established that the policies and activities of this period resulted in a re-ordering of society and economy. How it is to be interpreted and labelled still remains a matter of debate. What began as a study of these changes being seen as a counterpart to those taking place in Europe, and defining 'medievalism', has now taken on other dimensions. Some of these trends can be better recognized through comparisons that surface in the discussion of a feudal mode of production. Other trends become apparent through a different perspective. And above all there are variations. Variance would arise not only from the manner of structuring economic conditions of the time, but also from the intervention of caste as a system of organizing society, where enhancing the privileges of some and denying rights to others was implicit.

Despite the continuity in the forms developed during this period, the suggestion that there were two phases is worth reconsideration, although the characteristics may have differed from those originally suggested by Kosambi. The earlier phase saw the opening up of new areas, the creation of intermediaries and *kshatriyas*, with the stirring of religious practices in some ways different from the prevailing ones. The later phase saw the establishing of the new system. The change from the earlier to the later lay in the enhancement of grants of land, the revival and resurgence of commerce, increased conversion to caste and the formation of new religious sects. Each of these aspects would have modified or exaggerated the influence of the others. Thus if a decline in commerce characterizes a feudal society, then the resurgence of commerce would have changed some aspects of the feudal nature of society, and transregional trade might have interfered with inte-grative polities. Whether it is because the quantity and quality of source materials differs, it does seem that there might have been some justification for describing the earlier phase as witnessing change introduced by those in authority, but with the participation of those at the local level, whereas the later phase was characterized by the intervention of more ranks of intermediaries representing those at a local level and perhaps taking the initiative in creating a change. Whereas initially the intervention of the state led to the granting of land and a change in the economy, in the latter part of this period the initiative towards change came from the intermediaries aspiring to a higher status.

Theories of explanation have recognized that the structure of the state in post-Gupta times was different from that of pre-Gupta times. Although there were some states in areas where none had existed before, many were created from a realignment of existing administration. The state was now characterized by a distributive political economy where power, authority and resources were distributed through a chain of linkages rather than a one-to-one relationship with the state or its representatives. A major point of departure lay in the extensive grants of land that came to be seen as property, overriding the rights of others on the land. The increasing emphasis on the divinity of the king could also be viewed as expressive of his growing weakness, paralleled by the multiple centres of authority – the grantee, the tributary raja, the temple. The distribution was unequal because of the hierarchy and was expressed in tributary relations and claims to lineage connections. The insistence on *kshatriya* status points to caste statuses underlining inequality. Regional identities indicated differences, but similarities drew on the pattern of land grants requiring the intervention of the landed magnate and the suppression of the peasant, as well as on the spread of Sanskritic culture with attempts at cultural homogeneity.

Distributive Political Economies

The debate on the patterns of change has usefully introduced many themes that require closer examination, especially in the context of a multiplicity of states. Apart from grants of land to beneficiaries, the payment of salaries to officers in equivalent grants of revenue or land, rather than in cash, have been linked to the weakening of the sovereignty of the state and of a centralized bureaucratic system. This raises other questions. The explanation for introducing a system of granting land could relate to the decreasing authority of the king or, alternatively, the well-matched authority of a number of tributary rajas constantly reaching for suzerainty. Brahmans received land grants because they both legitimized the many new kings and claimed that they could avert the evil consequences of events such as eclipses – which they predicted – through performing the correct rituals as an antidote. Equally important, they were the settlers and pioneers in new lands. As landed intermediaries they became wealthy, in some cases functioning as *kshatriyas* when they established *brahma-kshatra* dynasties. Officers receiving grants of revenue from specific lands in lieu of cash salaries, may have spent more time and energy on their own estates than on the administration entrusted to them. The transference of administrative authority to the grantee would have made the grant more attractive.

A grant given for service, especially military service, could sometimes be revoked. Unfortunately there is less evidence available on the revoking of grants or reasons for doing so. To some extent this detracts from more specific information on the legal stipulations of the grant in terms of the definition and rights of property. A difference between ownership and rights of usage was recognized. Obviously not every governmental right was conceded, and therefore what was not conceded is a matter of interest. In land disputes involving a grant, the king's charter was the final authority. Where the grant could supposedly not be revoked it was stated that the grant should last as long as the moon and the sun endure, and here the right to inherit is implicit. The right to alienate may also be implied.

Other questions relate to the extension of cultivation through state action. Whereas earlier the Mauryan state settled cultivators on deserted lands or on lands newly developed for cultivation, or had such lands worked by prisoners of war, bringing the settlements under direct administrative control, this system gradually changed in the post-Mauryan period. The restructuring of the economy began with the increase in grants of land. New methods of expanding agriculture had to be found. The location of a land grant doubtless had to do with its intention: was it to reward brahmans; to intensify agriculture in areas already under cultivation; to clear forest land and start cultivation, converting the people of the forest into cultivators? Were there perhaps fewer people who could be forcibly settled on land or encouraged to settle, hence the resort to using grantees to enforce cultivation? Was there a growth in population but such that it was balanced by a growth in agricultural production, reducing the need for the peasant to migrate? Alternatively, was the possibility of migration prevented because the peasant was tied to the land through various controls, so that despite the burden of taxes in kind and in labour migration was not an easy solution?

The possibility of multiplying intermediaries at various points in the structure led to a wider diffusion of income from land. This weakened the king and placed him politically in a vulnerable position *vis-à-vis* the intermediaries, since he was dependent on their honouring their obligations. It is likely that the prosperity of intermediaries was at the expense of the peasants, with the demand from the landowner being as high as one-third in some cases. The peasants would also have had to cope with additional taxes imposed by intermediaries. These would have included cesses for the construction of irrigation works such as tanks, water-lifting devices and Persian wheels, or providing free labour on demand. Where the state constructed a major irrigation system it would initially have made demands of free labour. In the eleventh century the Paramara King Bhoj built an extensive reservoir with a dam (near Bhopal in Madhya Pradesh), which would have required a large investment of labour and possibly special taxes. That this was a normal procedure can be assumed by the specific mention in earlier records of this not being done when repairs were carried out to the dam on the Sudarshana Lake in western India.

Revenue was collected by the grantees, who were gradually empowered to carry out judicial functions and assert their authority in cases of dispute. The grantees therefore had both a political and administrative function. This did not eliminate the need for administrators controlled by the king and court, as evident from the functioning of various governments, but it could in theory reduce the number. The powers of the king's officers were specified even to the point of their not being allowed to enter the territory of some grantees. The area that was not given away in grants varied from kingdom to kingdom but was nevertheless substantial enough to constitute crown lands that were directly administered by the king.

Grants to brahmans were intended to bring religious merit to the king or to ward off an impending calamity. The grants reactivated to some extent the rural setting for Vedic practices and were often given to those who were specialists in Vedic ritual. Royal donors could claim that they were defending the norms of caste in governance, a statement that may not have been welcome in areas with a recent memory of a more egalitarian society. The brahmans performed sacrifices on behalf of the king who by accepted theory acquired one-sixth of the merit from such rituals. Kings were careful to patronize the brahmans, who in turn, to show their gratitude, composed fictitious genealogies for them to ensure their *kshatriya* status. The claim to this status even by intermediaries made them potential aspirants to kingship. Brahman landholders employed cultivators since caste laws forbade them to cultivate. Most such holdings were in fact large enough to require many tenants of various categories.

Among the *samantas* there was a premium on military achievements and heroic acts. The ideology of a warrior caste was current among those claiming *kshatriya* status. Frequent campaigns were essential to perpetuate this image and establish the reputation of military prowess. Where the desire for plunder was not in itself a sufficient excuse for war, an elaborate code of etiquette was established to justify response to the merest disparaging remark. War became a grand pageant, compared in one Chandella inscription to the performance of a Vedic sacrifice; in this kingdom villages were donated to maintain the families of those who had acquired the highest honour of death on the battlefield. This was also a means of encouraging the continuing flow of soldiers.

Village autonomy was naturally hampered by the privileges of the grantee but the relationship varied. The village headman, often a landholder, would have mediated where possible. Designations of such persons, for example *mahattaras* and *pattakilas*, have continued to the present in the *mehtas*, *mahtos*, *patels* and *patils*, some of whom retained this function until recently. There is a reference to a *thakkura* of a Chauhan village having to obtain the sanction of the village assembly to raise new dues for the village temple. But this need not have been a common practice. A smaller committee known as the *pancha-kula* – literally of five families – had some appointed members and some local representatives. They functioned as administrating committees both in towns and in rural areas, and on occasion collected the state revenue, recorded religious and secular grants, supervised the sale of goods and trade and acted as arbiters in disputes. These committees are suggestive of the institution of the *panchayat* whose membership was either of a locality or of a caste. Caste *panchayats* of professional castes carried elements of democratic functioning because the status of its members was relatively equal. Nevertheless, this was a limited practice since the wider context of caste was hierarchical. Long-established societies were habituated to accepting hierarchy, but would those freshly inducted into the caste system and more familiar with the egalitarian clan have acquiesced to the same degree?

Many issues have entered the discussion of whether or not this was feudalism. Among them are the ties of vassalage, the creation of fiefs and the existence of serfdom, all drawing from the debates on European feudalism. They assume not only an economic relationship but also the accommodation of a particular legal system. The numerical growth of *samantas* decreased the concentration of power at one central point. The grant was in a sense a contract between the king and the grantee but need not have created a condition of vassalage. In most regions grants for non-religious purposes were fewer than those for religious purposes. The grant to the brahman would not have required either homage or an oath of fidelity, both required of the European vassal, since the relationship between king and brahman was complementary. Fief has a special meaning in relation to the contract between the suzerain and the vassal, involving the kind of authority delegated over a region and a possible hereditary right which is not applicable arbitrarily to any grant of land, even for services rendered. Servile labour, however much it ties a peasant and may even prevent him from migrating, is not the same as serfdom. The latter requires a contractual relationship between the peasant and the landholder, which could include the cultivation of the latter's land. Servile labour need not always be linked to agricultural production as was serfdom. The use of the term *pida*, pain, for the taxes imposed on the peasant is different from the specific terms used earlier for taxes, such as *bali*, *bhaga*, *shulka* and *kara*. *Pida* indicates a burden, and it is interesting that it was used by those who imposed the burden. Another form of tying down the peasant was either pledging his field or his labour, imposed because of a failure to pay back a debt often arising out of rent or taxes. Bonded labour had continuity over generations.

Additional taxes would have required improvement in the use of resources, which would have involved agricultural technology and especially irrigation. There are texts that discuss soil, fertility and crops. Irrigation facilities were expanded in the form of wells, tanks and devices for lifting water. The *araghatta* was a water-wheel, but the gearing mechanism associated with the Persian wheel may have been introduced towards the latter part of this period. Land irrigated by this device was regarded as special, and the expense of constructing such a wheel may have been left to the landholder who would charge a tax on its use. A variety of people are said to have been involved in constructing irrigation tanks.

Land being an important economic asset, problems concerning the division of land and inheritance received special attention in contemporary *Dharma-shastras* and their commentaries. The texts discussed disputes over boundaries of fields, fallow and cultivated land, embankments and suchlike. An increase in such disputes might also point to a pressure on the land or even a rise in the population of some areas. The beginning of a more intensive use of land is also reflected in categories of fallow, some following one or two years. Land that had been fallow for five years was treated as having reverted to forest.

Kings and Politics

The genesis of dynasties differed. Some were built up by adventurers through raiding and conquest, others through intermediaries defying a suzerain and eventually being recognized as independent, while still others descended from recipients of grants of land or from administrators. Initially, power relations would have been determined by these origins, as well as the questions of fiscal and military agreements so essential to politics.

Almost in inverse ratio to their actual power, kings took exalted titles such as *maharajadhiraja*, *parameshvara*, *paramabhattaraka* and suchlike, which were generally embedded in eulogistic phraseology. Prithviraja III, the Chauhan King, was referred to as *bharateshvara*, 'the lord of Bharata'.

A twelfth-century ruler of Kanauj described himself as 'the most exalted, the great king of kings, the supreme lord, the king over horses, elephants and men, the sovereign of the three worlds'. Such statements were not to be taken literally as defining the geography of the kingdom, but as part of the rhetoric associated with royalty and their world of make-believe. Minor deeds were depicted as heroic acts. Flattery even of the most obvious kind became part of the courtly style, though admittedly the more intelligent rulers preferred subtler forms.

Relations between the king and the brahman, that had once included both dependency and competition, now tended to the former especially as there were tangible benefits for the brahman. Rituals intended to consecrate or empower kings were at one level aimed at balancing the competing authority between the two. Land grants enhanced the relations between patron and client: the brahman validated the king as a *kshatriya* or performed a similar act, and in return received wealth in the form of land. This carries echoes of the competition for power between the *raja* as chief and the brahman as priest that had accompanied the process of state formation in the early first millennium BC. With new states being created through a comparable but more complex process a millennium later, the potential of that relationship seems to have been revived. The analogy with the earlier system is, however, circumscribed. The wealth in earlier times had been movable and barely heritable, whereas now it was land and therefore immovable, permanent and heritable. There was also a competition over patronage among kings, where the most generous in granting land would be eulogized.

To the extent that land constituted property, it changed the politics of the balance. It allowed the brahman to appropriate the authority of the *kshatriya* and establish a ruling lineage. The branch lineages may not have been kin-related but the fiction of kinship had to be maintained, and this fiction attempted to follow the normative rules, thus adding to the emphasis on caste. In the earlier period the popularity of the Shramanic sects with their heterodox teachings probably led to more questioning of caste norms. Now, when the fiction was more apparent and the norms actually flaunted, with brahmans taking to kingship or trade, the theoretical reiteration of the norms nevertheless continued.

Kingdoms were less frequently named after founding clans than in the past and more frequently after territories. This would be expected, especially where the new state was part of an earlier kingdom or created with some additions of territory. This is suggested by the continuance of terms from earlier administrative units, such as *bhukti* and *vishaya* in the new names.

There was a re-mapping of territories based on dominance and alliances. Administrative structures are said to reflect links between territory and lineages, and although a regulated administration has been suggested it may not have been so regulated in practice. In some areas under Rajput control for instance, the territorial unit was said to be that of eighty-four villages – the *chaurasi* – and was furnished with a *garh* or fort as its nucleus. Those in authority owed allegiance to a Rajput king. Marriage alliances within Rajput families further demarcated the Rajput as a social category. At a wider level the change from clan to caste was not immediate, with those aspiring to high status restrained by having to retain their clan identity. Hence the seemingly contradictory references to brahmans and *shudras* carrying the same name, for instance, Abhira brahmans and Abhira *shudras*.

Grants of land, if of a sufficient size, were an avenue to power which reinforced the fact that political power was relatively open. Nevertheless, the argument that there was now a broader distribution of power through lineage links is perhaps not a sufficient explanation for change, since the reality of power also draws on access to resources and control of labour despite claims to divinity and other forms of legitimacy suggesting power. The nature of contractual relations between those contributing labour and others appropriating labour also have to be defined. Here perhaps the hierarchy of social relationships implicit in the listing of *jatis* would be a better clue than *varnas*, since regional differences discouraged a uniform pattern with regard to the latter. Service relationships based on caste status and the hierarchy implicit in the status would have locked in the obligations of each caste and the system would be subservient to the family that held the land. Where this prevailed the peasant was reduced to a condition of unfreedom. Migration, resorted to in the earlier period, was now difficult and wasteland could not be arbitrarily cleared and settled. Such service relationships were to be increasingly built into the structure of control of landed magnates and could extend to institutional landholders such as temples. The adoption of *varna* statuses sharpened the division between privileged castes and the rest, and between the free and the unfree.

This process marks a substantial departure in terms of differentiating between those who control the land and those who work it. On the first of these there have been many studies and differences of perception. On the second, the rights and terms relevant to the producers remain ambiguous, despite having been raised in the theory of the feudalization of Indian society. These have significance, irrespective of whether or not the grantee was a feudal lord. The nature of labour and its relations to other aspects of society and the economy have yet to be investigated in greater detail. A simple question of whether peasants had the right to present their complaints at court was mentioned, although infrequently, in the context of kings receiving complaints when travelling in rural areas. But there are folk-stories in which the peasant is anxious to do just that. This assumes that even if such an action was a distant wish in most cases, the peasant felt that he should be able to do so.

Whether the grants amounted to a decentralization of royal authority or a distribution of power to those identified as branch lineages, it involved a restructuring of the agrarian economy. The grant would have acted as a lever for extending agricultural produce not just by technical aids such as irrigation, but also through the concerned supervision of the grantee. The agricultural economy was placed in the hands of those who claimed the knowledge to improve it, namely officers of the administration and brahmans. Agriculture or even its technical supervision was not generally expected of brahmans. Nevertheless, texts dealing with agriculture, such as the *Krishiparashara* or parts of Varahamihira's *Brihatsamhita*, point to agriculture being included in their expertise. Manuals on agriculture would have been a primary requirement for brahman settlers, either to introduce cultivation or to increase the yield.

The focus on grants of land has diverted attention from pastoralism, prevalent in wooded areas and in the drier tracts. Admittedly not as significant as in the earlier period, pastoralism was nevertheless important in the interstices of agrarian areas and in some hill states. Cattle were widely used in rural areas, not only for traction of various kinds but also for providing power to work the water-wheels and mills to crush sugar cane. Pastoral clans were also among those who, like forest-tribes, were converted to castes when they became cultivators.

Grants of land promoted economic change with the sanction of the state, but through the agency of the grantee where the state was not the direct collector of revenue. Grantees had to organize the existing cultivators to their advantage or convert shifting cultivators to sedentary cultivation, adjusting their society to that of the grantee. According to the terms of the grant the state could concede administrative, fiscal and judicial rights to the grantee. These, together with the grant, became the nucleus of the authority of the grantee. The conversions to *jati* involved the creation of new castes which required some reshuffling of local caste hierarchies. The king, according to earlier texts, was to use *danda* or coercion to protect his subjects and to maintain the law. But it was now conceded that the law could vary according to *jati*, locality and occupation. The newly created *jatis* would continue to observe some of their previous customary law.

Urbanism in a New Context

In the immediate post-Gupta period commercial activity in some parts of northern India appears to have declined, even if produce from the land did not exclude other forms of economic exchange. Excavations of urban sites suggest that material culture in the Gupta period was of a lesser standard compared to the Kushana period, or that there was a desertion of some sites, although here again horizontal excavation would be more helpful in determining de-urbanization. Floods and environmental change have been given as the cause for the latter. Possible climatic changes occurred in the mid-first millennium AD, although the evidence for these is not conclusive. The Chinese Buddhist monk, Hsüan Tsang, mentioned passing through some deserted towns. Impressive monuments no longer marked the old trade routes. Declining trade in certain areas could well have been a cause. Towns became deserted when trade routes changed course and the location of markets shifted. Deserted towns have to be juxtaposed with new urban centres and such juxtaposition indicates that urban decline was not registered uniformly all over the subcontinent. Furthermore, courts were not invariably held in the capital. There were times during prolonged campaigns or tours of outlying areas when a royal court could take the form of a military camp, or was on the move, creating the impression of a deserted town.

Urban decline would have been caused by less availability of produce for exchange. This usually consisted of manufactured items or agricultural produce such as sugarcane, cotton and indigo, which also served rural markets. Trade would have shifted to other areas, with new towns replacing the older ones. Administrative centres attached to the courts of smaller kingdoms would have attracted trade and become commercial centres. Hsüan Tsang writes of Thanesar, Kanauj and Varanasi as commercial centres. The first two had earlier been administrative centres. Increased agricultural production would have required the creation of many more rural markets and while the existence of these may not have created a major commercial decline exchange of produce could have moved out of the older urban centres.

Ports and coastal towns appear to have been less affected by commercial decline, although references pick up from the ninth century. Debal in the Indus Delta, Veraval (the port for Somanatha) and Cambay in Gujarat, Thana and Sopara further south, and ports in the Ganges Delta, were mentioned. Cargoes were of goods either produced in India or brought by

Indian merchants from further east. Of the items imported, silk and porcelain came from China, while China imported cotton textiles, ivory, rhinoceros horn and a variety of precious and semi-precious stones from India. The exports westwards continued to be substantially pepper and spices, and textiles. Mention of improved technologies in the production of cotton probably register its importance to commerce. Merchants from west Asia and the eastern Mediterranean settled along the west coast, participating in the Indian trade with the west, and encroaching on the eastern trade as well. Arab merchants strove to replace Indian middlemen in the trade between India, south-east Asia and China by going directly to these places. The north Indian overland trade with central Asia met with vicissitudes owing to the movements of peoples such as the Turks and Mongols.

From the tenth century onwards, commercial exchange finds more frequent reference. Certain guilds continue to be mentioned, such as those of goldsmiths, the organizers of caravans, braziers, oil-pressers and stone-masons. These could of course have been based in the capitals of courts rather than in commercial centres. But some new items were introduced and routes seem to have changed. The most striking item was the import of horses on a large scale. A greater frequency of even small campaigns would have required more horses, which may have been accompanied by a greater dependence on the cavalry wing of the army. Metal stirrups, improved saddles and horse trappings converted the cavalry into a more formidable wing than it had been. The horse became a major item of trade, not only in the north-west but along the west coast down to south India. Indian horse-traders in the north, some of whom were brahmans, traded with merchants from the Indo-Iranian borderlands and the north-west, and doubtless with centres such as Ghazni or others further into central Asia. Commercial centres in India were often located at new sites such as Prithudaka/Pehoa in the Indo-Gangetic watershed, or others in the western Ganges Plain, and at Veraval and Cambay. New commercial centres in eastern India also became economically profitable.

Horse-dealers at Pehoa included brahmans who were defying the *Dharma-shastra* rule against brahmans living by trading in animals. Providing horses to the elite was doubtless too attractive a business proposition. The other traders involved in the commerce at Pehoa have names that seem to suggest they were non-brahmans. The management of the trade was handled by a committee. Donations were made to temples in Pehoa and Kanauj. Centres for the horse trade seem to have developed from the locations of animal fairs where horses were the prize animals. Horses were then sold in widely distributed markets. Pehoa was located at the point of entry to the Ganges Plain and was also linked to routes going south-west to Rajasthan and south to the Deccan. The latter would have cut through what had been regarded as areas of isolation. Markets along these routes also became instrumental in introducing caste society to these areas and impinged on those living in nearby forests. Bana's description in the *Harsha-charita* of a Shabara settlement in a Vindhyan forest touches on many nuances of this transition, even though it was written earlier in the seventh century.

An increase in the volume of trade was brought about by a variety of factors. The more obvious among them was the interest of Arab traders in Indian products, and in turn the interest of Indian traders in exchanges with south-east Asia. The initial Arab intention to conquer western India was probably motivated by the wish to control the hinterland of ports and trade centres, rather than merely territory. Where trade had already existed as a viable economic enterprise, as in Gujarat, there was less dependence on affluent landholders. But elsewhere, a less obvious though significant factor would have been a partial repetition of the earlier processes encouraging the evolution of towns. With the growth of the agrarian economy, through inputs by the state or by landholders, there was wealth available for investing in trade. Much of the agricultural surplus went not to those who laboured to produce it, but to those to whom the producers had to pay rent and labour taxes. Added to this were the many varieties of taxes collected from the sale or exchange of produce or from using the facilities provided, such as irrigation works, tools and mills. The existence of wealthy landholders encouraging exchange centres in rural areas led to consumer demand for locally produced items. Such a demand had already existed for necessities such as salt and metals, but now other items could be added.

This encouraged the setting up of rural exchange centres, such as the *hatta*. Some grew into towns trading in items from within the subcontinent, partly determined by the distribution of what was grown. Sugarcane, for example, required a place where the cane or molasses could be exchanged or sold, and the same applied to cotton. Places where the state administration collected its taxes and customs dues, the *mandapika*, were also potential towns. The location of temples and places of pilgrimage could encourage urbanization, such as the location of the Somanatha temple which adjoined the port of Veraval. Temples and shrines at such places were sometimes built or maintained by merchants, with those operating out of Pehoa, for instance, recorded as having made donations to the local places of worship.

Royal action could also be conducive to establishing a market. A ninth-century inscription of a Pratihara king in Rajasthan described the setting up of a market at a location near Jodhpur. Earlier occupied by the pastoral cattle-keeping Abhiras, it became the base for their looting the inhabitants of the area since it was not so accessible to policing by the administration. This was an activity frequently associated with Abhira pastoralists. The king, in a bold action, burnt their villages, took away their cattle and introduced the cultivation of sugarcane and the planting of fruit orchards in the area. The village of Rohinsakupa was converted into a market with a settlement of merchants. A Jaina temple was built and maintained by Jaina monks and merchants. An activity of a different kind that also led sometimes to the emergence of towns was associated with the court. Royal courts often preferred the sophistication of urban culture but sometimes had to make do with temporary, albeit elaborate, encampments. Some royal inscriptions were issued from temporary camps. Such locations, if visited regularly, could enter the network of urbanization. Terms for towns continued to be those used earlier – *pura*, *nagara*, *pattana*, and those of a larger size were *mahanagaras*.

Carriers of trade ranged from cattle-keepers to ship-owners. The *banjaras* were cattle-keepers who traversed various parts of the subcontinent and came to be widely used for transporting goods. Camel-herders transported goods across deserts and arid terrain. Such groups indulged in peddling and incipient trade, with occasional more complex commercial transactions. Cattle-herders also provided bullocks for carts, the most common form of transporting goods in the plains. Pack-asses were more frequent in steep, hilly areas. This was an informal arrangement compared to the professional caravans drawn by oxen, or in deserts by camels, and maintained by the *sarthavahas*. The term *shreshthi* for a merchant continued in use, as it does in the present day *setthi*. The *nauvittaka*, or its Arabic equivalent of *nakhuda*, referred to the particularly rich merchants who owned ships, pointing to the expansion of maritime trade. Some wealthy merchants of the thirteenth century, such as Vastupala and Jagadu, made their fortunes in overseas commerce and were admired for this, becoming respected members of the urban council at the Chaulukya capital at Anahilapattana. Jaina centres in western India received handsome donations from some among these merchants.

Interest on money lent, *kusida*, was handled professionally by the financier and moneylender, and was normally 15 per cent. But 25 per cent was known in the Rashtrakuta kingdom and other places. Rates varied according to the item, its method of transportation and the distance it travelled. Both compound interest and interest in kind were mentioned. Interest paid in kind could include commodities or labour. Caste considerations as applied to interest rates appear to have been regularized. Where the brahman was charged 2 per cent the *shudra* was charged 5 per cent or more on the same capital.

A paucity of coins from the seventh to the tenth century, and particularly the termination of good-quality gold coins after the Gupta period, has been cited as characteristic of a feudal economy. Whereas gold coins became less frequent in this period, the broader generalization is problematic, as there were regional variations and the intervention of monetization in various economies differed. A large variety of coins was referred to in the texts, particularly from the ninth century, although the quantity in circulation varied: *dramma, dinara, nishka, rupaka, gadyanaka, vimshatika, karshapana, gadhaiya, tanka* and so on. The mention of transactions in money would imply that coins were in use, the question being the degree of monetization. In some areas, such as the Punjab, Haryana, the north-west and Sind, the circulation of coins was common, and, interestingly, these are areas with few if any grants of land.

Indo-Sassanian coins circulated in large numbers from the fifth century onwards. *Gadhaiya* coins, although of low value, were also in circulation in post-Gupta times. From the eighth to the eleventh century, reference was made to the billon *drammas*, of mixed silver and copper, associated with the Gurjara Pratiharas, and to local issues of bimetallic or copper coins in Sind, the north-west and Kashmir. A tenth-century inscription from coastal western India referred to one gold *gadyanaka* being the tax on every ship that brought commercial goods, and this tax was to be given to the temple and its priests. Gold coins issued by the Ummayads were used in centres along the west coast. From the eleventh century onwards the bull-and-horseman billon coins were circulating in northern and western India and, to a lesser extent, some gold issues. In eastern India there were references to the widely used silver coinage of Harikela. Packets of silver- and gold-dust may also have circulated, despite being a clumsy method of exchange compared to coins. For lesser transactions copper coins were preferred and cowrie shells were normal for more localized exchange. In some cases coinage was debased.

Coins continued to be minted in the north-west and Sind, and their range of circulation would have included some other parts of north India. The Ganges heartland appears to have had a shorter supply of coins until the tenth century. The circulation of coins for the period from the seventh to the tenth century needs a more detailed regional study, focusing on mints, the weight of coins, material, design and legends. If a paucity of coins contributed to the creation of feudal conditions, then the increased use of coins after the tenth century in many parts of northern India would doubtless have brought about noticeable changes from the earlier pattern.

The Senas in eastern India introduced a cash assessment for revenue. In a thirteenth-century land-charter from western India a payment of three thousand *dramma* was required as revenue, together with various other sums in taxes. An earlier contract of a similar kind dates to the eighth century and suggests that coined metallic money was available. Gradually, gold coins were revived, with the need for high-value money in the purchase and sale of luxury commodities. Arab sources mentioned that Indian merchants bought horses for a large sum counted in *dirhams*, the money used by the Arabs. This may have been only an equivalent valuation in Arab money or else Arab high-value money may have been in use among Indian traders.

The increasing prosperity of merchants in the latter part of this period led to the acceptance of a larger presence of a commercial economy in the society of the time. Some merchants were given grants in the hope that they would revive deserted towns. Others were appointed to the *pancha-kulas* or committees that supervised the administration not only of urban centres, but also sometimes of the more important rural areas. Merchants recorded their donations in votive inscriptions and these included eulogies of the merchant's family as well as of the king. These brief genealogies are useful sources of information on social history. This was partly an attempt to establish status, but was also a way to keep track of dispersed merchant groups when commerce was no longer limited to a local area. Information on family histories and caste status were prime requirements in arranging marriages and establishing inheritance. Each keeper of a set of genealogies, whether brahman or bard, kept the record for specific families. The tradition continued even into the subsequent period of the Sultanate, evident in inscriptions found in the vicinity of Delhi. This becomes another way of articulating the importance of commerce in the polity.

There were close links between the merchants of Rajasthan and towns in western India, with the Oswals and Shrimals being mentioned in inscriptions at Mt Abu. An interesting overlap between the commercial professions and administration can be seen in persons from Jaina families employed at senior bureaucratic levels in western India. Literacy was at a premium in the Jaina tradition and their experienced handling of financial enterprises qualified them for service in the higher echelons of government. The Chaulukyas often had Jaina ministers, some of whom made greater contributions to the history of Gujarat than many of the rulers. Hemachandra was not only a scholar of extraordinary learning, but was also reputed to be an administrator of considerable ability.

At the close of this period Eurasian commercial connections, both overland and maritime, were emerging as a factor in bringing together the distant areas of the continents from the eastern Mediterranean and Byzantium to east Asia, via central Asia and the Indian Ocean. There were interconnected economic interests, commodities for exchange and competition for markets. The Arabs were moving towards controlling the maritime routes, while many others were involved in the overland trading circuits. The Indian merchant continued to play at least one traditional role – that of the middleman.

New Social Trends

A number of new groups entered the established hierarchy of castes. Perhaps the most visible were the new *kshatriya* castes. They were open to those who had acquired political authority and could claim the status through a genealogy or an appropriate marriage alliance. Other than those claiming connection with existing *kshatriya* castes, they were grantees in the category of *samantas* or chiefs that had been inducted into caste society. The new *kshatriyas* constituted an aristocracy but brought with them elements of their earlier practices that had to be adjusted, at least ostensibly, to the norms of caste society. Practices of the upper castes were imitated and the appropriate status claimed. Such claims enabled the new ruling class to enforce a hierarchy of dominance and subordination, drawing its strength from the changed land relations and the new foci of power. By the end of this period, designations such as *rauta*, *ranaka*, *thakkura* and suchlike were available to those who had received grants of land and become grantees.

Somewhat parallel to this was the even larger expansion of *shudra jatis*, through the incorporation of pastoralists and forest-peoples into caste society, often as peasant castes. Some associations of specialized craftsmen, gradually increasing with the demands of both rural markets and of urban commercial centres, also became the basis for *jati* identities. There was less reference to distinctions between *vaishyas* and *shudras*, and in some regions the *vaishya* category was virtually absent. Unlike the south, where rich peasants such as those among the *velalas* remained *shudras*, and where in the relative absence of the *kshatriya* and *vaishya* categories there was little need to seek a higher-caste status, in north India attempts were made by rich landholders to upgrade their caste to *kshatriya*. Lists of *shudra jatis* expanded so much that fresh categories had to be introduced. Apart from mixed castes, a distinction was made between the *sat*, true or pure *shudras*, and the *asat* or unclean *shudras*. The significance of this expansion of categories points not only to larger numbers being inducted, but also to some *shudra* categories moving to higher-status work, who therefore had to be differentiated from those still employed at lower levels.

Merchants consolidated their professional strength through various associations. The most familiar from earlier periods was the *shreni*, translated as 'guild'. According to one source it was a group of persons who performed the same professional work, either belonging to the same caste or to various castes. In the latter case they were doubtless related castes. The tendency would have been to prefer membership for those with *jati* connections. These associations enabled the merchants to organize their trade or crafts with some degree of autonomy. Rulers may well have accepted this, provided it did not interfere with their income from taxes on commerce, and it may even have increased the income. Influential merchants, sometimes included in the category of *mahajanas*, were appointed to various management committees, including those of temples. They were welcomed irrespective of their caste affiliation, perhaps because they made handsome donations.

Brahman castes covered a range of gradations. The most respected were the learned brahmans, the *shrotriyas*, who could have been from wealthy brahman settlements or *agraharas*. They were often named after their area of original domicile, such as Kanauj, Utkala, Gauda and Maithil. As recipients of substantial grants, they developed centres of Vedic learning and Sanskrit scholarship. Many migrated from their *agraharas* to seek employment in distant courts. Bilhana, for example, whose family migrated from Kanauj to Kashmir, travelled extensively in northern and western India before eventually settling at the Chaulukya court in the Deccan. Such employment carried grants and helped in the diffusion and establishing of Sanskritic culture. There were narrations of rivalries at these courts with Buddhist or Jaina scholars. The conversion to Jainism of Kumarapala, the Chaulukya king, asserted by Jaina authors, was contested by Shaivas. Lesser brahmans, such as those trading in horses, some categories of temple priests in small temples or village priests performing routine rites, had a lower status. Some may have dropped out from rigorous Sanskrit scholarship, while others were priests of local cults that had been incorporated into Puranic Hinduism.

Intermediate castes sometimes claimed high status. Among these were the *kayasthas*, the scribes of the administration who were responsible for writing documents and maintaining records. There was some confusion about where they should be ranked as a caste since some described them as *kshatriyas* who had fallen in status, others as descendants of a mixed-caste union of brahman and *shudra*, which would give them a low status. But contact with rulers improved their social standing and those who received grants of land and made donations became part of the elite. *Kayastha* ministers were mentioned in association with the Chandellas, Kalachuris and Gangas.

Some castes claimed origin from socially elevated ancestors but maintained that their status had been reduced through economic necessity or through a fault in the performing of a ritual. The *khatris*, an established caste of traders in northern India, claimed *kshatriya* origin in recent times, maintaining that their lowered status was purely a result of having had to work in commerce. Gurjaras, Jats and Ahirs also claimed *kshatriya* origin and conceded that they had lost this status. The emergence of new *jatis* had been a feature of caste society since its inception, but in the early agrarian communities it was probably slower since there had not been a pressure to convert non-caste groups to caste status. The restructuring of the agrarian economy in this period, the intensified mercantile activity and the dispersal of certain higher castes accelerated the process of conversion. Flexibility associated with upper-caste society did not exist for those at the lowest levels or those branded as beyond the pale of caste society. Despite some contestation of orthodox views on caste, these generally remained established among the upper castes.

Women of high status were expected to conform to patriarchal norms. Women of the lower *jatis* were often governed by the custom of the *jati*, which in some cases helped in distancing them from patriarchal pressures. Kinship patterns and gender relations would have differed between the major groups of castes and between regional practices. It is likely that in the initial stages of conversion to *jati* status, some customary practices from the previous status were retained. Gradually, however, these were either incorporated into the practices of the specific *jati*, or the proximity to caste society would have required greater conformity to existing caste rules. Thus, encouraging *kshatriya* women to become *satis* when their husbands died in battle or in a raid would have weakened support for practices such as *niyoga*, levirate, and widow remarriage. These practices, and other forms of marriage regarded as low in the normative texts, were not negated among the *shudras*. Cross-cousin marriage was known among some groups in western India, but was infrequently mentioned compared to its frequency in the south. Societies settled in the Himalayan borders continued their practice of fraternal polyandry, although such societies were more often Buddhist.

However, the imprint of the upper-caste model was clear. In the process of claiming higher status, patriarchal requirements would have been insisted upon, particularly in relation to upper-caste laws of marriage and inheritance. Groups in the process of being incorporated into caste status would all have experienced some tensions in this process of change. These groups would have included the forest-chiefs of central India, or those who assisted in the making of dynasties, such as the Bhillas who had associations with the Guhilas in Rajasthan, or the Gonds who were linked to the Chandellas. They were familiar with a relatively more egalitarian system that was also extended to women, so the need to conform to new social codes may have been a problematic transition.

Untouchables had little possibility of improving their status. They were regarded as outside the pale of caste society. Not only was their touch polluting, but even their shadow falling across the path of a brahman called for ritual ablution. They were sometimes assigned to the category of *mlechchha*, namely, those who could not be included in caste society and who differed in language and custom. Apart from the descendants of the existing untouchables, this category included tribes and peoples – sometimes of foreign origin – who were not eligible for a caste identity. How eligibility was determined remains somewhat unclear and was doubtless influenced, among other things, by the need for labour or profitable occupations. In terms of labour requirements, a permanent category of labour, bonded through both poor economic and low ritual status, was a substantial economic asset to the many dependent on this labour. The continued insistence that birth determined status ensured its permanency.

The status of untouchables was therefore immutable. In rural areas they were often the landless labour, put to any task. In urban settlements they were the scavengers who also maintained the cremation grounds, where proximity to death associated them with a high degree of ritual pollution. Therefore they had to live well away from the limits of normal habitation. Even the Buddhists and Jainas tacitly conceded associating pollution with untouchables in practice, although they otherwise argued against social distinctions determining the quality of a human being. However, other sects, such as some Tantrics and Aghoris, made a fetish of the performance of rites in cremation grounds and the breaking of caste rules, but these were not sects working towards changing the rules of social organization. Their concern was with breaking ritual taboos and orthodox rites.

Given the flux in society at some levels, existing social codes needed modification but doing so in a radical manner was avoided. The modification could take the form of commentaries on earlier *Dharma-shastras*. The more widely quoted were those of Medatithi, written in the tenth century on the highly authoritative text of Manu, and the thirteenth-century commentary of Kulluka. Such commentaries had to adjust the older norms to a changed situation of different practices. These would have been associated with the customary practice of the new *jatis* or with the rise in status of wealthy merchants and landholders. Since major changes were unacceptable within the framework of the normative texts, deviations and exceptions made earlier texts more relevant to contemporary situations.

Two systems of family law, *Dayabhaga* and *Mitakshara*, became basic to the upper castes and remained so until recent years. Both systems referred, among other things, to property held jointly by the male members of a family. According to the *Dayabhaga* system, which came to prevail in eastern India, only on the death of the father could the sons claim rights to property and partition the property. In what became the more widely prevalent *Mitakshara* system, the sons could claim this right even during the lifetime of the father. Doubtless, here too there would have been regional and caste differences. Where the system of cross-cousin marriage or matrilineal custom prevailed, the inheritance of the daughter had to be mentioned, as was sometimes done in inscriptions. In some areas, the wealth given and gifted specifically to a woman, her *stridhana*, could now include immovable property. In parts of Rajasthan and the Ganges Plain, the wives of rulers and subordinate lords received and held lands in their own right, and often the holdings were large enough to enable them to grant land to a religious beneficiary.

Learning and Literature

Among the more telling changes that emerged at this time were some new literary forms with an orientation towards historical perceptions in an attempt at capturing the past. The *Mahabharata* and the *Ramayana* constructed genealogies of the lineages presumed to be involved in the struggles narrated in the epics. These have parallels in the genealogical section of the early *Puranas*, where an attempt was made to provide the equivalent of a genealogical map of the lineages, actual and fictional, and a listing of the rulers in the dynasties up to the Guptas. But the earliest states in the Ganges Plain in the mid-first millennium BC, being the first of their kind, could not be valorized through precedents from the past.

Buddhist chronicles had had a different perspective on the past. The

Sangha as an institution was brought into juxtaposition with the state or other institutions, and their interdependence became part of the narrative. This is illustrated in the Pali chronicles from Sri Lanka, starting with the *Dipavamsa* and the *Mahavamsa* of the previous period, but continuing with others such as the *Chulavamsa* that focused on the relationship between the state and the Sangha. The chronicles of Ladakh and neighbouring areas, using the Tibetan Annals as their model, also described the establishment of Buddhism in the region often being accompanied by the emergence of a kingdom. There were some similarities between these and the chronicles in the Sanskritic tradition, but the latter had different concerns.

The formation of states in the post-Gupta period was an innovatory experience in some areas. For those forging this experience, a past was already recorded in various forms and used for validating the changes in the present. This became a signpost to authority. Drawing on the past as an indirect way of asserting authority was quickly comprehended. The section on historical succession in the *Vishnu Purana*, for instance, provided references to construct a variety of links encapsulating power that were based on the claims of contemporary rulers to connections with heroes from these genealogies. The *Puranas* referred to the creation of the new *kshatriyas* subsequent to Gupta rule. These were the kings who made a point of insisting on their upper-caste ancestry and on their duty to protect caste society. Genealogy took a linear, narrative form and dynastic change was measured in genealogical time.

The lists of dynasties in the *Puranas* petered out after the Guptas, and some post-Gupta dynasties began to write their own history. This was made available in the inscriptions issued by kings – in effect the annals of Indian history – or in the biographies of a few kings, or in the chronicles of regional kingdoms. The format of the inscriptions generally began with an evocation of the deity worshipped by the king and then proceeded to the origin myth, attempting to establish the high status of the dynasty. The earlier kings were often linked to the ancient heroes of the Puranic genealogies or the epics, which established the lineage as either solar or lunar, or occasionally an equivalent. Then followed the vignettes of the ancestors and a much fuller treatment of the reigning king.

The inscriptions incorporating land grants covered much the same ground to start with, including a list, sometimes rhetorical, of the king's many conquests and his upholding of caste society. This near formulaic section was followed by the practical and legal details of the grant: the origins of the grantee, his qualifications and achievements, that which was granted, the rights and obligations involved, tax exemptions if any and the dues and rents and other taxes he was permitted to collect. The text concluded with the list of witnesses who were often officials of the government, the names of those who composed and engraved the grant and finally a curse on anyone attempting to revoke the grant – if it was a grant not to be revoked. The charters were legal documents that had to be precise, whether engraved on stone and located in a temple or other monument, or engraved on copper plates.

Parallel to the inscriptions were some of the biographies or *charitas* that were eulogies of the kings. These need some decoding to understand their intention. The focus was often on a particular matter, crucial to the acquiring of power, which was expanded into a text. Bana's *Harsha-charita* had described Harsha's accession, which may have involved a usurpation of the throne and, if so, then a contravening of primogeniture. Bilhana's *Vikramankadeva-charita* explained why the king was advised by no less than Shiva himself to replace his reigning elder brother. Sandhyakara-nandin's *Rama-charita* centred his biography of the Pala King Ramapala on the revolt by the Kaivartas and his successful reassertion of power. In some biographies and inscriptions the king was described as an incarnation of Shiva or Vishnu, or at least as receiving instructions directly from the deity. This was yet another form of validating kingship. As a unit of time, the fragment of the lifetime could be extracted from cyclic cosmology, and to that extent it incorporated the more secular linear form.

Expanded versions of the format used in the inscriptions were paralleled in chronicles such as the *Rajatarangini*, the history of Kashmir, or the much shorter one of Chamba, as well as those of kingdoms in Nepal and Gujarat and others from the peninsula. But they provide more detailed histories of the rulers and attempt to present the dynasties and the region in an accessible fashion. They formed a category known as the *vamshavalis* and their theme was the history of a monastery, or a dynasty or a region. The presumed history of a temple, a sect or a place of pilgrimage was woven into myths and practices that were narrated in the *mahatmyas* and the *sthala-puranas*. The *Rajatarangini* is exceptional in the fact that Kalhana did search for reliable evidence on the past from a variety of sources, so his narrative is infused with events and their explanations, many of which are historically insightful. It is undoubtedly an unusual text, even if rooted in the *vamshavali* tradition, and his extraordinary sense of history may have evolved from a familiarity with Buddhist writing.

A characteristic of the inscriptions and some of the text is that they were dated in eras, the *samvat*. These were often a continuation from an earlier period, such as the Vikrama era of 58 BC, the Shaka era of AD 78 or the

Harsha era of 606. Sometimes they were started by contemporary kings, such as the Vikrama Chalukya era of 1075, or else arose from wider usage such as the Lakshmana era of 1119. The starting of eras became a sign of status, with the era sometimes named after the king or the dynasty. Calculations for starting an era could have been based on local oral and calendrical traditions, or on observations in astronomy. The frequent use of genealogies, dynasties, eras and chronicles was an indication of comprehending the historical importance of linear time. This was immediate, manageable time, largely dictated by human activities, and was distinctly different from the large cycles that went into the making of the time-cycle of the universe. The use of linear time within the cycle creates a fascinating intersection of cyclic and linear time. The intersection is apparent from the fact that the genealogies and dynastic lists were in linear time but were eventually enveloped in the time-cycle of cosmology.

Grants of land provided foundations for nuclei of brahmanical learning. The widespread distribution of these centres required texts and training that were met through the increasing numbers of *agraharas* and *mathas*. This encouraged the growth of lively locations for discourse, parallel to the monastic institutions of the Buddhists and Jainas. The network of brahmanical and heterodox learning expressed in Sanskrit gradually established dialogue between various schools. This led to some merging, although there were also accusations of borrowing ideas. Some were seen as brahmanical contestations of the Buddhist critique of Vedic thought. From this perspective there was much intellectual activity, although it may have been limited to the learned few. Of the various philosophical theories, Vedanta was gradually coming to the forefront alongside the teachings of Mimamsa and Nyaya.

There had been an extensive tradition of analytical grammars in Sanskrit. The interpretation of a word in a system of ideas often required grammatical explanation, which encouraged further interpretations and counter-interpretations. The dialectics of these reveal methods of enquiry. Grammar and etymology were essentially rational enquiries and this was conceded by both the orthodox and the heterodox. Both were now using the same language, which would have heightened their contributions to systems of knowledge.

The brahmanical endorsement of preserving texts continued, especially the Vedic corpus through the oral tradition, but was accompanied by a dependence on literacy. Sanskrit was the language of elite discourse and of literature. But in its more popular forms it carried elements of the local Prakrits. The latter are of linguistic interest. Although their use in creative literature was declining, they nevertheless fostered the emergence of Apa-brahmsha in some areas, and eventually some regional languages. The last of the major works in the older tradition of writing in Prakrit included the *Setubandha*, narrating the invasion of Lanka by Rama, Vakpati's *Gauda-vaho*, a biography of Yashovarman ruling in Kanauj, and Rajashekara's play, *Karpuramanjari*. Apabrahmsha, or 'falling away', was a form of Prakrit believed to have evolved in western India. When its speakers moved to more central locations they took the language with them. The Prakrit of Jaina writers sometimes had traces of Apabrahmsha forms and these created a link between the older and newer languages, especially in Gujarati and Maharashtri. Gujarati folk-poetry, particularly that depicting the loves of Krishna, became the nucleus of early Gujarati. Bengali, Assamese, Oriya and some Hindi dialects evolved at a later date from the Prakrits. The new religious sects helped accelerate the growth of regional languages, their compositions being in the language commonly used.

The translation of Sanskrit works into the regional languages was usually an adaptation, incorporating much of regional culture rather than invariably being literal. Narratives familiar from the epics were a constant source for themes to be elaborated upon and sometimes substantially altered in the new literature. Confidence in the regional language is apparent when inscriptions use it alongside Sanskrit, or when the Sanskrit used carries recognizable elements of the regional language. This would point to some bilingualism. Even if Sanskrit was the dominant language, it could not exclude the local linguistic idiom at court or elsewhere. Regional languages did not surface overnight. These were substratum languages spoken by many. When social groups using these languages rose in status, the status of their language also rose. Identities were gradually created out of multiple expressions in literature, the arts, intellectual discourse and daily functioning.

Migrant brahmans might have found it more expedient to be bilingual, especially in the peninsula. Or was the world of courtly literature trans-regional but limited to using Sanskrit? Further diversification would have followed from the recognition of the multiplicity of languages identified by location. The *Natya-shastra* listed such languages. The diversification was perceived in part as the function of language. Where the courts of new kingdoms responded to Sanskrit, the larger spectrum of society gradually began to respond to other languages. When chronicles of temples and dynasties were written in the regional language, these became signals of different cultural norms. The new languages often became the carriers of new ideas.

Kings were said to be authors of significant literary or scholarly works.

The training of future kings would have involved some intellectual expertise, but when literary forms became the mark of high culture it would be expected that they would be attributed to reigning kings, even if this were not the fashion earlier. Sanskrit was largely taught in institutions attached to temples, in *mathas* and monasteries, but princes of the royal family would have had special tutors.

Although the older system of training in guilds as apprentices to artisans continued for professionals, a number of technical books were written in Sanskrit on subjects such as agriculture, architecture, medicine and the veterinary sciences, pertaining especially to horses and elephants. This would suggest collaboration between those knowing Sanskrit and specialists in the profession. There was little embarrassment about scholars writing on seemingly mundane subjects, since some of these had become germane both to handling economic resources and kindling curiosity about knowledge and its applications. In each case the subjects treated pertained to practical knowledge for current requirements, such as temple-building or the care and maintenance of animals crucial to the army. Commentaries on earlier texts were another method of updating knowledge.

In studies of medicine the tendency was to write commentaries, for example those of Vagabhatta and Chakrapanidatta on Charaka. References to empirical knowledge in these areas were less common. Where experiments were made practical results ensued, such as the use of iron and quicksilver in medicine. The interest in magic among votaries of Tantric sects led to some experiments with chemicals and metals in particular. The Tantrics claimed that the taking of mercury in combination with certain other chemicals could prolong life. They must also have taken part in alchemical experiments, which became popular particularly during the latter part of this period.

Interest in astronomy was encouraged. At a scholarly level this was linked to advanced work in mathematics, which continued the studies of Aryabhatta and his successors. The study of numbers led to algebra and initiated aspects of the exact sciences. Algebra remained a significant contribution to mathematics and was a source of great interest to Arab mathematicians as had been medicine and astronomy earlier. The Arab interest in Indian sciences continued with some ideas being taken by them to Europe. Among the more brilliant mathematicians was Bhaskaracharya (not to be confused with the earlier Bhaskara), whose mathematical problems were sometimes set in unusual contexts. A problem from his famous work, the *Lilavati*, was set out as follows:

Whilst making love a necklace broke
A row of pearls mislaid.
One-sixth fell on the floor
One-fifth fell on the bed
The woman saved a third
One-tenth were caught by her lover.
If six pearls remained on the string
How many pearls were there altogether?

Quoted in Georges Ifrah,
The Universal History of Numbers
(London, 1998), p. 431

The presence of scholars from others parts of Asia and the subcontinent probably encouraged a more catholic outlook in the Buddhist monasteries compared to the *mathas*. Such monasteries survived mainly in eastern India. Nalanda was perhaps the best known, but the attack by the Turks virtually closed it. Jaina centres of education were closer in spirit to the Buddhist than the brahmanical, and these were concentrated in Gujarat, Rajasthan and, to a more limited extent, in Karnataka.

Both Buddhist and Jaina centres of learning were now using Sanskrit quite extensively. The Jainas were prolific in the writing of biographies, chronicles and narratives of kings and courts, in addition to texts on religion. Keeping track of the activities of various Jaina sects and their teachings gave some historical flavour to their narratives, as it had done earlier in the Buddhist tradition. Authors such as Hemachandra in the twelfth century, and Merutunga in the fourteenth century, contributed substantially to this genre of writing, and the Jaina tradition paralleled the concerns of the Buddhist tradition in many ways. The *Dvayashraya-kavya* was a fine example of sophisticated scholarship combining grammatical exegesis with some history, and the *Parishishtaparvan* and *Prabandhachintamani* drew on the *prabandha* or chronicle tradition. The writing of biographies and hagiographies included works on the life and activities of Mahavira, such as the *Mahavira-charita*. An interesting aspect of Jaina literature was the continuation of narratives about the story of Rama from the Jaina perspective. Texts, both by Jaina authors and others, often deviated to a lesser or a greater extent from the established versions, including the *Ramayana* of Valmiki. Other traditions drew upon the patriarchal and orthodox versions of the story, and changes had included Sita being eventually sent once again into exile; or a *shudra* being killed because he had dared to practise the austerities and rites permitted only to the upper castes.

The Jaina insistence on literacy required that texts be written, maintained and preserved as part of the *bhandara* or treasury of the Jaina temple. These developed into impressive libraries of manuscripts and remain so to this day. Texts were frequently written on palm leaves, but could also be on *bhurjapatra* or birchbark. The strips were written upon, and held together by cord passed through a hole in the strip. Wooden covers made the manuscript more secure and were occasionally painted in the current style. Specially prepared cloth could also be used, but generally only for a few purposes. Paper was a later, borrowed innovation. The scripts and styles of writing were still derived from the earlier *brahmi* script, although this had evolved into new forms, such as the *sharada* script, that were closer to the later *Devanagari*.

Poetry and prose romances were often embellishments of themes familiar from epic and Puranic legends, and the narrative aspect could be subordinated to the linguistic. Prosody and the technicalities of composition were studied in some detail. Anandavardhana and Abhinavagupta explored some of the ideas first mooted in the *Bharata Natya-shastra*, such as the suggestive meaning and sound of words, and the place of poetry in drama. Writers and poets were welcome at the new courts, evoking the court establishments of earlier times. An exception to the romantic courtly style was the eleventh-century anthology of prose stories, the *Kathasaritsagara* (*The Ocean of the Stream of Stories*), by Somadeva, with its mix of folk and courtly themes, some of which suggest commentaries on travels to distant places.

Drama, patronized by various courts, retained the individuality of earlier plays. A sharp edge to the dialogue was given by the religious sectarian rivalry that entered the better-known plays, such as Rajashekhara's *Karpura-manjari* and Krishna Mishra's *Prabodha-chandrodaya*. Satire was directed at Buddhist or Jaina monks and some Shaiva sects were pilloried for their anti-social behaviour. Occasional Shaiva ritual practices were regarded as abhorrent, a critique also extended to practices among some Kaula and Tantric sects. The new cults were probably discussed at court as much as among ordinary people.

Lyric poetry had a more personal appeal, although often couched in sophisticated form. Perhaps the most spontaneous was the outburst of erotic poetry, characteristic of this period, with a possible ancestry in the earlier single-stanza poems of Bhartrihari. Erotic mysticism, expressing the relationship between the individual and his deity, seems to have caught the imagination of people. Jayadeva's *Gita Govinda*, written in the twelfth century, describes the love of Krishna for Radha, the lyrical quality of the poetry being virtually unsurpassed. Bilhana, in his *Chaurapanchashika*, describes the love between a princess and a man who has broken into the palace, a theme where the erotic is inevitable.

Articulation of the erotic is evident in poetry and temple sculpture, perhaps released by the rituals and ideas current in Tantric belief and practice which were being assimilated among the elite. Nineteenth-century colonial authors wrote about it as the depravity of taste, the pandering to the sensuous and the degradation of morals in India – a view emerging largely out of Victorian definitions of morality. Possibly the absence of the imprint of 'original sin' may have encouraged a freer treatment of the erotic in India. The representation of erotic themes is striking, whether in the *Gita Govinda* or in the sculptures at Khajuraho. Some are sensitively rendered, others are more audacious. In some other societies elsewhere the expression of these were suppressed or sublimated, but in segments of Indian society they were a part of aesthetic expression. This may also have been a way of challenging social conventions.

Monuments and their Historical Role

Regional variation was not only expressed in the emergence of new languages, but was also visible in styles of architecture and in art. Temples grew in size from small places of worship to impressive, monumental structures, built in almost every region. The latter were built at times when, according to the chronicles of the Turkish rulers, raids on temples by the Turks were becoming more frequent. Curiously, there is little reference to such raids nor much concern that the temples being built should be specially protected.

The overall architectural requirements and their ground-plans evolved from the earlier temples. The flat-roofed forms had acquired a *shikhara* or central tower over the main shrine and now there were smaller *shikharas* over subsidiary shrines as well, sometimes adjoining the main shrine. The central tower was tall, often tapering slightly in a convex shape. This altered the elevation and provided scope for new styles and decorative features in the Nagara or north Indian style. But this did not exclude regional variation in the design of the elevation. The north Indian temples were also centres of civic and corporate life although the area enclosed by most was less than that of their southern counterparts. However, the component parts were the same. The *garbha-griha* was where the main image was placed and the *shikhara* was built over it. This location was approached through the *mandapas* – the halls or antechambers – some with open spaces, creating a play of light and shadows, and were used for various occasions.

The small, early temples were essentially places of worship, and were experimenting with new aesthetic forms. Temples of the later period were considerably larger and were the locations for major ceremonies of royal initiation and legitimation, linking the icon, the deity and the king. Such state spectacles required space. Sculptured panels often depicted state occasions such as the consecration of the king, and this was again the encapsulation of a sense of power. The earlier, smaller temples tended to fall into disrepair and only some were renovated. The later, larger ones were rich and therefore more frequently renovated, although their wealth made them potential targets for looting.

The Salt Range in the north-west was the site of temples rebuilt by the Hindu Shahiyas in the ninth and tenth centuries, such as Malot, their unusual architecture hinting at an almost Romanesque or even Baroque style in their fluted columns and decorative features. These could have evolved from earlier Gandhara forms and from the temples in Kashmir. The small Ambamata temple at Jagat (Rajasthan) is exquisitely proportioned. The early Shiva temple at Eklingji near Udaipur is plainer and housed the deity of the rulers of Mewar. The ninth-century Harshadmata temple at Abaneri in Rajasthan is among those that had fallen into disrepair, but despite this the sculpture is of an impressive quality. The Maladevi temple at Gyaraspur in Madhya Pradesh commands a view of the countryside from its location halfway up a hill, with an unusual form that is partly structural and partly rock-cut. The Mukteshvara and Gauri temples at Bhuvaneshwar in Orissa are also of this period. The temple to Surya – the Sun god – at Osian in Rajasthan points to the transition from early to late. This is also true of the Sun temple at Martand in Kashmir, which although of an earlier date than the one at Modhera in Gujarat, was equally renowned. During this period the construction of temples also began in the hills in Kumaon and Garhwal.

Among the temples of the later period, the Jaina temples at Mt Abu, built in white marble by Vastupala and Tejapala, ministers to the Chaulukyas, are representative of Jaina architecture in western India. They are richly adorned with sculpture, which, though profuse, is subsidiary to the architecture. The temples at Khajuraho – Lakshmana and Kandariya Mahadeo – are among the best examples of the Bundelkhand group in central India, and these too are rich in sculpture. They display a balance in size and form that makes of each an aesthetically remarkable structure. The erotic sculpture at Khajuraho, as at Konarak in Orissa, and the eagerness of visitors to see it and guides to show it, often diverts attention from the impressive qualities of both architecture and sculpture. Among the more dramatic structures is the unfinished Shaiva temple near Bhopal, started by the Paramara King Bhoja in the eleventh century. Engraved sketches of some parts of the temple-plans are visible near by, also the ramp used for transporting large stones. The temples of Orissa, particularly the Lingaraja at Bhuvaneshwar and the Sun temple at Konarak, are monumental. The Jagannath temple at Puri in Orissa, built in the twelfth century, gradually became even more monumental. The greater use of erotic sculpture was associated with fertility cults and with some Tantric concepts. Closer to the Shakta cults and contemporary with the earlier temples were the Yogini temples, sometimes in the vicinity of other temples as at Khajuraho and sometimes as centres on their own as at Hirapur in Orissa. Yogini temples tend to be clustered in central India.

Characteristic of Gujarat and parts of Rajasthan were the *vav* – the unique step-wells. A well of substantial size whose surface was located at a considerable depth was reached by flights of steps and enclosed by basement galleries. These were decorated with icons and scenes from mythology as in the Queen's step-well at Patan. The *vav* was a structure hewn out of the earth that went down, sometimes many storeys, instead of being built up. Such step-wells in their simpler forms were used for supplying water to places on the edge of the desert and also provided cool spaces during the heat of summer. Some were used for irrigating land, presumably in areas where the water table was low.

The construction of temples was supervised by the *sutradharas*. Manuals on construction – the *shilpa-shastras* – were now being used where large temples were constructed. Craftsmen associated with the building profession – carpenters, masons, stonecutters, sculptors – had a low status in the social codes and were often included as mixed castes. The question then is, who wrote the manuals? If the *sutradharas* were formally trained in Sanskrit this would have raised the status of their otherwise technical and professional education. Or were the manuals written in conjunction with brahmans? The need for manuals became apparent when every independent dynasty declared its presence through various activities, of which building stone temples in a recognized style would have been one. To follow the established norms of temple building required the supervision of a *sutradhara* and a manual. *Sutradharas* were being named in inscriptions, such as the references to Kokasa, and they were associated with particular temples. However, it is not clear whether they travelled between courts or whether each body of architects and builders was attached to one court. The formalization of architecture in a text disseminated a style and

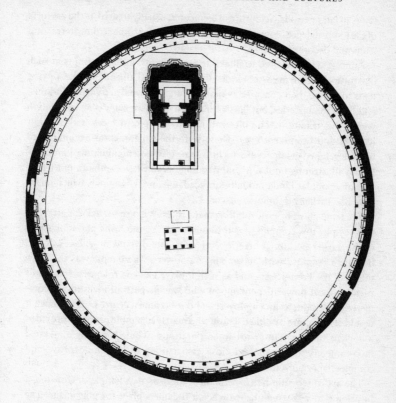

7. Circular Devi temple: plan

way of building, but it might also have acted as a check on experimentation.

As in earlier times, sculpture reflected the impact of regional styles. Eastern India produced a distinctive sculpture in stone and metal. The stone, dark grey or black, shone with a metallic lustre when polished. Buddhist icons at Nalanda set the standard and Pala patronage also extended to the sculpting of icons of Puranic Hinduism. Although used in other parts of north India, the choice of bronze as a medium for sculpture was put to particularly effective use in eastern India, Kashmir and Nepal, even though it did not attain the aesthetic brilliance of Chola bronze sculpture. The Indian contribution to the fine arts was primarily in sculpture. Had it preserved an independent form it might have continued to evolve its own style, but when reduced to architectural embellishment it declined aesthetically as did temple styles in later periods. Sculpture in terracotta, usually treated as the art form of the less privileged, continued to be the medium for some striking terracotta icons and decorative friezes.

Painting was now used to illustrate manuscripts. Initial attempts at such illustrations began in eastern India, Gujarat, Rajasthan and Nepal. Copying texts to ensure their constant availability was a normal activity in Buddhist and Jaina monasteries, but illustrating such manuscripts was an innovation within this tradition. The illustrations often depicted faces with angular features and prominent eyes. These were the experimental beginnings of what developed in later centuries into a fine tradition of miniature paintings, largely illustrating books. Mural painting became less common, but paintings of a popular kind gradually surfaced in painted hangings, which might have had earlier beginnings.

The temple was by now fulfilling many roles. Where a *matha* was attached to a temple, this complex was the counterpart to the *stupa* and monastery of the earlier period. Where it received grants of land or villages, it too became a landlord with accompanying powers. The temple was the institution of the Puranic sect and as such it played a civic role: as a symbol of royal or local power depending on who was its patron; investing in commerce and credit; as an employer; and if it became a centre of pilgrimage it would also acquire a market. Those who managed temple property provided a nucleus for agrarian or urban corporations. Where the temple invested in commerce, its priests had close associations with administrative and commercial organizations.

The act of worship had a permanent location in a temple or a shrine, a location that was strengthened when it became a place for pilgrimage. The location could include the worship of more than a single deity, although one was supreme. Flowers, fruit and grain were offered to the deity who was believed to sanctify the offering. The action was embedded in a ritual of worship – *puja* – that also encapsulated the personal tie between worshipper and deity. Worship included *vratas* or the observance of vows, fasts and other such acts seen as devotion to the deity. It was therefore different from the ritual of sacrifice performed according to Vedic rites. These were less frequent now. Vedic sacrifices no longer sufficed in claims to legitimacy. Other forms such as genealogies and patronage of temples became more immediate.

The temple, particularly the section that housed the image, was not open to every worshipper. The so-called unclean *shudra* castes and the untouchables were not permitted entry. They had their own separate cult shrines, generally in the section of the village or town that they inhabited.

Their deities were either different or were variant manifestations of the deities worshipped in the temple, and this was also the case with some of the rituals and offerings. Thus libations of alcohol were excluded in the temple and the sacrifice of animals, common to the ritual of the lower castes, was less frequent in temples, although those dedicated to Kali could make concessions to such offerings. This was a matter of caste, but the survival of places of worship was also dependent on environmental factors. Despite the imprint of Sanskritic culture many communities retained their earlier places of worship, which were small and less distinctive. Such temples would tend to merge into the landscape since they were constructed of locally available material and conformed to local architecture, function and climate. This also made them more susceptible to weathering and decline.

Because the temple received offerings and donations it was also a treasury and a financial centre. The giving of gifts – *dana* – to brahmans and to the temple was an appeal to the deity through an intermediary. A temple built through royal patronage was seen as symbolizing the power and well-being of the kingdom. This was demonstrated by the characteristics which accompanied the establishment of a state – the titles of the king accompanied by a genealogy and often the writing of a *vamshavali*, the building of a capital with a royal temple constructed according to the norms of the *shilpa-shastras*, and agricultural and commercial expansion. As an institution with managerial functions the reach of the temple included extensive areas surrounding it.

The temple as an institution not only employed a large hierarchy of priests and others with administrative skills, but also those who would have provided religious discourses and the recitation of religious texts. Thus, there were recitations by professional narrators, often with a commentary, of the *Puranas*, the *Ramayana* and *Mahabharata*, and other compositions now regarded as sacred. The adoration of the deity through music and dance meant that *devadasis* were also maintained. Occasions for pilgrimages were linked to festivals and the larger the number of such occasions the better, for pilgrims brought devotion and donations. At some temples, such as Somanatha, the pilgrims paid a pilgrim tax that provided a healthy income for the local raja, provided it had not already been looted from the pilgrim by other rajas, which was a common complaint.

Puranic Hinduism required a location where the deity could be established permanently in an appropriate building for worship. Even though the worship was devotional and awaited the grace of the deity, an icon could be the focus for devotion and the giving of gifts. An icon was not necessary for worship, but gradually became common. The centrality of the icon further distanced Puranic Hinduism from the Vedic religion. An object of worship, even aniconic and with no recognizable form, could be converted into a deity and sometimes at a later stage replaced by an anthropomorphic deity with a human form. If required, additions were made to this form in the shape of extra physical features – such as arms, generally symbolizing the attributes of the deity. The ritual was performed by brahmans who had conceded the importance of the object of worship and the rites connected with this, or by priests from the earlier form of the cult who were now recruited to the brahman fold. The *Puranas* and the *Agamas*, relating to both Shaiva and Vaishnava worship, were texts recording the mythology that were intended to explain the rites in the worship of a deity. The *Mahatmyas* and the *Sthala-puranas* narrated the supposed history, legends and myths of the place of worship, with further explanations for rituals and observances. Not every cult deity was converted in this manner. The choice had much to do with popular support, political clout and the advantages of incorporating the cult into mainstream worship.

Temples were also a signal of the upward social mobility of the patrons who financed the building. Vastupala and Tejapala, from a merchant family, had sufficient wealth to build temples at Mt Abu where they created a significant Jaina centre. This was on the scale of royal patronage. Their inscriptions at the site not only laud their own families but also indicate the status and power of their community of merchants. A signal of a different kind came from the Chandella dynasty. These kings narrated a complex origin myth linked to the lunar line in their inscriptions but their origin was also associated with the Gond tribes of central India. It is said that they originally worshipped a rock, Maniya Deo, installed in their earliest capital at Mahoba. Through the processes of acquiring Rajput status and subscribing to Sanskritic culture, which involved devotion to Puranic deities, they expressed this change by building the temples at Khajuraho which were distinctly different from the shrine of Maniya Deo. This illustrates a shift from a local cult to the patronage of a Puranic sect. Tribal priests could accompany such a transfer and eventually become priests of the Puranic sect with which the icon was associated. If the icon were linked to a Puranic deity this would assert the upper-caste status of the patron. This is also evident in the mutation of what appears to be a local cult associated with Vishnu-Jagannath in Orissa in the temple at Puri. When, in the thirteenth century, the king claimed to be the deputy of the god, the political dimensions of incorporating the territory where the god was worshipped were intermeshed with the requirements of belief and ritual. Such mutations have many layers of growth. The territory covered by the cult and its sacred geography became part of the circuit of pilgrimage. When such a cult acquired royal patronage, then the territory and the cult in turn became a base of support for its royal patron. The cult provided a hinterland of worshippers and a network of links, parallel in some ways to the network of grants of land. A comparable pattern can be seen in the western Deccan, with the worship of Vithoba as a manifestation of Vishnu at Pandharpur.

In eastern India Buddhist monastic complexes, some built under the patronage of the Palas, constituted monumental religious architecture. The more impressive of these were the monasteries at Mainamati and Vikrama-shila, and the magnificent Somapuri monastery at Paharpur. Structures at the Buddhist site of Ratnagiri in Orissa were renovated in the eleventh century and it became a centre for Tantric Buddhism. The monasteries at Nalanda were enlarged. This patronage may have been encouraged by the Buddhist association with the mercantile community active in south-east Asia, and in the increasingly profitable trade with Tibet.

These monumental structures of eastern and southern India already had parallels in some parts of south-east Asia, such as Cambodia and Java. The *stupas* at Pagan were closer in style to the south Asian ones but their clustering created a relatively different form. The linguistic linking of Sanskrit with Javanese can also be seen in Old Javanese, but here again, despite the closeness of Sanskrit, the assertion of a Javanese presence is unmistakable. The many versions of the story of Rama in south-east Asia, with local narrative traditions enveloping the kernel of the original story and creating a variety of renderings, were evocative of plural cultural strands. The links continued with areas of the subcontinent that had a strong interest in south-east Asian trade, such as Gujarat, the Coromandel coast and eastern India.

Forms associated with Islamic architecture, the most obvious of which were the true arch and the dome, would have been innovations. Early attempts at such buildings would have been in the north-west and probably also in the Arab settlements along the west coast. This is evident from the reference to the mosque at Cambay destroyed by the Paramara king and the Shia'h mosque at Mansura desecrated by Mahmud. The establishing of the Sultanate was marked at Delhi and at Ajmer by converting the existing temple into a mosque, doubtless to proclaim victory but also to appropriate sacred space.

Religions Mutations

Buddhism was a proselytizing religion and Buddhist monks and teachers had taken it to various parts of Asia. It was therefore not unexpected that monks from distant places in Asia came to Buddhist monasteries in India, attracted by the libraries of manuscripts and the potentialities of discourse. These monks linked the areas from where they came or from where they were trained to other centres of Buddhism. Atisha, for example, contributed to the evolution of Tibetan Buddhism in the eleventh century although he was from eastern India and, according to tradition, was trained in Suvarnadvipa, possibly Java. Buddhist monasteries had provided a support to the state, but the ideology of Puranic Hinduism gradually replaced the Buddhists. The Puranic ideology was now honed to efficiency in its additional role of converting groups into caste society and religious sects, necessary to the establishing of states in areas that hitherto had none. Hostility between the Buddhists and some sects of Shaivas grew from philosophical and religious contestation, as well as competition for patronage. There was a questioning of the Shramanic emphasis on renunciation, which was seen as too unrealistic for the ordinary person. Monkhood was sometimes caricatured as an idle and comfortable life, made possible by the work of others. Brahmans, familiar with migrating to distant parts of the subcontinent, had taken their promises of ritual status to lands still further away. The Indian connections in south-east Asia were not only of value in commercial matters, but also in the forging of cultural norms. These connections were also of assistance to the Arabs, enabling them eventually to capture much of the trade when they established trading settlements in south-east Asia. In Java and the Malay peninsula these settlements evolved into an impressive cultural interweaving of the local culture with beliefs and practices from India and west Asia.

By the end of this period, the Vaishnava, Shaiva and the Shakta-Tantric sects were dominant in northern India. Jainism was restricted to the west and Buddhism, which had been largely confined to the east, was declining. An attempt was made to assimilate the Buddha into the Vaishnava pantheon as an incarnation of Vishnu but this did not attract enthusiasm. The worship of the Buddha by non-Buddhists remained largely formal and deferential. The militaristic ethos of the Rajputs was incompatible with the emphasis on non-violence of the Shramanic religions, even though some Jainas distinguished themselves on the battlefield. Among those involved with Puranic Hinduism, the idea of non-violence was now closer to the teachings of a few *bhakti* sects who opposed violence for reasons largely similar to those of Mahavira and the Buddha.

Many of the changes introduced into Hinduism at this time resulted from a compromise between orthodox belief and a popular demand for a more personal religion. Image worship increased substantially and a multitude of new forms took shape, many basically anthropomorphic. Ritual was not confined to elaborate sacrifices, and was more commonly individual worship, even if the worship was channelled through a temple or a shrine. This reflects new patterns of thought, aspirations and connections, as well as a different historical situation. The mythologies associated with the gods had a wide reach through versions in the regional languages and oral recitation. These included narratives that grew out of cults incorporated into Puranic Hinduism, which became part of the texts of regional languages when they acquired a literary form. The multiple *Upapuranas* gave even greater flexibility to incorporating local custom into ritual and belief. The theory that deities could be incarnated in human form was used as a method of incorporation. Such incarnations also served a political purpose and helped in legitimizing those kings who claimed to be incarnations of deity.

The perception of deities became more complex. Krishna, for example, regarded as an incarnation of Vishnu, was viewed as a pastoral deity, the herdsman who spent his hours with the milkmaids and particularly with his beloved Radha. This became the source of intense devotional worship, celebrated in poetry from which the erotic was not always absent. But was he also the philosopher of the *Bhagavadgita*, carrying the universe, carrying time, defending virtue against evil and reiterating the codes of caste and behaviour? The name Krishna literally means 'dark' and he has been associated with the Tamil Mayon, 'the black one', also a herder of cattle. A number of traditions are reflected in the various manifestations of Vishnu, which may be one of the reasons for his popularity. However, the connection between the topography of modern Vrindavan near Mathura and the life of Krishna was introduced by sects of a later period, such as the followers of Chaitanya from eastern India. Similarly, the link between the topography of present-day Ayodhya and the life of Rama was referred to in the *Ayodhya Mahatmya* of the mid-second millennium AD and was established through the activities of the Ramanandin sect, drawing on the possible identity of Ayodhya with Saketa.

Minor sects and cults were not rejected out of hand by orthodoxy. Some were tolerated, while others were encouraged by priests who performed the ritual both as worship and livelihood. Local priests tended to be sympathetic to popular religion. The worship of the Sun-god Surya rose in popularity and received royal patronage in the form of magnificent temples, particularly in northern and western India – not to mention the vast complex at Konarak in Orissa. The popularity of Surya might have been due to what is believed to have been the migration into India of the Magha or Shakadvipi brahmans from across the north-western borders, perhaps reinforced by the presence of Zoroastrians in western India. But elsewhere it was a continuation of the earlier worship of the Sun. Existing deities took on fresh significance and new gods emerged. Ganesh or Ganapati, the elephant-headed god, rose further in status. In origin perhaps a totem god, he had been given a respectable parentage and described as the son of Shiva and his consort, Parvati. There was a more visible worship of the goddesses, often associated with the fertility cult.

Puranic Hinduism, apart from the assimilation of innumerable cults and deities, also shaped strong sectarian tendencies focusing on particular schools of thought. These two trends seem to be contradictory, but the contradiction is reconciled by the attempted formal organization of belief systems and philosophies through the sects. In common with the Shramanic religions, these teachings were closely related to the historical founders of sects, such as Shankaracharya, Ramanuja, Madhva and Basavanna, and sometimes to a believed succession of teachers, suggesting historicity. The history and evolution of the sect centred on the interpretations of what was said by the founders, a common occurrence in sectarian religions. Some of the sectarian teaching was intended to undermine the Shramanic sects, but at the same time it appears there were attempts to imitate them in various ways. The strength of the sect was dependent on patronage, particularly on the donation of property that allowed it to build an institutional base. This transformation of aspects of Puranic Hinduism into sectarian religions would also have contributed to the decline of the earlier sectarian religions – Buddhism and Jainism.

Sectarianism would have encouraged rivalry and hostility between sects. This was sometimes expressed by more than one sect claiming the same king as patron. For instance, there are contradictions between Shaiva and Jaina sources regarding whether Kumarapala, the Chaulukya King who had been a Shaiva, was actually converted to Jainism. A number of Jaina temples were attributed to his patronage; according to Jaina sources these were destroyed by his successor Ajayapala, who is described as hostile to the Jainas. Such hostilities did not, however, take on the dimensions of a holy war.

The term *pasamda* that referred to any kind of sect in the Ashokan edicts now came to mean 'heretic', and eventually 'fraud'. Thus the brahmans on

occasion refer to the Buddhists and Jainas as heretics and the latter sometimes use the same word for the former, in both cases infused with invective.
The sparring could be amusing, as in the courtly dramas of the *Mattavilsa-
prahasana* or the *Prabodha-chandrodaya*, but on other occasions it was
ruthless.

Sects with teachers and poets propagating *bhakti* began to find expression
in regions north of where they had originated. They were to become a
dynamic force in north India from the fourteenth century, playing much
the same catalytic role as they had done in the south. This was not a
proselytizing movement, but an expression of similar thoughts arising out
of not dissimilar conditions. It could draw on a variety of earlier religious
expression: the Shramanic sects, Vaishnava and Shaiva worship, as well as
the esoteric and popular levels of the Shakta tradition. But the *bhakti*
movement veered more towards an appeal to deity without the trappings of
elaborate ritual. Some among them were almost on the edge of being
puritanical protest.

Other popular cults and sects sometimes demonstrated their protest in a
more startling manner, such as the rites of the Shaiva Kalamukhas and
Kapalikas or the Kaulas, or certain kinds of Tantric rituals that often were
a deliberate reversal of upper-caste practice. Some of their rituals, however,
were rooted in those sections of society that had hardly known the Hinduism
formulated by the brahmans, and were therefore not protesting but worshipping in their own ways. The adjustment to this on the part of the orthodox
was either to exclude such groups from caste status or else, if they carried
social support and patronage, to make them respectable by slowly transforming them.

Tantrism, so-called after its compositions, the *Tantras*, influenced the
practices of virtually every older religion, apart from upholding a belief and
practice contrary to Vedic Brahmanism. Although originating earlier, it
became widely practised from about the eighth century when it gradually
surfaced throughout the subcontinent. In the east it had close ties with
Tibetan religious expression. Some of the ritual was similar, together with
the belief in the efficacy of *mantras* (prayers and mystical formulae), *mudras*
(hand gestures) and *mandalas* (magical diagrams representing the cosmos).
It was open to all castes and included women in the rituals, which identified
it with non-orthodox sentiment. Goddesses were accorded great veneration,
as is evident from the collection of legends in the *Devi-mahatmya*. The Devi,
or the goddess, had an individuality of her own and was worshipped for
this rather than merely as a consort of a god. The *sapta-matrikas*, or
seven mothers, were more closely associated with male counterparts. Since

goddesses could be created as and when occasion required it, there are large numbers of them.

The commanding position accorded to goddesses was sometimes the surfacing of a substratum religion, doubtless associated with the rise of subaltern groups who could with their new status elevate the worship of the goddess. The symbols associated with the worship of a Devi often derived from forms of fertility worship, which is not unexpected. At a conceptual level, but not in terms of introducing change into social codes, the worship of the goddess challenged patriarchy. Women were permitted to establish their own *ashramas*, to act as priestesses and to teach. This carried forward, as it were, some of the activities of the Buddhist or Jaina nuns and some of the sentiments of the women poets from the early *bhakti* tradition. Tantrism was also linked with the Shakta-Shakti cult that regarded female creative energy – *shakti* – as essential to any action.

Those desirous of joining a Tantric sect had to be initiated by a guru. Tantric ritual involved the ritual partaking of the five Ms – *madya*, alcohol, *matsya*, fish, *mamsa*, flesh, *mudra*, gestures, and *maithuna*, coition. In the final state of purification everything and everyone was equal. The ritual being what it was, secret meetings became necessary, especially when some other sects denounced its practices as being depraved. Gradually there was a bifurcation into the Left-Hand path that experimented with these practices, and the Right-Hand path that restricted itself to yoga and *bhakti*. Although Tantrism has often been condemned for its more extreme activities, it seems also to have been a vehicle for opposition to the brahmanical ordering of society. Elements of social radicalism in such movements become visible when the movement is viewed in the context of the broader social norms.

Vajrayana Buddhism had incorporated Tantric ideas and the Taras or saviouresses, spouses of the male *bodhisattvas*, received veneration similar to that of Shakti. Among the many magical formulae which Vajrayana Buddhism has popularized is the oft-repeated Tibetan prayer, *om mane padme hun*/behold the jewel is in the lotus, which is the symbolic representation of divine coitus. Buddhism had undergone many changes with the evolving of new sects and practices, but the incorporation of Tantric ideas made it less distinctive as a religion.

In western India where the Jainas grew in strength, their patrons were largely from the trading community, although royal patronage, especially from the Chaulukyas, provided them with an even more established position. Although small in numbers, they were prosperous and visible. Since they were forbidden agriculture as a profession for fear of injuring small creatures of the soil (although they accepted the occasional grant of land), their forte was commerce and their profits enabled them to become patrons of culture and learning. A further stabilizing factor was that since they were literate, financially astute and proficient in management they often found high office at royal courts. In spite of the destruction of Jaina temples by kings, both Hindu and Muslim, Jainism remained resilient.

Buddhism, however, was eventually to lose the status of even a minor religion. Its decline was gradual, but towards the thirteenth century became rapid. Its association with Tantric cults was confusing since much of its original ethical teaching, which had been its initial strength, was being submerged in the new ritual. The support of the Pala kings sustained Buddhism in eastern India and they doubtless used the religion as an avenue of control over trade, and in their diplomatic relations with Tibet and south-east Asia. Royal patronage kept it going in some other areas for brief periods. But the Buddhists did not always succeed in winning royal patronage. Confrontations with the growing strength of Puranic Hinduism, and its ability to incorporate new castes, was a fresh challenge to Buddhism.

The new landholders were either brahmans or patrons of the brahmans and of Puranic Hinduism. Buddhism and Jainism ceased to play a major role in the transformation of the polity except in limited areas. Where chiefs were being converted to landholders and other members of the clan to peasants, the introduction of caste was a useful mechanism of control over the new *kshatriyas* and *shudras*. The use of caste in this process came more easily to Puranic Hinduism than to the Shramanic sects. The new *kshatriyas* would not have been attracted to Buddhism. Unlike the Puranic texts authored by brahmans, Buddhist and Jaina texts had no extensive genealogies of the kind on to which the new *kshatriyas* could latch themselves and acquire status. Buddhist myths explaining the origin of government related it to a contract between an elected ruler and the people and were divorced from any divine sanction. The Buddhist *chakkavatti* with the symbol of the wheel of law was a distant concept from the models of conquest held up to the *kshatriyas* and Rajputs. Patronage therefore went to the ideology of Puranic Hinduism.

The Buddhist Sangha was best established in an area that had an existing, sedentary agricultural society, with a capacity to maintain the institutions, or where there was sufficient commercial activity for the community to maintain monastic centres. Even when Buddhist monasteries were given grants of revenue or land, these were more frequently villages or land already under cultivation. Monks were not supposed to pioneer agricultural change, although they did work as supervisors in various capacities relating to the income and the better functioning of the Sangha. Ideally, monks were expected to play the passive role of being recipients of alms and donations. This could have distanced, if not alienated, Buddhism from a society changing its systems. This was a contrast to brahman grantees where brahmans could be settlers and pioneers, could profitably restructure the landscape to agrarian requirements and, above all, could found dynasties.

The major successes of Buddhism, apart from periods when they received royal patronage, were in areas of existing agrarian societies that were also developing into centres of exchange or in areas where commerce was the primary activity. The thrust of trade carried it to distant places that in turn made it attractive to those who wished to profit by this trade. This is not to deny that in all periods there were conversions to Buddhism from religious conviction. But the decline of Buddhism virtually everywhere except in eastern India requires a wider explanation than just a change in the religion. Nor was the coming of Islam primarily responsible for Buddhist decline, despite the thirteenth-century Turkish attack on Nalanda. By the eighth century AD Buddhism was more prevalent in north-western India and eastern India than elsewhere. The conversion of these areas to Islam was a gradual process. The decline of Buddhism in the Ganges heartland and the peninsula occurred before the Turkish conquest.

The coming of the Arabs, Turks and Afghans brought a new religion to India that found roots in various ways in many communities. Islam was unable to create a homogeneous, monolithic community, and in this it was conditioned by the same segmentation that earlier religions in India had experienced. Apart from the Muslim theologians, an early impact of Islam was the arrival of Muslim mystics from Persia, distinct from and sometimes disapproved of by Muslim theologians. The Sufis first settled in Sind and the Punjab, from where their teaching travelled to Gujarat, the Deccan and Bengal. The amalgamation of Indian and Islamic mysticism evolved into new schools of Sufism different from those in Persia. Sufi ideas attracted an interest in India, particularly among those inclined to mystic teachings and asceticism, since much of the symbolism was similar. Their dialogue with the *bhakti* movement was to the advantage of both, as they questioned orthodoxy in their explorations of the meaning of religion and of the human condition. They attracted large followings which gave them a political potential that converted their *khanqahs* or hospices into centres of political discussion as well.

The period from the ninth century in the subcontinent, far from being 'dark', was a period of illumination as it was germane to many later institutions. The states that emerged, together with the new political economies, were characterized by a hierarchy of grants of land and accompanying land-holders that set the pattern for a few centuries. At the same time, Indian traders were active in the Indian Ocean and overland through central Asia to more distant markets than in the past. They were again significant participants in Asian trade. Together with the emergence of new *jatis*, there was also a reshuffling of castes, often ancestral to those that were registered in subsequent centuries. Regional linguistic roots of this period were seminal to the languages now used in various regions of India. Religious cults and sects, dominating the lives of rural and urban populations at a popular level today, link themselves to the religious expression of this time. Regional cultures were finding their shape within these changes. The greater range and amount of historical evidence available from this period compared with earlier ones has allowed the reconstruction of a more complete picture.

The most challenging and stimulating aspect of the history of this period is the interface between the emergence of regional cultures and the firming up of the contours of sub-continental cultures. The interplay of assertion and accommodation that this required led to significant new dimensions in Indian history.

Maps

Map 1 Geographical Features

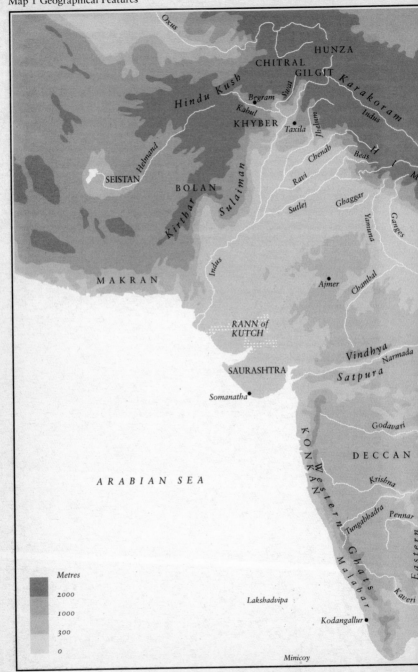

Oxus

HUNZA

CHITRAL

GILGIT

Hindu Kush

Begram

Kabul

Swat

Karakoram

Indus

KHYBER

Taxila

Jhelum

H

Chenab

M

Beas

SEISTAN

Helmand

Ravi

BOLAN

Ghaggar

Kirthar

Sulaiman

Sutlej

Yamuna

Ganges

Indus

MAKRAN

Ajmer

Chambal

RANN of
KUTCH

SAURASHTRA

Vindhya

Narmada

Satpura

Somanatha

Godavari

K
O
N
K
A
N

DECCAN

ARABIAN SEA

W
e
s
t
e
r
n

Krishna

Tungabhadra

Pennar

Eastern

Ghats

Malabar

Kaveri

Metres

2000

1000

300

0

Lakshadvipa

Kodangallur

Minicoy

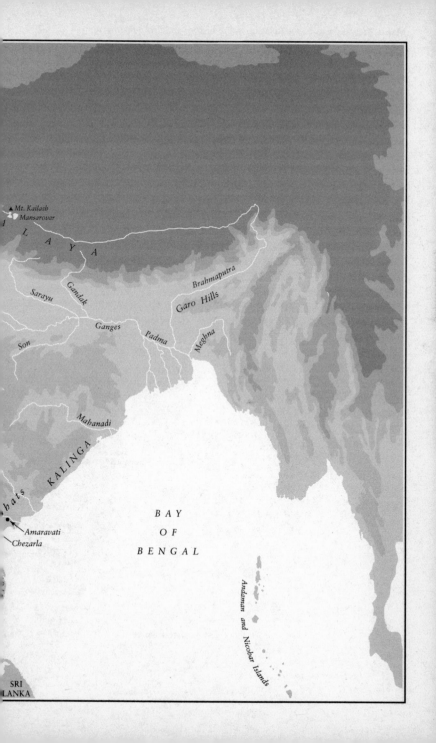

Map 2 Archaeological Sites Relating to Pre-history and Proto-history

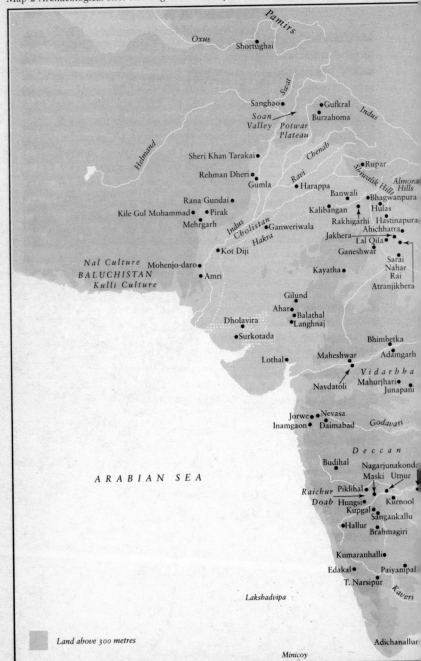

Map 3 Nothern India *c.* 1200 to 500 BC

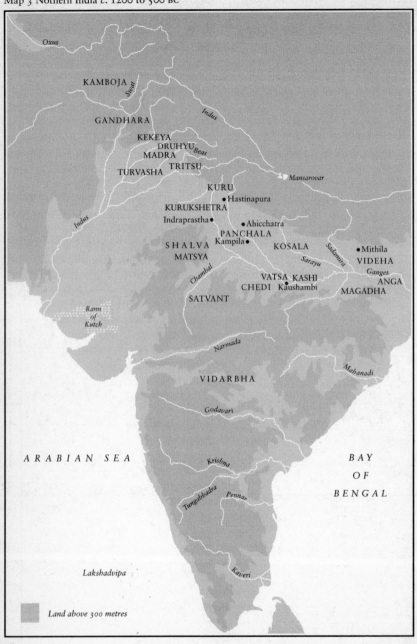

Oxus

KAMBOJA

Swat

Indus

GANDHARA

KEKEYA

DRUHYU

MADRA   Beas

TURVASHA   TRITSU

KURU   Mansarovar

KURUKSHETRA   ● Hastinapura

Indraprastha ●

                    ● Ahicchatra

              PANCHALA

              Kampila ●

SHALVA   KOSALA   ● Mithila

MATSYA   VIDEHA

                              Sarayu   Sadanira

                                            Ganges

              Chambal   VATSA KASHI   ANGA

                          CHEDI Kaushambi

                                            MAGADHA

              SATVANT

Rann
of
Kutch

                    Narmada

                                    Mahanadi

              VIDARBHA

                    Godavari

ARABIAN SEA   BAY

                                        OF

              Krishna   BENGAL

    Tungabhadra   Pennar

Lakshadvipa

                    Kaveri

Land above 300 metres

Map 4 Kingdoms and Chiefdoms: Mid-first Millennium BC

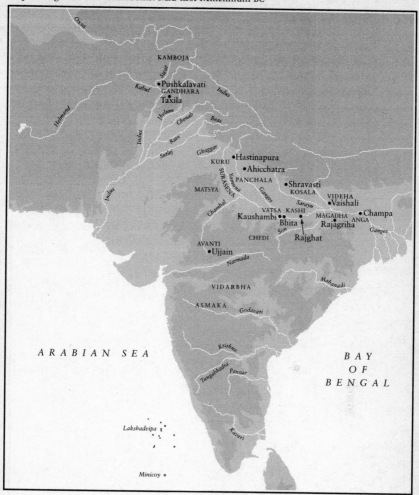

Map 5 Some Sites of the Mauryan Period

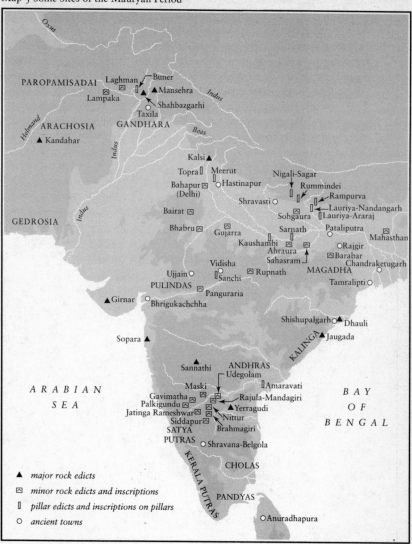

PAROPAMISADAI

Oxus

Laghman
Buner
▲ Mansehra
Lampaka ⊠
Shahbazgarhi
○ Taxila
Indus
ARACHOSIA
GANDHARA
Helmand
▲ Kandahar
Indus
Beas

Kalsi ▲
Topra ▯
Meerut ▯
Nigali-Sagar ▼
Rummindei
Bahapur (Delhi) ⊠
○ Hastinapur
Rampurva
GEDROSIA
Indus
Shravasti ○
Lauriya-Nandangarh
Bairat ⊠
Sohgaura
Lauriya-Araraj
Bhabru ⊠
Gujarra ⊠
Sarnath ▯
Pataliputra ○
Mahasthan
Kaushambi ⊠
Ahraura ⊠
○ Rajgir
Sahasram
⊠ Barabar
Chandraketugarh ○
Vidisha
Rupnath ⊠
MAGADHA
Ujjain ○
Sanchi ⊠
Tamralipti ○
PULINDAS
Panguraria ⊠
▲ Girnar
○ Bhrigukachchha
Shishupalgarh ○
▲ Dhauli
KALINGA
Sopara ▲
▲ Jaugada

A R A B I A N
S E A

ANDHRAS
▲ Sannathi
Udegolam
Maski ▲
Amaravati ▯
Gavimatha ⊠
Rajula-Mandagiri
Palkigundu ⊠
▲ Yerragudi
Jatinga Rameshwar ⊠
Nittur
Siddapur ⊠
SATYA
Brahmagiri
PUTRAS
○ Shravana-Belgola

B A Y
O F
B E N G A L

KERALA PUTRAS

CHOLAS

PANDYAS

▲ major rock edicts
⊠ minor rock edicts and inscriptions
▯ pillar edicts and inscriptions on pillars
○ ancient towns

○ Anuradhapura

Map 6 North India and West Asia *c.* 200 BC to AD 300

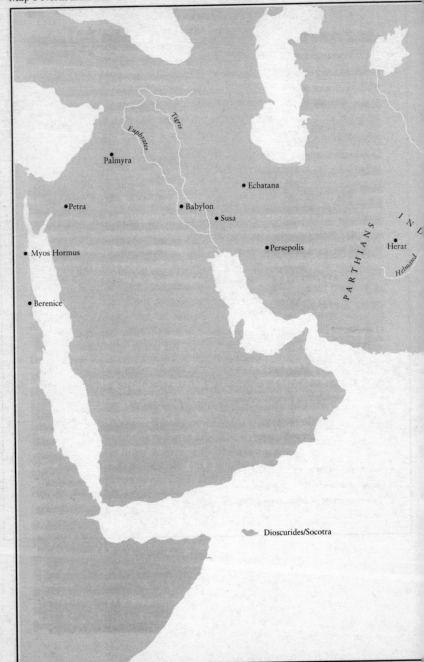

Palmyra

Euphrates

Tigris

Ecbatana

Petra

Babylon

Susa

Myos Hormus

Persepolis

PARTHIANS

IND

Herat

Helmand

Berenice

Dioscurides/Socotra

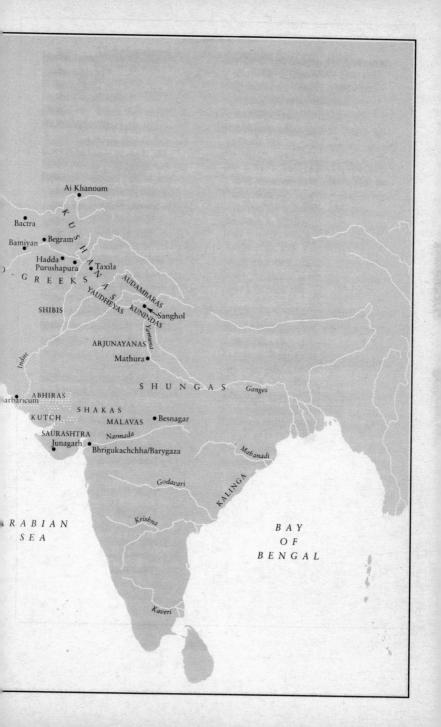

Ai Khanoum

Bactra

K U S H A N S

Bamiyan • Begram

Hadda
Purushapura • Taxila

• O - G R E E K S

AUDAMBARAS

SHIBIS YAUDHEYAS KUNINDAS • Sanghol

ARJUNAYANAS

Mathura •

S H U N G A S *Ganges*

ABHIRAS
arbaricum

KUTCH S H A K A S

MALAVAS • Besnagar

SAURASHTRA
Junagarh •

Bhrigukachchha/Barygaza *Narmada*

Mahanadi

Godavari KALINGA

Krishna

*RABIAN
SEA*

Indus

Yamuna

B A Y
O F
B E N G A L

Kaveri

MAP 7 Central Asia and China

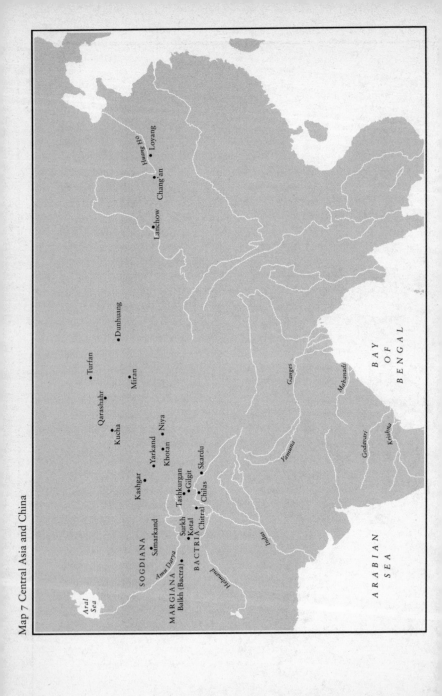

Map 8 The Indian Peninsula *c.* 200 BC to AD 300

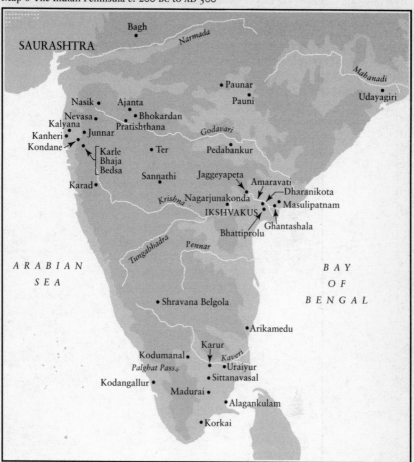

SAURASHTRA

Narmada

Mahanadi

Bagh

• Paunar

Pauni

Udayagiri

Nasik •

Nevasa •

• Ajanta

• Bhokardan

Kalyana •

Pratishthana

Kanheri •

• Junnar

Kondane

Godavari

Karle

Bhaja

Bedsa

• Ter

Pedabankur

Karad •

Sannathi

Jaggeyapeta

Amaravati

• Dharanikota

Nagarjunakonda

Krishna

• Masulipatnam

IKSHVAKUS

Bhattiprolu

• Ghantashala

Tungabhadra

Pennar

ARABIAN

SEA

BAY

OF

BENGAL

• Shravana Belgola

• Arikamedu

Karur

Kodumanal •

Kaveri

Palghat Pass

• Uraiyur

Kodangallur •

• Sittanavasal

Madurai •

• Alagankulam

• Korkai

Map 9 The Indian Subcontinent: Mid-first Millennium AD

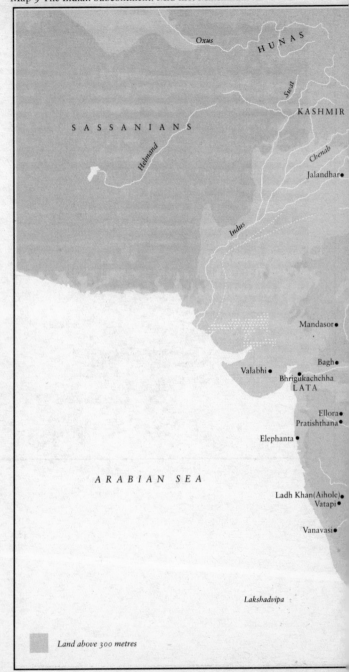

Oxus

HUNAS

Swat

KASHMIR

SASSANIANS

Helmand

Chenab

Jalandhar●

Indus

Mandasor●

Bagh●

Valabhi ●

Bhrigukachchha

LATA

Ellora●

Pratishthana●

Elephanta ●

ARABIAN SEA

Ladh Khan(Aihole)●

Vatapi●

Vanavasi●

Lakshadvipa

Land above 300 metres

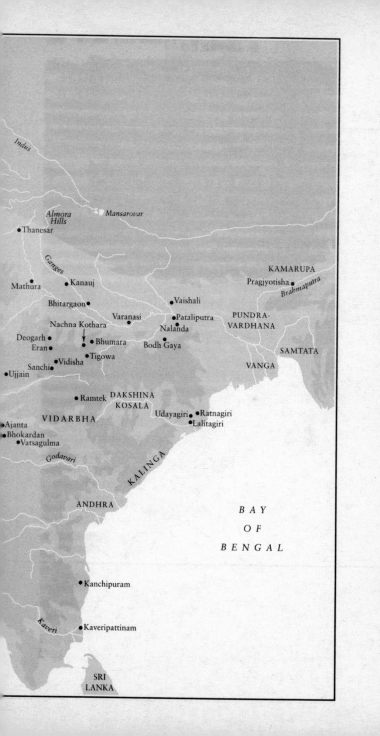

Map 10 Indian Contacts with South East Asia

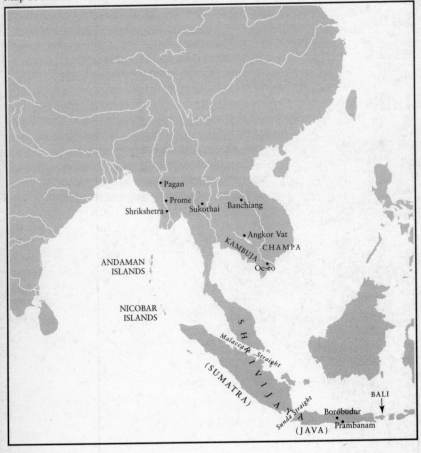

Map 11 The Indian Peninsula *c*. AD 700 to 1300

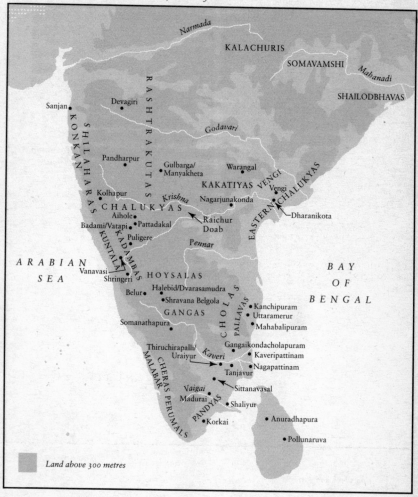

KALACHURIS

SOMAVAMSHI

Narmada

Mahanadi

SHAILODBHAVAS

Sanjan

Devagiri

Godavari

RASHTRAKUTAS

KONKAN

SHILAHARAS

Pandharpur

Gulbarga/
Manyakheta

Warangal

KAKATIYAS

VENGI

Vengi

Kolhapur

Krishna

Nagarjunakonda

EASTERN CHALUKYAS

CHALUKYAS

Dharanikota

Aihole

Raichur
Doab

KUNTALA

Badami/Vatapi

Pattadakal

Puligere

Pennar

KADAMBAS

ARABIAN
SEA

Vanavasi

HOYSALAS

BAY

Shringeri

Belur

Halebid/Dvarasamudra

OF

Shravana Belgola

Kanchipuram

BENGAL

GANGAS

CHOLAS

PALLAVAS

Uttaramerur

Somanathapura

Mahabalipuram

Gangaikondacholapuram

Thiruchirapalli/
Uraiyur

Kaveri

Kaveripattinam

CHERAS

Tanjavur

Nagapattinam

MALABAR

PERUMALS

Vaigai

Sittanavasal

Madurai

Shaliyur

PANDYAS

Anuradhapura

Korkai

Pollunaruva

Land above 300 metres

Map 12 Northern India *c.* AD 700 to 1100

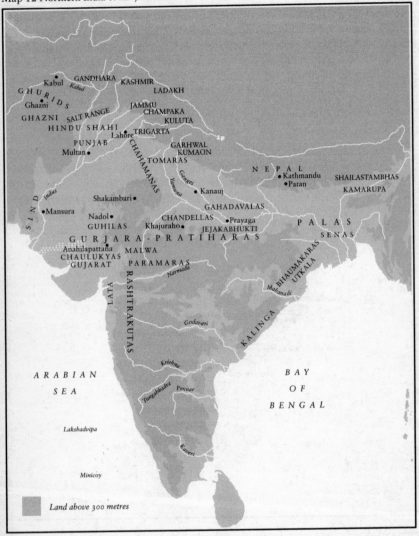

Kabul
GANDHARA
KASHMIR
LADAKH
GHURIDS
Ghazni
Kabul
GHAZNI
SALT RANGE
JAMMU
CHAMPAKA
KULUTA
HINDU SHAHI
TRIGARTA
Lahore
PUNJAB
GARHWAL
Multan
KUMAON
TOMARAS
CHAHAMANAS
Ganges
NEPAL
Kathmandu
Patan
SHAILASTAMBHAS
KAMARUPA
Yamuna
Shakambari
Kanauj
GAHADAVALAS
Indus
Mansura
Nadol
CHANDELLAS
Prayaga
PALAS
GUHILAS
Khajuraho
JEJAKABHUKTI
SENAS
GURJARA-PRATIHARAS
Anahilapattana
MALWA
CHAULUKYAS
PARAMARAS
GUJARAT
Narmada
BHAUMAKARAS
UTKALA
LATA
Mahanadi
RASHTRAKUTAS
KALINGA
Godavari
ARABIAN
SEA
Krishna
BAY
OF
BENGAL
Tungabhadra
Pennar
Lakshadvipa
Kaveri
Minicoy

Land above 300 metres

Map 13 Northern India *c.* AD 900 to 1300

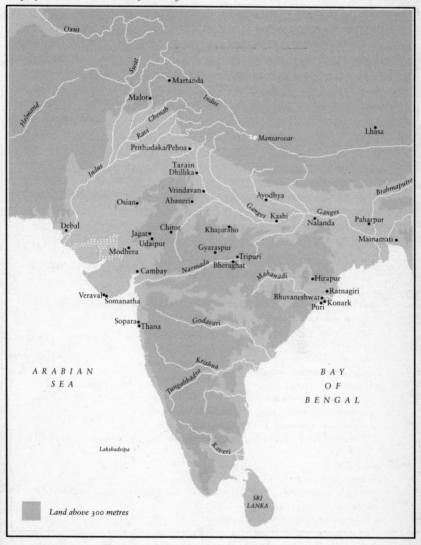

Oxus

Swat

• Martanda

Malot •

Indus

Chenab

Ravi

Helmand

Prithudaka/Pehoa •

Indus

Tarain
Dhillika •

Vrindavan •
Abaneri •

Osian •

Debal •

Chitor •

Jagat •
Udaipur •

Modhera •

• Cambay

Veraval •
Somanatha •

Sopara •
• Thana

Khajuraho •

Gyaraspur •

Narmada

Bheraghat •

• Tripuri

Godavari

Krishna

Tungabhadra

Kaveri

Ayodhya •

Ganges

Kashi •

Ganges

Nalanda •

Mansarovar

Lhasa •

Brahmaputro

Paharpur •

Mainamati •

Mahanadi

• Hirapur

• Ratnagiri
Bhuvaneshwar •
Puri • Konark

*ARABIAN
SEA*

*BAY
OF
BENGAL*

Lakshadvipa

*SRI
LANKA*

Land above 300 metres

Glossary

acharya teacher

adhyaksha superintendent/government official of importance

adivasi the indigenous inhabitant – now used sometimes for the Scheduled Tribes (ST) of India

agnikula ruling families claiming ancestry from a hero who sprang out of a sacrificial fire

agrahara donation of land or village to brahmans, usually by royalty

ahimsa non-violence

Ajivika a heterodox sect of the time of the Buddha

Alvar Vaishnava poets and composers of hymns belonging to the Tamil devotional movement

amatya designation of a high official

anuloma literally, in the direction of the body hair, therefore observing the caste hierarchy even in marriages across castes

apsara celestial woman/nymph

aranya forest/wilderness

artha livelihood/economy

aryavarta the land inhabited by *aryas*

ashrama hermitage/refuge; also used with reference to the four stages or *ashramas* of the human life-cycle – *brahmacharin*/studentship, *grihastha*/householdership, *vanaprastha*/initiating renunciation, *samnyasa*/asceticism

ashtakula-adhikarana administrative body

ashvamedha sacrifice performed by those desirous of being accorded royal status, and by kings

atman soul

ayukta official designation

banjaras generally cattle pastoralists who were also carriers of goods exchanged in trade

banya member of a trading community

Bhagavata associated with the worship of Vishnu

bhakti devotion, a characteristic feature of what modern historians have called the Bhakti movement, focusing on devotion to a deity *bhogta* one who enjoys: used by extension for those who enjoyed revenue rights over certain lands

bhukti administrative unit

bodhisattva one who works for the welfare of the world and voluntarily postpones release from rebirth; also refers sometimes to an incarnation of the Buddha prior to his own birth in the world

brahmacharin celibate studentship, the first of the four stages of the ideal life-cycle

brahmadeya village or land donated to a brahman, who received the revenue that came from it

brahma-kshatra the claim to an ancestry associated with both brahman and *kshatriya*

brahman the first in rank among the four *varnas* of Hindu society, frequently translated as caste, but in some contexts should more correctly be translated as ritual status; the brahman was primarily a ritual specialist and also provided the structures for formal education in Sanskrit

Brahmanas Vedic exegetical texts for rituals

brahmi the earliest deciphered script of India and dating to historical times

chaitya a sacred enclosure – later took the form of a hall and became an essential focus of Buddhist worship together with the *stupa*

chakravartin/chakravartigal/chakkavatti universal monarch

chandala a group from among the outcast section of society, gradually regarded as untouchable

Chandravamsha the lunar lineage, indicative of royal status

chetti/chettiyar merchants

daivaputra literally, the son of a deity; a royal title

dakshina sacrificial fee; the southern direction

dana donation/votive offering

danda force/coercion/punishment

dasa initially 'the Other' of the *arya* – later a slave or servant

desha territory or an administrative unit; a region

devadana usually land or revenue donated to a temple

devadasi female slave of the gods, used with reference to women dedicated to the temple

devanagari the later, evolved form of the *brahmi* script, also used for some modern Indian languages

Dhamma/dharma piety, morality, ethics, virtue/the social and religious order

Dharma-shastra texts attempting to codify the social and ritual duties, and obligations of the members of the four *varnas* and the relationship between them

Digambara literally, 'sky-clad', one of the two main Jaina schools

digvijayin the conqueror of the four quarters

dinara a coin based on the Roman *denarius*

doab the land between two rivers

dronavapa a measure of grain

dvija literally, the twice-born, refers to either the highest *varna* or the three upper *varnas* of Hindu caste society, where the first birth is the physical birth and the second is the initiation into *varna* status

eripatti land from which the revenue was used to maintain irrigation tanks

gahapati a landowner

gana-rajya oligarchy/chiefdom

garbha-griha literally, the womb-house, the sanctum sanctorum of the Hindu temple

gavunda categories of landowners; could be a member of a local administrative committee

ghatika an educational centre often attached to a temple

ghi clarified butter

grama village

guru teacher or guide

heggade a term used in the peninsula for a landowner

Hinayana The Lesser Vehicle, a major school of Buddhism

itihasa-purana sections of texts claiming to refer to events of the past

jana people, subjects, tribe, clan

janapada literally, where the clan or tribe places its foot; the territory initially occupied by a clan and which could evolve into a state

jati caste; a social segment identified by membership through birth, marriage circles, occupation, custom and location

jyestha elder, as in the guild-like organization of the *shreni*

kahapana/karshapana/pana widely used coin series, often silver

kakini copper coins

Kalamukha a Shaiva sect

kaliyuga the fourth and final age of the great cycle of time, the *mahayuga*

kalpa a frame of time-reckoning

kama desire

Kapalika a Shaiva sect

karma action or deed, and also used in the theory of future births being conditioned by the deeds of the present life

kassaka a cultivator, not as well-off as the *gahapati*

kayastha a caste, chiefly of scribes

kharoshthi a script used in north-west India and derived from the Aramaic script

kshatrapa associated with the administrative title of satrap, and used specifically for some rulers of western India

kshatriya the second in rank among the four *varnas*; included a warrior aristocracy, landowners and royalty

kshetra field

kula family

kuladevi clan goddess

kulyavapa a winnowing basket

kumaramatya a title of honour, often used for a prince

kutumbi householder

lingam the phallic symbol, associated with the worship of Shiva

mahadanas great gifts/donations

maharajadhiraja great king of kings

mahasamanta ruler or governor but subordinate to an overlord *mahasammata* 'the great elect', the person elected to rule and signifying the origin of government in Buddhist theory

mahasenapati commander-in-chief of the army

mahattara head of the village

Mahayana the Great Vehicle, a major school of Buddhism

mana a large unit of weight

mandala a cosmogram, projecting the universe in a geometric pattern, often concentric with indications of cardinal points and sometimes square; also refers to a theory of interstate relations where the king desirous of victory is at the centre and the pattern lays out potential allies and enemies.

mandalam an administrative unit

manigramam a formal association or guild of merchants

mantra sounds, words, verses associated with magical and religious connotations

marga the path/mainstream

matha a hospice or a monastery attached to a temple and often a centre of education

matsyanyaya a political theory where a parallel is drawn between a condition of drought when tanks dry up with the big fish eating the small fish, and a condition of political anarchy when the strong devour the weak

maya illusion

mlechchha outside the pale of caste society/impure

moksha liberation from rebirth

nadu a territorial unit in south India

nagarashresthin the chief merchant of the city

nataka dance, mime, drama

Nayanars Shaiva poets of Tamil devotionalism

nigama a market or a ward of a city

nirvana release from the cycle of rebirth

nishka a unit of value, later used for a coin

paan betel-leaf

Pali an Indo-Aryan language in which the Buddhist Canon of the Theravada sect was recorded

palli a hamlet, sometimes also a small market centre

panchakula administrative body

panchayat an administrative body, said to be a council of five

Pashupata a Shaiva sect

pipal ficus religiosa tree

pradesha an administrative unit

pratiloma literally, against the direction of the body hair, therefore against the hierarchy of castes in relation to marriage

purohita priest and mentor, especially in families of status

rajadhiraja royal title

rajasuya sacrifice performed to enhance royal or chiefly status

rajuka official designation

ranaka rank or status given to a landed intermediary

rasa a mood or an emotion evoked in creative literature, music and dance *rashtra* country/administrative unit

sabha an assembly, usually small and of special persons

samanta initially a term used for a neighbour; later it referred to a landed intermediary subordinate to the king

samiti an assembly

samnyasi ascetic

samsara used most commonly to refer to the cycle of transmigration

sangha frequently used to indicate the organizational Order in the Shramanic religions and more commonly in Buddhism

sankirna jati mixed caste

sarthavaha caravaneer

sati a virtuous woman; one who has immolated herself on the funeral pyre of her husband

setthi merchant

shakti power

Shangam assembly; more specifically the earliest literary corpus of Tamil poems

shastra texts on various subjects viewed as authoritative

shatamana coin

shikhara tower surmounting the sanctum of the temple

shraddha worship of the ancestors at a particular time of the year

shreni formal association of members of a profession; a guild

shudra the fourth and lowest *varna*

shunya the zero

Shvetambara literally, clad in white, one of the major Jaina schools

soma the plant from which the juice was prepared and drunk in a ritual context during some Vedic sacrifices, and thought to be a hallucinogen

stri-dhana the wealth of a woman given specifically to her for her own use

stupa tumulus-like structure containing relics of the Buddha or others and worshipped by Buddhists

Suryavamsha solar lineage

suvarna literally, of good colour and another name for gold

svyamavara the ceremony at which a princess chose her husband from among an assembly of suitors

thakkura the rank or status of a landed intermediary

Theravada an early Buddhist sect

tirtha literally a ford, more frequently a place of pilgrimage

tirthankara literally, a ford-maker; the teachers of Jainism

ur village assembly in south India

vaishya the third status in the *varna* hierarchy concerned theoretically with raising livestock, cultivation and trade

valanadu administrative unit in south India

vana forest

varna literally, colour; used for the four castes often as ritual statuses; the reference was not to skin pigmentation since in one text the four colours listed are white, yellow, red and black *varna-ashrama-dharma* upholding a society organized on the basis of *varna* and the social and sacred duties that this entailed

velala peasants or landowners of various categories

vihara Buddhist monastery

vina lyre

vishaya an administrative unit

vishti forced labour or labour in lieu of a tax, often compared to the corvée

vratya initially referring to those who were thought not to conform to orthodoxy, it came to mean degenerate forms in various categories

yaksha a demi-god

yoni female organs of generation

yuga a period of time

ziarat a place of pilgrimage

Select Bibliographies

1 Perceptions of the Past

COLONIAL CONSTRUCTIONS: ORIENTALIST READINGS

Jones, W., *Discourses Delivered before the Asiatic Society*, 2nd edn (London, 1824)

Inden, R., *Imagining India* (Oxford, 1990)

Drew, H., *India and the Romantic Imagination* (Delhi, 1987)

Leslie Willson, A., *A Mythical Image: The Ideal of India in German Romanticism* (Durham, 1964)

Leask, N., *British Romantic Writers and the East* (Cambridge, 1992)

Marshall, P. J., *The British Discovery of Hinduism in the Eighteenth Century* (Cambridge, 1970)

Mukherjee, S. N., *Sir William Jones: A Study in Eighteenth Century British Attitudes to India* (Delhi, 1983)

Said, E., *Orientalism* (New York, 1978)

Schwab, R., *The Oriental Renaissance: Europe's Discovery of India and the East 1680–1880* (New York, 1984)

Staal, F., *A Reader on the Sanskrit Grammarians* (Cambridge, Mass., 1972)

Teltscher, K., *India Inscribed: European and British Writing on India 1600–1800* (Delhi, 1995)

Thapar, R., *The Past and Prejudice* (Delhi, 1975)

Thapar, R., *Time as a Metaphor of History* (Delhi, 1996)

Thapar, R., *Interpreting Early India* (Delhi, 1992)

COLONIAL CONSTRUCTIONS: A UTILITARIAN CRITIQUE

Mill, J., *The History of British India*, 5th edn (New York, 1968)

Metcalfe, T. R., *Ideologies of the Raj* (Cambridge, 1995)

Majeed, J., *Ungoverned Imaginings. James Mill's The History of British India and Orientalism* (Oxford, 1992)

Philips, C. H. (ed.), *Historians of India, Pakistan and Ceylon* (London, 1962)

Smith, V., *Early History of India from 600 BC to the Muhammadan Conquest*, 4th edn (Oxford, 1957)

SELECT BIBLIOGRAPHIES

INDIA AS 'THE OTHER'

Weber, M., *The Religion of India*, repr. (Glencoe, 1967)

Kantowsky, D., *Recent Research on Max Weber's Studies of Hinduism* (London, 1986)

Durkheim, E., *The Elementary Forms of Religious Life: A Study in Religious Sociology* (London, 1915)

Hubert, H. and Mauss, M. *Sacrifice: Its Nature and Function* (tr.) (London, 1964)

Mauss, M., *The Gift*, repr. (New York, 1967)

Bougle, C., *Essays on the Caste System*, repr. (Cambridge, 1971)

'DISCOVERING' THE INDIAN PAST

Cumming, J. (ed.), *Revealing India's Past* (London, 1939)

Tod, J., *Annals and Antiquities of Rajastan* (Oxford, 1821)

Kejriwal, O. P., *The Asiatic Society of Bengal and the Discovery of India's Past, 1784–1838* (Delhi, 1988)

NOTIONS OF RACE AND THEIR INFLUENCE ON INDOLOGY

Poliakov, L., *The Aryan Myth* (London, 1974)

Max Müller, F., *Biographies of Words and the Home of the Aryas* (London, 1888)

Max Müller, F., *India What Can it Teach Us?* (London, 1883)

Trautmann, T. R., *Aryans and British India* (Delhi, 1997)

Robb, P. (ed.), *The Concept of Race in South Asia* (New Delhi, 1995)

HISTORY AND NATIONALISM

Jayaswal, K. P., *Hindu Polity*, 2nd edn (Bangalore, 1943)

Altekar, A. S., *State and Government in Ancient India* (Banaras, 1949)

Majumdar, R. C., Raychaudhuri, H. C. and Datta, K. K., *An Advanced History of India* (London, 1961; 3rd edn, Delhi, 1973)

THE SEEDING OF COMMUNAL HISTORY

Thapar, R., Mukhia H., and Bipan, Chandra, *Communalism and the Writing of Indian History*, repr. (Delhi, 2000)

Panikkar, K. N., *The Concerned Indian's Guide to Communalism* (Delhi, 1999)

Pandey, G., *The Construction of Communalism in Colonial North India* (Delhi, 1990)

MARXIST HISTORIES AND THE DEBATES THEY GENERATED

O'Leary, B., *The Asiatic Mode of Production: Oriental Despotism, Historical Materialism and Indian History* (Oxford, 1989)

Bailey, A. M. and Llobera, J. R. (eds), *The Asiatic Mode of Production. Science and Politics* (London, 1981)

Gough, K., *Rural Society in Southeast India* (Cambridge, 1981)

Anderson, P., *Lineages of the Absolutist State* (London, 1974)

Hobsbawm, E. J. (ed.), *Introduction to Pre-Capitalist Economic Formations* (London, 1984)

Wittfogel, K., *Oriental Despotism: A Comparative Study of Total Power* (New Haven, 1975)

Hobsbawm, E. J. (ed.), *Pre-Capitalist Economic Formations* (London, 1964)

Kosambi, D. D., *Introduction to the Study of Indian History* (Bombay, 1957)

Sharma, R. S., *Indian Feudalism* (Delhi, 1980)

Jha, D. N. (ed.), *Feudal Social Formation in Early India* (Delhi, 1987)

Byres, T. and H., Mukhia (eds), *Feudalism and non-European Societies* (London, 1985)

Chattopadhyaya, B. D., *The Making of Early Medieval India* (Delhi, 1994)

Stein, B., *Peasant State and Society in Medieval South India* (Delhi, 1980)

Karashima, N., *South Indian History and Society, Studies from Inscriptions AD 850–1800* (Delhi, 1984)

HISTORY AS A SOCIAL AND HUMAN SCIENCE

Burke, P. (ed.), *New Perspectives on Historical Writing*, 2nd edn (Cambridge, 2001)

Braudel, F., *On History* (Chicago, 1980)

Chakrabarti, D. K., *A History of Indian Archaeology from the Beginning to 1947* (Delhi, 1988)

Chakrabarti, D. K., *Theoretical Issues in Indian Archaeology* (Delhi, 1988)

Ucko, P. (ed.), *Theory in Archaeology* (London, 1995)

Heninge, D., *Chronology of Oral Tradition* (Oxford, 1974)

Vansina, J., *Oral Tradition as History* (Madison, 1985)

Wachtel, N., *The Vision of the Vanquished* (Hassocks, 1977)

Hivale, S., *The Pradhans of the Upper Narmada Valley* (Bombay, 1946)

Deshpande, M. M., *Sanskrit and Prakrit: Socio-linguistic Issues* (Delhi, 1993)

Chaudhuri, K. N., *Asia Before Europe. Economy and Civilisation of the Indian Ocean from the Rise of Islam to 1750* (Cambridge, 1990)

Abu-Lughod, J., *Before European Hegemony. The World System AD 1250–1350* (New York, 1989)

Reynolds, S., *Fiefs and Vassals: The Medieval Evidence Reinterpreted* (Oxford, 1994)

Wickham, C., *Land and Power* (London, 1994)

Klass, M., *Caste: The Emergence of the South Asian Social System* (Philadelphia, 1980)

Berreman, G., *The Hindus of the Himalayas* (Berkeley, 1963)

Srinivas, M. N., *Collected Essays* (Delhi, 2002)

Roy, K. (ed.), *Women in Early Indian Societies* (Delhi, 1999)

Sharma, R. S. and Jha, D. N. (eds), *Indian Society: Historical Probings. In Memory of D. D. Kosambi* (New Delhi, 1974)

Haskell, F., *History and its Images: Art and the Interpretation of the Past* (London, 1993)

Baxandall, M., *Painting and Experience in Fifteenth Century Italy* (Oxford, 1973)

Sebeok, T., *Current Trends in Linguistics*, vol. 5: *Linguistics in South Asia* (The Hague, 1969)

CULTURAL HISTORIES OF A DIFFERENT KIND

Evans, R. J., *In Defence of History* (London, 1997)

Skinner, Q., *The Return of Grand Theory in the Human Sciences*, repr. (Cambridge, 2000)

2 Landscapes and Peoples

TIME AND SPACE

Braudel, F., *On History* (Chicago, 1980)

Braudel, F., *The Mediterranean and the Mediterranean World in the Age of Philip II* (London, 1973)

Horden, P. and Purcell, N. *The Corrupting Sea* (Oxford, 2000)

Thapar, R., *Time as a Metaphor of History*, repr. (Delhi, 1992)

Law, B. C., *Historical Geography of Ancient India* (Paris, 1954)

Chattopadhyaya, B. D., *A Summary of Historical Geography of Ancient India* (Calcutta, 1984)

THE LANDSCAPE

Subba Rao, S., *The Personality of India* (Baroda, 1958)

Spate, O. H. K. and Learmonth, A. T. A., *India and Pakistan, a General and Regional Geography*, 4th edn (London, 1972)

Singh, R. L. (ed.), *India, a Regional Geography* (Varanasi, 1971)

Guha, R. (ed.), *Social Ecology* (Delhi, 1998)

Gadgil, M. and Guha, R. *The Fissured Land: an Ecological History of India* (New Delhi, 1992)

Reade, J. (ed.), *The Indian Ocean in Antiquity* (London, 1995)

FRONTIERS

Lattimore, O., *The Inner Asian Frontiers of China*, repr. (Oxford, 1988)

Khazanov, A. M., *Nomads and the Outside World*, 2nd edn (Madison, 1994)

Whittakar, R. C., *Frontiers of the Roman Empire* (London, 1994)

TRANSPORTATION

Deloche, J., *Transport and Communication in India Prior to Steam Locomotion*, vol.I: *Land Transport*; vol. II: *Water Transport* (Delhi, 1993; 1994)

POPULATION

Cavalli-Sforza, L. L., Piazza, A. and Menozzi, P., *The History and Geography of Human Genes* (New Jersey, 1994)

Guha, S., *Health and Population in South Asia* (Delhi, 2001)

CATEGORIES OF SOCIETIES – HUNTER-GATHERERS, PASTORALISTS, PEASANTS, TOWNSMEN

Sahlins, M., *Tribesmen* (New Jersey, 1968)

Kavoori, P. S., *Pastoralism in Expansion* (Delhi, 1999)

Sontheimer, G. D., *Pastoral Deities in Western India* (Delhi, 1993)

Diamond, J., *Guns, Germs and Steel* (New York, 1999)

Fried, M. H., *The Evolution of Political Society* (New York, 1967)

Claessen, H. J. M. and Skalnik, P. (eds), *The Early State* (The Hague, 1978)

Claessen, H. J. M. and Skalnik, P. (eds), *The Study of the State* (The Hague, 1981)

Allchin, B. (ed.), *Living Traditions: Studies in the Ethnoarchaeology of South Asia* (Delhi, 1994)

THE CREATION OF CASTES

Bose, N. K., *The Structure of Hindu Society* (Calcutta, 1975)

Klass, M., *Caste: The Emergence of the South Asian Social System* (Philadelphia, 1980)

Gupta, D. (ed.), *Social Stratification* (Delhi, 1992)

Mandelbaum, D., *Society in India*, vols I and II (Berkeley, Calif., 1970)

3 Antecedents

PREHISTORIC BEGINNINGS

Agrawal, D. P., *The Archaeology of India* (London, 1982)

Allchin, R. and Allchin, B., *Origins of a Civilization* (Delhi, 1997)

Chakrabarti, D. K., *India, An Archaeological History* (Delhi, 1999)

Ghosh, A. (ed.), *An Encyclopaedia of Indian Archaeology*, vols I and II (Delhi, 1989)

Neumayer, E., *Lines on Stone: Prehistoric Rock Art of India* (Delhi, 1993)

Mathpal, Y., *The Prehistoric Rock Art of Bhimbetka, Central India* (Delhi, 1984)

Possehl, G. L., *Radio-Carbon Dates for South Asian Archaeology* (Philadelphia, 1989)

Jacobson, J. (ed.), *Studies in the Archaeology of India and Pakistan* (New Delhi, 1986)

Kennedy, K. A. R. and Possehl, G. L. (eds), *Studies in the Archaeology and Palaeoanthropology of South Asia* (New Delhi, 1984)

THE FIRST URBANIZATION – CITIES OF THE INDUS CIVILIZATION

Possehl, G. L. (ed.), *Ancient Cities of the Indus* (Delhi, 1979)

Possehl, G. L. (ed.), *Harappan Civilization – a Recent Perspective*, 2nd edn (Delhi, 1993)

Meadow, R. (ed.), *Harappa Excavations 1986–1990: a Multi-Disciplinary Approach to Third Millennium Urbanism* (Madison, 1992)

Mughal, M. R., *Ancient Cholistan* (Lahore, 1997)

Parpola, A., *Deciphering the Indus Script* (Cambridge, 1944)

Mahadevan, I., 'The Indus Script: Texts, Concordance and Tables', in *Memoirs of the Archaeological Survey of India*, 77 (New Delhi, 1977)

Ratnagar, S., *Enquiries into the Political Organization of Harappan Society* (Pune, 1991)

Ratnagar, S., *The End of the Great Harappan Tradition* (Delhi, 2000)

Ratnagar, S., *Understanding Harappa* (Delhi, 2001)

Kohl, P. (ed.), *The Bronze Age Civilization of Central Asia* (New York, 1981)

NEOLITHIC AND CHALCOLITHIC CULTURES, OTHER THAN IN THE NORTH-WEST

Dhavlikar, M. K., *The First Farmers of the Deccan* (Pune, 1988)

Eliade, M., *Shamanism* (New Jersey, 1974)

Allchin, F. R., *Neolithic Cattle Keepers of South India* (Cambridge, 1963)

Roy, T. N., *The Ganges Civilization* (New Delhi, 1983)

Tripathi, V., *The Painted Grey Ware: An Iron Age Culture of Northern India* (Delhi, 1976)

Gaur, R. C., *Excavations at Atranjikhera* (New Delhi, 1983)

Chattopadhyaya, D. P., *History of Science and Technology in Ancient India* (Calcutta, 1986)

Atre, S., *The Archetypal Mother* (Pune, 1987)

MEGALITHIC BURIALS

Gururaja Rao, B. K., *The Megalithic Culture in South India* (Prasaranga, 1981)

Sundara, A., *The Early Chamber Tombs of South India* (Delhi, 1975)

Deo, S. B., *Problem of South Indian Megaliths* (Dharwar, 1973)

Moorti, U. S., *Megalithic Culture of South India* (Varanasi, 1994)

4 Towards Chiefdoms and Kingdoms

NARRATIVES OF BEGINNINGS

Brockington, J. L., *The Sanskrit Epics* (Leiden, 1998)

Brockington, J. L., *Righteous Rama* (Delhi, 1984)

Bulcke, C., *Ramakatha* (Varanasi, 1971)

Sukhthankar V. S., *On the Meaning of the Mahabharata* (Bombay, 1954)

Goldman, R. P., *Gods, Priests and Warriors. The Bhrigus of the Mahabharata* (New York, 1977)

Pargiter, F. E., *The Ancient Indian Historical Tradition* (London, 1922)

Deshpande, M. M. and Hook, P. (eds), *Aryan and Non-Aryan in India* (Ann Arbor, 1979)

Burrow, T., *The Sanskrit Language* (London, 1973)

Heninge, D. P., *The Chronology of Oral Tradition* (Oxford, 1974)

Ong, W. J., *Orality and Literacy* (London, 1982)

Lad, G., *Mahabharata and Archaeological Evidence* (Pune, 1983)

SELECT BIBLIOGRAPHIES

THE VEDIC CORPUS

Gonda, J., *Vedic Literature* (Wiesbaden, 1975)

Banerji, S. C., *Dharmasutras, A Study in their Origin and Development* (Calcutta, 1962)

Witzel, M. (ed.), *Inside the Texts Beyond the Texts: New Approaches to the Study of the Vedas* (Cambridge, 1997)

Tripathi, V., *The Painted Grey Ware: An Iron Age Culture of Northern India* (Delhi, 1976)

Raychaudhuri, H. C., *The Political History of Ancient India* (Delhi, 1996)

History and Culture of the Indian People, vol. 1: *The Vedic Age* (Bombay, 1965)

Dandekar, R. N., *Vedic Bibliography* (Pune, 1946)

Pollet, G. (ed.), *India and the Ancient World* (Leuven, 1987)

Caillat, C. (ed.), *Dialectes dans les littératures Indo-Aryennes* (Paris, 1989)

THE CONTEXT OF THE *RIG-VEDA*

Masica, C. P., *Defining a Linguistic Area: South Asia* (Chicago, 1976)

Mallory, J. P., *In Search of the Indo-Europeans: Language, Archaeology and Myth* (London, 1989)

Deshpande, M. M., *Sociolinguistic Attitudes in India: An Historical Reconstruction* (Ann Arbor, 1979)

Emeneau, M. B., *Language and Linguistic Area* (Stanford, 1980)

Kuiper, F. B. J., *Aryans in the Rigveda* (Amsterdam, 1991)

Rau, W., *The Meaning of 'Pur' in Vedic Literature* (Munich, 1976)

Lincoln, B., *Priests, Warriors and Cattle* (Los Angeles, 1981)

Bryant, E., *The Quest for the Origins of Vedic Culture* (Delhi, 2000)

SOCIETIES IN THE VEDIC CORPUS

Erdosy, G. (ed.), *The Indo-Aryans of Ancient South Asia: Language, Material Culture, Ethnicity* (Berlin, 1995)

Thapar, R., 'From Lineage to State', in *History and Beyond* (Delhi, 2000)

Trautmann, T. R., *Dravidian Kinship* (Cambridge, 1981)

Sharma, R. S., *Material Culture and Social Formation in Ancient India* (Delhi, 1983)

Chattopadhyaya, D. P., *History of Science and Technology in Ancient India*, vols I and II (Calcutta 1986; 1991)

Gaur, R. C., *The Excavations at Atranjikhera: Early Civilization in the Ganges Basin* (Delhi, 1983)

Kochar, R. *The Vedic People* (New Delhi, 2000)

CHIEFS AND KINGS

Gonda, J., *Ancient Indian Kingship from the Religious Point of View* (Leiden, 1969)

Roy, K., *The Emergence of Monarchy in North India* (Delhi, 1994)

Mauss, M., *The Gift* (New York, 1967)

Sharma, R. S., *Aspects of Political Ideas and Institutions in Ancient India*, 3rd edn (Delhi, 1991)

Singh, S. D., *Ancient Indian Warfare with Special Reference to the Vedic Period* (Leiden, 1965)

Earle, T. (ed.), *Chiefdoms: Power, Economy and Ideology* (Cambridge, 1991)

INCIPIENT CASTE

Kosambi, D. D., *Introduction to the Study of Indian History* (Bombay, 1956)

Karve, I., *Hindu Society – an Interpretation* (Poona, 1961)

Dumont, L., *Homo Hierarchicus* (Chicago, 1970)

SACRIFICE AS RITUAL AND AS A FORM OF SOCIAL EXCHANGE

Dandekar, R. N., *Vedic Mythological Tracts* (Delhi, 1979)

Staal, F., *Agni* (Berkeley, Calif., 1981)

Gonda, J., *The Ritual Sutras* (Wiesbaden, 1977)

Heesterman, J. C., *The Ancient Indian Royal Consecration* (The Hague, 1957)

Keith, A. B., *Religion and Philosophy of the Vedas and Upanishads* (Cambridge, Mass., 1925)

Hubert, H. and Mauss, M., *Sacrifice – its Nature and Function* (Chicago, 1964)

Lincoln, B., *Death, War and Sacrifice* (Chicago, 1991)

Some Sources in Translation

Griffiths, R. T. H., *Hymns of the Rigveda* (Varanasi, 1896–97)

Geldner, K. F., *Der Rigveda Samhita*, German text (Cambridge, Mass., 1951)

Keith, A. B., *The Rigveda Brahmanas* (Cambridge, Mass., 1920)

Eggeling, J., *Shatapatha Brahmana* (Oxford, 1898)

Radhakrishnan, S., *The Principal Upanisads* (London, 1953)

Olivelle, P., *The Dharmasutras* (Oxford, 1999)

Darmesteter, J., *The Zend Avesta*, repr. (Varanasi, 1969)

5 States and Cities of the Indo-Gangetic Plain

STATES AND CITIES

Thapar, R., *From Lineage to State*, 2nd edn (Delhi, 1996)

Makkhan Lal, *Settlement History and the Rise of Civilization in the Ganga-Yamuna Doab from 1500 BC–AD 300* (Delhi, 1984)

Sharma, R. S., *Material Culture and Social Formation in Ancient India* (Delhi, 1983)

Fried, M., *The Evolution of Political Society* (New York, 1967)

Claessen, H. J. M. and Skalnik, P. (eds), *The Early State* (The Hague, 1978)

Claessen, H. J. M. and Skalnik, P. (eds), *The Study of the State* (The Hague, 1981)

Law, B. C., *Geography of Early Buddhism*, repr. (Varanasi, 1973)

THE SECOND URBANIZATION: THE GANGES PLAIN

Allchin, F. R., *The Archaeology of Early Historic South Asia: The Emergence of Cities and States* (Cambridge, 1995)

Chakrabarti, D. K., *The Early Use of Iron in India* (Delhi, 1992)

Erdosy, G., *Urbanization in Early Historic India*, BAR (Oxford, 1988)

Ghosh, A., *The City in Early Historical India* (Shimla, 1973)

Jha, S. K., *Beginning of Urbanization in Early Historic India* (Patna, 1998)

Marshall, J., *Taxila* (Cambridge, 1951)

Sharma, G. R., *The Excavations at Kaushambi 1957–59* (Allahabad, 1960)

Roy, T. N., *The Ganges Civilization* (New Delhi, 1983)

Sarao, K. T. S., *Urban Centres and Urbanisation as Reflected in the Pali Vinaya and Sutta Pitakas* (Delhi, 1990)

Dani, A. H., *The Historic City of Taxila* (Paris, 1986)

Chakrabarti, D. K., *The Archaeology of Ancient Indian Cities* (New Delhi, 1995)

Thakur, V. K., *Urbanisation in Ancient India* (New Delhi, 1981)

GANA-SANGHAS – CHIEFDOMS AND OLIGARCHIES

Law, B. C., *Some Kshatriya Tribes in Ancient India*, repr. (Delhi, 1975)

Wagle, N. N., *Society at the Time of the Buddha*, 2nd edn (Bombay, 1996)

Chanana, D., *Slavery in Ancient India* (Delhi, 1960)

Sharma, R. S., *Sudras in Ancient India*, 2nd edn (Delhi, 1980)

Sharma, J. P., *Republics in Ancient India* (Leiden, 1968)

Jha, H. N., *The Licchavis* (Varanasi, 1970)

KINGDOMS AND THE PRE-EMINENCE OF MAGADHA

Raychaudhuri, H. C., *Political History of Ancient India* (Calcutta, 1965); with an update by B. N. Mukherjee (Calcutta, 1996)

Kosambi, D. D., *The Culture and Civilization of Ancient India in Historical Outline* (London, 1966)

Shrimali, K. M., *History of Pancala to c. AD 500*, vols I and II (Delhi, 1985)

NORTH-WEST INDIA AND ALEXANDER

Lane Fox, R., *Alexander the Great* (New York, 1974)

Smith, V., *Early History of India from 600 BC to the Muhammadan Conquest*, 4th edn (Oxford, 1957)

Bosworth, A. B., *A Historical Commentary on Arrian's History of Alexander* (Oxford, 1995)

EARLY TRADE

Allan, J., *Catalogue of Indian Coins in the British Museum. Coins of Ancient India*, repr. (London, 1967)

Mitchiner, M., *The Origins of Indian Coinage* (London, 1973)

Gupta, P. L. and Hardekar, T. R., *Indian Silver Punch-Marked Coins of the Magadha-Maurya-Karshapana Series* (Anjaner, 1985)

Fick, R., *Social Organization of North-eastern India in the Buddha's Time*, repr. (Delhi, 1972)

Nath, V., *Dana: Gift System in Ancient India (600 BC to AD 300)* (Delhi, 1987)

RELIGIONS AND IDEOLOGIES: QUESTIONS AND RESPONSES

Lamotte, E., *History of Indian Buddhism* (Louvain, 1976; 1988 (tr.))

Ling, T., *The Buddha* (Harmondsworth, 1988)

Bechert, H. (ed.), *The Dating of the Historical Buddha*, Vols 1–3 (Göttingen, 1992–97)

Chakravarti, U., *The Social Dimensions of Early Buddhism* (Delhi, 1987)

Frauwallner, E., *The Earliest Vinaya and the Beginnings of Buddhist Literature* (Rome, 1956)

Jayatilleke, K. N., *Early Buddhist Theory of Knowledge* (London, 1963; Delhi, 1983)

Pande, G. C., *Studies in the Origins of Buddhism* (Allahabad, 1957)

Horner, I. B., *Women under Primitive Buddhism* (London, 1930)

Dundas, P., *The Jainas* (London, 1992)

Basham, A. L., *The History and Doctrine of the Ajivikas* (London, 1951)

Chattopadhyoya, D. P. *Lokayata* (Delhi, 1955)

Some Sources in Translation

Woodward F. L., and Hare, E. M., *Anguttara Nikaya*, repr. (Oxford, 1995)

Max Müller, F., *Dhammapada*, repr. (Delhi, 1965)

Rhys Davids, T. W., *Digha Nikaya*, 3rd edn (London, 1951)

Oldenberg, H. and Rhys Davids, T. W., *Vinaya Pitaka*, repr. (Delhi 1965)

Jacobi, H., *Jaina Sutras*, repr. (Delhi, 1964)

McCrindle, J. W., *Ancient India as Described by Ktesias the Knidian*, repr. (Delhi, 1973)

McCrindle, J. W., *Ancient India as Described in Classical Literature* (Westminster, 1901)

McCrindle, J. W., *The Invasion of India by Alexander the Great*, repr. (New York, 1972)

Ghosh, A., *An Encyclopaedia of Indian Archaeology* (Delhi, 1989)

6   The Emergence of Empire: Mauryan India

THE MAURYAS AND THEIR WORLD

Nilakanta Sastri, K. A. (ed.), *The Age of the Nandas and Mauryas* (Varanasi, 1952)

Bongard-Levin, G., *Mauryan India* (Delhi, 1985)

Thapar, R., *Asoka and the Decline of the Mauryas*, 2nd edn (Delhi, 1997)

Dandamaev, N. A. and Lukonin, V. G., *The Culture and Social Institutions of Ancient Iran* (Cambridge, 1989)

Frye, R., *The History of Ancient Iran* (Munich, 1984)

Karttunen, K., *India in Early Greek Literature* (Helsinki, 1989)

Rostovtzeff, M. I., *The Social and Economic History of the Hellenistic World* (Oxford, 1941)

Sherwin-White, S. and Kuhrt, A. (eds), *From Samarkhand to Sardis* (London, 1993)
Chattopadhyaya, S., *The Achaemenids and India*, 2nd edn (Delhi, 1974)

THE POLITICAL ECONOMY OF EMPIRE

Trautmann, T. R., *Kautilya and the Arthasastra* (Leiden, 1971)
Kosambi, D. D., *Indian Numismatics* (Delhi, 1981)
Marshall, J., *Taxila* (Cambridge, 1951)
Salomon, R., *Indian Epigraphy* (Delhi, 1998)
Dani, A. H., *Indian Palaeography* (Oxford, 1963)
Gupta, P. L., *A Bibliography of the Hoard of Punch-Marked Coins in Ancient India* (Bombay, 1955)

WELDING A SUBCONTINENTAL SOCIETY

Thapar, R., *The Mauryas Revisited* (Calcutta, 1988)
Sharma, R. S., *Sudras in Ancient India*, rev. edn (Delhi, 1980)
Derret, J. D., *Religion, Law and the State in India* (London, 1968)
Lingat, R., *The Classical Law of India* (Berkeley, 1973)

ADMINISTRATION AND EMPIRE

Thapar, R., *The Mauryas Revisited* (Calcutta, 1988)
Ghoshal, U. N., *The Agrarian System in Ancient India* (Calcutta, 1930)
Fox, R. G., *Realm and Region in Traditional India* (New Delhi, 1977)
Claessen, H. and Skalnik, P. (eds), *The Early State* (The Hague, 1978)
Ray, N. R., *Maurya and Shunga Art* (Calcutta, 1945)

ASHOKA'S *DHAMMA*

Lingat, R., *Royautés Bouddhiques*, part 1 (Paris, 1989)
Sircar, D. C., *Ashokan Studies* (Calcutta, 1979)
Tambiah, S. J., *World Conqueror and World Renouncer* (Cambridge, 1976)
Mukherjee, B. N., *Studies in the Aramaic Edicts of Asoka* (Calcutta, 1984)

Some Sources in Translation

Kangle, R. P., *Kautiliya Arthasastra*, 3 vols (Bombay, 1965)
Strong, J. S., *The Legend of King Asoka* (New Jersey, 1983)
McCrindle, J. W., *Ancient India as Described by Megasthenes and Arrian* (Calcutta, 1877)
Bloch, J., *Les Inscriptions d'Asoka* (Paris, 1950)
Hultzsch, E., *Corpus Inscriptionum Indicarum*, vol. 1: *The Inscriptions of Asoka*, repr. (Delhi, 1969)
Pargiter, F. E., *The Purana Texts of the Dynasties of the Kali Age*, repr. (Varanasi, 1962)
Geiger, W., *The Mahavamsa* (London, 1964)
Przyluski, J., *La Légende de l'Empereur Açoka* (Paris, 1923)
Coulson, M., *Three Sanskrit Plays* (Harmondsworth, 1981)

7 Of Politics and Trade

SHUNGAS, KHARAVELA, OLIGARCHIES

Raychaudhuri, H. C., *Political History of Ancient India*, commentary B. N. Mukherjee (Delhi, 1996)

Lahiri, B., *Indigenous States of Northern India* circa *200 BC to 320 AD* (Calcutta, 1974)

Dasgupta, K. K., *A Tribal History of Ancient India: a Numismatic Approach* (Calcutta, 1974)

INDO-GREEKS AND SHAKAS

Narain, A. K., *The Indo-Greeks* (Oxford, 1957)

Guillaume, O., *Analysis of Reasonings in Archaeology* (Delhi, 1990)

Guillaume, O., *Graeco-Bactrian and Indian Coins* (Delhi, 1991)

Bernard, P. et al., *Fouilles d'Ai Khanoum*, vols I–VII (Paris, 1973–87)

Mukherjee, B. N., *Mathura and its Society – the Saka-Pahlava Phase* (Calcutta, 1981)

Van Lohuizen de Leeuw, J. E., *The Scythian Period* (Leiden, 1949)

SHAKAS, PARTHIANS, KUSHANAS AND KSHATRAPAS

Basham, A. L. (ed.), *Papers on the Date of Kaniska* (Leiden, 1968)

Gershevitch, I. (ed.), *The Cambridge History of Iran*, vol. II (Cambridge, 1985)

Jettmar, K. et al., *Rock Inscriptions in the Indus Valley. Antiquities of Northern Pakistan* (Mainz, 1989)

Liu Xinru, *Ancient India and Ancient China: Trade and Religious Exchanges AD 1–600* (Delhi, 1988)

Mukherjee, B. N., *The Rise and Fall of the Kushana Empire* (Calcutta, 1988)

Sharma, G. R. (ed.), *Kushana Studies* (Allahabad, 1968)

Sinor, D. (ed.), *The Cambridge History of Early Inner Asia* (Cambridge, 1990)

Khazanov, A. M., *Nomads and the Outside World* (Cambridge, 1984)

Seaman, G. (ed.), *Ecology and Empire. Nomads in the Cultural Evolution of the Old World*, vol. I (Los Angeles, 1989)

Colledge, M. A. R., *The Parthian Period* (Leiden, 1986)

Mukherjee, B. N., *An Agrippan Source. A Study in Indo-Parthian History* (Calcutta, 1969)

Bagchi, P. C., *India and Central Asia* (Calcutta, 1955)

SATAVAHANAS

Shastri, A. M., *Early History of the Deccan: Problems and Perspectives* (New Delhi, 1987)

Margabandhu, C., *Archaeology of the Satavahana and Kshatrapa Times* (New Delhi, 1985)

Yazdani, G. (ed.), *Early History of the Deccan* (Delhi, 1960)

Sircar, D. C., *The Successors of the Satavahanas in the Lower Deccan* (Calcutta, 1969)

Gupte, R. S., *Excavation at Bhokardan* (Nagpur, 1974)

Sarkar, H. and Nainar, S. P. *Amaravati* (New Delhi, 1972)

Knox, R., *Amaravati: Buddhist Sculpture from the Great Stupa* (London, 1992)

Sankalia, H. D. and Dikshit, M. G., *Excavation at Brahmapuri (Kolhapur) 1945–46* (Poona, 1952)

SOUTH INDIA

Abdul Majeed, A. et al., *Alagankulam: a Preliminary Report* (Madras, 1992)

Gurukkal, R. and Raghava Varier, M. R. (eds), *Cultural History of Kerala*, vol. I (Tiruvananthapuram, 2000)

Subrahmanian, N., *Sangam Polity: The Administration and Social Life of the Sangam Tamils*, repr. (Bombay, 1980)

Mahalingam, T. V., *Report on the Excavations in the Lower Kaveri Valley* (Madras, 1970)

Champakalakshmi, R., *Trade, Ideology and Urbanisation: South India 300 BC to AD 300* (Delhi, 1996)

Claessen, H. J. M. and Skalnik, P. (eds), *The Study of the State* (The Hague, 1981)

Kailasapathy, K., *Tamil Heroic Poetry* (Oxford, 1972)

Nagaswamy, R. (ed.), *Seminar on Inscriptions* (Madras, 1968)

Turner, P. J., *Roman Coins from India* (London, 1989)

NETWORKS OF ROUTES AND TRADING CENTRES

Deo, S. B. and Paddayya, K. (eds), *Recent Advances in Indian Archaeology* (Poona, 1988)

Parashar-Sen, A. (ed.), *Social and Economic History of the Early Deccan: Some Interpretations* (New Delhi, 1993)

De Romanis, F. and Tchernia, A. (ed.), *Crossings* (Delhi, 1997)

Deloche, J., *Transport and Communications in India*, vols 1 and 2 (Delhi, 1993)

Bagchi, P. C., *India and China*, 2nd edn (Calcutta, 1981)

Some Sources in Translation

Casson, L., *The Periplus Maris Erythraei*, text with introduction, translation and commentary (Princeton, 1989)

Rhys Davids, T. W., *The Questions of King Milinda* (Oxford, 1890–4)

Konow, S., *Corpus Inscriptionum Indicarum*, vol. II, repr. (Ootacamund, 1963)

Epigraphia Indica. vol VII: *Calcutta 1902–3*; vol. VIII: *Calcutta 1905–6*

Allan, J., *Catalogue of Coins in the British Museum, Ancient India*, repr. (London, 1967)

Smith, V., *Catalogue of Coins in the Indian Museum*, repr. (Delhi, 1972–6)

Rapson, E. J., *Catalogue of Coins in the British Museum, Andhras and Western Kshatrapas*, repr. (London, 1967)

Whitehead, R. B., *Catalogue of Coins in the Punjab Museum, Lahore* (London, 1914)

Gardner, P., *Catalogue of Coins in the British Museum, Greek and Scythic Kings* (London, 1886)

Rama Rao, M., *Satavahana Coins in the Andhra Pradesh Government Museum* (Hyderabad, 1961)

Shastri, A. M. (ed.), *Coinage of the Satavahanas and Coins from Excavations* (Nagpur, 1972)

Mahadevan, I., 'Corpus of the Tamil-Brahmi Inscriptions', in R. Nagaswamy (ed.), *Seminar on Inscriptions* (Madras, 1968)

Ghosh A. (ed.), *An Encyclopaedia of Indian Archaeology*, vols 1 and 2 (Delhi, 1989)

8   The Rise of the Mercantile Community

Most of the monographs listed for the previous chapter are also relevant to this chapter.

ECONOMIES OF EXCHANGE

Bernard, P. and Grenet, F. (eds), *Histoire et cultes de l'asie centrale pre-islamiques – sources écrites et documents archéologiques* (Paris, 1991)

Mukherjee, B. N., *The Economic Factors in Kushana History* (Calcutta, 1970)

Raschke, M. G., 'New Studies of Roman Commerce with the East', *Aufsteig und Neidergang der Romischer Welt* (Berlin, 1978)

Liu, Xinru, *Silk and Religion* (Delhi, 1996)

Dasgupta, K. K., *A Tribal History of India: A Numismatic Approach* (Calcutta, 1974)

Potts, D. T., *The Arabian Gulf in Antiquity* (Oxford, 1990)

Motichandra, *Trade and Trade Routes in Ancient India* (Delhi, 1977)

Miller, J. I., *The Spice Trade of the Roman Empire* (Oxford, 1969)

Begley, V. and De Puma, R. D., *Rome and India* (Delhi, 1992)

Begley, V., *Arikamedu*, vols I and II (Pondichery, 1995; forthcoming)

Chattopadhyaya, B. D., *Coins and Currency Systems in South India* (Delhi, 1977)

Bose, A., *Social and Rural Economy of Northern India*, vols I and II (Calcutta, 1942–45)

Pollet, G. (ed.), *India and the Ancient World: History, Trade and Culture before AD 650* (Leuven, 1987)

Higham, C., *The Archaeology of Mainland Southeast Asia* (Cambridge, 1989)

CULTURAL INTERACTIONS

Dani, A. H., *Chilas* (Islamabad, 1983)

Dani, A. H., *Recent Archaeological Discoveries in Pakistan* (Paris, 1988)

Errington, E. and J. Cribb (eds), *The Crossroads of Asia* (Cambridge, 1992)

Frye, R., *The Heritage of Central Asia* (Princeton, 1996)

Karttunen, K., *India and the Hellenistic World* (Helsinki, 1997)

Kuhrt, A. and Sherwin-White S. (eds), *Hellenism in the East* (London, 1987)

Marshall, J., *Taxila* (Cambridge, 1951)

Ray, H. P., *Monastery and Guild, Commerce under the Satavahanas* (New Delhi, 1986)

Wolters, O. W., *History, Culture and Region in Southeast Asian Perspectives* (Ithaca, 1999)

Mukherjee, R. K., *The History of Indian Shipping* (London, 1912)

EDUCATION, LITERATURE AND SYSTEMS OF KNOWLEDGE

Sivathamby, K. (ed.), *Drama in Ancient Tamil Society* (Madras, 1981)

Zvelebil, K., *Tamil Literature* (Weisbaden, 1974)

Takahashi, T., *Tamil Love Poetry and Poetics* (Leiden, 1995)

Chattopadhyaya, D. P., *Science and Society in Ancient India* (Calcutta, 1977)

Zysk, K. G., *Asceticism and Healing in Ancient India. Medicine in the Buddhist Monastery* (New York, 1991)

Pingree, D., *Jyotihsastra* (Wiesbaden, 1981)

Warder, A. K., *Indian Kavya Literature* (Delhi, 1972)

Bose, D. M. et al. (ed.), *A Concise History of Science in India* (New Delhi, 1971)

Zimmerman, F., *The Jungle and the Aroma of Meats* (Berkeley, Calif., 1987)

SOCIAL FORMS

Srinivasan, D. M. (ed.), *Mathura, A Cultural History* (Delhi, 1989)

Kosambi, D. D., *Myth and Reality* (Bombay, 1962)

Bhattacharya, S. C., *Some Aspects of Indian Society from c. second century BC to c. fourth century AD* (Calcutta, 1978)

Paul, D. Y., *Women in Buddhism*, 2nd edn (Berkeley, 1985)

Sharma, R. S., *Sudras in Ancient India*, 2nd edn (Delhi, 1980)

Chanana, D., *Slavery in Ancient India as Depicted in Pali and Sanskrit Texts* (Delhi, 1960)

ARCHITECTURE AND VISUAL EXPRESSION

Huntington, S., *The Art of Ancient India – Hindu, Buddhist, Jaina* (New York, 1985)

Nehru, L., *Origins of the Gandharan Style* (Delhi, 1989)

Rosenfield, O. M., *The Dynastic Arts of the Kushans* (Berkeley, 1967)

Sarkar, H. B., *Studies in Early Buddhist Architecture of India* (Delhi, 1966)

Dehejia, V., *Early Buddhist Rock Temples* (London, 1972)

Dehejia, V., *Discourse in Early Buddhist Art: Visual Narratives of India* (New Delhi, 1997)

Dhavlikar, M. K., *Sanchi. A Cultural Study* (Poona, 1965)

Krishnamurthy, K., *Nagarjunakonda: A Cultural Study* (Delhi, 1977)

Sundara, A., *The Early Chamber Tombs of South India* (Delhi, 1975)

Miller, B. (ed.), *The Powers of Art* (Delhi, 1992)

Sharma, R. C., *Buddhist Art of Mathura* (Delhi, 1984)

THE INTERMINGLING OF RELIGIOUS BELIEFS AND PRACTICES

Schopen, G., *Bones, Stones and Buddhist Monks* (Honolulu, 1997)

Salomon, R., *Ancient Buddhist Scrolls from Gandhara* (London, 1999)

Heitzman, J., *The Origin and Spread of Buddhist Monastic Institutions in South Asia, 500 BC to AD 300* (Philadelphia, 1980)

Raychaudhuri, H. C., *Early History of the Vaishnava Sect*, repr. (Delhi, 1975)

Medlycot, A. E., *India and the Apostle Thomas* (London, 1905)

Some Sources in Translation

Casson, L., *The Periplus Maris Erythraei. Text with Introduction, Translation and Commentary* (Princeton, 1989)

McCrindle, J. W., *Ancient India as Described by Ptolemy* (Calcutta, 1927)

Buehler, G., *The Laws of Manu*, repr. (Delhi, 1971)

Cowell, E. B., et al., *Buddhist Mahayana Sutras* (Oxford, 1894)

Suzuki, D. T., *The Lankavatara Sutra* (London, 1932)

Ramanujan, A. K., *Poems of Love and War* (New York, 1985)

9 Threshold Times

THE GUPTAS AND THEIR SUCCESSORS

Majumdar, R. C. and Altekar, A. S. (eds), *The Vakataka-Gupta Age* (Benaras, 1954)

Goyal, S. R., *History of the Imperial Guptas* (Allahabad, 1967)

Altekar, A. S., *The Coinage of the Gupta Empire and its Imitations* (Varanasi, 1957)

Gupta, P. L., *The Imperial Guptas*, 2 vols (Varanasi, 1974–9)

Shastri, A. M. (ed.), *The Age of the Vakatakas* (Delhi, 1992)

Devahuti, D., *Harsha, a Political Study*, 3rd edn (Delhi, 1998)

INDICATORS OF A CHANGING POLITICAL ECONOMY

Jha, D. N., *Revenue System in Post-Maurya and Gupta Times* (Calcutta, 1977)

Sircar, D. C., *Political and Administrative System of Ancient and Medieval India* (Delhi, 1974)

Maity, S. K., *Economic Life of Northern India in the Gupta Period AD 300–500* (Calcutta, 1958)

Sharma, R. S., *Aspects of Political Ideas and Institutions in Ancient India* (Delhi, 1968)

Sharma, R. S., *Indian Feudalism c. AD 300–1200* (Delhi, 1980)

Shrimali, K. M., *Agrarian Structure in Central India and the Northern Deccan* (Delhi, 1987)

URBAN LIFE

Thakur, V. K., *Urbanism in Ancient India* (New Delhi, 1981)

Sharma, R. S., *Urban Decay in India* (New Delhi, 1983)

Sharma, R. S., *Perspectives in Social and Economic History in Early India* (New Delhi, 1983)

Mukherjee, B. N., *Coins and Currency System in Gupta Bengal* (New Delhi, 1992)

Hourani, G. F., *Arab Seafaring*, expanded edn, J. Carswell (Princeton, 1995)

Hall, K. R., *Maritime Trade and State Development in Early South East Asia*, (Honolulu, 1984)

SOCIAL MORES

Smith, B. L. (ed.), *Essays on Gupta Culture* (Delhi, 1983)

Suryavamsi, B., *The Abhiras: Their History and Culture* (Baroda, 1962)

Gupta, C., *The Kayasthas: A Study in the Formation and Early History of a Caste* (Calcutta, 1996)

Altekar, A. S., *The Position of Women in Hindu Civilisation* (Varanasi, 1956)

SYSTEMS OF KNOWLEDGE

Cunningham, A., *The Book of Indian Eras* (London, 1889)

Ghosh, A., *Nalanda*, ASI, 6th edn (Delhi, 1971)

Sankalia, H. D., *The University of Nalanda* (Delhi, 1972)

Mookerji, R. K., *Ancient Indian Education: Brahmanical and Buddhist*, 3rd edn (Delhi, 1969)

Houben, J. E. M. (ed.), *Ideology and Status of Sanskrit: Contributions to the History of the Sanskrit Language* (Leiden, 1996)

Lingat, R., *The Classical Law of India* (Berkeley, 1973)

Matilal, B., *Perception* (Oxford, 1986)

Zimmerman, F., *The Jungle and the Aroma of Meats* (Berkeley, 1987)

Pargiter, F. E., *Purana Texts of the Dynasties of the Kali Age* (London, 1922)

Pathak, V. S., *Ancient Historians of India* (Bombay, 1966)

Radhakrishnan, S., *Indian Philosophy* (London, 1948)

Das Gupta, S. N., *History of Indian Philosophy*, vols I–V (Cambridge, 1923–49)

Bose, D. M. et al. (eds), *A Concise History of Science in India* (New Delhi, 1971)

CREATIVE LITERATURE

Warder, A. K., *Indian Kavya Literature*, 2nd edn (New Delhi, 1989)

Stoler Miller, B. (ed.), *Theatre of Memory* (New York, 1984)

Thapar, R., *Shakuntala: Texts, Readings, Histories* (Delhi, 1999)

Kosambi, D. D., *Myth and Reality: Studies in the Formation of Indian Culture* (Bombay, 1962)

Keith, A. B., *History of Sanskrit Literature* (Oxford, 1928)

ARCHITECTURE, ART AND PATRONAGE

Harle, J. C., *Gupta Sculpture: Indian Sculpture from the Fourth to the Sixth Centuries AD* (Oxford, 1974)

Williams, J., *The Art of Gupta India* (Princeton, 1982)

Asher, F. M., *The Art of Eastern India 300–800* (Minneapolis, 1980)

Stoler Miller, B. (ed.), *The Powers of Art: Patronage in Indian Culture* (Delhi, 1992)

Poster, G. A., *From Indian Earth: Four Thousand Years of Terracotta Art* (New York, 1986)

RELIGIOUS FORMULATIONS

Basham, A. L., *The Origins and Development of Classical Hinduism* (Delhi, 1990)

Rocher, L., *The Puranas* (Wiesbaden, 1986)

Hazra, R. C., *Studies in the Puranic Records on Hindu Rites and Customs* (Delhi, 1975)

Nath, V., *Puranas and Acculturation* (Delhi, 2000)

Jaiswal, S., *The Origin and Development of Vaishnavism*, 2nd edn (Delhi, 1981)

Bhandarkar, R. G., *Vaishnavism, Shaivism and the Minor Religious Sects* (Strasburg, 1913)

Chandra, K. R., *A Critical Study of the Paumacariyam* (Vaishali, 1970)

Coburn, T. B., *Devi Mahatmya: The Crystallisation of the Goddess Tradition* (Delhi, 1984)

Some Sources in Translation

Fleet, J., *Corpus Inscriptionum Indicarum*, vol. III, repr. (New Delhi, 1981)

Mirashi, V. V. (ed.), *Corpus Inscriptionum Indicarum*, vol. V, *Inscriptions of the Vakatakas* (Ootacamund, 1963)

Allan, J., *Catalogue of the Coins of the Gupta Dynasty in the British Museum*, repr. (London, 1967)

Altekar, A. S., *Catalogue of the Gupta Gold Coins in the Bayana Hoard* (Bombay, 1954)

Giles, H. A., *The Travels of Fa-hien* (London, 1959)

Stoler Miller, B. (ed.), *Theatre of Memory* (New York, 1984)

Wilson, H. H., *The Vishnu Purana*, repr. (Calcutta, 1961)

Lariveiere, R., *Narada Smriti*, parts 1 and 2 (Philadelphia, 1989)

Jolly, J. *The Institutes of Vishnu* (Oxford, 1880)

Cowell, E. B. and Thomas, F. W. *The Harsacarita of Bana*, repr. (Delhi, 1968)

Watters, T., *On Yuan Chwang's Travels in India*, repr. (Delhi, 1973)

Beal, S., *Si-yu-ki Buddhist Records of the Western World*, repr. (Delhi, 1969)

Beal, S., *Life of Hiuen Tsang by the Shaman Hwui Li* (London, 1911)

Doniger, W. and Kakar, S., *The Kamasutra* (New Delhi, 2002)

10   The Peninsula: Emerging Regional Kingdoms

PALLAVAS, CHALUKYAS AND RASHTRAKUTAS

Nilakanta Sastri, K. A., *A History of South India: From Earliest Times to Vijayanagar* (Madras, 1958)

Mahalingam, T. V., *Kanchipuram in South Indian History* (Bombay, 1969)

Mahalingam, T. V., *South Indian Polity*, 2nd edn (Madras, 1967)

Moraes, G. M., *The Kadamba Kula – A History of Ancient and Medieval Karnataka* (Bombay, 1931)

Ramesh, K. V., *History of South Kanara* (Dharwar, 1970)

Yazdani, G. (ed.), *The Early History of the Deccan*, repr. (Delhi, 1982)

Altekar, A. S., *The Rastrakutas and their Times*, rev. edn (Poona, 1967)

Sircar, D. C., *Successors of the Satavahanas in the Lower Deccan* (Calcutta, 1939)

POLITICAL ECONOMIES OF THE PENINSULA

Champakalakshmi, R., *Trade, Ideology and Urbanism* (New Delhi, 1996)

Ludden, D., *Peasant History in South India* (New Jersey, 1985)

Nagaswamy, R. (ed.), *Seminar on Hero Stones* (Madras, 1974)

Natana, K., *Hero Stones in Tamil Nadu* (Madras, 1978)

Setter, S. (ed.), *Memorial Stones* (Dharwar, 1982)

Stein, B., *Peasant State and Society in Medieval South India* (Delhi, 1980)

Banga, I. (ed.), *The City in Indian History: Urban Demography, Society and Politics* (Delhi, 1991)

Veluthat, K., *The Political Structure of Early Medieval South India* (Delhi, 1993)

Kulke, H., *Kings and Cults. State Formation and Legitimation in India and Southeast Asia* (New Delhi, 1993)

Chattopadhyaya, B. D., *Coins and Currency Systems in South India* (Delhi, 1977)

Parasher-Sen, A. (ed.), *Social and Economic History of the Early Deccan: Some Interpretations* (New Delhi, 1993)

Minakshi, C., *Administration and Social Life Under the Pallavas* rev. edn (Madras, 1977)

Nagaswamy, R., *Kaveripattinam – A Guide* (Madras, 1973)

LITERARY CULTURE

Zvelebil, K. V., *The Smile of Murugan: On the Tamil Literature of South India* (Leiden, 1973)

Aiyar, V. V. S., *Kamba Ramayana – A Study* (Bombay, 1965)

Peterson, I. V., *Poems to Shiva: The Hymns of the Tamil Saints* (Delhi, 1991)

Ramesh, K. V., *Jaina Literature in Tamil* (Delhi, 1974)

Sivathamby, K., *Drama in Ancient Tamil Society* (Madras, 1981)

Meenakshi, K., *Literary Criticism in Tamil and Sanskrit* (Chennai, 2000)

Ramanujan, A. K., *Hymns for the Drowning*, Poems for Visnu by Nammalvar (Princeton, 1981)

PHILOSOPHICAL AND RELIGIOUS CHANGES

Obeysekere, G., *The Cult of Goddess Patini* (Delhi, 1987)

Desai, B. P., *Jainism in South India and Some Jaina Epigraphs* (Sholapur, 1957)

Gunawardana, R. A. L. H., *Robe and Plough* (Tucson, 1979)

Shanta Kumari, L., *History of the Agraharas, Karnataka, 400–1300* (Madras, 1986)

Lorenzen, D., *The Kapalikas and Kalamukhas: Two Lost Shaivite Sects* (New Delhi, 1972)

Narayanan, M. G. S., *Cultural Symbiosis in Kerala* (Trivandrum, 1972)

Pande, G. C., *The Life and Thought of Shankaracharya* (Delhi, 1994)

Mayeda, S., *A Thousand Teachings* (Tokyo, 1979)

Clothey, F. W., *The Many Faces of Murugan: The History and Meaning of a South Indian God* (The Hague, 1978)

THE ROLE OF THE TEMPLE
Stein, B. (ed.), *South Indian Temples* (Delhi, 1978)
Tartakov, G. M., *The Durga Temple at Aihole* (Delhi, 1997)
Champakalakshmi, R., *The Hindu Temple* (Delhi, 2001)
Michell, G., *Pattadakal* (Delhi, 2002)

Some Sources in Translation
South Indian Inscriptions
Sewell, R. and Aiyangar, S. K. (eds), *Historical Inscriptions of South India* (Madras, 1932)
Pope, G. U., *The Sacred Kural* (London, 1888)
Parathasarathy, R., *The Tale of an Anklet* (New York, 1993)
Danielou, A., *Manimekhalai* (New Delhi, 1993)
Ryder, A. W., *Dandin's Dasakumaracharita* (Chicago, 1927)
Kingsbury, F. and Philips, G. E., *Hymns of the Tamil Shaivite Saints*, (Calcutta, 1921)

11   The Peninsula: Establishing Authorities and Structures

THE POLITICS OF THE PENINSULA
Nilakanta Sastri, K. A., *The Cholas*, repr. (Madras, 1975)
Subbarayalu, Y., *Political Geography of the Chola Country* (Madras, 1970)
Derrett, J. D. M., *The Hoysalas* (Oxford, 1957)
Sheikh Ali, B. (ed.), *The Hoysala Dynasty* (Mysore, 1972)
Spencer, G. W., *The Politics of Expansion. The Chola Conquest of Sri Lanka and Sri Vijaya* (Madras, 1983)
Talbot, C., *Pre-Colonial India in Practice* (Delhi, 2001)
Narayanan, M. G. S., *Perumals of Kerala* (Calicut, 1996)
Nilakantha Sastri, K. A., *The Pandyan Kingdom* (Madras, 1982)
Desai, B. P. (ed.), *A History of Karnataka* (Dharwar, 1970)
Altekar, A. S., *The Rashtrakutas and Their Times*, 2nd rev. edn (Poona, 1967)
Krishnan, K. G., *Studies in South Indian History and Epigraphy* (Madras, 1981)

STRUCTURES OF AN AGRARIAN SYSTEM
Gururajachar, S., *Some Aspects of Economic and Social Life in Karnataka (AD 1000–1300)* (Mysore, 1974)
Kuppuswamy, G. R., *Economic Conditions in Karnataka, AD 973–AD 1336* (Dharwar, 1975)
Stein, B., *Peasant State and Society in Medieval India* (Delhi, 1980)
Jha, D. N. (ed.), *Feudal Social Formation in Early India* (Delhi, 1987)
Karashima, N., *History and Society in South India*, repr. (Delhi, 2001)
Sundaram, K., *Studies in Economic and Social Conditions in Medieval Andhra* (Machilipatnam, 1968)

Parasher-Sen, A. (ed.), *Social and Economic History of the Early Decan: Some Interpretations* (New Delhi, 1993)

Ludden, D., *Peasant History in South India* (Princeton, 1985)

Chattopadhyaya, B. D., *Aspects of Rural Settlements and Rural Society in Early Medieval India* (Calcutta, 1990)

Gros, F. and Nagaswamy, R., *Uttaramerur: Légendes, Histoire, Monuments* (Pondicherry, 1970)

TOWNS AND MARKETS

Hall, K. R., *Trade and Statecraft in the Age of the Cholas* (Delhi, 1980)

Abraham, M., *Two Medieval Merchant Guilds of South India* (New Delhi, 1988)

Champakalakshmi, R., *Trade, Ideology and Urbanisation* (Delhi, 1996)

Ramaswamy, V., *Textiles and Weavers in Medieval South India* (New Delhi, 1985)

Goitein, S. D., *From the Mediterranean to India* (New Jersey, 1974)

Chattopadhyaya, B. D., *Coins and Currency Systems in South India* (New Delhi, 1977)

Mahalingam, T. V., *Kancipuram in Early South Indian History* (Bombay, 1969)

Srinivasan, C. R., *Kanchipuram Through the Ages* (Delhi, 1979)

THE TEMPLE AS AN INSTITUTION

Settar, S., *The Hoysala Temples* (Dharwar, 1992)

Meister, M. (ed.), *Encyclopaedia of Indian Temple Architecture*, vol. I, 1, *Lower Dravidadesa, 200 BC–AD 1324* (Philadelphia, 1983)

Sundaram, K., *The Simhachalam Temple* (Waltair, 1969)

Thapar, R., 'Cultural Transactions and Early India – Patronage', in *History and Beyond* (Delhi, 2000)

Pillai, K. K., *The Suchindaram Temple* (Madras, 1963)

Nagaswamy, R., *Gangaikondacholapuram* (Madras, 1970)

Stein, B. (ed.), *South Indian Temples. An Analytical Reconsideration* (New Delhi, 1978)

LANGUAGE AND LITERATURE

Meenakshi, K., *Literary Criticism in Tamil and Sanskrit* (Chennai, 2000)

Shulman, D. D., *The King and the Clown in South Indian Myth and Poetry* (Princeton, 1988)

Shulman, D. D., *Tamil Temple Myths. Sacrifice and Divine Marriage in the South Indian Saiva Tradition* (Princeton, 1980)

Peterson, I., *Poems to Siva, the Hymns of the Tamil Saints* (Princeton, 1989)

Zvelebil, K., *Companion Studies to the History of Tamil Literature* (Leiden, 1992)

RELIGIONS AND IDEOLOGIES

Ramaswamy, V., *Divinity and Deviance. Women in Vaishnavism* (Delhi, 1990)

Ramaswamy, V., *Walking Naked: Women, Society, Spirituality in South India* (Simla, 1997)

Zvelebil, K., *The Irulas of the Blue Mountains* (Syracuse, 1988)

Hardy, F., *Viraha-Bhakti: The Early History of Krsna Devotion in South India* (Delhi, 1983)

Lorenzen, D. N., *The Kapalikas and Kalamukhas: Two Lost Saivite Sects* (New Delhi, 1975)

Sontheimer, G. D., *Pastoral Deities in Western India* (New York, 1989)

Carman, J. B., *The Theology of Ramanuja. An Essay in Interreligious Understanding* (Yale, 1974)

Ayyar, C. V. N., *Origin and Early History of Shaivism in South India*, repr. (Madras, 1974)

Desai, P. B., *Jainism in South India and Some Jaina Epigraphs* (Sholapur, 1957)

Singh, R. B. P., *Jainism in Early Medieval Karnataka* (Delhi, 1975)

Some Sources in Translation

Epigraphia Indica

Epigraphia Carnatica

South Indian Inscriptions

Panchmukhi, R. S., *Karnataka Inscriptions* (Dharwar, 1941)

Rice, L., *Mysore and Coorg from the Inscriptions* (London, 1909)

Elliot, W., *Coins of Southern India*, repr. (Varanasi, 1970)

Biddulph, C. H., *Coins of the Cholas* (Varanasi, 1968)

12 The Politics of Northern India

THE STRUGGLE OVER THE NORTHERN PLAINS

Ray, H. C., *Dynastic History of Northern India*, vols I and II, repr. (New Delhi, 1973)

Puri, B. N., *The History of the Gurjara Pratiharas* (Bombay, 1957)

Fox, R. G. (ed.), *Realm and Region in Traditional India* (Delhi, 1977)

KINGDOMS BEYOND THE GANGES HEARTLAND

Maclean, D. N., *Religion and Society in Arab Sind* (Leiden, 1989)

Majumdar, A. K., *Chaulukyas of Gujarat* (Bombay, 1956)

Morrison, B., *Political Centres and Cultural Regions of Early Bengal* (Tucson, 1970)

Majumdar, R. C., *The History of Bengal*, vol. I, 2nd edn (Patna, 1971)

Singh Upinder, *Kings, Brahmanas and Temples in Orissa* (Delhi, 1993)

Mahtab, K. H., *The History of Orissa*, vols I and II (Cuttack, 1959–60)

Mitra, S. K., *The Early Rulers of Khajuraho* (Calcutta, 1958)

Goetz, H., *Studies in the History and Art of Kashmir and the Indian Himalayas* (Wiesbaden, 1969)

Barua, K. L., *Early History of Kamarupa*, 2nd edn (Gauhati, 1966)

RAJPUTS

Sharma, D., *Early Chauhan Dynasties* (Delhi, 1959)

Sharma, D. (ed.), *Rajasthan Through the Ages* (Bikaner, 1966)

Asopa, J. N., *Origin of the Rajputs* (Delhi, 1976)

Bhatia, P., *The Paramaras* (Delhi, 1970)

Chattopadhyaya, B. D., *The Making of Early Medieval India* (New Delhi, 1994)

THE CREATION OF NEW SETTLEMENTS

Sharma, R. S., *Aspects of Political Ideas and Institutions in Ancient India*, rev. edn (Delhi, 1991)

Sharma, R. S. and Jha, V. (eds), *Indian Society: Historical Probings* (New Delhi, 1974)

Pouchepadass, J. and Stern, H. (eds), *From Kingship to State, the Political in the Anthropology and History of the Indian World* (Paris, 1991)

CENTRAL ASIAN INTERVENTION

Wink, A., *Al-Hind, The Making of the Indo-Islamic World*, vol. I (Delhi, 1999)

Nazim, M., *The Life and Times of Sultan Mahmud of Ghazna*, 2nd edn (New Delhi, 1971)

Habib, M., *Sultan Mahmud of Ghazna*, 2nd edn (New Delhi, 1971)

Thapar, R., *Narratives and the Making of History*, two lectures (Delhi, 2000)

Bosworth, C. E., *The Ghaznavids: Their Empire in Afghanistan and Eastern Iran, 994–1040* (Edinburgh, 1963)

Bosworth, C. E., *The Medieval History of Iran, Afghanistan and Central Asia* (London, 1977)

Eaton, R. M., *Essays on Islam and Indian History* (Delhi, 2000)

Davis, R. H., *Lives of Indian Images* (Princeton, 1997)

Foltz, R. C., *Religions of the Silk Road* (London, 1999)

Rehman, A., *The Last Two Dynasties of the Shahis: an Analysis of their History, Archaeology, Coinage and Palaeography* (Islamabad, 1979)

THE COMING OF TURKISH RULE

Habibullah, A. B. M., *The Foundation of Muslim Rule in India* (Allahabad, 1961)

Gommand, J. J. L. and Kolff, D. H. A. (ed.), *Warfare and Weaponry in South Asia, 1000–1800* (Delhi, 2001)

Chattopadhyaya, B. D. *Representing the Other?: Sanskrit sources and the Muslims* (New Delhi, 1998)

Some Sources in Translation

Stein, M. A., *Kalhana's Rajatarangini, a Chronicle of the Kings of Kashmir*, repr. (Delhi, 1979)

Chachnama in Elliot, H. M. and Dowson, J., *The History of India as Told by its own Historians*, vol. I, repr. (Delhi, 1996)

Elliot, H. M. and Dowson, J., *The History of India as Told by its own Historians*, vols II and III, repr. (Delhi, 1996)

Sachau, E. C., *Alberuni's India*, vols I and II, repr. (Delhi, 1964)

13 Northern India: Distributive Political Economies and Regional Cultures

THEORIES OF HISTORICAL CHANGE

Sircar, D. C., *Landlordism and Tenancy in Ancient and Medieval India as Revealed by Epigraphical Records* (Lucknow, 1969)

Sharma, R. S., *Indian Feudalism* (Calcutta, 1965)

Sharma, R. S., *Social Changes in Early Medieval India* (circa AD 500–1200) (Delhi, 1969)

Sharma, R. S., *Urban Decay in India*, c. AD 300–c. 1000 (Delhi, 1987)

Sharma, R. S., *Early Medieval Indian Society* (Delhi, 2001)

Byres, T. J. and Mukhia, H. (eds), *Feudalism and non-European Societies* (London, 1985)

Jha, D. N. (ed.), *Feudal Social Formation in Early India* (Delhi, 1987)

Jha, D. N., *The Feudal Order* (New Delhi, 2000)

Chattopadhyaya, B. D., *The Making of Early Medieval India* (Delhi, 1994)

DISTRIBUTIVE POLITICAL ECONOMIES

Chattopadhyaya, B. D., *Aspects of Rural Settlements and Rural Society in Early Medieval India* (Calcutta, 1990)

Om, Prakash, *Early Indian Grants and State Economy* (Allahabad, 1988)

Raychaudhuri, T. and Habib, I. (eds), *Cambridge Economic History of India*, vol. I (Cambridge, 1982)

Singh, Upinder, *Kings, Brahmanas and Temples in Orissa* (Delhi, 1993)

Chaudhary, A. K., *Early Medieval Village in North-eastern India* (AD 600–1200) (Calcutta, 1971)

Gopal, L., *The Economic Life of Northern India* (Varanasi, 1965)

Chaudhuri, K. N., *Asia Before Europe* (Cambridge, 1990)

KINGS AND POLITICS

Kulke, H., *Kings and Cults. State Formation and Legitimation in India and Southeast Asia* (New Delhi, 1993)

Kulke, H. (ed.), *The State in India, 1000–1700* (Delhi, 1997)

Sinha, S. C., *Tribal Polities and State Systems in Pre-Colonial Eastern and North Eastern India* (New Delhi, 1987)

Morrison, B. M., *Lalmai, a Cultural Centre of Early Bengal* (Seattle, 1974)

URBANISM IN A NEW CONTEXT

Deyell, J. S., *Living Without Silver: The Monetary History of Early Medieval North India* (Delhi, 1990)

Jha, A. K., (ed.), *Coinage, Trade and Economy* (Nasik, 1991)

Jain, V. K., *Trade and Traders in Western India* (AD 1000–1300) (New Delhi, 1990)

Jain, K. C., *Ancient Cities and Towns of Rajasthan* (Delhi, 1972)

Mukherjee, B. N., *Post-Gupta Coinages of Bengal* (Calcutta, 1989)
Thakur, U., *Mints and Minting in Ancient India* (Varanasi, 1972)

NEW SOCIAL TRENDS

Yadava, B. N. S., *Society and Culture in Twelfth Century North India* (Allahabad, 1973)

Jha, D. N. (ed.), *Society and Ideology in India: Essays in Honour of Professor R. S. Sharma* (Delhi, 1996)

Gupta, C., *The Kayasthas: A Study in the Formation and Early History of a Caste* (Calcutta, 1996)

Sharma, R. S., *Social Changes in Early Medieval India*, c. AD 500–1200 (Delhi, 1969)

Dutta, S., *Migrant Brahmanas in Northern India and their Settlements and General Impact* c. AD 475–1030 (Delhi, 1989)

LEARNING AND LITERATURE

Lingat, C. R., *The Classical Law of India* (New Delhi, 1973)

Pathak, V. S., *Ancient Historians of India: A Study in Historical Biography* (Bombay, 1966)

Thapar, R., *Exile and the Kingdom: Some Thoughts on the Ramayana* (Bangalore, 1978)

Chattopadhyaya, D. P., *Science and Society in Ancient India* (Calcutta, 1979)

Sircar, D. C., *Indian Epigraphy* (Delhi, 1965)

Warder, A. K., *Indian Kavya Literature*, 4 vols (Delhi, 1972–83)

Dutta, B. B. and Singh, A. N., *History of Hindu Mathematics* (Lahore, 1935)

Ray, P. C., *A History of Hindu Chemistry*, 2 vols, 2nd edn (Calcutta, 1925)

MONUMENTS AND THEIR HISTORICAL ROLE

Michell, G., *The Hindu Temple: An Introduction to its Meaning and Forms* (Chicago, 1998)

Champakalakshmi, R., *The Hindu Temple* (New Delhi, 2001)

Stoller Miller, B. (ed.), *The Powers of Art: Patronage in Indian Culture* (Delhi, 1992)

Meister, M. and Dhaky, M. A., *Encyclopaedia of Indian Temple Architecture* vol. II. 1: *Foundations of a North Indian Style* c. 250 BC–AD 1100 (Delhi, 1980); vol. II.2: *Period of Early Maturity 700–900* (Delhi, 1971)

Handa, D., *Osian. History, Archaeology, Art and Architecture* (Delhi, 1984)

Desai, D., *Khajuraho* (Delhi, 2000)

Desai, D., *Erotic Sculpture of India* (New Delhi, 1975)

Dehejia, V., *Yogini Cult and Temples* (New Delhi, 1994)

Thakur, L. S., *Buddhism in the Western Himalaya* (Delhi, 2002)

RELIGIOUS MUTATIONS

Coburn, T., *Devi-Mahatmya: The Crystallisation of the Goddess Tradition* (Delhi, 1984)

Dehejia, V. (ed.), *Devi: The Great Goddess* (Ahmedabad, 1999)

Jaini, P. S., *Gender and Salvation: Jaina Debates on the Spiritual Liberation of Women* (Delhi, 1992)

Eischmann, A., Kulke, H. and Tripathi, G. C. (eds), *The Cult of Jagannath and the Regional Tradition of Orissa* (New Delhi, 1978)

Thapar, R., *Ancient Indian Social History: Some Interpretations* (Delhi, 1978)

Hazra, R. C., *Studies in the Puranic Records on Hindu Rites and Customs*, 2nd edn (Delhi, 1975)

Banerjea J. N., *The Development of Hindu Iconography* (Calcutta, 1956)

Woodroffe, J., *Shakti and Sakta* (Madras, 1956)

Bhattacharya, N. N., *History of the Tantric Religion* (New Delhi, 1992)

Bhattacharya, N. N., *History of the Sakta Religion*, 2nd edn (New Delhi, 1996)

Chakrabarti, K., *Religious Process, The Puranas and the Making of a Regional Tradition* (Delhi, 2001)

Banerjee, J. N., *Puranic and Tantric Religion* (Calcutta, 1966)

Gupta, S., et al., *Hindu Tantrism* (Leiden, 1979)

Some Sources in Translation

Majumdar, N. G., *Inscriptions of Bengal* (Rajashahi, 1929)

Mirashi, V. V., *Corpus Inscriptionum Indicarum*, vol. IV, parts 1 and 2: *Inscriptions of the Kalachuri-Chedi Era* (Ootacamund, 1929; 1955)

Trivedi, H. V., *Corpus Inscriptionum Indicarum*, vol. VII, parts 1–3, *Inscriptions of the Paramaras, Chandellas, Kachchhapagatas and Two Minor Dynasties* (generally texts only) (Delhi, 1991)

Nambiar, S. K., *Prabodhacandrodaya of Krsna Misra* (Delhi, 1971)

Majumdar, R. C., Basak, R. and Banerji, P. N., *The Ramacaritam of Sandhyakaranandin* (Rajashahi, 1939)

Ph. Vogel, *The Antiquities of Chamba State* (Calcutta, 1911)

Tawney, C. H. (tr.), *The Ocean of Story (Kathasaritasagara)*, repr. (Delhi, 1968)

Arnold, E., *The Chaurapanchashika* (London, 1986)

Jha, G., *Medhatithi Manubhashya* (Calcutta, 1922–29)

Stoler Miller, B., *Love Song of the Dark Lord: Jayadeva's Gita Govinda* (New York, 1977)

Tawney, C. H., *The Prabandhachintamani of Merutunga Acarya* (Calcutta, 1899)

Williams, A., *Tales from the Panchatantra* (Oxford, 1930)

General Bibliography

The exclusion of some of the older authors from this General Bibliography as well as from the bibliographies attached to each chapter is not because their writings are no longer important, but because they are still far better known than some of the recent studies and the latter require mention.

Basham, A. L. (ed.), *The Legacy of India* (Oxford, 1975)

Basham, A. L., *Studies in Indian History and Culture* (Calcutta, 1964)

Basham, A. L., *The Wonder That Was India*, 3rd edn (New York, 1971)

Bhattacharya, S. and Thapar, R. (eds), *Situating Indian History* (New Delhi, 1986)

Brough, J., *Selections from Classical Sanskrit Literature* (London, 1951)

Conze, E., *Buddhist Texts through the Ages* (Oxford, 1954)

Coomaraswami, A. K., *History of Indian and Indonesian Art*, repr. (Delhi, 1972)

Cunningham, A., *A Book of Indian Eras*, repr. (Varanasi, 1970)

Cunningham, A., *The Ancient Geography of India*, repr. (Varanasi, 1975)

Dani, A. H., *Indian Palaeography* (Oxford, 1963)

Datta, B. B. and Singh, A. N., *History of Hindu Mathematics* (Lahore, 1935)

Ghoshal, U. N., *History of Hindu Political Theories*, 2nd edn (Oxford, 1927)

Gupta, P. L., *Coins*, 4th edn (New Delhi, 1996)

Harle, J., *The Art and Architecture of the Indian Subcontinent* (London, 1986)

Huntington, S. L., *The Art of Ancient India* (New York, 1985)

Kane, P. V., *History of Dharmasastra*, vols I–V (Poona, 1968–75)

Kosambi, D. D., *An Introduction to the Study of Indian History*, repr. (Delhi, 1970)

Kosambi, D. D., *Myth and Reality* (Bombay, 1962)

Kosambi, D. D., *Combined Method in Indology and Other Writings* edited by B. D. Chattopadhyaya (Delhi, 2002)

Kulke, H. and Rothermund, D., *A History of India*, 3rd edn (London, 1998)

Jha, D. N., *Ancient India* (Delhi, 1998)

Lamotte, E., *History of Indian Buddhism* (Louvain, 1988)

Law, B. C., *Historical Geography of Ancient India* (Paris, 1954)

Meister, M. M. and Dhaky, M. A., *Indian Temple Architecture* (Delhi/Varanasi, 1983–)

Nilakanta Sastri, K. A., *A History of South India*, 4th edn (Madras, 1974)

Radhakrishnan, S., *Indian Philosophy* vols I and II (London, 1923–27)

Ray, N. R. et al., *A Sourcebook of Indian Civilisation* (Delhi, 2000)

Ray, P. C., *A History of Hindu Chemistry*, vols I and II (Calcutta, 1907–25)

Raychaudhuri, H., *Political History of Ancient India*, commentary B. N. Mukherjee, rev. edn (Delhi, 1996)

Salomon, R., *Indian Epigraphy* (Delhi, 1998)

Schwartzberg, J. E. (ed.), *A Historical Atlas of South Asia*, 2nd edn (Oxford, 1992)

Sharma, R. S., *Aspects of Political Ideas and Institutions in Ancient India*, 3rd edn (Delhi, 1991)

Sharma, R. S. and Jha, D. N. (eds), *Indian Society Historical Probings. Essays in memory of D. D. Kosambi* (New Delhi, 1974)

Singh, R. L., *India. A Regional Geography* (Varanasi, 1971)

Sircar, D. C., *Indian Epigraphy* (Delhi, 1965)

Sircar, D. C., *Epigraphical Glossary* (Delhi, 1966)

Spate, O. H. K. and Learmonth, A. T. A., *India and Pakistan, a General and Regional Geography*, 4th edn (London, 1972)

Subbarao, B., *The Personality of India*, 2nd edn (Baroda, 1958)

Thapar, R. (ed.), *Recent Perspectives of Early Indian History*, 2nd edn (Bombay, 1998)

Thapar, R., *Cultural Pasts* (Delhi, 2000)

Winternitz, M., *A History of Indian Literature* (Calcutta, 1933)

Journals

There are many journals and periodical publications that carry articles on the history of India or data on sources discussed in this book. References to articles in the bibliographies would have made the bibliographies for each chapter unwieldy. Those consulted more frequently are included in the following:

Acta Orientalia

Ancient India (Bulletin of the Archaeological Survey of India)

Ancient Pakistan

Annales

Annals of the Bhandarkar Oriental Research Institute

Annual Report of Indian Epigraphy

Antiquity

Archaeology

Artibus Asiae

Bulletin of the School of Oriental and African Studies

Burlington Magazine

Comparative Studies in Society and History

Contributions to Indian Sociology

Corpus Inscriptionum Indicarum/CII

East and West

Epigraphia Carnatica

Epigraphia Indica
History and Culture of the Indian People, vols I–V
History of Religions
Hyderabad Archaeological Series
Indian Antiquary
Indian Archaeology – a Review
Indian Economic and Social History Review
Indian Historical Review
Indian Studies: Past and Present
Indo-Iranian Journal
Journal Asiatique
Journal of Asian Studies
Journal of Indian History
Journal of the American Oriental Society
Journal of the Asiatic Society of Bengal
Journal of the Bihar and Orissa Research Society
Journal of the Bombay Branch of the Royal Asiatic Society
Journal of the Economic and Social History of the Orient
Journal of the Epigraphical Society of India
Journal of the Numismatic Society of India
Journal of the Royal Asiatic Society of Great Britain and Ireland
Man and Environment
Man in India
Memoirs of the Archaeological Survey of India
Modern Asian Studies
Pakistan Archaeology
Proceedings of the Indian History Congress
Purana
Silk Road Art and Archaeology
Social Science Probings
South Asia Research
South Asian Archaeology
South Asian Studies
South Indian Inscriptions
Sri Lanka Journal of the Humanities
Studies in History

Index